THE
NEW YORK PUBLIC LIBRARY
STUDENT'S
DESK
REFERENCE

THE
NEW YORK PUBLIC LIBRARY
STUDENT'S
DESK
REFERENCE

A STONESONG PRESS BOOK

Prentice Hall General Reference
New York London Toronto Sydney Tokyo Singapore

PRENTICE HALL GENERAL REFERENCE
15 Columbus Circle
New York, New York, 10023

Library of Congress Cataloging-in-Publication Data

The New York Public Library student's desk reference.
p.   cm.
"A Stonesong Press book."
Includes bibliographical references and index.
Summary: Provides information on our universe, the Earth, animals, plants,
mathematics, the fine arts, grammar, etiquette, and other areas.
ISBN 0-671-85013-X
1. Curiosities and wonders—Juvenile literature. 2. Questions and answers—Juvenile
literature. [1. Almanacs.] I. New York Public Library.
AG243.N49   1993   93-22842
031.02—dc 20

Designed by Irving Perkins Associates, Inc.
Manufactured in the United States of America
10 9 8 7 6 5 4 3 2 1
First Edition

A NOTE FROM THE EDITORS

Every attempt has been made to ensure that this publication is as accurate as possible and as comprehensive as space would allow. We are grateful to the many researchers, librarians, teachers, reference editors, and friends who contributed facts, figures, time, energy, ideas, and opinions. Our choice of what to include was aided by their advice and their voices of experience. The contents, however, remain subjective to some extent, because we could not possibly cover everything that one might look for in basic information. If errors or omissions are discovered, we would appreciate hearing from you, the user, as we prepare future editions. Please address suggestions and comments to The Stonesong Press in care of Prentice Hall, 15 Columbus Circle, 16th floor, New York, NY 10023.

We hope you find our work useful.

CONTENTS

PREFACE

In 1989, we published *The New York Public Library Desk Reference,* which presented in a single volume answers to adults' most common questions on basic subjects, drawn from the more than 5 million reference requests fielded every year by the branch libraries of The New York Public Library.

After the phenomenal success of the *Desk Reference,* we realized that there was a need for a similar volume for young people. So the idea was born for a brand-new *Student's Desk Reference,* intended especially for readers between the ages of nine and fourteen.

In planning *The New York Public Library Student's Desk Reference,* the Library and the editors of The Stonesong Press wanted a book that would satisfy the natural curiosity of young people, a volume that would delight as well as inform and be wide-ranging yet not overwhelming. Our first step was to consult children's and young adults' librarians and reference editors about what information students most often need and want to know. Informally, we also surveyed the young people in our private and professional lives, soliciting their advice. We have tried to incorporate the suggestions of both adults and children throughout this book.

For example, the book contains 24 subject categories that both these groups felt would encompass the interests of young readers. Entries range from an explanation of why dinosaurs became extinct to capsule biographies of sports champions and space explorers. However diverse, these entries all provide basic answers to the questions that young people commonly ask.

Like its parent, *The New York Public Library Desk Reference,* the *Student's Desk Reference* contains many basic facts that will remain unchanged, such as the signs of the Zodiac and the rules for the game Scrabble®. Of course, other information will change over time as a result of political activities or new inventions and discoveries. This volume will, we hope, become a standard reference to be revised and updated as necessary.

Since our audience consists of young people, we have tried to create a book that is not only easy to use but also fun. Boxes, lists, charts, graphs, tables, and drawings are included to make it as accessible as possible. At the end of every section, we have included a list of other worthwhile references for further research. Thus, we hope that *The New York Public Library Student's Desk Reference,* while answering young people's basic questions, won't mark the end of their inquiries, but rather will serve as a gateway for further exploration.

1

OUR UNIVERSE

THE SOLAR SYSTEM

The word *solar* means "of the sun." Our solar system contains the nine planets that revolve around the sun, plus their moons. It also contains minor planets called asteroids and comets, which are lumps of dust and ice. Just like the planets, asteroids and comets orbit the sun. The pulling force of the sun, or gravity, keeps the planets, comets, and asteroids in their orbits.

THE SUN AND OTHER STARS

There are billions of stars in space. One of them, which we call the sun, is the center of our solar system. Without the energy the sun sends out in the form of light and heat, there would be no life on Earth. It would simply be too dark and cold for animals and plants to survive.

Sun Fact File

- The sun is almost 865,400 miles in diameter, or 600 times larger than all the planets combined.
- The sun is about 93 million miles from Earth.

- The sun is middle-aged. About 4.6 billion years ago, it began burning up hydrogen gas, which it turns into energy. In around 5 billion years from now, the sun will die because it will run out of hydrogen fuel. Near the end of its life the sun will start to expand to 100 times its present size and become a red giant. After millions more years, the giant sun will cool and contract. It will become a white dwarf, a star that is only a few thousand miles across. As it cools down, the sun will no longer shine.
- The sun is hottest at its core and coolest at its surface. Temperature at the core can reach 27 million degrees Fahrenheit, while at the surface it can be 10,800°F. The sun is so hot at the core because great heat is produced as hydrogen gas changes into helium gas.

THE MOON

The moon is Earth's next-door neighbor in space. Scientists are not sure exactly how the moon formed, but they know it was created 4.6 billion years ago—the same time as Earth.

The Solar System

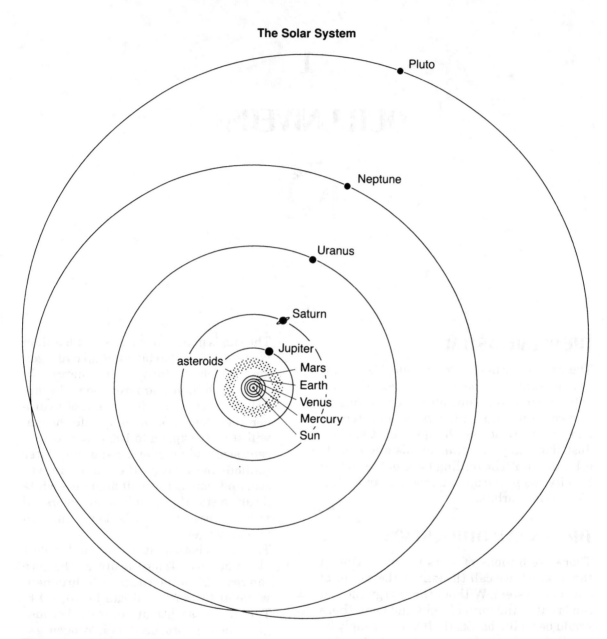

Phases of the Moon

Each time it orbits Earth, the moon spins once on its axis. This explains why we see only one face of the moon. But as it makes its 29½-day journey around Earth, the moon appears to change its shape. To understand why, we need to remember that the moon itself gives off no light but is lit by the sun. The moon seems to change shape because the one side that always faces us is lit by the sun from different angles during the moon's orbit. These changes in shape are called phases of the moon. The moon has four main phases:

1. new moon
2. first quarter
3. full moon
4. third quarter

Why Does the Sun Rise and Set?

Every day we see the sun travel across the sky between sunrise and sunset. But our eyes are deceiving us, because it is Earth that is always moving, not the sun. Earth takes a year to orbit the sun. During this time the planet itself is always spinning on an imaginary central line called its axis, which passes through the North and South poles. Earth completes one spin from west to east every 24 hours. So we see the sun rising in the east in the morning and setting in the west in the evening. When our part of Earth is turned away from the sun, we have night.

These phases are the result of the moon's orbit around Earth while the moon and Earth orbit the sun. Half of the moon is always in sunlight. However, we see varying amounts of the lighted part from Earth. During the orbits of both Earth and moon, more of the sunlit side is visible until it becomes a full moon. Then the sunlit side is decreasingly visible until the return of the dark new moon.

The Phases of the Moon

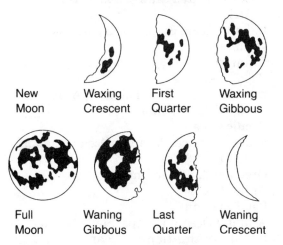

New Moon　　Waxing Crescent　　First Quarter　　Waxing Gibbous

Full Moon　　Waning Gibbous　　Last Quarter　　Waning Crescent

The Moon and Tides

Like Earth, the moon has gravity. It is this gravity that causes tides in Earth's oceans. The moon's gravity draws up the waters directly under it. As a result, two bulges called high tides are created in the sea. These tidal bulges journey from east to west as Earth spins on its axis and the moon rotates around the planet. So every day all parts of the seashore have two low tides and two high tides.

Moon Fact File

- The moon is 2,160 miles in diameter.
- The moon is 238,000 miles from Earth.
- One moon day equals 27.3 Earth days. As the moon revolves around Earth, the same side always faces us.
- The moon has no air, water, or wind.
- Temperatures can reach as high as 260°F, or as low as −280°F.
- The surface of the moon consists of mountains, craters, and plains of solid lava.
- The low gravity on the surface of the moon means that you would weigh about one-sixth of your Earth weight there.

ECLIPSES

An eclipse takes place when one body in space blocks our view of another body. Eclipses can be partial or complete. In a partial eclipse, our view is not completely blocked. In a total eclipse, it is. There are two kinds of eclipses: solar (sun) eclipses and lunar (moon) eclipses. Solar eclipses are caused when the orbiting moon passes in front of the sun. Lunar eclipses are caused when the full moon passes into Earth's shadow and appears reddish brown. A total lunar eclipse lasts more than 1½ hours. There may be as many as three eclipses of the moon in a year.

A Solar Eclipse

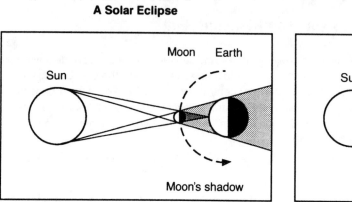

A Lunar Eclipse

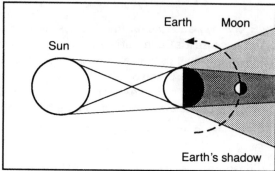

Total Eclipses of the Sun in the Twentieth Century

Date	Approximate duration (min:sec)	Maximum width (miles)	Location
1900 May 28	2:10	58	Mexico, United States, Spain, North Africa
1901 May 18	6:71	149	Indian Ocean, Sumatra, Borneo, New Guinea
1903 September 21	2:02	157	Antarctica
1904 September 9	6:19	146	Pacific Ocean
1905 August 30	3:46	123	Canada, Spain, North Africa, Arabia
1907 January 14	2:24	119	Soviet Union, China
1908 January 3	4:20	93	Pacific Ocean
1908 December 23	0:12	6	South America, Atlantic Ocean, Indian Ocean
1909 June 17	0:24	32	Greenland, Soviet Union
1910 May 9	4:14	. . .	Antarctica
1911 April 28	4:58	120	Pacific Ocean
1912 April 17	0:02	1	Atlantic Ocean, Europe, Soviet Union
1912 October 10	2:20	54	Brazil, South Atlantic Ocean
1914 August 21	2:15	113	Greenland, Europe, Middle East
1916 February 3	2:36	69	Pacific Ocean, South America, Atlantic Ocean
1918 June 8	2:23	70	Pacific Ocean, United States
1919 May 29	6:50	153	South America, Atlantic Ocean, Africa
1921 October 1	1:52	189	Antarctica
1922 September 21	6:39	142	Indian Ocean, Australia
1923 September 10	3:37	106	Pacific Ocean, Central America
1925 January 24	2:32	130	Northeast United States, Atlantic Ocean

Date	Approximate duration (*min:sec*)	Maximum width (*miles*)	Location
1926 January 14	4:11	92	Africa, Indian Ocean, Borneo
1927 June 29	0:50	48	England, Scandinavia, Arctic Ocean, Soviet Union
1928 May 19	. . .	. . .	(Umbra—shadow caused by eclipse— barely touched Antarctica)
1929 May 9	5:07	122	Indian Ocean, Malaya, Philippines
1930 April 28	0:01	1	Pacific Ocean, United States, Canada
1930 October 21	1:55	54	South Pacific Ocean
1932 August 31	1:45	104	Arctic Ocean, East Canada
1934 February 14	2:53	79	Borneo, Pacific Ocean
1936 June 19	2:31	83	Greece, Turkey, Soviet Union, Pacific Ocean
1937 June 8	7:04	156	Pacific Ocean, Peru
1938 May 29	4:04	. . .	South Atlantic Ocean
1939 October 12	1:32	276	Antarctica
1940 October 1	5:35	137	South America, Atlantic Ocean, Africa
1941 September 21	3:22	91	Soviet Union, China, Pacific Ocean
1943 February 4	2:39	146	Japan, Pacific Ocean, Alaska
1944 January 25	4:09	91	South America, Atlantic Ocean, Africa
1945 July 9	1:35	57	Canada, Greenland, Scandinavia, Soviet Union
1947 May 20	5:14	124	Argentina, Brazil, Central Africa
1948 November 1	1:56	53	Africa, Indian Ocean
1950 September 12	1:13	90	Arctic Ocean, Soviet Union, Pacific Ocean
1952 February 25	3:50	89	Africa, Arabia, Iran, Soviet Union
1954 June 30	2:35	96	United States, Canada, Scandinavia, Soviet Union
1955 June 20	7:08	159	Indian Ocean, Thailand, Pacific Ocean
1956 June 8	4:44	269	South Pacific Ocean
1957 October 23	. . .	. . .	(Umbra touched Antarctica)
1958 October 12	5:11	131	Pacific Ocean, Argentina
1959 October 2	3:01	76	Atlantic Ocean, Africa
1961 February 15	2:44	164	Europe, Soviet Union
1962 February 5	4:08	92	Borneo, New Guinea, Pacific Ocean
1963 July 20	1:40	63	Pacific Ocean, Alaska, Canada
1965 May 30	5:61	124	New Zealand, Pacific Ocean
1966 November 12	1:57	53	South America, Atlantic Ocean
1967 November 2	. . .	. . .	(Umbra touched Antarctica)
1968 September 22	0:40	68	Soviet Union
1970 March 7	3:28	99	Pacific Ocean, Mexico, Eastern United States
1972 July 10	2:36	111	Soviet Union, North Canada

(*continued*)

Total Eclipses of the Sun in the Twentieth Century (*continued*)

Date	Approximate duration (*min:sec*)	Maximum width (*miles*)	Location
1973 June 30	7:04	160	Atlantic Ocean, Central Africa, Indian Ocean
1974 June 20	5:08	216	Indian Ocean, Australia
1976 October 23	4:46	125	Africa, Indian Ocean, Australia
1977 October 12	2:37	63	Pacific Ocean, Colombia, Venezuela
1979 February 26	2:52	195	Northwest United States, Canada, Greenland
1980 February 16	4:08	93	Africa, Indian Ocean, India, China
1981 July 31	2:03	68	Soviet Union, Pacific Ocean
1983 June 11	5:11	125	Indian Ocean, New Guinea
1984 November 22	1:59	53	New Guinea, South Pacific Ocean
1985 November 12	1:59	. . .	Antarctica
1986 October 3	0:01	1	North Atlantic Ocean
1987 March 29	0:08	3	South Atlantic Ocean, Central Africa
1988 March 18	3:46	109	Sumatra, Borneo, Philippines
1990 July 22	2:33	130	Soviet Union, Pacific Ocean
1991 July 11	6:54	161	Hawaii, Mexico, South America
1992 June 30	5:20	186	South Atlantic Ocean
1994 November 3	4:51	119	Bolivia, Brazil, South Atlantic Ocean
1995 October 24	2:10	49	India, Southeast Asia, Indonesia
1997 March 9	2:50	231	Soviet Union, Arctic Ocean
1998 February 26	4:08	95	Pacific Ocean, Venezuela, Atlantic Ocean
1999 August 11	2:23	70	Central Europe, Middle East, India

THE PLANETS

Planets are the large bodies that orbit, or travel around, the sun in flattened circles called ellipses. In order of distance from the sun, the planets are

1. Mercury
2. Venus
3. Earth
4. Mars
5. Jupiter
6. Saturn
7. Uranus
8. Neptune
9. Pluto

Planets do not, like stars, give off their own light. Instead, they shine at night because they reflect light from the sun. Planets are divided into two groups.

The inner planets are the four small and rocky planets: Mercury, Venus, Earth, and Mars. These planets are closer to the sun than the tiny Pluto and the four giants: Jupiter, Saturn, Uranus, and Neptune.

The outer planets are the five planets that are beyond Mars: Jupiter, Saturn, Uranus, Neptune, and Pluto. Except for Pluto, these planets are composed mainly of gases.

Inner Planets

Mercury

The first planet from the sun, Mercury is composed of hot rock and has a cratered surface like that of the moon.

Mercury Fact File

- Only Pluto is smaller than Mercury, which is about 3,015 miles (4,850 kilometers) in diameter.
- Mercury is about 36 million miles (58 million kilometers) from the sun.
- One day on Mercury equals 59 Earth days. One year on Mercury equals 87.97 Earth days.
- Mercury has no atmosphere.
- At midday, Mercury is warmer than a furnace—about 660°F. But because Mercury does not have an atmosphere, the loss of heat makes the planet freezing at night.
- Mercury has no moons.

Venus

Venus is the second planet from the sun.

Venus Fact File

- Venus is 7,500 miles in diameter.
- Venus is 67 million miles from the sun.
- One day on Venus equals 24.3 Earth days. One year on Venus equals 224.7 Earth days.
- The atmosphere of Venus consists mainly of carbon dioxide gas.
- Because its dense carbon dioxide clouds trap the sun's heat, Venus is the hottest planet. Temperatures on it are as high as 896°F—hot enough to melt lead.
- Venus has no moons.
- Venus is the brightest planet. You can usually see it without a telescope during the early morning or early evening.

Earth

Earth is the third planet from the sun.

Earth Fact File

- Earth is 7,926 miles in diameter.
- Earth is 93 million miles from the sun.
- One day is 24 hours. One year is 365.26 Earth days.
- The atmosphere of Earth is composed of 78 percent nitrogen and 20 percent oxygen, plus small amounts of carbon dioxide and other gases, in addition to water vapor.
- Temperatures on Earth vary from the hottest of about 136°F (58°C) at the equator to −128°F (−89°C) at the North and South poles.
- In our solar system, Earth is the only planet that can support life as we know it.
- Earth has 1 moon.

Mars

Mars is the fourth planet from the sun.

Mars Fact File

- Mars is about 4,220 miles in diameter.
- Mars is about 142 million miles from the sun.
- One day on Mars equals 24 hours 37 minutes. One year on Mars is 687 Earth days.
- The thin atmosphere of Mars consists mainly of carbon dioxide.
- The temperature is always below the freezing point. Mars also has dust storms.
- Mars has 2 moons.
- The rocks on Mars contain rusted iron, which makes the planet appear red.

The Outer Planets

Jupiter

Jupiter is the fifth planet from the sun.

Jupiter Fact File

- At 88,700 miles in diameter, Jupiter is the largest planet.
- Jupiter is 483 million miles from the sun.

- One day on Jupiter equals almost 10 Earth hours. One year on Jupiter equals 4,322.7 Earth days.
- The atmosphere of Jupiter consists of hydrogen and helium.
- Jupiter has 16 moons. Its biggest moon is larger than the planet Mercury.
- Faint rings surround Jupiter.

Saturn

Saturn is the sixth planet from the sun.

Saturn Fact File

- Saturn is 74,980 miles in diameter.
- Saturn is 886 million miles from the sun.
- One day on Saturn equals nearly 11 Earth hours. One year on Saturn equals 10,759 Earth days.
- The atmosphere of Saturn consists of hydrogen and helium.
- Saturn has the most moons of any planet—24.
- Saturn has prominent rings.

Uranus

Uranus is the seventh planet from the sun.

Uranus Fact File

- Uranus is 32,490 miles in diameter.
- Uranus is 1.8 billion miles from the sun.
- One day on Uranus equals about 17 Earth hours. One day on Uranus equals 30,685 Earth days.
- The atmosphere of Uranus consists of hydrogen, helium, and methane.
- Uranus has 15 moons.
- Uranus is surrounded by 13 thin rings.

Neptune

Neptune is the eighth planet from the sun.

Neptune Fact File

- Neptune is 31,000 miles in diameter.
- Neptune is 2.8 billion miles from the sun.
- One day on Neptune equals about 16 Earth hours. One year on Neptune equals 60,190 Earth days.
- The atmosphere of Neptune consists of methane and other gases.
- Neptune has 8 moons.
- Neptune has rings.

Pluto

Pluto is usually the ninth planet from the sun. However, because its orbit now carries Pluto within the orbit of Neptune, Pluto will be closer to the sun than Neptune until 1999.

Pluto Fact File

- Pluto is 1,500 miles in diameter, making it the smallest planet.
- Pluto is 3.6 billion miles from the sun.
- One day on Pluto equals about 6.4 Earth days. One year on Pluto equals 90,800 Earth days.
- The atmosphere of Pluto is unknown.
- Because it is so far from the sun, Pluto is the coldest planet, with a temperature of 369°F below freezing.
- Pluto has 1 moon, named Charon.

STARS

A star is a body in space that gives off its own light and produces other kinds of energy.

Comets: Dirty Snowballs

Because comets are balls of ice and dust, astronomers call them "dirty snowballs." When a comet approaches the sun, its overwhelming heat begins to vaporize the icy comet. Solar wind blows the glowing stream of vapor outward in a tail. Sometimes the tail is so long that it becomes visible with the naked eye from Earth. But you need a telescope to see most comets.

There are around 200 billion stars in the known universe. Every star, including our sun, will go through various life stages from birth to death.

In the first stage, the new star develops inside a cloud of gas and dust called a nebula. In the second stage, the star emerges from its nebula. During this early stage, its color is a cool red. In the third stage, which lasts most of the star's life, it is yellow.

During its final stage, the star will be a white dwarf and run out of fuel. As a white dwarf it will become small, about the size of Earth, but remain very hot. It will then change from yellow to orange and then red before it fades away. Part of the star may survive as a neutron star. Most stars die as white dwarfs. They grow too dim for us to see without a telescope, and their surface temperature drops. But some stars called blue giants may suddenly explode in a great explosion called a supernova.

Star Fact File

- Neutron stars are the smallest stars. Their diameter is only around 10 miles. But neutron stars are extraordinarily dense.
- Red supergiants are the biggest stars. Some are 1,000 times larger than the sun.
- Blue supergiants are the hottest stars. They are 5 times hotter on their surfaces than the sun.
- Stars are not visible in the daytime because the light from the sun makes the sky so bright that the other stars are invisible.
- Some stars are as old as 15 billion years. Most stars are between 1 billion and 10 billion years old.
- The colors of stars can range from blue through white, yellow, and orange to red. The color of a star depends on its surface temperature.
- The nearest star, except for the sun, is Proxima Centauri, which is 4.3 light-years away.
- The brightest star, except for the sun, is Sirius, or the Dog Star.

Constellations

A constellation is a group of bright stars that makes a pattern in the sky at night. The stars in a constellation may appear close to each other, but they are often vast distances apart. Astronomers have named 88 constellations. You can see approximately 44 of them on a clear night. In the ancient world, stargazers named many constellations after gods, heroes, and animals.

Twelve Constellations of the Zodiac

Aquarius, the Water-Bearer
Aries, the Ram
Cancer, the Crab
Capricorn, the Goat
Gemini, the Twins
Leo, the Lion
Libra, the Balance or Scales
Pisces, the Fishes
Sagittarius, the Archer
Scorpio, the Scorpion
Taurus, the Bull
Virgo, the Virgin

Twenty-nine Constellations North of the Zodiac

Andromeda, the Chained Lady
Aquila, the Eagle
Auriga, the Charioteer
Bootes, the Wagoner
Camelopardalis, the Camelopard
Canes Venatici, the Hunting Dog
Cassiopeia, the Lady in the Chair
Cepheus, the King
Coma Bereniceses, Berenice's Hair
Corona Borealis, the Northern Crown
Cygnus, the Swan
Delphinus, the Dolphin
Draco, the Dragon
Equuleus, the Colt
Hercules (Kneeling)
Lacerta, the Lizard

Leo Minor, the Lesser Lion
Lynx, the Lynx
Lyra, the Lyre or Harp
Ophiuchus, the Serpent Holder (sometimes called Serpentarius)
Pegasus, the Winged Horse
Perseus, the Hero (with Medusa's head)
Sagitta, the Arrow
Scutum, the Shield
Serpens, the Serpent
Triangulum, the Triangle
Ursa Major, the Greater Bear
Ursa Minor, the Lesser Bear
Vulpecula, the Fox (and the Goose)

Forty-nine Constellations South of the Zodiac

Antila (Pneumatica), the Air Pump
Apus (Avis Indica), Bird of Paradise (or of India)
Ara, the Altar
Argo Navis, the Ship (may include Carina, the Keel; Malus, the Mast; Puppis, the Stern; Vela, the Sails)
Caelum (Sculptorium), the (Engraver's) Tool
Canis Major, the Greater Dog
Canis Minor, the Lesser Dog
Carina, the Keel (Argo Navis)
Centaurus, the Centaur
Cetus, the Whale
Chamaeleon, the Chameleon
Circinus, the Pair of Compasses
Columba (Noachi), (Noah's) Dove
Corona Australis, the Southern Crown
Corvus, the Crow
Crater, the Bowl
Crux Australis, the Southern Cross
Darado (Xiphias), the Gilthead or Swordfish
Eridanus, the River Po
Fornax (Chemicae), the (Chemist's) Furnace or Retort
Grus, the Crane
Horologium, the Clock
Hydra, the Water-Serpent or Hydra (fem.)
Hydrus, the Water-Snake or Sea-Serpent (masc.)

Indus, the Indian
Lepus, the Hare
Lupus, the Wolf
Malus, the Mast (Argo Navis)
Mensa (Mons Mensae), the Table Mountain
Microscopium, the Microscope
Monoceros, the Unicorn
Musca (Apis), the Fly or Bee
Norma, the Square or Rule
Octans, the Octant
Orion, the Hunter
Pavo, the Peacock
Phoenix, the Fabulous Bird
Pictor (Equuleus Pictorius), the Painter's Easel or Little Horse
Piscis Austrinus, the Southern Fish
Puppis, the Stern (Argo Navis)
Pyxis (Nautica), the (Ship's) Compass
Reticulum, the Reticule or Net
Sculptor (Apparatus Sculptorius), the Sculptor's Tools
Sextans, the Sextant
Telescopium, the Telescope
Triangulum Australe, the Southern Triangle
Tucana, the Toucan
Vela, the Sails (Argo Navis)
Volcans (Piscis Volans), the Flying Fish

THE MILKY WAY AND OTHER GALAXIES

Our solar system has many large clusters of stars. Some clusters contain hundreds of stars. Others, called galaxies, contain billions of stars. Astronomers have discovered millions of galaxies in distant space. The Milky Way galaxy is a huge group of stars, dust, and gases moving through space together. Our sun is one of more than 100 billion stars in the Milky Way. In fact, every star you see in the sky at night is in the Milky Way. The Milky Way is spiral-shaped. Galaxies can also be elliptical (oval) or irregular (unevenly shaped).

The two nearest galaxies to the Milky Way

are called the Magellanic Clouds. They are so far away that we measure the distance in light-years, which is the distance that light rays travel in one year. One light-year is 5.9 trillion (5,900,000,000,000) miles (9.5 billion kilometers).

TEN SCIENTISTS WHO CHANGED OUR VIEW OF THE UNIVERSE

Adams, John Couch (1819–1892) English astronomer. Adams and Urbain Jean Joseph Leverrier are credited with the discovery of the planet Neptune.

Copernicus, Nicholaus (1473–1543) Polish astronomer. Copernicus proposed that the sun is the center of the universe. Before Copernicus, people believed that Earth was the center and that the other planets revolved around Earth.

Einstein, Albert (1879–1955) German-born physicist. Einstein's theories of relativity changed our views about space, time, gravity, and the universe. His formula $E=mc^2$ (energy is equal to mass multiplied by the speed of light squared) explained the energy of the sun and stars.

Galilei, Galileo (1564–1642) Italian astronomer and physicist. Galileo was the first astronomer to use the telescope to observe the sky. With the telescope, Galileo discovered the four largest moons of Jupiter, the rings of Saturn, and sunspots. He also determined that stars make up the Milky Way.

Herschel, William (1738–1822) Amateur English astronomer who discovered the planet Uranus.

Kepler, Johannes (1571–1630) German astronomer who proposed that planets move in ellipses.

Leavitt, Henrietta Swan (1868–1921) American astronomer who found a way to measure distances in space.

Leverrier, Urbain Jean Joseph (1811–1877) French astronomer. Leverrier and John Couch Adams are credited with discovering the planet Neptune.

Newton, Sir Isaac (1642–1727) English physicist, mathematician, and theoretical astronomer. Newton recognized that every object in the universe attracts every other object. This attractive force he called gravity. Newton suggested that gravity is the force that moves the planets and holds the universe together. Newton also formulated the three laws of motion, which further explained the movement of objects in space.

Tombaugh, Clyde (1906–   ) American astronomer who discovered the planet Pluto.

SPACE FROM A TO Z

Here are some definitions you might find useful:

Apollo Program American space program with the goal of landing astronauts on the moon. There were 17 Apollo missions.

asteroid Small, planetlike body that circles the sun. Most asteroids orbit in a ring called the asteroid belt, which lies between the orbits of Mars and Jupiter.

astronaut Person trained to fly in a spaceship and perform tasks in space.

astronomy Scientific study of the stars, planets, and other bodies that make up our universe.

atmosphere Layer of gases around a planet.

binary star Pair of stars revolving around each other.

black hole Place in space from which nothing, even light, escapes. A black hole has very powerful gravity and can be caused by the collapse of a supergiant star.

cosmology Study of the history and structure of the universe.

cosmonaut Term used in the former Soviet Union for an astronaut.

Doppler effect A shift in frequency as a source goes farther away or gets closer. Just as the pitch of a siren or sound of a freight train changes from high to low as it passes an observer, the light waves emitted by a celestial body compress and grow shorter—shift to blue—as it approaches an observer on Earth. If a celestial object is going away from an Earth-bound observer, the light waves seem to grow longer—shift to red. The red shift or blue shift is a kind of light-wave speedometer because in a laboratory, an astronomer can tell how fast an object is traveling as well as whether it is coming closer toward us or growing more distant.

double star Pair of stars that appear close together in the sky as seen from Earth.

Explorer I First American satellite, launched on July 31, 1958.

galaxy Enormous group of stars, dust, and gases moving together through space. Millions of galaxies exist, some containing billions of stars.

gravity Invisible force of attraction between every object in the universe.

Halley's comet Comet named after the English astronomer Edmund Halley (1656–1742). Halley figured out that the orbit of the comet around the sun causes it to come close to Earth every 76 years. The last time Halley's comet appeared was 1985–86, which means it will not return until 2061–62.

Hubble space telescope Enormous telescope launched into orbit around Earth in 1990 by the *Discovery* space shuttle. Scientists hoped to obtain extremely clear photographs of the stars and distant galaxies because the telescope orbits above Earth's atmosphere. But problems with the telescope's design have made the Hubble telescope less useful than expected.

light-year Unit of measurement for enormous distances in space. It is the distance light travels in one year, or about 5.9 trillion (5,900,000,000,000) miles (9.5 billion kilometers).

magnitude Measurement of the brightness of an astronomical object.

Mariner Unmanned space probes for the purpose of studying Venus, Mercury, and Mars.

Mercury Project First American manned space program. John Glenn became the first United States astronaut to orbit Earth on February 20, 1962.

meteor Streak of light sometimes seen in the night sky. Meteors are created when small particles of rock or metal called meteoroids fall from space and burn up in Earth's atmosphere. Meteors are sometimes called shooting stars, but they are not stars.

meteorite Remains of a large meteoroid that survived the plunge to Earth. Geologists have found more than 120 meteorite craters on Earth.

mission control People who control a space mission from Earth.

nebula Cloud of gas and dust in space.

nova Exploding star. Because it flares up suddenly, the nova looks as if it is a bright, new star. *Nova* is the Latin word for "new."

pulsar Fast-burning neutron star that sends out regular bursts of radio waves.

quasar Powerful energy source in a very far galaxy.

red giant Enormous cool star that is in a late stage of its life cycle and, therefore, has very little nuclear fuel left. It is estimated that our sun will be a red giant in several billion years.

red shift Shift toward the red end of the spectrum, caused by a star moving away from Earth at tremendous speed. As an object moves away from an observer, all the wavelengths stretch and shift to the red end of the light spectrum—the color pattern that light makes as it goes through a prism. As they go through the prism, red light waves are longer, whereas blue light waves are shorter.

satellite Object in space that orbits a planet. A satellite is always smaller than the planet it orbits. The moon is a satellite of Earth.

space Everything in the universe beyond the atmosphere of Earth.

space shuttle Space transport that can be used and reused. Rockets lift the orbiter into space. After the mission is completed, the orbiter lands intact on Earth.

space station Large spacecraft orbiting Earth for a long period with astronauts working inside.

Sputnik Man-made satellite that orbits Earth. The first Sputnik was launched by the former Soviet Union on October 4, 1957.

star Any object in space that produces its own light and other types of energy. Our sun is a star.

sunspot Cool, dark patch on the surface of the sun.

telescope Instrument used to view distant objects in space, such as planets and stars.

Voyager 1* and *2 American space probes launched to study the outer planets. The probes have visited Jupiter, Saturn, Uranus, and Neptune. They are now beyond the nine planets in our solar system.

white dwarf Small, hot, dim star that is very dense. It has run out of nuclear fuel and shrunk down to about Earth's size. A teaspoonful of white-dwarf matter brought to Earth would weigh as much as a truck.

zero gravity State of weightlessness caused by traveling outside the gravitational pull of a planetary body like Earth.

INFORMATION, PLEASE

Asimov, Isaac, and Frank White. *Think about Space*. Walker, 1989.

Branley, Franklyn M. *Comets*. HarperTrophy, 1984.

———. *The Big Dipper*. HarperTrophy, 1991.

Gallant, Roy. *National Geographic Picture Atlas of Our Universe*. Rev. ed. National Geographic Society, 1986.

Krapp, E. C. *The Big Dipper and You*. William Morrow, 1989.

Lampton, Christopher. *Astronomy from Copernicus to the Space Telescope*. Franklin Watts, 1987.

Lewis, Richard S. *The Illustrated Encyclopedia of the Universe*. Harmony Books, 1983.

Rey, H. A. *Find the Constellations*. Rev. ed. Houghton Mifflin, 1988.

Simon, Seymour. *Space Words: A Dictionary*. HarperCollins, 1991.

Stacy, Tom. *Sun, Stars & Planets*. Random House, 1991.

Thompson, C. E. *Glow in the Dark Constellations: A Field Guide for Young Stargazers*. Grossett & Dunlap, 1989.

Trefil, James. *1001 Things Everyone Should Know about Science*. Doubleday, 1992.

2

PLANET EARTH

The study of the planet Earth is called earth science. It covers everything from the gaseous atmosphere that surrounds the earth to the earth's hard inner core.

EARTH FACTS

- The earth is composed primarily of rock, metal, and water.
- The earth's shape is spherical, or to be more exact, slightly ellipsoid.
- The earth is 7,907 miles (12,756 kilometers) in diameter.
- The earth's mass is sextillion metric tons. As a written number, that is 6,000, 000,000,000,000,000,000.
- The earth's circumference at the equator is 24,901.46 miles (40,075.02 kilometers).
- Earth orbits the sun at a speed of 66,000 miles per hour. It makes one circuit every 365¼ days.
- The earth spins on its own axis and completes one rotation every 23 hours, 56 minutes. Its axis is tilted at an angle of 23½ degrees.
- We live on the crust of the earth—an area so small compared to the earth's total volume and mass that it is like the skin of an apple.

THE ATMOSPHERE

The earth's atmosphere is a blanket of air that covers the planet. This outermost layer of our environment is composed of gases that keep us from burning to death during the day and freezing to death at night.

The atmosphere stretches 600 miles (1,000 kilometers) above us. Most of the atmosphere is calm, but the 6 miles right above us are constantly on the move. They produce our weather—tornadoes, monsoons, thunderstorms, and bright, clear days as well.

THE LAST FRONTIER: OCEANS

Three-fourths of the earth's surface is covered by water. Most of the water is in oceans, huge bodies of salt water. Even though people have given them separate names, the oceans are all connected.

Oceans were created when water filled the huge, low-lying basins between continents. The ocean basins consist of three main parts:

Continental shelf Forming the edge of the continents, the continental shelf is made of granite and stretches about 500 miles (180 kilometers) into the ocean. While

The Atmosphere

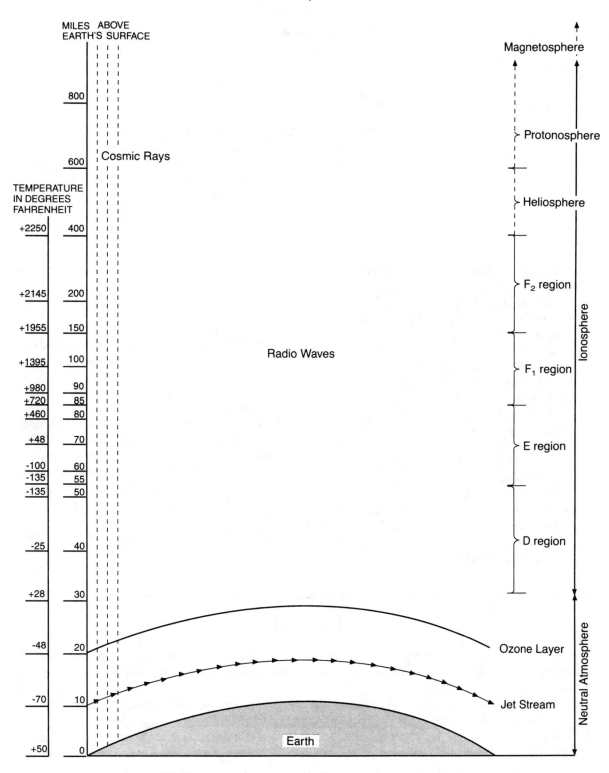

The Continental Shelf

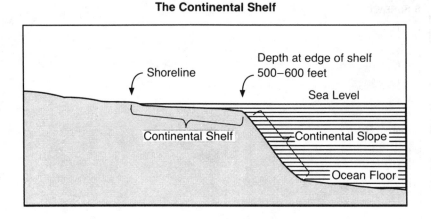

we once believed that the shelves were gradual declines into the ocean, we now know that they are rough and irregular. In some places, especially land that was once covered by glaciers, deep troughs exist close to shore. In other areas, the shelf is more gradual but is still filled with rock formations and sand ridges.

Continental slope The true beginning of an ocean, this is a sharp drop-off that is marked by still deeper canyons. The average depth of a canyon is about 1,000 feet (300 meters), but canyons twice as deep as the Grand Canyon have been found in the Atlantic Ocean.

Ocean floor This is a vast basinlike plain that can stretch to a depth of 10,000 feet (3,500 meters) and is composed primarily of fine, sandy sediment.

Ocean Facts

- Oceans cover 72 percent of the earth's surface.
- The deepest parts of the oceans are its trenches, which can be 7 miles (11,000 meters) deep. They are located near continents.
- The highest ridges are 4,000 feet (1,200 meters) from the ocean floor.
- Most of the ocean's resources—fish and petroleum—are found on the continental shelves.
- The oceans are far less explored than the land areas of earth. In fact, the oceans might be described as our last, great unexplored frontier.
- A sea, such as the Mediterranean or the Caribbean, is a region of an ocean.

Falling Up

Although most of the inhabitants of the ocean's basins are biologically engineered to withstand the tremendous pressure of the water, accidents do happen. Humans occasionally fall down, and deep-sea fish sometimes "fall up."

Fish that live on the bottom of the ocean survive only because they maintain an equilibrium with the water. The pressure inside their bodies equals the great pressure, or weight, of the water outside their bodies. If a deep-sea fish accidentally swims too high, though, the pressure inside its body changes. Its swimming bladder expands uncontrollably as it rises to the surface of the water—where it usually dies.

The World's Oceans (in descending order of area)

Pacific (70 million square miles; 181 million square kilometers)

Atlantic (36.3 million square miles; 94 million square kilometers)

Indian (28.2 million square miles; 73 million square kilometers)

Arctic (3.7 million square miles; 9.5 million square kilometers)

The Antarctic Ocean: Is It Really an Ocean?

The water around Antarctica is sometimes described as an ocean, but it has no obvious boundary on the north and is actually an extension of the Pacific, Atlantic, and Indian oceans.

WHERE WE STAND: CONTINENTS OF THE WORLD

Continents, the great land areas of the earth, form one-quarter of its surface. In contrast to the oceans, the continents are well explored.

Continents are made up of varied terrain —forests, plains, deserts, and mountain ranges. Most of the Arctic and Antarctica are frozen, uninhabitable terrain, but the rest of the continents, with few exceptions, are well populated by humans. Most of our food is produced on the continents.

The World's Continents and Their Land Areas (in square miles)

Asia	17,085,000
Africa	11,685,000
Europe	3,825,000
North America	9,420,000
South America	6,870,000
Australia	2,971,081
Antarctica	5,100,000

HIGHWAYS OF THE WORLD: RIVERS

Rivers are another great geographic feature found on continents. A river is an extraordinarily large stream of water. All rivers have a source, or starting place. It may be a glacier, a small spring, or a lake that overflows to form a river.

Rivers are important to people. They were

World's Longest Rivers (in miles/kilometers)

Nile	4,145/6,671	Northeast Africa
Amazon	4,000/6,437	South America
Yangtze	3,915/6,300	China
Huang He	2,903/4,672	China
Congo	2,900/4,667	Africa
Mekong	2,600/4,180	Asia
Niger	2,600/4,180	Africa
Mississippi	2,340/3,766	United States
Missouri	2,315/3,726	United States
Volga	2,194/3,531	Commonwealth of Independent States

the world's first highways and are still important transportation routes in some parts of the world. They provide people with water to grow crops, wash clothes, bathe, and sometimes to drink. Rivers have served as sources of energy as well, first for waterwheels and now for electricity. Rivers can sometimes be harmful to humans, as when they overflow into the flood plains where people live and farm.

Rivers may have the following parts:

Mouth The place where a river begins to slow down as it empties into another body of water.

Delta A soil-rich buildup of land that sometimes forms where a river joins a larger body of water.

Alluvial fan A wide, broad piece of land created when a river flows from a mountain down onto a large, flat plain.

Estuary A broad, deep mouth of a river. On these expanses of land, rivers deposit all the silt they have carried with them as they flowed.

Nile Delta

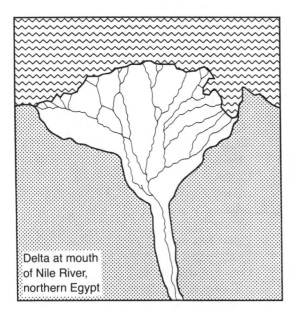

Delta at mouth of Nile River, northern Egypt

SOARING MAJESTY: MOUNTAINS

Mountains, with their varied sizes and shapes, are spectacular features of any continent. A mountain is a natural elevation rising to a great height, but what some people call a mountain, others may call a hill. Mountain's can be rocky and craggy, but they can also be softly rounded.

Mountains may stand alone or form parts of mountain ranges. Some are also parts of mountain systems, which include several mountain ranges. The Tethyan Mountain System stretches across three continents and includes such ranges as the Alps and the Carpathians in Europe; the Atlas Mountains of Africa; the Caucasus Mountains between Europe and Asia; and the Zagros Mountains, the Pamirs, the Karakoram Range, and the Himalaya in Asia.

Major Mountain Ranges of the World and Where They Are

Appalachian Mountains	United States and Canada
Rocky Mountains	United States
Pacific Mountain System	United States
Andes Mountains	South America
Tethyan Mountain System	Africa, Europe, Asia

Birth of a Mountain: Plate Tectonics

About thirty years ago, earth scientists developed a theory called plate tectonics to explain how mountains are formed. Scientists believe that the earth's crust is made up of seven large, rigid plates and several smaller ones. The continents and oceans ride on the plates, which move slowly all the time.

Two main kinds of mountains illustrate how plate tectonics works:

Fold mountains These are created when two plates meet head-on. Some fold

Climb Every Mountain: The World's Largest Mountains and Where They Are

Mountain	Height (ft./meters)	Location
WESTERN HEMISPHERE		
Aconcagua	22,831/6,959	Andes (Argentina)
Chimborazo	20,561/6,267	Andes (Ecuador)
Mt. McKinley	20,320/6,194	Alaska Range (Alaska)
Mt. Logan	19,524/5,951	St. Elias, Canada
Cotopaxi	19,347/5,897	Andes (Ecuador)
EASTERN HEMISPHERE		
Mt. Everest	29,028/8,848	Himalaya on Nepal-Tibet border
K2	28,250/8,611	Karakoram Range (also called Mustagh) in northern India
Mt. Kanchenjunga	28,208/8,598	Himalaya on Nepal-India border
Mt. Makalu	27,824/8,481	Himalaya on Nepal-India border
Annapurna	26,504/8,078	Himalaya in Nepal

Fold Mountains

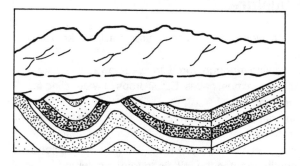

Fault-block Mountains

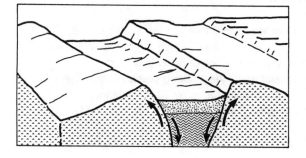

mountains are soft and roundly shaped, but others are sharply folded.

Examples: The Appalachians in the United States and the Alps in Europe.

Fault-block mountains These are created when two plates tilt or push against a fault, or crack, in one of the earth's plates. Fault-block mountains form sharp, rocky edges where the fault was pressed upward.

Examples: Sierra Nevada in California and Teton Range of Wyoming.

ROCKING AND ROLLING: EARTHQUAKES

An earthquake is a sudden shaking of the earth caused when shifts, collisions, splits, or slides occur along faults, breaks in the earth's plates. Faults are usually hidden inside the earth, but a large one, the San Andreas fault, is visible along the western edge of California.

Measuring an Earthquake's Strength

The severity of earthquakes is determined by measuring the waves that radiate away from the fault that moved. These are called seismic waves, from the Greek word *seismos*, meaning "earthquake." The farther a seismic wave travels from a fault, the less strength it has. Special seismographic stations have been set up around the world to record these waves. Seismologists watch the areas of the world where earthquakes are likely to happen, but they have not been able to predict with any exactness when they will occur.

The World's Major Earthquakes

EARTHQUAKES THAT HAVE KILLED MORE THAN 100,000 PERSONS.

Date	Location	Deaths
c. July 1201	Eastern Mediterranean	1,100,000
February 2, 1556	Shanxi Province, China	830,000
October 11, 1737	Calcutta, India	300,000
July 27, 1976	Tangshan, China	655,237
December 16, 1920	Gansu Province, China	180,000
September 1, 1923	Kanto Plain, Japan	142,807

Nature's Sculpture

If you have ever been in a cave, you may have seen huge, wonderful rock sculptures that look like giant icicles. These are called stalactites and stalagmites.

Caves are formed when water runs underground with enough force to wear away the rock. Eventually the stream of water runs out, but water still drips in most caves. Small drops of water cling to the ceilings of caves, sometimes dropping to the cave floor.

When the water evaporates, it leaves behind a tiny deposit of calcium carbonate, a substance in limestone. Each of these small drops gradually, over many years, builds up to form a solid shape—a stalactite or stalagmite. If the rock hangs from the ceiling, it is called a stalactite. If it forms from the floor, it is a stalagmite. Sometimes a stalactite and a stalagmite meet in the middle to form a column.

Cave Facts

World's deepest cave Reseau Jean Bernard in France is 5,256 feet, or almost a mile, deep.

World's longest cave The Mammoth Cave System in Kentucky, which is not yet completely explored, has thus far been proven to have more than 340 miles of passages.

World's largest cave chamber The Sarawak Chamber in the Lubang Nasib Bagus Cave, in Gunung Mulu National Park, Sarawak, Malaysia, is 2,300 feet long by 980 feet wide.

Deepest cave in U.S. The Lechuguilla Cave in Carlsbad Caverns National Park, New Mexico, is 1,565 feet deep.

World's longest free-hanging stalactite The 21-foot, 6-inch stalactite in the Poll an Ionain Cave in County Clare, Ireland, holds this record.

World's tallest stalagmite At about 105 feet tall, a stalagmite in the Krasnohorska Cave in the Czech Republic captures this prize.

Richter Scale

Scientist measure seismic waves by using the Richter scale. Each unit of magnitude is ten times greater than the one below it.

Magnitude	Effects
1	Detectable only by instruments.
2	Barely noticed by people at epicenter.
3	People feel slight tremors.
4.5	People within 20 miles (932 kilometers) of epicenter will feel shock; some minor damage may occur.
6	Moderately destructive.
7	Major earthquake.
8	Great earthquake.

Modified Mercalli Scale

The Modified Mercalli Scale, although unscientific, describes damage to objects, as well as what people experience during earthquakes.

Magnitude	Effects
I	Felt by only most sensitive person.
II	Felt by resting persons. Delicate hanging objects move.
III	Felt by some persons indoors. Objects as large as cars may move.
IV	Felt by most persons indoors. Awakens people from sleep. Windows and tabletop objects rock.
V	Felt by almost everyone. Plaster falls off walls, dishes break, and pendulum clocks stop.
VI	Felt by everyone, and people become frightened. Furniture moves.
VII	Everyone feels earthquake enough to take cover. Some structural damage to buildings.
VIII	People seriously alarmed. Water levels change in wells. Serious structural damage to weak buildings.
IX	People panic. Weak structures destroyed; strong structures, foundations, and underground pipes damaged. Ground cracks.
X	Panic. All but strongest buildings destroyed. Ground badly cracked. Railroad tracks bent. Water levels in rivers and lakes may rise dramatically.
XI	Panic. Few structures survive. Wide cracks in ground. Fault lines obvious.
XII	Devastating destruction. Ground is wavy, and people's lines of sight are distorted.

WINDOWS INTO EARTH: VOLCANOES

A volcano is a mountain with an opening in the crust of the earth. When it erupts, lava, gases, rocks, dust, and ash burst forth from the opening. The eruption is caused by magma.

Magma is molten (melted), liquid, flowing rock that comes from inside the earth. If it is still molten when it reaches the surface, magma is called lava. When lava is flowing, it is a dramatic, fiery red with a temperature as high as 2,000°F (over 1000°C), but when it cools, it hardens into a rocklike substance. Sometimes lava flows down the sides of the

Famous Volcanoes and the Damage They Did

Volcano	Height (in feet/meters)	Damage
Cotopaxi, in Ecuador	19,347/5,897	In 1877. 1,000 people killed; mudflow traveled 150 miles.
El Chichón, in Mexico	3,478/1,060	In 1982. 187 people killed; sent huge cloud of poisonous gases into atmosphere.
Hibokhibok, in Philippines	4,363/1,330	In 1951, 500 people killed by red-hot cloud of gases and dust.
Krakatoa, in Indonesia	2,667/813	In 1883, its greatest eruption was heard 3,000 miles from volcano's site, and sea waves caused by volcano led to drownings of 36,000 people on nearby islands.
Mauna Loa, in Hawaii	13,677/4,169	World's largest volcano, rising nearly 30,000 feet (9,100 meters) from ocean floor and 60 miles (97 kilometers) in diameter at base; frequently active.
Mont Pélee, in Martinique	4,583/1,397	In 1902, it erupted, killing 38,000 persons in minutes.
Mount Etna, in Sicily	11,122/3,390	In 1969, killed 20,000 people.
Mount St. Helens, Washington State	8,364/2,549	In 1980, it killed 57 people
Mount Tambora in Indonesia	9,350/2,850	In 1815, it killed 12,000 people in an explosion that released 6 million times more energy than an atomic bomb.
Nevado del Ruiz, in Colombia	17,717/5,400	In 1985, it killed about 25,000 people, many in the mudslides and floods triggered by the eruption.

mountain when the volcano erupts, and sometimes it explodes, blowing off part of the mountain.

Gases—composed chiefly of steam and a few chemicals such as carbon dioxide, nitrogen, and sulfur dioxide—also pour out of erupting volcanoes.

Volcanic ash and dust are sometimes carried around the world at high altitudes.

Some scientists believe they reduce the amount of sunlight that reaches earth and cause the vivid red sunsets that may be seen thousands of miles away from the site of an erupted volcano.

Some volcanoes are active and erupt every few months or years, while others are inactive and rarely, if ever, erupt.

Volcanoes have killed thousands of people

A Volcano

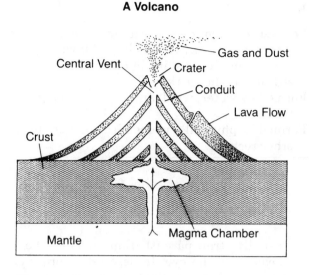

Gas and Dust
Central Vent
Crater
Conduit
Lava Flow
Crust
Mantle
Magma Chamber

Today, scientists study volcanoes to learn more about the interior of the earth. By measuring changes in a volcano, scientists are having some luck in predicting when it will erupt.

Earth's Interior

No one has ever explored the earth's innermost reaches, nor is anyone likely to. Even the deepest oil well goes only 5 miles into the earth. The inner core of the earth is very hot—10,000°F (5500°C). Most of what scientists have learned about the earth's interior has come from watching earthquakes and volcanoes. The earth's interior is made up of several layers:

Crust This outermost layer, composed of rock, is 22 miles (35 kilometers) deep.
Mantle Also made of rock, this layer is 1,800 miles (2,900 kilometers) deep.
Core This layer, 2,100 miles (3,400 kilometers) deep, is actually composed of two parts, an outer, liquid metal core and an inner, solid metal core.

who could not move out of the path of the lava; they have also wiped out entire towns. Perhaps the most famous town ever destroyed by a volcano was Pompeii in Italy. In A.D. 79, the volcano Vesuvius erupted, rapidly burying Pompeii and several other towns under ash and dust. Pompeii was rediscovered in 1748, and the preserved ruins, which have revealed many facts about life in ancient times, are now in a museum there.

ROCKY ROADS: THE STUDY OF GEOLOGY

Rock is a major substance on our planet and one that is constantly recycled. Rocks are always being made, and always being turned into other kinds of rocks. The study of rocks is called geology.

Rocks also contain minerals—natural inorganic materials with a variety of properties that make them useful in many ways. Gold and silver are minerals, for example, as are other metals. Most gemstones come from minerals. In addition to being valued for their beauty, minerals are important in manufacturing.

Rock Types

The three main kinds of rocks are each formed differently:

The Earth's Interior

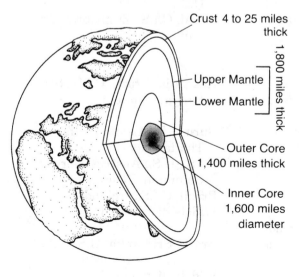

Crust 4 to 25 miles thick
Upper Mantle
Lower Mantle
1,800 miles thick
Outer Core 1,400 miles thick
Inner Core 1,600 miles diameter

Kind	Example	How Formed
igneous	balsalt, granite	Formed from molten material in the earth's interior, either by fast cooling of lava flows or by slow cooling of material while still inside the earth
sedimentary	sandstone, limestone	Formed by water, wind, and ice over a long time
metamorphic	marble, slate	Formed by physical and chemical changes to other rocks

Stones of Beauty: Gemstones

Gemstones are minerals that are relatively rare, unusually hard, and colored in a way (usually transparent) that makes them pleasing to the eye. In descending order of hardness, here are the ten main gemstones:

Name	Color	Major Sources
Diamond	Clear (pure), often with some yellow, brown, red, or black	South Africa, Namibia, Australia, Brazil
Ruby	Red	Brazil, Burma, Sri Lanka, Thailand, India, Australia
Sapphire	Blue	Brazil, Burma, Sri Lanka, Thailand, India, Australia, U.S.
Alexandrite (also known as Cat's Eye when brownish color)	Green and yellow shades	Brazil, C.I.S., Zimbabwe, Sri Lanka
Topaz	Colorless or pale blue, pale yellow, greenish, rarely pink	Australia, Brazil, C.I.S., Sri Lanka, Namibia
Spinel	Variable: commonly red	Burma, Sri Lanka, India, Thailand
Emerald	Green	C.I.S., U.S., Austria, Norway, Columbia, Zambia
Aquamarine	Pale blue-green	Brazil, C.I.S., Ireland
Zircon	Variable: light to reddish-brown common	Widely distributed
Tourmaline	Black, bluish-black; also reds and greens	Brazil, Sri Lanka, U.S., C.I.S.
Garnet	Varies greatly	Widely distributed

Starting a Rock Collection

What You Need to Get Started

This equipment can be purchased from a hardware store or a mineral dealer:

rock hammer—hammer with a pointed head on one side and a square head on the other, for loosening rocks from deposits and pounding them into small samples

chisel—also helps to remove rocks from deposits

magnifying glass—lets you view rock closely to choose best specimens

streak plate (piece of unglazed porcelain)—aids in recognizing minerals by their streak colors (colors obtained by rubbing a mineral across a hard, coarse substance)

pocketknife—to test mineral hardness

something to carry rocks in—a backpack works well

newspaper or tissue to wrap specimens in

some reference books with color pictures of rocks, or a reference collection of rocks—for identification of specimens

Showing Off Your Rocks

Most rock collectors like to show off their collections. Museums often have huge samples, but for home collections, rocks only a few inches in size are most practical. To display them, you need the following supplies:

bottle of white indelible ink
labels
blank record book
shallow, divided cardboard trays (homemade or purchased from a mineral dealer)

Here's how to proceed:
1. Use the hammer to trim the specimens to your desired size.
2. Clean specimens with soap and water and a brush if necessary. (Don't wash a specimen that contains rock salt; it will dissolve.)
3. Use the white ink to mark each specimen with a number.
4. Place a rock in one division of the tray. Write a label with the number of the rock and a brief description.
5. Write more detailed information, including where and when you found the rock, in the record book. Again, use the number of the rock for identification.

Best-Known Rock Collections in the United States

American Museum of Natural History, New York City
California Academy of Sciences, San Francisco
Field Museum of Natural History, Chicago
Cranbrook Institute of Science, Bloomfield Hills, Michigan
Harvard University Museum, Cambridge, Massachusetts
National Museum of Natural History, Washington, D.C.

What's Your Birthstone?

Month	Birthstone
January	garnet
February	amethyst
March	aquamarine or bloodstone
April	diamond
May	emerald
June	pearl, alexandrite, or moonstone
July	ruby
August	sardonyx or peridot
September	sapphire
October	opal or tourmaline
November	topaz
December	turquoise or lapis lazuli

WEATHER AND CLIMATE

Weather is the activity in the earth's atmosphere each day, and climate is the weather over a long period.

People like to know the weather each day because it helps them plan. Will they need to dress extra warmly because the weather today is especially cold? Will they need an umbrella tomorrow because the weather is going to be rainy?

Climate, or long-term weather, is equally important. It has the potential to affect our lives even more drastically than weather does. If a region does not receive enough rainfall, it may suffer from drought, or lack of rain. Crops and livestock may die, and if the drought is severe, as several recent African droughts have been, people suffer and sometimes also lose their lives.

The world is divided into several different climatic regions:

Regions	Climate
tropical forest	continually hot; heavy rainfall throughout year
savanna	hot summers, warm winters; wet in summer
tropical steppe	continually hot; little rainfall
continental steppe	warm summers, cold winters; little precipitation
tropical desert	continually hot; little rainfall
continental desert	hot summers, cold winters; little precipitation
subtropical	hot summers, mild winters; moderate precipitation
temperate	warm summers, cool winters; moderate precipitation
subarctic	short, cool summers, long, cold winters; little precipitation
tundra	short, cold summers, long, very cold winters; little precipitation
highland	cooler than surrounding areas
icecap	continually cold; little precipitation

Weather and climate are determined by the winds, temperature, and humidity (the amount of water in the air). Winds are the most important weather force, though, because they affect temperature and humidity.

The general circulation of the air in the earth's atmosphere creates a large, complicated pattern of wind movement. In addition, local wind patterns create local weather patterns.

Meteorologists, people who study the weather, divide the earth into several weather/climate zones, based on the kind of winds that dominate the region. The equatorial zone, which surrounds the equator, is dominated by trade winds, warm winds that move from north to south around the planet. Above the equatorial weather zones are two middle zones with temperate, or mild, winds, both warm and cool, depending on the season and the weather. Above the temperate zones are the polar zones, where the winds produce weather that is harsh and cold.

The winds control temperature, too. Warm winds heat the air, raising the temperature, and cool winds cool the air, causing the temperature to drop.

The winds also cause precipitation. Warm air collects moisture as it crosses large bodies of water. The moisture then cools as it reaches land. If there is enough moisture, it will form into drops of water. Depending on the temperature and how quickly the moisture was cooled when it reached land, this water, or precipitation, takes one of several forms: rain, snow, sleet, or hail.

People have not yet learned to control the weather, but they have learned how to predict it with some accuracy.

Water, Water, Everywhere: Kinds of Precipitation

Rain Liquid waterdrops.
Hail Large, round balls of ice. These are caused when moisture travels through hot and cold layers of air and snowflakes

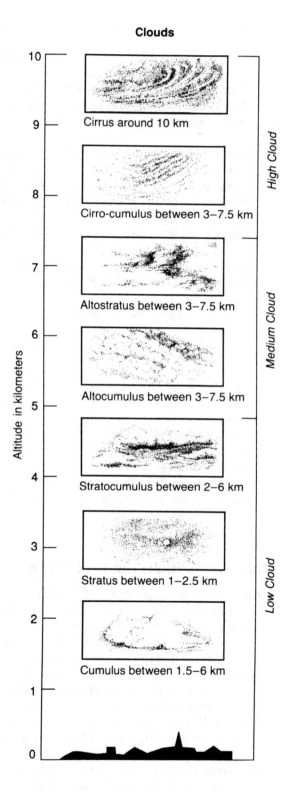

Clouds

Cirrus around 10 km

Cirro-cumulus between 3–7.5 km

High Cloud

Altostratus between 3–7.5 km

Altocumulus between 3–7.5 km

Medium Cloud

Stratocumulus between 2–6 km

Stratus between 1–2.5 km

Cumulus between 1.5–6 km

Low Cloud

Altitude in kilometers

Weather Records

Hottest temperature ever recorded Al'Aziziyah, Libya, 136.4°F, September 13, 1922.

Lowest temperature ever recorded Vostok, Antarctica, −128.6°F, July 21, 1983.

Most sunshine yearly Yuma, Arizona, is sunny 90 percent of the time, or more than 4,000 hours a year.

Least sunshine yearly The South Pole receives no sunshine for 190 days a year.

Most rainfall Forty-six inches of rain fell on July 14–15, 1911 in Baquio, Luzon, in the Philippines.

Biggest wind ever recorded Mt. Washington, New Hampshire, 231 miles per hour, April 12, 1934.

World's hottest place Dallol, Ethiopia, recorded an annual mean temperature of 94°F over a 6-year period between mid-1960 and mid-1966.

World's coldest place Polus Nedostupnosti, Pole of Inaccessibility, Antarctica, has an average annual temperature of −72°F.

World's rainiest place Mt. Wai'ale'ale, Kauai, Hawaii, endures 350 rainy days in an average year.

World's driest place The Desierto de Atacama, Chile, has no recordable rainfall in an average year.

World's biggest hailstones On April 14, 1986, 2¼-pound hailstones killed 92 people in Bangladesh.

combine with raindrops to form iceballs. Hail can range from ¼ inch to 4 inches in width.

Sleet Freezing raindrops. As these tiny raindrops hit the ground, they freeze into ice drops.

Snow Ice crystals or flakes. These are produced when the temperature is cold enough to freeze raindrops.

Many Winds Blow: Kinds of Winds

Chinook Warm, dry burst of air found on mountainsides. These winds bring warm temperatures and sometimes melt snow. They occur in the Alps and in the Rocky Mountains and are also called foehns.

Harmattan Dusty wind that blows from the Sahara across western Africa. It occurs during the cool, winter months.

Mistral Very dry, strong, cold wind that starts in the Alps and blows through southern France during the winter.

Monsoon Changing wind that starts over the sea and blows through countries north of the Indian Ocean. The wind is caused by the difference in temperature between the sea and the land. From April to October, monsoons are wet and bring heavy rain. From November to March, they bring cool, dry air.

Norther A cold, north, winter wind that causes sudden drops in temperature. It blows through the southwestern and south-central United States.

Simoom Saharan wind that begins when the sand and the air become very hot and dry. Simooms create the huge sand dunes seen in the Sahara.

Sirocco Warm wind that blows along the north side of the Mediterranean Sea. Like monsoons, sirocco winds can be either wet or dry.

Beaufort Scale of Winds

Winds are also measured in terms of their strength, ranging from Force 1 to Force 12. This scale was devised by Francis Beaufort (1774–1857). In 1955, the U.S. Weather Service added Forces 13 through 17, but these are not used internationally.

Force No.	Description	Miles per Hour/ Kilometers
0	calm	0–1/0–1
1	light air	1–3/1–5
2	light breeze	4–7/6–11
3	gentle breeze	8–12/12–19
4	moderate breeze	13–18/20–29
5	fresh breeze	19–24/30–39
6	strong breeze	25–31/40–50
7	near gale	32–38/51–61
8	gale	39–46/62–74
9	strong gale	47–54/75–87
10	storm	55–63/88–101
11	violent storm	64–73/102–117
12	hurricane	74+/119+

The Earth in Crisis

After many years of misuse, the earth is becoming damaged. People will have to change the way they live to help preserve it. Scientists are aware of several environmental crises occurring right now.

Greenhouse Effect

Some scientists believe the earth is growing warmer. They have named one of the causes of this the "greenhouse effect." A warmer world could be dangerous if the warmer temperatures caused the polar icecaps to melt. This water would flood such low-lying cities as New York, London, and Sydney.

Warmer temperatures have been caused by the increase of the gases carbon dioxide and methane in the atmosphere. Carbon dioxide comes from burning fuels such as coal, oil, and wood. Methane comes from the decay of plants and animals and is produced by swamps, farms, and large garbage dumps.

Ozone Hole

Ozone, a bluish gas that protects us from the sun's harmful rays, is decreasing in the earth's atmosphere. Each spring a hole has appeared over the Antarctic. In 1992, scientists announced that the hole had spread to the North American continent. The ozone hole may increase the number of people who will get skin cancer.

Acid Rain

Two gases—sulfur oxide and nitrogen oxide—are responsible for acid rain, which kills plants and changes the content of the soil. The gases are released by cars, factories, and electric power stations. When the gases mix with raindrops, they create an acid that is harmful to forests.

TRAILBLAZERS: GREAT EXPLORERS OF THE WORLD AND WHAT THEY FOUND

People have always been curious about their world. The first known explorers were the ancient Babylonians and Egyptians, whose travels took place more than four thousand years ago. Since then, humans have explored virtually the entire planet.

The first great age of exploration occurred during the Middle Ages, when westerners traveled east—and found the grandeur and riches of Asia. The culmination was the great age of European exploration, beginning in the 1400s, when voyagers traveled to North and South America, Africa, and India. At the same time, Europeans were also venturing into Australia, with its large central desert. By the early 1800s, people turned their attention to the polar continents, which proved to be both treacherous and uninhabitable.

We are now in another great age of exploration—beyond Earth and into space.

Trailblazers of the World

FAMOUS ANCIENT EXPLORERS

Name	Nationality	Years of Journeys	Area Explored
Leif Eriksson	Norwegian	c. 1000	Probably first European to reach North America
Marco Polo	Italian	1271–1295	Far East and India
Ibn Batuta	Arabian	1325–1354	China, Middle East, India

AGE OF EUROPEAN DISCOVERY

Vasco Núñez de Balboa	Spanish	1528–1536	Isthmus of Panama; first European to see Pacific Ocean from American side
Christopher Columbus	Italian	1492–1504	West Indies and Caribbean
Francisco de Coronado	Spanish	1540–1542	American Southwest
Vasco da Gama	Portuguese	1498	Reached India by sea
Bartholomeu Dias	Portuguese	1487–1488	First European to sail around Cape Hope
Sir Francis Drake	English	1577–1580	Sailed around the world
Ferdinand Magellan	Portuguese	1519–1521	First major worldwide voyage
Francisco de Orellana	Spanish	1541	Amazon River
Amerigo Vespucci	Italian	1499–1504	South America

EXPLORING NORTH AMERICA

Samuel de Champlain	French	1603–1616	North America and the St. Lawrence River
William Clark and Meriwether Lewis	U.S.	1804–1806	Rocky Mountains to Pacific

Name	Nationality	Years of Journeys	Area Explored
John Charles Fremont	U.S.	1680	American West
Sir Alexander MacKenzie	Canadian	1789–1793	Western Canada

EXPLORING AFRICA

Sir Richard Burton	English	1853–1858	Africa and Arabia
Mungo Park	Scottish	1795–1797	Niger River (Africa)

EXPLORING AUSTRALIA AND THE PACIFIC

Robert O'Hara Burke and William John Wills	Burke, Irish; Wills, English	1860–1861	Crossed Australia north to south
James Cook	English	1768–1779	South Pacific

POLAR EXPLORATION

Roald Amundsen	Norwegian	1911–1926	First to reach South Pole over land
Vitus Bering	Danish	1727–1729	Proved separation between Asia and North America
Robert Scott	English	1910–1912	Reached South Pole
Richard Byrd	American	1926, 1929	Flew over both poles
Robert Peary	American	1909	First to reach North Pole
Sir Ernest Shackleton	Irish	1907–1916	Antarctica

Your World or Mine: Earth Through Different Eyes

Ancient Babylonians They believed the earth was a hollow mountain supported and surrounded by the oceans. Inside the mountain was the world of the dead.

Egyptians They saw the earth as a resting god and the heavens as gods bending over the earth. Bet, the god of the atmosphere, held up the skies. They believed a sun god sailed through the heavens each day, causing sunrise, sunset, and sunshine in between.

Hindus Hindus, in India, believed the earth was held up by elephants, which caused earthquakes when they moved. The elephants stood on a turtle representing the god Vishnu, which stood on a cobra, the symbol of water.

Early Christians They believed the earth was composed of three continents. Jerusalem was at the center, and the Garden of Eden was located in Asia.

Early Europeans They believed the earth was flat and that one could sail off its edges if one roamed too far from home.

48 Places to See Earth's Natural Wonders

In the United States, a vast array of natural wonders can be explored in our 48 national parks.

Acadia National Park, Minnesota
Arches National Park, Utah
Badlands National Park, South Dakota
Big Bend National Park, Texas
Biscayne National Park, Florida
Bryce Canyon National Park, Utah
Canyonlands National Park, Utah
Capitol Reed National Park, Utah
Carlsbad Caverns National Park, New Mexico
Channel Islands National Park, California
Crater Lake National Park, Oregon
Denali National Park, Alaska
Everglades National Park, Florida
Gates of the Arctic National Park, Alaska
Glacier Bay National Park, Alaska
Glacier National Park, Montana
Grand Canyon National Park, Arizona
Grand Teton National Park, Wyoming
Great Basin National Park, Nevada
Great Smokey Mountains National Park, North Carolina and Tennessee
Guadalupe Mountains National Park, Texas
Haleakala National Park, Hawaii
Hawaii Volcanoes National Park, Hawaii
Hot Springs National Park, Arkansas
Isle Royale National Park, Michigan

Katmai National Park, Alaska
Kenai Fjords National Park, Alaska
Kobuk Valley National Park, Alaska
Lake Clark National Park, Alaska
Lassen Volcanic National Park, California
Mammoth Cave National Park, Kentucky
Mesa Verde National Park, Colorado
Mount Rainier National Park, Washington
North Cascades National Park, Washington
Olympic National Park, Washington
Petrified Forest National Park, Arizona
Redwood National Park, California
Rocky Mountain National Park, Colorado
Sequoia and Kinds Canyon National Parks, California
Shenandoah National Park, Virginia
Theodore Roosevelt National Park, North Dakota
Virgin Islands National Park, Virgin Islands
Voyageurs National Park, Minnesota
Wind Cave National Park, South Dakota
Wrangell-St. Elias National Park, Alaska
Yellowstone National Park, Wyoming, Montana, and Idaho
Yosemite National Park, California
Zion National Park, Utah

EARTH'S GUIDEBOOKS: FINDING YOUR WAY WITH MAPS

Maps are guides to Earth—or any other heavenly body, for that matter. Most maps are flat, although some have raised areas to show where hills and mountains are located. A globe is a "round map" that shows the shape of the world.

Maps are useful to travelers. They sometimes provide information about weather and climate, and they locate geographic features, such as oceans and mountains, or man-made features, such as the boundaries of countries.

Basic Kinds of Maps

Mobility maps Show roads and other paths of travel. Map A is a road map.
Thematic maps Show information about our world. Thematic maps can also show people's incomes, the population in var-

ious areas, how people vote, or other information.

Inventory maps Show the locations of specific features of a place. Inventory maps

represent different geographic features such as forestlands and urban areas.

Combined reference maps Show one or more political and geographic features.

INFORMATION, PLEASE

Asimov, Isaac. *ABCs of the Earth*. Walker, 1971.

Cosgrove, Brian. *Weather*. Knopf, 1991.

Parker, Steve. *Pond & River*. Knopf, 1988.

———. *Seashore*. Knopf, 1989.

Pough, Frederick H. *A Field Guide to Rocks and Minerals*. 4th ed. Houghton Mifflin, 1976.

Stangl, Jean. *Crystals and Crystal Gardens You Can Grow*. Franklin Watts, 1990.

Thackeray, John. *The Earth and Its Wonders*. Larousse, 1980.

3

THE ANIMAL WORLD

Human beings are members of the animal kingdom. And so are whales, lizards, lions, and hawks. Animals are classified into groups called classes. We belong to the class called mammals, the same class as dolphins, cats, elephants, gorillas, and many others. (Mammals are animals that nurse their young on milk.)

The smallest animal on earth is so tiny it can live inside a blood cell. The largest animal is one-third the size of a football field. The variety of animals, large and small, is almost endless. The one thing we share in common is that we're all connected. What people do to the environment affects animals and, in turn, we depend on animals for our own survival.

Creatures invisible without a microscope are so small that it's hard to tell whether they are animals or plants. With larger animals, you can see the difference in two ways. First, a living thing that moves independently is likely to be an animal. Second, if it eats—takes in and digests food—it is probably an animal.

On the planet we all inhabit, different types of animals live in different ways and in different places. Some animals burrow into the ground; some fly through the skies. Some like it cold; some like it hot. Different ani-

mals do things differently. Some eat tree bark, while others feast on each other. But all animals try to survive and to reproduce.

HABITATS: WHERE ANIMALS LIVE

Animals live everywhere on land and in the sea. They live in all climates, side by side with other animals. They have characteristics that enable them to survive in their environment—a polar bear's fur coat, for example. Some species have stayed in one place for thousands of years. Over time, they have developed bodies and ways of life well suited to that environment.

Animals live in six basic types of environments, or habitats: deserts, forests, grasslands (or prairies), mountains, polar regions, and oceans.

Animals of the Desert

Deserts are hot and dry, with few trees. Most animals that live there have small bodies, which makes it easier to find shade from the scorching sun in a place where the plants are small, too.

- Some desert animals dig into the sand to escape the daytime sun. Others find

Fish Alert!

The United States Government is concerned that many species of fish are being caught faster than they can replace themselves. The following list shows some of these endangered fish:

Northeast

Atlantic cod	Hard clams
Atlantic halibut	Large coastal sharks
Atlantic menhaden	Lobster
Atlantic salmon	Pollock
Flounder	Redfish
Haddock	Sea scallops

Southeast

Atlantic swordfish	King mackerel
Bluefin tuna	Red drum
Caribbean reef fish	Red snapper
Grouper	Spiny lobsters

Pacific

Abalone	Pacific striped bass
Albacore tuna	Perch
Blue marlin	Rockfish
	Salmon; all except Alaskan

shade under rocks or brush. Some reptiles—such as snakes, lizards, and tortoises—enjoy the high temperatures, but even they go for cover when it's hottest.

- Deserts can be very cool after sunset. That's the time when desert animals search for food. They also come out during and after the infrequent rains. Some desert insects experience their entire lifetime during and immediately after a desert storm. In that brief span of time, they come to life, reproduce, and die in the returning sun.
- Most desert animals don't need much water. Some have the ability to store it in their bodies. Most can live without water for several days. That's why the camel has been used for travel in the desert: It doesn't have to drink for many days.
- Other large desert animals include the mule deer, coyote, bobcat, and kit fox. The rabbit, gila monster, mouse, kangaroo rat, cactus wren, and bat are among the small desert animals.

Animals of the Forests

Very different animals live in forests, depending on the climate. There are two basic kinds of forest, temperate and tropical.

Temperate forests are neither very hot nor very cold. They are found primarily in North America, Asia, and Europe.

- Most of the animals depend in some way on the ponds, lakes, and streams.

Animal S.O.S.: Some Endangered Species

Animal species have become extinct throughout the history of the earth. But over the past 300 years, the speed of extinction has quickened. The cause of this speedup is human activity. Hunters have legally overhunted some animals, such as many species of pheasants. Other animals have been hunted illegally, including African elephants. Commercial fishing has endangered still other species, such as certain dolphins. Garbage, chemical wastes, and pesticides have killed some species of pelicans. The destruction of their habitat has been a major source of animal extinction.

A species is said to be endangered when more animals die than are replaced through reproduction. The following lists describe some currently endangered species.

Common name

Animals	*Range*	*Survival problems*
American crocodile	Mexico, Florida, Central and South America, Caribbean islands	Habitat destroyed; overhunted for its hide
Asiatic lion	India	Habitat destroyed; overhunted for sport
Black-footed ferret	Seen only in captivity	Poisoning of prairie dogs, its main prey
Black rhinoceros	South of Sahara (Africa)	Habitat destroyed; overhunted for horn
Blue whale	Every ocean	Overhunted for blubber, food, and oil
Brown pelican	California, North Carolina to Texas, West Indies, coastal Central and South America	Food supply contaminated with pesticides
California condor	Seen only in captivity	Habitat destroyed; hunted for sport; eggs overcollected for food
Imperial parrot	Dominica, West Indies	Habitat destroyed; illegal capture for pets
Ivory-billed woodpecker	Cuba, South-central and Southeastern United States	Habitat destroyed; overcollected for museums
Orangutan	Sumatra, Borneo	Habitat destroyed; overcollection of young for zoos
Red wolf	Southeastern United States to central Texas	Habitat destroyed; hunted, trapped, and poisoned by people who saw it as a pest
Snow leopard	Central Asia	Overhunted for fur
Tiger	Temperate and tropical Asia	Habitat destroyed; overhunted for sport

- The large animals found there include bear, deer, and moose, but most of the animals have small bodies so they can move easily through the underbrush. Small creatures include the raccoon, squirrel, chipmunk, skunk, porcupine, and opossum.
- Some animals live both on land and in the water. These include the beaver, turtle, frog, otter, muskrat, and salamander.
- Many birds, such as the owl, hawk, and wild turkey, nest in temperate forests. Insects and worms live in the rich soil and among the plants, providing food for the birds.

Extinct Animals

Certain animals have already lost the fight for survival. The following is a list of some animals no longer seen on Earth. The number next to the name of an animal tells how many species of that animal are extinct.

Birds

- Duck (2)
- Finch (5)
- Macaw (4)
- Ostrich, Arabian
- Owl (10)
- Parakeet (8)

Mammals

- Arizona jaguar
- Bali tiger
- Bear (3)
- Greenland tundra reindeer
- Lion (2)
- Rat (12)

Fish

- Minnow (2)
- Thicktail chub

Reptiles

- Gecko (2)
- Iguana (2)
- Lizard
- Tortoise (11)
- Tree snake (2)

Amphibians

- Palestine painted frog
- Vegas Valley leopard frog

Tropical forests are found primarily in South America and Africa. Lightly wooded areas in some tropical forests have only moderate rainfall. Other tropical forests are dense with trees and foliage, and the rainfall is heavy. These are called tropical rain forests.

- In tropical forests, the tigers, leopards, anteaters, and other resident animals have had to adjust to a climate that stays hot all year long.
- In tropical rain forests, vines and the treetops form a thick canopy overhead, where monkeys, sloths, and other climbing animals live. Apes, such as gibbons and orangutans, swing from the trees.
- Exotic birds, such as brightly colored parrots, nest there. The birds feed mostly on ants and other insects.
- The environment in tropical rain forests is so lush with food and foliage that some snakes and spiders grow bigger there than their relatives in the temperate forests. Boa constrictors and tarantulas can be of gigantic size.

Animals of the Grasslands and Prairies

Grasslands and prairies are vast stretches of open country.

- Most of the world's largest animals, including the elephant and the hippopotamus, live on the grasslands.
- Some of the fastest runners—the zebra, ostrich, blackbuck, and pronghorn among them—live there, too.
- Africa has more grassland animals than any other continent. The lion hunts in Africa, and the giraffe feeds off the tops of trees there.
- Only Australia's grasslands have kangaroo.

- Smaller grassland animals include the vulture, the secretary bird, and the aardvark.
- Among the many small animals that dig tunnels for homes is the prairie dog of North America.

Animals of the Mountains

Animals live on every mountain level. On the peaks of snow-covered mountains, insects and spiders may be found. Below the snowy peaks, sure-footed goats and sheep roam the rocky cliffs and crags. Many birds also build their nests at this level. On nearly every mountain level there are grassy slopes and plateaus or valleys covered with forests. Here grazing animals such as yaks and vicuñas live. Many mountain animals travel between levels searching for food as the seasons change.

Animals of the Polar Regions

Polar regions have ice and snow year-round.

- Few land animals but lots of fish live in polar regions.
- Most animals depend on the fish for food. In the far North, polar bears living on arctic ice floes eat fish. Southern polar seas provide food for penguins and other antarctic birds.
- Many animals of the polar regions live in the arctic tundra. Caribou and musk ox graze over these swampy plains of northern Asia, Canada, and Europe.
- Grizzly bears, foxes, lemmings, and ermines live in the arctic also.
- Arctic birds are the loon, sandhill crane, snowy owl, and rock ptarmigan.

Animals of the Ocean and Seashore

Seawater covers 70 percent of the surface of the earth, and animals live at every depth.

- Whales, the biggest animals in the world, live in vast oceans. The food of most whales—a mass of organisms called plankton—is made up of tiny animals that drift with the ocean currents and tides. However, most sea animals are active swimmers, like fish.
- Most of the fish in the sea stay near the landmasses of the continents, but some, like flying fish, swim in the open seas. Brightly colored fish live close to tropical reefs.
- Some sea animals with shells, such as marine clams and sea urchins, live on the ocean floor. Others, such as abalone and crab, live mainly under rocks near the shoreline.
- Small sea animals are often the food of the larger sharks, sting rays, and octopuses.

HOW ANIMALS REPRODUCE

All types of animals create more of their own kind. They reproduce in two main ways: asexual reproduction and sexual reproduction.

Asexual Reproduction

Only one parent creates the offspring in asexual reproduction. In the process called fragmentation, the animal breaks its body into two or more pieces. The flatworm reproduces in this way, usually dividing into two halves. Then each half grows the body parts it is missing and becomes a new flatworm.

Another asexual process is budding, whereby an animal puts out bud extensions from its own body. When a bud forms its own feeding organs, it can break off from the parent and become a new individual. Hydras and corals create more of their own kind by budding.

In addition, some animals are able to reproduce by regeneration. New individuals form from parts of their bodies that have broken off. Lost parts of certain animal bodies

---

The Smallest Mammals

- The pygmy shrew, which lives in Africa and Europe, is the smallest land animal. It is 1½ inches (3.8 centimeters) long and weighs as much as a Ping-Pong ball.
- The bumblebee bat is the smallest flying mammal. When its wings are spread, this bat is about the size of a big butterfly.
- The chihuahua is the smallest breed of dog.
- The smallest sea mammal is the Commerson's dolphin. An adult weighs between 55 and 77 pounds (25 to 35 kilograms).

The Biggest Mammals

- The blue whale is the biggest mammal that ever lived. One female caught in 1922 in the Atlantic Ocean was more than 110 feet (33 meters) long. Blue whales are also the heaviest mammals. One can weigh as much as 2,000 men combined. Baby blue whales are the largest mammal babies. At birth a calf can be more than 25 feet (7 meters) long and weigh over 2 tons.
- The African elephant is the biggest land mammal. An adult bull is about 10½ feet tall and weighs over 6 tons.
- The capybara, found in South America, is the biggest rodent. It can weigh as much as 250 pounds (113 kilograms) and is about the size of a sheep.

---

can also be replaced by regeneration. For example, crabs and lobsters can grow new claws. A salamander that loses a leg can grow a new one.

Other animals that reproduce asexually include

sponges
jellyfish
sea squirts

Sexual Reproduction

Most animals that reproduce sexually must pair up with a mate to do so. These animals have special cells that combine to produce their young. The female sex cells are called eggs. The male sex cells are called sperm.

When eggs and sperm unite, the process is called fertilization.

Many animals reproduce sexually. They include

humans
fireflies
whales
pelicans

Some animals, such as birds, lay eggs, from which their young hatch after a period of time. Other animals, called mammals, give birth from the womb of the female and nurse their young on milk. The period during which the offspring grow in the womb is called gestation. The average gestation period for human beings is nine months.

Animal Life Spans

Some animals live to a very old age, while others have only a short life span. Below are the average life spans of some animals.

Human being	60–80 years	Giraffe	15–25 years
Asian elephant	70–75 years	Gray kangaroo	15–29 years
Killer whale	50–79 years	Dog (domestic)	12–20 years
Rhinoceros	20–50 years	Cat (domestic)	12–28 years
Arabian camel	25–40 years	Rabbit (domestic)	5–13 years
Chimpanzee	30–40 years	Rat	4 years
Bottle-nosed dolphin	25–40 years	Mole	3–4 years
Zebra	20–30 years	Long-haired shrew	12–18 months

Mammals and Their Babies

Animal	Average gestation	Typical number of young
Asian elephant	20 months	1
Giraffe	15 months	1
Blue whale	11 months	1
Human being	9 months	1
Chimpanzee	8 months	1
Dog	2 months	3–6
House mouse	19 days	4–32
American opossum	13 days	10

NEWBORN ANIMALS

Some baby animals can care for themselves as soon as they are born. Other animals rely on their parents to feed and protect them until they can care for themselves.

Many water animals get along by themselves from birth. They include most types of

starfish
mollusks
sea urchins
salmon
sea turtles
frogs and toads
insects

Kangaroos and opossums care for their young by keeping them in a pouch on the mother's body after they are born. Other animals that take care of their offspring include

sea horses
ants
bees
wolves
deer
monkeys

Animal parents train their offspring, too. Some teach them how to hunt, to find food, to recognize danger and run away, and to keep warm. They communicate with them through sounds and other signals.

WHAT ANIMALS EAT

All animals need food to survive. The types of food are as various as the types of animals.

- Some animals eat many different kinds of food. Others stick to just one kind.
- Some animals, such as lions, hunt other animals for their meat. Other animals eat nothing but plants. Koala bears, for example, eat the leaves of certain kinds of trees.
- Many underwater animals capture smaller animals for food by a process called filter feeding. They make currents of water that bring them victims. Clams, oysters, and certain kinds of worms are filter feeders.

- The one-celled amoeba can change its shape. It eats simply by surrounding smaller animals and digesting them.

HOW ANIMALS MOVE

All animals move at one time or another. They do so in many different ways, depending on what their bodies are like and where they live. People live on land, so they walk and run primarily. Birds spend most of the time in the air, so they fly. Fish live in the water, so they swim. What do the rest of the animals do to move? It depends mostly on the element in which they live:

On Land	In the Air	In the Water
walk	fly	swim
run	glide	row
jump	soar	ride
climb		jet propel
creep		
crawl		
wriggle		
swing		

Animal Baby Names

Animals are known by special names when they are young. Here are some of them:

bunny: rabbit
calf: cattle, elephant, antelope, rhino, hippo, whale
chick, chicken: fowl
cockerel: rooster
colt: horse (male)
cub: lion, bear, shark, fox
cygnet: swan
duckling: duck
eaglet: eagle
fawn: deer
filly: horse (female)
flapper: wild fowl
fledgling: bird
foal: horse, zebra
fry: fish

gosling: goose
heifer: cow
joey: kangaroo
kid: goat
kit: fox, beaver, rabbit
kitten, kitty: cat
lamb: sheep
nestling: bird
owlet: owl
piglet: pig
pullet: hen
pup: dog, seal, sea lion, fox
puss, pussy: cat
squab: pigeon
tadpole: frog

- Most animals use a combination of several of these ways to get from place to place. Monkeys, for example, are land animals that walk and run. But they do much of their traveling by swinging from tree to tree.
- Some animals divide their time between two or more elements. Animals that live both in water and on land (amphibians) move in different ways in each element. Frogs, for example, jump on land but swim in water. Most birds live at least in two elements. But some birds, like geese, live part of their lives in all three—on the water, in the air, and on land.
- Animals that divide their time between two or more elements move better in some than others. Ducks fly and swim very well. But they walk . . . well, like a duck.
- Each element—land, water, or air—presents its own set of challenges. In motion, animals may shine in one element and just get by in another.

Land Animals

Most mammals (animals that suckle their young on milk) live on land, with some exceptions. (The whale is a mammal and it lives in water.) How do animals move on land? They use their legs, feet, hands, paws, and claws. Legs are very important for most land animals. Legs lift the body's weight against gravity and move the body above the ground.

- Most land animals do some form of walking, running, or jumping to get from place to place. Whether small or large, they have clever ways of moving. Some combine climbing, digging, pulling, and even eating to make their way. Even some big animals, such as bears, can climb. Monkeys use their hands and tails to climb, jump, and swing from tree to tree.

- Animals that live in the ground work harder but move more slowly. Moles dig their way along. Earthworms dig and pull their way through loose soil, but they have to eat through hard ground.
- For animals of the air, wings are the key to flying, but no creature can stay in the air all the time. That is why a flying animal needs legs as well as wings—so when it lands it can walk about on the ground.
- Some animals without wings can move short distances in the air—some squirrels, fish, frogs, and lizards. But they are gliding, not really flying. A lizard that lives in Asia and the East Indies is called the flying dragon. It can spread out folds of its skin to act like wings, which it uses to glide through the air from tree to tree.

How Do Animals Walk?

This is how four-legged animals walk on land:

Three feet (or hooves or paws) must be on the ground in order to walk without falling.

The center of the body weight must be over the three feet before the fourth is lifted off the ground.

One leg swings after the other in a certain order.

Stopping How do animals keep from falling down? Dogs, elephants, and salamanders are all four-legged creatures. They need to walk but they need to stop, too. How do animals stop without losing their balance? In walking, if the left front leg moves first, the right rear leg swings into position next. Then the right front leg steps, followed by the right rear leg. This balancing of left and right sides means that any four-footed animal can stop suddenly without falling down.

Funny walking When is walking more like wriggling? For salamanders. Their legs are at their sides, not underneath their bodies. Unable to stand on their legs, they can't walk on them either. On land they move their bodies and tails from side to side, the way they do in water. They almost "swim" on land: Their legs catch on the ground as they wriggle, moving the salamander along.

How Do Animals Run Fast?

The strong legs of most mammals give them support and a method of travel. Long, strong legs under a relatively lean, small body make for speed. That's why a horse can run as fast as fox or a rabbit, but an elephant can't. This is how a four-footed animal runs:

It lifts each foot just before putting down the one ahead of it.

Only two feet are on the ground at the same time, but two feet cannot support the body weight for long. Because running is so fast, the other two legs take the weight before the animal loses its balance and falls.

Each complete running movement is called a stride. The running speed of an animal depends on the length and rate of its stride. With its long legs, a giraffe has a long stride, but its legs move slowly. A mouse's legs move quickly, but they are short. A horse has the right leg combination for running: long, fast-moving legs.

Speed demons Who's the fastest runner of all? In general, the fastest animals are those with the longest legs in relation to their body size. Antelope, deer, horses, zebras, and ostriches—at more than 50 miles per hour—can outdistance almost anything. But the cheetah is the fastest runner of all over short distances.

Relative speed Who is faster—a mouse or a spider? To go faster, a few pairs of longer legs are usually better than lots of short legs. Spiders, with four pairs of legs, move across the floor faster than centipedes, with 15 pairs of legs. But more speedy than a spider is a mouse, with its two pairs of legs.

Balancing Who has the best balance? The longer the legs in relation to the body, the faster the animal. But the longer and fewer the legs, the better the body must be balanced. Insects probably have the best balance. With six legs in all, they use three legs to steady the body while moving with the other three. A pair of claws end each leg, and sometimes a sticky pad, too. All this makes for ease of walking upside down on ceilings without falling on their heads. But for speed, other leg arrangements work better.

Flying Animals

Only animals with wings can truly fly. These include

bats
most birds
many insects

- Bats are the only mammals with wings, and the only mammals that fly. Long ago, flying reptiles, such as pterodactyls, were among the animals of the air. But they died out with the dinosaurs.
- Each group of flying animals has its own type of wing. The wings of bats, birds, and flying reptiles all have bones. The wings of insects are different. Like their bodies, their wings have no bones. Veins make an insect's wing strong. These veins are really air tubes with sturdy walls.
- Insects take off from the ground much more easily than birds. Because they are very small and light, it takes less lift to make them airborne. Some insects can hover like a hummingbird.

Bat Facts

- Bats are the only mammals that fly.
- There are more than 900 species.
- Bats live everywhere except very cold places.
- Bats hear better than any other land mammal.
- Bats live between 10 and 20 years.
- Vampires are the most dangerous bats because they spread rabies and other diseases. Legends used to be spread that vampires were really evil people who could transform themselves into bats and then suck other people's blood. People believed that wearing a garlic necklace or showing a crucifix scared vampires away.
- Bats hunt at night and sleep during the day.
- During the winter many species hibernate in caves, hanging upside down from their cave's ceiling.

Insect Facts

- There are about 1 million kinds of animals. Over 800,000 of these species are insects.
- Insects live everywhere, but only a few can be found in oceans.
- Insects may be annoying, but they also help us. They pollinate crops, provide us with honey, and are a food source for birds, fish, and other animals.
- Insects have lived on Earth for at least 400 million years.
- The life span of insects ranges from a few days or hours to 50 years for a queen termite. But most insects die within a year.
- Most insects are tiny, measuring less than $1/4$ inch (6.4 millimeters) in length. But some insects are much larger, like the Goliath beetle, which is more than 4 inches (10 centimeters) in length.
- Insects have a dazzling range of colors.
- Insects have a huge variety of special structures and shapes, which help them survive in their natural environment. Some insects look like dry leaves, while others look like thorns.

How Do Birds Fly?

Birds fly by beating their wings against the air.

Moving the air upward and downward, wings lift the body against the pull of gravity.

The faster the wings beat, the higher a bird can fly.

Wings drive the body forward through the air, too.

Getting ready

How do birds get ready for takeoff? By flapping their wings. It's the air rushing over the wings that creates the lift they need to take off. Then they get up air speed by continuing to flap. The smaller the bird, the faster its wings can flap, and the more lift it gets. Taking off from the ground is easier for a small, light creature, like an insect, than for a bird.

The great blue heron is four feet long. It can flap its wings only two times a second.

- One of the heaviest birds that can fly is the male trumpeter swan. It weighs 38 pounds and must run at least 100 feet to gather enough speed to take off. Flamingos, which are heavy birds, need a long runway, too.
- Smaller birds, like sparrows, jump into the air and they're off.
- The hummingbird can rise straight up like a helicopter.

Gliding Why do birds glide? To keep up in the air. The bird stretches out its wings, moving them only to change the wing shape or angle. Holding them this way, the bird glides. It keeps moving forward with very little sinking and little effort. The bird always sinks, or falls, a bit when gliding, especially in still air. Hawks glide for long periods, circling in search of prey. Keen eyesight enables them to spot reptiles and snakes from very high in the sky.

Mini super flyer What is the smallest bird in the world? The bee hummingbird— only two inches long. This tiny creature can flap its wings more than 50 times per second. It can hover to suck the nectar from a flower by changing the angle and motion of its wings. The hummingbird can also fly backward.

Water Animals

Numerous animals live in water, because nearly 70 percent of the earth's surface is covered with water.

- Fish, shellfish, and many tiny creatures spend their whole lives in water. Some mammals, such as whales and dolphins, do, too.
- Others, such as seals and sea lions, spend most of their time in the water but come out to sun themselves on the shore.

- Frogs, alligators, crocodiles, and other amphibians spend a good deal of time in or near the water.
- Fish can be airborne for short periods. "Flying" fish are actually gliding in the air, not flying. Some leap from the water and stay aloft as far as 150 feet.

How Do Animals Move in the Water?

The various ways water animals move include

swimming
jet propulsion
rowing
riding

Swimming Most kinds of animals move in water by swimming, and most of these animals belong to the class of fishes. How does a fish swim? By moving its tail fin to propel its body through the water. Its body is very streamlined and flexible. So even if it loses its fins, a fish can swim by pushing itself through the water and twisting its body from side to side. Side fins allow some fish to move forward or backward.

Jet propulsion How do squids and cuttlefish move through the water? By jet propulsion. They suck water into their bodies, then squirt it out, and this shoots them ahead. Jellyfish move by jet propulsion, too. They slowly open their jellylike umbrellas, then rapidly close them. This forces out a stream of water, pushing the jellyfish forward.

Rowing What about creatures with tiny hairs (cilia) or ones with whiplike threads? Those with oarlike cilia row themselves through the water. Those with threads on their bodies pull themselves forward.

Riding How do water animals ride? A few hitch a ride on other animals to get from place to place. For example, the remora, or shark sucker, has a sucker on top of its head. This fish attaches its sucker to a bigger fish, like a shark. After the shark kills another fish for food, the animal riding on it gets off and has a meal, too.

ANIMAL DEFENSES: FIGHT, FLEE, OR FAKE IT?

Every animal has the instinct to survive and has ways of defending itself against enemies. The first way, usually, is to run away. The second best choice is to hide. The third is to fight.

Faking It

Many animals fool their enemies by hiding or seeming to disappear. They do this by using their natural color or shape, or by changing their color. Animals that look like their surroundings simply blend in with the background. By remaining motionless, the animal can become very difficult to see. An enemy does not notice it, or loses interest and goes away.

The ways an animal defends itself by hiding its real appearance are called

camouflage
protective coloration
protective resemblance

Playing dead is another way an animal defends itself. Some attackers that would pounce on live prey don't pay any attention to dead animals. The opossum fakes death by letting its body go limp and closing its eyes when threatened. Some beetles, a type of adder (a snake), and the hognose snake also fake death.

Concealment can work in favor of the hunter as well as the hunted. Camouflaged, a tiger's stripes blend in with the shadows of tall grass. The white polar bear seems to disappear in the snow, so it can sneak up on its prey.

Flee

Animals try to get away from danger if they can, as fast as they can. As prey for other animals, some try to outrun their attackers. Long-legged types, such as deer, antelope, kangaroo, and horses, can run far and fast. Those with short legs can flee quickly, but they cannot sustain their speed over great distances. Right away, these animals head for cover where their enemies cannot follow:

- The prairie dog rushes into a hole in the ground.
- Small birds dart into thick bushes.
- Larger birds take flight into the air when they are threatened.

Fight

Animals usually fight only when there is no other choice. They fight to protect their young or when they are cut off from escape.

Sometimes animals fight each other to win a mate. But these fights are mostly ritualized battles to prove which male is stronger and deserves the chance to reproduce. Usually these are not fights to the death. Still, sometimes the animals do die from their injuries.

Domestic cats hiss and yowl to protect their territory, and their fur stands on end. But most of their conflicts are more noisy than bloody; so, too, the conflicts between other animals of the same species. With their own kind, animals have ways to say "you win" without fighting it out. The wolf, for example, turns over on its back and bares its neck to the victor.

Animals usually don't attempt to fight, but when they have to, they can use parts of their bodies as weapons. They bite, gore, claw, kick, suffocate, or poison their enemies.

- Elk, moose, and other deer use their antlers.
- Ostriches and kangaroos can rip open an enemy with a sharp claw on their toe.
- Horses kick with their hooves and bite with their teeth.

- Hawks, eagles, and owls fight with their claws and curved beaks.
- Baboons and large cats are armed with powerful jaws full of strong teeth.
- Large snakes, such as pythons, boa constrictors, and anacondas, wrap their entire bodies around an enemy so that it cannot breathe.
- Certain animals produce chemical weapons that they inject by piercing the hide of an enemy. Some snakes and spiders use fangs to administer the poison. Bees, wasps, and ants use stingers. The skunk squirts a strong-smelling fluid from glands near its tail. The sickening odor cannot kill intruders, but it keeps them far away.

DINOSAURS

Dinosaurs in All Sizes and Shapes

Why did dinosaurs rule the earth for 140 million years? One possible reason is that they came in a huge range of sizes and shapes. Here are some of the hundreds of species of dinosaurs.

Herrerasaurus The first known dinosaur. The 10-foot-long Herrerasaurus lived

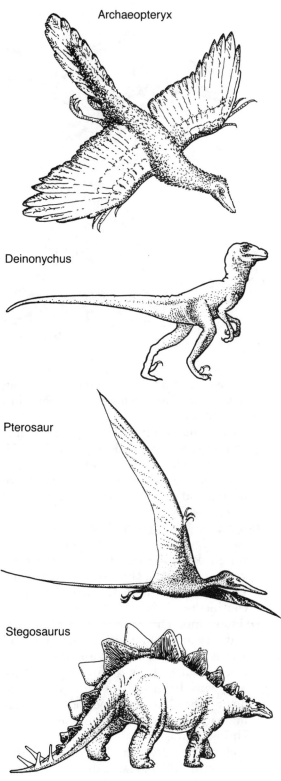

Archaeopteryx

Deinonychus

Pterosaur

Stegosaurus

Ankylosaurus

Apatosaurus

Triceratops

Dimetrodon

220 million years ago during the Triassic period. It had pointed teeth and a big lower jaw. Fossil remains were found in Argentina.

Apatosaurus Brontosaurus/Apatosaurus was 110 feet long and weighed about 30 tons. It lived 150 million years ago in the Jurassic period. Fossil remains have been found in South Africa, Europe, and the Americas.

Iguanodon A huge herbivore, or plant-eater. Iguanodon was 30 feet long and weighed up to 5 tons. It lived 144 million years ago during the Cretaceous period. Fossil remains have been found on all continents.

Deinonychus The most dangerous dinosaur. Deinonychus was between 8 and 13 feet in length and it hunted in packs. It used sharp claws to kill its prey. Deinonychus lived 140 million years ago during the Cretaceous period. Fossil remains have been found in the western United States.

Troodon The most intelligent dinosaur. The brain of Troodon can be compared with that of birds and mammals living today. Troodon was perhaps 8 feet (2.4 meters) in length. This small hunter used its 3-fingered hands to grasp prey. Troodon lived 75 million years ago during the Cretaceous period. Fossil remains have been discovered in North America.

Tyrannosaurus rex The largest meat-eating dinosaur. Tyrannosaurus rex was about 39 feet (12 meters) in length and had very sharp teeth. It lived 67 million years ago during the Cretaceous period. Fossil remains have been found in North America and Eastern Asia.

Nanotryannus The smallest tryannosaur. Nanotryannus had a keen sense of smell, excellent vision, and a big brain. It lived 65 million years ago. Fossil remains have been found in Montana.

Dinosaur Questions and Answers

When did dinosaurs first appear, and when did they disappear?

The first dinosaurs appeared more than 210 million years ago. They lived on Earth for more than 150 million years. Then, around 64 million years ago, they mysteriously disappeared.

What were dinosaurs?

Most dinosaurs were reptiles. Like all reptiles, these dinosaurs had scaly skins. One dinosaur, called **Stegosaurus**, had a double row of bony plates covering its skin. Recent theories, however, indicate that some dinosaurs were not reptiles, but warm-blooded animals.

How did dinosaurs get their name?

The name was made up by English scientist Richard Owen in 1841 from the Greek word *dinosauria*, meaning "fearfully great lizard."

Were all dinosaurs gigantic?

Many were huge, but other dinosaurs were the size of a chicken.

What was the biggest dinosaur?

The biggest dinosaur was **Seismosaurus.** Seismosaurus weiged up to 90 tons and was 140 feet long. This plant-eater lived 154 million years ago during the Jurassic period. Fossil remains were found in New Mexico.

What was the smallest dinosaur?

The chicken-sized **Compsognathus** was probably the smallest dinosaur.

Were all dinosaurs meat-eating?

No. Some dinosaurs ate meat, others ate plants, and still others ate both meat and plants. All dinosaurs in the group called Theropoda (beast-footed) ate meat.

Some of the meat-eating dinosaurs were called carnosaurs, or flesh-eaters. Carnosaurs had big heads, long jaws, and huge, sharp teeth. The other meat-eaters were called **Coelurosaurs.** They ran quickly and had long arms and narrow jaws. Their speed helped them catch prey.

Many dinosaurs were plant-eaters. Even some of the biggest dinosaurs ate plants. These dinosaurs were peaceful creatures that ate leaves off the tops of trees.

How did dinosaurs move?

Some dinosaurs walked on two rear legs, while other dinosaurs used all four legs.

Where did dinosaurs live?

Most of them lived on land, but some went into such waters as rivers and swamps.

Why did dinosaurs disappear?

Many scientists believe that changes in the earth's landscape and climate caused the dinosaurs to die out. Previously, an inland sea covered most of North America, and dinosaurs lived in this sea, in its swamps, or on its banks. In other parts of the world, dinosaurs lived in similar conditions. But then the American inland sea began to fill in. The Atlantic Ocean widened, moving Europe and Africa farther from this continent. Because of these changes, sea levels rose. The areas where the dinosaurs lived were flooded. In addition, the climate became colder and more changeable, perhaps because a giant meteoid struck Earth and threw up huge clouds of dust to hide the sun. The types of vegetation also changed. The new flowering plants were leafless for half the year, which caused the plant-eaters to die out from lack of food. Their death caused the meat-eaters to starve, since they preyed on the plant-eaters. All these changes caused the extinction of the dinosaurs.

How do we know that dinosaurs ever existed?

People began discovering dinosaur fossils perhaps as early as the 1700s. Dinosaur fossils take the form of bones, eggs, and footprints and skin impressions in rock. In the 1800s scientists began to study these remains and decided that they belonged to some giant extinct creatures, which Dr. Owen named in 1841.

ANIMALS FROM A TO Z

Adaptation Special characteristics that enable animals to survive. Examples include the thick fur that polar bears have to protect them from the cold.

Amphibians Any members of a class of animals that are born with gills but later develop lungs. Examples are frogs and salamanders.

Amphibious animals Animals that can live on the land and in water.

Anthropods Members of the superfamily that includes humans and great apes, such as chimpanzees and gorillas, and their ancestors.

Camouflage Marking or color that helps some animals hide from their enemies.

Carnivore Animal that eats meat.

Carrion Flesh of a dead animal.

Classification The arrangement of animals to show their evolutionary relationship to each other. The levels of classification are from the most general to the most specific. For example, the chimpanzee is classified in the following way:

> kingdom—Animals
> phylum—Chordata
> class—mammalia
> order—primates
> family—Pongidae
> genus—*Pan troglodytes*
> species—chimpanzee

Cold-blooded animal Animal that cannot regulate its own body temperature. Cold-blooded animals have to absorb heat from their environment to keep warm. Examples include reptiles, fish, and amphibians.

Colonization Process by which animals move or are transported to a new area in order to survive and reproduce.

Conservation The protection of animals and their habitats.

Crustacean Any members of a class of invertebrates that are basically aquatic. Crustaceans have lungs, hard but flexible skeletons, and two pairs of antennae. Examples include shrimp and lobsters.

Dinosaurs Subclass or superorder of animals that lived on Earth for more than 150 million years. Dinosaurs became extinct around 64 million years ago. Many dinosaurs were huge.

Ecosystem Major subdivision of the biosphere (part of the earth where life can exist) in which a number of plants and animal species interact with each other and their physical environment.

Endangered species Animal species that are in danger of becoming extinct.

Evolution The process by which species develop new physical traits through genetic change. Over long periods, new species develop.

Extinct animals Animals that no longer exist.

Food chain Feeding pattern in which species in an ecosystem eat other species. At the bottom of the food chain are producer plants. At the next step up are herbivorous animals. At the highest step are carnivorous animals.

Gestation Length of time a mother carries offspring in her womb.

Gills Blood-filled organs that allow an animal to absorb oxygen from water. Fish of all kinds have gills.

Habitat The specific environment in which an animal or plant lives. Examples include desert, jungle, mountains, and grassland.

Herbivore An animal that eats plants. An example is the elephant.

Hibernation A deep sleep or period of inactivity during which an animal saves energy in winter. Examples of animals that hibernate are bears and chipmunks.

Incubation Process by which animal eggs are kept warm so that the embryo inside can develop until it hatches. Eggs can be incubated by the parent, the sun's rays, or decaying vegetation.

Insects Any members of a class of small animals that have three pairs of legs, hard outer skeletons, and three body segments.

Invertebrates Animals without a backbone and with an outer skeleton. Insects are examples of invertebrates.

Larva Immature, wormlike form of a newly hatched insect.

Mammals Any members of a class of warm-blooded animals that nurse their young.

Marsupials Order of animals whose tiny young grow further in the mother's abdominal pouch after they are born. Examples include kangaroos.

Migration Periodic movement of groups of animals to a better climate or a location with more food.

Molting Process during which animals periodically shed and then regrow their feathers, hair, or skin.

Niche A role in the ecosystem for a particular species.

Nocturnals Animals that hunt for food at night and rest during the day. Examples include bats.

Omnivore Animal that eats both plants and meat.

Parasite Animal that lives on or in another animal, called a host, from which it gets food. A parasite usually harms its host and may kill it.

Predator Animal that hunts and eats other animals. Wolves and lions are examples.

Prehensile tail The tail of some primates and marsupials that is able to grasp and support.

Primates Order of mammals that includes humans, apes, and monkeys.

Raptor Any bird of prey. Examples include hawks and vultures.

Reptiles Any members of a class of cold-blooded animals that have scaly skins or hard plates. Examples include snakes and alligators.

Rodents Order of mammals with front teeth used for gnawing and large back molars for grinding. Examples include rats and chipmunks.

Ruminants Even-toed hoofed mammals that chew the cud and have stomachs with three or four chambers. Examples include sheep, deer, and camels.

Scavenger Animal that lives off carrion.

Symbiosis Close relationship between two species from which both benefit.

Territory An area "possessed" by an animal or group of animals that defend it against other animals.

Troglophiles Animals that live in caves but leave them to search for food. Bats are examples.

Vertebrate Any animal that has a backbone and an internal skeleton. Reptiles, birds, mammals, and amphibians are vertebrates.

Warm-blooded animal Animal that has a constant body temperature that is usually warmer than its surroundings.

MAJOR ZOOS IN THE UNITED STATES AND CANADA

Zoos, or zoological gardens, are private or public parks where animals of all sorts are exhibited and studied. Zoos have existed in one form or another for thousands of years, from ancient China, Egypt, and Rome to the present. Most major cities throughout the world have zoos, and they vary widely. Petting zoos allow contact between children and animals. Amusement parks may put on shows with trained porpoises.

The following list of major zoos is arranged by state, zone, and province. The name and address of each zoo is given, as well as the number of species and specimens. Where it is available, the zoo's specialty is also given. Special zoos are marked with an asterisk.

United States

ALABAMA

Birmingham Zoo
2630 Cahaba Road
Birmingham, AL 35223

263 species, 893 specimens

ARIZONA

Phoenix Zoo
60th Street & East Van Buren
P.O. Box 5155
Phoenix, AZ 85010

353 species, 1,277 specimens
Specialty: Arabian oryx

Arizona-Sonora Desert Museum
Tucson Mountain Park
P.O. Box 5607
Tucson, AZ 85703

194 species, 722 specimens
Specialty: Sonoran desert fauna and flora and earth sciences

Animal Collection

When a group of animals join together, the members are called by a special name. The following are the words that describe these groups:

bale of turtles	leash of greyhounds, foxes
band of gorillas	litter of pigs
bed of clams, oysters	mob of kangaroos
brace of ducks	murder of crows
brood of chicks	muster of peacocks
cloud of gnats	nest of vipers
colony of ants	pack of hounds, wolves
crash of rhinoceroses	pod of whales, seals
cry of hounds	pride of lions
drift of swine	school of fish
drove of cattle, sheep	shoal of fish
flight of birds	skein of geese
flock of sheep, geese	skulk of foxes
gaggle of geese	sleuth of bears
gang of elks	span of mules
grist of bees	swarm of bees
herd of elephants	team of ducks, horses
horde of gnats	troop of monkeys
leap of leopards	yoke of oxen

ARKANSAS

Little Rock Zoological Gardens
1 Jonesboro
Little Rock, AR 72205

76 species, 286 specimens

CALIFORNIA

Roeding Park Zoo
894 West Belmont Avenue
Fresno, CA 93728

243 species, 728 specimens

T. Wayland Vaughan Aquarium-Museum
Scripps Institute of Oceanography
University of California
La Jolla, CA 92037

203 species, 1,402 specimens
Specialty: marine fish of Southern
    California

The Los Angeles Zoo
5333 Zoo Drive
Los Angeles, CA 90027

763 species, 2,387 specimens

Oakland Baby Zoo
9777 Golf Links Road
Oakland, CA 94605

32 species, 116 specimens
Specialty: baby animals

Marine World/Africa USA
Marine World Parkway
Redwood City, CA 94065

115 species, 7,570 specimens

San Diego Zoological Garden
Zoological Society of San Diego
Balboa Park
P.O. Box 551
San Diego, CA 92112

1,112 species, 3,988 specimens
Specialties: lemurs, tortoises, marsupials

Sea World
1720 South Shores Road
Mission Bay
San Diego, CA 92109

594 species, 9,150 specimens
Specialties: trained marine mammals,
   waterfowl

San Francisco Zoological Gardens
Zoo Road and Skyline Boulevard
San Francisco, CA 94132

314 species, 1,050 specimens
Specialties: primates, bears, cats,
   waterfowl

Prentice Park Zoo
1700 East First Street
Santa Ana, CA 82703

98 species, 326 specimens
Specialty: children's petting zoo

CANAL ZONE

Summit Gardens and Zoo
P.O. Box 973
Balboa Heights
Panama Canal Zone

128 species, 232 specimens
Specialty: Panamanian animals

COLORADO

Cheyenne Mountain Zoological Park
P.O. Box 158
Colorado Springs, CO 80901

220 species, 854 specimens
Specialties: giraffes, primates, large cats

Denver Zoological Gardens
City Park
Denver, CO 80205

369 species, 1,482 specimens
Specialty: waterfowl

CONNECTICUT

Beardsley Zoological Gardens
Bridgeport, CT 06610

56 species, 235 specimens
Specialty: fauna of North and
   South America

DISTRICT OF COLUMBIA

The National Aquarium
Commerce Building
Washington, DC 20230

380 species, 2,000+ specimens

National Zoological Park
Smithsonian Institution
Washington, DC 20009

627 species, 2,618 specimens

FLORIDA

Jacksonville Zoological Park
8605 Zoo Road
Jacksonville, FL 32218

268 species, 932 specimens

Crandon Park Zoo
4000 Crandon Boulevard
Key Biscayne
Miami, FL 33140

280 species, 988 specimens
Specialty: aardvarks

Marineland of Florida
RFD 1, Box 122
St. Augustine, FL 32084

106 species, 613 specimens
Specialty: performing dolphins

Busch Gardens Zoological Park
P.O. Box 9158
Tampa, FL 33674

410 species, 2,736 specimens
Specialties: African hoofed mammals,
   parrots

Dreher Park Zoological Gardens
P.O. Box 6597
1301 Summit Boulevard
West Palm Beach, FL 33405

49 species, 105 specimens

GEORGIA

Atlanta Zoological Park
800 Cherokee Avenue, SE
Atlanta, GA 30315

401 species, 1,037 specimens
Specialties: amphibians and reptiles

Yerkes Regional Primate Research Center
Emory University
Atlanta, GA 30322

26 species, 1,310 specimens
Not open to the public

HAWAII

Honolulu Zoo
Waikiki Beach
Kapiolani Park
Honolulu, HI 96815

341 species, 1,568 specimens
Specialty: Galapagos tortoise

IDAHO

Boise City Zoo
Julia Davis Park
Boise, ID 83706

81 species, 245 specimens

ILLINOIS

Chicago Zoological Park (Brookfield Zoo)
Brookfield, IL 60513

531 species, 2,100+ specimens
Specialty: dolphins

John G. Shedd Aquarium
1200 South Lake Shore Drive
Chicago, IL 60605

477 species, 4,786 specimens

Lincoln Park Zoological Gardens
100 West Webster Avenue
Chicago, IL 60614

593 species, 2,036 specimens
Specialties: great apes, large cats,
   toothless mammals

INDIANA

Mesker Park Zoo
Bement Avenue
Evansville, IN 47712

192 species, 589 specimens
Specialty: large geographic exhibits

Fort Wayne Children's Zoological Gardens
3411 North Sherman Street
Fort Wayne, IN 46808

Indianapolis Zoological Park
3120 East 30th Street
Indianapolis, IN 46218

156 species, 404 specimens

IOWA

Upper Mississippi River Fishery
   Management Station
Iowa Conservation Commission
P.O. Box 250
Guttenberg, IA 52052

68 species, 260 specimens
Specialty: fish and reptiles of the
   Mississippi River

KANSAS

Topeka Zoological Park
635 Gage Boulevard
Topeka, KS 66606

217 species, 520 specimens

KENTUCKY

Louisville Zoological Garden
1100 Trevilian Way
Louisville, KY 40213

158 species, 498 specimens

LOUISIANA

Greater Baton Rouge Zoo
P.O. Box 458
Baton Rouge, LA 70821

136 species, 471 specimens

Audubon Park Zoo and Odenheimer
   Aquarium
P.O. Box 4327
New Orleans, LA 70118

216 species, 800+ specimens

MARYLAND

Baltimore Zoo
Druid Hill Park
Baltimore, MD 21217

336 species, 1,061 specimens

MASSACHUSETTS

Franklin Park Zoo and Children's Zoo
Dorchester, MA 02110

New England Aquarium
Central Wharf
Boston, MA 02110

464 species, 7,416 specimens
Specialty: fish of the Atlantic Ocean

Aquarium of the National Marine
   Fisheries Service
Albatross Street
Woods Hole
Falmouth, MA 02543

43 species, 228 specimens
Specialty: local fauna

MICHIGAN

Detroit Zoological Park and Belle Isle
   Aquarium
8450 West 10 Mile Road
P.O. Box 39
Royal Oak, MI 48068

543 species, 4,656 specimens

Potter Park Zoo
1301 South Pennsylvania Avenue
Lansing, MI 48933

103 species, 415 specimens

Saginaw Children's Zoo
1461 South Washington
Saginaw, MI 48605

85 species, 326 specimens

MINNESOTA

Duluth Zoo
7210 Fremont Street
Duluth, MN 55807

89 species, 285 specimens

St. Paul's Como Zoo
Midway Parkway and Kaufman Drive
St. Paul, MN 55103

134 species, 454 specimens
Specialties: large cats, great apes

MISSISSIPPI

Jackson Zoological Park
2918 West Capitol Street
Jackson, MS 39209

181 species, 752 specimens

MISSOURI

Kansas City Zoological Gardens
Swope Park
Kansas City, MO 64132

174 species, 586 specimens

St. Louis Zoological Park
Forest Park
St. Louis, MO 63139

731 species, 2,216 specimens

MONTANA

Red Lodge Zoo
Box 820
Red Lodge, MT 59068

77 species, 210 specimens

NEBRASKA

Lincoln Municipal Zoo
1300 South 27th Street
Lincoln, NE 68502

146 species, 464 specimens

Henry Doorly Zoological Gardens
Riverview Park
Omaha, NE 68107

136 species, 486 specimens
Specialties: rare hoofed mammals, great
   apes, large cats

NEW JERSEY

Turtle Back Zoo
560 Northfield Avenue
South Mountain Reservation, NJ 07052

256 species, 817 specimens
Specialty: turtles

NEW MEXICO

Rio Grande Zoological Park
903 10th Street, SW
Albuquerque, NM 87102

184 species, 691 specimens
Specialty: hoofed mammals

NEW YORK

International Wildlife Conservation Park
   (Bronx Zoo)
185th Street and Southern Boulevard
Bronx, NY 10460

675 species, 3,200+ specimens

Buffalo Zoological Gardens
Delaware Park
Buffalo, NY 14214

340 species, 877 specimens

Staten Island Zoo
614 Broadway
Staten Island, NY 10310

430 species, 960 specimens
Specialty: reptiles

NORTH DAKOTA

Dakota Zoo
Dakota Zoological Society
P.O. Box 711
Bismarck, ND 58501

109 species, 430 specimens
Specialty: North American fauna

OHIO

Zoological Society of Cincinnati
3400 Vine Street
Cincinnati, OH 45220

564 species, 1,627 specimens

Cleveland Aquarium
Gordon Park
601 East 72nd Street
Cleveland, OH 44109

Cleveland Zoological Park

Brookside Park
P.O. Box 09040
Cleveland, OH 44109

299 species, 1,010 specimens

Columbus Zoological Gardens and Arthur
   C. Johnson Aquarium
9990 Riverside Drive
Powell, OH 43065

671 species, 3,399 specimens
Specialties: gorillas, reptiles, cichlids

Toledo Zoological Gardens
2700 Broadway
Toledo, OH 43609

477 species, 2,085 specimens

OKLAHOMA

Oklahoma City Zoo
Oklahoma City, OK 73112

510 species, 1,801 specimens

Tulsa Zoological Park
5701 East 36th Street North
Tulsa, OK 74115

238 species, 660 specimens

OREGON

Aquarium-Museum
Oregon State University Marine Science
 Center
Marine Science Drive
Newport, OR 97221

165 species, 2,500 specimens
Specialty: marine animals of Oregon

Portland Zoological Gardens
4001 SW Canyon Road
Portland, OR 97221

123 species, 368 specimens
Specialty: elephants

PENNSYLVANIA

Philadelphia Zoological Gardens
34th Street and Girard Avenue
Philadelphia, PA 19104

536 species, 2,079 specimens
Specialties: waterfowl, great apes, reptiles

Pittsburgh Zoological Gardens
P.O. Box 5072
Pittsburgh, PA 15206

633 species, 2,817 specimens

RHODE ISLAND

Roger Williams Park Zoo
Roger Williams Park
Providence, RI 02905

102 species, 237 specimens

SOUTH CAROLINA

Columbia Zoological Park
Riverbanks Park
P.O. Box 1143
Columbia, SC 29202

234 species, 922 specimens

Brookgreen Gardens
Murrells Inlet, SC 29576

23 species, 162 specimens
Specialty: fauna of southeastern United
 States

SOUTH DAKOTA

Great Plains Zoo
15th and Kiwanis
Sioux Falls, SD 57102

83 species, 230 specimens
Specialty: animals of the North American
 Great Plains

TENNESSEE

Knoxville Zoological Park
915 Beaman Street at Chilhowee Park
Knoxville, TN 37914

128 species, 519 specimens

Overton Park Zoo and Aquarium
Memphis, TN 38112

425 species, 1,964 specimens
Specialties: aquatic animals, rare
 ruminants

TEXAS

Abilene Zoological Gardens
Box 60
Abilene, TX 79604

130 species, 438 specimens

Dallas Aquarium
Fair Park
First and Forest Avenue
Dallas, TX 75226

464 species, 5,859 specimens

Dallas Zoo in Marsalis Park
621 East Clarendon Drive
Dallas, TX 75203

714 species, 2,168 specimens

Fort Worth Zoological Park and James R.
  Record Aquarium
2727 Zoological Park Drive
Forest Park
Fort Worth, TX 76110

791 species, 3,894 specimens

Houston Zoological Gardens
Hermann Park
P.O. Box 1562
Houston, TX 77001

507 species, 1,605 specimens

San Antonio Zoological Garden and
  Aquarium
3903 North St. Mary's
San Antonio, TX 78212

775 species, 7,457 specimens

Caldwell Children's Zoo
P.O. Box 428
Tyler, TX 75701

102 species, 361 specimens

Central Texas Zoological Park
Zoo Park Drive
Waco, TX 76708

115 species, 505 specimens

UTAH

Hogle Zoological Gardens
2600 Sunnyside Avenue
P.O. Box 2337
Salt Lake City, UT 84110

333 species, 1,062 specimens

VIRGINIA

Lafayette Zoological Park
3500 Granby Street
Norfolk, VA 23501

71 species, 195 specimens

WASHINGTON

Woodland Park Zoological Gardens
5500 Phinney Avenue, N
Seattle, WA 98103

278 species, 912 specimens

WISCONSIN

Henry Vilas Park Zoo
500 South Randall
Madison, WI 53715

207 species, 834 specimens

Milwaukee County Zoological Park
10001 West Bluemound Road
Milwaukee, WI 53226

636 species, 5,130 specimens

Racine Zoological Park
2131 North Main Street
Racine, WI 53402

143 species, 543 specimens

Canada

ALBERTA

Calgary Zoo and National History Park
St. George's Island
Calgary 21
Alberta T2G 3H4

356 species, 1,191 specimens

Alberta Game Farm
RR 4
Sherwood Park
Edmonton
Alberta T5E 5S7

180 species, 3,400 specimens

BRITISH COLUMBIA

Stanley Park Zoo
Stanley Park
Vancouver 5
British Columbia V6E 1V3

117 species, 515 specimens
Specialties: North American mammals
  and birds

Vancouver Public Aquarium
Stanley Park
P.O. Box 3232
Vancouver 3
British Columbia V6B 3X8

492 species, 11,115 specimens
Specialty: marine life of the northeast
  Pacific

MANITOBA

Assiniboine Park Zoo
2355 Corydon Avenue
Winnipeg
Manitoba R3P 0R5

296 species, 1,156 specimens
Specialty: Nearctic animals

ONTARIO

Metro Toronto Zoo
P.O. Box 280
West Hill
Toronto
Ontario M1E 4R5

444 species, 3,666 specimens

QUEBEC

Société Zoologique de Granby
303 rue Bourget O
Casse Postale 514
Granby, PQ
Québec J2G E8

140 species, 940 specimens

Montreal Aquarium
St. Helen's Island
Montréal, PQ H3C 1A0
Québec

313 species, 2,244 specimens

Aquarium de Québec
1675 Avenue du Parc
Québec, PQ G1W 453

325 species, 2,324 specimens

Jardin Zoologique de Québec
8191 Avenue du Zoo
Orsainville, PQ G1G 4G4
Québec

286 species, 1,081 specimens
Specialty: North American fauna

INFORMATION, PLEASE

American Kennel Club. *The Complete Dog Book*. 17th ed. Howell House, 1985.

Burnie, David. *Bird*. Knopf, 1988.

Chrystie, Frances N. *Pets: A Complete Handbook on the Care, Understanding and Appreciation of All Kinds of Animal Pets*. 3d rev. ed. Little, Brown, 1974.

Dangerfield, Stanley. *The International Encyclopedia of Dogs*. Howell, 1974.

Encyclopedia of the Animal World. 12 vols. Facts on File, 1988–1990.

Encyclopedia of Tropical Fishes: With Special Emphasis on Techniques of Breeding. 27th ed. T.F.H., 1983.

Lambert, David. *A Field Guide to Dinosaurs: The First Complete Guide to Every Known Dinosaur*. Avon, 1983.

————. *The Field Guide to Early Man*. Facts on File, 1987.

Lampton, Christopher. *Endangered Species*. Watts, 1988.

Lily, Kenneth. *Kenneth Lily's Animals*. Lothrop, Lee & Shepard, 1988.

Mound, L. A. *Insect*. Knopf, 1990.

Norman, David. *Dinosaur*. Knopf, 1989.

Parker, Steve. *Fish*. Knopf, 1990.

————. *Pond and River*. Knopf, 1988.

————. *Seashore*. Knopf, 1989.

Sattler, Helen R. *The New Illustrated Dinosaur Dictionary*. Lothrop, Lee & Shepard, 1990.

Taylor, Paul D. *Fossil*. Knopf, 1990.

Whalley, Paul Ernest Sutton. *Butterfly & Moth*. Knopf, 1988.

4

THE PLANT WORLD

Whereas most animals stop growing when they reach maturity, plants, which are non-animal organisms, grow constantly. Plants also make their own food and reproduce by growing seeds, which then grow into other plants. The study of plants is called botany.

THE WORK OF PLANTS: PHOTOSYNTHESIS

The cells of most green plants contain chlorophyll, a chemical. By a process called photosynthesis, a plant uses this chemical, the energy from sunlight, plus water from the plant roots to manufacture food. The food, called glucose, is a type of sugar. Without photosynthesis, animals could not live, since plants are the beginning of the food chain on which all animal life depends. As a by-product, plants also release oxygen into the air, which animals use to breathe.

HOW PLANTS REPRODUCE

Most plants contain both male and female reproductive organs in the same individual. These organs are found in the plant's flowers.

Plants reproduce when pollen, which is grown on the anther, or male part of the plant, is transferred via the stigma to the

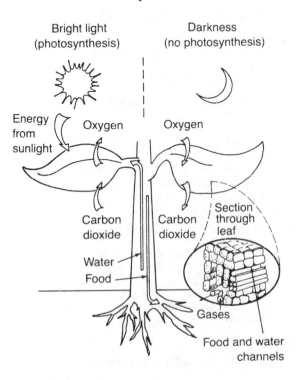

Photosynthesis

Bright light (photosynthesis)

Darkness (no photosynthesis)

Energy from sunlight

Oxygen

Oxygen

Carbon dioxide

Carbon dioxide

Section through leaf

Water

Food

Gases

Food and water channels

Parts of a Flower

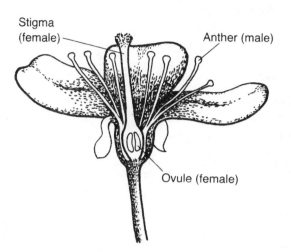

Stigma (female)

Anther (male)

Ovule (female)

also carries pollen. After a plant has been pollinated, the female part of the plant grows seeds, which are then transported to a new location by insects, birds, animals, wind, or water. In their new site, the seeds take root and grow a new plant.

TREES

Trees, the largest kind of plants, are made up of a single, reedy stem that is typically at least 3 to 4 inches (8 to 10 centimeters) in diameter. In some trees, the central stem is very large, typically three to seven or more feet around. Twenty people holding hands barely reach around a giant sequoia. These trees, which grow in northern California, are also the world's largest trees, at a height of 200 feet.

Trees are also among the longest-lived plants. Some California bristlecone pines are 4,000 to 5,000 years old, and some sequoias are 3,500 years old.

ovule, or female parts of the same or a different plant. This process is called pollination.

Pollen is carried from one plant to another by insects, especially bees, which are drawn by a sticky substance called nectar. Wind

Germinating Seeds

If you give a plant water, light, and air, it will grow from a seed. Try to germinate some seeds by following the directions below.

What You Need

    package of seeds (such as radishes or some other vegetable or flower)
    egg carton or paper cups
    tray
    soil
    water

Soak the seeds overnight to help them sprout faster. Poke a hole in each egg compartment or cup. Fill the egg cartons or cups with some of the soil. Now carefully place three or four seeds in each container. Cover them with more soil, to a depth of about 1 inch. Place the container on the tray. Water the seedlings thoroughly so the soil is wet but has no pools of water resting on it. The extra water will drain off through the holes in the bottom.

Place the tray on a windowsill and keep the seeds moist until they germinate, or begin to grow.

What's Your Birth Flower?

Lots of people know what their birthstone is, but did you also know that you have a birth flower?

Month	Flower
January	snowdrop
February	primrose
March	violet
April	daisy
May	hawthorn
June	rose
July	water lily
August	poppy
September	morning glory
October	hops
November	chrysanthemum
December	holly

Kinds of Trees

Although more than 20,000 different kinds of trees exist, most trees fall into one of three groups. They are broadleaf, coniferous, or tropical.

Broadleaf trees
Leaves are flat and broadly shaped
Variety of shapes, but often oval or round
Favor warmer climates
Produce flowers and seeds
Seeds are in nuts or fruit
Shed their leaves every autumn
The main trunk divides into spreading branches
Typical species: oak, beech, ash, maple, ginkgo

Coniferous trees
Leaves are needles or scales
Variety of shapes, but often triangular
Grow in cold climates, in North America, Scandinavia, and Siberia
Coniferous; that is, they produce cones instead of flowers
Are evergreen; that is, they do not shed their leaves in autumn

Short side branches coming out of main trunk
Typical species: Scotch pine, blue spruce, cypress

Tropical trees
Often have long, pointed leaves
Canopy-shaped, with long, straight main trunk, and a canopy of leaves at top
Grow in warm climates
Produce flowers, which become nuts and fruits
Some shed their leaves seasonally to survive droughts, while others have leatherlike leaves that resist drought
Upward growth pattern, with main trunk growing first and leaves shooting out last
Typical species: palms, eucalyptus, tree fern, banyan

From Acorn to Oak: How Trees Grow

All plants start in the same way, from a tiny sprout. Even the mighty oak tree, which grows to a height of 100 feet, starts life as a small acorn. The acorn, which is a seed, is

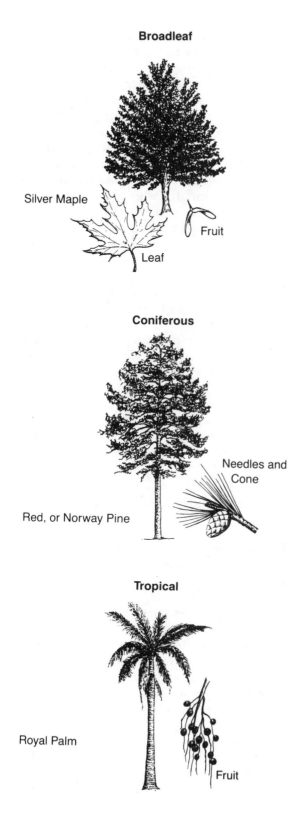

Broadleaf

Silver Maple

Fruit

Leaf

Coniferous

Needles and Cone

Red, or Norway Pine

Tropical

Royal Palm

Fruit

transported, usually by wind or water, away from its parent tree to a new spot. After lying on the ground absorbing moisture for a few days or weeks, the acorn splits open and sends out two sets of shoots. One set of shoots becomes the tree's roots; the other becomes the trunk and leaves. The roots bring water to the trees, and the leaves make food, which all plants need to survive.

Inside Story: Tree Trunks

The woody stem inside a tree reveals many interesting things. A tree trunk is composed of several layers:

Bark The outermost layer, which protects the tree as our skin protects us. Smooth when the tree is young, bark develops characteristics unique to that type of tree as it ages. The bark of a birch tree is strong, thin, and white. An ash tree has diamond-shaped bark, and the black locust's bark has deep ridges.

Cambium The growing part of the tree. Each year, the cambium does its work

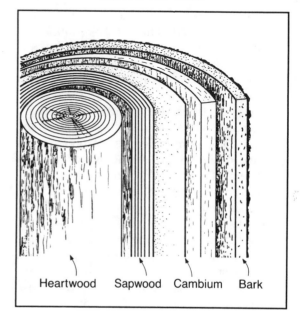

Inside a Tree Trunk

Heartwood   Sapwood   Cambium   Bark

and then dies, building a new layer of bark on its outside and a layer of wood on its inside.

Sapwood The inside layer of cambium, sapwood is made up of cells that carry the tree's food—minerals from the soil and water—to all parts of the tree. When sapwood dies each spring, it leaves another ring in the tree's trunk. That's why you can tell how old a tree is by counting its rings.

Heartwood Dead sapwood, this innermost layer of a tree trunk takes on a darker color. Although the heartwood is dead, it is very strong. Its job is to support the tree.

Tree Insurance: How Trees Adapt to Their Environment

Since trees cannot flee when they are in danger the way animals can, they have devised other ways of adapting to their environment and protecting themselves from their enemies, which include insects, animals, and adverse weather and climate conditions.

Bark A tree's tough bark is a defense against insects. The giant sequoias may have lived so long because their bark is as much as 1 foot thick in places, helping to protect them from insects and forest fires.

Leaves A tree's leaves are high above ground, so animals can't feast on them. The long, pointed leaves of tropical trees are designed to let the water roll off them. Trees in dry areas have thick, tough coverings to help keep them from drying out.

Trunks The baobab tree, which grows in Africa and lives for several thousand years, has developed an enlarged trunk that stores water and helps it survive droughts. The trunks of pine trees protect them from insects by producing a sticky substance called resin. The ombu of Argentina has a trunk too moist to burn and too spongy to cut down.

Roots Some trees develop large, twisted, above-ground roots, called buttress roots, which are designed to support their great weight. Some trees, growing in areas where there is not enough water, have roots that can split a rock probing for water. The banyan tree, found in tropical climates where the soil may be too soggy to hold roots in the ground, develops roots called pillars, which grow off the branches of the main tree, into air. The roots of some banyan trees cover acres of ground.

Shape The wind can blow so hard that it kills all the branches and leaves on one side of a tree. Some trees compensate by growing sideways away from the wind.

Size Trees grow very small on mountaintops, where the cold and wind sap their energy, and at the beach, where the soil is too sandy to anchor a tree securely. In tropical rain forests, where vegetation is dense, trees grow very tall to reach the sunlight.

Tires and Books: How Humans Use Trees

Without trees, humans would not survive, nor would they live so safely and comfortably as they do.

Trees are an important building material. They are used in the framing and also as the outside covering of houses.

Trees are a source of food. We eat their berries, fruits, and nuts.

Trees are used as fuel. For most of human existence, wood has been an important source of fuel.

Trees play a role in spreading knowledge. Without trees, we would know far less about our world, because wood chips are used to make paper, which in turn,

Food from Trees and Other Plants: Fruit

Flowering plants produce fruit, which usually encloses the seeds of the plant. There are many different kinds of fruit, and many of the foods that we may think of as vegetables—peas, lima beans, and tomatoes, for example—are actually fruit. Nuts are also fruits.

Nonflowering plants, called conifers, produce their seeds in cones, which remain tightly closed against the elements—the cold, snow, and ice—until the seeds are fully matured. Then the cones open and the seeds are released. Cones take almost two years to grow seeds, longer than most other plants, which typically grow new seeds every year, usually in the late summer and early fall. People have long grown trees for food.

Twelve Major Categories of Fruit

Aggregates Fruits that typically grow in small clusters, such as strawberries, blackberries, and raspberries.

Berries Fleshy fruits with seeds embedded, such as tomatoes and grapes.

Capsules Fruits with seeds enclosed in a pod with compartments, such as okra.

Caryopsis Fruit with seeds enclosed in tough, outer skin, such as corn.

Drupes Fleshy fruits with thin outer skin and a large seed, called a pit or a stone, at center, such as peach, nectarine, or plum.

Dry fruits This group includes the fruits of grains, flowers, and other plants, such as wheat or oats.

Hesperidium Fruits encased in a tough outer skin, called a peel, with a moist inner sac to hold seeds, such as lemon and grapefruit.

Legumes Fruits with seeds encased in a single pod without compartments, such as peas, lima beans, and peanuts.

Multiple fruits Fruits formed from multiple flowers, such as pineapples.

Nuts Dry fruits encased in a hard outer shell enclosing a single seed, which is itself usually wrapped in a thin, dry husk.

Pepos Firm fruits wrapped in a tough outer peel that protects many interior seeds, such as cucumbers, pumpkins, and squash.

Pomes Fleshy fruits with thick outer skin and a seed compartment at the center, such as apples and pears.

becomes books, magazines, and newspapers.

Trees are one of the world's major sources of medicines. Parts of various trees are used to make medicines that treat many diseases.

Trees provide us with a variety of other useful products. Rubber trees produce latex, which is used to make balls, weatherproof coats, and most important, tires. Maple trees are a source of maple sugar, which is converted to maple syrup and candy. In the southern United States, the sap of longleaf and slash pines is used to make turpentine. In Central America, the sapodilla tree's sap is used in chewing gum.

PLANTS

The term *plant* includes the huge variety of flowers, herbs, mosses, and ferns that also make up the plant world but are not trees. There are 350,000 known species of plants.

Plants exhibit an amazing range of shapes and sizes. Some grow under water and some, such as water lilies, grow on water. Other plants grow in deserts, where there is almost no water. Some grow on trees or other plants and require no soil. Some are so tiny they are barely visible to the human eye, while others have flowers that are several feet across.

Plants are divided into two main groups:

Flowering This group reproduces through its flowers.

Nonflowering This group, which includes mosses, ferns, and gynospheres (conifers), reproduces in a variety of other ways.

The Parts of a Flowering Plant

Flowering plants, of which over 250,000 species have been discovered, are typically composed of four main parts:

Flowers Often a showy display that makes plants spectacular to look at, flowers produce the seeds that the plant uses for reproduction.

Leaves They produce the food the plant needs to survive.

Stems They carry the food to all parts of

Parts of a Root

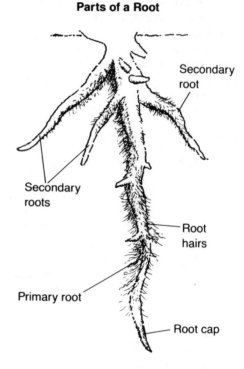

Fascinating Facts

World's oldest plant A creosote plant found growing in southern California was in 1980 estimated to be 11,700 years old.

World's smallest flowering plant Only 0.0236 inches long and 0.0129 inches wide, and weighing about 1/100,0000 ounce, the aquatic duckweed of Australia is the world's smallest plant. Its fruit, which resembles a fig, weighs about 1/400,0000 ounce.

World's fastest growing plant One *Hesperoyucca whipplei*, a member of the lily family, grew 12 feet in 14 days in 1978 in Great Britain.

World's slowest flowering plant A rare Bolivian herb, *Puya raimondii*, grows for 80 to 150 years, blooms once, then dies.

World's largest flowers The stinking corpse lily, which grows in Asia, typically produces flowers 3 feet across and 15 pounds in weight. Although it would be impossible to say for sure, this may also be the world's worst-smelling plant.

Most nutritious fruit The avocado, with 741 calories per pound and a healthy dose of vitamins A, C, and E, is the most nutritious fruit if not necessarily the best choice for dieters.

Least nutritious fruit Cucumbers, with only 73 calories per pound, are the least nutritious fruit.

the plant and also support the flowers, seeds, berries, nuts, and fruit.

Roots They bring in moisture and other nutrients from the soil.

Some seeds have a longer germination time than others. If you are growing your own, read the back of the package to find out how quickly your seeds can be expected to grow.

Plant Protection: How Plants Adapt to the Environment

Like trees, other plants have developed a variety of ingenious ways to protect themselves from climate and enemies. Here are the some of the ways plants protect themselves and adapt to their environment:

Hair Many plants are covered with a fine, dense hair that traps insects.

Chemicals Some plants, such as the stinging nettle, protect themselves with chemicals. Nettles produce a combination of chemicals that spring into action when someone brushes past the plant—and sting the intruder.

Poisons Many plants—such as the lovely lily of the valley, dumbcane, mountain laurel, larkspur, and English ivy—contain poisons that make them dangerous to eat.

Crystals Even though humans eat its roots, the large, inviting leaves of the tropical taro plant contain many small crystals that feel like thousands of piercing, small needles when enemies bite into them.

Thorns and thistles Many plants, including the beautiful rose, have thorns that serve as protection against animal invaders. Screw pines, a tropical plant, have hard, pointed leaves with large thorns on them. The thistle flower is especially well defended, with spines on its stems and leaves.

Alliances against enemies The acacia tree forms an alliance with stinging ants that keeps other animals from feasting on its leaves. The ants eat the pith of the acacia tree's thorns and then nest in them, viciously attacking any animal that comes near their home.

Drowning enemies Some plants drown their enemies. The teasel's leaves form a V-shaped well that fills with water. When the insects and snails that like to feed on the plant appear, they risk drowning in the plant's tiny moat.

Storage reservoirs Cacti adapt to living in the desert by storing water in their fleshy spines. Then they develop bristles that protect them from animals that might want to drink from their reservoir.

Location Lichen and moss that live on mountains survive frosts that kill other plants by growing under large rocks. Many other mountain plants also grow close to the ground and around big rocks.

Don't Eat! Don't Touch!

Some plants are dangerous to humans and animals. If you eat them, you could become very sick—or even die. Some plants are harmful if touched, or even if you breathe the fumes when they are burned.

The most common plant that causes rashes and skin disturbances is poison ivy. It grows throughout the United States, Mexico, Canada, Japan, and China. A saying helps you identify this plant: "Leaves of three, let it be." Poison ivy and its relative, poison oak, can be identified by the way their leaves grow in groups of three.

Another plant that causes skin rashes is poison sumac. It grows mostly in the southern United States.

The following chart lists some common plants that are poisonous. It tells which portions of the plant are toxic, describes symptoms of the illnesses they cause, and indicates which plants are or may be fatal, that is, may cause death if eaten.

Dangerous Plants

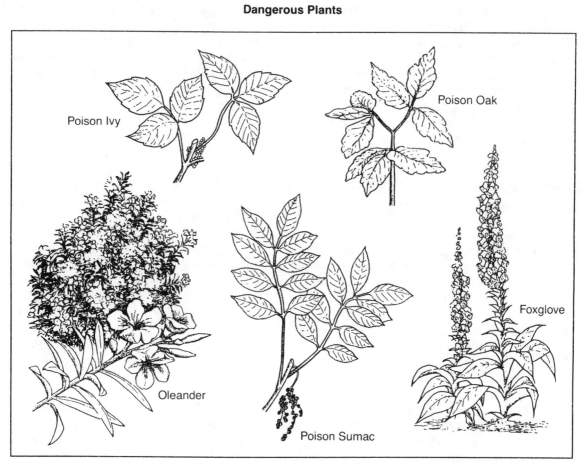

Plants	Toxic Portions	Symptoms of Illness; Degree of Toxicity
Autumn crocus	Bulbs	Nausea, vomiting, diarrhea; can cause death
Azalea	All parts	Nausea, vomiting, depression, breathing difficulty, coma; can cause death
Belladonna	Young plants, seeds	Nausea, twitching muscles, paralysis; can cause death
Bittersweet	Leaves, seeds, roots	Vomiting, diarrhea, chills, convulsions, coma
Buttercups	All parts	Harm digestive system
Caladium	All parts	Intense burning and irritation of the tongue and mouth; can be fatal if the base of the tongue swells, blocking air passage of the throat
Castorbean	Seeds, foliage	Burning in mouth, convulsions; can cause death
Daffodil	Bulbs	Nausea, vomiting, diarrhea; may cause death

Plants	Toxic Portions	Symptoms of Illness; Degree of Toxicity
Daphne	Berries (red or yellow)	Severe burns to mouth and digestive tract followed by coma; can cause death
Delphinium	Young plants, seeds	Nausea, twitching muscles, paralysis; can cause death
Dumbcane (Dieffenbachia)	All parts	Intense burning and irritation of the tongue and mouth; fatal if the base of the tongue swells, blocking air passage of the throat
Elderberry	Roots	Nausea and upset stomach
Elephant ear	All parts	Intense burning and irritation of the tongue and mouth; fatal if the base of the tongue swells, blocking air passage of the throat
English holly	Berries	Severe stomach upset
English ivy	Leaves, berries	Stomach pains, labored breathing, possible coma
Foxglove	Leaves, seeds, flowers	Irregular heartbeat and pulse, usually accompanied by digestive upset and mental confusion; may cause death
Goldenchain	All parts, especially seeds	Excitement, staggering convulsions, coma; may cause death
Horse chestnut	All parts	Nausea, twitching muscles, sometimes paralysis
Hyacinth	Bulbs	Nausea, vomiting, diarrhea; may cause death
Hydrangea	Buds, leaves, branches	Severe stomach upset, gasping, convulsions; may cause death
Iris	Fleshy underground portions	Severe stomach upset
Jack-in-the-pulpit	All parts, especially roots	Intense irritation and burning of the tongue and mouth
Jimsonweed (thorn apple; datura)	All parts	Abnormal thirst, blurred vision, mental confusion, coma; may cause death
Larkspur	Young plants, seeds	Nausea, twitching muscles, paralysis; can cause death
Laurel	All parts	Nausea, vomiting, depression, breathing difficulty, coma; can cause death
Lily of the valley	Leaves, flowers	Irregular heartbeat and pulse usually accompanied by stomach upset and mental confusion; may cause death
Mayapple	Unripe apples, leaves, and roots	Diarrhea, severe stomach upset
Mistletoe	All parts, especially berries	Causes death
Monkshood	All parts, especially roots	Stomach upset and nervous excitement; juice in plant parts can cause death

(continued)

Plants	Toxic Portions	Symptoms of Illness; Degree of Toxicity
Morning glory	Seeds	Large amounts can cause severe mental disturbances; can cause death
Mushrooms, wild	All parts of many varieties	Causes death
Narcissus	Bulbs	Nausea, vomiting, diarrhea; may cause death
Nightshade	All parts, especially unripe berries	Intense digestive disturbances and nervous symptoms; often causes death
Oak	Foliage, acorns	Gradual kidney failure
Oleander	All parts	Severe stomach upset, heart trouble, skin rash; can cause death
Philodendron	All parts	Intense burning and irritation of the tongue and mouth; fatal if the base of tongue swells, blocking air passage of the throat
Poinsettia	All parts	Severe stomach upset; can cause death
Poison hemlock	All parts	Stomach pains, vomiting, paralysis of the central nervous system; may cause death
Poison ivy and oak	All parts	Intense itching, watery blisters, red rash
Poppy	Foliage, roots	Nervous symptoms, convulsions
Potato	Foliage, green parts of vegetable	Intense stomach disturbances, nervous symptoms
Privet	Berries, leaves	Mild-to-severe stomach disturbances; may cause death
Rhododendron	All parts	Nausea, vomiting, depression, breathing difficulty, coma; can cause death
Rhubarb	Leaf blade	Kidney disorder, convulsions, coma; can cause death
Rosary pea	Seeds, foliage	Burning in mouth, convulsions; can cause death
Snowdrop	Bulbs	Vomiting, nervous excitement
Tomato	Vines	Stomach upset, nervous disorders
Wisteria	Seeds, pods	Mild-to-severe stomach disturbances

Painkillers and Potatoes: How Humans Use Plants

Plants other than trees have been put to use by humans to supply countless needs, from clothing to food to medicine.

Plants are a primary source of food. Around the world, people rely on corn, oats, rice, and wheat as staple foods. We grow and eat many parts of plants: the leaves of cabbages, lettuce, and spinach; the stems of asparagus and celery; and the roots of potatoes, carrots, and beets. When we eat cauliflower and broccoli, we are eating flowers. Coffee, tea, and many soft drinks are made from plants.

Plants are food for animals. Cows, sheep, and goats eat grass and other plants in

Life Savers: Medicines We Get from Trees and Plants

People have used trees and other plants to cure illnesses for thousands of years. Originally, the plants themselves were used. But today, scientists are often able to re-create the plants' healing substances in their laboratories. This way, much larger batches of medicine can be made without destroying plants. Without the original plants, though, researchers would not have known about these medicines.

- An African plant called strophanthus contains a chemical that was initially used in cortisone, a medicine that helps people suffering from arthritis.
- A drug called reserpine, which calms people and lowers blood pressure, was originally found in snakeroot, a plant that grows on mountainsides.
- Opium, which is used to make morphine, a painkiller, comes from the poppy flower.
- The bark of the cinchona tree, which grows in Peru, was for many years the source of quinine, the only known treatment for the dangerous fever of malaria. Without quinine, a malaria sufferer would eventually become so weakened by the recurring fevers that he might die.
- Ancient peoples knew that the fruit of the chaulmoogra tree could cure leprosy, a dreaded skin disease. But this cure was known only in a few parts of the world. In the mid-eighteenth century, British doctors traveling in India heard about this miraculous cure. They were able to buy the seeds of the tree in markets, but they never could find the tree. Many years later, they located the tree in Burma, where it grows naturally, and transported some seeds to Hawaii, where they are now cultivated.

order to produce milk. Plants are a primary source of food for many other animals and insects as well.

Plants are a primary source of clothes. Linen comes from the flax plant, and cotton provides cotton clothes. Rope and twine are made from hemp and other plants. Even silk comes indirectly from plants—silkworms must eat the leaves of the mulberry tree in order to make strong silk thread for their cocoons, which humans then make into beautiful material.

Plants are a source of fuel. They play a role in creating our most basic fuels— coal, oil, and natural gas. These fuels are derived in part from decayed plants that mixed with soil and water and were compressed for many thousands of years until they changed form.

Plants are an important source of medicine. They are so important that scientists are concerned about the huge number of undiscovered medicines that are being lost every day as the rain forest, one of the world's richest collections of plant life, is being destroyed.

INFORMATION, PLEASE

Burnie, David. *Eyewitness Books: Plant.* Knopf, 1988.

————. *Eyewitness Books: Tree.* Knopf, 1989.

Cosgrove, Margaret. *Wonders of the Tree World.* Dodd, Mead, 1970.

Edlin, Herbert L. *Atlas of Plant Life.* Crowell, 1973.

Venning, Frank D. *Wildflowers of North America.* Golden Press, 1984.

5

WEIGHTS AND MEASUREMENTS

Weights and measurements are used often in our daily lives. They are the standards people use to discover the weights and sizes of things, as well as other information. For example, we buy fruit by the pound, race a certain distance, and figure out how tall we are.

There are two systems of measurement. People in the United States and several other countries use the **customary**, or **English system of measurement.** The customary system was created in England over a long period, starting around the 1200s. Today England and most other countries use a newer system of measurement called the **metric system.** The metric system was developed in France during the 1790s. In 1975 the United States Congress passed the Metric Conversion Act, which called for a voluntary conversion to the metric system.

Why have most countries adopted the metric system? It is simpler for everyday measurements than the customary system for two reasons:

1. The metric system is based on the decimal system. This means that metric units increase or decrease by tens. For example, a meter has 10 parts called **decimeters.** A decimeter has 10 parts

called **centimeters.** In the customary system the units do not have any single number relationship between them. For example, pints and quarts are related by twos, (2 pints = 1 quart), but pints and gallons are related by fours (4 pints = 1 gallon).

2. The customary system uses more than 20 base units for common measurements, and additional base units for special measurements. The metric system uses only the following 7 base units to measure everything:

The unit of length is the *meter.*
The unit of mass is the *kilogram.*
The unit of temperature is the *kelvin.*
The unit of time is the *second.*
The unit of electric current is the *ampere.*
The unit of light intensity is the *candela.*
The unit of substance amount is the *mole.*

Both the customary and metric systems measure everyday things such as length or distance, area, volume and capacity, weight, time, and temperature.

Length or distance The measurement between two points, such as Paris and New York or our head and our toes.

Eleven Quick Ways To Measure When You Don't Have a Ruler

1. Most credit cards are $3\frac{3}{8}$ inches by $2\frac{1}{8}$ inches.
2. Standard business cards are printed $3\frac{1}{2}$ inches wide by 2 inches long.
3. Floor tiles are usually manufactured in 12-inch-by-12-inch squares.
4. U.S. paper currency is $6\frac{1}{8}$ inches wide by $2\frac{5}{8}$ inches long.
5. The diameter of a quarter is approximately 1 inch, and the diameter of a penny is approximately three-quarters of an inch.
6. A standard sheet of paper is $8\frac{1}{2}$ inches wide and 11 inches long.

Each of the following five items can be used as a measuring device by multiplying its length by the number of times it is used to measure an area in question.

7. A shoelace
8. A tie
9. A belt
10. Your feet—placing one in front of the other to measure floor area (equals about one foot).
11. Your outstretched arms from fingertip to fingertip (equals about one yard).

Largest, Tallest, Longest, Biggest

The largest cake The largest cake ever baked weighed 128,238 pounds, 8 ounces, including 16,209 pounds of icing. The cake was made to celebrate the 100th birthday of Fort Payne, Alabama, on October 18, 1989.

The tallest candle The tallest candle ever made was 80 feet high and $8\frac{1}{2}$ feet in diameter. It was made for the 1897 Stockholm Exhibition in Stockholm, Sweden.

The largest greeting card The largest greeting card ever made was 37 feet, 3 inches by 54 feet, 9 inches. The card was created by the Oceanway P.T.A., Jacksonville, Florida, on April 21, 1989.

The tallest basketball player The tallest basketball player was Suleiman Ali Nahnush, who was 8 feet when he played for a Libyan team in 1962.

The longest walk The longest walk was completed by Thomas Carlos Pereira of Argentina. He spent 10 years walking 29,825 miles around 5 continents between April 1968 and April 1978.

The biggest hamburger The biggest hamburger weighed 5,520 pounds. It was made at the Outagamie County Fairgrounds in Wisconsin on August 5, 1989.

The longest home run during a regular season major league game The longest home run was 537 feet and was hit by Chicago White Sox player Dave Nicholson on May 6, 1964, in Comiskey Park, Chicago.

The largest diamond The largest diamond is the 3,106-carat Cullinan diamond. It was found in Pretoria, South Africa, on January 25, 1905, and named after the mine's discover, Sir Thomas Cullinan.

The highest temperature The highest temperature ever recorded on Earth was 136.4°F (58°C) on September 13, 1922, in Al'Aziziyah, Libya.

The coldest place The coldest permanently inhabited place on Earth is Oymyakon, a village in the former Soviet Union, where the temperature reached −90°F (−32°C) during the winter of 1933.

Area The measurement of a surface, such as a tennis court.

Volume and capacity The measurement of the space something occupies or encloses. For example, a volume measurement shows the size of a bottle, and a capacity measurement shows how much the bottle can contain.

Weight The measurement of the pressure something puts on whatever supports it from below. For example, a dog's weight is measured by the amount of pressure its body puts on a scale.

Time The metric and customary systems have the same measurements for time longer than a second.

Temperature The heat of something.

Avoirdupois Weights The customary system for measuring weight includes
The apothecaries' system for weighing drugs and medicines, but today rarely used

The troy system for weighing precious metals
The avoirdupois system for weighing everyday objects:

$27^{11}/_{32}$ grains	= 1 dram
16 drams	= 1 ounce
16 ounces	= 1 pound
100 pounds	= 1 hundredweight
20 hundredweights	= 1 ton
	= 2,000 pounds

Miscellaneous Weights and Measures This table shows some other common customary measures.

3 inches	= 1 palm
4 inches	= 1 hand
6 inches	= 1 span
18 inches	= 1 cubit
$2^{1}/_{2}$ feet	= 1 military pace

COMMON U.S. WEIGHTS AND MEASURES

Circular Measures In the table below, a sextant is $1/_6$ of a circle and a quadrant is $1/_4$ of a circle.

60 seconds	= 1 minute
60 minutes	= 1 degree
30 degrees	= 1 sign
60 degrees	= 1 sextant
90 degrees	= 1 quadrant
4 quadrants	
or	
360 degrees	= 1 circle

Cloth Measures In the table below, a nail is also equal to $1/_{16}$ of a yard.

$2^{1}/_{2}$ inches	= 1 nail
4 nails	= 1 quarter
4 quarters	= 1 yard

Square Measures Square measures are area measures. An area does not have to be square in order for us to find out how many square units fit into it.

144 sq. inches	= 1 sq. foot
9 sq. feet	= 1 sq. yard
40 sq. rods	= 1 road
4 roads	= 1 acre
4,840 sq. yards	= 1 acre
640 acres	= 1 sq. mile

Cubic Measures Cubic units measure both volume and capacity, both of which combine length, width, and depth. Some cubic units, such as the liter and the quart, do not include the word *cubic*.

1,728 cu. inches	= 1 cu. foot
5.8 cu. feet	= 1 bulk barrel
27 cu. feet	= 1 cu. yard
128 cu. feet	= 1 cord (wood)
40 cu. feet	= 1 ton (shipping)
2,150.42 cu. inches	= 1 standard bushel
231 cu. inches	= 1 standard gallon

Liquid Measures Liquid measures are volume measures because they tell us how much material a container can hold. For example, we buy a quart or a gallon container of milk.

A Pinch of Salt: Household Conversion Table

This table may be useful around the house, for example, in baking a cake or mixing juices.

From	To	Multiply by	From	To	Multiply by
dozens	units	12	pints	cups	2
baker's dozens	units	13	pints	liters	0.47
teaspoons	milliliters	4.93	pints	quarts	0.50
teaspoons	tablespoons	0.33	quarts	cups	4
tablespoons	milliliters	14.79	quarts	gallons	0.25
tablespoons	teaspoons	3	quarts	liters	0.95
cups	liters	0.24	quarts	pints	2
cups	pints	0.50	gallons	liters	3.79
cups	quarts	0.25	gallons	quarts	4

1 fluid dram	= 60 minims or $1/8$ fluid ounce
1 teaspoon (tsp.)	= $1/3$ tablespoon or $1/8$ fluid ounce
1 tablespoon (tbs.)	= 3 teaspoons or $1/2$ fluid ounce
1 fluid ounce (fl. oz.)	= 2 tablespoons or 6 teaspoons
1 gill (gi.)	= $1/2$ cup or 4 fluid ounces
1 cup (c.)	= 16 tablespoons or 8 fluid ounces
1 pint (pt.)	= 2 cups or 4 gills or 16 fluid ounces
1 quart (qt.)	= 2 pints or 4 cups or 32 fluid ounces
1 British imperial quart	= 1.20095 U.S. quarts
1 gallon (gal.)	= 4 quarts or 8 pints or 16 cups
1 British imperial gallon	= 1.20095 U.S. gallons
1 barrel	= 31.5 U.S. gallons (a petroleum barrel = 42 U.S. gallons)

COMMON METRIC WEIGHTS AND MEASURES

Linear Measures

10 millimeters (mm = 1 centimeter (cm)
10 centimeters = 1 decimeter (dm)
10 decimeters = 1 meter (m)
10 meters = 1 dekameter (dam)
10 dekameters = 1 hectometer (hm)
10 hectometers = 1 kilometer (km)
10 kilometers = 1 myriameter (mym)

Area Measures

100 sq. millimeters (mm^2) = 1 sq. centimeter (cm^2)
10,000 sq. centimeters = 1 sq. meter (m^2)
100 sq. meters = 1 are (a)
100 acres = 1 hectare (ha)
100 hectares = 1 sq. kilometer (km^2)

Fluid Volume Measure

10 milliliters (ml) = 1 centiliter (cl)
10 centiliters = 1 deciliter (dl)
10 deciliters = 1 liter (l)
10 liters = 1 dekaliter (dal)
10 dekaliters = 1 hectoliter (hl)
10 hectoliters = 1 kiloliter (kl)

Weights

10 milligrams (mg) = 1 centigram (cg)
10 centigrams = 1 decigram (dg)
10 decigrams = 1 gram (g)
10 grams = 1 dekagram (dag)
10 dekagrams = 1 hectogram (hg)
10 hectograms = 1 kilogram (kg)
1,000 kilograms = 1 metric ton (t)

Cubic Measures

1,000 cu. millimeters (mm^3) = 1 cu. centimeter (cm^3)
1,000 cu. centimeters = 1 cu. decimeter (dm^3)
1,000 cu. decimeters = 1 cu. meter (m^3 = 1 stere

Metric Prefixes

The prefixes below, in combination with the basic metric units such as meter, gram and liter, provide the multiples in the International System. For example, centi + meter = centimeter, or one one-hundredth of a meter.

Prefix	Symbol	Multiples	Equivalent
exa	E	10^{18}	quintillionfold
peta	P	10^{13}	quadrillionfold
tera	T	10^{12}	trillionfold
giga	G	10^9	billionfold
mega	M	10^6	millionfold
kilo	k	10^3	thousandfold
hecto	h	10^2	hundredfold
deka	da	10	tenfold

Prefix	Symbol	Submultiples	Equivalent
deci	d	10^{-1}	tenth part
centi	c	10^{-2}	hundredth part
milli	m	10^{-3}	thousandth part
micro	u	10^{-6}	millionth part
nano	n	10^{-9}	billionth part
pico	p	10^{-12}	trillionth part
femto	f	10^{-15}	quadrillionth part
atto	a	10^{-18}	quintillionth part

Watch Those Prefixes!: Prefixes in the Metric System

Remember that the metric system is a decimal system. A unit in a decimal system is always 10 times larger than the next smaller unit.

Most metric units use prefixes to describe the relationship between that unit and the base unit. Greek prefixes show multiples of a base unit that make every base unit larger. For example, *hecto-* makes any base unit 100 times larger, and *kilo-* makes any unit 1,000 times larger. Latin prefixes show submultiples of a base unit that make every base unit smaller. For example, *centi-* makes a unit a hundred times smaller, and *milli-* makes a unit a thousand times smaller.

Metric Conversion Table

Use this table to change customary measurements to and from metric units.

	When You Know:	You Can Find:	If You Multiply By:
LENGTH	inches	millimeters	25
	feet	centimeters	30
	yards	meters	0.9
	miles	kilometers	1.6
	millimeters	inches	0.04
	centimeters	inches	0.4
	meters	yards	1.1
	kilometers	miles	0.6
AREA	square inches	square centimeters	6.5
	square feet	square meters	0.09
	square yards	square meters	0.8
	square miles	square kilometers	2.6
	acres	square hectometers (hectares)	0.4
	square centimeters	square inches	0.16
	square meters	square yards	1.2
	square kilometers	square miles	0.4
	square hectometers (hectares)	acres	2.5
MASS	ounces	grams	28
	pounds	kilograms	0.45
	short tons	megagrams (metric tons)	0.9
	grams	ounces	0.035
	kilograms	pounds	2.2
	megagrams (metric tons)	short tons	1.1
LIQUID VOLUME	ounces	milliliters	30
	pints	liters	0.47
	quarts	liters	0.85
	gallons	liters	3.8
	milliliters	ounces	0.034
	liters	pints	2.1
	liters	quarts	1.06
	liters	gallons	0.26

Miles-to-Kilometers and Kilometers-to-Miles

Miles	Kilometers	Kilometers	Miles
1	1.6	1	0.6
2	3.2	2	1.2
3	4.8	3	1.8
4	6.4	4	2.4
5	8.0	5	3.1
6	9.6	6	3.7
7	11.2	7	4.3
8	12.8	8	4.9
9	14.4	9	5.5
10	16.0	10	6.2
20	32.1	20	12.4
30	48.2	30	18.6
40	64.3	40	24.8
50	80.4	50	31.0
60	96.5	60	37.2
70	112.6	70	43.4
80	128.7	80	49.7
90	144.8	90	55.9
100	160.9	100	62.1
1,000	1,609.0	1,000	621.0

Measuring Temperature

The metric system of temperature measurement is in Celsius degrees. The customary system of temperature measurement is in Fahrenheit degrees. Both scales are shown below, along with their freezing and boiling points.

To convert degrees Fahrenheit to degrees Celsius, first subtract 32, and then multiply by $5/9$. To convert Celsius to Fahrenheit, multiply by $5/9$, and then add 32.

WEIGHTS AND MEASUREMENTS FROM A TO Z

10 Special Weights and Measures

acre 43,560 square feet, which also equals about 70 square yards.

ampere Unit of electric current, often called amp.

bale Large bundle of goods. In the United States a bale of cotton weighs about 100 pounds.

carat or karat 20 milligrams or 3,086 troy. The carat is a measure of the amount of alloy per 24 parts of gold. For example, a 24-carat gold ring is pure gold and an 18-carat gold ring is $3/4$ gold and $1/4$ alloy.

decibel Unit of comparative loudness. The smallest amount of change in loudness the human ear can detect is 1 decibel (db). A 20-decibel sound is 10 times as loud as a 10-decibel sound.

10 decibels—a light whisper
20 decibels—quiet conversation
30 decibels—normal conversation
40 decibels—light traffic
50 decibels—a typewriter; loud conversation
60 decibels—a noisy office
70 decibels—normal traffic; a quiet train
80 decibels—raucous music; the subway
90 decibels—heavy traffic; thunder
100 decibels—a plane at takeoff

Fahrenheit and Celsius Temperature Scales

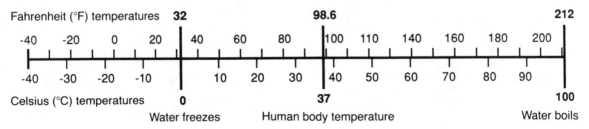

Fahrenheit (°F) temperatures 32   98.6   212
-40 -20 0 20 | 40 60 80 |100 110 140 160 180 200

Celsius (°C) temperatures 0   37   100
-40 -30 -20 -10 | 10 20 30 |40 50 60 70 80 90

Water freezes   Human body temperature   Water boils

gross 12 dozen, or 144, objects.

hand Unit of measure that equals 4 inches. This unit is used to measure the height of horses.

horsepower Power needed to lift 33,000 pounds a distance of 1 foot in 1 minute. Horsepower is used to measure the power of engines, for example.

knot Rate of speed of 1 nautical mile per hour. Knots are used to measure the speed of ships. (A nautical mile is longer than a land, or statute, mile.)

light year Unit of length equal to the distance that light travels in one year in a vacuum, or about 5,900,000,000,000 miles (9.5 billion kilometers).

Ancient and Historic Weights and Measures

Units of Weight	Location	Customary	Metric
amphora	Greece	10.3 gal.	38.8l
amphora	Rome	6.84 gal.	26l
bath	Israel	2,250 cu. in.	37l
ephah	Israel	1.1 bu.	40l
gallon, beer	England	282 cu. in.	4.62l
hekat	Israel	291 cu. in.	4.77l
tun	England	252 gal.	954l

Units of Weight	Location	Customary	Metric
carat	England, U.S.	3$^1/_6$ grains	206 mg
denarius	Rome	0.17 oz.	4.6 g
dinar	Arabia	0.15 oz.	4.2 g
drachma	Greece	0.154 oz.	4.36 g
livre	France	1.08 lb.	490 g
livre (demikilo)	France	1.10 lb.	500 g
mite	England	0.05 grain	3.24 mg
obol	Greece	11.2 grains	0.73 g
pfund	Germany	1.1 lb.	500 g
pound, tower:	England		
12 oz.		5,400 grains	350 g
15 oz.		6,750 grains	437 g
16 oz.		7,200 grains	465 g
shekel	Israel	0.5 oz.	14.1 g
shekel, trade	Babylonia	0.3 oz.	8.37 g

Units of Length	Location	Customary	Metric
cubit	Greece	18.3 in.	46.5 cm
	Rome	17.5 in.	44.4 cm
hand	England, U.S.	4 in.	10.2 cm
stadion	Greece	622 ft.	190 m
stadium	Rome	606 ft.	185 m

Ancient Rules of Thumb

Some ancient civilizations based their measuring units on certain parts of a man's body.

- To measure length, the ancient Egyptians used the cubit, which was the length from a man's elbow to the tip of his middle finger.
- To measure length, the Romans used the unica, which was the width of a thumb. Twelve unica equaled one foot. A foot was about the length of a man's foot. Three feet was a yard, or the distance from a man's nose to the tip of the middle finger when his arm was outstretched.

INFORMATION, PLEASE

To understand more about weights and measures you may want to read:

Bendick, Jeanne. *How Much and How Many?* Watts, 1989.

_____. *Mathematics Illustrated Dictionary: Facts, Figures, and People*. Rev. ed. Watts, 1989.

Taylor, Barbara. *Weight and Balance*. Watts, 1990.

6

TIME AND DATES

People have always needed to know how to tell time. For example, prehistoric people needed to know when the seasons would change and the animals they hunted would migrate from one location to another. When humans began to grow crops, they needed to know when to plant seeds so they would have enough sunlight and warmth to grow. The ancient Egyptians needed to know when the Nile River would flood each year so they could evacuate.

As humans began clustering in communities, they needed to be able to measure time so they could celebrate religious holidays. They needed to know when to schedule market days and when to pay—or collect—bills.

People learned to tell time by watching the sun, moon, and stars. Days were known as suns, and the periods of darkness between them became known as nights.

People also noticed that the moon passed through regular cycles. Sometimes there was a full moon, while at other times, the moon was only a sliver. These lunar cycles became months, each cycle lasting 29¼ days.

Observation of the sun and stars led to the discovery of the solar cycle. People observed that the setting and rising sun seemed to move around the twelve constellations known as the zodiac, and they called this cycle a year. Each solar cycle lasts 365¼ days.

The week was probably the first unit of time that did not depend on the movement of bodies in the solar system. Weeks undoubtedly originated when people began to grow more crops than they could eat. The solution was to sell or barter them with others. People began to meet every few days to do this, so the crops wouldn't spoil. Thus, weeks were probably used to mark the amount of time between market days.

TIME FROM A TO Z

ante meridiem, A.M. The twelve hours between midnight and noon, as in 1 A.M. or 4 A.M.

calendar Chart for keeping time. Records the days, weeks, and months in a year.

day 1. The period between sunrise and sunset. 2. The period during which the earth completes one complete rotation on its axis.

daylight saving time Block of time during which clocks are set one hour ahead of standard time in order to have more useful hours of daylight in each day.

equinox One of the two days each year when day and night are of equal length; the day the sun crosses the equator.

Greenwich mean time Average solar time at the prime meridian in Greenwich, England; used to calculate time throughout the world.

holiday Special day set aside for civic or religious celebration.

hour One of 24 parts of a day.

international date line Imaginary line that runs down the earth at 180 degrees longitude. East of the date line, it is one day earlier than to the west. Directly opposite, that is, 180 degrees from the international date line, is the prime meridian.

latitude Imaginary lines running around the earth at every 15 degrees, parallel to the equator; used to tell time and to calculate position when traveling by air or sea.

leap year Span of 366 days occurring in years divisible by four, such as 1988 and 1992. Even century years, such as 2000, must be divisible by 400 to be leap years. Dates in ordinary years move forward a single day each year (so if a holiday is on a Monday one year it will be on a Tuesday the next year), but in leap years, they leap forward two days following February 29, leap day.

longitude Imaginary lines running up and down the earth, perpendicular to the equator, every 15 degrees; used to tell time and to calculate position when traveling by air or sea.

lunar year The period equal to twelve cycles of the moon.

mean solar day An average of all the sun's daily trips across the sky during one year.

meridian Imaginary circle on the earth used to measure time and space.

minute One of 60 parts in an hour.

month One of twelve divisions in a year, divided into weeks and days.

post meridiem, P.M. The twelve hours between noon and midnight, as in 6 P.M. or 8 P.M.

prime meridian The beginning meridian, from which all longitudes are measured. Directly opposite, that is, 180 degrees from the prime meridian, is the national date line.

second One of 60 parts in a minute.

solstice Two days each year (one in summer and one in winter) when the sun is farthest from the equator.

week One of 52 measures in a year, divided into days.

year Period of time when Earth completes one revolution around the sun, consisting of approximately 365 days.

Divisions of Time

Unit	Duration	Abbreviation
second		sec., s., "
minute	60 seconds	min., m., '
hour	60 minutes	hr., h., hrs.
day	24 hours	da., d.
week	7 days	wk., w., wks.
fortnight	2 weeks	
month	30 days (generally)	mo., m., mos.
year	12 months; 52 weeks; 365 days	yr., yrs.
olympiad	4 years	
decade	10 years	
century	100 years	cen., c.
millenium	1,000 years	

Words to Describe Time

annual	yearly
biannual	twice a year (at unequally spaced intervals)
bicentennial	relating to a period of 200 years
biennial	relating to a period of two years
bimonthly	every two months; twice a month

biweekly	every two weeks; twice a week
centennial	relating to a period of 100 years
decennial	relating to a period of 10 years
diurnal	daily; of a day
duodecennial	relating to a period of 12 years
millennial	relating to a period of 1,000 years
novennial	relating to a period of nine years
octennial	relating to a period of eight years
perennial	occurring year after year
quadrennial	relating to a period of four years
quadricentennial	relating to a period of 400 years
quincentennial	relating to a period of 500 years
quindecennial	relating to a period of 15 years
quinquennial	relating to a period of five years
semiannual	every six months (at equally spaced intervals)
semicentennial	relating to a period of 50 years
semidiurnal	twice a day
semiweekly	twice a week
septennial	relating to a period of seven years
sesquicentennial	relating to a period of 150 years
sexennial	relating to a period of six years
thrice weekly	three times a week
tricennial	relating to a period of 30 years
triennial	relating to a period of three years
trimonthly	every three months
triweekly	every three weeks; three times a week

undecennial	relating to a period of 11 years
vicennial	relating to a period of 20 years

FROM DAWN TO DUSK: DAYS AND HOURS

A day is the amount of time Earth takes to spin once on its axis. Because the sun takes a longer period to cross the sky during the summer, and far less time in winter, the length of a day is calculated using a yearly average of the sun's daily trips; this is called the mean solar day.

Names of the Days

The names of the days are based on old English or Latin names for the gods and the planets.

English	Latin	Saxon
Sunday	Dies Solis (Sun)	Sun's Day
Monday	Dies Lunae (Moon)	Moon's Day
Tuesday	Dies Martis (Mars)	Tiw's Day
Wednesday	Dies Mercurii (Mercury)	Woden's Day
Thursday	Dies Jovis (Jupiter)	Thor's Day
Friday	Dies Veneris (Venus)	Frigg's Day
Saturday	Dies Saturni (Saturn)	Saterne's Day

Hours of the Day

Days are divided into hours, minutes, and seconds. Before mechanical clocks were invented, people divided days into different lengths of time. The Greeks, Romans, and Egyptians had 24-hour days, which they divided into twelve hours of day and twelve hours of night. But because days and nights are shorter in the winter and longer in the summer, the hours were of different lengths during the different seasons of the year. When mechanical clocks were invented in the Middle Ages, hours could be measured in equal lengths.

1 day	= 24 hours
1 hour	= 60 minutes
1 minute	= 60 seconds

When Does a Day Begin?

Throughout most of the world, a day is measured from midnight to midnight. Some groups, such as Jews and Muslims, still measure days from sunset to sunset for their religious holidays.

Counting the Hours

Some parts of the world count the hours of a day in two 12-hour parts, while others measure days in one 24-hour part.

The 12-Hour Day

The United States uses the 12-hour system of counting hours:

| Midnight | = 12 A.M. or 12 M |
| Noon | = 12 P.M. or 12 N |

A.M. is the abbreviation for the Latin *ante meridiem,* and means "before noon."
P.M. is the abbreviation for the Latin *post meridiem,* and means "after noon."

The 24-Hour Day

The U.S. military and much of Europe uses the 24-hour system of counting hours:

0 hour	= midnight	0600	= 6 A.M.
0100	= 1 A.M.	0700	= 7 A.M.
0200	= 2 A.M.	0800	= 8 A.M.
0300	= 3 A.M.	0900	= 9 A.M.
0400	= 4 A.M.	01000	= 10 A.M.
0500	= 5 A.M.	01100	= 11 A.M.
01200	= noon	1900	= 7 P.M.
1300	= 1 P.M.	2000	= 8 P.M.
1400	= 2 P.M.	2100	= 9 P.M.
1500	= 3 P.M.	2200	= 10 P.M.
1600	= 4 P.M.	2300	= 11 P.M.
1700	= 5 P.M.	2400	= 12 MID- NIGHT

The Time of Your Life: Standard Time Around the World

Because of the earth's rotation on its axis, it is daytime in some parts of the world when it is night in others. If everyone used the same time, 12 noon would fall in the middle of the night for some people. For several hundred years, people solved the problem by following their own "local" time, so that noon was always when the sun was directly overhead.

When trains began to travel across entire continents, though, so many individual time zones threatened to make travel impossible. A train traveling across the United States might have traveled literally through hundreds of different time zones to reach its destination. No one would know when a train would arrive or depart from any one community. To solve this problem, in 1883 the world was divided into standard time zones.

Imaginary lines called meridians, occurring every 15 degrees on the globe, were used to create the new time zones. The meridians run from the top to the bottom of the globe and are called longitudes. The world is thus divided into 24 time zones, each one hour apart. For political reasons, such as national boundaries, the time zones do not always fall exactly every 15 degrees, but sometimes zigzag around borders.

Greenwich Mean Time and the Prime Meridian

Obviously, some place in the world had to be the beginning, or zero meridian. Greenwich, England, was chosen, and Greenwich furnished the world with its prime, or zero, meridian.

The United States has four different meridians and four different time zones, at 75, 90, 105, and 120 degrees west of Greenwich, England.

Summer Time: Daylight Saving Time

Although Benjamin Franklin had suggested that people might benefit from resetting their clocks in summer so they could enjoy more hours of useful daylight, daylight saving time was not invented until before World War I. An Englishman, William Willett, made the first formal proposal for daylight saving time in a booklet entitled *Waste of Daylight*. He suggested that clocks be set forward 1 hour in the spring, so that the sun would rise later by the clock and set later, giving people another hour of useful daylight.

In 1916, Germany went on the new "summer time" in order to save electricity. Great Britain and western Europe followed soon after, and in 1917, the United States and Canada initiated daylight saving time as a wartime measure to save power.

Generally, western Europe goes on daylight time on the last Sunday in March and changes back on the last Sunday in September. Russia and the Commonwealth of Independent States stay on "advanced time" year-round. China, by government order, operates as one time zone even though it should, geographically, be in 11 different zones. For religious reasons, Israel is approximately two hours behind the rest of its time zone. This means that the sun may be setting there as early as 3:30 P.M.

Paraguay, Ireland, and the Dominican Republic adjust their clock time in winter instead of summer. Thus, their time is aptly known as winter time.

How Times Flies: Crossing the International Date Line

An international date line became necessary when people found themselves able to fly around the world. If you flew west with the sun for twenty-four hours in a plane, you would have arrived at your destination on the same day you left. But for the people on the ground at your destination, it would have

---

Ship's Bells

Aboard ship, a sailor has an assigned duty period called a watch. A day on most ships consists of six 4-hour watches. The watches change at 8 A.M., noon, 4 P.M., 8 P.M., midnight, and 4 A.M. At each of these hours, some sailors go off duty and are replaced by other crew members. A chime indicates each half hour on a watch. During a 4-hour watch, one bell chimes at the first half hour. Then two bells chime the second half hour, and so on up to the eighth half hour. The sequence begins over again when the next watch starts, according to the following schedule:

1 bell	12:30 or 4:30 or 8:30 A.M. or P.M.			5 bells	2:30	6:30	10:30
2 bells	1:00	5:00	9:00	6 bells	3:00	7:00	11:00
3 bells	1:30	5:30	9:30	7 bells	3:30	7:30	11:30
4 bells	2:00	6:00	10:00	8 bells	4:00	8:00	12:00

The ship's whistle is blown at noon on many boats. On some ships, a single, soft chime is sounded 15 minutes before the change of watch.

Standard Time Zones in Continental United States

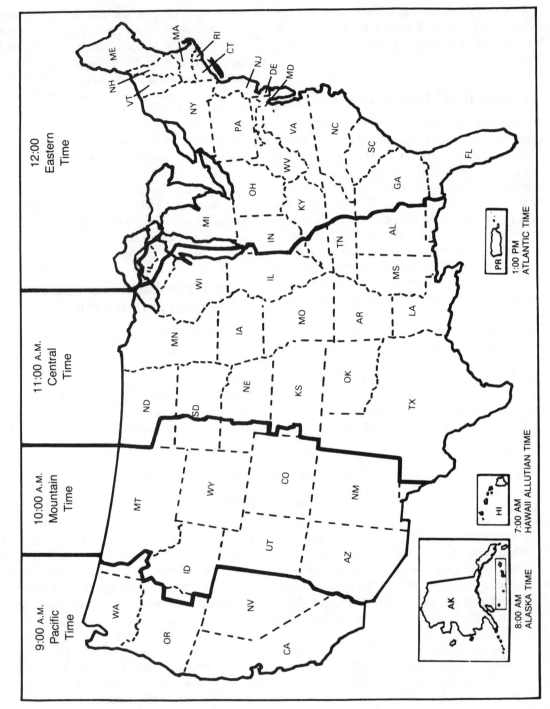

been the next day. To avoid this confusion, an imaginary line set at 180 degrees longitude—directly opposite Greenwich, England—now divides the earth, creating two separate days. If you travel on Sunday, for example, the day will instantly become Monday when you cross the international date line. And when you return, you will recover the "lost" day.

TICKING TIME: A HISTORY OF CLOCKS

The need to tell time ever more accurately led to the development of timepieces, or clocks. People probably first got the idea to make a timekeeping device when they watched the shadows of trees move to different positions as the day progressed.

Shadow Clocks

Used by Egyptians, the first shadow clocks were poles or dials that cast shadows, which moved as the sun moved through the heavens. A sundial is a kind of shadow clock, and Romans soon gave it a face with numbers to mark the hours. The word *dial* comes from the Latin *dies*, meaning "day." Cleopatra's Needle in Central Park in New York City is an example of a obelisk shadow

clock. Shadow clocks were used from the fifteenth century B.C. through the nineteenth century, when clockmakers still used sundials to set watches. Shadow clocks have a serious drawback, though: They work only on sunny days.

A sundial showing 2:45 P.M.

Water Clocks

Called clepsydras, water clocks consisted of two vessels with a small opening between them. Water dripped from one vessel to another over the course of 24 hours. But water clocks had their drawbacks, too: They were difficult to move, and they froze in cold weather. Despite these problems, cities of

Growing Young in Space

Scientists used to think that time moved at the same speed everywhere in our universe. But the brilliant scientist Albert Einstein suggested that time is in fact relative, or different in different places.

Under Einstein's theory, time would slow down for a person traveling in space as the speed of light is approached, because the person would become both heavier and smaller. If time slows down, in theory, the person would age more slowly.

Scientists demonstrate this theory with an example called the twin paradox. Suppose that one twin traveled in space while the other twin stayed on Earth. As the space-traveling twin approached the speed of light, that person would begin to age more slowly. At home, however, the twin would continue aging at the usual rate. Upon return home, the adventuring twin would actually be younger than the stay-at-home twin, even though they were born at the same time.

any size boasted a large, public (and carefully guarded) clepsydra. For the 2,000 years of their use (until the sixteenth century), water clocks were continuously improved, primarily throught the development of gears or mechanisms that made them more accurate.

Hourglasses

Called a sandglass or cleosamia, the hourglass was a portable clock that was unaffected by freezing spells and didn't require the sun to operate. Like the water clock, it was developed in Egypt thousands of years ago and was used as recently as 1839 by the British navy. Hourglasses could measure specific amounts of time—an hour, a half hour, 8 minutes, or 3 minutes. But they needed to be turned over at the end of the period.

An Hourglass

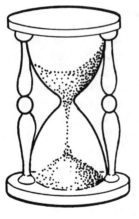

Sound Clocks

Taking a cue from the mechanisms in water clocks, during the Middle Ages inventors came up with the first mechanical clock—a gear-driven timekeeper. Monasteries were the first to have this new invention, but soon every town sported these huge clocks, which sat in their own towers. Sound clocks did not have faces. Instead, they rang bells to announce the quarter hour, half hour, and hour. These clocks, which were the first ornamental timepieces, charmed people with their hourly displays. When the clocks chimed, dancing bears or dashing knights on horseback came into view as the time was rung.

Pendulum Clocks

In 1656 a Dutch astronomer, Christian Huygens, invented the pendulum clock, which had a face to record time. A spring mechanism coiled and uncoiled, while the pendulum marked seconds.

Pendulum Clock

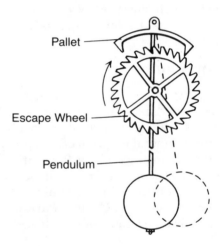

Pallet

Escape Wheel

Pendulum

Watches

People did not have watches until around 1500 when a German, Peter Henlein, invented timekeeping devices that people could wear. These watches were beautiful jewelry, but they didn't keep very accurate time.

Chronometer

Although pendulum clocks and watches worked fine for the average person, some people—most notably scientists and sail-

Time and Space Together

Time and space are intertwined. In fact, time is necessary to measure space. Scientists, for example, calculate how far away a star is by measuring the time it takes light to travel from the star to Earth.

Even on Earth, time is used to measure space. In the great seagoing age of the seventeenth and eighteenth centuries, sailors desperately needed a way to measure longitude; so they could measure the distance they had traveled east or west. Latitude had easily been measured by means of a sextant to mark the distance between the ship and the sun or several designated stars. Special charts were then used to pinpoint the ship's location north and south. But east-west distance could not be measured in this way, and it remained a problem for many years until someone came up with the idea of using time to measure longitude.

Sailors now measure longitude by figuring out how far east or west they have traveled from the prime meridian in Greenwich, England. If they are three hours away, they know, for example, that they are at longitude 45 degrees. Earth turns 360 degrees every 24 hours, so lines of longitude are 15 degrees apart.

ors—needed more accurate clocks than had yet been produced. In the great seagoing age of the eighteenth and nineteenth centuries, sailors required a clock to help them measure longitude and thus determine their exact position. Reward money was offered to the person who could invent an accurate seagoing clock. Such a clock was invented around 1721 by John Harrison, an Englishman who then spent a lifetime perfecting a system of springs and balances that lost only 5 seconds per 1,000 miles at sea. He claimed the reward and his invention, which was called a chronometer.

Electric Clocks

Not surprisingly, electricity led to the development in the 1930s of the electric clock, which was small enough to set on a desktop. The electric clock is motor-powered. Current is the regulator, just as the balance is the regulator in a spring-and-balance clock. Even early electric clocks were accurate to a few seconds a day.

Atomic Clocks

Astronomers and physicists, who often measure one-thousandths or even billionths of a second, needed clocks that were even more accurate. In 1956, the first atomic clock—the world's most accurate clock to date—was built. These clocks are too big and expensive to be used in anyone's home, but they do the job and are accurate to $3/1,000,000$ of a second per year. Two atomic clocks, in Ft. Collins, Colorado, and Kauai, Hawaii, have been the official timekeepers of the United States since 1971. Radio transmissions announce the accurate time to the rest of the country.

CHARTING TIME: A HISTORY OF THE CALENDAR

A calendar is a chart for counting time. For thousands of years, in many parts of the world, calendars were based on lunar cycles. Lunar calendars are still used to record religious holidays in some parts of the world, such as the Middle East. Gradually, though the world's calendars shifted to a solar cycle.

Mayan

Invented around the sixth century B.C., this calendar was more accurate than its western counterpart, the Julian calendar (see below). It used 18 months of 20 days each. Five "unlucky" days brought the year in line with the solar year. It also included an ingenious method to add the leftover time needed to complete the 365¼-day solar year.

Aztec

With their 365-day solar year (18 months of 20 days each), the Aztecs borrowed heavily from the Mayan calendar. A special calendar of 260 days was used to mark religious celebrations. The Aztec calendar, which was based on the sun, the moon, and the stars, worked for 52 years before the seasons occurred at the wrong time. The Aztecs then started another 52-year cycle.

Babylonian

Originating in 3000 B.C., this was a 354-day calendar with 12 months of either 29 or 30 days. Extra months were added every few years to compensate for the 11½ days the calendar was short. This was one of the first calendars to have a 7-day week.

Egyptian

This early lunar calendar was tied to the flooding of the Nile, which happened every 365 days, when the star Sirius rose on the horizon. The calendar began with the first new moon after the sighting of Sirius, and consisted of 12 months of 29½ days each for a year of 354 days, 11 short of 365. To update the calendar, an extra month was added as needed.

The Egyptians also created a solar calendar consisting of 12 months of 30 days each, with 7-day weeks. They saw the need for leap years, but the priests forbade the adding of days to calendars, so the solar calendar could not be used.

Chinese

Predating written history, this is the oldest continuously used calendar. Consisting of a 354-day lunar year with 12 months of 29 to 30 days in length, the calendar repeated in 60-year cycles, with 5 smaller cycles of 12 years each. Each of the 12 years is named for an animal. Modern Chinese use the Gre-

---

Remnants of Time

Around the world, ruins testify to humans' earliest attempts to tell time.

Stonehenge, England Huge stones were arranged in prehistoric times to measure the summer and winter solstices. At about June 21, the sun is at its farthest point from the equator in England.

Great Pyramid of Cheops, near Cairo, Egypt Built around 2600 B.C., it has east and west faces that are touched by the rising and setting sun. The pyramid was also used to mark the equinoxes.

Gateway of Kalasasaya In the Bolivian Andes stands a pre-Incan ruin that is the world's oldest calendar. The year is divided into 12 months, which were probably not the same as our months. The stone reads the hours, days, and moon's phases.

Chichén Itzá, Yucatán, Mexico This and other Mayan observatories throughout Central and South America recorded the positions of the sun, moon, and stars with scientific accuracy.

gorian calendar (see below), but the Chinese calendar is still used for New Year and special events. The Chinese count time from 2698 B.C., so the current year must be added to this figure to calculate the Chinese year.

Cycles of the Chinese Calendar

1991	4689	Sheep
1992	4690	Monkey
1993	4691	Rooster
1994	4692	Dog
1995	4693	Pig
1996	4694	Rat
1997	4695	Ox
1998	4696	Tiger
1999	4697	Hare
2000	4698	Dragon
2001	4699	Snake
2002	4700	Horse

Julian

Julius Caesar revised the Roman calendar in 49 B.C. and gave it his name. The Roman calendar was a confusing chart that had been constantly revised from its first use around 660 B.C. Its major contribution was to give us the names of the months that we use today. The Julian calendar, in contrast, was simple and fairly accurate. The first perpetual calendar, it consisted of 365¼ days and began on the same day each year. A day was added every 4 years (during leap year).

This became the Christian calendar in A.D. 325 under Constantine, who also instituted a 4-week month rather than the Roman three-week month (Kalends, Nones, and Ides). The idea for a 4-week calendar was probably borrowed from the Hebrew calendar.

The seven-day week created some problems, which Constantine ignored. Because, it provided for a 52-week year plus 1 day, every year a day had to be borrowed from the first week of the new year. As an example, consider that January 1 was a Sunday in 1989, a Monday in 1990, a Tuesday in 1991, and a Wednesday in 1992; 1992 was a leap year, so February gained a day, and 1993 skipped a day and began on Friday. Problems like this destroyed the perpetual Julian calendar, which, despite Constantine's changes, continued to go by this name until the Gregorian calendar came into use.

The Magic of the 7-Day Week

Throughout history people used weeks of different lengths. Some African tribes followed a four-day week, while some Central Americans established a five-day week. The Incas had a 10-day week. Ancient Assyrians developed a six-day week, and ancient Romans made their week eight days long.

Eventually, seven days became the accepted length of the week around the world. Why did people settle on seven days when there were so many different lengths for weeks? A week is approximately one-fourth of a lunar cycle, but if people wanted the week to correspond to the lunar cycle they could as easily have picked eight as seven days.

Some historians believe the world settled on a seven-day week because of the special meaning that the number seven has in many cultures and religions. It was an ancient symbol of perfection. In Japanese culture, there are seven gods of happiness. Rome is built on seven hills. Early Christians counted seven deadly sins and seven virtues.

Other experts believe the seven-day week developed because of the makeup of our planetary system. At the time the week became common, people believed the planetary system consisted of the sun, the moon, and five planets—Mercury, Venus, Mars, Jupiter, and Saturn.

HOLIDAYS AROUND THE WORLD

Major U.S. Holidays

*January 1	New Year's Day	Third Sunday in June	Father's Day
*January 15	Martin Luther King, Jr.'s Birthday	*July 4	Independence Day
January 19	Robert E. Lee's Birthday (Southern States)	*First Monday in September	Labor Day
January 20	Inauguration Day	September 17	Citizenship Day
February 2	Groundhog Day	Fourth Friday in September	American Indian Day
February 12	Lincoln's Birthday	*October 12	Columbus Day
February 14	Valentine's Day	October 24	United Nations Day
February 22	Washington's Birthday	October 31	Halloween
March 17	St. Patrick's Day	First Tuesday after the first Monday in November	Election Day
March or April	Easter Sunday	*November 11	Veterans' Day
April 1	April Fools' Day	*Fourth Thursday in November	Thanksgiving Day
April 14	Pan American Day	*December 25	Christmas Day
May 1	May Day		
Second Sunday in May	Mother's Day		
Third Saturday in May	Armed Forces Day		
*Last Monday in May	Memorial Day		
June 3	Jefferson Davis's Birthday (Southern states)		
June 14	Flag Day		

* These are the officially designated national holidays, but with three modifications: the days honoring Martin Luther King, Jr., George Washington, Christopher Columbus, and Memorial Day are observed not on the indicated dates, but on the Mondays closest to those dates on the calendar.

Major Canadian Holidays

January 1	New Year's Day	Second Monday in October	Thanksgiving Day
March or April	Good Friday		
	Easter Monday	November 11	Remembrance Day
First Monday Before May 25	Victoria Day	December 25	Christmas Day
		December 26	Boxing Day
July 1	Canada Day		
First Monday in September	Labor Day		

Major Foreign Holidays

January 1	New Year's Day throughout the Western world and in India, Indonesia, Japan, Korea, the Philippines, Singapore, Taiwan, and Thailand; founding of Republic of China (Taiwan)

January 2	Berchtoldstag in Switzerland
January 3	Genshi-Sai (First Beginning) in Japan
January 5	Twelfth Night (Wassail Eve or Eve of Epiphany) in England
January 6	Epiphany, observed by Catholics throughout Europe and Latin America
Mid-January	Martin Luther King, Jr.'s birthday on the third Monday in the Virgin Islands
January 15	Adults' Day in Japan
January 20	St. Agnes Eve in Great Britain
January 26	Republic Day in India
January 29	Australia Day in Australia
January/February	Chinese New Year and Vietnamese New Year (Tet)
February	Hamstrom on the first Sunday in Switzerland
February 3	Setsubun (Bean-throwing Festival) in Japan
February 5	Promulgation of the Constitution Day in Mexico
February 11	National Foundation Day in Japan
February 27	Independence Day in the Dominican Republic
March 1	Independence Movement Day in Korea; Constitution Day in Panama
March 8	Women's Day in many socialist countries
March 17	St. Patrick's Day in Ireland and Northern Ireland
March 19	St. Joseph's Day in Colombia, Costa Rica, Italy, and Spain
March 21	Benito Juarez's Birthday in Mexico
March 22	Arab League Day in Arab League countries
March 23	Pakistan Day in Pakistan
March 25	Independence Day in Greece; Lady Day (Quarter Day) in Great Britain
March 26	Fiesta del Arbol (Arbor Day) in Spain
March 29	Youth and Martyrs' Day in Taiwan
March 30	Muslim New Year in Indonesia
March/April	Carnival/Lent/Easter: The pre-Lenten celebration of Carnival (Mardi Gras) and the post-Lenten celebration of Easter are movable feasts widely observed in Christian countries.
April 1	Victory Day in Spain; April Fools' Day (All Fools' Day) in Great Britain
April 5	Arbor Day in Korea
April 6	Van Riebeeck Day in South Africa
April 7	World Health Day in U.N. member nations
April 8	Buddha's Birthday in Korea and Japan; Hana Matsuri (Flower Festival) in Japan
April 14	Pan American Day in the Americas
April 19	Declaration of Independence Day in Venezuela
April 22	Queen Isabella Day in Spain
April 23	St. George's Day in England
April 25	Liberation Day in Italy; ANZAC Day in Australia and New Zealand
April 29	Emperor's Birthday in Japan
April 30	Queen's Birthday in The Netherlands; Walpurgis Night in Germany and Scandinavia
May	Constitution Day on first Monday in Japan
May 1	May Day/Labor Day in the C.I.S. and most of Europe and Latin America
May 5	Children's Day in Japan and Korea; Victory of General Zaragosa Day in Mexico; Liberation Day in The Netherlands

May 8	V-E Day in Europe
May 9	Victory over Fascism Day in the C.I.S.
May 31	Republic day in South Africa
June 2	Founding of the Republic Day in Italy
June 5	Constitution Day in Denmark
June 6	Memorial Day in Korea; Flag Day in Sweden
June 8	Muhammad's Birthday in Indonesia
June 10	Portugal Day in Portugal
June 12	Independence Day in the Philippines
Mid-June	Queen's Official Birthday on second Saturday in Great Britain
June 16	Soweto Day in U.N. member nations
June 17	German Unity Day in Germany
June 20	Flag Day in Argentina
June 22	Midsummer's Day in Finland
June 24	Midsummer's Day in Great Britian
June 29	Feast of Saints Peter and Paul in Chile, Colombia, Italy, Peru, Spain, and Venezuela
July 1	Half-year Holiday in Hong Kong; Bank Holiday in Taiwan
July 5	Independence Day in Venezuela
July 9	Independence Day in Argentina
July 10	Bon (Feast of Fortune) in Japan
July 12	Orangemen's Day in Northern Ireland
July 14	Bastille Day in France
Mid-July	Feria de San Fermin during second week in Spain
July 17	Constitution Day in Korea
July 18	National Day in Spain
July 20	Independence Day in Colombia
July 21–22	National Holiday in Belgium
July 22	National Liberation Day in Poland
July 24	Simón Bolívar's Birthday in Ecuador and Venezuela
July 25	St. James Day in Spain
July 28–29	Independence Day in Peru
August	Bank Holiday on first Monday in Fiji, Grenada, Guyana, Hong Kong, Ireland, and Malawi; Independence Day on first Tuesday in Jamaica
August 1	Lammas Day in England; National Day in Switzerland
August 5	Discovery Day in Trinidad and Tobago
August 9	National Day in Singapore
August 10	Independence Day in Ecuador
August 12	Queen's Birthday in Thailand
August 14	Independence Day in Pakistan
August 15	Independence Day in India and Korea; Assumption Day in Catholic countries
August 16	National Restoration Day in the Dominican Republic
August 17	Independence Day in Indonesia
August 31	Independence Day in Trinidad and Tobago
September	Rose of Tralee Festival in Ireland
September 7	Independence Day in Brazil
September 9	Choxo-no-Sekku (Chrysanthemum Day) in Japan

September 14	Battle of San Jacinto Day in Nicaragua
Mid-September	Sherry Wine Harvest in Spain
September 15	Independence Day in Costa Rica, Guatemala, and Nicaragua; Respect for the Aged Day in Japan
September 16	Independence Day in Mexico and Papua New Guinea
September 18–19	Independence Day in Chile
September 28	Confucius's Birthday in Taiwan
October 1	National Day in People's Republic of China; Armed Forces Day in Korea; National Holiday in Nigeria
October 2	National Day in People's Republic of China; Mahatma Gandhi's Birthday in India
October 3	National Foundation Day in Korea
October 5	Proclamation of the Portuguese Republic Day in Portugal
October 9	Korean Alphabet Day in Korea
October 10	Kruger Day in South Africa; Founding of Republic of China in Taiwan
October 12	Columbus Day in Spain and widely throughout Latin America
October 19	Ascension of Muhammad Day in Indonesia
October 20	Revolution Day in Guatemala; Kenyatta Day in Kenya
October 24	United Nations Day in U.N. member nations
October 26	National Holiday in Austria
October 28	Greek National Day in Greece
November 1	All Saints' Day, observed by Catholics in most countries
November 2	All Souls' Day, in Ecuador, El Salvador, Luxembourg, Macao, Mexico, San Marino, Uruguay, and Vatican City
November 4	National Unity Day in Italy
November 5	Guy Fawkes Day in Great Britain
November 11	Armistice Day in Belgium, France, French Guiana, and Tahiti
November 12	Sun Yat-sen's Birthday in Taiwan
November 15	Proclamation of the Republic Day in Brazil
November 17	Day of Penance in Federal Republic of Germany
November 19	National Holiday in Monaco
November 20	Anniversary of the Revolution in Mexico
November 23	Kinro-Kansha-No-Hi (Labor Thanksgiving Day) in Japan
November 30	National Heroes' Day in the Philippines
December 5	Discovery by Columbus Day in Haiti
December 6	Independence Day in Finland
December 8	Feast of the Immaculate Conception, widely observed in Catholic countries
December 10	Constitution Day in Thailand; Human Rights Day in U.N. member nations
Mid-December	Nine Days of Posada during third week in Mexico
December 25	Christmas Day, widely observed in all Christian countries
December 26	St. Stephen's Day in Austria, Ireland, Italy, Lichtenstein, San Marino, Switzerland, and Barcelona (Spain); Boxing Day in Great Britain and Northern Ireland
December 28	National Day in Nepal
December 31	New Year's Eve throughout the world; Omisoka (Grand Last Day) in Japan; Hogmanay Day in Scotland

Religious Holidays

Holy Days of Obligation

Members of the Roman Catholic faith are required to attend Mass on Sundays and also on Holy Days of Obligation. Saturday evening Masses also fulfill the Sunday obligation in the United States. Rome recognizes 10 days of devotion (technically called "solemnities"), but canon law permits some local selectivity regarding their observance. In this chart the starred* entries are days of obligation for Catholics in the United States.

Holy Day	Date	First Observed
**Solemnity of Mary	January 1	1970*
Epiphany of Our Lord	January 6	third century
St. Joseph	March 19	fifteenth century
*Ascension of the Lord	forty days after Easter	first (?) century
Corpus Christi	Thursday after Trinity Sunday	1246
Saints Peter and Paul	June 29	third century
*Assumption of Mary	August 15	seventh century
*All Saints' Day	November 1	835
*Immaculate Conception	December 8	1854
*Christmas	December 25	fourth (?) century

**The Solemnity of Mary replaces the Feast of the Maternity of Mary, which had been observed on October 11. In falling on January 1, it also replaces the feast of the Circumcision of Christ, which was celebrated on that day until 1970.

Major Jewish Holidays

Name	Approximate Date	Hebrew Date
Purim (Lots)	March	14 Adar
Pesach (Passover)	March/April	14–21 Nisan
Shavuot (Pentecost)	May/June	6 Sivan
Tisha b'Av (Ninth of Av)	Mid-July	9 Av
Rosh Hashana (New Year)	September	1, 2 Tishri
Yom Kippur (Day of Atonement)	September/October	10 Tishri
Succot (Tabernacles)	September/October	15–22 Tishri
Hanukkah (Dedication)	November/December	25–3 Tevet Kislev

INFORMATION, PLEASE

Apfel, Necia H. *Calendars*. Franklin Watts, 1985.

Burns, Marilyn. *This Book Is About Time*. Little, Brown, 1978.

Fisher, Leonard Everett. *Calendar Art: Thirteen Days, Weeks, Months, and Years from Around the World*. Four Winds Press, 1987.

Pere, Lila. *Blue Monday and Friday the Thirteenth*. Ticknor, 1986.

Ziner, Feenie and Elizabeth Thompson. *Time*. Children's, 1982.

7

SIGNS AND SYMBOLS

Signs and symbols take the place of words. In our daily lives we are surrounded by signs and signals. Traffic signs tell drivers and pedestrians when to stop and when to go. Question marks and periods inform us we're at the end of a sentence. In math, a plus sign instructs us to add and a minus sign tells us to subtract. In a store window a dollar sign lets us know how much something costs. A skull with crossbones on a bottle warns that the contents are poisonous.

Signs and symbols are a kind of universal language. A Japanese boy and a French girl both understand that an arrow directs them where to go. The following are some of the many universal signs that people around the world use to communicate with each other.

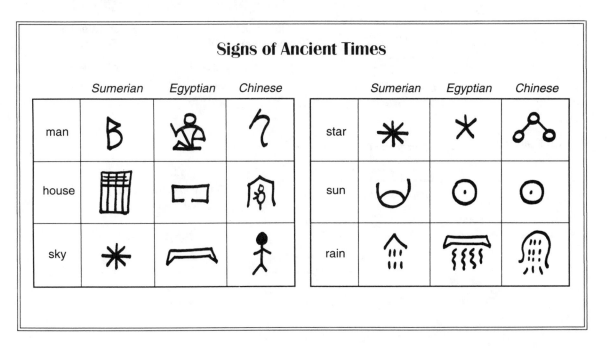

MAP AND CHART SYMBOLS

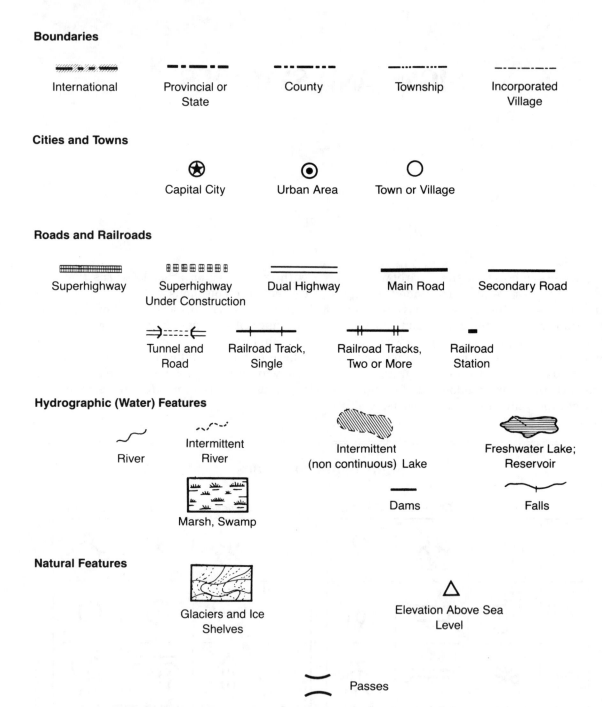

Boundaries

International

Provincial or State

County

Township

Incorporated Village

Cities and Towns

Capital City

Urban Area

Town or Village

Roads and Railroads

Superhighway

Superhighway Under Construction

Dual Highway

Main Road

Secondary Road

Tunnel and Road

Railroad Track, Single

Railroad Tracks, Two or More

Railroad Station

Hydrographic (Water) Features

River

Intermittent River

Intermittent (non continuous) Lake

Freshwater Lake; Reservoir

Marsh, Swamp

Dams

Falls

Natural Features

Glaciers and Ice Shelves

Elevation Above Sea Level

Passes

International Road Signs and Travel Symbols

Danger Signs

Curve	Intersection	Opening bridge	Road works	Tunnel	Pedestrian crossing	Danger

Watch out for children	Animals crossing	Road narrows	Slippery road	Main road ahead	Stop at intersection

Prohibition Signs

No entry	Road closed	Closed to motor vehicles	Closed to motorcycles	Closed to pedestrians

No left (or right) turns	No U turns	Overtaking prohibited	Speed limit	End of speed limit

Mandatory Signs (signs that must be in place)

Direction to follow	Traffic circle	Parking	Hospital	Mechanical help

Telephone	Filling station	Camping site	Caravan site	Youth hostel

CULTURAL, HISTORICAL, AND RECREATIONAL SYMBOLS

■ Points of interest

 Winter sports areas

 Ruins

 National Wildlife Refuge

▲ Campsites

State monuments, memorials, and historic sites

 Ranger Station

WEATHER SYMBOLS

Weather Conditions

Clear sky

Cloudy (partly)

Cloudy (completely overcast)

Drizzle

═ Fog (light)

≡ Fog (heavy)

∞ Haze

Rain

Ⓗ High

Ⓛ Low

Hurricane

Lightning

Sandstorm or dust storm

Hail showers

Rain showers

△ Sleet

✳ Snow

Snow (drifting, slight to moderate)

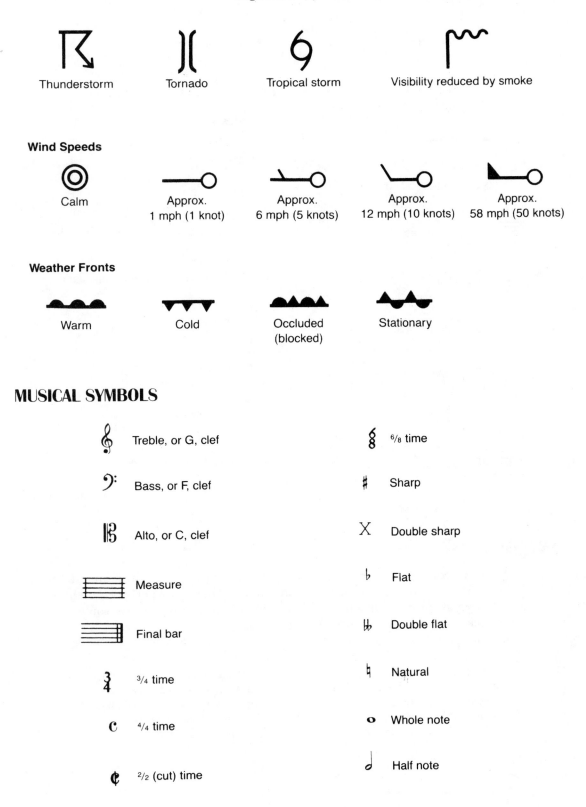

Thunderstorm Tornado Tropical storm Visibility reduced by smoke

Wind Speeds

Calm

Approx.
1 mph (1 knot)

Approx.
6 mph (5 knots)

Approx.
12 mph (10 knots)

Approx.
58 mph (50 knots)

Weather Fronts

Warm Cold Occluded (blocked) Stationary

MUSICAL SYMBOLS

Treble, or G, clef

Bass, or F, clef

Alto, or C, clef

Measure

Final bar

$3/4$ time

$4/4$ time

$2/2$ (cut) time

$6/8$ time

Sharp

Double sharp

Flat

Double flat

Natural

Whole note

Half note

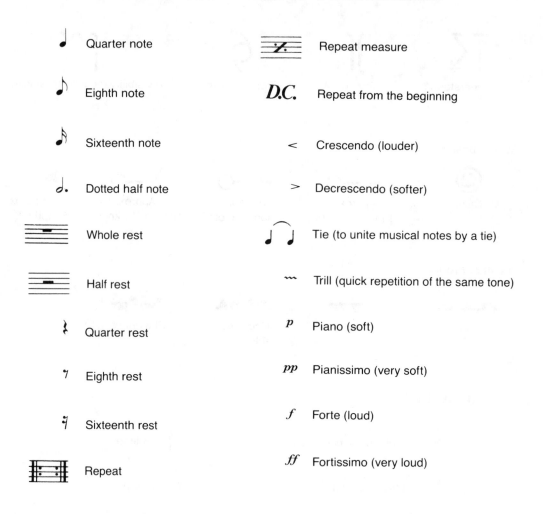

♩ Quarter note	Repeat measure
♪ Eighth note	*D.C.* Repeat from the beginning
♬ Sixteenth note	< Crescendo (louder)
♩. Dotted half note	> Decrescendo (softer)
Whole rest	Tie (to unite musical notes by a tie)
Half rest	Trill (quick repetition of the same tone)
Quarter rest	*p* Piano (soft)
Eighth rest	*pp* Pianissimo (very soft)
Sixteenth rest	*f* Forte (loud)
Repeat	*ff* Fortissimo (very loud)

ACCENT MARKS

Most languages have certain accent marks that, when placed near a phonetic character or characters, change the pronunciation. For example, this mark (˘) is called a breve. A breve placed over a vowel indicates that that vowel is "short." English is one of the few languages that does not use accent marks widely. The following are some common accents:

- ´ Acute accent (as in *café*)
- ˘ Breve (pronunciation symbol that indicates a short vowel)
- ¸ Cedilla (as in *François*)
- ^ Circumflex (as in *château*)

- ¨ Diaeresis or umlaut (as in *Köln*)
- ` Grave accent as in *à la carte*)
- – Macron (pronunciation symbol that indicates a long vowel)
- ~ Tilde (as in *São Tomé*)

RELIGIOUS SYMBOLS

Buddhism

Buddha

Lotus

The wheel

Christianity

Celtic cross

Latin cross

Orthodox cross

Agnus Dei
(Lamb of God)

Descending dove;
Holy Spirit

Chi Rho
(Christian monogram
formed from the
first two letters
X and P of
the Greek word
for Christ)

Hinduism

Mandala

Om

Shiva

Islam

Star and crescent

Judaism

Menorah

Star of David

Ten commandments

Shinto

Torii

Taoism

Water: life-giving source

Yin-yang

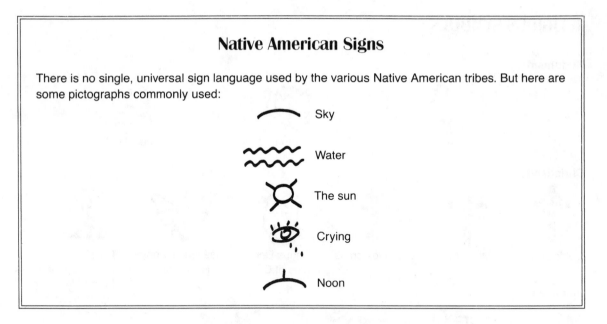

Native American Signs

There is no single, universal sign language used by the various Native American tribes. But here are some pictographs commonly used:

Sky

Water

The sun

Crying

Noon

ZODIAC SIGNS

 *or*

Aries
The Ram
Mar. 21–Apr. 19

 *or*

Cancer
The Crab
June 22–July 22

 or

Taurus
The Bull
Apr. 20–May 20

or

Leo
The Lion
July 23–August 22

 or

Gemini
The Twins
May 21–June 21

 or

Virgo
The Virgin
Aug. 23–Sept. 22

or

Libra
The Scales
Sept. 23–Oct. 23

 or

Capricorn
The Goat
Dec. 22–Jan. 19

 or

Scorpio
The Scorpion
Oct. 24–Nov. 21

 or

Aquarius
The Water Carrier
Jan. 20–Feb. 18

 *or*

Sagittarius
The Archer
Nov. 22–Dec. 21

Pisces
The Fishes
Feb. 19–Mar. 20

LANGUAGE CODES AND SIGNS

International Radio Alphabet and Morse Code

A: Alpha · —
B: Bravo — · · ·
C: Charlie — · — ·
D: Delta — · ·
E: Echo ·
F: Foxtrot · · — ·
G: Golf — — ·
H: Hotel · · · ·
I: India · ·
J: Juliet · — — —
K: Kilo — · —
L: Lima (leema) · — · ·
M: Mike — —
N: November — ·
O: Oscar — — —

P: Papa · — — ·
Q: Quebec (kaybec) — — · —
R: Romeo · — ·
S: Sierra · · ·
T: Tango —
U: Uniform · · —
V: Victor · · · —
W: Whiskey · — —
X: X-ray — · · —
Y: Yankee — · — —
Z: Zulu — — · ·
1: · — — — —
2: · · — — —
3: · · · — —

4: · · · · —
5: · · · · ·
6: — · · · ·
7: — — · · ·
8: — — — · ·
9: — — — — ·
10: — — — — —
period: · — · — · —
comma: — — · · — —
question mark: · · — — · ·
semicolon: — · — · — ·
colon: — — — · · ·
hyphen: — · · · · —
apostrophe: · — — — — ·

Semaphore Code

Semaphore is a system of signaling with two
flags, one held in each hand.

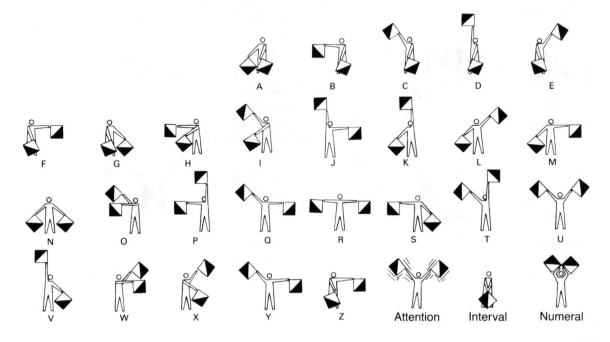

Distress Signals

I	**II**	**X**	**F**	**≋**	**K**
Need doctor	Need medicine	Cannot proceed	Need food and water	Need weapons	Indicate direction

↑	**D**	**⌐**	**△**	**LL**	**L**
Going this way	Aircraft damaged	Attempting take-off	Safe to land	All well	Need fuel and oil
N	**Y**	**JL**	**W**	**□**	**⁝**
No	Yes	Don't understand	Need engineer	Need compass and map	Need signal lamp

Manual Alphabet (Sign Language)

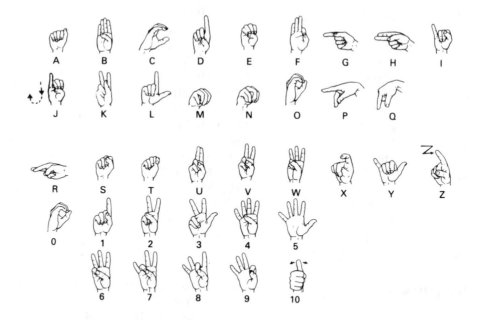

Braille Alphabet and Braille Numbers

In the Braille system, the dots are raised so the visually impaired are able to "read" them with their fingers.

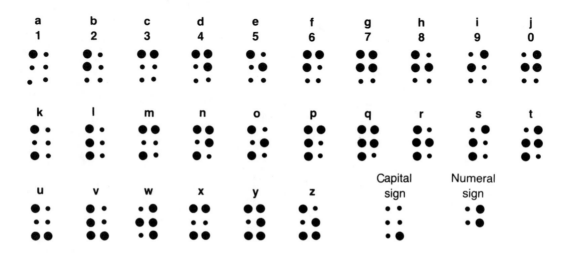

ROMAN NUMERALS

1 I	70 LXX	1,910 MCMX
2 II	80 LXXX	1,920 MCMXX
3 III	90 XC	1,930 MCMXXX
4 IV	100 C	1,940 MCMXL
5 V	150 CL	1,950 MCML
6 VI	200 CC	1,960 MCMLX
7 VII	300 CCC	1,970 MCMLXX
8 VIII	400 CD	1,980 MCMLXXX
9 IX	500 D	1,990 MCMXC
10 X	600 DC	2,000 MM
15 XV	700 DCC	3,000 MMM
20 XX	800 DCCC	4,000 MMMM or $M\overline{V}$
25 XXV	900 CM	5,000 $\overline{V}$
30 XXX	1,000 M	10,000 $\overline{X}$
40 XL	1,500 MD	100,000 $\overline{C}$
50 L	1,900 MCM or	1,000,000 $\overline{M}$
60 LX	MDCCCC	

INFORMATION, PLEASE

Adkins, Jan. *Symbols: A Silent Language.* Walker and Company, 1984.

Campbell, Joseph, and M. J. Abadie. *The Mythic Image.* Princeton University Press, 1981.

Cooper, J. C. *An Illustrated Encyclopedia of Traditional Symbols.* Thames and Hudson, 1987.

DeSola, Ralph. *Abbreviations Dictionary.* New York: Elsevier, 1985.

Dreyfuss, Henry, ed. *Symbol Sourcebook: An Authoritative Guide to International Graphic Symbols.* Van Nostrand Reinhold, 1984.

Fisher, Leonard. *Symbol Art.* MacMillan, 1985.

Helfman, Elizabeth S. *Signs and Symbols.* Lothrop, Lee and Shepard, 1967.

Modley, Rudolf, and William R. Meyers. *Handbook of Pictorial Symbols.* Dover, 1976.

8

MATHEMATICS

Most of us need some basic, working knowledge of math to get through our day-to-day lives and perform well on the job. Mathematics is the science of numbers. The most commonly used branches of mathematics are arithmetic, algebra, and geometry.

ARITHMETIC

Of all the branches of mathematics, arithmetic is the one we use most often. It deals with the ways in which numbers are used in calculations and problem solving.

Addition

Addition lets you find the total, or sum, of a series of numbers.

If, for example, one softball team has 3 catcher's mitts and another has 2, how many catcher's mitts are there?

$$3 + 2 = 5$$

Subtraction

Subtraction is the opposite of addition. In subtraction, you take away a number or numbers from another number. Subtraction is also used to show how many more objects there are in one group than in another.

For example, if you have 4 marbles and you give 1 to a friend, how many marbles are left?

$$4 - 1 = 3$$

Multiplication

Multiplication is a shortcut for addition. Let's say you have 4 groups of pencils, with 3 pencils in each group. What is the total number of pencils?

To get the answer, you can add all the groups:

$$3 + 3 + 3 + 3 = 12$$

Or you can multiply:

$$4 \times 3 = 12$$

Division

Division lets you separate a number into a group of smaller, equal parts. Let's say you have 42 chairs that you must place equally among 7 tables. How many chairs will go at each table?

$$42 \div 7 = 6$$

Fractions

Fractions are parts of numbers. Here are some common fractions and their decimal and percentage equivalents:

Fraction	Decimal	Percent (%)	Fraction	Decimal	Percent (%)
$1/32$	0.03125	3.125	$17/32$	0.53125	53.125
$1/16$	0.0625	6.25	$9/16$	0.5625	56.25
$3/32$	0.09375	9.375	$19/32$	0.59375	59.375
$1/10$	0.1	10	$3/5$	0.6	60
$1/8$	0.125	12.5	$5/8$	0.625	62.5
$5/32$	0.15625	15.625	$21/32$	0.65625	65.625
$3/16$	0.1875	18.75	$2/3$	0.6666+	66.666+
$1/5$	0.2	20	$11/16$	0.6875	68.75
$7/32$	0.21875	21.875	$7/10$	0.7	70
$1/4$	0.25	25	$23/32$	0.71875	71.87
$9/32$	0.28125	28.125	$3/4$	0.75	75
$3/10$	0.3	30	$25/32$	0.78125	78.125
$5/16$	0.3125	31.25	$4/5$	0.8	80
$1/3$	0.3333+	33.333+	$13/16$	0.8125	81.85
$11/32$	0.34375	34.375	$27/32$	0.84375	84.375
$3/8$	0.375	37.5	$7/8$	0.875	87.5
$2/5$	0.4	40	$9/10$	0.9	90
$13/32$	0.40625	40.625	$29/32$	0.90625	90.625
$7/16$	0.4375	43.75	$15/16$	0.9375	93.75
$15/32$	0.46875	46.875	$31/32$	0.96875	96.875
$1/2$	0.5	50			

Here are the basic rules and formulas of fractions:

Addition and subtraction of fractions: (Start with a common denominator)

$$\frac{2}{3}+\frac{4}{5}=\frac{10}{15}+\frac{12}{15}=\frac{22}{15}=1\frac{7}{15}$$

$$\frac{4}{5}-\frac{2}{3}=\frac{12}{15}-\frac{10}{15}=\frac{2}{15}$$

Multiplication of fractions:

$$\frac{2}{5}\times\frac{7}{4}=\frac{14}{20}=\frac{7}{10}$$

Division of fractions:

$$\frac{1}{2}-2=\frac{1}{2}\times\frac{1}{2}=\frac{1}{4}$$

Fractions to decimals:

$$\frac{3}{10}=0.3;\ \frac{3}{100}=0.03;\ \frac{3}{1,000}=0.003$$

ALGEBRA

This is the branch of mathematics in which symbols, usually letters, stand in for unknown numbers. All the operations—addition, subtraction, multiplication, and division—can be performed on all the numbers and symbols:

Number added to an unknown:

$$x + 3 = 10$$
$$x = 10 - 3$$
$$x = 7$$

Number subtracted from an unknown:

$$3 - y = 1$$
$$-y = 1 - 3$$
$$-y = -2$$
$$y = -(-2)$$
$$y = 2$$

Number multiplied using an unknown:

$$5x + 5 = 25$$
$$5x = 20$$
$$x = \frac{20}{5}$$
$$x = 4$$

Number divided by unknown:

$$20 \div y = 5$$
$$20 = 5y$$
$$4 = y$$

GEOMETRY

Geometry is the mathematics of measurements. It provides a way to measure surfaces and solid areas of objects and to calculate the relationships between angles, points, lines, and surfaces.

Magic Squares

Magic squares are sets of numbers arranged within a square in which all the rows—vertical, horizontal, and diagonal—add up to the same total.

Magic squares aren't new. In fact, they were discovered in India over 2,000 years ago. Probably the best known magic square is the one below, which uses all the numbers from 1 to 9.

2	9	4
7	5	3
6	1	8

There are also magic squares with four numbers in a row. In these squares, the 4 adjoining squares in the corners add up to the same numbers.

1	15	14	4
12	6	7	9
8	10	11	5
13	3	2	16

What You See Isn't What You Get: Penrose's Triangle

British mathematician Roger Penrose and his father discovered this triangle, which is now named after them. Study it carefully. Does it look strange to you?

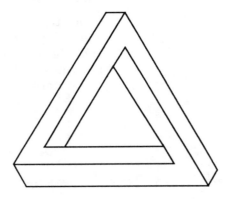

That's because the Penrose triangle could never exist, except as a drawing. It would be impossible to construct an object with surfaces that look like this.

Here are some formulas for measuring area and volume:

Area of a square:

Area = length × width, or length of one side (χ) squared (χ^2)

Area of a rectangle:

Area = length × width

Area of a triangle:

Area = $^1/_2$ × base × perpendicular height

Area of a pentagon (5 sides):

Area = square of the length of one side × 1.720

Area of a hexagon (6 sides):

Area = square of the length of one side × 2.598

Area of octagon (8 sides):

Area = square of the length of one side × 4.828

Area of a cube:

Area = square of the length of one side × 6

Area of a sphere (solid circle):

Area = square of the diameter × pi (3.1416)

Area of a circle:

Area = square of the radius × pi (3.1416)

Area of an ellipse:

Area = long diameter × short diameter × 0.7854

Circumference of a circle:

Circumference = diameter × pi (3.1416)

Volume of a cube:

Volume = cube (χ^3) of the length (χ) of one side

Volume of a pyramid:

Volume = area of the base × height × ⅓

Volume of a cylinder:

Volume = square of the radius (r^3) × pi (3.1416) × height

Volume of a sphere:

Volume = cube of the radius (r^3) × pi (3.1416) × ⁴⁄₃

Volume of a cone:

Volume = square of the radius (r^2) of the base × pi (3.1416) × height × ⅓

Volume of a rectangular solid:

Volume = length × width × height

Parts of a Circle

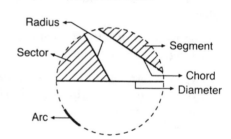

Sphere

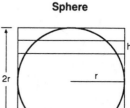

Cube

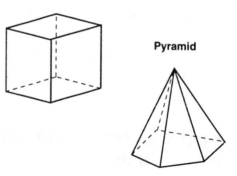

Pyramid

Cylinder

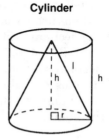

Here are two methods for measuring triangles:

For all triangles, the sum of the angles of a triangle = 180 degrees.

Pythagorean theorem: The square of the hypotenuse of a right-angled triangle is equal to the sum of the squares of the other two sides.

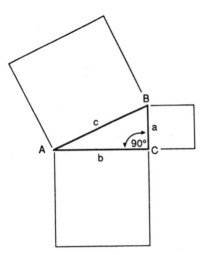

WHAT IF WE HAD EIGHT FINGERS?: BASE SYSTEMS

Because we probably used our hands when we first started to count, many of the world's number systems are based on 10 digits. This is called the decimal system and consists of the digits 0, 1, 2, 3, 4, 5, 6, 7, 8, and 9.

In the decimal system, the position of the digit determines its value. For example, in each of these numbers, the *1* symbolizes the value of the number:

1	symbolizes the ones place
10	symbolizes the tens place
100	symbolizes the one hundreds place
1,000	symbolizes the one thousands place
10,000	symbolizes the ten-thousands place
100,000	symbolizes the one-hundred-thousands place
1,000,000,000	symbolizes the one-millions place

But what if we'd had four fingers on each hand? Then we would most likely have a number system with eight digits. There is nothing magical about ten digits, and there is no reason that a different set of base numbers could not be used if it would be helpful. Scientists and mathematicians, in fact, have sometimes done just that.

Computer scientists work in base two, which is also called the binary system. The binary system consists of two digits: 0 and 1. It counts numbers from the left instead of from the right, and ignores zeros in calculations. In the decimal system, place values move up by a factor of 10, but in the binary system, they move up by a factor of 2. Moving from left to right the place values are:

1	symbolizes the ones place
10	symbolizes the twos place
100	symbolizes the fours place
1,000	symbolizes the eights place
10,000	symbolizes the sixteens place

The chart that follows compares decimal and binary numbers 1–10.

Decimal	Binary
1	1
2	10
3	11
4	100
5	101
6	110
7	111
8	1000
9	1001
10	1010

Mathematicians also use octal, or base 8, and hexadecimal, or base 16, systems for certain calculations. In base 8, the numbers 0–7 are used. In base 16, the numbers 0 through 9 are typically used along with the letters A through F. Count on your fingers, and you will find that 0 through 9 plus A through F equal 16.

UNDERSTANDING NUMBERS BETTER: SET THEORY

Set theory provides us with another way of looking at mathematics. Set theory is used in algebra, geometry, and logic, which is the study of reasoning.

Just as learning grammar helped you to understand English, set theory can help you understand mathematics by explaining numbers in a different way.

The Language of Sets

There are several different kinds of sets.

Finite/Infinite

A finite set has a limited number of members, whereas an infinite set has no limit on the number of members.

If you have three balls to play basketball with, you have a finite set. It would be described this way:

{ Ball A, Ball B, Ball C }

What's Your Lucky Number?

Like many people, you may have a "lucky number." Certain numbers have been considered lucky for thousands of years.

- The ancient Greeks and the Chinese believed numbers were either masculine or feminine. The odd numbers were masculine, and the even numbers were feminine. The numbers 2 and 3 were thought to be lucky because they were the lowest feminine and masculine numbers.
- Three has been a lucky number in many cultures. This probably derives from the Greek and Roman trios of deities, the three Fates and Graces. There were also three Harpies, Sirens, and Furies. Later, after Christianity was founded, the number three took on special meaning because it symbolized the Trinity.
- Four has been considered lucky because it symbolizes the forces of nature: earth, fire, water, and air.
- Five was lucky to ancient Greeks, especially when associated with marriage, because it was the total of the first masculine and feminine numbers.
- The ancient Greeks also considered 6 lucky because it is the first perfect number. A perfect number is a number that is equal to the sum of all its factors (excluding the number itself). In the case of 6: 1 + 2 + 3 = 6.
- Seven probably has special significance in more cultures than any other number. It was an ancient symbol of perfection. Before all the planets were discovered, there were thought to be seven bodies in our solar system—the sun, the moon, and five planets. In Japanese culture, there are seven gods of happiness. In Christianity, there are seven virtues—and, unfortunately, seven deadly sins.

Empty

Set having no members, usually indicated by the symbol ø. If you had no balls to play with, you would describe the situation this way:

Basketballs available = { } = ø

Single Element

Set with only one member, indicated as follows:

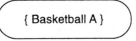

{ Basketball A }

Equivalent

Two or more sets having the same number of members, usually indicated by arrows, as

A ◀──▶ B

Equal

Two or more sets that have exactly the same members, usually indicated by arrows or written as an equation.

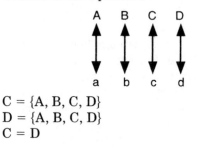

C = {A, B, C, D}
D = {A, B, C, D}
C = D

Overlapping

Two or more sets that share some members in common, indicated by overlapping circles. Let's say that two basketball teams each own two balls and borrow two additional balls, which they must share when they practice together. These sets would look like this:

Ball A   Ball B   Ball C   Ball D   Ball E   Ball F

Disjoint

Two or more sets with no members in common. If there is no way the two teams will share the basketballs, the sets would be described like this:

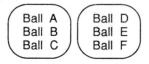

Ball A   Ball D
Ball B   Ball E
Ball C   Ball F

Universal

These are sets made up of all the members that can be considered at any one time, usually indicated by the letter U. It would be described like this:

U = {Basketball A, Basketball B, Basketball C}

Subset

Often groups of sets exist within other sets. For example, consider odd and even numbers as two different subsets of numbers. They would be described this way:

U = 1 through 10
Subset A = {1,3,5,7,9} Subset B = {2,4,6,8,10}

To write this as an equation, you would use the symbol ⊂, which means "is included in." For example:

A ⊂ U
B ⊂ U

Set Pictures: Diagramming Sets to Understand Them

Just as you sometimes diagram a sentence so you can better understand the relationships among various words, phrases, and clauses, you can also use diagrams to describe sets and explain the relationships among them. Most set diagrams consist of a rectangle and several other symbols and units depicting sets.

Universal Set

Subsets

In the diagram, U is a set. A is a subset of U, and B is a subset of A.

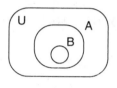

Equal Sets

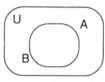

Overlapping Sets

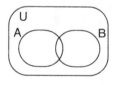

Disjoint Sets

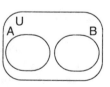

THE HISTORY OF NUMBERS

In the very early part of our history, humans had no need to write down numbers or give them names. But gradually, counting became important. People wanted to know how many goats or sheep they owned. They needed to count their baskets of grain to be sure they had enough to survive the winter.

People must have started counting on their fingers, and then moved on to using small stones, twigs, and even rope. The Incas of Peru devised a complex system of counting with knots tied in hanging cords. The kind of knot and its position on the cord indicated a specific number. With their knot system, they kept detailed records of dates and were able to work with large sums. We know about the Incan system because some of their *quipus*, or knot-records, have survived.

Among other ancient cultures, the Egyptians and the Sumerians devised their own ways of writing numbers at about the same time, 5,000 years ago. Phoenicians originated another system, which the Greeks followed. The Romans used their own system, called Roman numerals.

Our numbers, which are called Arabic, really came from the Hindus in India. The first Hindu numbers, like most numbers, were little more than lines. But gradually those lines were joined to form the figures that became known to us as Arabic numbers. Here is what Hindu numbers would have looked like about 2,000 years ago:

Egyptian Numbers

The Egyptians created written numbers more than 5,000 years ago, using hieroglyphics to form a decimal system. As was the case with many other early number systems, there was no zero. Egyptian numbers looked like this:

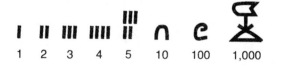

Like many of the earliest originators of number systems, the Egyptians wrote big numbers by grouping small numbers together. The Egyptian number for 436 looked like this:

$$\text{eeeennn}^{|||}_{|||}$$

This method of grouping numbers worked well when the world was still a simple place, mathematically speaking—before, let's say, any human could dream of accumulating more than a thousand of anything, let alone a million. But can you imagine writing a number like 984,452 in Egyptian numbers?

Roman Numerals

One ancient numbering system—that of the Romans—is still used today. Roman numerals can be seen on clocks and watches and in cornerstones of public buildings. The copyright date on old movies is often in Roman numerals.

The Romans used letters to make numbers. For example, *C* stood for *centum*, the Latin word for 100; *M* stood for *mille*, the Latin word for 1000. Roman numerals look like this:

I	II	III	IV	V	VI	VII	VIII
1	2	3	4	5	6	7	8

IX	X	L	C	D	M
9	10	50	100	500	1,000

The problem with Roman numerals is that, like Egyptian numbers, they are grouped

numbers. Thus, large numbers become awkward to work with. For example, 3351 looks like this:

MMMCDLI

Chinese Numbers

The Chinese have an ancient system of counting that involves the use of small sticks, arranged to represent various numbers. Initially, their stick system looked like this:

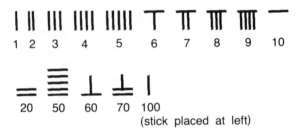

Today, modern Chinese numbers still resemble these ancient marks:

一　二　三　四　五　十　十
1　　2　　3　　4　　5　　10　　13
(10 plus 3)

INFORMATION, PLEASE

Bendick, Jeanne. *Mathematics Illustrated Dictionary.* Rev. ed. Watts, 1989.

Considine, Douglas. *Van Nostrand's Scientific Encyclopedia.* Van Nostrand Reinhold, 1982.

Fisher, Leonard Everett. *Number Art.* Four Winds Press, 1982.

Helfman, Elizabeth S. *Signs and Symbols Around the World.* Lothrop, Lee and Shepard, 1967.

9

THE BASIC SCIENCES: CHEMISTRY AND PHYSICS

Chemistry and physics are often referred to as the "basic" sciences because they explain so much about our world, and because they are used in so many other sciences.

WHAT IS CHEMISTRY?

Chemistry is the study of the composition, structure, properties, and reactions of matter. Matter is any substance that has weight (when it is in a gravitational field) and fills space. It exists as either a solid, a liquid, or a gas. The purpose of chemistry is to understand the chemical changes that happen to matter.

Chemists try to ask and answer these questions:

• What are the basic elements that make up the earth?
• In what quantities are they found on the earth?
• In what ways can they be combined? What happens when they are combined?

ELEMENTS: THE WORLD'S BUILDING BLOCKS

The most basic substances on the earth are the chemical elements. They are often called the "building blocks" of our world because they cannot be reduced chemically to any other substance.

So far, 92 natural elements have been discovered, and 15 more have been created in a laboratory. You already are familiar with some elements, such as gold, iron, or carbon.

So that scientists don't have to write an element's name in full every time they work with one, the name is expressed by a symbol. Carbon, for example, is identified as C. The chemical name of iron is Fe.

The chart that follows, called the periodic table, shows all the chemical elements, with their symbols, and other important information about them that will be explained below.

Periodic Table of the Elements

Element*	Symbol	Valence	Atomic Number
Actinium	Ac	3	89
Aluminum	Al	3	13
Americium	Am	3, 4, 5, 6	95
Antimony	Sb	3, 5	51
Argon	Ar	0	18
Arsenic	As	3, 5	33
Astatine	At	1, 3, 5, 7	85
Barium	Ba	2	56
Berkelium	Bk	3, 4	97
Beryllium	Be	2	4
Bismuth	Bi	3, 5	83
Boron	B	3	5
Bromine	Br	1, 3, 5, 7	35
Cadmium	Cd	2	48
Calcium	Ca	2	20
Californium	Cf	3	98
Carbon	C	2, 4	6
Cerium	Ce	3, 4	58
Cesium	Cs	1	55
Chlorine	Cl	1, 3, 5, 7	17
Chromium	Cr	2, 3, 6	24
Cobalt	Co	2, 3	27
Columbium	(see Niobium)		
Copper	Cu	1, 2	29
Curium	Cm	3	96
Dysprosium	Dy	3	66
Einsteinium	Es		99
Erbium	Er	3	68
Europium	Eu	2, 3	63
Fermium	Fm		100
Fluorine	F	1	9
Francium	Fr	1	87
Gadolinium	Gd	3	64
Gallium	Ga	2, 3	31
Germanium	Ge	4	32
Glucinum	(see Beryllium)		
Gold	Au	1, 3	79
Hafnium	Hf	4	72
Helium	He	0	2
Holmium	Ho	3	67
Hydrogen	H	1	1
Indium	In	3	49
Iodine	I	1, 3, 5, 7	53
Iridium	Ir	3, 4	77

Element*	Symbol	Valence	Atomic Number
Iron	Fe	2, 3	26
Krypton	Kr	0	36
Lanthanum	La	3	57
Lawrencium	Lw		103
Lead	Pb	2, 4	82
Lithium	Li	1	3
Lutetium	Lu	3	71
Magnesium	Mg	2	12
Manganese	Mn	2, 3, 4, 6, 7	25
Mendelevium	Md		101
Mercury	Hg	1, 2	80
Molybdenum	Mo	3, 4, 6	42
Neodymium	Nd	3	60
Neon	Ne	0	10
Neptunium	Np	4, 5, 6	93
Nickel	Ni	2, 3	28
Niobium	Nb	3, 5	41
Nitrogen	N	3, 5	7
Nobelium	No		102
Osmium	Os	2, 3, 4, 8	76
Oxygen	O	2	8
Palladium	Pd	2, 4, 6	46
Phosphorus	P	3, 5	15
Platinum	Pt	2, 4	78
Plutonium	Pu	3, 4, 5, 6	94
Polonium	Po	2, 4	84
Potassium	K	1	19
Praseodymium	Pr	3	59
Promethium	Pm	3	61
Protactinium	Pa		91
Radium	Ra	2	88
Radon	Rn	0	86
Rhenium	Re		75
Rhodium	Rh	3	45
Rubidium	Rb	1	37
Ruthenium	Ru	3, 4, 6, 8	44
Samarium	Sm	2, 3	62
Scandium	Sc	3	21
Selenium	Se	2, 4, 6	34
Silicon	Si	4	14
Silver	Ag	1	47
Sodium	Na	1	11
Strontium	Sr	2	38
Sulfur	S	2, 4, 6	16

(*continued*)

Periodic Table of the Elements (*continued*)

Element*	Symbol	Valence	Atomic Number
Tantalum	Ta	5	73
Technetium	Tc	6, 7	43
Tellurium	Te	2, 4, 6	52
Terbium	Tb	3	65
Thallium	Tl	1, 3	81
Thorium	Th	4	90
Thulium	Tm	3	69
Tin	Sn	2, 4	50
Titanium	Ti	3, 4	22
Tungsten	W	6	74
Uranium	U	4, 6	92
Vanadium	V	3, 5	23
Xenon	Xe	0	54
Ytterbium	Yb	2, 3	70
Yttrium	Y	3	39
Zinc	Zn	2	30
Zirconium	Zr	4	40

* The 103 chemical elements known at present are included in this table. Some of those recently discovered have been obtained only as unstable isotopes.

ATOMS: THE PARTICLES THAT MAKE UP ELEMENTS

The elements are composed of atoms, which are the smallest particles that can be involved in a chemical reaction. Atoms, in turn, are made up of still smaller particles called protons, neutrons, and electrons. All the atoms in an element have the same number of protons.

Protons and neutrons form the nucleus, or center, of an atom, which contains most of

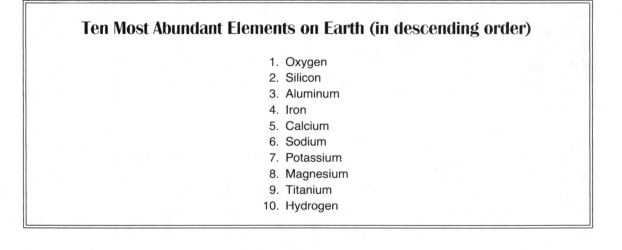

Ten Most Abundant Elements on Earth (in descending order)

1. Oxygen
2. Silicon
3. Aluminum
4. Iron
5. Calcium
6. Sodium
7. Potassium
8. Magnesium
9. Titanium
10. Hydrogen

its weight. Electrons, which revolve around the nucleus, give the atom its chemical properties—that is, its atomic weight, its softness or hardness, and its boiling and freezing points.

An Atom

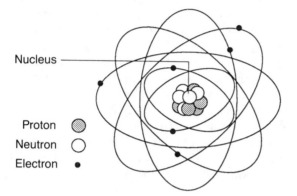

Nucleus

Proton ⊗
Neutron ○
Electron ●

Protons and electrons are electrically charged. Protons have a positive electrical charge, and electrons have a negative charge. (Neutrons are neutral.) Since opposite electrical charges attract, the positively charged protons in the nucleus of the atom help to keep the negatively charged electrons in the atom. The more energy an electron has, though, the more it can resist the force of the protons, and the farther away from the nucleus it is likely to be.

The electrical forces also act on atoms to create chemical bonds that cause two or more atoms to join together to form a molecule. A molecule is a basic unit of two or more atoms that cannot be subdivided.

Atoms and Isotopes

Even though all atoms are tiny, they have many different characteristics. The lightest atom, for example, is hydrogen, which has one electron and one proton. The heaviest atom is uranium, with 92 electrons, 92 protons, and 146 electrons.

In addition to the names of the elements and their symbols, the periodic table on pages 120 to 122 lists several measures of atoms:

- The atomic number is the number of protons in an atom's nucleus.
- The valence describes the ability of an element to combine with another to form molecules. Electrons are usually arranged in layers, or shells, around the nucleus. The outer electrons are the ones that are acted on in chemical changes.

Substances that contain the same number of protons but a different number of neutrons are different forms of the same element; they are called isotopes. All elements have isotopes. Hydrogen, for example, has three isotopes, which scientists call hydrogen 1, 2, and 3, or protium, deuterium, and tritium.

ACTION AND REACTION: CHEMICAL CHANGES IN MATTER

Most chemical changes either form a new substance (action) or destroy an old one (reaction).

A chemical action or reaction is not the same as a physical action, but an under-

---

Highest, Lowest, Hottest, Coldest: More About Elements

- Carbon is the element with the highest melting point, at about 3550 degrees Centigrade.
- Helium has the lowest melting point, at somewhere lower than −272.2 degrees Centigrade.
- Tungsten has the highest boiling point, at 5660 degrees Centigrade.
- Hydrogen has the lowest boiling point, at −252.87 degrees Centigrade.

Isotopes of Hydrogen

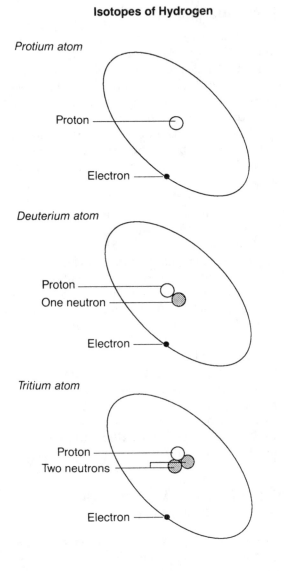

sulfuric acid, a key component in acid rain. These are chemical changes.

Although elements are substances that cannot be reduced physically, they can be changed chemically. You cannot break iron and oxygen down into anything smaller than iron and oxygen, for example, but you can change them chemically into rust.

Chemical change occurs on several levels. Two or more atoms can combine to form a molecule, a basic unit of matter that cannot be broken down into anything but atoms without losing its characteristics. Molecules can consist of atoms from the same element or ones from different elements.

When two or more elements are combined, their atomic structures merge to form a compound. When carbon is combined with oxygen, it merges to form a new chemical substance called carbon dioxide.

Chemical Equations

Chemists describe chemical changes in formulas. For example, the merging of carbon and oxygen is written this way:

$$C + O_2 \rightarrow CO_2$$

In this equation, the number 2 indicates the number of atoms in the molecule.

DATING DINOSAURS AND CATCHING CROOKS: THE USES OF CHEMISTRY

Through their many discoveries about atoms and elements, chemists have changed our world, and they continue to do so by using chemistry to create new products and processes. Here are some of the ways chemistry has changed our lives:

• Chemistry is used to convert raw products into glass, paper, and metals.
• Chemistry is used to control pollution and find better ways to manage waste materials, sometimes by converting them into new products.

standing of physical actions helps us to understand chemical ones. A physical action might consist, for example, of pulling apart two wooden blocks that are stuck together. Two objects are together, but when they are taken apart, they become separate objects.

Chemical actions create changes in matter's atoms. For example, when the two elements iron and oxygen combine, they form a new substance called rust. When sulfur trioxide gas combines with water, it produces

- Chemistry is used to produce and process foods.
- Chemistry is widely used in medicine to diagnose, treat, and cure a variety of illnesses.
- Chemistry plays a role in combating cancer, as biochemists study agents that cause molecular changes in cells.
- Chemistry has been responsible for creating new sources of energy—through the use of gasoline and solar and nuclear power, for example.
- Chemistry has been used to create better fertilizers and pesticides for farmers.
- Chemistry is used to manufacture everything from plastics, rubber, and synthetic fibers to soaps and household cleansers.
- Chemistry is used by museum workers to determine the age of works of art, archaeological objects, and the remains of plants and animals—including dinosaurs.
- Chemistry is used in law enforcement when fibers from criminals' clothing and/or blood left at the scene of a crime are identified and traced to their original sources.

SUPERSCIENTISTS: CHEMISTS WHO MADE A DIFFERENCE

Among the important scientists who contributed major ideas that advanced chemistry, are the following:

The French chemist *Antoine Lavoisier*, who lived in the 1700s, studied chemical processes and taught the world to view them in a new light. For example, he proved that the respiration process in animals is similar to the chemical process of combustion. He also helped to establish the naming system for chemicals that is still in use today.

In 1803 the English chemist *John Dalton* developed the theory that atoms exist. He proved the theory that when the atoms of one substance combine with the atoms of another substance, they form compounds. Dalton was also the first to calculate atomic weights.

In 1869 the Russian chemist *Dmitri Mendeleev* discovered what is known as the *periodic law*. He used it to arrange the periodic table. By placing elements according to their atomic weights, he was able to group similar elements together. Mendeleev even left gaps in the table, where he predicted—accurately, as it turns out—that newly discovered elements would be placed.

CAREERS IN CHEMISTRY

Many different careers are open to someone who wants to become a chemist. Here are some of the specialties:

analytical chemistry The study of the characteristics of substances, such as the way they can be combined to form compounds.

applied chemistry The study of the practical uses of chemistry, especially in agriculture, the environment, and industry.

astrochemistry The study of chemical changes in outer space.

biochemistry The study of actions and reactions in living organisms.

geochemistry The study of chemistry in geological matter, especially as it relates to mining and oil production.

inorganic chemistry The study of actions and reactions on nonliving matter.

nuclear chemistry The study of atomic structure, especially as it applies to the uses of nuclear energy.

physical chemistry The study of chemical processes and how they relate to the physical properties of matter, such as their weight, mass, heat, and radiation. This specialty explores the theories upon which many other specialties then build.

WHAT IS PHYSICS?

Physics is the study of what happens to matter physically, as opposed to chemically. It is the study of how energy of various kinds—

The Ways of Working Scientists: Using the Scientific Method

Did you know that science is a highly creative endeavor? A scientist looks at something—even something so obvious as light or sound, for example—and suddenly realizes that it can be used in a new way. At first, though, the scientist has nothing but an idea or theory about how the new product or process might work. The task of testing the validity of the theory remains ahead of him or her and the other scientists who follow.

Chemists and physicists were among the first scientists to develop specialized techniques to use in proving or disproving a theory or idea. These techniques, which vary little from science to science, are called the scientific method. Here are the steps most scientists follow in pursuing their theories:

1. *Observe the data.* This is one of the oldest techniques, dating back to the ancient peoples who observed the movement of the heavenly bodies and formed some theories based on what they saw.
2. *Classify the data.* Naturalists, for example, observed the many kinds of plants and animals, and began to sort them into groups and subgroups, called kingdom, phylum (or division), class, order, family, genus, and species. In this way, biologists were able to see that small domestic cats are related to the large wild cats. In another example, mathematicians have borrowed from scientists to develop set theory, which enables them to see relationships among various kinds of groups.
3. *Propose a hypothesis.* When chemists had studied enough atoms, they were able to devise a hypothesis about how atoms act and react. They did not have to study every atom in existence (an impossible task) to draw some conclusions.
4. *Conduct experiments.* Experiments are necessary to prove the validity of a theory. Galileo was one of the first scientists to recognize the need to conduct experiments. He rolled balls down differently angled planes to test his theory that all objects move at the same speed regardless of weight unless they are acted upon by an outside force.
5. *Formulate a theory.* In this step, the scientist proposes an explanation for his theory—based on either his original hypothesis or a revised one. By using logic to formulate a theory, chemists were able to say that they believed if one atom behaved in a certain way, then it was reasonable to assume that other atoms would also behave that way. Once a theory has been formulated, other scientists can test its validity. When enough people have found that it is correct, it will be accepted by the scientific world.

gravitational, electrical, and nuclear—acts on matter.

The four basic kinds of atoms

1. gravitational
2. electromagnetic
3. strong nuclear
4. weak nuclear

The gravitational force is the attraction between any two bodies that have mass, includ-ing atoms. (Virtually all matter has mass. The only exception

, such as protons and electrons. The strong and weak nuclear forces act only at the nuclear level of an atom.

The physicist, like the chemist, looks for patterns in the way matter acts and reacts and then writes laws that describe those patterns.

BRIDGES AND TRANSISTORS: HOW PHYSICS CHANGES OUR LIVES

Without the laws of physics applied to the following fields, our lives would be far different.

building construction Architects and engineers use physics in designing roads, bridges, and other structures.

communication Plasma physicists have pioneered the use of optic cable to convey telephone messages.

fuels Thermodynamics are used to design engines that use fuel more efficiently and to develop new fuels.

manufacturing Physics gave us the semiconductor industry, which has led to improved electronics for everything from stereos to computers. Lasers and fiber optics are changing the face of many industries.

medicine Physics played a role in the development of radiation therapy, X-rays, and medical-imaging systems, such as CAT scans and magnetic resonance imaging (MRI) systems, and will probably provide even more advanced imaging systems in the future.

optics Optics physicists design eyeglasses and contact lenses, as well as telescopes and microscopes.

transportation Automotive engineers and designers use the principles of mechanics to design engines and vehicles. One day in the future, physicists may give us superfast trains that ride on magnetic fields.

weaponry Physicists developed the atomic and hydrogen bombs.

MASTERS OF THE UNIVERSE: GALILEO, KEPLER, NEWTON

Three scientists who worked in the 1600s—*Galileo, Johannes Kepler,* and *Sir Isaac Newton*—made invaluable contributions to the basic sciences. Not only did their discoveries open a path to future research, but more important, they showed—for the first time—that the universe is an orderly place, and that there are laws that govern its physical actions. Their discoveries and research are invaluable to chemists and physicists.

All three men worked to discover the laws of motion. Galileo uncovered the natural laws that govern falling bodies and the motion of a swinging pendulum. Building on Galileo's work, Kepler established the laws that control the movement of the planets around the sun. Finally, Newton confirmed these earlier findings and proposed three laws of motion that apply to all matter:

1. An object in motion or at rest will remain in motion or at rest until it is acted upon by an outside force.
2. The acceleration, or rate of the change of the speed, of an object is directly related to the force that acts upon it.
3. For every action, there is an opposite and equal reaction.

CAREERS IN PHYSICS

Many different careers are open to someone who wants to become a physicist. Here are some of the specialties:

acoustics The study of sound.

atomic physics The study of atoms.

biophysics The study of physics applied to living organisms.

fluid physics The study of liquids and gases.

mechanics The study of matter in its three forms—liquid, gas, and solid—and motion. This is the major discipline of physics. Two subdivisions of this specialty are dynamics, which is the study of matter in motion, and statics, the study of matter at rest.

molecular physics The study of molecules.

nuclear physics The study of the atom's nucleus, especially as it relates to nuclear reactions and their uses.

optics The study of light and motion.

particle physics The study of the elementary particles—electrons, neutrons, and protons—and how they behave.

plasma physics The study of special gases called plasma.

quantum physics The study of electromagnetic radiation and matter.

solid-state physics The study of solid materials.

thermodynamics The study of heat and motion.

SCIENCE FROM A TO Z

acceleration Change in rate of velocity, or rate of speed, with respect to time. If an object moves faster in a specific amount of time, it is said to have accelerated.

acid Substance that, in liquid form, will turn blue litmus paper red, react with alkalis (bases) to form salts, and dissolve metals to form salts.

alkali Any compound that has the chemical qualities of a base, such as reacting with acids to form salts.

atom Smallest particle that can be acted on chemically.

atomic number Number of protons in an atom of an element.

base An alkaline substance that will accept or receive a proton from another chemical unit.

bond A strong electrical force that holds atoms together in molecules, crystals, and other combinations.

catalyst A substance that accelerates a chemical reaction without becoming part of the end product of the reaction. A catalyst can usually be found in its original form after the reaction has occurred.

compound A substance formed by combining two or more chemical elements.

conduction Transfer of heat by molecular motion from its source to a cooler region. The tendency is to create the same temperature throughout the substance.

convection In physics, the mechanical transfer of heated molecules of a gas or liquid from a source to another region, as when an entire room is warmed by the movement of molecules heated by a radiator.

electrolyte Any chemical, such as a mineral, that conducts electric current when melted or dissolved in water.

electromagnetic force Energy exerted by magnetism that occurs when an electric charge is in motion.

electromotive force Force that causes the movement of electrons through an electrical circuit.

electron A negatively charged particle that moves in orbit around the nucleus of an atom.

element Basic substance that cannot be reduced physically but can be acted upon chemically.

energy The ability to perform work. Energy can be changed from one form to another, as from heat into light, but it cannot be created or destroyed.

force In physics, the influence on a body that causes it to accelerate.

gas State of matter that is neither liquid nor solid, and which lacks definite shape and volume, diffuses easily, and readily resists flowing when pressure is applied.

gravity A force in nature that pulls bodies with enough mass together.

heat Form of energy that results from the disordered motion of molecules. As the motion becomes more rapid and disordered, the amount of heat is increased.

isotope One of two or more atoms with the same atomic number but a different mass number. Alternate forms of the same element.

liquid State of matter that is neither solid nor gas, that flows, or pours, easily and does not resist flowing when pressure is applied.

mass number Number of protons and neutrons in an atom of an element.

matter Anything that has weight or fills space, such as a solid, gas, or liquid.

Science Projects: How to Organize Them

Science projects help you learn about science. Usually a project involves a written paper and some kind of physical demonstration: either performing an experiment, building a model, or forming a collection. Here are the main steps required to do a successful science project:

1. *Develop an idea.* Your teacher will help you. Remember the project has to be something that is feasible. You may be interested in nuclear reactors, but it won't be practical to build one as a science project. Similarly, if you choose a science project that involves a live animal, you cannot make it ill or otherwise harm it.
2. *Do background reading.* Read what has been written about your chosen subject.
3. *Formulate a thesis.* In one or two sentences, write down what you are going to attempt to do or prove—your thesis, in other words. Remember that you will usually be following in someone else's footsteps. Much of the work that scientists do consists of proving or disproving the work of other scientists.
4. *Acquire the materials and equipment you need.* Draw up lists of what you need before acquiring them.
5. *Prepare any visual and support materials.* Do you need to prepare a poster showing the steps of the experiment you are conducting? Perhaps you need to copy an article that has been important in guiding your research? Support materials should help your audience understand your project.
6. *Do the actual project.* Build the model, assemble the collection, or conduct the experiment. Especially if you are doing an experiment, you may need to practice several times before doing it publicly.
7. *Write the paper.* Science projects should be backed up with a paper explaining what you intended to do, how you went about doing it, and whether your project was a success or not, scientifically speaking. Remember, the true success of a science project lies in the efficiency and organization you bring to the project—not in whether you prove or disprove your thesis.

molecule Basic unit that cannot be subdivided without losing its characteristics; molecules consist of 2 or more atoms.

nuclear force Energy exerted by atoms.

oxidation Any chemical reaction that increases the number of oxygen atoms in a compound, or in which the positive valence is increased by a loss of electrons.

power Rate at which work is performed.

solid State of matter having a definite shape and volume.

valence The ability of an element to combine with another to form molecules. It is measured by the number of hydrogen or chlorine atoms it will combine with.

weight In physics, the force on a body produced by the downward pull of gravity on it.

INFORMATION, PLEASE

Apfel, N. H. *It's All Elementary: From Atoms to the Quantum World of Quarks.* Lothrop, 1984.

_____. *It's All Relative: Einstein's Theory of Relativity.* Lothrop, 1981.

Asimov, Isaac. *Asimov's New Guide to Science.* Basic Books, 1984.

_____. *How Did We Find Out About Atoms?* Walker, 1976.

McGraw-Hill Encyclopedia of Science and Technology. 5th ed. 5 vols. McGraw-Hill, 1982.

Taylor, Ron. *The Invisible World.* Facts on File, 1985.

Weast, Robert. *Handbook of Chemistry and Physics.* 69th ed. CRC Press, 1988.

10

COMPUTERS

A computer is a machine that takes in information, processes it, stores it, and gives it back on request. Because computers do all this electronically, they are able to work with amazing speed—far faster than the human mind. Computers are probably the most important invention in the last century, if not since the printing press.

Computers have changed our lives. The uses that humans have devised for computers are truly amazing. As individuals, we use computers for an array of activities from writing letters to playing games to balancing our checkbooks. But computers have also proved invaluable in science, engineering, finance, medicine, the humanities, and the military—virtually every area of human endeavor.

Ten Things Computers Can Do Now

1. Find you when you are lost. SARSATS are search-and-rescue satellites operated by computers. They circle the earth, and pick up signals from downed planes or distressed ships.
2. Fly planes.
3. Operate radio stations.
4. Predict the weather.
5. Operate robots.
6. Tell farmers when to plant crops.
7. Test your blood samples.
8. Design and draw a house's floor plan.
9. Help sports agents write contracts by taking a player's statistics and calculating his worth to a team.
10. Give you money at a bank.

COMPUTERS IN OUR LIVES

- Scientists use computers to solve equations and other numerical problems, which computers do far faster and more accurately than humans.
- Engineers use computers to predict how a new airplane will fly.
- Bankers use computers to show how savings will grow at different rates of interest.
- Researchers and librarians use computers to store information, including entire libraries.
- Governments use computers to store data—including the entire U.S. Census report.
- Writers use computers to write, edit, and rewrite entire books.
- Doctors use computers to make images of the human body.
- Space agencies use computers to guide rockets to their destination.

LIFE IN MICROLAND

Not until the microcomputer was invented in 1975 was it possible for everyone to have a computer on her desk—or in his pocket. But what exactly is a microcomputer? It is a personal computer, or PC, as it is frequently called. PCs come in three forms:

desktop These are meant to sit on desks. They weigh about 25 pounds and usually have to be plugged into an electrical outlet.

laptop These small computers, which weigh 8 to 10 pounds, are portable and can operate on batteries. The screen displays less text than a desktop screen, but laptops are not necessarily less powerful than desktops. Some laptops easily outperform some desktops.

pocket Weighing only a few ounces and about the size of a woman's pocketbook, these baby PCs usually function as address books, dictionaries, and game-boards. A few pocket PCs are general-purpose, but these aren't as powerful as either desktops or laptops.

THE PARTS OF A COMPUTER

Most people use the word *computer* when what they really mean is "computer system." A computer system has three main parts:

processor This unit takes in information and acts on it.

memory This unit records information, holds it until needed, and then retrieves it.

input/output equipment These tools, which include the monitor, printer, modem, and disks, enable the user and computer to communicate with each other.

Hardware and Software: Another Way of Looking at Computers

hardware The physical equipment a computer uses. This consists of the processor, the memory, and the input-output devices, such as the monitor, printer, floppy disks, modem, and cassette tapes.

software Sets of instructions, usually on floppy disks and accompanied by instruction books, that tell the computer what to do with the information it receives. Also called *programs*.

BINARY DANCE: HOW A COMPUTER WORKS

Computers use symbols to read information. The symbols they use are the numbers 0 and 1, but they could as easily be any other symbols.

The reason a computer uses this binary, or two-number, system, is convenience. It is easy to build electronic switches—like light switches—that have two positions, "on" and "off." Computers make use of numerous

Six Things Computers Will Do in the Future

1. Control your television. There will be more than 1,000 stations to choose from, and you'll use a database to order individual shows.
2. Use virtual reality to go into computer-generated worlds where you'll be able to interact with characters and other people.
3. Respond to your voice. You will simply speak to your computer to tell it to turn on, find a document, or print a document.
4. Help the blind "see." Shoulder-mounted computers will produce mental images to help blind persons know in what direction they are moving or how far away an obstacle is.
5. Build other computers. Computer-generated robots will be able to build other robots, which will then be used to build products such as houses and televisions.
6. Fit in your pocket. Really powerful computers will be the size of credit cards.

Computer Parts

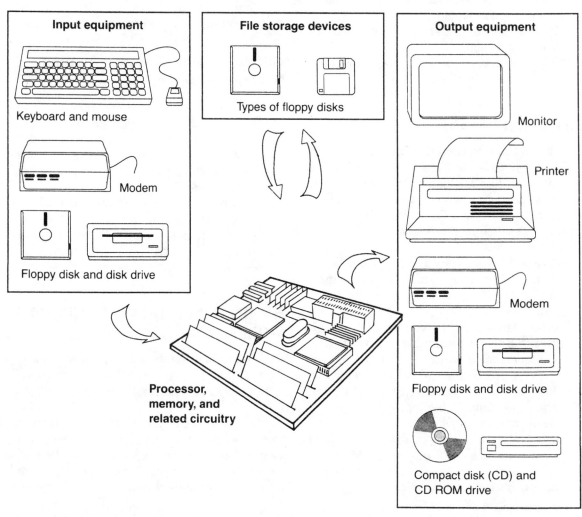

Input equipment

Keyboard and mouse

Modem

Floppy disk and disk drive

File storage devices

Types of floppy disks

Output equipment

Monitor

Printer

Modem

Floppy disk and disk drive

Compact disk (CD) and CD ROM drive

Processor, memory, and related circuitry

electronic switches based on this principle. An electronic switch is called a *binary digit*, or *bit* for short.

Using only two number symbols, a computer can read an infinite amount of numbers or words. It reads the number 32,800, for example, as 1000000000100000. This is a lot of digits, but the computer processes the information extremely quickly. A computer also uses numbers to describe letters and words. A is represented by 010001, while B is 010010, and C is 010011. Each of these combinations is called a *byte*.

The computer takes in, or *inputs*, the bytes, processes them, and then converts them back to, or *outputs*, letters or numbers that mean something to you.

In order for the computer to know what to do with the information, it must have software. One program might tell a computer how to do mathematical calculations. Another might tell it how to do word processing. Some software consists of games. Using the software, the computer can perform all sorts of tasks.

Here are some common symbols and their 7-bit computer codes:

0	0000000	F	1010110	$	0101011
1	1000001	G	0010111	*	1101100
2	1000010	H	0011000	)	0101101
3	0000011	I	1011001	;	0101110
4	1000100	&	1011010	'	1101111
5	0000101	.	0011011	+	0110000
6	0000110	]	1011100	/	1110001
7	1000111	(	0011101	S	1110010
8	1001000	<	0011110	T	0110011
9	0001001	\	1011111	U	1110100
[	0001010	↑	1100000	V	0110101
#	1001011	J	0100001	W	0110110
@	0001100	K	0100010	X	1110111
:	1001101	L	1100011	Y	1111000
>	1001110	M	0100100	Z	0111001
?	0001111	N	1100101	←	0111010
(space)	1010000	O	1100110	,	1111011
A	0010001	P	0100111	%	0111100
B	0010010	Q	0101000	=	1111101
C	1010011	R	1101001	"	1111110
D	0010100	–	1101010	!	0111111
E	1010101				

THE DEVELOPMENT OF COMPUTERS

Like many major inventions, the computer developed over a long period and drew on the principles that led to several other inventions.

One of the most important things a computer does, for example, is store large amounts of information in its memory. Thus the computer's development was helped along by the invention of the Jacquard loom, which used cards with holes punched in them to create patterns for woven material. Similar cards with holes punched in them were used to feed information into early computers. The invention of binary math was another important step that was necessary in order for computers to be developed.

But an ancient device called the abacus,

Ancient Abacus

An ancient Chinese counting device called an abacus, which is still used today in some parts of the world, is credited with giving early computer scientists an idea about how to store information in a computer's memory. Abacuses are used not only for counting but also as a memory aid for the user who is counting large numbers.

Drawing A shows the place values of an abacus.

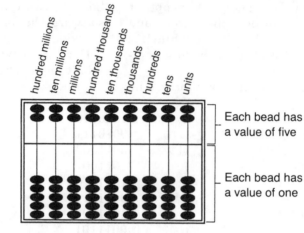

a

Each bead has a value of five

Each bead has a value of one

Drawing B shows the number 10,555.

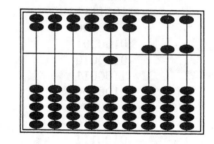

b

The bead below the horizontal marker in the fifth place from the left has been moved up to represent 10,000. Beads in the last three rows have been moved down to represent, correspondingly, 500, 50, and 5. The number, as you can see, is read on the horizontal line across the abacus.

Drawing C: What number is represented on the abacus?

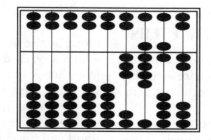

c

Answer: 3962.

invented by the Chinese and used for thousands of years, was the first counting machine that could handle really large numbers, and it is credited with giving early computer scientists the idea of storing numbers.

Time Line for Computer Development

Date	Event
Ancient times	Abacus, a calculating device used for thousands of years by the Chinese, assists people in processing numbers into the hundred millions.
1801	Jacquard loom is invented. This leads to development of punch cards that are later used to program the first computers.
1830s	Charles Babbage designs the first computer, which he calls an "analytical machine." It contains the components of all the later computers: storage, memory, and a system for coordinating the two. The machine is never completed enough to be mass-manufactured, largely because people do not yet understand how electricity works, nor do they have the technology to make the complicated parts required to manufacture computers.
Mid-1800s	Binary math is invented by George Boole. Complex math operations can now be done using only two digits.
1888	Herman Hollerwirth creates a punch-card computer system that is used to process the U.S. census report.
1947	Transistors are invented to replace vacuum tubes. This means that the size of computers can be reduced.
1960s	Transistor chips become specialized. Some hold memory; some form the processor. Eventually one chip will become the entire microprocessor in a desktop computer.
1975	First desktop computer is invented. Computer technology will soon be available to everyone. Businesses that cannot afford to buy their own mainframes can afford these smaller computers.
1977	Steven Jobs and Stephen Wozniak found Apple Computers and begin to market desktop models to individuals at a reasonable price.
1981	IBM, the biggest manufacturer of mainframes, introduces its own desktop computers. Many other manufacturers now compete with Apple and IBM.
Mid-1980s	A small (10 pounds or under) portable computer dubbed a "laptop" is introduced. Now the race is on to create even smaller, more powerful computers.

COMPUTERS FROM A TO Z

artificial intelligence A computer that will be able to make decisions based on information fed into it. It is unclear whether computers will be able to do this.

binary number Two-digit number system, usually consisting of the number symbols 0 and 1.

bit Smallest piece of information a computer can process, either 1 or 0.

byte A basic unit of computer informa-

Computer Jargon

Like any other group of specialists, computer users speak their own special language. Here are some of the words computer users love to use:

gronked	inoperative
cuspy	excellent
dink	modify
mung	change
bagbiter	failure
deadlock	jammed
gigo	garbage in, garbage out
wysiwyg	what you see is what you get

tion, usually 8 digits, such as that for a short word.

CPU Central Processing Unit, the part of the computer that processes and stores information.

cursor A mark, either a line or a small block, that appears on the monitor's screen to indicate where the next piece of information will be input.

database Large body of information, such as a library or newspaper, that the computer can read and output.

disk *See* **floppy disk** and **hard disk**.

disk drive Hardware unit that holds portable disk (such as a floppy). The disk drive can read information from the disk and can copy information onto the disk.

down time Period when a computer is not working.

floppy disk A portable device for storing information that is separate from the computer.

hard copy Printed information from a computer. The output of a printer.

hard disk A part of the computer that stores far more information than a floppy disk. Unlike a floppy disk, it cannot be removed from the computer.

hard drive *See* **hard disk.** Also called fixed disk.

hardware The physical parts of a computer system, including the computer, the monitor, modem, printer, disks, etc. *See also* **software**.

input The information that is fed into a computer, which it then processes, stores, and returns on request. *See also* **output**.

interface A piece of equipment that is used to connect the computer to other hardware, such as a printer, a mouse, or an external modem.

joystick An external hardware tool; a lever that is used to move the cursor.

keyboard An input hardware tool that enters information typed on it into the computer.

language Software information that tells the machine what to do with the information it receives. Popular languages are BASIC, COBOL, and FORTRAN.

mainframe computer A large computer that can store enormous amounts of information and perform sophisticated tasks. Used by governments and major companies. *See also* **personal computer**.

modem Stands for MOdulator DEModulator; a device used to carry computer information over telephone wires anywhere in the world.

Users and Abusers in the Land of Hackerdom

In computer jargon, the growing numbers of persons with desktop computers are called end users, or more simply, users. The majority of users do not understand the operating software and tend to use the machine only for work-related activities.

In the land of hackerdom, though, live the hackers, also known as gweeps and lurkers—persons who live with their computers. *Lurkers* are those shy souls who go to electronic meetings and don't say anything—and also those who break into other people's computers.

In fact, the term *hacker*, initially used to describe a genuine computer enthusiast, is more often used these days to describe someone who misuses a computer—to tap into the Pentagon's computer, as has happened, or search through other sensitive, closed networks. It is legal for hackers to use their computers to share information, but illegal to tap into the databases of businesses and governments.

Sophisticated hackers can indeed do just about anything they want to do with their computers, including reading electronic mail and credit reports. Real hackers, however, devote their lives to exploring the infinite wonders of their computing machines without violating the privacy of others.

mouse An external hardware tool that has a ball used to move the cursor.

off-line Computer jargon for turning off the computer, as in "I'm going off-line now."

on-line Computer jargon for using the computer. Computer users say they are "on-line" when they are working at a computer.

output The information that a computer feeds out, after it has finished processing. Output is usually displayed on a monitor or a printout.

personal computer Microcomputer that functions fully without being attached to a mainframe computer.

printout Printed version of data; also called hard copy.

RAM Random-access memory. One of several levels of computer memory; changing data in computer. Also called main memory because it is where the current program and data that the user is working with are stored.

ROM Read-only memory; unchanging data in a computer. One of several levels of computer memory. ROM is what is stored and stays in the computer after it has been turned off.

software Programs that tell the computer what to do.

spreadsheet A program that calculates numbers; the user can create, edit, and revise budgets, estimates, and other calculations with it.

terminal A keyboard and monitor, typically one that has no permanent record of the data. Data is stored in a main computer that is elsewhere but connected to the terminal.

transistor Small electronic switch. A major part of the internal structure of a computer.

video display terminal (VDT) Also called a monitor; unit that displays computer data on a screen.

word processor A software program that works with words, enabling the user to create, edit, and revise documents.

ELECTRONIC VILLAGE: NETWORKING NOW AND IN THE FUTURE

Computers are linking humans all over the world into an "electronic village" where information is available to anyone who has the equipment. In theory, every computer in the world could be linked to every other

Byte into Bulletin Boards

Virtually every city of any size in the United States now has one or more computer bulletin boards, usually sponsored by the local computer club. Major databases also sponsor bulletin boards, but these tend to be about specific subjects. For example, there are forums for every interest, be it photography, chess, journalism, astronomy, or electronics, to name but a few.

Members "post" messages for one another, and often use the bulletin boards for announcements and sale notices. Bulletin board messages are transmitted to a central computer, which sends and receives information to and from the members, who go on-line by using a communications software program plus a modem.

computer, and all the information that exists in libraries, universities, newspapers, and museums could be shared.

Here are just a few ways that people are already sharing information:

- Two doctors, hundreds of miles apart, can look at the same CAT Scan at the same time and discuss the diagnosis for a patient.
- A travel agent in Indianapolis, Indiana, in a matter of seconds reserves rooms for a party of 5 to stay in the Serengetti game reserve in Africa for two weeks.
- A scholar in San Diego, California, gets information from a library in London, a school in Rio de Janeiro, and another scholar in New York.
- You want to ask your dad when the Cubs last won a pennant, but you live in Des Moines, Iowa, and he is in Chicago on business. You send an electronic message to his laptop and within seconds have his answer on your desktop com-

Libraries of the Mind

If computers in theory can provide access to all the information in the world, then where should all the information be stored? In one big museum or library, in individual ones? At learning centers around the world? This is one of the big questions computer experts are attempting to answer.

First, though, all the world's printed information—all the books, newspapers, magazines, and files—must be rewritten in digital form so that computers can read them. In the future, virtually all information will be available electronically. When you subscribe to a magazine, it will arrive on a floppy disk. Or you may read the morning newspaper on your computer.

Some kinds of information already have been gathered in databases, which are electronic collections of information organized for computer users. Lawyers and doctors, as well as many other professionals, have their own specialized databases. Some of the encyclopedias that you use to do your homework are already in electronic databases, as are dictionaries and thesauruses. These databases are nothing compared with the ones of the future. No one knows where they will be located, but one thing is certain. Someday you will be able to turn on your computer and ask it to gather information for a term paper you are writing on, say, the Impressionist artist Claude Monet. The computer could go to five libraries in five countries, and in three minutes you could have all the information you need to write your report.

puter screen. He tells you to look it up in your electronic encyclopedia and then get busy with your homework.

Computer experts are currently working on the best ways to share information, including

modems Many computers are already hooked up to modems and share information over the telephone lines. But while this is good for sharing short pieces of information, sending, for example, an entire book over the telephone takes a long time and is expensive.

satellites A satellite can send information around the world in seconds, by picking up radio signals from one location and transmitting them to another. Information is already being relayed from one computer to another in this manner.

fiber optics Fiber optic cable is already in use in many parts of the world. These pure glass threads, laid in underground cables, transmit light signals that convey information at great speed.

INFORMATION, PLEASE

Berger, Melvin. *Computers in Your Life*. Crowell, 1981.

Greene, Laura. *Computer Pioneers*. Watts, 1985.

Laurie, Peter. *The Joy of Computers*. Little, Brown, 1989.

Long, Larry, and Nancy Long. *Computers*. Prentice Hall, 1986.

Neill, Shirley Boes, and George W. Neill. *Only the Best: The Cumulative Guide to Highest-Rated Educational Software, Preschool–Grade 12*. Bowker, 1989.

Pizzey, Steve, and Sheila Snowden. *The Computer in Society*. Watts, 1986.

Shulman, Elayne Engelman. *Data Bases for Beginners*. Watts, 1987.

Spencer, Donald D. *Computer Dictionary*. Camelot, 1990.

11

INVENTIONS AND SCIENTIFIC DISCOVERIES

What is the difference between an invention and a discovery? An invention is something, created by one or more people, that never existed before. A discovery is something that existed but was not known before. In the table below, *c.* means "around or about that time."

Inventions That Changed the World

Year	Invention	Inventor/Origin
B.C.		
c. 1,750,000	Flint tools	
c. 3500	First writing system	Mesopotamia
c. 3000	Wheel	Sumer & Syria
c. 2000	Ox-drawn plow	Egypt
c. 1300	Musical notation	Ugarit, Syria
c. 1300	32-letter alphabet	Ugarit, Syria
c. 1100	Phoenician alphabet (22 letters)	
c. 221	Gunpowder	China
c. 200	Archimedes' screw	Archimedes, Greece
c. 200	Pump (for lifting up liquids)	Archimedes, Greece
A.D.		
c. 10	Paper	Ts'ai Lun, China
c. 520	Decimal number system	Aryabhata Varamihara, India
c. 580	Iron suspension bridge	China
640	Windmill	Persia
1045	Movable type	Bi Sheng, China
c. 1100	Magnetic compass	China
1250	Magnifying glass	Roger Bacon, England

Year	Invention	Inventor/Origin
1360	Mechanical clock	Henri de Vick of Württemberg for King Charles V of France
c. 1438	Printing press, using movable metal type	Johannes Gutenberg, Germany
1550	Screwdriver	Gunsmiths & armorers (location unknown)
1565	Graphite pencil	Konrad Gesner, Switzerland
1590	Compound microscope	Zacharius Janssen, Holland
1608	Telescope	Hans Lippershey, Holland
1609	Astronomical telescope	Galileo Galilei, Italy
1616	Medical thermometer	Santorio Santorio, Italy
1643	Barometer	Evangelista Torricelli, Italy
1667	Blood transfusion (lamb to boy)	Jean-Baptiste Denys, France
1690	Steam engine	Denis Papin, France
1715	Fahrenheit temperature scale	Daniel Gabriel Fahrenheit, Poland
1742	Celsius temperature scale	Anders Celsius, Sweden
1764	Spinning jenny	James Hargreaves, England
1780	Artificial insemination	Lazzaro Spallanzani, Italy
1787	First workable steamboat	John Fitch, United States
1793	Cotton gin	Eli Whitney, United States
1799	Metric system	French Academy of Sciences
1800	Electric battery	Alessandro Volta, Italy
1804	Steam locomotive	Richard Trevithick, England
1810	Canned food	Peter Durand, England
1816	Stethoscope	René Laënnec, France
1826	Photograph	Joseph-Nicéphore Niepce, France
1827	Modern matches	John Walker, England
1831	Reaping machine	Cyrus McCormick, United States
1831	Generator	Michael Farraday, England
1833	Calculating machine	Charles Babbage, England
1837	Braille system	Louis Braille, France
1838	Morse code	
		United States
1847	Nitroglycerin	Ascanio Sobrero, Italy
1849	Safety pin	Walter Hunt, United States
1850	Foucault's pendulum (proving Earth's rotation)	Jean-Bernard-Léon Foucault, France
1853	Gasoline engine	Eugenio Barsanti & Felice Matteucci, Italy
1853	Safety elevator	Elisha G. Otis, United States
1861	Machine gun	Richard Jordan Gattling, United States
1863	Subway train	George Pearson, England
1867	Dynamite	Alfred Nobel, Sweden

(*continued*)

Inventions That Changed the World (*continued*)

Year	Invention	Inventor/Origin
1867	Typewriter	Christopher Latham Sholes, Carlos Glidden, & Samuel W. Soulé, United States
1874	Barbed wire	Carlos Glidden, United States
1876	Telephone	Alexander Graham Bell, United States
1877	Phonograph	Thomas Alva Edison, United States
1879	Incandescent light bulb	Joseph Wilson Swan, England, & Thomas Alva Edison, United States
1885	Skyscraper	Louis Sullivan, United States
1884	Fountain pen	Lewis Edson Waterman, United States
1884	Linotype machine (speeded up typesetting)	Ottmar Mergenthaler, Germany-United States
1884	Viscose rayon (first manufactured fiber)	Hilaire de Chardonnet, France
1885	Gasoline-engine automobile	Gottlieb Daimler, Wilhelm Mayback, & Karl Friedrich Benz, Germany
1888	Kodak box camera	George Eastman, United States
1891	Zipper	Witcombe L. Judson, United States
1897	Diesel engine	Rudolf Diesel, Germany
1894	Radio	Guglielmo Marconi, Italy
1895	Telegraph (wireless)	Guglielmo Marconi, Italy
1895	Motion pictures	Jean and Auguste Lumière, France
1895	Escalator	Jesse W. Reno, United States
1898	Tape recorder	Vlademar Pulsen, Denmark
1901	Alkaline battery	Thomas Alva Edison, United States
1901	Electric hearing aid	Miller Reese Hutchinson, United States
1906	Motion pictures with sound	Eugene-Augustin Lauset, France
1911	Air conditioning	Willis H. Carrier, United States
1926	Liquid-fueled rocket	Robert H. Goddard, United States
1926	Television, Color television	John Logie Baird, Scotland
c. 1935	Fluorescent light	Arthur H. Compton & George Inman, United States
1939	Jet aircraft	Hans von Ohain, Germany
1939	Helicopter	Igor Sikorsky, Russia-United States
1940	Radar	Robert A. Watson-Watt, Scotland
1945	Atomic bomb	J. R. Oppenheimer, Arthur H. Compton, & Leo Szilard, United States, & Enrico Fermi, Italy-United States
1947	Transistor	William Shockley, United States
1949	Jet airliner	R. E. Bishop & team, United States
1950	Xerographic copying machine	Haloid Co., United States
1952	Hydrogen bomb	Edward Teller & team, United States
1956	Plastic contact lens	Norman Bier, United States
1957	Sputnik (artificial satellite)	U.S.S.R.

Year	Invention	Inventor/Origin
1957	FORTRAN computer language	John Backus & team for IBM, United States
1957	Intercontinental ballistic missile	U.S.S.R.
1958	Laser	Charles H. Townes, United States
1958	Communications satellite	SCORE, United States
1962	Minicomputer	Digital Corp. & IBM, United States
1963	Cassette audiotapes	Philips Co., Holland
1964	Laser eye surgery	H. Vernon Ingram, Germany-England-United States
1965	Word processor	IBM, United States
1969	Cassette videotape	Sony, Japan
1970	Computer floppy disk	IBM, United States
1971	Earth-orbiting space station	U.S.S.R.
1971	Pocket calculator	Texas Instruments, United States
1972	Video disk	Philips Co., Holland, & Sony, Japan
1972	Video game	Noland Buschnel, United States
1977	Space shuttle	NASA, United States
1979	Compact disk player	Sony, Japan, & Philips Co., Holland
1984	Megabit computer chip	IBM, United States

Discoveries That Changed the World

Year	Discovery	Discoverer/Origin
B.C.		
c. 12,000	Fire	Unknown
c. 10,000	Zero (nothing)	Hindu priests
A.D.		
c. 80	Magnetism	China
c. 200	Blood circulation	Galen, Greece
1538	Optic nerve	Constanzo Vardio, Italy
1531		
		Bartholin, Denmark
1658	Red blood cells	Jan Swammerdam, Holland
1661	Wood (methyl) alcohol	Robert Boyle, England
1682	Halley's comet	Edmond Halley, England
1684	Theory of gravity	Isaac Newton, England
1690	Speed of light	Ole Römer, Denmark
1694	Plant pollen	Rudolph Jakob Camerarius, Germany
1756	Carbon dioxide	Joseph Black, Scotland

(continued)

Discoveries That Changed the World (*continued*)

Year	Discovery	Discoverer/Origin
1772	Nitrogen & oxygen	Daniel Rutherford & Joseph Priestly, England, & Karl Wilhelm Scheele, Sweden
1781	Uranus	William Herschel, England
1793	Astigmatism (nearsightedness)	Thomas Young, England
1796	Smallpox vaccine	Edward Jenner, England
1801	Asteroids	Guiseppe Piazzi, Italy
1801	Wave theory of light	Thomas Young, England
1801	Ultraviolet light	Johann Wilhelm Ritter, Germany, & William Hyde Wollaston, England
1803	Atomic theory	John Dalton, England
1807	Sensory-motor nerve system	Charles Bell, Scotland
1807	Potassium & sodium	Humphrey Davy, England
1811	Iodine	Bernard Courtois, France
1821	Caffeine	Pierre-Joseph Pelletier, France
1824	Electromagnetism	William Sturgeon, England
1827	Electrical resistance	Georg Simon Ohm, Germany
1828	Cocoa	Conrad van Houten, Holland
1838	Plant cells	Matthias Jakob Schleiden, Germany
1839	Animal cells	Theodor Schwann, Germany
	Protoplasm	Jan Evangelista Porkyne, Austro-Hungarian Empire (Czechoslovakia)
1840	Ozone	Christian Friedrich Schonbein, Germany
1842	Ether anesthesia	Crawford Long, United States
1852	Fluorescence	George Gabriel Stokes, England
1854	Paleozoic fossils	Adam Sedgwick, England
1858	Atomic & molecular weights	Stanislao Cannizzaro, Italy
1859	Evolution theory	Charles Darwin, England
1861	Speech center of brain	Pierre-Paul Broca, France
1864	Electromagnetic wave transmission	Mahlon Loomis, United States
1864	Pasteurization	Louis Pasteur, France
1865	Laws of genetics	Gregor Johann Mendel, Austro-Hungarian Empire (Czechoslovakia)
1869	Periodic law	Dmitri Ivanovich Mendeleyev, Russia
1873	Electromagnetic radiation	James Clerk Maxwell, Scotland
1880	Inoculation	Louis Pasteur, France
1882	Tuberculosis bacillus	Robert Koch, Germany
1884	Local anesthesia (affects specific area only)	Carl Koller, Austria-United States
1891	Submarine	John Philip Holland, United States
1892	Viruses	Dmitri Iosifovich Ivanovsky, Russia
1894	Helium	William Ramsay, Scotland
1895	X-rays	Wilhelm Konrad von Roentgen, Germany

Year	Discovery	Discoverer/Origin
1896	Electron	Joseph John Thomson, England
1898	Neon	William Ramsay, Scotland, & Morris William Travers, England
1898	Spinal anesthesia	Karl Bier, Germany
1900	Quantum theory	Max Karl Ernst Planck, Germany
1901	Blood groups	Karl Landsteiner, Austria-United States
1902	Hormones	William Maddock Bayliss & Ernest Henry Starling, England
1902	Radium	Pierre & Marie Curie, France
1905	Theory of relativity	Albert Einstein, Germany-Switzerland-United States
1911	Cosmic rays	Victor Franz Hess, Austria
1911	Theory of atomic structure	Ernest Rutherford, England
1912	Thiamine (vitamin B)	Casmir Funk, Poland
1913	Vitamin A	Thomas Burr Osborne, Lafayette Benedict Mendel, Elmer V. McCollum, & Marguerite Davis, United States
1918	Vitamin D	Edward Mellanby, England
1918	Insulin	Frederick G. Banting & Charles Best, Canada
1922	Vitamin E	Herbert McLean Evans, United States
1928	Penicillin	Alexander Fleming, England
1930	Pluto	Clyde Tombaugh, United States
1932	Neutron	James Chadwick, England
1938	Cortisone	Edward Calvin Kendall, United States
1940	Plutonium	Glen Theodore Seaborg & Edwin Mattison McMillan, United States
1953	DNA	Francis H. Crick, England, & James D. Watson, United States
1953	Measles vaccine	John F. Enders & team, United States
1956	Human growth hormone	Choh Hao Li, China-United States
1957	Polio vaccine	Albert B. Sabin, United States
1963	Measles vaccine	John F. Enders & team, United States
1982	Abnormal cancer-causing genes	Robert Weinberg & team, United States
1984	Top quark (subatomic particle)	Carlo Rubbia, Italy
1985	Anxiety chemical (human brain)	Alessandro Guidotti & Erminio Costa, Italy
1985	Diminished ozone shield	Susan Solomon, National Oceanic Atmospheric Administration, United States

Clothes Call: 7 Inventions That You Wear

1. *Shoes*   2000 B.C.   Near East.
   The oldest shoe is the sandal, made of woven papyrus. In the ancient world sandals were the most popular shoes for people living in hot regions.
2. *Buttons*   200 B.C.   Southern Asia.
   The earliest buttons did not fasten clothes but served as decorations. They were carved from sea shells into circles or triangles. Early buttons had two holes so they could be sewn onto clothes.
3. *Lace handkerchiefs*   Late 1400s   England.
   The first handkerchiefs had the name of a loved one sewn on them. A tassel or cord hung from one corner. The English called these square bits of lace "true love knots."
4. *Bathing suits*   Mid-1850s   Europe.
   The first bathing suits for women were high-necked flannel, with sleeves to the elbow and knee-length skirts. Women wore bloomers (full, loose pants) and black stockings under a bathing suit. Mens' bathing suits also covered much of the body.
5. *Jeans*   1860s   San Francisco.
   A tailor named Levi Strauss sewed the first jeans. Strauss made denim pants for miners who needed work clothing. He dyed the neutral-colored denim blue to hide mud and earth stains.
6. *Sneakers*   1912   U.S. Rubber.
   The first popularly marketed sneakers were called Keds. They were brown canvas with black soles.
7. *Zippers*   1914   Witcomb Judson, United States.
   The first zippers were made of rows of hooks and eyes (loops to catch hooks). A person pulled a slide to lock the hooks and eyes together.

Food for Thought: 7 Inventions That You Eat

1. *Pie*   The first was baked by Greeks sometime during the fifth century B.C. They called their meat-hash pie an *artocreas.* Early pies had only a bottom crust.
2. *Ice cream*   The Chinese made the first ice cream around 2000 B.C. It consisted of overcooked rice, spices, and milk and was packed in snow. Only nobles ate this special treat.
3. *Sausage*   The first sausage was eaten in Babylonia around 1500 B.C. The Babylonians stuffed spiced meats into animal intestines.
4. *Ketchup*   The first ketchup was made around 300 B.C. in Rome. It contained vinegar, oil, peppers, and dried anchovy paste. The Romans named this mixture *liquamen* and poured it over fish and fowl.
5. *Cookie*   The first cookie was baked in the third century B.C. in Rome. Roman cookies were thin, hard, square wafers without much taste. Romans dipped their cookies in wine to soften them.
6. *Hamburger*   The first hamburger was cooked in Germany before the fourteenth century. The Germans combined shredded beef and spices. In the town of Hamburg, they called this new meat dish "Hamburg steak."
7. *Potato chip*   The first potato chip was fried by the chef George Crum in 1853 in Saratoga Springs, New York. When a guest at the resort where Crum worked objected that the French fries were too thick, Crum fried the thinnest and crispest fries he could. Soon all the guests at the resort were asking for these potato "chips."

Ready, Set, Go: 6 Inventions You Have Fun With

1. *Marbles*   3000 B.C.   Egypt.
   In the ancient world, marbles were made of semi-precious stones or ordinary clay. Romans used clear glass for marbles.
2. *Kites*   2000 B.C.   China.
   The first kites were used as military signals from one camp to another. The pattern, color, and movement of a kite communicated messages in code.
3. *Checkers*   c. 2000 B.C.   Egypt.
   In ancient Egypt, checkers was a game used to predict events in wartime. Two players played the game across a checker board. Each player had up to 12 pieces.
4. *Yo-yo*   1100 B.C.   China.
   The first yo-yos had two ivory disks connected by a peg. A silk cord was wound around the peg.
5. *Roller skates*   1759   Belgium.
   The first roller skates were constructed by Joseph Merlin, who made musical instruments. His skates had two wheels each. Merlin built the skates so that he could enter a costume party on them.
6. *Crossword puzzle*   1913   New York.
   The first crossword puzzle was created by journalist Arthur Wynn. His boss asked Wynn to come up with a new entertainment feature for the *New York World*. Wynn's puzzle appeared in the December 21, 1913 issue of the newspaper.

INFORMATION, PLEASE

Asimov, Isaac. *Asimov's Chronology of Science and Discovery*. Harper & Row, 1982.

Bender, Lionel. *Eyewitness Books: Invention*. Knopf, 1991.

Panati, Charles. *Extraordinary Origins of Everyday Things*. Harper & Row, 1987.

12

FINE ARTS

PAINTING AND SCULPTURE IN TIME

Painting and sculpture have evolved over time, and can be divided into historical periods. Each period is marked by its own characteristic styles or movements, some of which overlap in time.

Ancient Art—3000 B.C.–A.D. 100

Three major ancient civilizations that produced works of art were Egypt, Greece, and Rome.

Egyptian—3000 B.C.–A.D. 525

Much of Egyptian art was used to decorate tombs. These tomb paintings show people and objects related to the dead. After a tomb was sealed, the art inside was not supposed to be seen by the living again.

- Heads and feet of people always face to the side. The shoulders and body face frontward.
- Powerful and important people are portrayed larger than ordinary people.
- Art remains nearly unchanged for more than three thousand years because artists obeyed strict rules for painting and sculpture.

Examples: Sculpture—*Queen Nofretet* (c. 1360 B.C.); painting—*Grape Harvest* (c. 1425 B.C.)

Greek—c. 1100 B.C.–A.D. 30

Greek art developed through three main styles: archaic (700 B.C.–c. 480 B.C.), classical (c. 480 B.C.–300 B.C.), and Hellenistic (323 B.C.–30 B.C.). When most people think of Greek art, they usually think of the classical period. In the classical style:

- Bodies are perfectly proportioned. No human body is quite as symmetrical or well built as a Greek statue.
- Faces and bodies are never flawed as in real life. They are created according to the Greek idea of beauty. Gods look like people and people look godlike.
- There is an impression of life and grace in the statues.

Examples: Sculpture—*Hermes* by Praxiteles (c. 300–320 B.C.); painting—Attic white-ground vase by the Achilles Painter (c. 440–430 B.C.)

Roman—100 B.C.–A.D. 315

Portraits and busts (heads and shoulders) are now made from marble instead of wax and look like the people they represent, not like the ideal of beauty.

- Historical events are shown.
- Storytelling is emphasized.
- Most paintings are frescoes; they are painted in fresh plaster before it hardens.

Examples: Sculpture—*Equestrian Statue of Marcus Aurelius* (A.D. 161–80); painting—*The Punishment of Ixion* (A.D. 63–79)

Middle Ages—4th to 13th Century

The three major styles of art during the Middle Ages are Byzantine, Romanesque, and Gothic. Byzantine art is the art of Christian artists of eastern Europe and the Near East. Romanesque and Gothic art was produced in western Europe. The Byzantine, Romanesque, and Gothic styles differ in some ways but are also similar. Some similarities:

- The chief subject of art is the Christian religion.
- Most art is produced for religious purposes, such as to decorate churches. In the West, medieval art also appears in religious books called illuminated manuscripts.
- Art is symbolic. For example, a gold sky symbolizes God's heavenly kingdom.
- Perspective is ignored because artists are not interested in depicting the real, or three-dimensional, world. So paintings lack a sense of depth, which partly explains why scientific perspective in painting is not discovered until after the Middle Ages, around 1435.

Byzantine—323–1453

- In the earlier Byzantine era, figures are tall, magnificently costumed, and solemn but not lifelike. Later figures show a kind of noble suffering.
- Faces are dominated by large eyes, which stare ahead.
- Gestures are not lifelike and natural but

represent certain ideas that the medieval viewer would have understood.

- Artists work in mosaics—pictures made by putting small pieces of stone or glass into cement on walls, floors, and ceilings. They also continue to paint and sculpt.

Example: Painting—*Madonna Enthroned* (late 13th century)

Romanesque—1000–1100

- Figures are sturdy, solid, and very large.
- Faces express certain set emotions.
- Line in painting and sculpture does not have to represent the natural world. Lines are used to create pattern and design and seem to have a life of their own. Later in this era, line is once again used to make forms more lifelike—it "follows" form.
- In both painting and sculpture, works tend to be crowded with figures and full of frantic movement.

Examples: Sculpture—*Apostle* (c. 1090), St.-Sernin, France; painting—*St. John the Evangelist,* from the *Gospel Book of Abbot Wedricus* (shortly before 1147)

Gothic—1150–1420

The greatest achievements in Gothic sculpture occur between 1220 and 1420. In contrast, Gothic painting reaches its creative peak between 1300 and 1350 in central Italy.

- In painting, bright colors, such as those used in stained glass, dominate.
- Figures become natural, free, and graceful, expressing a range of emotions. They also show human warmth.
- Early Gothic statues are calm and poised. The drapery or clothing suggests the form of the human body beneath. They hold symbolic objects (such as a book or a lamb), the meaning of which would have been clear to the medieval churchgoer. Late Gothic sculpture is more true to life. Figures are no longer

stiffly vertical, and they bend and twist with lifelike movement. Drapery is more detailed. The body beneath the clothes seems to disappear.

- Painters paint church altar panels, stained glass windows, and frescoes. They also decorate religious manuscripts.
- The Italian painter Giotto creates figures that seem three-dimensional.

Examples: Sculpture—*Annunciation* and *Visitation*, center portal of west facade, Reims Cathedral (c. 1225–45), Reims, France; painting—*Christ's Entry into Jerusalem* (1305–06) by Giotto, *Christ Entering Jerusalem* (1308–11) by Duccio

Renaissance—1400–1600

The Renaissance began in Italy and spread throughout western Europe. The Italian Renaissance is usually divided into two phases, the Early Renaissance and the High Renaissance (1495–1600).

In the Early Renaissance the Italian city of Florence and the northern European region called Flanders are the main centers of art. In the High Renaissance in Italy, Rome replaces Florence as the center of Italian art, with Venice as a second center. In the North, the centers of art are Germany, France, and The Netherlands.

Early Renaissance in Italy—1400–1500

- Figures are three-dimensional. Their faces express real emotion, and are positioned naturally.
- The figures are more perfectly formed than real-life models. The arrangement of colors, figures, and lines is more calm. Ideas about art are influenced by the ideals of classical Greek artists.
- Greek and Roman myths and human beings are now considered appropriate subjects, in addition to religious subjects.
- Scientific perspective based on geometrical principles is introduced. With per-

spective, figures and architecture in paintings and sculpture now appear three-dimensional.
- Realism is emphasized. Paintings are filled with everyday details, for example.
- Painters begin to use oil paints, which enable them to create a wide variety of effects, such as new soft, dark shades of color.

Examples: Sculpture—*St. George* (c. 1415–17) by Donatello, *Putti with Dolphin* (c. 1470) by Andrea del Verrocchio; painting—*The Holy Trinity* (1425) by Massacio, *The Annunciation* (c. 1450) by Fra Angelico, *The Birth of Venus* (c. 1480) by Sandro Botticelli

Early Renaissance in Flanders—1400–1500

- Painters use oil paint instead of tempera (powdered pigment mixed with egg yolk). With oil, Flemish painters can render objects in precise detail and rich, dark shades.
- Real life and symbols are depicted in the same artwork.
- Flemish figures are on a smaller scale and are modeled after everyday people. Even Christ and his apostles in religious paintings have the familiar quality of people next door.
- Architectural details in paintings are based on Gothic art, rather than on ancient Roman art.

Examples: Painting—*Wedding Portrait* (1434) by Jan van Eyck, *The Descent from the Cross* (c. 1435) by Rogier van der Weyden

The High Renaissance in Italy—1495–1600

- Painters use a method called *chiaroscuro* (which means "light and dark") by which varying degrees of light, rather than outline, create a three-dimensional effect.
- Composition—the way objects, figures, patterns of color, light, and shadow are arranged in an artwork—is balanced

and harmonious. Everything seems to be in its proper place, like in a well-ordered room.
- Figures can be heroic, dramatic, or graceful.
- Ancient Roman realism, which showed people as they really are, is a model.
- Venetian painters are more interested in color, and their paintings are meant to please viewers, rather than encourage them to act nobly.

Examples: Sculpture—*David* (1501–04) by Michelangelo, *Tomb of Giuliano de' Medici* (1524–34) by Michelangelo; painting—*Mona Lisa* (1503–05) by Leonardo da Vinci, Ceiling of the Sistine Chapel (1508–12) by Michelangelo, *The School of Athens* (1510–11) by Raphael, *The Tempest* (c. 1505) by Giorgione, *Man with the Glove* (c. 1520) by Titian

The High Renaissance in Northern Europe—1495–1600
- Many different kinds of art emerge, instead of a single style.
- In Germany, one trend is toward larger-than-life figures that have great energy and movement. They are copied from nature but also symbolize particular ideas.
- In the Netherlands, artists replace traditional religious themes with those drawn from everyday life, like hunting or farming or doing business. Portraits are of ordinary middle-class people.
- In France, clean, simple lines and forms are favored.

Examples: Sculpture:—*Fountain of the Innocents* (1548–49) by Jean Goujon; painting—*The Isenheim Altarpiece* (c. 1509–15) by Matthias Grünewald, *Self Portrait* (1500) by Albrecht Durer, *The Return of the Hunters* (1565) by Pieter Bruegel the Elder

Mannerism—1525–1600

The next important style of art to develop after the High Renaissance is Mannerism. In Mannerism:

- Figures have exaggerated poses.
- Figures are distorted and unbalanced.
- Composition appears arbitrary.
- In painting, lighting is harsh instead of natural.
- Later Mannerism is more elegant.

Examples: Sculpture—*Saltcellar of Francis I* (1539–43) by Benevenuto Cellini; painting—*The Last Supper* (1592–94) by Tintoretto, *The Burial of Count Orgaz* (1586) by El Greco

Baroque—1600–1800

Around 1600, a new style of art starts to develop in Rome and spreads to Spain, Flanders, and Holland. In the Baroque style:

- Paintings and sculptures have great movement and are dramatic and natural-looking. They are larger than life in emotion and scale.
- Ordinary poor people are subjects for art.
- Figures seem to move the way real people do.
- Art is designed mainly to appeal to emotions and senses.
- Painters prefer brilliant colors.
- Intense lighting is used to increase drama.

Examples: Sculpture—*David* (1623) by Gianlorenzo Bernini, *The Ecstasy of St. Theresa* (1645–52) by Gianlorenzo Bernini; painting—*The Calling of St. Matthew* (c. 1596–98) by Caravaggio, *Judith and Maidservant* (c. 1625) by Artemesia Gentileschi, *Marie de' Medici, Queen of France, Landing in Marseilles* (1622–23) by Peter Paul Rubens, *The Maids of Honor* (1656) by Diego Velazquez

Dutch Painting—Late 1600s

In Holland, Baroque art consists mainly of painting, with some unique characteristics:

- Religion is emphasized less.
- "Genre painting," or the realistic depiction of everyday subjects, develops.

- Subjects are usually middle-class people.
- Tavern and domestic scenes are favorite subjects.
- Still-life painting of everyday objects becomes popular.
- Great attention is paid to the realistic depiction of objects, such as earrings, maps, windows, and so forth.
- Paintings are often small in size.

Examples: Painting—*Banquet of Officers of the Civic Guard of Saint George at Haarlem* (1616) by Frans Hals, *Self-Portrait* (c. 1660) by Rembrandt, *The Letter* (1666) by Jan Vermeer

Classicism—1660–1685

The Classic style refers to the style in French art during the reign of Louis XIV.

- Art is characterized by balanced, calm composition, in which figures, lines, or patterns in one area of the artwork are balanced by similar groupings in other areas. Figures are graceful.
- Artists attempt to imitate the style and subject matter of ancient art.

Examples: Sculpture—*Model for Equestrian Statue of Louis XIV* (c. 1687) by François Girardon; painting—*Joseph the Carpenter* (c. 1645) by Georges de La Tour, *Landscape with the Burial of Phocion* (1648) by Nicolas Poussin

Rococo—Late 1600s–c. 1780

The next painting style to develop in France is the Rococo. In the Rococo:

- Works of art are smaller than in ancient Greek Classical art.
- Everything seems relaxed, light-hearted, and playful.
- Curves and bright surfaces are emphasized.

Examples: Paintings—*A Pilgrimage to Cythera* (1717) by Antoine Watteau; *The Swing* (c. 1768) by Jean-Honoré Fragonard, *Princess de Polignac* (1783) by Marie-Louise-Elizabeth Vigée-Lebrun

The Modern Era—1776–Present

In the Modern Era, painting and sculpture usually follow the same path. But especially in the twentieth century, styles of sculpture sometimes go their own independent way. So you may not see examples here from the work of some famous sculptors from our own century. The list of major painters and sculptors later in this chapter does include brief descriptions of major sculptors, however.

Neoclassicism—c. 1750–1850

- Scenes from Roman history become common subjects. Roman virtues such as self-discipline and a high standard of morality are used to appeal to the patriotism of viewers.
- In painting, forms are simple and solid, with bright colors.
- Composition is balanced and clear.

Examples: Sculpture—*Voltaire* (1781) by Jean-Antoine Houdon; painting—*The Death of Socrates* (1787) by Jacques-Louis David

Romanticism—Late 1700s–1900

- Violent activity is emphasized.
- In painting, vigorous brush strokes are combined with rich colors and deep shadows.
- Art is supposed to appeal to the senses, not the mind.
- The individual is glorified.

Examples: Sculpture—*La Marseillaise* (1833–36) by François Rude; painting—*The Third of May, 1808* (1814–15) by Franciso Goya, *Odalisque* (1814) by Jean-Auguste-Dominique Ingres, *Greece Expiring on the Ruins of Missolonghi* (1827) by Eugène Delacroix, *The Slave Ship* (1840) by Joseph Mallord William Turner

Realism—1849–c. 1870

- Nature is observed honestly and unsentimentally.
- Artists rely on their own experience and observation of nature for inspiration.

Examples: Sculpture/painting—*The Stone Breakers* (1849) by Gustave Courbet

Pre-Raphaelites—c. 1848–c. 1853

- Painters attempt to imitate the "pure" and "innocent" style of Italian painters before Raphael.
- Paintings tend to have a moral or religious purpose.

Examples: Painting—*Ecce Ancilla Domini* (c. 1850) by Dante Gabriel Rossetti, *Ophelia* (1852) by John Everett Millais

Impressionism—c. 1868–c. 1910

Impressionism is basically a style of painting, although there are some sculptures that may be considered Impressionistic.

- Painters observe nature directly and carefully analyze and study the details.
- Painters attempt to capture the momentary and changing nature of light.
- Paintings depend on light and shimmering, luminous colors.
- Paintings do not try to tell a story.
- Subjects of paintings are often middle-class people.
- In sculpture forms are simplified. The artist does not try to disguise or erase the process or way that he has made the sculpture. The outward appearance is left unfinished, and sometimes part of the original uncut stone or marble is left in its original, unpolished state with the figure emerging from it.

Examples: Sculpture—*The Thinker* (1879–89) by Auguste Rodin; painting—*A Bar at the Folies Bergères* (1881–82) by Edouard Manet, *Young Woman Behind a Blind* (1878) by Berthe Morisot, *Le Moulin de la Galette* (1876) by Auguste Renoir, *At the Milliner's* (c. 1882) by Edgar Degas; *Water Lilies* (1907) by Claude Monet

Postimpressionism—c. 1886–c. 1920

- Artists focus on the solid structure of objects or figures and not on the light that falls on them.
- For painters, the color of the objects, or even made-up color, becomes more important than the light that falls on the objects. Paintings begin to look "flatter" and less three-dimensional.

Examples: Sculpture—*Seated Woman* (c. 1901) by Aristide Maillol; painting—*Fruit Bowl, Glass, and Apples* (1879–92) by Paul Cézanne, *Self-Portrait* (1889) by Vincent van Gogh, *The Yellow Christ* (1889) by Paul Gauguin

Fauvism—1903–1907

- Emphasis is on pleasure and joy.
- Bright colors are used. For example, a woman may have blue skin.
- Forms are distorted.
- Line and color are arranged in repeated patterns on the flat plane or surface of the picture.

Examples: Sculpture—*The Kiss* (1908) by Constantin Brancusi; painting—*The Joy of Life* (1905–06) by Henri Matisse, *The Last Supper* (1909) by Emil Nolde

Cubism—c. 1905–c. 1939

- Objects are shown as basic geometric shapes.
- Several views of the subject appear in the same painting.
- In the first phase of Cubism, called analytic cubism (1910–12), artists use sober colors, such as grays and browns.
- The second phase of Cubism, called synthetic cubism (1912–c. 1939), brighter colors and more varied shapes appear.
- The technique of collage—pasting various materials onto a flat surface—is introduced.

Examples: Painting—*Les Demoiselles d'Avignon* (1907) by Pablo Picasso, *Le Courrier* (1913) by Georges Braque, *Three Musicians* (1921) by Pablo Picasso

Expressionism—c. 1905–1939

- The feeling of the artist as he or she looks at the world becomes more important to express than copying the world as it really appears.

Example: Painting—*The Kiss* by Edvard Munch

Futurism—1909–1919

- Painters convey the fast-paced, whirlwind activity of machinery and the new twentieth-century technology in their artwork.
- Painting attempts to show the glories of war.
- The birth and excitement of the machine age inspires artists of all media.

Example: Sculpture—*Unique Forms of Continuity in Space* (1913) by Umberto Boccioni; painting—*Dynamism of a Cyclist* (1913) by Umberto Boccioni

Dadaism—1916–1922

- Everyday objects are used in unusual ways or settings to make fun of the idea that art means anything or has a purpose.

Example: Collage—*I Copper Plate I Zinc Plate I Rubber Plate 2 Calipers I Drainpipe Telescope I Piping Man* (1920) by Max Ernst; Painting—*The Bride* (1912) by Marcel Duchamp

Surrealism—1924–1930s

- Emphasis is placed on the unconscious, often using images from dreams.
- Images are placed next to each other without any logical connection.

Examples: Sculpture—*The Palace at 4 A.M.*

(1932–33) by Alberto Giacometti; mobile—*Lobster Trap and Fish Tail* (1939) by Alexander Calder; painting—*The Persistence of Memory* (1931) by Salvador Dalí, *Painting* (1933) by Joan Miró

Abstract Expressionism—c. 1943–Present

Abstract Expressionists usually belong to one of two schools—action painting or field painting.

- Painters do not try to represent reality.
- Action painters are interested in the physical act of applying, dripping, or spraying paint on their canvas. The process of making the painting is as important as the painting itself. Therefore, the action painter leaves a visible trail of how he created his work. Sometimes action painters are abstract, using no recognizable figure or image. Sometimes they are "figurative" and their subject matter is landscape or the human form.
- Field painters apply paint to large surfaces using colors that subtly relate to each other. They are very careful which colors they put next to each other. They use either simple geometric forms—like stripes and squares of luminous color—or softer-edged shapes resembling those found in nature.

Examples: Painting—*One (Number 31, 1950)* (1950) by Jackson Pollock, *Earth and Green* (1955) by Mark Rothko, *Celebration* (1959–60) by Lee Krasner, *Woman II* (1952) by Willem de Kooning

Pop Art—Late 1950s–Present

- Common objects, such as cans of soup, are used as subjects.
- Commercial images also become subjects.

Examples: Sculpture—*Giant Ice Bag* (1969–70) by Claes Oldenburg; painting—*Three Flags* (1958) by Jasper Johns

Minimalism—1960s–Present

- Art is reduced to its simplest elements such as line, color, a white canvas or wall, or a repeated pattern.
- The art object does not mean anything beyond what the eye of the viewer sees: color, shape, and pattern.

Examples: Sculpture—*Cigarette* (1967) by Tony Smith; painting—*Jasper's Dilemma* (1963) by Frank Stella, *Red, Blue, Green* (1963) by Ellsworth Kelly.

Postmodernism—1980s–Present

- Artists are working in a wide variety of styles and materials.
- Neoexpressionsts record uncomfortable and disturbing emotions.

Examples: Sculpture—*Dragons* (1981) by Judy Pfaff; painting—*Untitled* (1983) by Francesco Clemente, *Mondrian* (1983–84) by Susan Rothenberg

MAJOR PAINTERS AND SCULPTORS AND THEIR WORKS

American

Albers, Josef (1888–1976), b. Germany. Painter and designer. He taught at the famous German art school, the Bauhaus. Albers wrote books about the workings of color in art that people still study. He is best known for his *Homage to the Square* series of paintings begun in 1949.

Calder, Alexander (1898–1976), b. Pennsylvania. Sculptor. He made playful wire constructions of circuses. Much of his later work is large, heavy sculpture made for public spaces.

Cassatt, Mary (1845–1926), b. Pennsylvania. Painter. She was an Impressionist and spent much of her life in Paris. Her best-known paintings show women with children, such as *The Bath* (1892), and etchings, such as *The Letter* (1891).

Cornell, Joseph (1903–72), b. New York State. Collage artist and sculptor. He constructed small and large boxes and filled them with found objects and delicate collages. Some of his best-known works are *Medici Slot Machine* (1942) and *Hotel du Nord* (1953).

Davis, Arthur Bowen (1862–1928), b. New York State. Painter. He was a member of a rebellious group of early-twentieth-century painters called The Eight. He also helped organize the historic 1913 Armory Show in New York City. His paintings include mysterious and symbolic landscapes, such as *Unicorns* (1906).

Davis, Stuart (1894–1964), b. Pennsylvania. Painter. Inspired by jazz, Davis developed his own American version of Cubism in his brightly colored paintings, such as *Hot Still-Scape for Six Colors* (1940) and *Colonial Cubism* (1954).

de Kooning, Willem (1904–1989), b. The Netherlands. Painter. De Kooning is a leader of the Abstract Expressionist movement and was best known for his very large, cartoonlike *Woman* paintings, which he began in the early 1950s.

Demuth, Charles (1883–1935), b. Pennsylvania. Painter. His paintings were inspired by the geometric shapes and patterns of the industrial landscape. One of his best-known works is *I Saw the Figure 5 in Gold* (1928).

Dove, Arthur (1880–1946), b. New York State. Painter. Dove made the forms of nature, such as clouds and mountains, into simplified, abstract shapes. *Waterfall* (1925) and *Rise of the Full Moon* (1937) are well-known examples of his landscapes.

Eakins, Thomas (1844–1916), b. Pennsylvania. Painter. Eakins was famous for his portraits and for his teaching, but he was criticized when he introduced the European practice of working from live, nude models in the classroom. His best-known works are *The Gross Clinic* (1875), which shows an operation in progress, and *Max Schmitt in a Single Scull* (1871).

Feininger, Lyonel (1871–1956), b. New York State. Painter. He taught at the German art school, the Bauhaus, and he painted delicate geometric forms inspired by the way light falls on buildings. A famous painting is *Church at Gelmeroda* (1936).

Frankenthaler, Helen (1928–   ), b. New York State. Painter. Frankenthaler is the most famous woman Abstract Expressionist. She invented a new way of painting by staining her large canvases with splashes of rich, vibrant color, as in her abstract paintings *Mountains and Sea* (1952) and *Arden* (1961).

Gorky, Arshile (1904–48), b. Armenia. Painter. Gorky painted abstract biomorphic forms (shapes inspired by living creatures, such as cells, microscopic animals, and tree limbs) in brilliant, glowing colors, as in *The Liver is the Cock's Comb* (1944).

Henri, Robert (1865–1929), b. Ohio. Painter and influential teacher. He was a member of The Eight, a group of painters who rebelled against the accepted art of the time. He is best known for his book *The Art Spirit*, which has inspired generations of young painters, as well as for his dramatic portraits, such as *Woman in Manteau* (1898), *Himself* (1913), and *Herself* (1913).

Hoffman, Hans (1880–1966), b. Germany. Painter and teacher. He founded two important U.S. art schools where most of the notable Abstract Expressionists were his students. He used bold areas of vivid color and strong patterns in his paintings. *Effervescence* (1944) and *The Gate* (1959) are two good examples.

Homer, Winslow (1836–1910), b. Massachusetts. Painter. Homer is one of the most famous nineteenth-century Ameri-

can painters. He created dramatic seascapes, such as *West Point, Prout's Neck, Maine* and *On a Lee Shore* (both 1900).

Hopper, Edward (1882–1967), b. New York State. Painter. Hopper painted lonely street scenes and interiors. He used glowing color and paid careful attention to patterns of light and shadow. *Nighthawks* (1942) and *Early Sunday Morning* (1930) are good examples.

Indiana, Robert (1928–   ), b. Indiana. Painter and sculptor. He is best known for his bold and vivid paintings that look like signs and for sculptures, such as the *Love* series, which he began in 1966.

Johns, Jasper (1930–   ), b. Georgia. Painter and sculptor. Johns is a founder of Pop Art and uses everyday signs, symbols, and found objects—flags, targets, beer cans—in his paintings and sculpture. He has also revived the ancient practice of painting in encaustic. In encaustic, paint pigments are dissolved in hot wax and then applied to the canvas. One of his best-known paintings is *Three Flags* (1958).

Kline, Franz (1910–62), b. Pennsylvania. Painter. Kline's work is a perfect example of Abstract Expressionism. He painted large black-and-white paintings using bold, free brushstrokes. Good examples of his work include *White Forms* (1955) and *Mahoning* (1956).

Lichtenstein, Roy (1923–   ), b. New York State. Painter. He is one of the Pop Artists who use the images and themes of popular culture in their work. His paintings are based on comic strips. Good examples are *Masterpiece* (1962) and *Good Morning Darling* (1964).

Louis, Morris (1912–62), b. Maryland. Painter. He soaked canvases with paint until they were dyed with color. His work includes the *Veil* series (1954, 1958) and the *Unfurled* series (1960–61).

Moses, Grandma (Anna Mary Robertson Moses) (1860–1961), b. New York State.

Painter. She was a farmer's wife who began painting in her seventies. Her simple, colorful pictures of farm life, such as *Sugaring Off* (1943), are very popular.

Motherwell, Robert (1915–91), b. Washington State. Painter and writer. He painted large vague shapes in bleak colors. He is an Abstract Expressionist best known for the series *Elegy for the Spanish Republic*, begun in 1949.

Nevelson, Louise (1900–88), b. Russia. Sculptor. She made large sculptures out of painted wood, metal, and found objects. *Sky Cathedral* (1958) and *World* (1966) are good examples of her work.

Newman, Barnet (1905–71), b. New York State. Painter and sculptor. His most famous paintings use areas of flat color interrupted by thin, vertical stripes. Two famous works are *Onement I* (1948) and *Concord* (1949).

Noguchi, Isamu (1904–88), b. California. Sculptor. He created abstract pieces for public spaces, such as the sculpture garden for the UNESCO building in Paris (1958) and the entrance for the Museum of Modern Art in Tokyo (1969).

O'Keeffe, Georgia (1887–1987), b. Wisconsin. Painter. She lived in New Mexico and often used elements of the southwestern landscape, including mountains, skulls, and bones, in her work. *Cow's Skull, Red, White, and Blue* (1931) is a good example of her painting.

Oldenburg, Claes (1929–), b. Sweden. Sculptor. He is a leader of the Pop Art movement. He makes giant sculptures of common objects, such as *Dual Hamburger* (1962) and *Lipstick* (1969).

Parrish, Maxfield (1870–1966), b. Pennsylvania. Painter and illustrator. He created colorful, decorative posters, magazine covers, and book illustrations.

Pollock, Jackson (1912–56), b. Wyoming. Painter. A pioneer of Abstract Expressionism, Pollock was the first action painter. He dripped, poured, and threw paint onto very large canvases. *Number 1* (1948), *Number 32* (1950), and *Blue Poles* (1953) are some of his works.

Prendergast, Maurice Brazil (1859–1924) b. Canada. Painter. He was a member of The Eight, a group of artists who rebelled against the accepted art of their time. He painted decorative, colorful landscapes and figures, as in *The Promenade* (1913).

Rauschenberg, Robert (1925–), b. Texas. Painter and collage artist. His "combine paintings" are made up of painted images and actual objects from everyday life, such as window shades, pieces of fabric, ribbons, paper doilies, toys, and photographs. His work bridges Abstract Expressionism and Pop Art, and includes *Bed* (1955) and *Monogram* (1959).

Reinhardt, Ad (Adolph) (1913–1967), b. New York State. Painter. Reinhardt painted large canvases using mainly one color of paint. He is a Minimalist and is best known for his *Black Paintings*, begun in 1960.

Remington, Frederic (1861–1909), b. New York State. Painter, sculptor, illustrator, and writer. He portrayed frontier life on the plains of the West. His works include the sculpture *Bronco Buster* (1895) and the painting *Evening on a Canadian Lake* (1905).

Rivers, Larry (1923–), b. New York State. Painter and sculptor. He is inspired by the popular images of advertising and uses "visual quotations" from art masterpieces of the past in his own paintings, which include *Washington Crossing the Delaware* (1953) and the *Dutch Masters* series (1963).

Rockwell, Norman (1894–1978), b. New York State. Illustrator. He is best known for his *Saturday Evening Post* covers (1916–63). His images of small-town America are colorful and lifelike. *The Four Freedoms* (1943) is among his most famous paintings.

Rothko, Mark (1903–1970), b. Russia. Painter. He is a famous Abstract Expressionist, who covered his large canvases with glowing rectangles of richly colored paint. His work includes *No. 10* (1950) and a series of murals for an ecumenical chapel in Houston (1967–69).

Sargent, John Singer (1856–1925), b. Italy. Painter. He is best known for his vivid portraits of wealthy Americans, such as *The Daughters of Edward D. Boit* (1882) and *Madame X* (1884). He also painted impressionistic landscapes using watercolors.

Segal, George (1924–   ), b. New York State. Sculptor. He is a Pop Artist who uses plaster to sculpt realistic human figures in settings from daily life. Good examples are *Woman in Restaurant Booth* (1961) and *Cinema* (1963).

Shahn, Ben (1898–1969), b. Lithuania. Painter and illustrator. He was moved by the social and political injustices he saw in his world. His paintings tell people's stories without preaching. In the early 1930s, he did a series of 23 paintings based on the Sacco-Vanzetti trial in Boston.

Sheeler, Charles (1882–1965), b. Pennsylvania. Photographer and painter. He made photographs and paintings of the industrial landscape of America. His more famous paintings include *Ballardvale Revisited* (1949) and *Steel-Croton* (1953).

Smith, David (1906–65), b. Indiana. Sculptor. He welded metal together into abstract shapes. He worked on his large *Cubi* series from the late 1950s until he died.

Stella, Frank (1936–   ), b. Massachusetts. Painter. He uses bright colors and intricate patterns to create large works on irregularly shaped surfaces—canvas, wood, or paper. These paintings are sometimes three-dimensional. *Empress of India* (1965) is painted with a series of angular stripes. *Guadalupe Island* (1979) uses arches and wildly exuberant color.

Stuart, Gilbert (1755–1828), b. Rhode Island. Painter. He was one of the most outstanding portrait painters of his time. His most famous portraits were of George Washington.

Sully, Thomas (1783–1872), b. England. Painter. He painted portraits of many important people in the early history of this country. His most famous work is *Washington's Passage of the Delaware* (1819).

Warhol, Andy (1930–87), b. Pennsylvania. Painter and illustrator. He began the Pop Art movement, where images from the popular culture and everyday life are the subject matter for art. His works repeat familiar images, such as Campbell's soup cans, or figures from popular culture, such as Marilyn Monroe (both series begun in the 1960s).

Whistler, James Abbott McNeill (1834–1903), b. Massachusetts. Painter and graphic artist. His beautifully designed and subtly colored paintings include *The White Girl: Symphony in White No. 1* (1862) and *The Artist's Mother: Arrangement in Gray and Black* (1871). His series of *Nocturnes* were abstract nighttime landscapes painted long before abstract art became popular or accepted.

Wood, Grant (1891–1942), b. Iowa. Painter. He is best known for his stern, stiff figures and landscapes of the rural Midwest. His *American Gothic* (1930) is one of the most famous American paintings.

Wyeth, Andrew (1917–   ), b. Pennsylvania. Painter. He paints lifelike rural landscapes and portraits with great detail. His best-known work is *Christina's World* (1948).

Belgian: *See* Flemish, Belgian

British

Bacon, Francis (1909–92), b. Ireland. He was an Expressionist painter of nightmarish images. *Three Studies at the Base of a Crucifixion* (1944) and his series based on the famous Spanish painter Velazquez's *Pope Innocent X* portrait, which Bacon began in the 1950s, are good examples of his work.

Blake, William, (1757–1827). Painter, engraver, and poet. Blake illustrated the Book of Job from the Bible (1818–20), Dante's *Divine Comedy* (1824–27), and his own books of poems, with unearthly, mysterious images.

Constable, John (1776–1837). Painter. In landscapes, including *The White Horse* (1819), *The Hay Wain* (1821), and *Salisbury Cathedral* (1827), he made careful observations of nature and the way light changes from moment to moment.

Gainsborough, Thomas (1727–88). Painter. His best-known portraits include *Mr. and Mrs. Robert Andrews* (1748) and *Mrs. Siddons* (1785). His most famous painting is *The Blue Boy* (1770).

Hogarth, William (1697–1764). Painter and engraver. He satirized the social customs of his times in paintings that tell a story in a series of scenes. Good examples are *The Rake's Progress* (1733–35) and *Marriage a la Mode* (1743–45).

Moore, Henry (1898–1986). Sculptor. He abstracted and simplified the human figure into smooth, rounded shapes and hollows. He often sculpted a family group consisting of a man, woman, and child. Moore had many commissions for public spaces, including works for the Time-Life Building in London (1952–53) and for Lincoln Center for the Performing Arts in New York City (1962–65).

Reynolds, Sir Joshua (1723–92). Reynolds was the first president of the Royal Academy of Arts in London. He painted portraits of almost every important figure of his day. His works include *Commodore Keppel* (1753) and *Mrs. Siddons as the Tragic Muse* (1784).

Rossetti, Dante Gabriel (1828–82). Painter and poet. He was one of the original Pre-Raphaelites, a group of English artists who rebelled against the art establishment in 1848. His rich and symbolic works include *The Annunciation* (1850) and *Beata Beatrix* (1864).

Turner, Joseph Mallord William (1775–1851). Painter. Turner is one of the greatest English landscape painters. His canvases glow with light and rich color, as in *Calais Pier* (1803) and *The Grand Canal* (1835).

Dutch

Bosch, Hieronymous (Jerom Bos) (c. 1450–1516). Painter. He created bizarre and colorful religious fables on canvas, with grotesque figures and animals seemingly out of a nightmare. His works include *The Garden of Earthly Delights* (c. 1505–10) and *The Temptation of St. Anthony* (c. 1500).

Hals, Frans (c. 1580–1666). Painter. His lively, realistic portraits and scenes from everyday life sparkle with vivid color. His works include *The Banquet of the Officers of the St. George Militia* (1616) and *The Laughing Cavalier* (1624).

Mondrian, Piet (1872–1944). Painter. Mondrian was part of a Dutch abstract art movement called *de Stijl*. He favored abstract geometric shapes in his mature paintings. His works often consist of primary (red, blue, or yellow) squares bounded by black outlines, as in *Composition in Yellow and Blue* (1929) and *Red, Yellow, and Blue Composition* (1930).

Rembrandt Harmenszoon van Rijn (1606–69). Painter. This master of the Dutch school produced some 600 paintings. His work is distinguished by its deep humanity. Some examples are *The Anatomy Lesson of Dr. Tulp* (1632), *The Blinding of Samson* (1636), and *The Night Watch* (1642). Rembrandt painted nearly 100 self-portraits, dating from the 1620s to his last years.

Van Gogh, Vincent (1853–90). Painter. Van Gogh has become one of the most influential nineteenth-century artists. Many of his vibrant, expressive paintings were produced in the 29 months before his suicide. Van Gogh's most famous works include *The Potato Eaters* (1885), *The Night Café* (1888), *Starry Night* (1889), and a number of self-portraits.

Vermeer, Jan (Johannes) (1632–75). Painter. Vermeer painted solitary figures inside softly lit rooms. His careful study of light, attention to detail, and use of subtle colors give his work the clarity of photographs. His paintings include *Head of a Girl* (c. 1665), *Woman Weighing Pearls* (c. 1665), and *The Letter* (1666).

Flemish, Belgian

Bruegel, Pieter, the Elder (c. 1525–69). Flemish painter. He painted peasants at work and play, scenes of daily life, landscapes, and illustrations of proverbs. His works include *The Corn Harvest* (1565) and *The Peasant Wedding* (c. 1567).

Ensor, James (1860–1949). Belgian painter and etcher. Ensor's nightmarish compositions, such as *The Temptation of St. Anthony* (1887) and *The Entry of Christ into Brussels* (1888), opened the way for the Surrealist movement.

Limbourg, Herman, Jean, and Pol (active 1380–1416). Flemish painters and illustrators. These brothers worked in France for the Duke of Berry, a famous patron of the arts. They painted colorful, intricate illustrations for the duke's prayer book called *Les Très Riches Heures du Duc de Berry* (1413–16). This illuminated manuscript shows activities of daily life in the Middle Ages.

Magritte, René (1898–1967). Belgian painter. His Surrealist works, such as *The Key of Dreams* (1930) and *The Human Condition* (1934), are odd fantasies based on everyday situations. Often Magritte makes fun of the relationships between pictures and words.

Rubens, Peter Paul (1577–1640). Flemish painter. Rubens was a major Baroque artist. He worked with great freedom and vitality, producing dynamic, large paintings. His works include *The Raising of the Cross* (1610–11) and *The Judgment of Paris* (1638–39).

van der Weyden, Rogier (c. 1400–64). Flemish painter. His religious works, such as *The Descent from the Cross* (1435) and *The Last Judgment* (c. 1450), are large in size and deeply emotional. His penetrating portraits include *Francesco d'Este* (c. 1455).

Van Dyck, Sir Anthony (1599–1641). Flemish painter. Van Dyck's many portraits of the aristocracy include a number of Charles I of England, his royal patron from 1632 on. One such is *Portrait of Charles I Hunting* (c. 1635). This major Baroque artist also painted religious works, such as the *Lamentation* (1635).

Van Eyck, Jan (c. 1390–c. 1441). Van Eyck was one of the earliest masters of oil painting. By using thin layers of paint in such works as the church altarpiece in Ghent (1426–32) and the *Arnolfini Wedding Portrait* (1434), he brought a new depth of color and light to the art of painting.

French

Arp, Jean (Hans) (1887–1966). Painter, sculptor, and collage artist. His abstract paintings, sculptures, and collages use organic forms, such as *Squares Arranged According to the Laws of Chance* (1916–17) and *Navel, Shirt, and Head* (1926). Arp was one of the Dadaists and Surrealists.

Bonnard, Pierre (1867–1947). Painter, lithographer, and illustrator. He excelled at homey interiors with subtle lighting effects. His colorful work includes *Bowl of Fruit* (1933).

Braque, Georges (1882–1963). Painter. With Picasso, he started the Cubist movement. His works include *Large Nude* (1907–08) and *Woman with a Mandolin* (1937).

Cézanne, Paul (1839–1906). Painter. This Postimpressionist master built his landscapes, still lifes, and portraits from careful brushstrokes of richly colored paint. He simplified the shapes of nature into geometric forms, such as the cube, the cylinder, and the cone. His works include *The Card Players* (1890–92) and *Bathers* (1898–1905). Cézanne has had an enormous influence on twentieth-century art, especially Cubism.

Chardin, Jean-Baptiste-Siméon (1699–1779). Painter. Chardin was a master of everyday scenes and still lifes. His style is subtle, delicate, and unsentimental. His works include *Return from Market* (1739) and *Saying Grace* (c. 1740).

Corot, Jean-Baptiste-Camille (1796–1875). Painter. This influential artist made careful observations of nature and painted delicately lit landscapes, such as *View of the Forest of Fontainebleau* (1831) and *View of Avray* (c. 1840).

Courbet, Gustave (1819–77). Painter. Courbet revolted against political authority and believed in painting the world as it is, not as it should be. His works include *The Stone Breakers* (1849) and *The Artist's Studio* (1854–55).

Daumier, Honoré (1808–79). Painter, lithographer, and sculptor. Daumier satirized the social customs of his time. He made some 4,000 lithographs, such as *Transnonain Street* (1834), *14 April, 1834* (1834) and *The Legislative Belly*.

David, Jacques-Louis (1748–1825). Painter. David's paintings shows his passion for the ideals of the French Revolution and for classical art. This leading Neoclassical painter's works include *The Oath of the Horatii* (1784) and *The Death of Marat* (1793).

Degas, Edgar (1834–1917). Painter and sculptor. He exhibited with the Impressionists, but he preferred to paint in his studio, not outdoors. City nightlife interested him more than landscapes, and he perfected the art of painting with pastel chalks. His paintings often reveal very modern methods of composing figures and objects on canvas. Good examples of his works are *The Bellini Family* (1858–59) and *The Glass of Absinthe* (1876).

Delacroix, Eugène (1798–1863). Painter. Delacroix was inspired by the Romantic ideals of his time. His lively, freely painted, and richly colored works include *The Death of Sardanapalus* (1827) and *Liberty Leading the People* (1830).

Dubuffet, Jean (1901–85). Painter and sculptor. He created semiabstract, primitive works. He often used mixed media, such as asphalt, pebbles, and glass to texture the surfaces of his paintings. His works include the *Topographies* and *Texturologies* series (1957–59).

Duchamp, Marcel (1887–1968). Painter and sculptor. He created Cubist works and also cofounded Dadaism, a movement that made fun of all established values. His "ready-mades" are everyday objects exhibited as art. His works include the painting *Nude Descending a Staircase* (1912), the ready-made *Fountain* (1917), and the construction *The Bride Stripped Bare by Her Bachelors, Even* (1915–23).

Dufy, Raoul (1877–1953). Painter, illustrator, and decorator. He painted brightly colored Fauvist landscapes, seascapes, and portraits of society, including *Riders in the Wood* (1931) and *Cowes Regatta* (1934).

Fragonard, Jean-Honoré (1732–1806). Painter. This Rococo artist painted playful, romantic scenes in delicate colors. His works include *The Swing* (1769) and four *Progress of Love* paintings (1771–73).

Gauguin, Paul (1848–1903). Painter. At 35, he left his career and family to devote himself to painting. His best-known works have a two-dimensional feeling, with strong figures and bright colors. Much of his work was done in Tahiti and includes *Nevermore* (1897) and *Where Do We Come From? What Are We? Where Are We Going?* (1897).

Géricault, Théodore (Jean-Louis-André Théodore) (1791–1824). Painter. His works, based on events of his time, were done in the powerful, spontaneous style that French painters of the Romantic era liked. They include *A Cavalry Officer* (1812) and *The Raft of the Medusa* (1819).

Ingres, Jean-Auguste-Dominique (1780–1867). Painter. Ingres was deeply influenced by Raphael and by ancient Greek artists. His works include *La Grande Odalisque* (1814), *La Comtesse d'Haussonville* (1845), and *The Turkish Bath* (1859–62).

Léger, Fernand (1881–1955). Painter. He worked using flat areas of color and the simplified geometric shapes of machines. His paintings include *The City* (1919) and *Le Grand Déjeuner* (1921).

Lorrain, Claude (1600–82). Painter. He captured the changes of light and atmosphere in his sensitive landscape paintings, such as *The Embarkation of the Queen of Sheba* (1648) and *The Expulsion of Hagar* (1668).

Maillol, Aristide (1861–1944). Sculptor, painter, and woodcut artist. His best-known works are his calm, large-scale female nudes, such as *The Mediterranean* (c. 1901).

Manet, Édouard (1832–83). Painter. He introduced new themes and pioneered new painting techniques. His *Luncheon on the Grass* and *Olympia* (both 1863) are paintings of women of his own time in a realistic way. His works also include *A Bar at the Folies-Bergères* (1881).

Matisse, Henri (1869–1954). Painter, sculptor, lithographer, and collage artist. Matisse was a master of vivid color and line used in decorative patterns. His paintings include *La Joie de Vivre* (1905–06) and *The Dance* (1910).

Millet, Jean-François (1814–75). Painter. He painted scenes of peasant life as it really was, including *The Sower* (1850) and *The Angelus* (1855–57).

Monet, Claude (1840–1926). Painter. His work *Impression—Sunrise* (1872) gave the name to the Impressionist movement. This master's works include many series of the same subject seen under different atmospheric and lighting conditions, such as haystacks (1891), the Rouen Cathedral (1892–94), and water lilies (1899–1926).

Morisot, Berthe (1841–95). Painter. Morisot was the first woman Impressionist. Her paintings reveal a delicate, light-filled style and smooth brushwork. They include *The Cradle* (1873) and *Young Woman at the Dance* (1880).

Pissarro, Camille (1830–1903), b. Virgin Islands. Painter. He was an Impressionist landscape painter who was later influenced by Pointillism. His works include *Red Roofs* (1877) and *The Boulevard Montmartre at Night* (1897).

Poussin, Nicolas (1594–1665). Painter. He set standards for French Classical art based on the ideas of ancient Greece. His quiet, carefully painted works include *The Rape of the Sabine Women* (1636–67) and *The Holy Family on the Steps* (1648).

Renoir, Pierre-Auguste (1841–1919). Painter. He created warm, joyous, light-filled works, such as *Moulin de la Galette* (1876), *The Bathers* (1884–87), and *Luncheon of the Boating Party* (1881).

Rodin, Auguste (1840–1917). Sculptor. Many of his most famous works, such as *The Thinker* (1879–1900) and *The Kiss*

(1886–98), are enlarged figures from his great unfinished *Gates of Hell* (begun 1880). Other well-known works include *The Burghers of Calais* (1884–86) and *Balzac* (1892–97).

Rouault, Georges (1871–1958). Painter. This Expressionist artist was also associated with the Fauves. His subjects in paintings such as *Little Olympia* (1906), *Three Judges* (1913), and *Christ Mocked* (1932), were prostitutes, corrupt judges, and Christ.

Rousseau, Henri (1844–1910). Painter. He was self-taught. His colorful works, often of jungle scenes and animals, include *Sleeping Gypsy* (1897) and *The Dream* (1910).

Rousseau, Théodore (1812–67). Painter. He was a leading figure of the Barbizon School, a group of landscape painters who portrayed nature in a very lifelike manner. His landscape *Descent of the Cattle* (1835) is a good example of his intense and serious style.

Seurat, Georges (1859–91). Painter. He developed Pointillism, the technique of using small dots of pure color on his canvas. His works include *Bathing at Asnières* (1883–84) and *A Sunday Afternoon on the Island of La Grande Jatte* (1885–86).

Toulouse-Lautrec, Henri de (1864–1901). Painter and lithographer. He painted music halls, cabarets, and brothels in a realistic way, as in *At the Moulin de la Galette* (1892) and *In the Parlor at the Rue des Moulins* (1894).

Vuillard, Édouard (1868–1940). Painter and lithographer. He is famous for his interiors and his use of flat patterns, as in *Mother and Sister of the Artist* (c. 1893) and *Sitting Room with Three Lamps* (1899).

Watteau, Jean-Antoine (1684–1721). Painter. In such works as *A Pilgrimage to Cythera* (1717) and *La Toilette* (1720), he painted graceful scenes in delicate colors.

German

Beckmann, Max (1884–1950). Painter. His highly personal style reflected the misery of events that happened during his lifetime in Germany. His works include *The Night* (1918–19) and a series of nine triptychs, including *Departure* (1932–35).

Dürer, Albrecht (1471–1528). Painter and engraver. Dürer, a master of the German school, is known for his technical mastery and his use of the ideas of the Italian Renaissance. His works include the *Apocalypse* woodcuts (1498), the engraving *St. Jerome in His Study* (1514), and the painting *Four Apostles* (1526).

Ernst, Max (1891–1976). Painter. He was one of the founders of Dadaism and Surrealism. His nightmarish, sometimes whimsical, paintings include *Two Children Are Threatened by a Nightingale* (1924) and *The Temptation of St. Anthony* (1945).

Grosz, George (1893–1959). Painter. He painted savage caricatures of the post–World War I German middle class, such as *The Suicide* (1916) and *Eclipse of the Sun* (1926). He left Germany for the United States in 1933.

Grünewald, Mathias (Mathis Gothardt Neithardt) (c. 1475–1528). Painter. He was an unusually expressive artist. One of his favorite subjects was the crucifixion of Christ. His masterpiece is the Isenheim altarpiece (1515).

Holbein, Hans, the Younger (c. 1497–1543). Painter. This Northern Renaissance master painted portraits and religious subjects. His works include *Sir Thomas More* (1527) and the *Madonna of the Burgomeister Meyer* (c. 1528).

Kollwitz, Käthe Schmidt (1867–1945). Graphic artist and sculptor. Her works show her socialist and pacifist political views. They include the etching series *Peasants' War* (1902–08) and two lithography series, *The War* (1923) and

Death (1934–35). She also made many self-portraits.

Italian

Angelico, Fra (Guido or **Guidolino di Pietro,** also known as **Giovanni da Fiesole)** (c. 1400–55). Painter. A master of graceful line and color, he expressed great religious feeling in his paintings. His works encompass the frescoes for San Marco in Florence, including *The Annunciation* (c. 1447), and scenes from the lives of Saints Stephen and Lawrence in the Vatican (c. 1447–49).

Bellini, family of Renaissance painters. **Jacopo** (c. 1400–70) ran a workshop in Venice with his sons, **Gentile** (1429–1507) and **Giovanni** (c. 1430–1516). Jacopo's work includes *The Madonna and Child with Lionello d'Este* (c. 1441). Gentile was best at showing the Venetian ceremonies of his day. An example is *The Procession in the Piazza San Marco* (1496). Giovanni, probably the most talented, produced expressive works, such as *St. Francis in Ecstasy* (c. 1475) and the San Zaccaria altarpiece (1505).

Bernini, Giovanni Lorenzo (Gianlorenzo) (1598–1680). Sculptor, architect, and painter. His dramatic, masterful sculptures include *David* (1623) and *The Ecstasy of St. Theresa* (1645–52). Among his paintings is *Saints Andrew and Thomas* (1627).

Boccioni, Umberto (1882–1916). Painter and sculptor. This major figure of Futurist art was inspired by the technology of the machine age. His works include the painting *The City Rises* (1910) and the sculpture *Unique Forms of Continuity in Space* (1913).

Botticelli, Sandro (Alessandro di Mariano Filipepi) (c. 1444–1510). Painter. This Renaissance painter was a favorite of the Medici. He had a wonderful sense of color and was a master of line. He is

known for his mythological scenes, such as *Primavera* (c. 1478) and *The Birth of Venus* (c. 1482).

Canova, Antonio (1757–1822). Sculptor. His graceful works include the tomb of Pope Clement XIV (1783–87) and *Pauline Borghese as Venus* (1805–07).

Caravaggio, Michelangelo Merisi da (c. 1573–1610). Painter. He used bold, dramatic contrasts of light and dark in his masterpieces. They include *The Calling of St. Matthew* (c. 1598) and *The Conversion of St. Paul* (1600–01).

Carracci, family of painters. The brothers **Annibale** (1560–1609) and **Agostino** (1557–1602) and their cousin **Ludovico** (1555–1619) established an important painting school in Bologna. Annibale, the most talented, and Agostino painted richly decorative frescoes for the Farnese Palace in Rome (1597–1600). Annibale also painted landscapes, such as *Landscape with the Flight into Egypt* (1604).

Cellini, Benvenuto (1500–71). Sculptor, metalsmith, and author. His works include the gold and enamel saltcellar of Francis I (1540) and his masterpiece, *Perseus with the Head of Medusa* (1545–54).

Chirico, Giorgio de (1888–1978), b. Greece. Painter. His best-known paintings show deep perspective and solitary figures. They include *Mystery and Melancholy of a Street* (1914) and *Disquieting Muses* (1916–17).

Correggio (Antonio Allegri) (c. 1494–1534). Painter. Inspired by myths, he painted graceful, delicately lit works, such as *Jupiter and Io* (c. 1530), and ceiling frescoes, such as *The Assumption of the Virgin* for the cathedral in Parma (1526–30).

da Vinci, Leonardo *See* **Leonardo da Vinci.**

della Robbia, Florentine family of sculptors and ceramicists known for their brightly colored glazed terra-cotta. **Luca**

(c. 1400–82) founded a workshop; his works include *The Resurrection* and *The Ascension* (both late 1440s) for the Florence Cathedral. His nephew **Andrea** (1435–1525) made sculptures for the foundling hospital in Florence. Andrea continued the workshop with his sons, **Luca II, Giovanni,** and **Girolamo.**

Donatello (Donato di Niccolo di Betto Bardi) (c. 1386–1466). Sculptor. Donatello's powerful and expressive sculptures include *David* (c. 1408), *St. George* (c. 1415), and *Mary Magdelene* (c. 1456).

Ghiberti, Lorenzo (1378–1455). Sculptor. His two pairs of bronze doors for the Florence Baptistery, with their finely sculpted scenes inspired by stories from the Bible, are his masterpieces (1403–24 and 1425–52). His life-size bronzes include *St. John the Baptist* (1412–16) and *St. Matthew* (1419).

Giorgione (Giorgione da Castelfranco) (c. 1476–1510). Painter. His poetic and warmly colored works had a major influence on Venetian painting. They include *The Tempest* (c. 1500–10), *The Three Philosophers* (c. 1505–10), and *Sleeping Venus*, which was completed by Titian (c. 1510).

Giotto (Giotto di Bondone) (c. 1266–c. 1337). Painter. His large figures and lifelike way of painting space as the eye sees it were important. His works include the *Ognissanti Madonna* (c. 1310), frescoes in the Arena Chapel, Padua (finished 1313), and frescoes in the Bardi and Peruzzi chapels, Santa Croce, Florence (1320s).

Leonardo da Vinci (1425–1519). Painter, sculptor, architect, engineer, and scientist. His peaceful, beautiful paintings are great examples of High Renaissance art. Leonardo's studies of perspective and anatomy influenced generations of artists. His paintings include *The Virgin of the Rocks* (1483–85), *The Last Supper* (1495–98), and the *Mona Lisa* (1503–06).

Lippi, family of Florentine painters. **Fra Filippo** (c. 1406–69) was an important early Renaissance artist. Major works include *The Coronation of the Virgin* (1441) and the frescoes for the Prato Cathedral (1452–65). His son, **Filippino** (c. 1457–1504), painted a group of frescoes for the Strozzi Chapel, Santa Maria Novella, Florence (1495–1502).

Mantegna, Andrea (1431–1506). Painter and engraver. This early Renaissance painter used large-scale figures in his painting. Examples of his works include frescoes for the Ovetari Chapel, Church of the Eremitani, Padua (1448–57) and the San Zeno altarpiece (1456–59).

Masaccio (Tommaso Guidi) (1401–c. 1428). Painter. He revolutionized the way space was drawn in a painting. He painted the human body with new true-to-life proportions. His works include *The Expulsion from Eden* (c. 1427), one of the frescoes for the Brancacci Chapel, Santa Maria del Carmine, Florence (c. 1425–28).

Michelangelo Buonarroti (1475–1564). Sculptor, painter, architect, and poet. His influence on Western art was supreme. Michelangelo's works, all in a heroic, larger-than-life style, include the sculptures *Pietà* (1499), *David* (1501–04), *Moses* (1513–16), and the tombs of Lorenzo and Giuliano de' Medici (1519–34); the Sistine Chapel's ceiling (1508–12) and its *Last Judgment* fresco (1534–41).

Modigliani, Amedeo (1884–1920). Painter and sculptor. His portraits and nudes are painted with long, smooth lines. Some good examples are the paintings *Jeanne Hébuterne* (1919) and *Reclining Nude* (1919).

Piero della Francesca (c. 1420–92). Painter. This major Renaissance artist used detailed and exact perspective in his work. His paintings are very symmetrical. They include frescoes of *The Legend of the True Cross* in the Church of San

Francesco, Arezzo (1452–64), and *The Flagellation of Christ* (c. 1456).

Pisano, family of sculptors. **Nicola** (c. 1220–c. 1284) made pulpits for the Pisa Baptistery (finished 1260) and Siena Cathedral (1265–68). His son, **Giovanni** (c. 1250–1314), created the decorative facade, Siena Cathedral (1284–96), and the pulpit, Pisa Cathedral (1302–10).

Raphael (Santi or **Sanzio)** (1483–1520). Painter. His exquisitely balanced paintings are excellent examples of High Renaissance art. They include frescoes for the Stanza della Segnatura, including *The School of Athens* (finished 1511), which is in the Vatican, and *The Sistine Madonna* (1512).

Tintoretto (Jacopo Robusti) (1518–94). Painter. He used dramatic light and color in his paintings. A group of his works in the Scuola di San Rocco, Venice, include an enormous *Crucifixion* (1564–87), and *The Last Supper* (1592–94).

Titian (Tiziano Vecellio) (c. 1490–1576). Painter. This High Renaissance painter's expressive use of color influenced many other artists. His works include *The Assumption of the Virgin* (1516–18), *Pope Paul III and His Grandsons* (1546), and the *Pietà* (1576).

Uccello, Paolo (c. 1396–1475). Painter. He was an early master of perspective. His colorful, decorative works include three panels of *The Battle of San Romano* (c. 1455) and a cycle of frescoes for Santa Maria Novella, Florence (c. 1445).

Veronese, Paolo (Paolo Caliari) (1528–88). Painter. His large works show scenes of sumptuous ceremonies and are painted in rich colors. They include *The Marriage at Cana* (1562), *The Feast in the House of Levi* (1573), and decorative paintings for the Ducal Palace, Venice (1577–82).

Verrocchio, Andrea del (Andrea di Michele di Francesco di Cioni) (1435–88). Sculptor and painter. His sculptures include

The Doubting of Thomas (1465); among his paintings is *The Baptism of Christ* (1472), in which he was assisted by his pupil, Leonardo da Vinci.

Mexican

Kahlo, Frida (1907–54). Painter. Her vivid self-portraits express psychic and physical pain. They include *Frida and Diego Rivera* (1931) and *The Love Embrace of the Universe, the Earth (Mexico), Diego, Me and Señor Xolotl* (1949).

Orozco, José Clemente (1883–1949). Muralist. His large-scale wall paintings express concern for human rights. His murals are in the New School for Social Research, New York City (1931) and Dartmouth College, New Hampshire (1932–34).

Rivera, Diego (1886–1957). Painter and muralist. He founded the Mexican mural Renaissance. His works pay homage to Mexico's history and workers. They include *The History of Mexico*, National Palace of Mexico City (1929–36), and a series at the Detroit Institute of Arts (1933).

Siqueiros, David Alfaro (1896–1974). Muralist. His paintings express revolutionary political ideas. Siqueiros's murals include a series at the Plaza Art Center, Los Angeles (1932) and *The Liberation of Chile* at the Mexican School, Chillán, Chile (1942).

Tamayo, Rufino (1899–1991). Painter. His richly colored and decorative works are influenced by Cubism, Fauvism, and themes from Mexican folklore. They include *Sleeping Musicians* (1950) and a series of murals at Smith College, Massachusetts (1943).

Spanish

Dalí, Salvador (1904–89). Painter. He painted hallucinatory images in a clean, precise, Surrealistic style. They can be seen in *The Persistence of Memory* (1931), *Crucifixion* (1951), and *The Last Supper* (1955).

El Greco *See* **Greco, El.**

Goya y Lucientes, Francisco José de (1746–1828). Painter and graphic artist. His expressive works often make fun of the political and social customs of his time. They include the paintings *Nude Maja* and *Clothed Maja* (both c. 1804) and *Charles IV and His Family* (1800); and a number of etching series, such as *Los Caprichos* (1799) and *Disasters of War* (1810–14).

Greco, El (Domenikos Theotokopoulos) (1541–1614), b. Crete. Painter. He painted dramatic religious scenes peopled by long, thin figures. His work makes use of strong contrasts of light and shadow. Some good examples are *The Disrobing of Christ* (1577–79), *The Burial of Count Orgaz* (1586), and *View of Toledo* (1600).

Gris, Juan (José Victoriano González) (1887–1927). Painter and collage artist. This Cubist used simple forms and repeated patterns in his paintings and collages. His works include *Homage to Picasso* (1911–12), *The Violin* (1916), and *Violin and Fruit Dish* (1924).

Miró, Joan (1893–1983). Painter. He painted colorful amoebalike shapes in a playful, lyrical style. This Surrealist's works include *Harlequin's Carnival* (1924–25), *Dog Barking at the Moon* (1926), and ceramic murals for the UNESCO building, Paris (1955–58).

Murillo, Bartolemé Estéban (1618–82). Painter. His important works include a series for the Charity Hospital in Seville (1671–73), many versions of the Immaculate Conception, and portraits.

Picasso, Pablo (Pablo Ruiz y Picasso) (1881–1973). Painter, sculptor, graphic artist, and ceramicist. Picasso was able to master any art form or medium. He produced an enormous number of paintings, drawings, and sculptures and is

one of the masters of twentieth-century art. His *Les Desmoiselles d'Avignon* (1907) is one of the most important Cubist works. Other major paintings include *The Three Musicians* (1921) and *Guernica* (1937).

Ribera, Jusepe de (1591–1652). Painter. He painted mainly religious subjects. His lifelike yet mystical works include *The Martyrdom of St. Bartholomew* (c. 1630) and *The Mystic Marriage of St. Catherine* (1648).

Velázquez, Diego Rodríguez de Silva y (1599–1660). Painter. This master painted brilliantly colored canvases with great feeling and expression. His works include *The Surrender of Breda* (1634–35), *Pope Innocent X* (1650), and *The Maids of Honor* (1656).

Zurbarán, Francisco de (1598–1664). Painter. He was inspired by religious subjects. His paintings have an intensely serious feeling. They include *The Apotheosis of St. Thomas Aquinas* (1631) and *St. Serapion* (1628).

Other

Brancusi, Constantin (1876–1957), b. Romania. Sculptor. He sculpted with clean, simple lines and influenced other sculptors of his time. His works include *Bird in Space* (1919) and the immense *Endless Column*, erected in a park near his birthplace (1937).

Chagall, Marc (1887–1985), b. Russia. Painter. He lived mainly in France. His poetic, colorful, and symbolic works are often based on Jewish folklore. They include *I and the Village* (1911), *Self-Portrait with Seven Fingers* (1911), and murals for the Metropolitan Opera House, New York City (installed 1966).

Gabo, Naum (Naum Nehemia Pevsner) (1890–1977), b. Russia. Sculptor. His works include *Column* (1923) and *Kinetic Construction* (1920), a sculpture with a motor. In his *Realist Manifesto*, he proposed that the ideas of time and space be included in art.

Giacometti, Alberto (1901–66), b. Switzerland. Sculptor and painter. He sculpted elongated figures of animals and people, such as *The Forest* (1950) and *Walking Man* (1960).

Kandinsky, Wassily (1866–1944), b. Russia. Painter. He was a founder of the avant-garde *Blaue Reiter* (Blue Rider) group and a teacher at the Bauhaus, a German art school. His series of *Compositions, Improvisations,* and *Impressions*, beginning in 1910, are often seen as the first purely abstract works in the history of Western art.

Klee, Paul (1879–1940), b. Switzerland. Painter. His works, such as *Twittering Machine* (1922) and *Park Near L(ucerne)* (1938), combine abstraction with playful, childlike inventiveness. Klee was associated with the *Blaue Reiter* group.

Klimt, Gustav (1862–1918), b. Austria. Painter. He was part of the Art Nouveau movement in Vienna at the turn of the century. His exotic, symbolic works include *Death and Life* (1908).

Kokoschka, Oskar (1886–1980), b. Austria. Painter. This Expressionist artist produced many portraits and landscapes, such as *Le Marquis de Montesquieu* (1909–10) and *Jerusalem* (1929–30), as well as a series of self-portraits.

Malevich, Kasimir Severinovich (1878–1935), b. Russia. Painter. He created sparse paintings based on geometric forms. His works include *Black Square* (1915) and the *White on White* series (c. 1918). He described his theories in the book *The Non-Objective World* (1915).

Munch, Edvard (1863–1944), b. Norway. Painter and graphic artist. His work looked forward to Expressionism with its powerful images of terror, despair, and isolation, as in the paintings *The Scream* (1893) and *Vampire* (1895).

Phidias (Pheidias) (c. 500–c. 432 B.C.), b. Greece. Sculptor. One of the greatest ancient Greek sculptors, although none of his original works survive. He sculpted the enormous *Athena Parthenos*, Athens, and the *Zeus,* Olympia, one of the Seven Wonders of the Ancient World.

Praxiteles (c. 370–330 B.C.), b. Greece. Sculptor. His *Hermes with the Infant Dionysus* is the only existing original work by an ancient master. He also sculpted the *Aphrodite of Cnidus.*

Schiele, Egon (1890–1918), b. Austria. Painter and graphic artist. He used mainly lines and hard angles in his work. Many of his works are nudes, often in disturbing poses. His paintings include *The Embrace* (1917) and *Paris von Gütersloh* (1918).

Tatlin, Vladimir Evgrafovich (1885–1953), b. Russia. Sculptor and designer. This artist was a founder of Constructivism, a Russian geometric abstract art movement. His works include the *Relief Constructions* series (begun 1913) and the *Corner Reliefs* (begun 1915).

ART TERMS FROM A TO Z

acrylic Water-based paint made from pigments and a plastic binder. When dry they will not dissolve in water.

aquatint An etching method in which a solution of asphalt or resin is used on the metal plate. It produces prints with rich, gray tones.

caricature An artwork that humorously exaggerates the qualities, defects, or peculiarities of a person or idea.

cartoon A humorous sketch or drawing that tells a story or makes fun of some person or action. In fine arts, a sketch or design for a picture to be transferred to a fresco or tapestry.

carving In sculpture, the cutting of a form from a solid, hard material, such as stone or wood.

casting In sculpture, a technique for making copies of a work by pouring into a mold a substance such as plaster or molten metal, which then hardens.

chiaroscuro The use of light and shade in painting; the subtle gradations and marked variations of light and shade for dramatic effect.

collage A composition made by cutting and pasting different materials on a flat surface, sometimes with images added by the artist.

colors, complementary Two colors at opposite points on the color scale, for example, orange and blue, green and red.

colors, primary Red, yellow, and blue, the mixture of which will give all other colors but which cannot be produced themselves through a mixture of other colors.

colors, secondary Orange, green, and purple. These colors are made by mixing two primary colors.

composition The way light, color, and shapes are organized in an artwork.

drypoint A technique of engraving. A sharp-pointed needle is used to draw a picture on the plate. It produces a furrowed edge. Prints made from drypoint have soft, velvety lines.

encaustic Painting technique using pigments dissolved in hot wax.

engraving A method of printing in which designs are cut into wood or metal blocks or plates. The plates are then inked and printed.

etching The technique of printing designs from a metal plate. The plate is put into a corrosive acid bath, inked, and printed.

figure A representation of a human or an animal form.

foreshortening Perspective used to make a single form, for example, a foot or hand, appear three-dimensional on a flat surface.

fresco Meaning "fresh" in Italian, the technique of painting on moist lime plaster with colors ground in water.

frieze A band of painted or sculpted decoration, often at the top of a wall.

genre painting A realistic style of painting subject matter from everyday life, in contrast to subjects from religion or history.

gesso Ground chalk or plaster mixed with glue, used as a base coat for tempera and oil paintings on hard surfaces, such as wood or board.

gouache Opaque watercolors. The paints are prepared with a more gluey base than watercolors. The effect is less transparent.

highlight The point of most intense light on any object or figure.

impasto Paint applied very thickly. It often projects from the picture surface.

landscape Painting in which natural scenery is the subject.

lithography A printing process in which ink impressions are taken from a flat stone or metal plate prepared with a greasy substance, such as an oily crayon.

modeling In sculpture, the building up of form using a soft medium such as clay or wax. In painting and drawing, the use of color and light to make something look three-dimensional.

monochrome A painting or drawing in a single color.

monotype A single print made from a metal or glass plate on which an image has been drawn in paint or ink.

mural A large painting or decoration done on a wall.

oil A method of painting with pigments mixed with oil. It can produce a wide range of effects of light, color, and texture.

palette A flat board used by a painter to mix and hold colors. A portable palette is traditionally rounded and oblong, with a hole for the thumb. A palette is also a range of colors used by a particular painter.

pastel A soft, subdued color; a drawing stick made of ground pigments, chalk, and gum water.

perspective A way of representing three-dimensional forms and deep space on a

The First Famous Woman Artist

During the Middle Ages the majority of artists were anonymous. Women artists began to be identified about 1550, but they were allowed to paint only portraits, still lifes, and genre scenes.

The major obstacle women artists faced was that they usually were not permitted to draw from the nude model in art classes. Society considered the female sex too modest to see such a sight. This restriction meant that they were unable to learn how to depict the human body, one of the main subjects of painting and sculpture. The few exceptions to this practice first appeared in the seventeenth century in Italy.

The first woman artist to become famous in her own time was Artemisia Gentileschi, who was born in Rome in 1593. Her father was a follower of the famous artist Caravaggio. Gentileschi's love of dramatic subjects was typical of her time.

The artist's favorite subjects included two tragic heroines from the Bible, Judith and Bathsheba. According to the Old Testament, Bathsheba was loved by King David, while Judith saved her people by beheading the general Holofernes. In her painting *Judith and Maidservant with the Head of Holofernes* (c. 1625), Gentileschi reveals Judith's emotions after the murder.

---

flat surface to produce an effect similar to what we see with our own eyes.

polychrome Of many or various colors.

polyptych In painting, a work made of several panels or scenes joined together. A diptych has two panels; a triptych, three.

primary colors *See* **colors, primary.**

relief In sculpture, an image or form that projects, or sticks out, from its background. Sculpture formed in this manner is described as high relief or low relief (bas-relief) depending on how much it projects.

secondary colors *See* **colors, secondary.**

stenciling A method of producing images or letters from sheets of cardboard, metal, or other materials from which forms have been cut out.

still life The representation of inanimate objects in painting, drawing, or photography.

tempera A painting technique using pigments mixed with egg yolk and water. It produces clear, pure colors.

texture The visual quality and feel of a work of art based on the particular way the materials are handled or the kinds of materials that are used. Texture also means the distribution of tones or shades of a single color.

tone The effect of the harmony of color and values in a work.

trompe l'oeil Meaning "fool the eye" in French. In painting, the fine, detailed rendering of objects to convey the illusion that the painted forms are real and three-dimensional.

values In painting, the degree of lightness or darkness in a color.

wash In painting, a thin layer of translucent color.

watercolor Painting in pigments suspended in water. It can produce brilliant and transparent colors.

woodcut The image carved on a wood block. It is then inked to produce a print.

INFORMATION, PLEASE

Beckett, Wendy. *Contemporary Women Artists*. Universe, 1988.

Fletcher, Banister. *Sir Banister Fletcher's History of Architecture*. 19th ed. Edited by John Musgrove. Butterworths, 1987.

Gardner, Helen. *Art through the Ages*. 9th ed.

Revised by Horst de la Croix et al. Harcourt Brace Jovanovich, 1990.

Gloag, John. *Guide to Western Architecture.* Macmillan, 1958.

Gombrich, Ernst Hans. *Story of Art.* 15th ed. Abrams, 1987.

Goulart, Ron. *The Great Comic Book Artists.* St. Martin's, 1988.

Greenberg, Jan, and Sandra Jordan. *The Painter's Eye.* Delacorte, 1991.

Honour, Hugh and John Fleming. *The Visual Arts: A History.* Prentice Hall, 1991.

Janson, H. W. *History of Art for Young People.* 3rd ed. Abrams, 1987.

13

MUSIC AND DANCE

Western music can be divided into two categories:

Classical Orchestral music, chamber music, and opera. Although classical composers are at work today, the main body of this music is historical, having been written one hundred or more years ago. The eighteenth century was, most music experts agree, a period of unsurpassed creativity in this music.

Popular Folk, country, jazz, rock, and theater music make up this category. Although folk and country repertoires contain tunes dating back hundreds of years, this music has, for the most part, been written recently.

CLASSICAL MUSIC

Prior to 1600, most music was written for the Roman Catholic church. It was primarily choral, with instruments playing little or no role. The musical forms that we are most familiar with—those we hear in symphony halls today—can be traced to four musical periods, the first of which began around 1600.

Baroque—1600–1760

- Religious music gives way to secular music, with the purpose of entertaining or amusing the listener.
- Italy is the world's music center.
- Musicians, especially composers, are often supported by wealthy private patrons or royal courts.
- The modern scale system comes into use.
- The musical forms called the sonata and the concerto are developed, and opera is emerging.
- Individual sections, or movements, within longer pieces of music are relatively brief.
- The keyboard, especially the harpsichord, is a dominant instrument.

Classical—1730–1820

- New musical forms—the string quartet, the symphony, and the piano sonata—emerge.
- Vienna, home to Haydn, Mozart, and Beethoven, is the musical center of Europe.
- Individual movements become longer.

Fascinating Musical Facts

Most popular songs In English the three most often-performed songs are "Happy Birthday," "For He's a Jolly Good Fellow," and "Auld Lang Syne."

Richest concert tour Mick Jagger and the Rolling Stones mounted the most successful concert tour ever, the 1989 "Steel Wheels" tour, which earned approximately $310 million and was attended by over 3.2 million people.

Biggest rock concert Pink Floyd's "The Wall" concert, held July 21, 1990, in Potsdamer Platz, a plaza spanning East and West Berlin, involved 600 people on a stage that was 551 by 82 feet tall and was attended by 200,000 people celebrating German reunification.

Biggest classical concert The New York Philharmonic Concert on July 5, 1986, on the Great Lawn in Central Park in New York City was attended by an estimated 80,000 people celebrating Statue of Liberty Weekend.

Oldest national anthem The Japanese national anthem, *"Kimigayo,"* has words dating to the ninth century; the music was written in 1881. The Dutch national anthem, *"Vilhelmus,"* has the oldest music, dating from around 1570.

Most expensive classical instrument A 1720 Stradivarius violin sold for $1.76 million in 1990.

Most expensive rock instrument Jimi Hendrix's guitar, a Fender Stratocaster, sold for $338,580 in 1990.

Longest musical performance Of music that is frequently performed, the longest musical piece is the opera *Die Meistersinger von Nürnberg* by Richard Wagner. A normal uncut performance runs about 5 hours and 15 minutes.

- The keyboard disappears as a staple instrument. Whole symphonies are written that do not call for a keyboard instrument, and the harpsichord almost vanishes from musical composition.
- There is little experimentation in form, in contrast to earlier and later eras; boundaries are maintained and rules followed.

Romantic—1815–1910

- This is a great age of individualism in music. Musicians break free from the demands of patrons and compose for their own—and their audiences'—pleasure.
- Music becomes more dramatic.
- Symphonies and sonatas continue to be composed and played but with a new emphasis on conveying a story idea or suggesting pictorial scenes. The term "symphonic poem" is used to describe some of the new musical compositions.

- Opera becomes more serious and more dramatic.
- Nationalism is a force in music, and composers often incorporate folk music into their work.

Modern—1900s–Present

- Music, like art and literature, makes a startling break with the past.
- The primary development is the introduction of dissonance, or playing together two or more tones that clash.
- Musical compositions are often harsh, jarring, unharmonious.
- Traditional forms are sometimes maintained and sometimes ignored. Movements can be long or short—or nonexistent.

MAJOR COMPOSERS
American

Barber, Samuel (1910–81), b. Pennsylvania. Winner, Pulitzer Prize, for the opera *Vanessa* (1957) and Piano Concerto (1963). His works also include two symphonies, the overture to *The School for Scandal, Dover Beach,* and the popular *Adagio for Strings.*

Bernstein, Leonard (1918–90), b. Massachusetts. Conductor and music director of the New York Philharmonic 1958–69. He composed symphonies, songs, ballets, and musicals, including *West Side Story* (1957).

Cage, John (1912–92), b. California. Originator of controversial and experimental music, including the *Music of Changes,* derived from the ideas of *I Ching, 4'33",* and *Imaginary Landscape No. 4* for 12 radios tuned randomly. Cage collaborated with dancer Merce Cunningham, artist Marcel Duchamp, and others.

Copland, Aaron (1900–90), b. New York State. Composer of *Appalachian Spring* (1944) and two other symphonies, a piano concerto, other orchestral works, chamber music, and ballets. The developer of a distinctly American music, Copland received the Pulitzer Prize in 1945.

Gershwin, George (1898–1937), b. New York State. Composer of music in a distinct blend of classical, popular, and jazz styles. Gershwin's works include numerous popular songs and musical comedies and more ambitious concert pieces—*Rhapsody in Blue* (1924), *An American in Paris* (1928), and the jazz opera *Porgy and Bess* (1935).

Ives, Charles (1874–1954), b. Connecticut. Composer of advanced and innovative works and winner of the Pulitzer Prize in 1947. Ives wrote *Holiday Symphony* and three other symphonies, chamber and choral music, songs, and piano works.

Menotti, Gian Carlo (1911–   ), b. Italy. Composer of ballets, a piano concerto, and the operas *Amelia Goes to the Ball, The Island God, The Medium, Amahl and the Night Visitors* (1951), and *The Saint of Bleecker Street* (1954). He founded the Festival of Two Worlds in Spoleto, Italy and Spoleto Festival in Charleston, S.C.

Schoenberg, Arnold (1874–1951), b. Austria. Originator of a revolutionary new system of music. The theory is shown in his works *Five Pieces* for piano, *Serenade* for seven instruments and bass baritone, and *Variations* for orchestra.

Thomson, Virgil (1896–1989), b. Missouri. Music critic and composer. His works include two operas (with librettos by Gertrude Stein), a ballet, choral and chamber music, pieces for theater and film (among them *The River,* 1937), keyboard music, and songs. He is the author of *The State of Music* (1939), *The Musical Scene* (1945), and *The Art of Judging Music* (1948).

Austrian

Bruckner, Anton (1824–96). Organist and composer of Romantic music. Principal works include nine symphonies, choral works, and chamber music for string quintet.

Haydn, Franz Joseph (1732–1809). Outstanding artist of the Classical style. Among his works are more than 100 symphonies, numerous concertos, 20 operas (five are lost), oratorios, church music, string quartets, piano trios, keyboard sonatas and variations, and many songs. Haydn is credited with inventing the string quartet and playing a central role in the invention of the symphony.

Mahler, Gustav (1860–1911). Conductor of the Hamburg and Vienna operas and the Metropolitan Opera in New York. He composed nine symphonies, as well as songs, in a Romantic style, including the

Resurrection Symphony (1894) and *Symphony of a Thousand* (1907).

Mozart, Wolfgang Amadeus (1756–91). Master of the Classical style in all its forms of his time. Mozart began to compose and perform at the age of six; at 11 he had composed three symphonies and 30 other works and arranged some piano concertos of J. S. Bach. His principal works include the operas *The Marriage of Figaro* (1786), *Don Giovanni* (1787), and *The Magic Flute* (1791); chamber music; piano sonatos and fantasias; symphonies; and church music, including the *Requiem* (1791).

Schubert, Franz Seraph Peter (1797–1828). Composer of numerous symphonies, masses, quartets, and sonatas, but most notably of songs in the spirit of early Romantic poetry. His works include the No. 9 C-Major Symphony ("The Great") (1825), the piano sonatas, the A-Minor (1824) and G-Major Quartets (1826), and the Trios in B flat (1826) and E flat (1827).

Strauss, family of Viennese musicians. **Johann I** (1804–49) was the composer of waltzes famous throughout Europe. He was the father of **Johann II** (1825–99), who became his rival, composer of over 400 waltzes, including *The Blue Danube* (1866) and *Tales from the Vienna Woods* (1868), as well as operettas. His brothers, **Josef** (1827–70) and **Eduard I** (1835–1916), were also successful composers and conductors.

Webern, Anton von (1883–1945). Editor, conductor, and composer in the 12-tone system of Arnold Schoenberg. Webern wrote a symphony for small orchestra, three cantatas, a string quartet, a concerto for nine instruments, songs, and other works.

British

Britten, (Edward) Benjamin (1913–76). Major twentieth-century composer. His operas include *Peter Grimes, The Rape of Lucretia, Billy Budd,* and *The Turn of the Screw.* Among his most popular works are *A Ceremony of Carols* (1942), *A Young Person's Guide to the Orchestra* (1945), and the *War Requiem* (1962).

Elgar, Sir Edward (1857–1934). Composer with a unique personal style. His works include *The Light of Life* (1896), *Scenes from the Bavarian Highlands* (1896), and *King Olaf* (1896), for chorus; orchestra works, including *Serenade for Strings* (1893), two symphonies, and concertos; and music for brass band, chamber music, organ sonatas, and songs.

Purcell, Henry (c. 1659–95). Organist at Westminster Abbey and composer of music for more than 40 plays, including *The Fairy Queen* (1692) and *The Tempest* (1695); and odes, songs, cantatas, church music, chamber music, and keyboard works.

Sullivan, Sir Arthur (1842–1900). Conductor, organist, and composer. His works include the grand opera *Ivanhoe* (1891); ballads; oratorios; cantatas, including *The Golden Legend*; church music; a symphony; songs; and works for piano. He is best known for his light operas to librettos by W. S. Gilbert.

Vaughan Williams, Ralph (1872–1958). Composer noted for his adaptations of folk music. Pincipal compositions include *A London Symphony* (1913), *Norfolk Rhapsodies* (1906), and *The Lark Ascending* (1914), all for orchestra; *A Sea Symphony* (1911) and *Five Mystical Songs* (1911) for chorus; the operas *Hugh the Drover* (1914), *Riders to the Sea* (1932), and *The Pilgrim's Progress* (1951); and works for stage, chamber music, and songs.

French

Berlioz, Hector (1803–69). Conductor and composer of Romantic works. Berlioz is best known for the *Fantastic Symphony* (1830). He also wrote the symphonic work *Harold in Italy*, the opera *Damnation of Faust*, and the oratorio *Childhood of Christ* (1850–54).

Bizet, Georges (1838–75). Composer best known for the operas *The Pearlfishers* (1836), *The Young Maid of Perth* (1867), *Djmileh* (1872), and *Carmen* (1875). His Symphony in C Major (1868) is highly regarded.

Boulez, Pierre (1925–   ). Composer of works using serialism, including *The Hammer Without a Master* (1953–54) and *Memorials* (1975). He served as music director of the New York Philharmonic 1971–77.

Debussy, Claude (1862–1918). Composer noted for his Impressionist style. Orchestral works include *The Sea* (1905) and *Nocturnes* (1899); piano works include *Moonlight* (*Clair de lune*), preludes, études, arabesques, and *The Children's Corner*. Debussy also wrote choral works, an opera, and the well-known tone poem *Prelude to the Afternoon of a Faun* (1894).

Fauré, Gabriel (1845–1924). Organist and composer who excelled in song writing. He wrote the operas *Prometheus* (1900) and *Penelope* (1913), orchestral music, chamber works, and piano and church music. Fauré was the teacher of Maurice Ravel.

Massenet, Jules-Émile-Frédéric (1842–1912). Best known for his operas *The King of Lahore* (1877), *Manon* (1884), and *Werther* (1892). Massenet also wrote oratorios, orchestral works, concertos, and songs.

Offenbach, Jacques (1819–80). Composer of 90 operettas, including the popular *Orpheus in the Underworld* (1858), *Beautiful Helen* (1864), and *The Parisian Life* (1866). His best work is thought to be *The Tales of Hoffmann* (1881).

Ravel, Maurice (1875–1937). Leading exponent of Impressionism. Ravel's principal works include *Spanish Rhapsody* (1908) and *Bolero* (1928), for orchestra, and *Waltz Noble and Sentimental* (1911) and *The Tomb of Couperin* (1917), for piano.

Saint-Saëns, Charles-Camille (1835–1921). Pianist and composer. Saint-Saëns began performing at the age of 10 and later composed symphonic poems under the influence of Franz Liszt; operas, including *Samson and Delilah* (1877); and concertos.

German

Bach, Johann Sebastian (1695–1750). Baroque organist and composer, and one of the greatest creators of Western music. In his early years as an organist, Bach wrote mostly keyboard music, such as *The Well-tempered Clavier* and his many fugues and suites. Later he composed instrumental works, including the *Brandenburg* concertos, and superb religious works, such as *The St. Matthew Passion*. He had 20 children, 10 of whom survived, including **Wilhelm Friedemann** (1710–84), organist and composer; **Johann Christoph Friedrich** (1732–94), composer; and **Johann Christian** (1735–82), composer of 11 operas, church music, symphonies, piano concertos, chamber music, and songs.

Beethoven, Ludwig van (1770–1827). Composer of instrumental works, particularly symphonies. Beethoven was a student of Mozart and Haydn, whose influence is seen throughout his early works. By 1824 he had lost his hearing, but he continued to compose. His works include *Fidelio*, an opera; a violin concerto and five piano concertos; the *Egmont* overture; 32 piano sonatas, including the *Apassionata*; 16 string quartets; the Mass in D (*Missa Solemnis*); and nine symphonies, the best known of which are the Third (*Eroica*), the Fifth (*Victory*), the Sixth (*Pastoral*) and the Ninth (*Choral*). The Ninth, completed in 1823, is considered the greatest of his works.

Brahms, Johannes (1833–97). Developer of a Romantic style. His principal works include the *Tragic Overture,* two piano concertos, and serenades, for orchestra; *Renaldo* and *Song of Destiny*, for chorus; chamber music; piano solos; and many songs.

Gluck, Christoph Willibald von (1714–87). Composer of more than 100 operas, among them *Orpheus and Euridice* (1762) and *Alcestis* (1767), which established a new style of Italian opera; 11 symphonies; instrumental trios; music for solo voice and keyboard; and a flute concerto.

Handel, George Frideric (1685–1759). Baroque composer most famous for the oratorio *Messiah* (1742). Trained in law and music in Germany, Handel produced his operas in Italy and London, incorporating German, Italian, and English styles. Among his works are many operas, including *Almira* (1705), *Flavio* (1723), and *Orlando* (1733); *Music for the Royal Fireworks* (1749) and the *Water Music* (1717); suites for harpsichord; chamber music; and many Italian cantatas.

Humperdinck, Engelbert (1854–1921). Composer of six operas, including the popular *Hansel and Gretel* (1893); vocal works; and songs.

Mendelssohn, Felix (1809–47). Composer of orchestral works, including five symphonies and the overture *A Midsummer Night's Dream* (1826); choral works, including the oratorios *St. Paul* (1836) and *Elijah* (1846); operas, including *Son and Stranger* (1829); piano works; and songs.

Schumann, Clara Josephine née Wieck (1819–96). Pianist and composer of piano works and songs. She often played the works of other composers, particularly those of her husband, Robert Schumann.

Schumann, Robert (1810–56). Composer of piano music and of orchestral works. His piano compositions include *Scenes from Childhood, Album for the Young,* and Piano Concerto in A Minor (1845). The *Rhemish Symphony* (1850) combined the Classical and Romantic styles.

Strauss, Richard (1864–1949). Composer of many operas, including the famous *The Rose Bearer* (1909); two ballets; tone poems for orchestra; concertos; chamber music; songs; and piano works.

Wagner, Richard (1813–83). Composer of many operas, the most famous of which is *The Ring of the Nibelung,* a cycle of four operas—*The Rheingold, The Valkyrie, Siegfried, The Twilight of the Gods.* These are based on German mythology, a favorite topic of Wagner. Wagner did most of his later work under the sponsorship of Ludwig II, the young king of Bavaria. He also helped the composer build a theater in the town of Bayreuth. The Bayreuth Wagner Festival, still sponsored in part by Wagner's descendants, continues today as a major music gala.

Italian

Bellini, Vincenzo (1801–35). Composer of operas, including *The Foreign Woman* (1829), *The Sleepwalker* (1831), *Norma* (1831), and *The Puritans* (1835).

Boccherini, Luigi (1743–1805). Cellist and composer. His principal compositions are for chamber music. Boccherini also wrote symphonies, concertos, and vocal music.

Corelli, Arcangelo (1653–1713). Violinist and composer. His music, written mainly for the violin, established a style that was frequently copied.

Donizetti, Gaetano (1797–1848). Composer of operas. His best-known works included *Lucrezia Borgia* (1833), *The*

Favorite (1840), and the comic operas *The Elixir of Love* (1832) and *Don Pasquale* (1843).

Leoncavallo, Ruggiero (1857–1919). Composer of operas. His most successful was *Pagliacci* (1892). He wrote his own librettos, a ballet, and a symphonic poem.

Mascagni, Pietro (1863–1945). Opera composer and conductor. His most famous work is *Rustic Chivalry* (1890).

Monteverdi, Claudio (1567–1643). Ordained priest and composer of church music, including Masses, vespers, madrigals, magnificats, and motets. He also wrote secular vocal music, at least 12 operas, and ballets.

Palestrina, Giovanni Pierluigi da (Johannes Praenestinus) (c. 1525–94). Organist, choirmaster, and composer of church music, including Masses and motets.

Puccini, Giacomo (1858–1924). Composer of many operas. Best known are *La Bohème* (1896), *Tosca* (1899), and *Madame Butterfly* (1904). *Turandot* was completed after his death by Franco Alfano.

Respighi, Ottorino (1879–1936). Composer of operas, tone poems, and other orchestral works, chamber music, concertos, and songs. Among his most popular works are *The Fountains of Rome* (1917) and *The Pines of Rome* (1924), both symphonic poems.

Rossini, Gioacchino (1792–1868). Composer of operas. The best known are *William Tell* and *The Barber of Seville*. Rossini also wrote cantatas, songs, piano pieces, and woodwind quintets.

Scarlatti, Alessandro (1660–1725). Conductor and the most prolific composer of Italian operas of his time. In addition to 115 operas, he wrote 20 oratorios, some 600 cantatas, 10 Masses, a Passion, motets, and other church music, chamber pieces, concertos, and works for harpsichord.

Scarlatti, (Giuseppe) Domenico (1685–1757). Greatest Italian composer for harpsichord of his time. He wrote 550 pieces, now called sonatas, as well as concertos, operas, cantatas, Masses, a *Stabat Mater*, and two *Salve Reginas*.

Verdi, Giuseppe (1813–1901). Foremost composer of operas. They include *Rigoletto* (1851), *The Wayward Woman* (1853), *Othello* (1887), and *Falstaff* (1893). Verdi also composed church music, including the *Requiem* (1874), *Ave Maria* (1889), *Stabat Mater* (1898), and *Te Deum* (1898).

Vivaldi, Antonio (1678–1741). Violinist, composer, and ordained priest. Master of the Italian Baroque, Vivaldi is best known for his instrumental music and the concertos *The Four Seasons*. He also wrote church music, an oratorio, and operas.

Russian

Moussorgsky, Modest (1839–81). Composer of operas and orchestral works. Moussorgsky is best known for his outstanding operas *Boris Gudunov* (1868) and *Khovanshchina* (1886), as well as for *Pictures at an Exhibition* (1874) for piano and *Night on Bald Mountain* (1860–66) for orchestra.

Prokofiev, Sergei (1891–1953). Composer, pianist, and conductor. His principal compositions are the operas *Love for Three Oranges* (1921) and *War and Peace* (1942); *Peter and the Wolf* (1936), for orchestra and narrator; and seven symphonies, piano concertos, ballets, and piano sonatas.

Rachmaninoff, Sergei (1873–1943). Composer, pianist, and conductor. Rachmaninoff emigrated to the United States at age 17. His compositions include three operas; orchestral works, including the tone poem *Isle of the Dead* (1907); four concertos; choral works; chamber music; and songs.

Rimsky-Korsakov, Nicolai (1844–1908). Composer of operas and orchestral works. His greatest works are the operas

Mlada (1890), *Christmas Eve* (1895), *Sadko* (1896), and *The Golden Cockerel* (1907). His orchestration influenced the work of Igor Stravinsky and others.

Shostakovich, Dmitri (1906–75). Composer of chamber and symphonic works. Shostakovich's works include 11 symphonies, among them *May the First* (1930) and the outstanding *Ninth Symphony* (1940); operas; the ballet *The Golden Age* (1930); piano works; sonatas; and string quartets.

Stravinsky, Igor (1882–1971). Composer of the strikingly modern ballet *Rite of Spring*. Later works, such as *The Soldier's Tale*, for narrator and instruments, and the ballet suite *Apollon Musagete*, are more solemn. Stravinsky settled in the United States in 1941, where he experimented with 12-tone composition, as in the *Cantata* (1952).

Tchaikovsky, Peter Ilyich (1840–93). One of the most important Russian composers, Tchaikovsky is best known for his ballet music, including *The Nutcracker* (1892), *Swan Lake* (1876), *The Sleeping Beauty* (1889), and his operas *Eugene Onegin* (1878) and *Queen of Spades* (1890). He also wrote symphonies, including the popular Fifth Symphony (1888), chamber music, and choral works, and published books on harmony, autobiographical essays, and translations.

Other

Bartók, Béla (1881–1945). Hungarian pianist and composer who studied and collected Hungarian folk music. His principal works include orchestral pieces; the opera *Duke Bluebeard's Castle;* the ballet *The Wooden Prince;* the pantomime *The Miraculous Mandarin;* chamber music; piano works, including the *Mikrokosmos;* and arrangements of folk songs. He emigrated to the United States in 1940.

Chopin, Fréderic François (1810–49). Polish composer and pianist. Called "the poet of the piano," he composed hundreds of pieces for that instrument, most notably two piano concertos.

Dvořák, Antonín (1841–1904). Czech composer of works in a nationalist spirit, including the *Symphonic Variations, Slavonic Rhapsodies,* and the opera *The Peasant Rogue* (1877). His best-known work, the symphony *From the New World* (1893), combines Czech and American music.

Grieg, Edvard (1843–1907). Norwegian composer, conductor, and pianist. Principal works include the overture *I Host* (1866), two suites from *Peer Gynt* (1888, 1891), *At a Southern Convent Gate* (1871) for chorus, and *Lyric Pieces* for piano.

Liszt, Franz (1811–86). Hungarian com-

Choose Your Weapon: Kinds of Instruments

Instruments are grouped into four main classes:

Stringed
Wind
Percussion
Keyboard

Musical Instruments

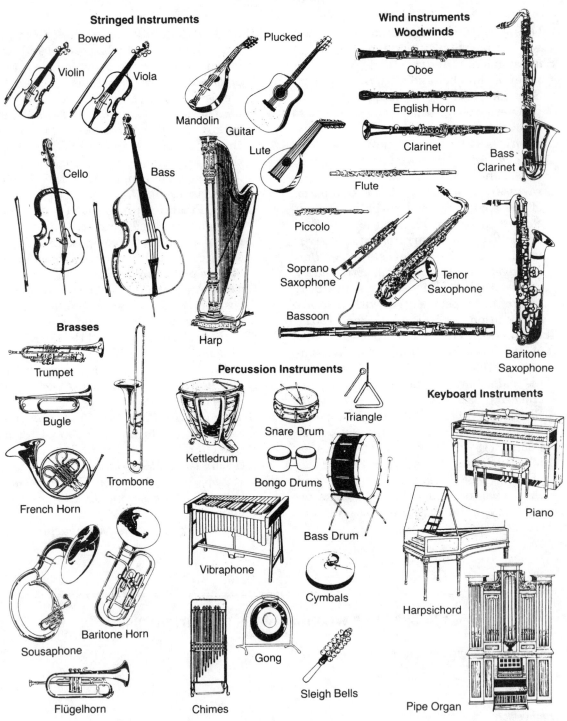

Stringed Instruments

Bowed

Violin

Viola

Cello

Bass

Plucked

Mandolin

Guitar

Lute

Harp

Wind instruments
Woodwinds

Oboe

English Horn

Clarinet

Bass Clarinet

Flute

Piccolo

Soprano Saxophone

Tenor Saxophone

Bassoon

Baritone Saxophone

Brasses

Trumpet

Bugle

French Horn

Trombone

Sousaphone

Baritone Horn

Flügelhorn

Percussion Instruments

Kettledrum

Snare Drum

Triangle

Bongo Drums

Bass Drum

Vibraphone

Cymbals

Chimes

Gong

Sleigh Bells

Keyboard Instruments

Piano

Harpsichord

Pipe Organ

The Makeup of a Symphony Orchestra

Not all these players are needed every time an orchestra plays. The number of players depends upon the piece of music being played, but these are the maximum number of players who would make up a typical orchestra.

Strings
32 violins, divided equally into firsts and seconds—the instruments are the same, but firsts and seconds play different music
12 violas
12 cellos
10 string basses (double bass, bass viol)
2 harps (often listed separately from other strings)

Woodwinds
3 flutes
1 piccolo
3 oboes
1 English horn
3 clarinets
1 bass clarinet
3 bassoons
1 contrabassoon

Brass
3 trumpets
4 French horns
3 trombones
1 tuba

Percussion
tympani
bass drum
cymbals
triangle
snare drums
glockenspiel (bells)
xylophone
piano (considered a percussion instrument in modern score with exception of piano concertos)
celesta (small keyboard instrument that sounds like soft bells)

Note: One percussionist plays tympani, one pianist plays piano and celesta, and two or three other percussionists divide the remaining instruments, often playing them interchangeably.

poser who spent time in Paris and Rome. He was an unsurpassed virtuoso pianist and a composer of symphonies, including *Faust* (1853); symphonic poems; piano concertos, études, and 19 *Hungarian Rhapsodies*; choral pieces; fantasia and fugues for organ; and songs.

Sibelius, Jean (1865–1957). Finnish composer. Sibelius attempted to create a national music, as in *A Tale* (1893) and *The Return of Lemminkäinen* (1895), based on the Finnish epic the *Kalevala*. Notable works include *Valse Trsite* (1903) and *Finlandia* (1899).

POPULAR MUSIC

Unlike classical music, popular music cannot be easily divided into historical periods. Some of its styles are old and others are newer, but it is a completely contemporary form of music that is constantly rewriting itself. All the types described below continue to coexist today.

Country

Folk music of rural, southern American whites. Simple harmony and tunes. Its recording center is Nashville, Tennessee, and the music is performed live at the Grand Ole Opry, also in Nashville. This form changes little over time. The guitar is the predominant instrument, along with vocalists.

Folk

The traditional music of rural people around the world. May be instrumental or vocal, or a combination of the two. Instruments vary widely, depending on the location. With its simple harmony and tunes, folk music is handed down orally from generation to generation. Like country music, folk changes little over time.

Jazz

This complex music, which began in black, southern American communities in the late 1800s, merges Western and African music. Its harmonies and tunes have always been complex, and it has over the years become one of the most sophisticated forms of Western popular music. Unlike country and folk, jazz has changed and continues to change today as new forms are introduced.

Rock

This music is a spinoff of blues (another black American musical form) and folk and jazz. Rock began in the late 1950s, when it was called rock and roll, and has continued to change forms with amazing frequency, probably because it is the music of youth. Rock has a strong beat and a simple melody, with repeated harmony. Electric guitar is the predominant instrument, along with vocalists, bass, drums, and sometimes piano and woodwinds.

Theater Music

This song-and-dance music makes up a small but influential portion of Western music. It is written for the theater, and its centers are New York and London. Musical theater reached its height in popularity in the 1940s. In the 1960s rock briefly merged with musical theater to produce such rock musicals as *Hair, Godspell,* and *Jesus Christ Superstar.*

LISTENING TO DIFFERENT DRUMMERS: MUSIC AROUND THE WORLD

For many years Western music has been adopted around the world, but that does not mean that other cultures do not have their own, often unique forms of music. Thanks to a new mood of international cooperation, Westerners are becoming more familiar with other people's music.

African Music

The music of people who live south of the Sahara is already familiar to Westerners,

Rockin' Along: A Minihistory of Rock Styles

1950s
Rock and roll begins and is popularized by such performers as Elvis Presley, Chubby Checker, Chuck Berry, and Buddy Holly.

1960s
Rock enters mainstream popular music, thanks to the stunning success of such musicians as the Beatles, the Fifth Dimension, the Supremes, and Simon and Garfunkel.

1970s and 1980s
Rock becomes less mainstream, and there are many diverse styles as it seeks to recapture its offbeat creativity:

heavy metal These groups consist primarily of loud guitar duels, played by such groups as Led Zeppelin, AC-DC, and Kiss.

fusion jazz Rock and jazz merge under the guidance of such musicians as James Taylor and Paul Simon.

disco A rare form of rock in that it is rarely performed live. It is recorded in studios. This was the dance music craze of the 1970s. No major groups leave a lasting imprint.

punk rock This form emerged in the mid-70s as a rebellious kind of music that sought to reenergize rock. Although no groups made their mark in a lasting way, punk rock left a legacy of simpler, faster music that many later artists incorporated.

new wave A direct descendent of punk, this more mainstream rock form produced such major artists as Devo and Blondie.

rap The latest wave in rock music, rap began in black discos in the mid-1970s, although the first rap records were not cut until 1979, and rap did not cross over to mainstream musical culture until the late 1980s. The voice is the primary instrument, and it chants in rhythm and rhyme over the music. Rap is a dance music with its own routines, such as double Dutch rhythms and hiphop. Major rappers include Grandmaster Flash and the Furious Five, Dave D with Kurtis Blow, Funky Four Plus One, and Brother D. Rap has political overtones, as exemplified in such songs as Brother D's "How We Gonna Make the Black Nation Rise?" and Grandmaster Flash and the Furious Five's "The Message."

since African music has long been present in such Western forms as jazz, gospel, and rock. Drums are the most important instrument, backed up by flutes, xylophones, and stringed instruments that are plucked rather than bowed. Bells and clapping hands are other popular instruments, along with vocalists. The rhythms are complex and some include harmony. African music is often used in religious worship and practice.

Asian Music

Best known to most Westerners through the music of China and Japan, Asian music sounds different to the Western ear because the scales, instruments, and compositions are unlike those of Western music.

In Chinese music, the principal instruments are the *jin* and the *pipa*, both plucked strings. Chinese music also uses bowed strings, flutes, percussion, and bells.

Japanese music employs bamboo flutes, gongs, drums, and the *samisen* and *koto,* two plucked instruments. The music has no harmony, but there is free rhythm and microtones, which are smaller spaces between notes than those found in Western music.

Asian music is used in religious worship, but it is primarily music for theater and performance.

Indian Music

The music of India has enjoyed popularity in the United States for many years. Its primary instruments are the voice, strings, drums, and a uniquely Indian lutelike instrument called a *tambura.* Indian scales are arranged in *ragas,* which may be associated with seasons, hours, moods, or emotions. Indian music began in the courts of the maharajahs, or rulers, and is largely a performance art.

Arabian Music

This is the music of the Middle East and northern Africa. Flutes and drums, along with two special stringed instruments, the *oud* and the *ganun,* predominate. Instrumental music is banned in Muslim worship, but vocal music in the form of chants and calls to prayer are part of the religious ritual.

Native American Music

The music of the Native peoples of North and South America is used primarily for religious rituals. Combined with dancing, it employs drums, rattles, and the voice as the primary instruments. Some Native American music employs a five-note scale that gives it its distinctive sound.

MUSIC FROM A TO Z

a cappella Vocal music without accompaniment (literally, "in the church style").

accent The stress given to one tone over another.

accompaniment Secondary instrument(s) or background vocal added to the principal instrument or soloist.

acoustics The science of sound, which deals with intensity, quality, resonance, pitch, tone, etc.

adagietto A direction to play slightly faster than adagio.

adagio A direction to play slowly.

adagissimo A direction to play very slowly.

ad libitum A direction to interpret, improvise, or omit, according to the player's preference.

agitato A direction to play in an "agitated," restless, hurried manner.

air A tune or melody. The French eighteenth-century term for song; also, an

---

Weighing In: Musical Scales Around the World

Musical scales—the series of ascending or descending musical notes marked with defined intervals (or spaces) between the notes—are not the same everywhere in the world. And that fact is largely what makes Asian music sound different from African or Western music.

- The Western scale has 12 notes.
- The Arabian scale has 17 notes.
- The Indian scale has 22 steps.
- The scale used by many Native Americans has 5 notes.

Some Types of Western Scales

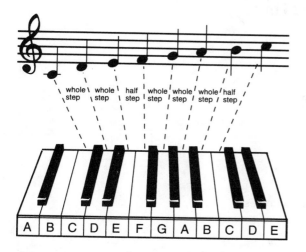

The C major scale has a half step between its third and fourth notes and between its seventh and eighth notes. You hear it when you play the white keys from C to C on the piano.

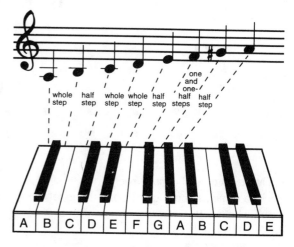

The harmonic minor scale has one and one half steps between its sixth and seventh notes. This wide leap provides a bridge to the *tonic*, or main note, at the octave.

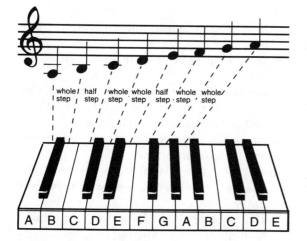

The natural minor scale follows a pattern of one whole step, one half step, two whole steps, one half step, and two whole steps. This scale is often used in folk music.

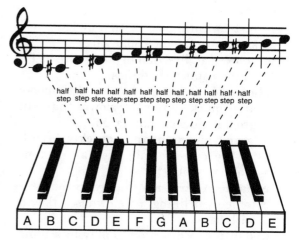

The chromatic scale consists entirely of half steps and has 12 notes to an octave. You hear this scale when you play all the white and black keys from C to C on the piano.

Highs and Lows:

Musical Notes

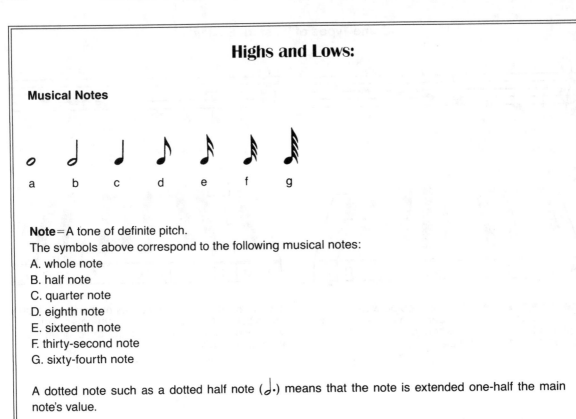

Note=A tone of definite pitch.
The symbols above correspond to the following musical notes:
A. whole note
B. half note
C. quarter note
D. eighth note
E. sixteenth note
F. thirty-second note
G. sixty-fourth note

A dotted note such as a dotted half note ($\downarrow$•) means that the note is extended one-half the main note's value.

---

instrumental piece with a melodic style similar to that of a solo song.

alla breve A direction to play twice as fast as the notation signifies.

allegretto A direction to play with moderately quick movement, slower than allegro but quicker than largo.

allegro A direction to play quickly, briskly.

alto The lowest female voice; also, a tenor violin or viola.

andante A direction to play in moderate tempo, inclining to slowness, flowing with ease.

andantino A direction to play in a tempo slightly quicker than andante.

animato A direction to play with animation.

anthem A choral piece for use in church services; also a song of praise or joy.

arabesque A lyrical, or dramatically expressive, piece in a fanciful style; a term first used by Schumann and later by Debussy.

aria A long vocal solo in an opera or oratorio.

arpeggio The technique of playing the notes of a chord one after the other, rather than at the same time.

aubade Morning music, in contrast to *serenade,* or evening music.

auxiliary note Usually, a grace note one degree above or below a principal note.

ballad A song that tells a story, originally accompanied by dancing; also, an instrumental piece in ballad style.

bar A line drawn vertically across the staff to divide it into measures.

baritone A high bass voice; also, any musical instrument between bass and tenor.

bass The lowest male voice, or lowest part

in a musical composition; also, short for the double bass or bass tuba.

beat A unit of measurement indicated by the conductor's gesture.

bolero A Spanish dance accompanied by castanets.

buffa In the comic style.

buffo The male singer of a comic part.

cadenza An ornamental passage near the end of a composition or movement.

canon A contrapuntal composition in which one part is echoed by one or more other parts, so that the statements overlap.

cantata A piece that is sung, in contrast to a *sonata,* which is played. The term now refers to choral works accompanied by orchestra, similar to the oratorio but shorter.

canto The part of a choral work that carries the melody.

capo The beginning.

capriccio A short composition in free form.

catch A round for three or more voices.

chamber music Music suitable for a small hall; instrumental music in the sonata form.

chant A sacred song, the oldest form of choral music.

chorale. A psalm or hymn tune sung in church; also, a harmonization of a chorale melody.

chord The combination of three or more tones played at once.

clef A symbol that indicates the pitch of a particular line on a stave.

coda A passage at the end of a piece or movement that brings it to a conclusion.

common time Four-four ($^4/_4$) time—that is, four quarter notes to a measure.

concertmaster The leader of the first violins, next in rank to the conductor.

concerto A composition for solo instrument, usually with orchestral accompaniment.

concerto grosso A composition for orchestra with passages for a group of solo instruments.

console The part of the organ from which the player controls the instrument—the keyboard, pedals, etc., as distinguished from the pipes.

continuo The bass, or lowest, line of a composition.

contralto The range of a low female voice; alto.

contrapuntal In counterpoint.

counterpoint The combination of two or more individual but related parts.

crescendo A direction to increase the volume.

da capo A direction to repeat from the beginning.

decrescendo A direction to decrease the volume.

diminuendo Diminishing; getting softer.

discord, dissonance A combination of tones that are unharmonious, jarring.

divertimento Originally, a suite of movements for chamber ensemble, designed for entertainment; a short symphony.

divertissement A fantasia on well-known tunes.

do The first note of the scale.

dot Written after a note, an indication to prolong its length by $^1/_2$; the double dot means to prolong it by $^3/_4$. Above or below the note, the dot indicates staccato.

duet A composition for two players or two voices, with or without accompaniment.

eighth A note with the value of $^1/_8$ whole note.

étude A study; a practice exercise for a solo instrument.

expression marks Marks used to aid in the interpretation of a work; they indicate *forte, allegro,* etc.

fa The fourth note of the scale.

falsetto The false voice; used to sing notes above the normal range.

fantasia A piece in which the composition follows the imagination rather than any traditional form.

finale The last movement of a work of several movements; for example, the conclusion of a concerto or the last act of an opera.

flat The sign ♭ , indicating the pitch is to be lowered by half step.

form The pattern of a work; its basic elements are repetition, variation, and contrast in the areas of harmony, rhythm, and tone.

forte A direction to play loudly.

forte piano A direction to play loudly, then softly.

fortissimo A direction to play very loudly.

fundamental The lowest tone of a chord when the chord is founded on that tone.

glee A simple part-song, generally for three of more male voices.

glissando Sliding the finger rapidly up or down the musical scale across keys or strings.

grace note An ornamental note not essential to the melody and not counted as part of the measure.

grave A direction to play slowly, solemnly.

Gregorian chant A style of church music for unaccompanied voices, without definite rhythm.

half note A note held half as long as a whole note and twice as long as a quarter note.

harmony The structure and relationships of chords.

impresario The conductor or manager of an opera or concert company.

impromptu A piece of music without a fixed form.

incidental music Music for performance during the action of a play.

interlude A short piece played between the acts of a drama; the verses of a song, parts of a church service, or sections of a cantata.

intermezzo A play with music, performed between the acts of an opera or drama; a short movement in a symphony.

interval The distance in pitch between two notes.

key A series of notes forming a major or minor scale; also, a lever on a keyboard instrument.

key signature Sharps or flats placed at the beginning of a composition to indicate its key.

la The sixth note of the scale.

largo A direction to play more slowly than adagio but not as slowly as grave.

legato A direction to play smoothly and continuously.

lento A direction to play slowly, but not as slowly as largo.

libretto The words of an opera or oratorio.

madrigal An unaccompanied song for three or more voices using counterpoint and imitation.

major scale A scale in which the half steps occur between the third and fourth and the seventh and eighth tones.

march A composition with a strong beat for a procession or parade.

measure A unit of rhythm, indicated by bars on the staff.

melody A succession of single tones, in contrast to *harmony,* which refers to chords.

meter A scheme of accents; a grouping of beats into units of measure.

mezzo Medium, half; moderate.

mezzo forte A direction to play moderately loudly.

mezzo soprano The female voice between soprano and alto.

mi The third note of the scale.

middle C The C note that is nearest the middle of the piano keyboard.

minor Intervals, scales, keys, and chords having intervals a semitone less than major.

minor scale A scale with half steps between tones two and three and between five and six.

minuet A slow, graceful dance of French origin in triple time; a composition in this rhythm.

movement A distinct division of a composition with its own key, themes, rhythm, and character.

natural The sign ♮ , indicates that a previous sharp or flat is not to be used, or cancelled.

nocturne A serenade, or evening music; a melody over an accompaniment of chords.

note A tone of definite pitch.

obbligato Indispensable; the opposite of *ad libitum.*

octave The interval between a note, or tone, and the eighth above it; all the tones within the interval.

octet A composition for eight parts or voices; also, the group of its performers.

opera A drama set to music performed with scenery and costumes; among its elements are arias, recitatives, duets, and choruses.

operetta A light, amusing opera that includes spoken dialogue.

opus A musical work or composition.

oratorio A long, dramatic musical composition for an orchestra and singers, based on a scriptural text set and performed without costumes, scenery, or action.

orchestra A group of musicians playing various instruments.

overture An introduction to a large composition, such as an opera or oratorio; however, it can be independent or precede a symphonic poem.

part A series of notes for voice, instrument, or group, to be performed with other parts or in solo.

part-song A contrapuntal composition for three or more voices, unaccompanied.

pastorale A musical composition suggestive of rural life.

pianissimo A direction to play very softly.

piano quartet A term usually applied to quartets for piano, violin, viola, and cello.

piano quintet A combination of piano with string quartet.

polka A lively dance in $^2/_4$ time that originated in Bohemia c. 1830.

polonaise A Polish dance in a stately rhythm adopted as a musical form by Chopin.

prelude An introductory movement; a short piano piece in one movement.

program music Music intended to depict, or "tell," a story.

quartet A composition for four parts or voices; the performers of a four-part composition.

quintet A composition for five voices or instruments; also, the performers of a five-part composition.

re The second note of the scale.

recitative A style of singing resembling speech.

refrain Repeated lines that occur at the end of each stanza of a poem or song.

requiem A Mass for the dead; also, a musical setting for such a Mass.

rest A symbol indicating pause or silence.

rhapsody A title given to compositions of a heroic or dramatic character, sometimes based on folk song.

romance A freestyle vocal or instrumental composition of romantic character.

rondo A form of instrumental composition with a leading theme that is repeated.

root The fundamental tone of a chord.

round A canon for three or more voices.

scale A series of tones arranged according to rising pitches.

scherzo A playful, humorous instrumental composition.

semitone Half a whole step.

septet A composition for seven voices or instruments.

serenade A spur-of-moment vocal or instrumental performance, often outdoors and in the evening.

sharp The sign ♯ , indicates the pitch is to be raised by a half-step.

signature Directions placed on the staff at the beginning of a piece that show the key and the rhythm.

slur A curved line over or under a series of notes indicating a smooth flow between them.

sol The fifth note of the scale.

solo Performed alone.

sonata An instrumental composition of three or four movements in related keys and in different forms and character.

sonatina A short, simple sonata.

soprano The highest female or boy's voice.

staccato An instruction to play notes distinctly without holding on to them; the opposite of *legato*.

staff The five horizontal lines on and between which notes are written.

suite An instrumental composition consisting of a series of movements or distinct pieces.

symphonic poem A large orchestral work that "tells" a story in one movement.

symphony A sonata for orchestra, usually in four movements.

syncopation A shift in rhythm or from a strong to a weak beat.

tempo The speed at which a piece is played, indicated by terms such as *adagio*.

tenor A high male voice; also, an instrument with a high range.

theme A musical subject.

ti The seventh note of the scale.

tone A sound of definite duration and pitch; a note.

transpose To change the key of a composition.

treble The highest voice in a choir or part; soprano; G clef.

tremolo Rapid repetition of a note to resemble trembling.

trio A composition for three parts or voices; the second part of a minuet or march.

triple time Time in which there are three beats to a measure.

twelve-tone music A method of composition based on a scale of 12, rather than 8, tones, developed by Arnold Schoenberg.

variation Development of a theme through a variety of forms; differences in rhythm, key, harmony, etc.

volume Fullness of a tone; loudness.

waltz A round dance in triple rhythm performed by couples; also, music in this rhythm.

whole note The longest note in common use.

KINDS OF DANCE

Dance is the rhythmic movement of the body, usually in time to music. Dance can be divided into two major categories:

Theatrical Dancing performed to entertain an audience. Ballet, modern dance, tap dancing, and musical comedy dances are examples of dance entertainments.

Social Dancing performed for the participant's own pleasure. There are many social dances, each with its own steps and rhythms.

MAJOR DANCERS, CHOREOGRAPHERS, AND PRODUCERS OF THE NINETEENTH AND TWENTIETH CENTURIES

Ailey, Alvin (1931–89). American choreographer. Ailey formed the American Dance Theater and is noted for dramatic works and use of African elements, as in *Creation of the World* (1954) and *Revelations* (1960).

Alonso, Alicia (1921–   ). Cuban dancer and choreographer. Alonso soloed with companies including the American Ballet Theater (1939) and danced on Broadway. She has formed her own company, now the National Ballet of Cuba.

Ashton, Sir Frederick (1906–88). British choreographer and director of Sadler's Wells (now Royal) Ballet (1935–70). His works include *Cinderella, Ondine,* and *A Month in the Country*.

Astaire, Fred (1899–1987). American actor and dancer in numerous musical comedies, such as *Over the Top* and *The Bandwagon,* and films, including *Top Hat* (1935) and *Shall We Dance?* (1937). Astaire costarred with Judy Garland, Rita Hayworth, and Ginger Rogers and was noted for his original and graceful tap dancing.

Balanchine, George (1904–83). American choreographer and dancer (b. Russia).

Balanchine danced with Sergei Diaghilev's Ballets Russes (1924–28); was ballet master, Royal Opera, Copenhagen; organized the Ballets Russes de Monte Carlo (1934); directed the Metropolitan Opera Ballet (1934–37); and served as principal artistic director and choreographer of the New York City Ballet (1948–82). His major works include *Serenade* and *Agon*.

Baryshnikov, Mikhail (1948–   ). Soviet choreographer and dancer who emigrated to the West. Baryshnikov was a soloist with the Kirov Ballet (1969–74), a member of the American Ballet Theater (1974–78), and later its director (1980–*). A leading male dancer of the early 1980s, he appeared in the film *The Turning Point* (1977).

Béjart, Maurice (1928–   ). French director of the Ballets de l'Étoile, Paris (1954–   ). Béjart organized the influential Ballet of the 20th Century, Brussels. His works incorporate nontraditional elements, such as jazz, avant-garde music, and acrobatics.

Cunningham, Merce (1922–   ). American dancer and choreographer. A soloist with the Martha Graham Company, Cunningham formed his own company and experimented in multimedia works, with music by John Cage and others. His works include *Symphony by Chance* and *Square Game*.

d'Amboise, Jacques (1934–   ). American soloist with the New York City Ballet and choreographer. D'Amboise is known for his roles in American-theme works, such as *Western Symphony*. His own works include the ballets *The Chase* and *Irish Fantasy*. He now teaches dance to children and teenagers.

De Mille, Agnes (c. 1908–   ). American choreographer and dancer. De Mille created the first American ballet, *Rodeo* (1942), and *Fall River Legend* (1948), and brought ballet techniques to musicals such as *Oklahoma!* (1943).

Diaghilev, Sergei Pavlovich (1872–1929). Russian impresario and founder of the Ballets Russes, Paris (1909), whose productions revolutionized ballet.

Duncan, Isadora (1878–1927). American dancer who greatly influenced modern dance. Her works, based on Greek classical art, used free-flowing movements and barefoot dancers. Duncan founded schools in Berlin (1904), Paris (1914), and Moscow (1921).

Fokine, Michel (1880–1942). Russian-American choreographer for Nijinsky and Diaghilev. Fokine is considered the founder of modern ballet. His works include *Firebird* and *Petrouchka*.

Fonteyn, Dame Margot (1919–1991). English star of the Royal Ballet. Her major roles were in *Sleeping Beauty, Firebird,* and *Petrouchka*. Fonteyn was the partner of Rudolf Nureyev after 1962.

Graham, Martha (1895–1991). American dancer and choreographer. Graham formed her own company in 1929. Her works include *Appalachian Spring* and *Archaic Hours*. Her dances use the entire body to reveal the inner feelings of the characters she portrays.

Ivanov, Lev (1834–1905). Russian choreographer of the *Nutcracker* (1892) and leading figure of Russian Romanticism.

Joffrey, Robert (1930–88). American choreographer. Joffrey formed his own company, the City Center Joffrey Ballet, in 1954. He choreographed works for the New York City Opera, including Douglas Moore's *The Devil and Daniel Webster* and Marc Blitzstein's *Regina*.

Jooss, Kurt (1901–79). German artist noted for his antiwar *Green Table*. Jooss worked in England with the Ballet Jooss during the Hitler era. He is noted for introducing psychological themes into ballet.

Karsavina, Tamara (1885–1978). Russian member of Diaghilev's Ballets Russes. Karsavina created principal roles in *Firebird* and *Petrouchka* with her partner Nijinsky. She incorporated the theories of Fokine.

Kirstein, Lincoln (1907–   ). American cofounder, with Balanchine, of the School of American Ballet (1934). Kirstein was the director of the New York City Ballet (1948–   ) and a promoter of an authentic American style.

Makarova, Natalia (1940–   ). Russian member of the Kirov Ballet (1959–70) and the American Ballet Theater (1970–72). Makarova was noted for outstanding dramatic technique.

Massine, Léonide (1896–1979). Russian-American principal dancer and choreographer of Diaghilev's company (1914–20) and the Ballets Russes de Monte Carlo (1932–42). His choreographed works include *Parade* and the film *The Red Shoes* (1948).

Mitchell, Arthur (1934–   ). American soloist with the New York City Ballet and founder of the Dance Theater of Harlem (1968), the first black classical dance company.

Nijinsky, Vaslav (1890–1950). Russian premier dancer with Diaghilev's Ballets Russes. Nijinsky created some of the greatest ballet roles, as in *Petrouchka* and *Afternoon of a Faun*. He is considered by many to be the greatest dancer of the twentieth century.

Nureyev, Rudolf (1938–93). Russian soloist with the Kirov Ballet (1958) and leading classical dancer of his generation. Nureyev, often partner to Dame Margot Fonteyn in the Royal Ballet, defected to the West in 1961.

Pavlova, Anna Matveyevna (1881–1931). Russian member of Diaghilev's Ballets Russes, Pavlova toured widely. Considered the greatest ballerina of her generation, she is noted for her role in *Dying Swan*.

Petipa, Marius (1822–1910). French creator of modern classical ballet. Petipa introduced European technique to the St. Petersburg Imperial Theater. His works include *La Bayadère* (1874) and *Sleeping Beauty* (1890).

Robbins, Jerome (1918–   ). American dancer and choreographer of musical comedies and ballets; member of the American Ballet Theater and the New York City Ballet (1969–   ). Robbins is noted for his roles in *Fancy Free* and for his choreography and direction of *West Side Story*. His works include *Dances at a Gathering*.

Taglioni, Maria (1804–84). Italian major ballerina of the Romantic period, noted for her exquisite style and outstanding performances, as in *La Sylphide*, Paris Opera (1832).

Tallchief, Maria (1925–   ). American prima ballerina with the Ballets Russes de Monte Carlo (1942–47) and the New York City Ballet. She promoted American ballet through television appearances and tours.

Taylor, Paul (1930–   ). American dancer with Merce Cunningham and Martha Graham. Taylor formed his own company of innovative modern dance in 1954.

Tharp, Twyla (1941–   ). American innovative dancer (1962–65) and choreographer. Tharp was the director of the Netherlands Dance Theater (1969) and the Stuttgart Ballet (1974–76). She later formed her own company.

Vestris, Gaetan (1729–1808). Italian dance master to Louis XVI; considered the greatest dancer of his time.

BALLET

Ballet was first performed in the Italian royal courts during the late 1400s. It spread to France after 1547. Following are some of the main developments of ballet, some of which overlapped in time, as changes occurred gradually.

1600s–1700s

- Louis XIV of France (1638–1715) founded the Royal Academy of Dancing, the first school to train professional dancers. They performed for the king and his court.
- French dancers began to perform in theaters.
- A form of dramatic ballet that told a story, called the *ballet d'action,* was developed. Most of these ballets were about Greek gods and goddesses.
- Women dancers shortened their skirts to midcalf and began performing in shoes without heels.

1800–1900

- Dramatic ballets told stories about common people and were set in foreign lands or dreamlike worlds.
- Women dancers danced on their toes and wore tutus, or fluffy calf- or knee-length skirts.
- In dance, women became idealized creatures. The main role of male dancers was to lift the leading women dancers, or ballerinas.
- In Russia, the French choreographer Marius Petipa introduced fairy tales as the subject of ballet.

1900–Present

- Sergei Diaghilev founded the famous Russian dance company Ballets Russes (1909–1929). Before the Ballets Russes, dances were choreographed for the purpose of showing off dancers' techniques. The Ballets Russes, however, used technical skills to express emotion and character. The company also emphasized the role of male dancers.
- During the mid-1900s many choreographers developed dances based on dramatic action.
- Most contemporary ballets have no story. Plotless ballets explore certain aspects of movement or express the music through the dance.
- Contemporary ballets combine styles and techniques from many sources, including jazz, modern dance, and rock.

THE POSITIONS OF THE FEET AND LEGS

Each ballet movement and pose starts and ends with the feet in one of these five positions. The arabesque is a ballet pose in which the dancer's leg is raised straight.

BALLET FROM A TO Z

attitude A pose in which the leg is bent and raised in front or behind the dancer.

ballerina A leading female dancer.

barre A wooden or metal rail attached to a wall that dancers use to support themselves during ballet exercises.

corps de ballet A group of dancers who perform together.

danseur A male dancer.

divertissement A series of dances to show technique. A divertissement has no relation to the plot, but often appears in a story ballet.

entrechat During this straight-up jump, the dancer swiftly crosses the legs before and behind each other.

jeté A jump from two feet to one foot in any direction.

labanotation A system for recording choreography in writing.

pas de deux A dance for two persons.

pirouette A complete turn on one foot.

plié A movement in which the knees are bent outward and the back is held straight.

sur les pointes On the toes.

tour en l'air A full turn in the air after the dancer springs straight up.

The Five Positions of the Feet

1st Position

2nd Position

3rd Position

4th Position

5th Position

1st Arabesque

Arabesque Allongée
(Arabesque
leaning forward)

turnout A position in which the legs are turned outward from the hip socket as far to the side as possible. The turnout is the basis of the five positions of the dancer's feet.

MODERN DANCE

The modern dance movement developed during the early 1900s. Its leaders rebelled against what they saw as the artificiality, rigidity, and superficiality of classical ballet. They sought more personal forms of movement and ways to express ideas through dance.

Since the 1940s, modern dance has shifted from emotional and personal expression. Today modern dancers explore movement in itself. For example, dancers may walk, perform cartwheels, or make patterns with their bodies. Ballet companies have also absorbed some techniques of modern dance, as modern dance choreographers increasingly work with them. Therefore, the distinction between modern dance and classical ballet has gradually blurred.

TYPES OF SOCIAL DANCING

Unlike classical dance, social dancing cannot be divided into historical periods. Sometimes the period when a social dance first appears is known. Other times it is not. Some social dances disappear permanently from fashion, such as the minuet, while others, such as the waltz, continue to exist today.

Folk A traditional form of social dancing performed by a particular nation or ethnic group. The square dance, the polka, and the Irish jig are examples of folk dancing. Usually, the dancers make a basic pattern, such as a circle or a line. Most folk dances developed over time in villages and were passed on from generation to generation. Consequently, the basic steps may remain the same, but variations appear over time.

Popular Dancing that people do for fun and relaxation, for example, at parties and discos. Unlike folk dances, popular dances have been taught by professionals in every generation since the 1400s. Popular dances include the latest youth craze dances as well as older dances that have survived, such as the tango, fox-trot, and cha-cha.

SOCIAL DANCING FROM A TO Z

ballroom dances Social dances usually performed by couples, including the fox-trot, waltz, tango, rumba, and cha-cha.

cha-cha A fast, rhythmic ballroom dance of Latin-American origin with a basic three-step pattern and a shuffle.

conga A ballroom dance of Afro-Cuban origin, in which dancers step to the first three beats and kick to the fourth.

country dance A traditional English dance in which dancers form two facing lines.

flamenco A Sevillian gypsy dance; also, all nonformal Spanish dances.

fox-trot A ballroom dance of American origin, named after the trotting gait of a horse.

gallop A quick dance popular in the nineteenth century, named after the galloping gait of a horse.

jitterbug A dance to syncopated music, especially popular in the 1940s. (Syncopation is a shift in rhythm from a strong to a weak beat.)

mazurka A Polish national dance.

minuet A slow, graceful dance of French origin.

polka A Bohemian folk dance around 1839, popular throughout central and Eastern Europe.

reel A popular dance in Scotland for two couples. The Virginia reel is a variant for a large group of dancers.

rumba A ballroom dance of Cuban origin with strong hip movements.

square dance An American folk dance in

Disappearing Dances

You may think the dances you do with your friends will be popular forever, but in fact, most social dances are passing fads. Dance crazes are created by the young, and each generation seems to need to create its own. These dances were all once the hottest dances around.

cakewalk (around 1900)
tango (early 1900s)
Charleston (1920s)
black bottom (1920s)
big apple (1940s)
jitterbug (1940s)
stroll (late 1950s)
twist (early 1960s)
pony (early 1960s)

---

which an even number of dancers participate, arranged in the form of a square.

two-step A ballroom dance; the forerunner of the fox trot.

waltz An elegant ballroom dance performed by couples.

DANCING TO DIFFERENT DRUMMERS: DANCE AROUND THE WORLD

Western dance has been imported to non-Western nations. But these cultures have their own, unique forms of dance.

African Dance

Accompanies all major life events. Dancers may don masks and paint their bodies. African dance may consist of six rhythms at the same time, with each part of a dancer's body following the rhythm of a different instrument. African dance emphasizes the uninterrupted natural flow of movement.

Asian Dance

In most of Asia, traditional forms of theater combine dance with drama and opera. Performers often wear masks, heavy makeup,

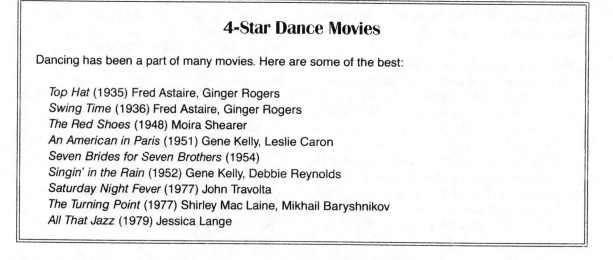

4-Star Dance Movies

Dancing has been a part of many movies. Here are some of the best:

Top Hat (1935) Fred Astaire, Ginger Rogers
Swing Time (1936) Fred Astaire, Ginger Rogers
The Red Shoes (1948) Moira Shearer
An American in Paris (1951) Gene Kelly, Leslie Caron
Seven Brides for Seven Brothers (1954)
Singin' in the Rain (1952) Gene Kelly, Debbie Reynolds
Saturday Night Fever (1977) John Travolta
The Turning Point (1977) Shirley Mac Laine, Mikhail Baryshnikov
All That Jazz (1979) Jessica Lange

and richly ornamented costumes. In Asian dance even the slightest movement conveys meaning. Dance themes usually concern magic and religion, and may recount a historical event, a myth, or legend.

Indian Dance

Indian dancers use *mudras,* or hand gestures, whose meaning is universally recognized by their audience.

Balinese Dance

The people of this Southeast Asian island perform trance dances. These combine Buddhist, Hindu, and Islamic beliefs and rituals with superstitions.

INFORMATION, PLEASE

Apel, Willi, ed. *The Harvard Dictionary of Music.* Rev. enl. ed. Harvard University Press, 1969.

Ardley, Neil. *Music.* Knopf, 1989.

Balanchine, George. *Balanchine's Complete Stories of the Great Ballets.* Doubleday, 1977.

Chujoy, Anatole, and P. W. Manchester, eds. *The Dance Encyclopedia.* Simon & Schuster, 1967.

Haskins, James. *Black Dance in America.* Crowell, 1992.

Kobbe, Gustav. *The Definitive Kobbe's Opera Book.* Edited, revised, and updated by the Earl of Harewood. Putnam, 1987.

Murphy, Howard. *Music Fundamentals: A Guide to Musical Understanding.* Sam Fox, 1962.

Nelson, Havelock, and Michael Gonzales. *Bring the Noise.* Harmony, 1991.

Pareles, Jon, and Patricia Romanowski. *The Rolling Stone Encyclopedia of Rock & Roll.* Summit, 1983.

Stanley, Sadie, ed. *The New Grove Dictionary of Music and Musicians.* 20 vols. Macmillan, 1980.

14

WORDS

etc.

Can you imagine a world without words? How could you tell anyone anything or they tell you? It would be very hard to communicate with your family and friends, teachers, and strangers without words. And there would be no books or radio or television to tell you what's going on. Words exist so that we can communicate ideas, feelings, and information.

COMMON ABBREVIATIONS

An **abbreviation** is a shortened form of a word or phrase. Some abbreviations, such as Mr. and Mrs., always substitute for the longer form. Abbreviations are not limited to, but frequently are used for, titles, academic degrees, organizations, measurements, and scientific words.

a	acre
A.B.	*artium baccalaureus* (Latin, bachelor of arts)
A.D.	*anno domini* (Latin, in the year of the Lord)
AFL	American Federation of Labor
AIDS	acquired immune deficiency syndrome
A.L.	American League (baseball)
A.M.	*ante meridiem* (Latin, before noon)

AMA	American Medical Association
anon.	anonymous
ASAP	as soon as possible
b.	born
B.A.	bachelor of arts
B.C.	before Christ
B.C.E.	before the common era
biol.	biology
B.S.	bachelor of science
B.S.A.	Boy Scouts of America
bu.	bushel
C	centigrade, Celsius
c., ca.	*circa* (Latin, about)
CARE	Cooperative for American Relief Everywhere
cf.	*confer* (Latin, compare)
chap.	chapter
CIA	Central Intelligence Agency
CIO	Congress of Industrial Organizations
cm	centimeter
co.	company
c/o	in care of
COD	cash on delivery
col.	column
coll.	college
cont.	continued
CORE	Congress of Racial Equality

corp.	corporation
CPR	cardiopulmonary resuscitation
CPU	central processing unit (computers)
CST	Central Standard Time
cu.	cubic
d.	died, daughter
D.A.	district attorney
D.D.S.	doctor of dental surgery
dept.	department
DOA	dead on arrival
doz.	dozen
DST	daylight saving time
D.V.M.	doctor of veterinary medicine
ed.	editor
EEO	equal employment opportunity
e.g.	*exempli gratia* (Latin, for example)
EPA	Environmental Protection Agency
EST	eastern standard time
et. al.	*et alii* (Latin, and others)
etc.	*et cetera* (Latin, and others)
ex.	example
F	Fahrenheit
FAA	Federal Aviation Administration
ff.	and following
FBI	Federal Bureau of Investigation
FCC	Federal Communications Commission
FDA	Food and Drug Administration
FDIC	Federal Deposit Insurance Corporation
FHA	Federal Housing Administration
fig.	figure
Fr.	French
FRS	Federal Reserve System
f/t	full time
ft.	foot
FTC	Federal Trade Commission
FYI	for your information
geom.	geometry
Ger.	German
Gk.	Greek
GMT	Greenwich mean time
G.O.P	Grand Old Party (Republican party)
GPO	Government Printing Office: general post office
G.S.A.	Girl Scouts of America
H.M.S.	his/her majesty's ship
HQ	headquarters
H.R.	House of Representatives
H.R.H.	his/her royal highness
HUD	(Department of) Housing and Urban Development
ibid.	*ibidem* (Latin, in the same place)
ICC	Interstate Commerce Commission
i.e.	*id est* (Latin, that is)
IHS	Jesus (Greek contraction)
in.	inch
Inc.	incorporated
INS	Immigration and Naturalization Service
IOU	I owe you
I.Q.	intelligence quotient
IRS	Internal Revenue Service
ISBN	international standard book number
It.	Italian
Jr.	junior
K	1,000
k.	karat
kg	kilogram
km	kilometer
kw.	kilowatt
kwh.	kilowatt-hour
l	liter
lat.	latitude
Lat.	Latin
lb.	pound
l.c.	lower case (printing)
L.C.	Library of Congress

lit.	literally	**PA**	public address
long.	longitude	**PC**	personal computer
L.P.N.	licensed practical nurse	**par.**	paragraph
		pk.	peck
m	meter	**pl.**	plural
MC	master of ceremonies	**P.M.**	*post meridiem* (Latin, after
M.D.	*medicinae doctor* (Latin, doctor		noon); prime minister
	of medicine)	**prep.**	preposition
memo	memorandum	**pron.**	pronoun
mgr.	manager	**pro tem.**	*pro tempore* (Latin, for the time
mi.	mile		being)
misc.	miscellaneous	**P.S.**	postscript
ml	milliliter	**p/t**	part time
mm	millimeter	**pt.**	pint
M.O.	money order; *modus operandi*	**PTA**	Parent-Teacher Association
	(Latin, mode of operation)		
M.P.	member of Parliament; mili-	**Q.E.D.**	*quod erat demonstrandum*
	tary police		(Latin, which was to be
mph	miles per hour		proved)
M.S.	master of science	**qt.**	quart
ms., mss.	manuscript, manuscripts	**q.v.**	*quod vide* (Latin, which see)
Ms.	miss or missus		
MSG	monosodium glutamate	**R.**	*rex, regina* (Latin, king, queen)
		rbi	runs batted in (baseball)
N/A	not applicable; not available	**R & D**	research and development
N.A.	North America	**REM**	rapid eye movement
NAACP	National Association for the Ad-	**Rev.**	Reverend
	vancement of Colored People	**RFD**	rural free delivery
NASA	National Aeronautics and	**RIP**	*requiescat in pace* (Latin, rest
	Space Administration		in peace)
NATO	North Atlantic Treaty Organi-	**RN**	registered nurse
	zation	**ROTC**	Reserve Officers' Training Corps
N.B.	*nota bene* (Latin, note well)	**rpm**	revolutions per minute
N.B.A.	National Basketball Association	**RR**	railroad
NFL	National Football League	**R & R**	rest and relaxation (military)
N.L.	National League (baseball)	**R.S.V.P.**	*répondez s'il vous plaît* (French,
no.	number		please respond)
NOW	National Organization for	**Rx**	prescription
	Women		
NRA	National Recovery Administra-	**s**	seconds
	tion; National Rifle Association	**S.A.**	South America; Salvation Army
NSC	National Security Council	**S.A.S.E.**	self-addressed stamped envelope
		s.c.	small capitals (printing)
ob., obit.	died	**SDI**	Strategic Defense Initiative
op. cit.	*opere citato* (Latin, in the work	**SEC**	Securities and Exchange
	cited)		Commission
oz.	ounce	**sec.**	seconds
		Sen.	Senate
p.	page	**seq.**	*sequentes* (Latin, the following)

86 Acceptable Two-Letter Scrabble™ Words

aa	ba	er	is	no	oy	us
ad	be	es	it	nu	pa	ut
ae	bi	et	jo	od	pe	we
ah	bo	ex	ka	oe	pi	wo
ai	by	fa	la	of	re	xi
am	da	go	li	oh	sh	xu
an	de	ha	lo	om	si	ya
ar	do	he	ma	on	so	ye
as	ef	hi	me	op	ta	
at	eh	ho	mi	or	ti	
aw	el	id	mu	os	to	
ax	em	if	my	ow	un	
ay	en	in	na	ox	up	

S.O.S.	international distress signal, often incorrectly thought to stand for "Save Our Ship"
Sp.	Spanish
SPCA	Society for the Prevention of Cruelty to Animals
SPQR	*Senatus Populusque Romanus* (Latin, the Senate and the Roman people)
sq.	square
SS.	saints
SS	Social Security; steamship
St.	saint
T	ton
TD	touchdown (football)
T.N.T.	trinitrotoluene
trans.	translated
treas.	treasurer
TVA	Tennessee Valley Authority
u.c.	upper case (printing)
U.K.	United Kingdom
UFO	unidentified flying object
U.N.	United Nations
UNESCO	United Nations Educational, Scientific, and Cultural Organization
UNICEF	United Nations International Children's Emergency Fund

univ.	university
U.S.	United States
U.S.A.	United States of America; United States Army
U.S.A.F.	United States Air Force
U.S.C.G.	United States Coast Guard
U.S.I.A.	United States Information Agency
U.S.M.C.	United States Marine Corps
U.S.N.	United States Navy
U.S.S.	United States ship
v., vs.	versus
VA	Veterans Administration
V.F.W.	Veterans of Foreign Wars
V.I.P.	very important person
viz.	*videlicet* (Latin, namely)
V.P.	vice president
vol.	volume
w	watt
Xmas	Christmas
yd.	yard
Y.M.C.A., Y.W.C.A.	Young Men's (Women's) Christian Association
Y.M.H.A., Y.W.H.A.	Young Men's (Women's) Hebrew Association
yr.	year

U.S. POSTAL SERVICE ABBREVIATIONS

Two-Letter State and Territory Abbreviations

Alabama	AL	Kentucky	KY	Ohio	OH
Alaska	AK	Louisiana	LA	Oklahoma	OK
Arizona	AZ	Maine	ME	Oregon	OR
Arkansas	AR	Marshall Islands	TT	Palau	TT
American Samoa	AS	Maryland	MD	Pennsylvania	PA
California	CA	Massachusetts	MA	Puerto Rico	PR
Colorado	CO	Michigan	MI	Rhode Island	RI
Connecticut	CT	Minnesota	MN	South Carolina	SC
Delaware	DE	Mississippi	MS	South Dakota	SD
District of Columbia	DC	Missouri	MO	Tennessee	TN
Federated States of		Montana	MT	Texas	TX
Micronesia	TT	Nebraska	NE	Utah	UT
Florida	FL	Nevada	NV	Vermont	VT
Georgia	GA	New Hampshire	NH	Virginia	VA
Guam	GU	New Jersey	NJ	Virgin Islands	VI
Hawaii	HI	New Mexico	NM	Washington	WA
Idaho	ID	New York	NY	West Virginia	WV
Illinois	IL	North Carolina	NC	Wisconsin	WI
Indiana	IN	North Dakota	ND	Wyoming	WY
Iowa	IA	Northern Mariana			
Kansas	KS	Islands	CM		

Geographic Directional Abbreviations

North	N
East	E
South	S
West	W
Northeast	NE
Southeast	SE
Southwest	SW
Northwest	NW

Street Designators (Street Suffixes)

Word	Abbreviation	Word	Abbreviation	Word	Abbreviation
Alley	ALY	Ford	FRD	Oval	OVAL
Annex	ANX	Forest	FRST	Park	PARK
Arcade	ARC	Forge	FRG	Parkway	PKY
Avenue	AVE	Fork	FRK	Pass	PASS
Bayou	BYU	Forks	FRKS	Path	PATH
Beach	BCH	Fort	FT	Pike	PIKE
Bend	BND	Freeway	FWY	Pines	PNES
Bluff	BLF	Gardens	GDNS	Place	PL
Bottom	BTM	Gateway	GTWY	Plain	PLN
Boulevard	BLVD	Glen	GLN	Plains	PLNS
Branch	BR	Green	GRN	Plaza	PLZ
Bridge	BRG	Grove	GRV	Point	PT
Brook	BRK	Harbor	HBR	Port	PRT
Burg	BG	Haven	HVN	Prairie	PR
Bypass	BYP	Heights	HTS	Radial	RADL
Camp	CP	Highway	HWY	Ranch	RNCH
Canyon	CYN	Hill	HL	Rapids	RPDS
Cape	CPE	Hills	HLS	Rest	RST
Causeway	CSWY	Hollow	HOLW	Ridge	RDG
Center	CTR	Inlet	INLT	River	RIV
Circle	CIR	Island	IS	Road	RD
Cliffs	CLFS	Islands	ISS	Row	ROW
Club	CLB	Isle	ISLE	Run	RUN
Corner	COR	Junction	JCT	Shoal	SHL
Corners	CORS	Key	KY	Shoals	SHLS
Course	CRSE	Knolls	KNLS	Shore	SHR
Court	CT	Lake	LK	Shores	SHRS
Courts	CTS	Lakes	LKS	Spring	SPG
Cove	CV	Landing	LNDG	Springs	SPGS
Creek	CRK	Lane	LN	Spur	SPUR
Crescent	CRES	Light	LGT	Square	SQ
Crossing	XING	Loaf	LF	Station	STA
Dale	DL	Locks	LCKS	Stream	STRM
Dam	DM	Lodge	LDG	Street	ST
Divide	DV	Loop	LOOP	Summit	SMT
Drive	DR	Mall	MALL	Terrace	TER
Estates	EST	Manor	MNR	Trace	TRCE
Expressway	EXPY	Meadows	MDWS	Track	TRAK
Extension	EXT	Mill	ML	Trail	TRL
Fall	FL	Mills	MLS	Trailer	TRLR
Falls	FLS	Mission	MSN	Tunnel	TUNL
Ferry	FRY	Mount	MT	Turnpike	TPKE
Field	FLD	Mountain	MTN	Union	UN
Fields	FLDS	Neck	NCK	Valley	VLY
Flats	FLT	Orchard	ORCH	Viaduct	VIA

(*continued*)

Street Designators (Street Suffixes) (*continued*)

Word	Abbreviation	Word	Abbreviation	Word	Abbreviation
View	VW	Vista	VIS	Wells	WLS
Village	VLG	Walk	WALK		
Ville	VL	Way	WAY		

250 COMMONLY MISSPELLED WORDS

accept/except
accessory
accidentally
accommodate
accompany
acquaintance
acquire
address
advise/advice
affect/effect
aisle/isle
allege
allot/a lot
all right
already
amateur
antarctic
antecedent
apparent
arctic
argument
arithmetic
asparagus
asthma
athletic
attendance
attorney

banana
baptize
bargain
bazaar
beginning
believe
biscuit
bizarre
bookkeeper

bureau
burglar

calendar
cantaloupe
capital/capitol
cashmere
caterpillar
ceiling
cellar
cemetery
cereal/serial
chandelier
changeable
chauffeur
chief
cinnamon
circuit
circumference
cocoa
colonel/kernel
committee
compliment/complement
concede
conceive
conscience
conscious
convenient
corduroy
correspondent
cough
counterfeit

debt
definite
dependent
design

desirable
desperately
dessert/desert
devise/device
dictionary
disappear
disappoint
dispel
dissatisfied

effect/affect
eighth
embarrass
environment
equipped
erroneous
especially
etiquette
exaggerate
exceed
excel
existence
expense

familiar
fascinate
fatigue
February
fiancé (man)
fiancée (woman)
forehead
foreign
foreword/forward
formerly/formally
forth/fourth
fragile
freight

gauge
glacier
government
grammar
grease
guarantee
guess
guest

handkerchief
harass
height
heir
hygiene

idol/idle
incite/insight
independence
Indispensable
irresistible
isthmus
its/it's

judgment

khaki

laboratory
laugh
league
library
license
licorice
literature
lose/loose
lying

maintenance
manual
mathematics
mattress
minuscule
mischief
missionary
misspell
misstate
molasses
mortgage
mosquitoes

necessary
neighbor
niece
noticeable
nuisance

obedience
occasion
occur
occurred
occurrence
o'clock
offense
omitted

parallel
parliament
phenomenon
physician
plaid
pneumonia
politically
possess
potatoes/potato
prairie
precede/proceed
preferred
principle/principal
privilege
probably
pseudonym
psychology

quiet/quite

raspberry
receipt
receive
recess
recognize
recommend
reference
rendezvous
repellent
resemblance
reservoir
resume
rhyme
rhythm
ridiculous

sandwich
satellite
scissors
secretary
seize
separately
siege
sieve
similar
sincerely
special
squirrel
stationary/stationery
straight/strait
strengthen
succeed
success
suit/suite
superintendent
supersede
susceptible
synagogue
syringe

tariff
tenement
than/then
their/there
tobacco
tomatoes
to/too/two
tragedy
truly
Tuesday

usually

vaccinate
vacuum
villain
vinegar

warrant
Wednesday
weird
wholly
whose/who's
withhold
yolk
your/your're

Common Phrases: Major European Languages

English	French	German	Italian	Spanish
Hello/good day	Bon jour	Guten tag	Buon giorno	Buenas dias
Please	S'il vous plaît	Bitte	Per favore	Con su permiso por favor
Thank you	Merci	Danke schön	Grazie	Gracias
Excuse me/ pardon me	Excusez-moi pardonnez-moi	Entschuldigen sie mir	Mi scusi	Perdóne
Yes	Oui	Ja	Si	Sí
No	Non	Nein	No	No
Goodbye/ so long	Au revoir/ à bientôt	Auf wiedersehen	Arrivederci	Adiós; hasta la vista

FREQUENTLY USED FOREIGN WORDS AND PHRASES

à bas (F) — down with
ab ovo usque ad mala (L) — from soup to nuts (lit., "from the egg to the apples")
a cappella (It) — in the church style (vocally)
ad astra per aspera (L) — to the stars through difficulties
adagio (It) — slowly
ad hoc (L) — for a particular purpose (lit., "to this")
ad infinitum (L) — forever
ad nauseam (L) — to the point of disgust
aficionado (Sp) — enthusiast, fan
alma mater (L) — old school (lit., "fostering mother")
aloha (Hw) — greeting or farewell
amor vincit omnia (L) — love conquers all
anno domini; A.D. (L) — in the year of the Lord
a priori (L) — deductive (lit., "from what comes before")
ars gratia artis (L) — art for art's sake
ars longa, vita brevis (L) — art is long, life is short
au contraire (Fr) — on the contrary
au courant (Fr) — up-to-date, contemporary
au naturel (Fr) — nude, plain
avant-garde (Fr) — forward, advanced, vanguard

beau geste (Fr) — noble gesture
bête noire (Fr) — pet peeve (lit., "black beast")
billet doux (Fr) — love letter
Blitzkrieg (Gr) — lightning war
bon marché (Fr) — inexpensive (lit., "good market")
bon mot (Fr) — clever expression

bonne chance (Fr)	good luck
bon vivant (Fr)	partygoer; one who enjoys life
bon voyage (Fr)	have a good journey
carpe diem (L)	seize the day
carte blanche (Fr)	free hand, no restrictions (lit., "white card")
cause célèbre (Fr)	notorious controversy
caveat emptor (L)	let the buyer beware
c'est la vie (Fr)	that's life
chacun à son goût (Fr)	each to his own taste; to each his own
chef d'œuvre (Fr)	masterpiece
chutzpah (Y)	gall, daring, nerve
ciao (It)	good-bye, so long
circa (c., ca.) (L)	about, approximately
cogito ergo sum (L)	I think, therefore I am
comme il faut (Fr)	proper, appropriate
con mucho gusto (Sp)	with pleasure
corpus delicti (L)	evidence (lit., "body of the crime")
coup de grâce (Fr)	final blow
coup d'état (F)	overthrow of government
cul-de-sac (Fr)	dead end, blind alley (lit., "bottom of the bag")
cum grano salie (L)	with a grain of salt
da capo (It)	from the top
de facto (L)	in fact
de jure (L)	in law
Deo gratias (L)	thanks be to God
deus ex machina (L)	desperate or contrived solution (lit., "god from the machine")
enfant terrible (Fr)	brat; prodigy
en passant (Fr)	in passing; by the way
entre nous (Fr)	privately, between us
e pluribus unum (L)	from many, one
ersatz (Gr)	fake, imitation
et cetera (etc.) (L)	and others
Eureka! (Gk)	I've found it!
exempli gratis (e.g.) (L)	by way of example
ex post facto (L)	after the fact
fait accompli (Fr)	accomplished fact
faux pas (Fr)	social error (lit., "false step")
femme fatale (Fr)	alluring, dangerous woman
fin de siècle (Fr)	end of century
glasnost (R)	openness
goy (Y)	gentile

(*continued*)

FREQUENTLY USED FOREIGN WORDS AND PHRASES (*continued*)

habeas corpus (L)	writ requiring a court appearance (lit., "[that] you have the body")
hoi polloi (Gk)	common people, mob
hubris (Gk)	immoderate pride, arrogance
idée fixe (Fr)	fixed idea, obsession
id est (i.e.) (L)	that is
in loco parentis (L)	in the place of parents
in medias res (L)	in the middle of things
ipso facto (L)	by the fact itself
joie de vivre (Fr)	good spirits, exuberance (lit., "joy of living")
kamikaze (J)	suicide pilot (lit., "divine wind")
klutz (Y)	clumsy person
kvetch (Y)	complain, carp
laissez-faire (Fr)	noninterference (lit., "let [people] do [as they wish]")
lingua franca (It)	common language (lit., "French language")
magnum opus (L)	major work
mañana (Sp)	tomorrow
maven (Y)	expert, authority
mazel tov (Y)	congratulations, good luck
mea culpa (L)	my fault
mens sana in corpore sano (L)	a sound mind in a sound body
meshuggah (Y)	crazy
modus operandi (M.O.) (L)	method of operation
ne plus ultra (L)	the best
n'est-ce pas? (Fr)	isn't that true?
noblesse oblige (Fr)	the responsibility of noble birth
nom de plume (Fr)	pen name
non sequitur (L)	something that does not follow
nosh (Y)	nibble, eat
nota bene (N.B.) (L)	note well
par excellence (Fr)	above all, preeminently
par exemple (Fr)	for example
per diem (L)	by the day
per favore (It)	please
perestroika (R)	restructuring
persona non grata (L)	unwanted person
pièce de résistance (Fr)	showpiece item

pied à terre (Fr)	in-town apartment; temporary lodging
por favor (Sp)	please
prego (It)	you're welcome
prima facie (L)	on the face of it; at first sight
prix fixe (Fr)	fixed price
pro bono publico (L)	for the public good
quid pro quo (L)	fair exchange; tit for tat
quién sabe? (Sp)	who knows?
raison d'être (Fr)	reason for being
reductio ad absurdum (L)	reduction to absurdity (in logical argument)
répondez s'il vous plaît (R.S.V.P.) (Fr)	please respond
requiescat in pace (R.I.P.)	rest in peace
salaam aleicham (A)	peace to you
sanctum sanctorum (L)	holy of holies
savoir faire (Fr)	social savvy (lit., "to know what to do")
schlemiel (Y)	unlucky person, loser
schmaltz (Y)	excessive sentimentality
schtick (Y)	gimmick; a performer's idiosyncrasy
semper fidelis (L)	always faithful
shalom (H)	greeting or farewell (lit., "peace")
sic (L)	thus
sic transit gloria mundi (L)	thus passes the glory of the world
sine qua non (L)	something indispensable (lit., "without which not")
sotto voce (It)	softly (lit., "in a soft voice")
status quo (L)	current state of affairs
Sturm und Drang (Gr)	storm and stress
tabula rasa (L)	clean slate (lit., "erased tablet")
tempus fugit (L)	time flies
terra firma (L)	solid ground
terra incognita (L)	unknown territory
tête-à-tête (Fr)	intimate conversation (lit., "head to head")
tout de suite (Fr)	immediately
tout le monde (Fr)	everyone
trompe-l'œil (Fr)	optical illusion (lit., "fool the eye")
vaya con Dios (Sp)	go with God
veni, vidi, vici (L)	I came, I saw, I conquered
verboten (Gr)	forbidden
vox populi, vox Dei (L)	the voice of the people, the voice of God
Wanderlust (Gr)	desire to travel
Wunderkind (Gr)	prodigy
yenta (Y)	gossip or busybody

Key to abbreviations:

A	Arabic	H	Hebrew	lit.	literally
Fr	French	Hw	Hawaiian	Sp	Spanish
Gk	Greek	It	Italian	R	Russian
Gr	German	L	Latin	Y	Yiddish

ACRONYMS

Acronyms are pronounceable formations made by combining the initial letters or syllables of a string of words.

AIDS	acquired immune deficiency syndrome
ALCOA	Aluminum Company of America
AMEX	American Express Company
ARC	AIDS-related complex
ASCAP	American Society of Composers, Authors, and Publishers
AWOL	absent without leave
BAM	Brooklyn Academy of Music
BART	Bay Area Rapid Transit
BASIC	Beginner's All-purpose Symbolic Instruction Code (computer language)
CARE	Cooperative for American Relief Everywhere
CAT (scan)	computerized axial tomography
CLASSMATE	Computer Language to Aid and Stimulate Scientific, Mathematical and Technical Education
COBOL	Common Business-Oriented Language
COMEX	Commodity Exchange (New York)
CORE	Congress of Racial Equality
DOS	disk operating system
EPCOT (Center)	Experimental Prototype Community of Tomorrow
FICA	Federal Insurance Contributions Act (Social Security)
FORTRAN	formula translation (programming language)
GIPSY	General Information Processing System
HART	Honolulu Area Rapid Transit
INTERPOL	International Criminal Police Organization
INTERTELL	International Intelligence Legion
IRA	individual retirement account; Irish Republican Army
LASER	Light Amplification by Stimulated Emission of Radiation
LILCO	Long Island Lighting Company

Most-Used Letters of the Alphabet

The normal frequencies with which letters of the English alphabet occur (from most to least frequent) are: E, T, A, O, I, N, S, H, R, D, L, U, C, M, P, F, Y, W, G, B, V, K, J, X, Z, Q.

Some Common Oxymorons or Pairing of Contradictory or Incongruous Words

almost perfect	instant classic	original copies
bad health	jumbo shrimp	pretty ugly
bittersweet	larger half	real potential
clearly confused	least favorite	rock opera
constant variable	liquid gas	same difference
definite maybe	minor miracle	sweet sorrow
deliberately thoughtless	modern history	taped live
exact estimate	near miss	terribly enjoyable
extensive briefing	nondairy creamer	tragic comedy
genuine imitation	old news	working vacation
good grief	only choice	
holy war	open secret	

LORAN	Long-range Aid to Navigation
LSAT	Law School Admission Test
MADD	Mothers Against Drunk Driving
MASH	mobile army surgical unit
MOMA	Museum of Modern Art (New York)
NASA	National Aeronautics and Space Administration
NASCAR	National Association of Sports Car Racing
NATO	North Atlantic Treaty Organization
NOW	National Organization for Women
OPEC	Organization of Petroleum Exporting Countries
OXFAM	Oxford Famine Relief
PAC	political action committee
PATH	Port Authority Trans-Hudson
PEN	Poets, Playwrights, Editors, Essayists, and Novelists (organization)
PIN	personal identification number; Police Information Network
QUICKTRAN	Quick FORTRAN (computer language)
RADAR	radio detecting and ranging
RAM	random-access memory
RIF	Reading Is Fundamental
ROM	read-only memory
ROTC	Reserve Officer's Training Corps
SADD	Students Against Drunk Driving
SCUBA	Self-Contained Underwater Breathing Apparatus
SEATO	Southeast Asia Treaty Organization
UNESCO	United Nations Educational, Social, and Cultural Organization

(continued)

| UNICEF | United Nations International Children's Emergency Fund (now shortened to United Nations Children's Fund) |
| UNIVAC | universal automatic computer |

VISTA	Volunteers in Service to America
WHO	World Health Organization
YUPPIE	young urban professional
ZIP	zone improvement plan (U.S. Postal Service)

COMMON WORD FORMATIONS

Prefixes from Greek Words

Prefix	Meaning in English
a-	not
acous-	hearing
acro-	top, tip
aero-	air, gas
allo-	other
amphi-	both, around
an-	not
ana-	again, thorough, thoroughly
andro-	man
anthropo-	human
anti-	against
arch(i)-	chief
arche(o)-, archae(o)-	old, ancient
arthro-	joint
aster-, astro-	star
atmo-	vapor
auto-	self
baro-	weight
batho-, bathy-	deep
biblio-	book
bio-	life
bracchio-	arm
broncho-	throat
cardio-	heart
cath-, cato-	down, thorough, thoroughly
cephalo-	head
chiro-	hand
chloro-	green
chole-, cholo-	bile

Prefix	Meaning in English
choreo-	dance
chrom(at)o-	color
chrono-	time
cosmo-	universe
cranio-	skull
crypto-	hidden
cyto-	cell
dactylo-	finger
deca-	ten
dendro-	three
dermo-, dermato-	skin
deutero-	second
di(s)-	apart
dia-	through
dino-	terrible
diplo-	double
dodeca-	twelve
dyna-, dynamo-	force, power
dys-	bad, difficult
echino-	spiny
ecto-	outside, external
el-, em-, en-	in, into
encephalo-	brain
ennea-	nine
entero-	gut
ento-	inside, interior
entomo-	insect
eph-, epi-	on
ergo-	work
erythro-	red
ethno-	race, nation
eu-	good

Prefix	Meaning in English	Prefix	Meaning in English
ex-	out	meta-	beyond, after, changed
exo-	outside, external		
		metro-	measure
gastro-	stomach	micro-	small
geo-	earth, land	miso-	hatred
geronto-	old age	mono-	one, single
glosso-	tongue	morpho-	shape
gluc-, glyc-	sweet		
grapho-	writing	necro-	dead
gynec(o)-,		neo-	new
gynaec(o)-	woman	neuro-	nerve
		noso-	sickness
haemato-	blood		
hagio-	holy	octa-, octo-	eight
halo-	salt, sea	odonto-	tooth
haplo	simple	oligo-	few
hecto-	hundred	ombro-	rain
helico-	spiral	onto-	being
helio-	sun	ophthalm(o)-	eye
hema-, haema-	blood	ornitho-	bird
hemi-	half	oro-	mouth
hepato-	liver	ortho-	straight
hepta-	seven	osteo-	bone
hetero-	different	oto-	ear
hexa-	six	oxy-	sharp
holo-	whole, complete		
homeo-	similar, like	pachy-	thick
homo-	same	paleo-, palaeo-	ancient, old
hydro-	water	pan-	all
hyper-	above	para-	close, beside
hypno-	sleep	patho-	suffering, disease
hypo-	under	pedo-	child
		penta-	five
iso-	equal	peri-	around, very
		petro-	stone
kinesi-, kineto-	movement	phago-	eating
		phono-	sound
leuko-	white	photo-	light
litho-	stone	phreno-	brain
logo-	word	phylo-	species
lyo-, lysi-	dissolving	physio-	nature
		phyto-	plant
macro-	large	pluto-	riches
mega-, megalo-	great	pneumato-	breath, spirit
melano-	black	pneumo-	lung
meso-	middle	poly-	many

(continued)

Prefixes from Greek Words (*continued*)

Prefix	Meaning in English	Prefix	Meaning in English
pro-	before, forward	stylo-	pillar
proto-	first	sy-, syl-, sym-, syn-	with
pseudo-	false		
psycho-	mind, spirit, soul	tele-	distant
ptero-	wing	teleo-	final
pyro-	fire	telo-	distant, final
		thanato-	death
rhino-	nose	theo-	god
		thermo-	heat
sacchro-	sugar	topo-	place
sarco-	flesh	toxico-	poison
schisto-, schizo-	split	trachy-	rough
somato-	body		
speleo-	cave	xeno-	foreign
spermato-	seed		
stato-	position	zo-, zoo-	living
steno-	short, narrow	zygo-	double
stereo-	solid, three-dimensional		

Suffixes from Greek Words

Suffix	Meaning in English	Suffix	Meaning in English
-algia	pain	-iasis	disease
-androus	man	-iatrics, -iatry	medical treatment
-archy	rule, government	-itis	inflammation
-biosis	life	-kinesis	movement
-cephalic, -cephalous	head	-lepsy	seizure, fit
-chrome	color	-lith	stone
-cracy, -crat	rule, government	-logy	science of, list
-derm	skin	-machy	battle, fight
-drome, -dromous	run (race)	-mancy, -mantic	foretelling
		-mania(c)	craving
		-mere, -merous	part
-emia	blood	-meter, -metry	measure
-gamy	marriage	-morphic, -morphous	shape
-gen(ous), -geny, -gony	giving birth to, bearing	-nomy	science of, law of
-gnomy, -gnosis	knowledge		
-gon	angle	-odont	tooth
-gram, -graph(y)	writing	-oid	like, similar
		-opia	eye, sight
-hedral, -hedron	side, sided	-opsia	sight

Suffix	Meaning in English	Suffix	Meaning in English
-pathy	suffering, disease	-scope, -scopy	observation
-phage, -phagous	eating	-sect, -section	cutting
-phany	manifestation	-soma, -some	body
-phobe, -phobia	fear	-sophy	wisdom
-phone, -phony	sound		
-phyte	plant	-taxis, -taxy	order
-plasia, -plasis	growth	-tomy	cutting
-plasm	matter	-trophy	feed
		-tropous, -tropy	turned
-saur	lizard		

Prefixes from Latin Words

Prefix	Meaning in English	Prefix	Meaning in English
a-, abs-	from	dorsi-, dorso-	back (of body)
ac-, ad-, af-, ag-, al-, an-, ap-, as-, at-	to, toward	e-, ec-, ef-	out
alti-, alto-	high	equi-	equal
ambi-	both	ex-	out
ante-	before	extra-	outside, external
aqua-, aque-, aqui-	water		
arbori-	tree	ferri-, ferro-	iron
audio-	hearing	fissi-	split
avi-	bird	fluvio-	river
brevi-	short	igni-	fire
		il-, im-, in-	not, against, in, into, on
centi-	hundred	inter-	between
cerebro-	brain	intra-, intro-	inside, interior
cervico-	neck	ir-	not, against, in, into, on
circum-	around		
cirro-	curl		
cis-	near, on the near side of	juxta-	close, near, beside
co-, col-, com-, con-, cor-	with, thorough, thoroughly	labio-	lip
		lacto-	milk
contra-	against	ligni-	wood
cruci-	cross	luni-	moon
cupro-	copper, bronze		
		magni-	great
de-	not, down	mal(e)-	bad, evil
deci-	tenth	multi-	many
demi-	half		
denti-	tooth	naso-	nose
di(s)-	apart	nati-	birth
digit(i)-	finger	nocti-	night

(*continued*)

Prefixes from Latin Words (*continued*)

Prefix	Meaning in English	Prefix	Meaning in English
ob-, oc-	against	re-	again
octa-, octo-	eight	recti-	straight
oculo-	eye	retro-	backward
of-, op-	against		
oleo-	oil	sacro-	dedicated
omni-	all	sangui-	blood
oro-	mouth	se-	apart
ossi-	bone	septi-	seven
ovi-, ovo-	egg	sidero-	star
		somni-	sleep
pari-	equal	spiro-	breath
per-	through, very	stelli-	star
pisci-	fish	sub-, suc-, suf-,	
plano-	flat	sum-, sup-	under
plumbo-	lead (metal)	super-, supra-	above
pluvio-	rain		
post-	after	terri-	land, earth
pre-	before	trans-	through, on the far side of
preter-	beyond		
primi-	first		
pro-	for, forward	ultra-	beyond
pulmo-	lung	uni-	one, single
quadri-	four	vari(o)-	different
quinque-	five		

Suffixes from Latin Words

Suffix	Meaning in English	Suffix	Meaning in English
-cidal, -cide	kill	-grade	walking
-fid	split	-vorous	eating
-fugal, -fuge	run away from		

INFORMATION, PLEASE

Buchanan-Brown, John, et al. *Le Mot Juste: A Dictionary of Classical and Foreign Words and Phrases.* Vintage Books, 1981.

Chapman, Robert L., ed. *New Dictionary of American Slang.* Harper & Row, 1986.

———. *Roget's International Thesaurus.* 5th ed. HarperCollins, 1992.

Ciardi, John. *The Complete Browser's Dictionary: The Best of John Ciardi's Two Browser's Dictionaries in a Single Compendium of Curious Expressions and Intriguing Facts.* Harper & Row, 1988.

Costello, Elaine. *Signing.* Bantam, 1983.

DeSola, Ralph. *Abbreviations Dictionary.* 7th ed. Elsevier, 1986.

Fisher, Leonard Everett. *Alphabet Art.* Four Winds Press, 1978.

Laird, Charlton, ed. *Webster's New World Thesaurus.* Rev. ed. Prentice Hall, 1985.

MacMillan Dictionary for Children. Second Revised ed. MacMillan, 1989.

Hebrew Alphabet

Letters	Names	English Sounds	Letters	Names	English Sounds
א	aleph	n.a.	ל	lamed	l
ב	bet	b (v)	ם מ	mem	m
ג	gimel	g (g)	ן נ	nun	n
ד	dalet	d (d)	ס	samekh	s
ה	he	h	ע	ayin	n.a.
ו	vav	w	ף פ	pe	p (ph)
ז	zayin	z	ץ צ	tsadi	ts
ח	het	h	ק	koph	q
ט	tet	t	ר	resh	r
י	yod	y	שׂ	sin	s
כ ך	kaf	k (kh)	שׁ	shin	sh
			ת	tav	t

Like the Arabic alphabet, the Hebrew alphabet is made up mainly of consonants. Vowels usually do not appear in Hebrew writing. But for educational purposes they are indicated by vowel points—dots or strokes—that are used with a consonant, such as יוֹם, which would read *day.* Five of the consonants—*kaf, mem, nun, pe,* and *tsadi*—look different when they appear at the end of a word. By themselves, the consonants *aleph* and *ayin* are silent.

Russian Alphabet

Letters	English Sounds	Letters	English Sounds
А а	a	С с	s
Б б	b	Т т	t
В в	v	У у	u
Г г	g	Ф ф	f
Д д	d	Х х	kh
Е е	e	Ц ц	ts
Ж ж	zh	Ч ч	ch
З з	z	Ш ш	sh
И и Й й	i, y	Щ щ	shch
К к	k	Ъ ъ	n.a.
Л л	l	Ы ы	y
М м	m	Ь ь	n.a.
Н н	n	Э э	e
О о	o	Ю ю	yu
П п	p	Я я	ya
Р р	r		

The Russian, or Cyrillic, alphabet is based on the Greek alphabet. In modern Russian, the ъ is rare.

When Is "Was" a "Saw"?

Palindromes

A palindrome can be a single word, a verse, a sentence, a series of sentences, or a number that reads the same forward and backward. Palindromic sentences often become jokes when meanings are ascribed to them and when punctuation is added. For example, the best-known English palindrome is "Madam, I'm Adam," which is fun to think of as Adam's introduction to Eve. Madam is a palindromic word, but whole sentences are more fun:

Enid and Edna dine
A man, a plan, a canal—Panama!
Draw, O Caesar, erase a coward.
Al lets Della call Ed Stella.
Dennis sinned.
Naomi, did I moan?
Niagara, O roar again!
He lived as a devil, eh?
Able was I ere I saw Elba.

And here is a palindromic conversation between two owls:

"Too hot to hoot!"
"Too hot to woo!"
"Too wot?"
"Too hot to hoot!"
"To woo!"
"Too wot?"
"To hoot! Too hot to hoot!"

McCrum, Robert, et al. *The Story of English.* Sifton/Viking, 1986.

Random House Dictionary of the English Language. 2nd ed. Random House, 1987.

Urdang, Laurence. *A Basic Dictionary of Synonyms and Antonyms.* Lodestar Books, 1979.

Urdang, Laurence, ed. *The New York Times Everyday Reader's Dictionary of Misunderstood, Misused and Mispronounced Words.* Rev. ed. Times Books, 1985.

Webster's Compact Rhyming Dictionary. Merriam-Webster, 1987.

Webster's New World Crossword Puzzle Dictionary. Prentice Hall, 1983.

Webster's New World Dictionary, Third College Ed. Prentice Hall, 1988.

Webster's Ninth New Collegiate Dictionary. Merriam-Webster, 1985.

15

GRAMMAR AND PUNCTUATION

WHAT IS GRAMMAR AND WHY IS IT NECESSARY?

People use language to communicate with each other. *Grammar* is a set of rules that tells people the way words can and cannot be used. These rules are necessary so that speakers will use their language in the same way, so they can understand each other easily.

Each language has its own grammar, or rules. For example, English grammar stresses word order. In Chinese, the pitch of the speaker's voice can determine the meaning of the words.

Grammar is learned gradually from everyday speech and writing. This daily usage explains why people may understand the grammar of their language even without knowing every rule. For example, all English speakers do not have to learn the rules of word order to understand that the sentence should ordinarily be "You go home," not "Home go you." Nevertheless, sometimes we may not know if we are using our language in an acceptable way. The following English grammar basics should help in such cases.

THE PARTS OF SPEECH

Parts of speech are categories of words that are used in particular ways to express thoughts and ideas in sentences. The English language has 8 parts of speech:

noun
verb
conjunction
pronoun
adverb
interjection
adjective
preposition

Noun

A *noun* names a person, place, thing, quality, act, or feeling, such as boy, home, doll, beauty, execution, sadness. Nouns can be proper and common, singular and plural.

Proper noun A proper noun names a specific someone or something. Proper nouns are always capitalized (Elizabeth, Roger).

Common noun A common noun is any

noun that is not a proper noun (girl, dinner).

Singular noun A singular noun names *one* person, place, thing, quality, act, or feeling (doll, truck).

Plural noun A plural noun names more than one person, place, thing, quality, act, or feeling (times, troubles).

How to Form Plural Nouns

- Add -s to form the plural of most nouns (dogs).
- Add -es for nouns ending in -s, -x, -z, -sh, or -ch (wishes).
- Add -s for nouns ending with a vowel followed by a -y (keys).
- Change -y to -i and add -es for nouns ending with a consonant and -y (babies).
- Some nouns do not fit any rules for forming plurals. Here are 12 nouns that form irregular plurals:

fish-fish	child-children
mouse-mice	ox-oxen
man-men	foot-feet
wife-wives	tooth-teeth
person-people	deer-deer
woman-women	sheep-sheep

Possessive Noun

A **possessive noun** shows ownership (Michael's glove).

How to Form Possessives:

- Add -'s to form the possessive of most singular nouns (Dylan's videocassette).
- Add -' to form the possessive of plural nouns that ends in -s (boys').
- Add -'s to form the possessive of plural nouns that do not end in -s (children's).

Pronoun

A *pronoun* is a word that takes the place of a noun.

Personal Pronouns

A *personal pronoun* refers to a specific person or thing (he, it).

Singular pronouns refer to one person or thing (she, it). Plural pronouns refer to more than one person (they).

First-person pronouns refer to the person who is speaking or writing (I, we).

Second-person pronouns refer to the person being spoken or written to (you).

Third-person pronouns refer to any other person or object (them).

Subject pronouns replace a noun that is the subject of the sentence (*She* dances).

Possessive pronouns replace a possessive noun (*Her* tutu).

Object pronouns replace a noun that is receiving the action of a sentence (Tom bumped *him*).

Relative Pronouns

A *relative pronoun* introduces a subordinate clause. (The boy *who* sang yesterday is here.) There are three forms of relative pronouns: subjective, objective, and possessive. When a relative pronoun functions as the object of a preposition, it takes the objective form. (The boy to *whom* you sang is here.)

Subjective	Possessive	Objective
who	whose	whom
what	(no form)	what
that	(no form)	that
which	whose	which
whichever	(no form)	whichever
whoever	whosever	whomever

Interrogative Pronouns

An *interrogative pronoun* is a relative pronoun that introduces a question. (*Who* saw Kate enter the room?)

Demonstrative Pronouns

A *demonstrative pronoun* points out the thing to which it refers. (*This* makes me happy.) Other demonstrative pronouns are *these* and *that*.

Indefinite Pronouns

An *indefinite pronoun* refers to an unspecific

Personal Pronouns

| | SINGULAR | | | PLURAL | | |
	Subject	*Possessive*	*Object*	*Subject*	*Possessive*	*Object*
First Person	I	my mine	me	we	our ours	us
Second Person	you	your yours	you	we	your yours	you
Third Person	he she it	his her(s) its	him her it	they	their	them

person or thing (*Someone* is going to get in trouble). Here are 16 indefinite pronouns:

anybody	everyone	nothing
somebody	no one	whatever
everybody	anything	whoever
nobody	something	one
anyone	everything	you
someone		

Reflexive Pronouns

A *reflexive pronoun* refers back to the subject. Reflexive pronouns can be singular and plural:

myself
yourself
himself
itself
ourselves
yourselves
themselves

Adjective

An *adjective* describes or modifies (limits the meaning of) a noun or pronoun. (Four *happy* kids were singing. He was *sad* to hear the news.)

An *article* is one of these three words: *a, an,* and *the.* Articles are *limiting adjectives* because they point out one noun.

- Use the definite article *the* to refer to a specific noun. (I can't find *the* hat I was wearing.)
- Use the indefinite article *a* before singular nouns beginning with a consonant. (I need *a* raise in my allowance.)
- Use the indefinite article *an* before singular nouns beginning with a vowel. (Please buy *an* apple.)

Comparison of Adjectives

Adjectives can show differences in amount or degree by changes in form or by addition of the words *less, least, more,* and *most.*

How to Form Comparative and Superlative Adjectives

- Add -er or -est to form the comparative and superlative of most adjectives of one or two syllables:

Jason is smart.
Claire is smart*er* than Jason.
Molly is the smart*est* of the three.

- Add function words to form comparative and superlative of adjectives of more than two syllables:

Sean is generous.
Leslie is *more* generous than Sean.

Bill is the *most* generous guy in the school.

- A few common adjectives form irregular comparatives and superlatives:

bad, worse, worst
good, better, best
little, less, least,
many, more, most

Verb

A *verb* expresses action such as (read, run) or a state of being (is, were). A verb may consist of one word (dance) or a group of words (has been dancing).

- *Transitive verbs* need an object of an action, such as the word *ball* in the sentence: I hit the ball.
- *Intransitive verbs* need only a subject, such as the word *sun* in the sentence: The sun rises.
- *Linking verbs* connect the subject with a predicate noun, pronoun, or adjective that completes the meaning of the subject (I am Carol).

Verb Phrase

A *verb phrase* consists of a main verb and one or more helping verbs. In the following verb phrase, the main verb is *work* and the helping, or auxiliary, verb is *may*. (Mike may work.)

Some common helping verbs are *can, may, should, might,* and *must.*

The verbs *be, have, do* can stand by themselves as base verbs (We *have* it). But in some sentences they serve as auxiliary verbs. (We *have been* working.)

Verb Tenses

Verb tenses show different time, or tense. There are three divisions of time: present, past, and future. English makes use of six tenses within these categories: present, past,

future, present perfect, past perfect, and future perfect.

The simple tenses express the simple present, past, or future.

Present participles show action continuing in the present. They always end in -ing (Ray is *smiling*). *Past participles* show completed action (Brenda has *read* two books).

present tense:	Brandon smiles. He is smiling.
past tense:	Brandon smiled. He was smiling.
future tense:	Brandon will smile.

The perfect tenses express actions or states of being that do not occur in the simple present, past, or future.

- The *present perfect tense* shows an action or state of being that began in the past and extends to the present: Brenda has read two books by now.
- The *past perfect tense* shows an action completed in the past: Brenda had read one book yesterday.
- The *future perfect tense* shows an action to be completed in the future: Brenda will have read a third book by tomorrow.

Finite and Nonfinite Verbs

A *finite verb* is a verb that can form a complete sentence when combined with a subject. (Sara swims.)

A *nonfinite verb,* or *verbal,* is derived from a verb but is used as another part of speech. The three forms of verbals are gerunds, infinitives, and participles.

- A *gerund* acts as a noun. (*Swimming* is easy.)
- An *infinitive* (*to* + verb) can be used as a noun, adjective, or adverb. (*To swim* (noun) is fun; She is the person *to see* (adjective); Sam practiced *to become* (adverb) a better swimmer.)
- A *participle* serves as an adjective. (Ray joined the *swimming* team.)

Contractions

Contractions are formed with nouns or pronouns and auxiliary verbs or verbs which express a state of being or having. An apostrophe (') replaces the omitted letter or letters.

I am—I'm	*I have—I've*	*I will—I'll*
you are—you're	*you have—you've*	*you will—you'll*
she is—she's	*she has—she's*	*she will—she'll*
he is—he's	*he has—he's*	*he will—he'll*
it is—it's	*it has—it's*	*it will—it'll*
we are—we're	*we have—we've*	*we will—we'll*
they are—they're	*they have—they've*	*they will—they'll*

I had—I'd	*I would—I'd*	*is not—isn't*
you had—you'd	*you would—you'd*	*are not—aren't*
she had—she'd	*she would—she'd*	*was not—wasn't*
he had—he'd	*he would—he'd*	*were not—weren't*
it had—it'd	*it would—it'd*	*will not—won't*
we had—we'd	*we would—we'd*	*would not—wouldn't*
they had—they'd	*they would—they'd*	*cannot—can't*
		could not—couldn't
		should not—shouldn't
		has not—hasn't
		have not—haven't
		had not—hadn't
		does not—doesn't
		do not—don't
		did not—didn't

Regular and Irregular Verbs

Regular verbs are verbs that form the past and perfect tenses by adding -ed to the base form (walk*ed*). Most verbs are regular verbs: I walk (present), I walked (past), I have walked (perfect).

Irregular verbs are verbs that form the past and perfect tenses in a variety of ways.

50 of the Most Common Irregular Verbs

Present	Past	Perfect
begin	began	begun
bend	bent	bent
break	broke	broken

Present	Past	Perfect
blow	blew	blown
bring	brought	brought
buy	bought	bought
choose	chose	chosen
come	came	come
dive	dived, dove	dived
do	did	done
draw	drew	drawn
drink	drank	drunk
drive	drove	driven
eat	ate	eaten
fall	fell	fallen
fly	flew	flown
freeze	froze	frozen

(continued)

50 of the Most Common Irregular Verbs (*continued*)

Present	Past	Perfect
get	got	gotten
go	went	gone
grow	grew	grown
hang	hung	hung
hide	hid	hidden
is/are	was/were	been
know	knew	known
lay	laid	laid
lead	led	led
leave	left	left
lend	lent	lent
lie	lay	lain
read	read	read
ride	rode	ridden
ring	rang	rung
rise	rose	risen
see	saw	seen
shake	shook	shaken
show	showed	shown
shrink	shrank	shrunk
sing	sang	sung
sink	sank	sunk
slide	slid	slid
speak	spoke	spoken
spring	sprang	sprung
steal	stole	stolen
swear	swore	sworn
swim	swam	swum
take	took	taken
tear	tore	torn
wear	wore	worn
wind	wound	wound
write	wrote	written

Adverb

An *adverb* modifies (qualifies, or adds to the meaning of) a verb, an adjective, or another adverb. Adverbs usually tell when, where, how, or to what extent, such as now, inside, quickly, much.

Preposition

A *preposition* is a word or phrase that shows the relationship of a noun to a verb, an adjec- tive, or another noun. In the following list, we can see that some prepositions consist of more than one word.

48 Common Prepositions

about	beside	near
above	besides	next to
according to	between	of
across	beyond	on
after	by	onto
against	down	over
ahead of	during	through
along	except	throughout
among	for	to
around	from	toward
at	in	under
because of	in back of	until
before	in front of	up
behind	instead of	with
below	into	within
beneath	like	without

Conjunction

A *conjunction* is a word that connects other words, phrases, or sentences: and, but, or, so, if, however, therefore, because, except, though, although, unless, when.

Interjection

An *interjection* is a word, phrase, or sound used to express strong emotion or to attract attention. Most interjections are followed by commas or exclamation points.

> *Oh! Hey! Ouch!*
> *Oh,* I guess you're right.
> *Well,* we'll see you soon.
> *Say,* that's a great idea.
> *Why,* you're so smart.

WORDS INTO SENTENCES

Individual words do not communicate very much by themselves. They must be combined in some way to have meaning. The *sentence* is a group of words arranged to express a complete idea. It is the basic unit of grammar. A sentence opens with a capital letter and ends with a punctuation mark, such as a period or a question mark. Every sentence must have a subject and a predicate. There are four types of sentences:

- *Declarative sentences* make statements. (Karen bought ice cream.)
- *Interrogative sentences* ask questions. (Did Karen buy ice cream?)
- *Imperative sentences* give commands or make requests. (Give me ice cream.)
- *Exclamatory sentences* express a strong feeling. (How lucky Karen was to have ice cream!)

Subject and Predicate

A *subject* of the sentence is the part about which something is said. It consists of a noun or some other word that is used like a noun, such as a pronoun, plus the noun's modifiers, if there are any.

Example: In "The newest computer arrived today," the subject is *computer*. The modifier is *The newest*. Together, these three words form the complete subject.

A *predicate* tells something about the subject. It consists of a finite verb, plus its object and its modifiers, if there are any.

Example: In "Michael dribbled the basketball," the subject is *Michael*, and the predicate is *dribbled the basketball*.

A *compound subject* consists of two words that are both the subjects of a single verb. (Denise and Jodie saw the movie.)

A *compound predicate* consists of two or more finite verbs. (She *cooks and bakes*.)

Object

An *object* is a complement (a word or words that complete the meaning begun by the subject and verb) that does not refer to the subject. A sentence does not have to contain an object, but many sentences do.

- A *direct object* is a noun or a word used like a noun that is directly acted on by the subject through the verb's action. (Jamie won the *prize*.)
- An *indirect object* is a noun or a word used like a noun that identifies for whom or for which or to whom or to which the action of a verb is performed. (Jasmine sent *him* a card.)
- A *prepositional object* is a noun or a word used like a noun that follows a preposition and completes the prepositional phrase. (She coughed in *his face*.)

CLAUSE OR PHRASE?

A lot of people mix up clauses and phrases. Both express a single idea, so what is the difference between a clause and a phrase?

A *clause* is a group of words containing a subject and a predicate. A complete sentence is known as a *main*, or *independent*, clause. (He was sleeping.)

A *subordinate*, or *dependent*, clause begins with a subordinating conjunction, such as *while*, *unless*, or *because*; or with a relative pronoun, such as *who*, *which*, or *that*. (*Because it's sunny*, he is going to the beach.)

The two kinds of subordinate clauses are called *restrictive* and *nonrestrictive*. A restrictive clause cannot be omitted without changing the meaning of the sentence. In "The girl who was crying awakened the baby," the subordinate clause *who was crying* is restrictive because it is needed to tell us who awakened the baby.

A *nonrestrictive* clause can be omitted without changing the meaning of the sentence. In "Tara, who was crying, awakened the baby," the clause *who was crying* is nonrestrictive because "Tara" tells us who awakened the baby. Note that a nonrestrictive clause just adds extra information and that it is enclosed by commas. A restrictive clause has no commas around it.

A *phrase* is a combination of words that express a single idea. For example, in the sentence "The tall biker laughed," the phrase *The tall biker* functions the same as the one-word noun *Karen* in "Karen laughed." But a phrase does not contain a subject and a predicate because it has no verb.

A common phrase is the *prepositional phrase*. It consists of a preposition, the object of the preposition, and any words that modify them. (Tim ate *in silence*.)

PUNCTUATION

Punctuation is the use of certain marks to make the writer's meaning clear.

4 Punctuation Marks That Signal the End of a Sentence

- The *period* (.) is used at the end of a statement or a command. (Joe lied. Get up.)
- The *question mark* (?) is used after a question. (Did Fido bark?)
- The *exclamation point* (!) is used after an expression of strong feeling. (We won!)
- Four *ellipsis points* (. . . .) at the end of a sentence show that a sentence is incomplete. (If Justine is wrong. . . .)

Pauses Within a Sentence

Some punctuation marks show where to pause within a sentence.

Comma

The *comma* (,) is the most commonly used mark within a sentence. There are ten uses for a comma:

1. Use it after words, phrases, and clauses in a series. (The pencils were red, green, brown, and blue.)
2. Use it to separate the main clauses of a compound sentence except if it is brief. (We were happy to see the movie, but we felt tired afterward.)
3. Use it after addresses and dates. (They lived at 21 Jobs Lane, Southampton, New York, until July 4, 1990.)
4. Use it to set off a word or phrase that

explains a word, (Paul, the company's president, took a vacation.)
5. Use it to set off words like *yes*, *no*, and nouns of address. (No, we missed the party. Caroline, are you okay?)
6. Use it around certain adverbs, phrases, and conjunctions, such as *however* and *for example*. (They wanted, however, to buy more than one lamp.)
7. Use it after words, phrases, and clauses at the beginning of sentence. (If you miss me, send a card.)
8. Use it to set off quotations. ("May I," he asked, "borrow a pen?" "Yes," she answered.")
9. Use it to set off nonrestrictive clauses from the rest of the sentence. (Your mother, who had been laughing, stopped.)
10. Use it to prevent misunderstanding when the words could have more than one meaning. (*Some days after he left for Los Angeles* does not mean the same as *Some days after, he left for Los Angeles*.)

Semicolon

The *semicolon* (;) signals a longer pause than the comma:

- Use it in a compound sentence between two main clauses not joined by a conjunction. (Pink is in fashion this year; black is out.)
- Use it between the two main clauses of a compound sentence joined by a conjunction if they contain commas and the meaning is unclear. (We invited Joan, Larry, and Val; and Elliot will ask Barbara.)

Colon

The *colon* (:) calls attention to what comes next:

- Use it in a business letter following the salutation. (Dear Mr. Jones:)
- Use it after expressions like *as follows* or

the following list. (My favorite sports are as follows: tennis, swimming, baseball, and basketball.)

Dash

The *dash* (—) marks a sudden break in thought.

- Use it to separate a clause or phrase from the rest of the sentence. (You want—admit it—my help.)
- Use it to set off any definition or enumeration or listing within a sentence. (My favorite singers—Madonna and Whitney Houston—will be on the show.)

Ellipsis

Three *ellipsis points* (. . .) are used to indicate missing words or, in dialogue, hesitation. (We asked him to . . . and he refused. "Yes . . . I guess so.")

[] () ' - " " ' ' or 6 Other Punctuation Marks

1. *Parentheses* ( ) enclose explanatory words or phrases which may sometimes be omitted: Our dog (I can't remember when I gave him a bath) needs more exercise. Parentheses also enclose numbers in lists of points: She hopes to (1) win the race; (2) bring the trophy back to America; and (3) set a world record.
2. *Brackets* [ ] set off a writer's explanations, comments, or corrections about what is written within parentheses. (His main point [See previous speech] is that our team can't win.)

Sweet Talk: American Dialects

A *dialect* is a variation of a language spoken by a particular group. All dialects involve differences in pronunciation and vocabulary. In the United States, various regions have different dialects. The following are some examples of American dialects.

New England

A *grinder* is a hero sandwich; a *cabinet* is a milkshake; a *body* means a person; *up and died* means died; the *show* is the movies; and a *yardman* is a gardener.

Southern

A *haint* is a ghost; a *lick* is a blow; a *mess* is a quantity of something; *light bread* is store-bought bread; *comin' up a cloud* means it's going to rain; and *snap beans* are string beans.

Southern Mountains (Hillbilly Speech)

A *man-child* is a baby boy; the *Good-Man* is God; *kinfolks* are relatives; the *mully-grubs* are the blues; *play pretties* are children's toys; *treads* are steps, and *wax* is chewing gum.

Hawaiian

A *bla* is a brother; *bedclothes* are pajamas; a *package* is a bag; *small-little* is small; *fire* is burn; *broke* is tore, and *lab* is bathroom.

American English and British English

It has been said that the United States and Great Britain are two nations divided by a single language. This is true in a number of ways. In the first place, spellings of the same words can be decidedly different. The following list shows some common examples of the variances between American and British spellings.

American	British	American	British
center	centre	jewelry	jewellery
check		labor	labour
(money)	cheque	organization	organisation
color	colour	pajamas	pyjamas
connection	connexion	peddler	pedlar
curb	kerb	program	programme
gray	grey	realize	realise
honor	honour	recognize	recognise
inquire	enquire	theater	theatre
jail	gaol		

The two versions of the English language also differ when it comes to the names for many everyday objects and events. It is easy for a visitor from across the Atlantic to provoke amusement from the natives by calling a cloth used to wipe one's mouth a *napkin* in England, or by asking an American waiter for the *W.C.* The following is a list of some common American terms and their counterparts in the United Kingdom.

American	British	American	British
apartment	flat	line	queue
bathroom	toilet, W.C., or loo	napkin	serviette
candy	sweets	oven	cooker
checkers	draughts	round-trip	
closet	cupboard	ticket	return ticket
corn	maize	suspenders	braces
cracker	biscuit	truck	lorry
diaper	nappy	trunk (of car)	boot
drugstore	chemist's	underpass	subway
faucet	tap	undershirt	vest
gas,		vacation	holiday
gasoline	petrol	vest	waistcoat
hood (of car)	bonnet		

As if confusion about spelling and word choice were not enough, the quotation mark is also used in a substantially different way in the United States and Great Britain. Whereas U.S. usage dictates the use of double quotation marks to indicate speech, British usage employs single quotes. And whereas Americans put periods and commas at the end of a quote within their double quotation marks, the British do just the opposite, placing them outside their single quotation marks.

3. The *apostrophe* (') takes the place of a letter omitted in contractions (they're, can't, he'll). Apostrophes also show possession (the girl's trendy haircut).
4. The *hyphen* (-) links the elements of a compound word (thirty-four). Hyphens are also used to split syllables at the end of a line when space runs out and part of a word must go on the next line (com-puter, elec-tronic).
5. *Quotation marks* (" "), or *double quotation marks*, enclose the direct words of a speaker. (His mom said, "Don't be home too late."). They also enclose the titles of short stories, articles, songs, book chapters, TV and radio shows, poems, and lectures. In addition, they set off unusual uses of words, such as her "best" friend, or a nickname. (They called him "Hoop" because he was a great basketball player.) Quotation marks are also used to set off material taken directly from another source. For example, a writer uses quotation marks to enclose text from another author.
6. Quotations within quotations are set off in *single quotation marks* (' '). ("He said, 'My name is Ted,' and I didn't know what to say," she told her friends.)

WHICH COMES FIRST? HOW TO ALPHABETIZE

In the dictionary, which comes first, *sea gull* or *seafood*? There are two ways of alphabetizing a list of words. Both methods are equally acceptable. Both compare the first letter, then the second letter, and so forth, of the words on a list. In a word-by-word list, only the first word of each entry counts and hyphens are ignored. In the letter-by-letter list, it does not matter if the entry consists of one word or more than one, and spaces and hyphens are ignored.

The *word-by-word system* was used to alphabetize the following list:

sea
sea gull
Sea Side Heights
seafood
seal
seaside
season ticket
seasoning
second best
second name
secondary

Winning Words

The following are the last words given in each of the years since 1965 at the National Spelling Bee. They were all correctly spelled by the student under age 16 who became the national champion.

1965—eczema	1972—macerate	1979—maculature	1986—odontalgia
1966—ratoon	1973—vouchsafe	1980—elucubrate	1987—staphylococci
1967—chihuahua	1974—hydrophyte	1981—sarcophagus	1988—elegiacal
1968—abalone	1975—incisor	1982—psoriasis	1989—spoliator
1969—interlocutory	1976—narcolepsy	1983—Purim	1990—fibranne
1970—croissant	1977—cambist	1984—luge	1991—antipyretic
1971—shalloon	1978—deification	1985—milieu	

Here the same words were alphabetized by using the *letter-by-letter system*:

sea
seafood
sea gull
seal
seaside
Sea Side Heights
seasoning
season ticket

secondary
second best
second name

SPELLING TIPS

In English, there are many different ways of spelling the same sound. The following table shows the ways various common English sounds can be spelled.

Sound	Spellings
a	s*a*t, mer*i*ngue, s*a*lmon, l*au*gh
ah	f*a*ther, *au*nt, c*a*lm, s*e*rgeant, Afrik*aa*ns
aw	s*aw*, c*au*ght, *o*rder, *ough*t, w*a*lk
ay	f*a*de, *ae*robic, pl*ai*n, c*ay*, br*ea*k, n*eig*h, wh*ey*, r*e*gime
ch	*c*ello, *ch*ip, ques*ti*on, na*t*ure
e	*a*ny, g*ue*ss, l*eo*pard, fr*ie*nd, br*ea*d
ee	m*e*, s*ee*, l*ea*, sk*i*, *ei*ther, *Ae*sop, ver*y*, bel*ie*ve, ph*oe*nix
er	*ea*rth, j*er*k, st*ir*, t*ur*n, auth*or*
f	*f*all, tele*ph*one, rou*gh*
ih	h*i*t, *E*nglish, w*o*men, b*u*sy, cabb*a*ge, b*ui*ld, carr*ia*ge, s*ie*ve
i	*i*ce, sl*y*, g*ey*ser, h*i*gh, b*uy*, d*ie*, papa*ya*, *eye*
j	*j*am, le*dg*e, tra*g*edy
k	*k*elp, *ch*aracter, sla*ck*, a*c*re, a*q*ua, a*cc*ount
n	*n*ap, *k*now, *p*neumonia, *g*naw
oh	b*o*ne, *oa*t, s*ou*l, *oh*, f*o*lk, br*oo*ch, cr*ow*, th*ough*, bur*eau*
oo	d*o*, l*oo*, bl*ew*, s*ue*, *you*, cr*ui*se, b*eau*ty
ow	c*ow*, b*ough*, s*au*erkraut

Some Commonly Confused Words

accept to receive; to respond positively

except to leave out (verb); with the exclusion of (preposition)

affect to influence; to pretend

effect a result, an influence, an impression (noun); to bring about (verb)

anxious worried, unhappy

eager pleased but impatient

brake to stop

break to separate

capital a city; money; an uppercase letter

Capitol the building in which the U.S. Congress meets

compare to examine differences and similarities

Some Commonly Confused Words (*continued*)

contrast to examine differences

diagnosis the identification of a disease

prognosis the likely course of a disease

dinner the main meal of the day, at noontime or in the evening

supper the evening meal

dyeing coloring with dye

dying ceasing to live

emigrate to leave a country to live elsewhere

immigrate to enter a country to live there

further an extension in time or degree

farther more distant in space

guerrilla a warrior

gorilla an ape

hole a space, a void

whole complete, intact

its belonging to it

it's it is (contraction)

lay to put; to set down

lie to rest in a horizontal position; to make an untrue statement

liable responsible, likely

libel a defamatory statement

majority more than half

plurality more votes than any other candidate; the margin of victory

peace harmony; the absence of war

piece part of a whole

personal intimate; having to do with a specific person

personnel the employees of a company or organization

pray to address God

prey a victim

principle a moral rule; a law

principal main (adjective); the person in charge; money lent or borrowed (noun)

put (someone) on to mislead someone

put (someone) down to make fun of someone

re-collect to collect again

recollect to remember

sail to ride in a wind-powered boat

sale a discounted offering

stationary not moving

stationery writing materials

talk to to address others

talk with to converse together

whose of which

who's who is (contraction)

your belonging to you

you're you are (contraction)

INFORMATION, PLEASE

Bernstein, Theodore, M. *The Careful Writer: A Modern Guide to English Usage*. Atheneum, 1977.

The Chicago Manual of Style. 13th ed. University of Chicago Press, 1982.

Morris, William, and Mary Morris. *Harper Dictionary of Contemporary Usage*. 2d ed. HarperCollins 1985.

Strunk, William, Jr., and E. B. White. *The Elements of Style*. 3d ed. Macmillan, 1979.

16

LITERATURE

FORMS OF LITERATURE

Authors throughout the ages have used a variety of forms to write about their own experiences, either real or imagined.

Fiction

Writing invented by the author's imagination includes the following major literary forms:

novel A long work about events in the lives of real or imaginary characters. There are many different types of novels, dealing with a wide variety of subjects.

short story A short work usually focusing on one event. Most short stories have fewer characters and simpler plots than novels.

fable A brief story about animals that speak and act like humans. Every fable teaches a moral lesson. The most famous collection of fables is *Aesop's Fables*, created by a Greek slave, Aesop, around 600 B.C. In Aesop's fable about the race between the hare and the tortoise, the lesson is: *Slow and steady wins the race.*

poetry A composition that usually contains meter and rhyme. *Meter* is the arrangement of words in a definite rhythmical pattern. *Rhyme* is the repetition of sounds at the ends of lines or within lines. *Free verse* is a poem without regular rhyme or meter. The three main types of poetry are narrative, dramatic, and lyric.
Narrative poems tell a story. *Epics* are long narrative poems that describe the deeds of a legendary hero, such as the Greek general Odysseus. *Ballads* recount the actions of more popular folk figures, such as Robin Hood and Barbara Allen.
Dramatic poems are poems in which characters tell the story. Dramatic poems with one speaker are called *dramatic monologues*.
Lyric poems are brief, songlike poems. The focus of a lyric poem is on the thoughts and feelings of the poet or speaker.

drama A story consisting of dialogue or conversation that is intended for performance on stage by actors; a play. Most dramas contain stage directions, which describe the settings, characters and their actions. Comedy and tragedy are the two main types of drama.

Comedies are light, amusing dramas that end happily. *Satires* makes fun of the foolish things people do and say. A *comedy of manners* mocks the behavior of a particular social group.

Tragedies are serious dramas that end sorrowfully or disastrously.

A *tragicomedy* describes a serious situation that has a happy ending.

Nonfiction

All writing that is not fiction, including most writing in newspapers, textbooks, and magazines:

history A description of the life of a group of people, a nation, an instutition, or of the events of a certain period.

biography A record of the life of one person.

autobiography A person's own account of his or her life.

diary A person's daily autobiography written as the events occur.

essay An author's opinions and point of view about a subject.

LITERATURE FOR YOUNG PEOPLE

Many literary works are created especially for young people, from preschoolers to teenagers. Other books written for adults are also read by many young people. Examples of adult literature many young people enjoy include the *Iliad*, by the ancient Greek poet Homer, and *The Adventures of Sherlock Holmes*, by Arthur Conan Doyle.

There are several main kinds of literature written for young people, including the following:

Poetry

Many children are introduced to literature through nursery rhymes. These short, simple poems contain lots of action, humor, and musical language. One example of a nursery rhyme book is *The Random House Book of Mother Goose* (1986).

After you outgrow nursery rhymes, you may discover poems written particularly for you. These poems often describe animals and children humorously. The deliberately silly and illogical language, situations, and characters of *nonsense verse* make this kind of humorous poem especially appealing. Two of the best authors of nonsense verse were the English writers Edward Lear (1812–1888) and Lewis Carroll (1832–1898).

Folk literature

Folk literature includes myths, ballads, epics, fairy tales, and folk tales. Most of folk literature was created for adults, but young readers enjoy its simplicity and directness.

Folk literature is one of the oldest forms of literature, existing since prehistoric times. People of long ago told these stories orally, passing them from generation to generation. Therefore, we do not know the identity of the authors who created many of these tales. Only after the invention of the printing press was much folk literature written down.

myths Early peoples created stories called myths to answer questions about the world, such as Why do the seasons change? In these myths, gods and heroes control natural forces.

ballads Ballads are often changed from verse into prose for young people. Wandering minstrels or singers performed early ballads. They kept changing as each generation of minstrels retained the basic stories but added popular heroes of their own time. American ballad heroes include the railroad engineer Casey Jones.

epics Like ballads, epics are often changed into prose for children. Examples of epics you may find appealing are those about the English King Arthur and his Knights of the Round Table.

fairy tales Fairy tales are brief stories

Kids' Magazines

Most of the following magazines can be found in your local library.

Cobblestone
Child Life
Faces
Highlights for Children
Humpty Dumpty's Magazine
Jack and Jill
Kid City
Odyssey
Chickadee
Owl
National Geographic World
Ranger Rick
Zillions

---

about creatures with magical powers, such as fairies, elves, and witches. Cinderella is one of the best-loved fairy tales.

folktale Folktales are brief stories that illustrate the customs, superstitions, and beliefs of ordinary people. One group of American folktales concerns the actions of the legendary lumberjack Paul Bunyan.

Fiction

Here are some of the main kinds of fiction for children:

adventure stories Action-filled stories featuring courageous heroes and cunning villains. An example of an adventure story is Robert Louis Stevenson's *Kidnapped* (1886).

historical fiction Stories that take place in the past. This past can be as long ago as Ancient Greece or as recent as the 1950s. In her novel *Slave Runner* (1973), Paula Fox describes the American slave trade through the eyes of a young boy serving on the crew of a slave ship in 1840.

mysteries and detective fiction Mysteries are stories that usually deal with the solution of a mystery or a crime, while detective stories focus on the investigator who solves the crime. In *The Man in the Woods* (1984) by Rosemary Wells, a girl witnesses a crime and then turns detective when nobody believes her.

fantasies Stories that describe events, situations, and characters that cannot exist in the real world. In L. Frank Baum's *The Wonderful World of Oz* (1900), a Kansas farm girl named Dorothy journeys to see the Wizard.

animal stories Stories in which animals play a major role. Marguerite Henry's *King of the Wind* (1948) describes the adventures of a horse during his journey to England.

science fiction Adventures on other planets and in outer space. Many science fiction stories occur in the future. Other stories involve a time shift, in which a hero or heroine visits the past or the future. In Madeline L'Engle's *A Wrinkle in Time* (1962), a brother and sister are transported to someplace else in the universe.

realistic issues and problems Contemporary fiction that explores serious personal problems or social issues. In Judy Blume's *Are You There God? It's Me, Margaret* (1970), a young girl attempts to solve her religious doubts and personal problems.

Biography

Descriptions of the lives of important or famous people. James Haskins's *I am Somebody!* (1992) describes the life of African-American Reverend Jesse Jackson.

Informational Books

Non-fiction works that teach about almost every subject. Christopher Lampton's *Astronomy* (1987) describes the major discoveries in astronomy throughout history.

Newbery Medal Books

The Newbery Medal is awarded each year by the Association for Library Service to Children to the author of the most distinguished contribution to American literature for children. Here are the award winners:

Year Awarded	Book, Author	Year Awarded	Book, Author
1922	*The Story of Mankind*, Hendrik Willem van Loon	1934	*Invincible Louisa*, Cornelia Lynde Meigs
1923	*The Voyages of Dr. Dolittle*, Hugh Lofting	1935	*Dobry*, Monica Shannon
1924	*The Dark Frigate*, Charles Boardman Hawes	1936	*Caddie Woodlawn*, Carol Ryrie Brink
1925	*Tales from Silver Lands*, Charles Joseph Finger	1937	*Roller Skates*, Ruth Sawyer
1926	*Shen of the Sea*, Arthur Bowie Chrisman	1938	*The White Stag*, Kate Seredy
1927	*Smoky, the Cowhorse*, Will James	1939	*Thimble Summer*, Elizabeth Enright
1928	*Gay-Neck*, Dhan Gopal Mukerji	1940	*Daniel Boone*, James Daugherty
1929	*The Trumpeter of Krakow*, Eric P. Kelly	1941	*Call It Courage*, Armstrong Sperry
1930	*Hitty, Her First Hundred Years*, Rachel Field	1942	*The Matchlock Gun*, Walter D. Edmonds
1931	*The Cat Who Went to Heaven*, Elizabeth Coatsworth	1943	*Adam of the Road*, Elizabeth Janet Gray
1932	*Waterless Mountain*, Laura Adams Armer	1944	*Johnny Tremain*, Esther Forbes
1933	*Young Fu of the Upper Yangtze*, Elizabeth Foreman Lewis	1945	*Rabbit Hill*, Robert Lawson
		1946	*Strawberry Girl*, Lois Lenski
		1947	*Miss Hickory*, Carolyn S. Bailey
		1948	*Twenty-One Balloons*, William Pène Du Bois

Newbery Medal Books (*continued*)

Year Awarded	Book, Author	Year Awarded	Book, Author
1949	*King of the Wind*, Marguerite Henry	1971	*The Summer of the Swans*, Betsy Byars
1950	*The Door in the Wall*, Marguerite de Angeli	1972	*Mrs. Frisby and the Rats of NIMH*, Robert C. O'Brien
1951	*Amos Fortune, Free Man*, Elizabeth Yates	1973	*Julie of the Wolves*, Jean Craighead George
1952	*Ginger Pye*, Eleanor Estes	1974	*The Slave Dancer*, Paula Fox
1953	*Secret of the Andes*, Ann Nolan Clark	1975	*M. C. Higgins the Great*, Virginia Hamilton
1954	*. . . And Now Miguel*, Joseph Krumgold	1976	*Grey King*, Susan Cooper
1955	*The Wheel on the School*, Meindert DeJong	1977	*Roll of Thunder, Hear My Cry*, Mildred D. Taylor
1956	*Carry On, Mr. Bowditch*, Jean Lee Latham	1978	*Bridge to Terabithia*, Katherine Paterson
1957	*Miracles on Maple Hill*, Virginia Sorensen	1979	*The Westing Game*, Ellen Raskin
1958	*Rifles for Watie*, Harold Keith	1980	*A Gathering of Days*, Joan Blos
1959	*The Witch of Blackbird Pond*, Elizabeth George Speare	1981	*Jacob Have I Loved*, Katherine Paterson
1960	*Onion John*, Joseph Krumgold	1982	*A Visit to William Blake's Inn: Poems for Innocent and Experienced Travelers*, Nancy Willard
1961	*Island of the Blue Dolphins*, Scott O'Dell		
1962	*The Bronze Bow*, Elizabeth George Speare	1983	*Dicey's Song*, Cynthia Voigt
1963	*A Wrinkle in Time*, Madeleine L'Engle	1984	*Dear Mr. Henshaw*, Beverly Cleary
1964	*It's Like This, Cat*, Emily Cheney Neville	1985	*The Hero and the Crown*, Robin McKinley
1965	*Shadow of a Bull*, Maja Wojciechowska	1986	*Sarah, Plain and Tall*, Patricia MacLachlan
1966	*I, Juan de Pareja*, Elizabeth Borton de Trevino	1987	*The Whipping Boy*, Sid Fleischman
1967	*Up a Road Slowly*, Irene Hunt	1988	*Lincoln: A Photobiography*, Russell Freedman
1968	*From the Mixed-Up Files of Mrs. Basil E. Frankweiler*, E. L. Konigsburg	1989	*Joyful Noise: Poems for Two Voices*, Paul Fleischman
		1990	*Number the Stars*, Lois Lowry
1969	*The High King*, Lloyd Alexander	1991	*Maniac Magee*, Jerry Spinelli
1970	*Sounder*, William H. Armstrong	1992	*Shiloh*, Phyllis Reynolds Naylor

HISTORY OF LITERATURE

Like the other arts, literature has developed over time.

The Beginnings—late 3000s B.C.

- The ancient Sumerians who live in the region now called Iraq become the first writers of literature.
- Other early Middle Eastern peoples creating literature include the Babylonians, Egyptians, Hebrews, and Assyrians. They write fables, hymns, myths, epics, and histories.

Example: The Old Testament of the Bible.

Ancient Literature in Greek and Rome—900 B.C.–A.D. 300

- Greek literature has several major periods: the Epic Age (its peak c. 700 B.C.), the Lyric Age (c. 800 to 475 B.C.), the Attic Age (about 475 B.C. to 300 B.C.), and the Alexandrian Age (c. 300 B.C. to 146 B.C.). The literary period after the Romans conquer Greece is called the Greco-Roman Age (146 B.C. to A.D. 529).
- In the *Epic Age*, poets create long narrative poems about legendary heroes and the gods and goddesses.

Example: *The Odyssey* (late 8th century B.C.) by Homer

- In the *Lyric Age*, poets write love poems and odes, songs in praise of Greek military victories.

Example: *Odes* (498 B.C.–446 B.C.) by Pindar

- In the *Attic Age*, dramatists compose tragedies and comedies. Thuycidides creates the first "scientific" history, a description of the Peloponnesian War (c. 460 B.C.–c. 399 B.C.). The philosophers Plato (427 B.C.–347 B.C.) and Aristotle (384 B.C.–322 B.C.) write during this period.

Examples: plays—*Prometheus Bound* (date uncertain) by Aeschylus, *The Clouds* (423 B.C.) by Aristophanes, *Medea* (431 B.C.) by Euripedes, *Antigone* (441 B.C.) by Sophocles; philosophical works—*The Republic* (date unknown) by Plato

- In the Alexandrian Age, poets write pastoral poems that describe and praise rural life.

Example: *Idylls* (date unknown) by Theocritus

- In the *Greco-Roman Age*, the Romans copy the main Greek styles in literature. Latin dramatists model their comedies on Greek plays. Latin poets retell Greek myths or write epic poems based on the *Iliad* and the *Odyssey*. Roman leaders compose speeches and histories based on their own experiences that mirror the concerns and values of Roman society.

Examples: plays—*Andria* (166 B.C.) by Terrence; poetry—The *Aeneid* (29 B.C.–19 B.C.) by Virgil, *Metamorphosis* (c. A.D. 2) by Ovid; memoirs—*Commentaries on the Gallic War* (probably 51 B.C.) by Julius Caesar

The Middle Ages—c. 400–c. 1400

- In A.D. 400 Rome falls to the Goths. These groups do not depend on ancient literature since they have their own literary traditions.
- Epic poets record oral legends.
- Narrative stories, or romances, of knightly love, fantasy, and adventure become popular from 900 to 1300. The characters in romances display the chivalric codes associated with feudalism.
- Wandering minstrels compose and entertain noblemen and their ladies with songs of love.
- The Italian poet Dante Allighieri writes the first non-Latin poem. Dante's great work the *Divine Comedy* (1308–21) is the

first poem in a modern language (Italian).

Examples: epic poems—*Boewulf* (c. 700, author unknown); romances—Various tales of King Arthur and the Knights of the Round Table; *Canterbury Tales* (probably 1387) by Geoffrey Chaucer

Renaissance—1300–1600

- Writers rediscover Greek and Roman classics.
- Writers use new literary forms, such as the novel and the sonnet (a fourteen-line poem).

Examples: novels—*Don Quixote* (1605 and 1615) by Miguel de Cervantes; stories—*Decameron* (1349–53) by Giovanni Boccaccio; poetry—*Book of Songs* (c. 1340) by Petrarch, *The Faerie Queen* (1590–96), by Edmund Spenser, plays—*Hamlet* (1599–1601) by William Shakespeare; essays—*Essais* (1580) by Michel de Montaigne

The Age of Reason—1600–1800

- Writers attempt to achieve the clarity and simplicity of Greek and Roman classics. This is called neoclassicism, or the new classicism.
- In France, neoclassicism reaches its peak in drama.

Examples: the tragedies of Pierre Corneille (*Médéé*, c. 1634) and Jean-Baptiste Racine, (*Phèdre*, 1677), and the comedies of Molière (*School for Wives*, 1663).

- Many European writers emphasize reason or logical thinking instead of religious authority. Later, this attitude encourages the development of modern science.

Examples: plays—*Le Cid* (1637) by Pierre Corneille; philosophical romance—*Candide* (1759) by Voltaire.

- But in England, the Civil War (1642–1660) produces works with a strong religious flavor, followed by satires.

Examples: poems—*Paradise Lost* (1667) by John Milton, *The Rape of the Lock* (1712) by Alexander Pope; satires—*Gulliver's Travels* (1726) by Jonathan Swift

Romanticism—1750s–1850s

- Writers turn inward and examine their own feelings. A favorite literary emotion is a sense of melancholy or sadness.
- Nature becomes an important subject. Writers praise its beauty, unity, and goodness.
- Natural human instincts are valued.
- Poetry and novels flourish.

Examples: novels—*Ivanhoe* (1819) by Walter Scott, *Jane Eyre* (1847) by Charlotte Brontë, *Les Misérables* (1862) by Victor Hugo; short stories—*The Fall of the House of Usher* (1839) by Edgar Allan Poe; poetry—*Lyrical Ballads* (1798) by William Wordsworth and Samuel Taylor Coleridge, *The Eve of St. Agnes* (1819) by John Keats

Realism—1850s–1900

- Writers emphasize truthful and accurate descriptions of real life.
- Novels and plays are the dominant literary forms.

Examples: novels—*David Copperfield* (1849–50) by Charles Dickens, *War and Peace* (1863–69) by Leo Tolstoy, *Portrait of a Lady* (1881) by Henry James, *Adventures of Huckleberry Finn* (1884) by Mark Twain; plays—*A Doll's House* (1879) by Henrik Ibsen, *Major Barbara* (1905) by George Bernard Shaw; poetry—*Leaves of Grass* (1855) by Walt Whitman.

The Modern Age—1900–Present

- Writers experiment with many forms and techniques. World War I (1914–1918) and the study of the unconscious mind by the Austrian physician Sigmund Freud (1856–1939) cause writers to rebel against old ideas.
- In the 1920s, rootless and disillusioned characters dominate literature.
- In the 1930s, the Great Depression causes writers to focus on unjust social conditions.
- In the 1950s, Japanese and Latin American writers achieve international fame.

Examples: novels—*Ulysses* (1922) by James Joyce, *The Great Gatsby* (1925) by F. Scott Fitzgerald, *The Sun Also Rises* (1926) by Ernest Hemingway, *One Hundred Years of Solitude* (1968) by Gabriel García Marquez; plays—*The Cherry Orchard* (1904) by Anton Chekhov, *The Glass Menagerie* (1944) by Tennessee Williams, *Death of a Salesman* (1949) by Arthur Miller, *Waiting for Godot* (1955) by Samuel Beckett, *Long Day's Journey into Night* (1956) by Eugene O'Neill; poetry—*The Wasteland* (1922) by T. S. Eliot, *Cantos* (1925 and later) by Ezra Pound, *The Shield of Achilles* (1955) by W. H. Auden, *The Dolphin* (1973) by Robert Lowell

IMPORTANT U.S. AND CANADIAN AUTHORS AND THEIR WORKS

Any list of "important" authors is subject to debate. The following list includes writers who have had a substantial impact on American and Canadian literature, whether as a result of a single work or an entire oeuvre. This list is not all-inclusive, but it does contain most of the authors who are generally considered to have made a substantial contribution to American and Canadian literature.

The titles and dates of first publication of each author's major works are given. An asterisk (*) before a book title designates a book that was awarded a Pulitzer Prize in literature. An asterisk before an author's name indicates that he or she has written a book or books of particular interest to young people. A plus sign (+) indicates that the work was awarded a National Book Award. A dagger (†) indicates that the author was awarded a Nobel Prize in Literature. In those instances where an author is known by a pseudonym, he or she is listed by that pseudonym with the real name in brackets. The letter C. inside the parenthesis indicates that the author is Canadian.

*Agee, James (1909–55): *Let Us Now Praise Famous Men* (1941), **A Death in the Family* (1957), *Agee on Film* (1958)

Aiken, Conrad (1889–1973): *The House of Dust: A Symphony* (1920), **Selected Poems* (1929), *Conversation; or, Pilgrim's Progress* (1940), *The Soldier* (1944), *The Kid* (1947), *UShant: An Essay* (1952)

*Alcott, Louisa May (1832–88): *Little Women* (1868–69), *Little Men* (1871), *Silver Pitchers and Independence* (1876), *Spinning-Wheel Stories* (1884)

Algren, Nelson (1909–81): *The Man with the Golden Arm* (1949), *A Walk on the Wild Side* (1956)

*Anderson, Sherwood (1876–1941): *Winesburg, Ohio* (1919)

*Asimov, Isaac (1920–92): *Foundation* (1951), *Foundation and Empire* (1952), *Second Foundation* (1953), *Opus 200* (1979), *Foundation Edge* (1983), *Prelude to Foundation* (1989), *Forward the Foundation* (1993)

Atwood, Margaret (C. 1939–): *The Circle Game* (1966), *Surfacing* (1972), *Selected Poems* (1976), *Dancing Girls* (1977), *Life Before Man* (1979), *Bodily Harm* (1981), *The Handmaid's Tale* (1985), *Cat's Eye* (1988)

Auchincloss, Louis [Stanton] (1917–): *Portrait in Brownstone* (1962), *The Winthrop Covenant* (1976), *Life, Law and Letters* (1979), *Diary of a Yuppie* (1987)

Auden, W(ystan) H(ugh) (1907–73): *Spain

(1937), *For the Time Being* (1945), **The Age of Anxiety: A Baroque Eclogue* (1948), *Collected Shorter Poems, 1930–44* (1950), *Making, Knowing and Judging* (1956), *The Dyer's Hand* (1962), *Collected Poems* (1976)

Audubon, John James (1785–1851): *The Birds of America* (1827–38)

Austin, Mary (1868–1934): *Isidro* (1905), *A Woman of Genius* (1912), *The Ford* (1917), *Earth Horizon* (1932)

Baldwin, James (1924–87): *Go Tell It on the Mountain* (1953), *Notes of a Native Son* (1955), *Nobody Knows My Name* (1961), *Another Country* (1962), *Just Above My Head* (1979)

Baraka, Imamu Amiri (formerly LeRoi Jones, 1934–   ): *Dutchman* (1964), *The Slave* (1964), *The Toilet* (1964), *Black Music* (1967), *Black Magic . . .* (1969), *Selected Plays and Prose* (1979), *Selected Poetry* (1979)

Barth, John [Simmons] (1930–   ): *The Sot-Weed Factor* (1960), *Giles Goat-Boy* (1966), *Chimera* (1972), *The Last Voyage of Somebody the Sailor* (1991)

Barthelme, Donald (1931–89): *Come Back, Dr. Caligari* (1964), *Snow White* (1967), *City Life* (1970), *Sixty Stories* (1982)

Bartlett, John (1820–1905): *Familiar Quotations* (1855)

*Baum, Lyman Frank (1856–1919): *The Wonderful Wizard of Oz* (1900)

Beattie, Ann (1947–   ): *Distortions* (1976), *Chilly Scenes of Winter* (1976), *Where You'll Find Me* (1986), *Picturing Will* (1990)

Bellow, Saul (1915–   )†: *Dangling Man* (1944), *+The Adventures of Augie March* (1953), *Henderson the Rain King* (1959), *+Mr. Sammler's Planet* (1971), *Herzog* (1964), *More Die of Heartbreak* (1987), **Humboldt's Gift* (1975), *The Dean's December* (1982)

Benchley, Robert (1889–1945): *Love Conquers All* (1922), *My Ten Years in a Quandary* (1936), *Benchley Beside Himself* (1943)

Benét, Stephen Vincent (1898–1943): **John Brown's Body* (1928), *Ballads and Poems, 1915–30* (1931), *Thirteen O'Clock* (1937), **Western Star* (1943)

Benét, William Rose (1886–1950): *Oxford Anthology of American Literature* (editor, 1938), **The Dust Which Is God* (1941)

Bierce, Ambrose (1842–1914?): *Tales of Soldiers and Civilians* (1891), *Can Such Things Be?* (1893), *The Devil's Dictionary* (1911)

Bontemps, Arna (1902–73): *God Sends Sunday* (1931), *Drums at Dusk* (1939), *Sam Patch* (1951), *One Hundred Years of Negro Freedom* (1961)

Boyle, Kay (1903–   ): *Wedding Day* (1930), *Plagued by the Nightingale* (1931), *Death of a Man* (1936), *Thirty Stories* (1946), *The Underground Woman* (1975), *Fifty Stories* (1980)

*Bradbury, Ray (1920–   ): *The Martian Chronicles* (1950), *The Illustrated Man* (1951), *Fahrenheit 451* (1953), *Something Wicked This Way Comes* (1962), *I Sing the Body Electric* (1969)

Bradstreet, Anne (1612–72): *The Tenth Muse Lately Sprung Up in America* (1650)

Brooks, Gwendolyn (1917–   ): **Annie Allen* (1949), *In the Mecca* (1968), *Family Pictures* (1970)

*Buck, Pearl (1892–1973)†: **The Good Earth* (1931), *My Several Worlds* (1954), *Imperial Woman* (1956), *Command the Morning* (1959), *A Bridge for Passing* (1962)

Burroughs, Edgar Rice (1875–1950): *Tarzan of the Apes* (1914)

Burroughs, William S. (1914–   ): *The Naked Lunch* (1959), *Nova Express* (1964), *Cities of the Red Night* (1981)

Capote, Truman (1924–84): *Other Voices, Other Rooms* (1948), *The Grass Harp* (1951), *Breakfast at Tiffany's* (1958), *In Cold Blood* (1966)

*Cather, Willa (1873–1947): *O Pioneers!* (1913), *The Song of the Lark* (1915), *My*

Antonia (1918), **One of Ours* (1922), *Shadows on the Rock* (1931)

Chandler, Raymond (1888–1959): *The Big Sleep* (1939), *Farewell, My Lovely* (1940), *The Long Goodbye* (1954)

Cheever, John (1912–82): *+The Wapshot Chronicle* (1957), *The Wapshot Scandal* (1964), *Falconer* (1977), **The Stories of John Cheever* (1978)

Chopin, Kate (1851–1904): *Bayou Folk* (1894), *The Awakening* (1899)

[Connor, Ralph] Gordon, Charles William (c. 1860–1937): *Black Rock: A Tale of the Selkirks* (1898), *The Sky Pilot: A Tale of the Foothills* (1899), *The Men from Glengarry: A Tale of the Ottawa* (1901), *Glengarry School Days: A Story of Early Days in Glengarry* (1902), *The Foreigner: A Tale of Saskatchewan* (1909), *The Sky Pilot in No Man's Land* (1919)

*Cooper, James Fenimore (1789–1851): *The Spy* (1821), *The Pioneers* (1823), *The Pilot* (1823), *The Last of the Mohicans* (1826), *The Prairie* (1827), *The American Democrat* (1838), *The Pathfinder* (1840), *The Deerslayer* (1841)

*Crane, Stephen (1871–1900): *Maggie: A Girl of the Streets* (1893), *The Red Badge of Courage* (1895), *The Black Riders* (1895), *The Open Boat* (1898), *The Monster* (1899)

*cummings, e.e. [Edward Estlin] (1894–1962): *The Enormous Room* (1922), *&* (1925), *is 5* (1926), *50 Poems* (1940), *I × I* (1944), *95 Poems* (1958), *Poems 1923–1954* (1955)

Davies, Robertson (C. 1913–): *A Mixture of Frailties* (1958), *Fifth Business* (1970), *The Rebel Angels* (1981), *What's Bred in the Bone* (1985), *Murther and Walking Spirits* (1991)

*Dickinson, Emily (1830–86): *Poems* (1890), *Poems: Second Series* (1891), *Poems: Third Series* (1896), *The Single Hound* (1914)

Didion, Joan (1934–): *Slouching Towards Bethlehem* (1968), *The White Album* (1979), *Play It As It Lays* (1970), *Democracy* (1984)

Dillard, Annie (1945–): **Pilgrim at Tinker Creek* (1974), *Teaching a Stone To Talk* (1982), *The Living* (1992)

Doctorow, E(dgar) L(awrence) (1931–): *The Book of Daniel* (1971), *Ragtime* (1975), *Loon Lake* (1980), *World's Fair* (1986), *Billy Bathgate* (1989)

Dos Passos, John (1896–1970): *Manhattan Transfer* (1925), *The 42nd Parallel* (1930), *1919* (1932), *The Big Money* (1936)

Dreiser, Theodore (1871–1945): *Sister Carrie* (1900), *The Financier* (1912), *The Titan* (1914), *The Genius* (1915), *An American Tragedy* (1925)

Edel, Leon (1907–): **+Henry James: A Life* (5 vols, 1953–72), *Bloomsbury, A House of Lions* (1979), *Stuff of Sleep and Dreams* (1982)

Eliot, T(homas) S(tearns) (1888–1965)†: *Prufrock and Other Observations* (1917), *The Waste Land* (1922), *Murder in the Cathedral* (1935), *Four Quartets* (1943)

Ellison, Ralph (1914–): *+Invisible Man* (1952)

Emerson, Ralph Waldo (1803–82): "Nature" (1836), "The American Scholar" (1837), *Essays: First Series* (1841), *Essays: Second Series* (1844), *Conduct of Life* (1860), *Society and Solitude* (1870)

Faulkner, William (1897–1962)†: *Soldier's Pay* (1926), *Sartoris* (1929), *The Sound and the Fury* (1929), *As I Lay Dying* (1930), *Absalom, Absalom!* (1936), *The Hamlet* (1940), **A Fable* (1954), **The Reivers* (1962)

Fitzgerald, F. Scott (1896–1940): *Tales of the Jazz Age* (1922), *The Great Gatsby* (1925), *Tender Is the Night* (1934), *The Last Tycoon* (1941)

Franklin, Benjamin (1706–90): *Poor Richard's Almanack* (1733–58), *Autobiography* (1771–88)

*Frost, Robert (1874–1963): *North of Boston* (1914), *Mountain Interval* (1916), **New Hampshire* (1923), **Collected Poems* (1930), **A Further Range* (1936), **A Witness Tree* (1942), *In the Clearing* (1962)

Gardner, John (1933–82): *Grendel* (1971), *October Light* (1976), *Freddy's Book* (1980)

Ginsberg, Allen (1926–   ): *Howl and Other Poems* (1956), *Kaddish and Other Poems* (1961), +*The Fall of America: Poems of These States* (1973)

*****Hammett, Dashiell** (1894–1961): *The Maltese Falcon* (1930), *The Thin Man* (1932)

Hawkes, John (Clendennin Burne, Jr.) (1925–   ): *The Lime Twig* (1961), *The Blood Oranges* (1971), *Death, Sleep and the Traveler* (1974)

*****Hawthorne, Nathaniel** (1804–64): *Twice-Told Tales* (1837; enlarged 1842), *The Scarlet Letter* (1850), *The House of the Seven Gables* (1851)

*****Heinlein, Robert A.** (1907–88): *Stranger in a Strange Land* (1961), *Time Enough for Love* (1973)

Heller, Joseph (1923–   ): *Catch-22* (1961), *Something Happened* (1974), *Good as Gold* (1979)

Hellman, Lillian (1905–84): *An Unfinished Woman* (1969), *Pentimento* (1973), *Scoundrel Time* (1976)

Hemingway, Ernest (1899–1961)†: *The Sun Also Rises* (1926), *A Farewell to Arms* (1929), *To Have and Have Not* (1937), *For Whom the Bell Tolls* (1940), **The Old Man and the Sea* (1952), *A Moveable Feast* (1964)

*****Henry, O. [William Sydney Porter]** (1862–1910): *Cabbages and Kings* (1904), *The Four Million* (1906), *The Trimmed Lamp* (1907), *The Voice of the City* (1908), *Whirligigs* (1910), *Strictly Business* (1910), *Sixes and Sevens* (1911), *Rolling Stones* (1913), *Postscripts* (1923)

Hersey, John [Richard] (1914–   ): **A Bell for Adano* (1944), *Hiroshima* (1946), *The Wall* (1950)

Howells, William Dean (1837–1920): *The Rise of Silas Lapham* (1885), *A Traveler from Altruria* (1894)

*****Hughes, Langston** (1902–67): *The Weary Blues* (1926), *The Ways of White Folks* (1934), *Shakespeare in Harlem* (1941), *Ask Your Mama* (1961)

*****Hurston, Zora Neale** (1891–1960): *Mules and Men* (1935), *Their Eyes Were Watching God* (1937), *Dust Tracks on a Road* (1942)

*****Irving, Washington** (1783–1859): *History of New York* (1809), *The Sketch Book* (1819–20), *The Crayon Miscellany* (3 vols., 1835)

Jackson, Shirley (1919–65): *The Lottery* (1949), *The Bird's Nest* (1954), *The Haunting of Hill House* (1959), *We Have Always Lived in the Castle* (1962)

James, Henry (1843–1916): *The American* (1877), *The Europeans* (1878), *Daisy Miller* (1879), *The Portrait of a Lady* (1881), *The Bostonians* (1886), *Embarrassments* (1896), *The Two Magics* (1898), *The Awkward Age* (1899), *The Ambassadors* (1903), *The Golden Bowl* (1904)

*****Jarrell, Randall** (1914–65): *Selected Poems* (1955), +*The Woman at the Washington Zoo* (1960)

Kerouac, Jack (1922–69): *On the Road* (1957), *The Dharma Bums* (1958), *Desolation Angels* (1965)

Kosinski, Jerzy (1933–91): *The Painted Bird* (1965), +*Steps* (1968), *Being There* (1971), *Cockpit* (1975), *The Hermit of Sixty-Ninth Street* (1988)

Lardner, Ring (1885–1933): *You Know Me, Al: A Busher's Letters* (1916), *How to Write Short Stories* (1924), *The Love Nest and Other Stories* (1926)

Leacock, Stephen (1869–1944): *Literary Lapses* (1910), *Nonsense Novels* (1911), *Sunshine Sketches of a Little Town* (1912), *Arcadian Adventures with the Idle Rich* (1914), *My Discovery of the West* (1937)

*****Lewis, Sinclair** (1885–1951)†: *Main Street* (1920), *Babbitt* (1922), **Arrowsmith* (1925), *Dodsworth* (1929)

*****London, Jack** (1876–1916): *The Call of the Wild* (1903), *The Sea-Wolf* (1904), *White Fang* (1906), *The Iron Heel* (1908), *Martin Eden* (1909)

*****Longfellow, Henry Wadsworth** (1807–82): *Voices of the Night* (1839), *Ballads and*

Other Poems (1841), *Hiawatha* (1855), *The Courtship of Miles Standish* (1858), *The Tales of a Wayside Inn* (1863)

Lowell, James Russell (1819–91): *A Fable for Critics* (1848), *The Vision of Sir Launfal* (1848), *The Cathedral* (1869)

Lowell, Robert (1917–77): *Land of Unlikeness* (1944), *Lord Weary's Castle* (1946), *The Mill of the Kavanaughs* (1951), *Old Glory* (1964), *Dolphin* (1973)

Mailer, Norman (1923–   ): *The Naked and the Dead* (1948), *An American Dream* (1965), *The Armies of the Night* (1968), *The Executioner's Song* (1979), *Ancient Evenings* (1983), *Tough Guys Don't Dance* (1987), *Harlot's Ghost* (1990)

Malamud, Bernard (1914–86): *The Natural* (1961), *+The Fixer* (1967), *+The Magic Barrel* (1958), *The Tenants* (1971), *God's Grace* (1982), *A New Life* (1988)

McCarthy, Mary (1912–89): *The Groves of Academe* (1952), *Memories of a Catholic Girlhood* (1957), *The Group* (1963), *Cannibals and Missionaries* (1979), *Intellectual Memoirs: New York, 1936–1938* (1992)

*McCullers, Carson** (1917–67): *The Heart is a Lonely Hunter* (1940), *Member of the Wedding* (1946), *Clock Without Hands* (1961)

*Melville, Herman** (1819–91): *Typee* (1846), *Omoo* (1847), *White-Jacket* (1850), *Moby-Dick* (1851)

Mencken, H(enry) L(ouis) (1880–1956): *The American Language* (1919, revised 1921, 1923, 1936; supplements in 1945, 1948)

Michener, James (1907–   ): *Tales of the South Pacific* (1947), *Hawaii* (1959), *The Drifters* (1971), *Chesapeake* (1978), *Alaska* (1988), *Mexico* (1992)

Miller, Henry (1891–1980): *Tropic of Cancer* (1934), *Tropic of Capricorn* (1939)

Mitchell, Margaret (1900–49): *Gone With the Wind* (1936)

*Montgomery, Lucy Maude** (C. 1874–1942):

Anne of Green Gables (1908), *Emily of New Moon* (1923), *The Blue Castle* (1926), *A Tangled Web* (1931), *Jane of Lantern Hill* (1937)

Morrison, Toni [Chloe Anthony Wofford] (1931–   ): *The Bluest Eye* (1970), *Sula* (1973), *+Song of Solomon* (1977), *Tar Baby* (1981), *Beloved* (1987), *Jazz* (1992)

Munro, Alice (C. 1931–   ): *Dance of the Happy Shades* (1968), *Lives of the Girls and Women* (1971), *Who Do You Think You Are* (1978), *The Progress of Love* (1986)

Oates, Joyce Carol (1938–   ): *A Garden of Earthly Delights* (1967), *Expensive People* (1968), *+them* (1969), *Bellefleur* (1980), *On Boxing* (1987), *You Must Remember This* (1988), *American Appetites* (1989), *Black Water* (1992)

Paine, Thomas (1737–1809): *Common Sense* (1776), *The Age of Reason* (1794–95)

Parker, Dorothy (1893–1967): *Men I'm Not Married To* (1922), *Women I'm Not Married To* (1922), *Laments for the Living* (1930), *After Such Pleasures* (1933), *Here Lies* (1942), *Collected Poems: Not So Deep as a Well* (1937)

Percy, Walker (1916–90): *+The Moviegoer* (1961), *The Last Gentleman* (1966), *Love in the Ruins* (1971), *The Thanatos Syndrome* (1987)

Plath, Sylvia 1932–63): *The Colossus* (1960), *The Bell Jar* (1963), *Ariel* (1965), *Collected Poems* (1981)

*Poe, Edgar Allan** (1809–49): *Poems by Edgar A. Poe* (1831), *Tales of the Grotesque and Arabesque* (1840), *Tales* (1845), *The Raven and Other Poems* (1845)

Porter, Katherine Anne (1890–1980): *Flowering Judas* (1930), *Pale Horse, Pale Rider* (1939), *The Leaning Tower* (1944), *Ship of Fools* (1962), *Collected Stories* (1965)

Pound, Ezra (1885–1972): *Cantos* (1970)

Pratt, E. J. (C. 1882–1964): *The Witches'*

ATLAS

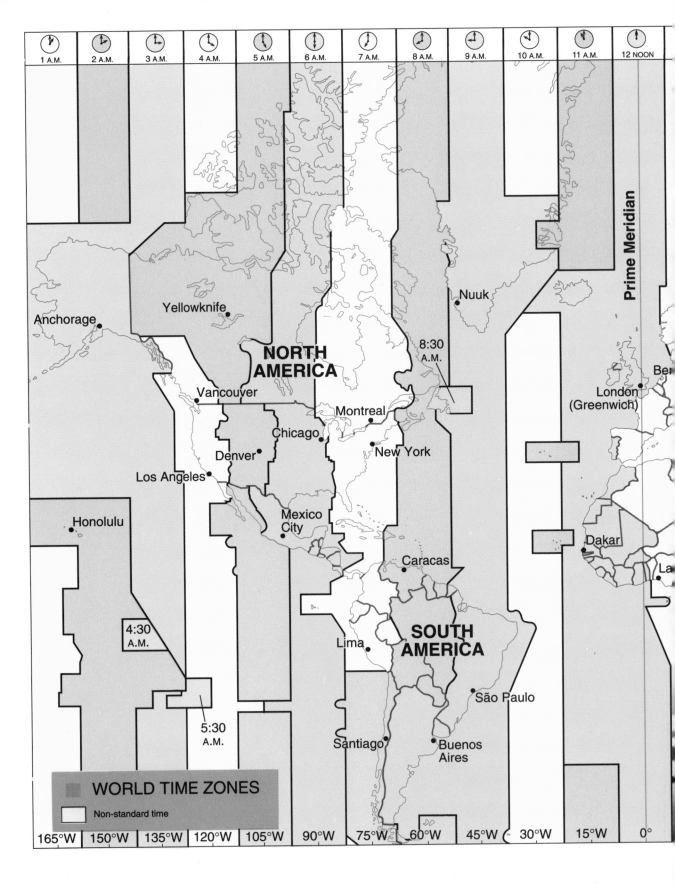

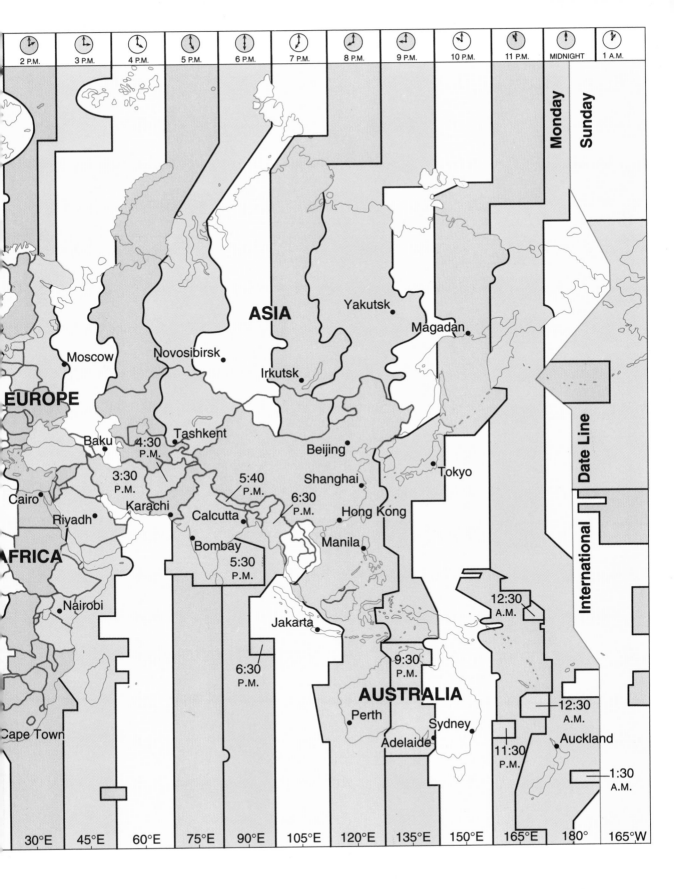

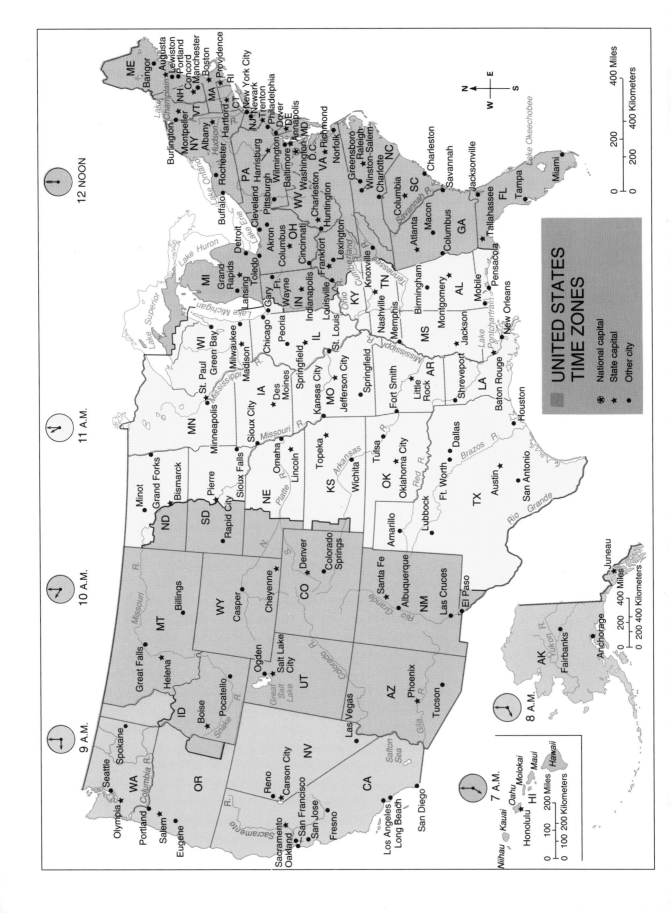

UNITED STATES
TIME ZONES

National capital ⊛
State capital ★
Other city •

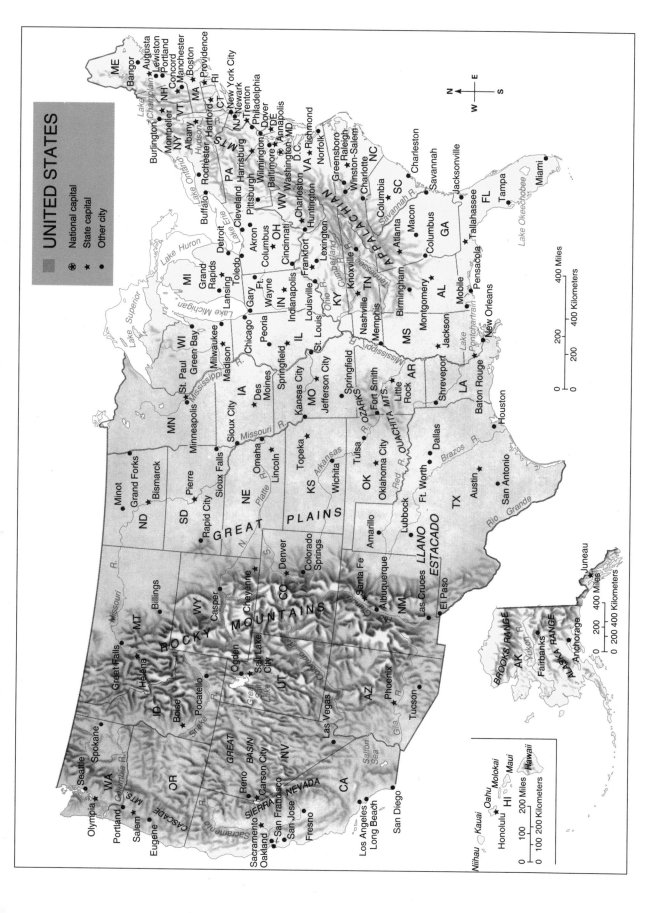

UNITED STATES

⊛ National capital
★ State capital
• Other city

N E
W S

400 Miles
0
0   200   400 Kilometers
0   200   400

200 Miles
0   100   200 Kilometers
0   100   200

ALASKA

BROOKS RANGE
Yukon R.
AK
Fairbanks
ALASKA RANGE
Anchorage
Juneau ★

0   200   400 Miles
0   200   400 Kilometers

HAWAII

Niihau   Kauai
Oahu   Molokai
Honolulu ★   HI   Maui
Hawaii

0   100   200 Miles
0   100   200 Kilometers

Seattle
Spokane
WA
Olympia ★
Portland
Salem ★
Eugene
OR
CASCADE MTS.
Columbia R.
Boise ★
Pocatello
ID
Great Falls
Helena ★
MT
Billings
ROCKY MOUNTAINS
Snake R.
GREAT BASIN
Carson City ★
Reno
NV
Sacramento ★
San Francisco
San Jose
Oakland
SIERRA NEVADA
Fresno
CA
Los Angeles
Long Beach
San Diego
Las Vegas
Salton Sea
AZ
Phoenix
Tucson
Gila R.
Salt Lake City ★
Ogden
Great Salt Lake
UT
Colorado R.
Santa Fe ★
Albuquerque
NM
Las Cruces
El Paso
Denver ★
Colorado Springs
CO
Cheyenne ★
Casper
WY
Great Falls
Rapid City
SD
Pierre ★
Minot
Grand Forks
Bismarck ★
ND
Missouri R.
GREAT PLAINS
LLANO ESTACADO
Amarillo
Lubbock
TX
Austin ★
San Antonio
Houston
Rio Grande
Brazos R.
Red R.
Dallas
Ft. Worth
Oklahoma City ★
OK
OUACHITA MTS.
Tulsa
Wichita
KS
Topeka ★
Lincoln ★
Omaha
NE
Platte R.
Sioux Falls
Sioux City
Des Moines ★
IA
Minneapolis
St. Paul ★
MN
Mississippi R.
WI
Green Bay
Milwaukee
Madison ★
Chicago
Peoria
Springfield ★
IL
Kansas City
MO
Jefferson City ★
St. Louis
Springfield
OZARKS
Fort Smith
Little Rock ★
AR
Shreveport
LA
Baton Rouge ★
New Orleans
Lake Pontchartrain
Arkansas R.
Mississippi R.
MS
Jackson ★
Memphis
Nashville ★
TN
Birmingham
Montgomery ★
AL
Mobile
Pensacola
Tennessee R.
Cumberland R.
KY
Frankfort ★
Louisville
Lexington
Knoxville
IN
Indianapolis ★
Ft. Wayne
Gary
Ohio R.
Cincinnati
Columbus ★
OH
Akron
Cleveland
Toledo
Detroit
Lansing ★
Grand Rapids
MI
Lake Michigan
Lake Superior
Lake Huron
Lake Erie
Lake Ontario
APPALACHIAN MTS.
WV
Charleston ★
Huntington
Pittsburgh
PA
Harrisburg ★
VA
Richmond ★
Norfolk
Greensboro
Raleigh ★
Winston-Salem
Charlotte
NC
Columbia ★
SC
Charleston
GA
Atlanta ★
Columbus
Macon
Savannah
Savannah R.
Jacksonville
Tallahassee ★
FL
Tampa
Lake Okeechobee
Miami
New Orleans

Bangor
ME
Augusta ★
Lewiston
Portland
Concord ★
NH
Manchester
Boston ★
MA
Providence ★
RI
Hartford ★
CT
New York City
Newark
NJ
Trenton ★
Philadelphia
Dover ★
DE
Baltimore
Annapolis ★
MD
Washington D.C. ⊛
Wilmington
Montpelier ★
VT
Burlington
Albany ★
NY
Rochester
Buffalo
Lake Champlain
Hudson R.
Lake Erie

400 Miles
0
0   200   400 Kilometers
0   200   400

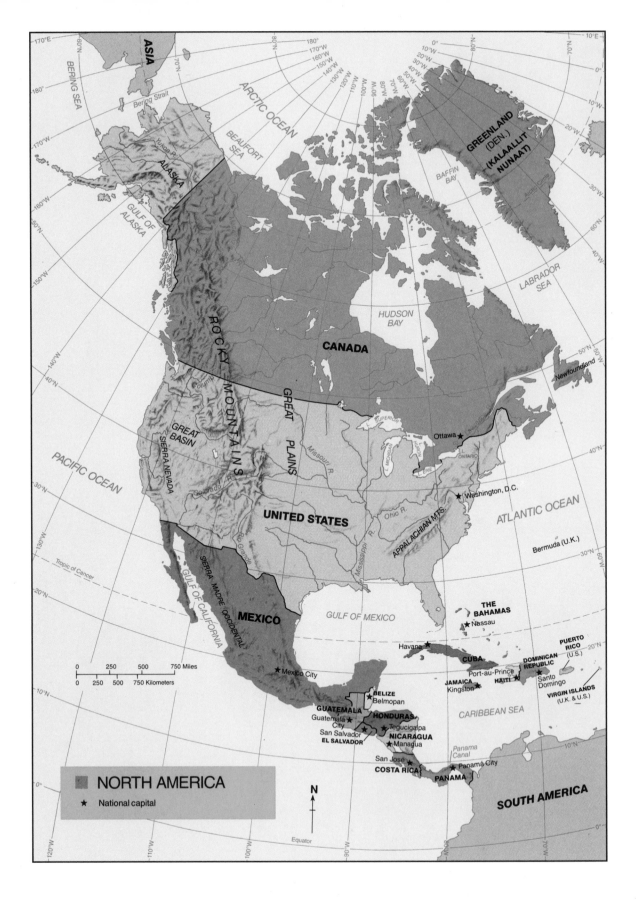

ASIA

BERING SEA

ARCTIC OCEAN

BEAUFORT SEA

ALASKA

GULF OF ALASKA

GREENLAND (DEN.) (KALAALLIT NUNAAT)

BAFFIN BAY

LABRADOR SEA

HUDSON BAY

CANADA

Newfoundland

PACIFIC OCEAN

R O C K Y   M O U N T A I N S

GREAT PLAINS

GREAT BASIN

SIERRA NEVADA

Ottawa ★

ONTARIO

Columbia R.

Missouri R.

UNITED STATES

Colorado

Washington, D.C. ★

Ohio R.

APPALACHIAN MTS.

ATLANTIC OCEAN

Mississippi R.

Rio Grande

Tropic of Cancer

SIERRA MADRE OCCIDENTAL

GULF OF CALIFORNIA

Bermuda (U.K.)

MEXICO

GULF OF MEXICO

THE BAHAMAS
★ Nassau

PUERTO RICO (U.S.)

Havana ★

CUBA

DOMINICAN REPUBLIC

Mexico City ★

Port-au-Prince ★

Santo Domingo

JAMAICA
Kingston ★

HAITI ★

VIRGIN ISLANDS (U.K. & U.S.)

BELIZE
★ Belmopan

GUATEMALA
★ Guatemala City

HONDURAS ★ Tegucigalpa

CARIBBEAN SEA

San Salvador ★
EL SALVADOR

NICARAGUA
★ Managua

Panama Canal

San José ★
COSTA RICA

★ Panamá City

PANAMA

SOUTH AMERICA

0   250   500   750 Miles
0   250   500   750 Kilometers

■ NORTH AMERICA

★ National capital

N

Equator

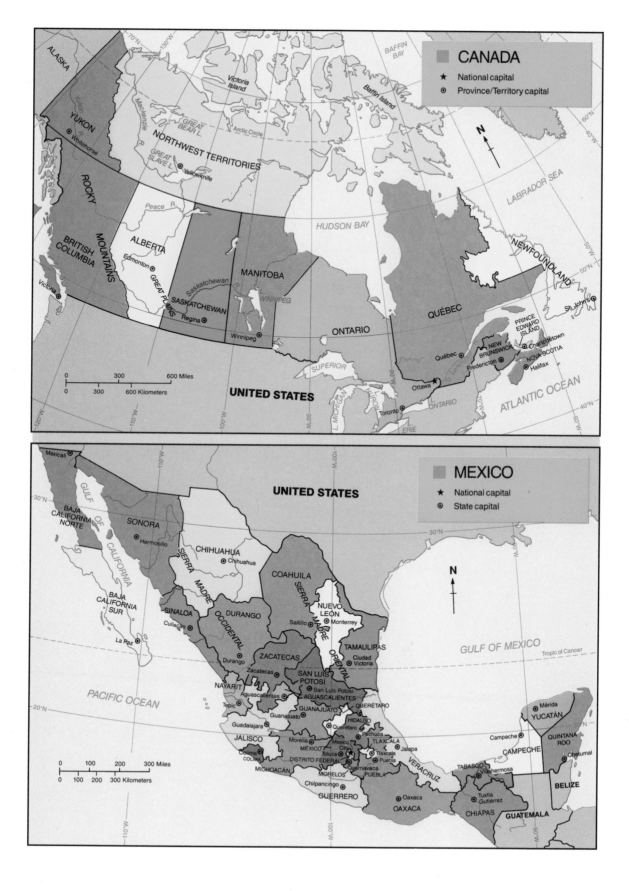

CANADA

★ National capital
⊙ Province/Territory capital

ALASKA

BAFFIN
BAY

Victoria
Island

Baffin Island

YUKON

Whitehorse ⊙

Mackenzie R.

GREAT
BEAR L.

Arctic Circle

NORTHWEST TERRITORIES

GREAT
SLAVE L.

Yellowknife ⊙

LABRADOR SEA

ROCKY

MOUNTAINS

BRITISH
COLUMBIA

Peace R.

ALBERTA

Edmonton ⊙

GREAT PLAINS

Saskatchewan R.

HUDSON BAY

NEWFOUNDLAND

MANITOBA

Victoria ⊙

SASKATCHEWAN

Regina ⊙

WINNIPEG

Winnipeg ⊙

QUÉBEC

St. John's ⊙

ONTARIO

PRINCE
EDWARD
ISLAND

Charlottetown ⊙

0   300   600 Miles

0   300   600 Kilometers

SUPERIOR

UNITED STATES

L. MICHIGAN

HURON

Québec ⊙

NEW
BRUNSWICK

Fredericton ⊙

NOVA SCOTIA

Halifax ⊙

Ottawa ★

L. ONTARIO

Toronto ⊙

ERIE

ATLANTIC OCEAN

MEXICO

★ National capital
⊙ State capital

Mexicali ⊙

UNITED STATES

GULF OF CALIFORNIA

BAJA
CALIFORNIA
NORTE

SONORA

Hermosillo ⊙

CHIHUAHUA

Chihuahua ⊙

COAHUILA

GULF OF MEXICO

BAJA
CALIFORNIA
SUR

SIERRA

MADRE

SIERRA

MADRE

ORIENTAL

NUEVO
LEÓN

Saltillo ⊙

Monterrey ⊙

La Paz ⊙

SINALOA

Culiacán ⊙

OCCIDENTAL

DURANGO

Durango ⊙

ZACATECAS

Zacatecas ⊙

TAMAULIPAS

Ciudad
Victoria ⊙

Tropic of Cancer

PACIFIC OCEAN

NAYARIT

Tepic ⊙

Aguascalientes ⊙

SAN LUIS
POTOSÍ

San Luis Potosí ⊙

AGUASCALIENTES

GUANAJUATO

Guanajuato ⊙

QUERÉTARO

Querétaro ⊙

HIDALGO

Pachuca ⊙

MÉRIDA

Mérida ⊙

YUCATÁN

Campeche ⊙

QUINTANA
ROO

Chetumal ⊙

Guadalajara ⊙

JALISCO

Morelia ⊙

MÉXICO

Mexico
City

Toluca ⊙

DISTRITO FEDERAL

TLAXCALA

Tlaxcala ⊙

Jalapa ⊙

Puebla ⊙

CAMPECHE

Colima ⊙

COLIMA

MICHOACÁN

Cuernavaca ⊙

MORELOS

PUEBLA

VERACRUZ

TABASCO

Villahermosa ⊙

BELIZE

0   100   200   300 Miles

0   100   200   300 Kilometers

Chilpancingo ⊙

GUERRERO

Oaxaca ⊙

OAXACA

Tuxtla
Gutiérrez ⊙

CHIAPAS

GUATEMALA

SOUTH AMERICA

★ National capital

NORTH
AMERICA

CARIBBEAN SEA

20°N

10°N

VENEZUELA

★ Caracas

Orinoco R.

GUIANA-HIGHLANDS

★ Georgetown

GUYANA

Paramaribo

SURINAME

★ Cayenne

FRENCH
GUIANA

★ Bogotá

COLOMBIA

0°

Galápagos
Islands (E.C.)

Quito ★

ECUADOR

AMAZON

BASIN

Negro R.

Amazon R.

Equator

PERU

PACIFIC
OCEAN

Lima ★

10°S

BRAZIL

A N D E S

Titicaca

La Paz ★

BOLIVIA

Sucre ★

Madeira R.

São Francisco R.

Brasília ★

BRAZILIAN
HIGHLANDS

20°S

Tropic of Capricorn

CHILE

GRAN CHACO

M O U N T A I N S

PARAGUAY

Paraguay

ATLANTIC
OCEAN

Asunción ★

Paraná R.

30°S

N

ARGENTINA

Santiago ★

PAMPAS

Buenos
Aires ★

URUGUAY

★ Montevideo

40°S

PATAGONIA

0   200   400   600 Miles

0   200   400   600 Kilometers

50°S

Strait of
Magellan

Falkland
Islands
(U.K.)

South
Georgia
Island
(U.K.)

Tierra Del
Fuego

Cape
Horn

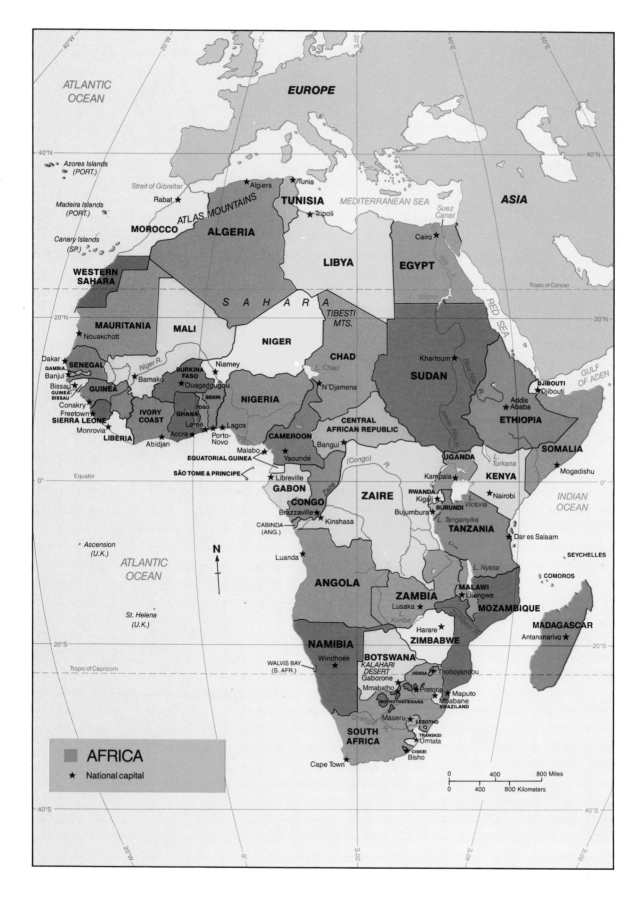

ATLANTIC
OCEAN

Azores Islands
(PORT.)

Madeira Islands
(PORT.)

Canary Islands
(SP.)

EUROPE

MEDITERRANEAN SEA

ASIA

Strait of Gibraltar

★ Algiers

★ Tunis

TUNISIA

Rabat ★

ATLAS MOUNTAINS

★ Tripoli

Suez
Canal

MOROCCO

ALGERIA

LIBYA

EGYPT

Cairo ★

Nile R.

Tropic of Cancer

WESTERN
SAHARA

S A H A R A

L. Nasser

RED SEA

40°N

20°N

MAURITANIA

MALI

TIBESTI
MTS.

Nouakchott

NIGER

GULF
OF ADEN

CHAD

Khartoum ★

Dakar ★

Niamey ★

L. Chad

SUDAN

DJIBOUTI ■

SENEGAL

Bamako ★

BURKINA
FASO

Djibouti

GAMBIA

Niger R.

★ Ouagadougou

N'Djamena ★

Addis
Ababa ★

Banjul

Bissau ★

BENIN

NIGERIA

CENTRAL
AFRICAN REPUBLIC

ETHIOPIA

GUINEA

TOGO

GUINEA-
BISSAU

IVORY
COAST

GHANA

Blue Nile R.

White Nile R.

Conakry ★

Lomé ★

★ Lagos

SOMALIA

Freetown ★

Accra ★

Porto-
Novo

Bangui ★

UGANDA

SIERRA LEONE

Abidjan ★

CAMEROON

Mogadishu ★

Monrovia ★

LIBERIA

Malabo ■

Kampala ★

L.
Turkana

Yaoundé ★

KENYA

EQUATORIAL GUINEA

INDIAN
OCEAN

SÃO TOMÉ & PRINCIPE

Equator

Libreville ★

RWANDA

Nairobi ★

0°

GABON

ZAIRE

Kigali ★

(Congo) R.

CONGO

BURUNDI

L.
Victoria

Ascension
(U.K.)

Brazzaville ★

Bujumbura ★

Zaire R.

Kinshasa ★

L. Tanganyika

TANZANIA

CABINDA
(ANG.)

Dar es Salaam ★

ATLANTIC
OCEAN

N

Luanda ★

SEYCHELLES

L. Nyasa

COMOROS

St. Helena
(U.K.)

ANGOLA

ZAMBIA

MALAWI

Lilongwe ★

MOZAMBIQUE

Lusaka ★

MADAGASCAR

Kariba

Antananarivo ★

20°S

NAMIBIA

ZIMBABWE

Harare ★

Tropic of Capricorn

WALVIS BAY
(S. AFR.)

Windhoek ★

BOTSWANA

KALAHARI
DESERT

VENDA

Thohoyandou ★

Gaborone ★

Mmabatho ★

Pretoria ★

Maputo ★

BOPHUTHATSWANA

Mbabane ★

SWAZILAND

Orange R.

Maseru ★

LESOTHO

TRANSKEI

SOUTH
AFRICA

Umtata ★

CISKEI

Bisho ★

Cape Town ★

AFRICA

★ National capital

0   400   800 Miles

0   400   800 Kilometers

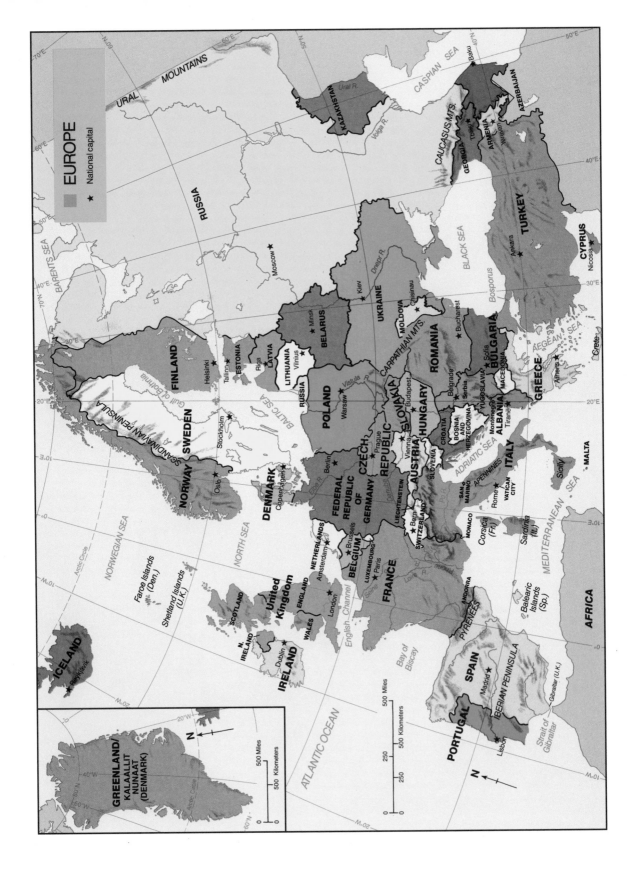

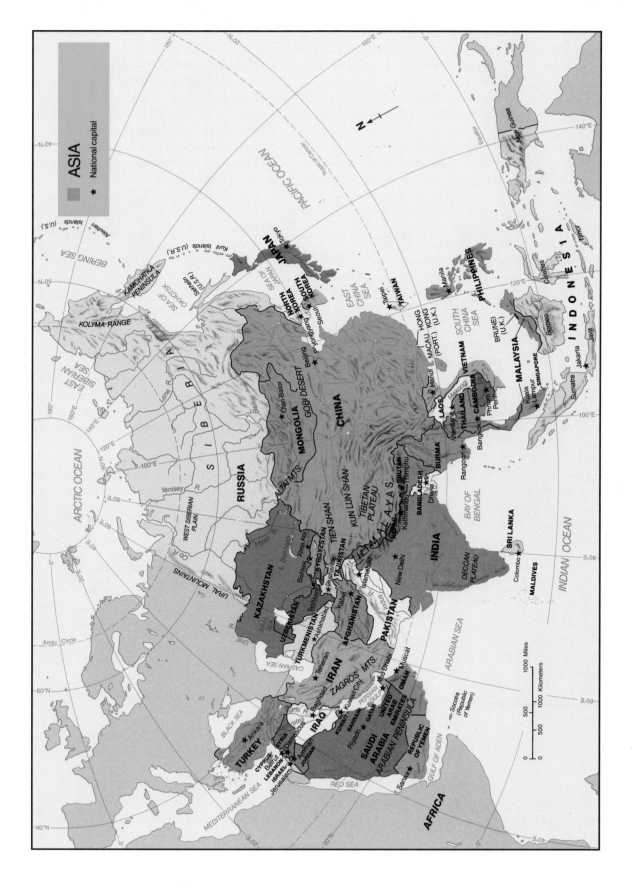

ASIA

★ National capital

N

PACIFIC OCEAN

Tropic of Cancer

Equator

Aleutian Islands (U.S.)

BERING SEA

Kuril Islands (U.S.S.R.)

Sakhalin (U.S.S.R.)

KAMCHATKA PENINSULA

KOLYMA RANGE

SEA OF OKHOTSK

EAST SIBERIAN SEA

S I B E R I A

Lena R.

★ Tokyo

JAPAN

SEA OF JAPAN

NORTH KOREA ★ P'yongyang

SOUTH KOREA ★ Seoul

★ Beijing

EAST CHINA SEA

Taipei ★ TAIWAN

HONG KONG (U.K.)

MACAU (PORT.)

Manila ★ PHILIPPINES

SOUTH CHINA SEA

BRUNEI (U.K.)

Celebes

New Guinea

I N D O N E S I A

Timor

ARCTIC OCEAN

Arctic Circle

Yenisey R.

WEST SIBERIAN PLAIN

Ob R.

RUSSIA

Baikal

Ulan Bator ★

MONGOLIA

GOBI DESERT

ALTAI MTS.

C H I N A

TIBETAN PLATEAU

KUN LUN SHAN

H I M A L A Y A S

Irtysh

URAL MOUNTAINS

Ural

ARAL SEA

L. Balkhash

KAZAKHSTAN

Alma Ata ★

Bishkek ★ KYRGYZSTAN

★ Tashkent

UZBEKISTAN

★ Dushanbe

TAJIKISTAN

TIEN SHAN

BURMA

Rangoon ★

Mekong

LAOS

★ Vientiane

THAILAND

★ Bangkok

VIETNAM

★ Hanoi

CAMBODIA

Phnom Penh ★

MALAYSIA

Kuala Lumpur ★

SINGAPORE ★

Sumatra

Jakarta ★

Borneo

Java

CASPIAN SEA

TURKMENISTAN

★ Ashkhabad

IRAN

★ Tehran

ZAGROS MTS.

AFGHANISTAN

★ Kabul

Indus

PAKISTAN

★ Islamabad

New Delhi ★

I N D I A

DECCAN PLATEAU

NEPAL

★ Kathmandu

BHUTAN

★ Thimphu

BANGLADESH

Dhaka ★

BAY OF BENGAL

SRI LANKA

Colombo ★

MALDIVES

INDIAN OCEAN

BLACK SEA

Ankara ★

TURKEY

CYPRUS

Beirut ★ SYRIA ★ Damascus

LEBANON

ISRAEL ★ Amman

Jerusalem ★ JORDAN

MEDITERRANEAN SEA

Tigris

Euphrates

★ Baghdad

IRAQ

Kuwait City ★ KUWAIT

BAHRAIN ★

QATAR ★

PERSIAN GULF

SAUDI ARABIA

★ Riyadh

UNITED ARAB EMIRATES

★ Abu Dhabi

OMAN

★ Muscat

ARABIAN PENINSULA

REPUBLIC OF YEMEN

★ Sanaa

RED SEA

GULF OF ADEN

Socotra (Republic of Yemen)

ARABIAN SEA

AFRICA

1000 Miles

1000 Kilometers

500

500

0

0

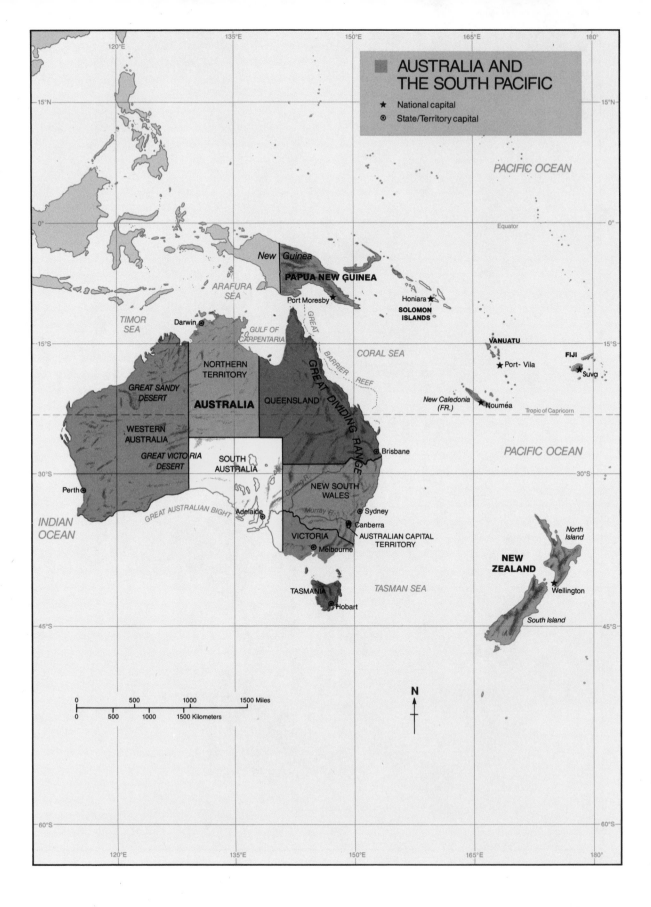

AUSTRALIA AND
THE SOUTH PACIFIC

★ National capital
⊙ State/Territory capital

PACIFIC OCEAN

New Guinea

PAPUA NEW GUINEA

*ARAFURA
SEA*

Port Moresby ★

Honiara ★

**SOLOMON
ISLANDS**

*TIMOR
SEA*

Darwin ⊙

*GULF OF
CARPENTARIA*

CORAL SEA

VANUATU

★ Port- Vila

FIJI

★ Suva

15°S

NORTHERN
TERRITORY

*GREAT
BARRIER
REEF*

*New Caledonia
(FR.)*

★ Nouméa

Tropic of Capricorn

*GREAT SANDY
DESERT*

AUSTRALIA

QUEENSLAND

GREAT DIVIDING RANGE

PACIFIC OCEAN

**WESTERN
AUSTRALIA**

*GREAT VICTORIA
DESERT*

SOUTH
AUSTRALIA

⊙ Brisbane

30°S

Perth ⊙

GREAT AUSTRALIAN BIGHT

Adelaide ⊙

Darling R.

NEW SOUTH
WALES

Murray R.

⊙ Sydney

*INDIAN
OCEAN*

VICTORIA

Canberra
AUSTRALIAN CAPITAL
TERRITORY

⊙ Melbourne

*North
Island*

**NEW
ZEALAND**

TASMANIA

TASMAN SEA

★ Wellington

⊙ Hobart

South Island

45°S

0   500   1000   1500 Miles

0   500   1000   1500 Kilometers

N
↑

Brew (1925), *Titans: Two Poems* (1926), *The Fable of the Goats and Other Poems* (1932), *The Titanic* (1935), *Brebeuf and His Brethren* (1940), *Towards the Last Spike* (1952), *The Collected Poems of E. J. Pratt* (1958)

Pynchon, Thomas (1937–): *V* (1963), +*Gravity's Rainbow* (1973), *Vineland* (1990)

Rand, Ayn (1905–82): *The Fountainhead* (1943), *Atlas Shrugged* (1957)

Richler, Mordecai (C. 1931–): *A Choice of Enemies* (1957), *The Apprenticeship of Duddy Kravitz* (1959), *Cocksure* (1968), *St. Urbain's Horseman* (1971), *Solomon Gursky Was Here* (1989)

Roberts, Sir Charles G. D. (C. 1860–1943): *Orion, and Other Poems* (1880), *In Divers Tones* (1887), *Songs of the Common Day* (1893), *Earth's Enigmas* (1896), *The Vagrant of Time* (1927), *The Iceberg, and Other Poems* (1934), *Further Animal Stories* (1936)

Roth, Philip (1933–): +*Goodbye, Columbus* (1959), *Letting Go* (1962), *Portnoy's Complaint* (1969), *The Great American Novel* (1973), *The Ghost Writer* (1979), *The Counterlife* (1987), *The Facts: A Novelist's Autobiography* (1988), *Deception* (1991)

*Salinger, J. D. (1919–): *The Catcher in the Rye* (1951), *Franny and Zooey* (1961)

Sandburg, Carl (1878–1967): *Chicago Poems* (1916), **Cornhuskers* (1918), **Complete Poems* (1950)

Saroyan, William (1908–81): *The Daring Young Man on the Flying Trapeze* (1934), *The Human Comedy* (1943), *One Day in the Afternoon of the World* (1964)

Sexton, Anne (1928–74): **Live or Die* (1966), *Love Poems* (1969)

Singer, Isaac Bashevis (1904–91)†: *Satan in Goray* (1935), *The Family Moskat* (1950), *Gimpel the Fool* (1957), *The Spinoza of Market Street* (1961), *Old Love* (1979), *The King of the Fields* (1988)

Stein, Gertrude (1874–1946): *Three Lives*

(1909), *The Autobiography of Alice B. Toklas* (1933), *Yes Is for a Very Young Man* (1946)

*Steinbeck, John (1902–68)†: *Tortilla Flat* (1935), *Of Mice and Men* (1937), *The Long Valley* (1938), **The Grapes of Wrath* (1939), *East of Eden* (1952)

*Stowe, Harriet Beecher (1811–96): *Uncle Tom's Cabin* (1852)

Styron, William (1925–): *Lie Down in Darkness* (1951), **The Confessions of Nat Turner* (1967), *Sophie's Choice* (1979)

*Thoreau, Henry David (1817–62): *Civil Disobedience* (1849), *Walden* (1854), *The Maine Woods* (1864)

*Twain, Mark [Samuel Langhorne Clemens] (1835–1910): *The Innocents Abroad* (1869), *Roughing It* (1872), *The Adventures of Tom Sawyer* (1876), *The Adventures of Huckleberry Finn* (1884), *Following the Equator* (1897)

Tyler, Anne (1941–): *A Slipping-Down Life* (1970), *Searching for Caleb* (1976), *Morgan's Passing* (1980), *Dinner at the Homesick Restaurant* (1982), *The Accidental Tourist* (1985), **Breathing Lessons* (1988), *Saint Maybe* (1991)

Updike, John (1932–): *Rabbit, Run* (1960), *Couples* (1968), **Rabbit Is Rich* (1981), *The Witches of Eastwick* (1984), *Rabbit at Rest* (1991)

Vonnegut, Kurt, Jr. (1922–): *Cat's Cradle* (1963), *Slaughterhouse-Five; or The Children's Crusade* (1969), *Breakfast of Champions* (1973), *Bluebeard* (1987)

Walker, Alice (1944–): *Meridian* (1976), **The Color Purple* (1982), *The Temple of My Familiar* (1988)

Warren, Robert Penn (1905–89): **All the King's Men* (1946), **Promises* (1957), *The Cave* (1959)

Webster, Noah (1758–1843): *An American Dictionary of the English Language* (2 vols., 1828)

Welty, Eudora (1909–): *The Bride of the Innisfallen* (1955), *Thirteen Stories*

(1965), *The Optimist's Daughter* (1970), *The Collected Stories of Eudora Welty* (1980), *One Writer's Beginnings* (1984)

*Wharton, Edith (1862–1937): *Ethan Frome* (1911), *Xingu and Other Stories* (1916)

White, E. B. (1899–1985): *One Man's Meat* (1942), *Here Is New York* (1949), *Charlotte's Web* (1952), (with Will Strunk) *The Elements of Style* (1959)

Whitman, Walt (1819–92): *Leaves of Grass* (1855), *Drum-Taps* (1865), *Passage to India* (1871), *Two Rivulets* (1876), *November Boughs* (1888)

Wilson, Edmund (1895–1972): *Axel's Castle* (1931), *The Wound and the Bow* (1941), *Patriotic Gore* (1962)

Wolfe, Thomas (1900–38): *Look Homeward, Angel* (1929), *Of Time and the River* (1935), *The Web and the Rock* (1939)

Wolfe, Tom [Thomas Kennerly Wolfe, Jr.] (1931–   ): *The Pump House Gang* (1968), *The Electric Kool-Aid Acid Test* (1968), *The Right Stuff* (1975), *The Bonfire of the Vanities* (1988)

Wouk, Herman (1915–   ): *The Caine Mutiny* (1951), *Marjorie Morningstar* (1955), *The Winds of War* (1971), *War and Remembrance* (1978)

Wright, Richard (1908–60): *Native Son* (1940), *Black Boy* (1945), *The Outsider* (1953)

IMPORTANT BRITISH, EUROPEAN, AND RUSSIAN AUTHORS AND THEIR WORKS

This list of important British, European, and Russian authors includes European writers who have made major contributions to the literature of their countries, their continent, and the world at large.

The years of first publication are given in parentheses. Authors known by their pseudonyms are so listed, with their real names given in brackets. An asterisk (*) before an author's name indicates that he or she has written a book of particular interest to young people. A dagger (†) indicates that the author was awarded a Nobel Prize in Literature.

Note: *See also* the section on major playwrights.

Amis, Kingsley (English, 1922–   ): *Lucky Jim* (1953), *One Fat Englishman* (1989), *The Folks That Live on the Hill* (1991)

*Andersen, Hans Christian (Danish, 1805–75): *Fairy Tales for Children* (1835–42), *Tales and Stories* (1839), *New Fairy Tales* (1843–47), *New Tales and Stories* (1858–67)

*Austen, Jane (English, 1775–1817): *Sense and Sensibility* (1811), *Pride and Prejudice* (1813), *Emma* (1816), *Persuasion* (1818)

Balzac, Honoré de (French, 1799–1850): *Droll Tales* (1832–37), *The Human Comedy* (1842–53)

Baudelaire, Charles-Pierre (French, 1821–67): *Les fleurs du mal* (1857), *Les paradis artificiels* (1860), *Les épaves* (1861), *Nouvelles fleurs du mal* (1866), *Petits poèmes en prose* (1869)

*Belloc, Joseph Hilaire Peter (English, 1870–1953): *The Bad Child's Book of Beasts* (1896), *On Nothing* (1908), *Cautionary Tales for Children* (1908), *On Everything* (1909), *On Anything* (1910)

*Blake, William (English, 1757–1827): *Poetical Sketches* (1783), *Songs of Innocence* (1789), *The Marriage of Heaven and Hell* (1793), *The Visions of the Daughters of Albion* (1793), *Songs of Experience* (1794), *Milton* (1804)

Blasco Ibañez, Vicente (Spanish 1867–1928): *The Mayflower* (1896), *The Cabin* (1898), *Reeds and Mud* (1902), *The Fruit of the Vine* (1905), *Blood and Sand* (1908)

Blok, Alexander Alexandrovich (Russian, 1880–1921): *Verses About the Beautiful Lady* (1904), *The Puppet Show* (1906), *A Frightful World* (c. 1910), *Dances of Death* (c. 1910), *Black Blood* (c. 1910), *The Twelve* (1918)

Boccaccio, Giovanni (Italian, 1313–75): *Decameron* (1351–53)

Böll, Heinrich (German, 1917–   )†: *Traveler, If You Come to Spa* (1950), *Adam, Where Art Thou?* (1951), *Billiards at Half-past Nine* (1959), *The Clown* (1963), *Group Portrait with Lady* (1971), *The Lost Honor of Katharina Blum* (1974), *The Safety Net* (1982)

Boswell, James (English, 1740–95): *The Life of Samuel Johnson* (1791)

*****Brontë, Charlotte** (English, 1816–55): *Jane Eyre* (1847)

*****Brontë, Emily** (English, 1818–48): *Wuthering Heights* (1847)

*****Browning, Elizabeth Barrett** (English, 1806–61): *The Seraphim and Other Poems* (1838), *Sonnets from the Portuguese* (1850), *Aurora Leigh* (1857), *Last Poems* (1862)

Browning, Robert (English, 1812–89): *Bells and Pomegranates* (1841–46), *Dramatic Lyrics* (1842), *Dramatic Romances and Lyrics* (1845), *Christmas Eve and Easter Day* (1850), *Men and Women* (1855), *Dramatis Personae* (1864)

Bulgakov, Mikhail (Russian, 1891–1940): *The Master and Margarita* (1967), *The Heart of a Dog* (1968)

Burgess, Anthony (English, 1917–   ): *A Clockwork Orange* (1962), *Napoleon Symphony: A Novel in Four Movements* (1974), *Earthly Powers* (1980), *Enderby's Dark Lady* (1984)

Burns, Robert (Scottish, 1759–96): *Poems, Chiefly in the Scottish Dialect* (1786), *The Scots Musical Museum* (1787–96)

Byron, Lord [George Gordon] (English, 1788–1824): *Childe Harold's Pilgrimage*, Cantos I and II (1812), *Childe Harold*, Cantos III and IV (1816, 1817), *The Prisoner of Chillon* (1816), *Manfred* (1817), *Don Juan* (1819–24)

*****Calvino, Italo** (Italian, 1923–85): *Italian Folktales* (1971)

Camus, Albert (French, 1913–60)†: *The Stranger* (1942, revised 1953), *The Myth of Sisyphus and Other Essays* (1942),

Caligula (1944), *The Plague* (1947), *The Rebel* (1951), *The Fall* (1956), *Exile and the Kingdom* (1957)

Canetti, Elias (German, 1905–   )†: *Auto-da-Fé* (1936), *Crowds and Power* (1960)

Capek, Karel (Czech, 1890–1938): *R.U.R.* (1921), *Tales from One Pocket* (1929), *Tales from the Other Pocket* (1929), *Hordubal* (1933), *Meteor* (1934), *An Ordinary Life* (1934)

*****Carroll, Lewis [Charles Lutwidge Dodgson]** (English, 1832–98): *Alice's Adventures in Wonderland* (1865), *Through the Looking Glass* (1871)

Catullus (Roman, c. 84 B.C.–54 B.C.): verse

Cavafy, C. P. (Egyptian, 1863–1933): *Poems* (1935)

*****Cervantes Saavedra, Miguel de** (Spanish, 1547–1616): *Don Quixote* (1605–15)

Chaucer, Geoffrey (English, c. 1340–1400): *The Canterbury Tales* (after 1387)

Chekhov, Anton Pavlovich (Russian, 1860–1904): *Motley Tales* (1886), *The Duel* (1892), *Uncle Vanya* (1896), *The Seagull* (1896), *Three Sisters* (1900), *The Cherry Orchard* (1904)

*****Christie, Agatha** (English, 1891–1976): *The Murder of Roger Ackroyd* (1926), *Murder on the Orient Express* (1934), *Death on the Nile* (1937), *And Then There Were None* (1940), *The Pale Horse* (1961)

Coleridge, Samuel Taylor (English, 1772–1834): *Lyrical Ballads* (1798), *Sybilline Leaves* (1817), *Biographia Literaria* (1817), *The Poetical Works* (1834)

Colette [Sidonie-Gabrielle Colette] (French, 1873–1954): *Claudine* (1900–03), *The Vagrant* (1910), *Mitsou* (1918), *Chéri* (1920), *A Lesson in Love* (1928), *Gigi* (1944)

Conrad, Joseph (English, 1857–1924): *Lord Jim* (1900), *Typhoon* (1902), *Nostromo* (1904), *Chance* (1914), *Victory* (1915)

Dante Alighieri (Italian, 1265–1321): *Divine Comedy* (c. 1310–20)

*****Defoe, Daniel** (English, 1660–1731): *Robinson Crusoe* (1719), *Moll Flanders* (1722)

*Dickens, Charles (English, 1812–70): *Oliver Twist* (1838), *Nicholas Nickleby* (1839), *A Christmas Carol* (1843), *David Copperfield* (1850), *Bleak House* (1853), *A Tale of Two Cities* (1859), *Great Expectations* (1861), *Edwin Drood* (1870)

*Dinesen, Isak [Karen Christence Dinesen, Baroness Blixen-Finecke] (Danish, 1885–1962): *Seven Gothic Tales* (1934), *Out of Africa* (1937), *Winter's Tales* (1942), *Last Tales* (1957)

Donne, John (English, 1572–1631): *The Anniversaries* (1611, 1612), *Songs and Sonnets* (1633)

Dostoyevsky, Fyodor Mikhailovich (Russian, 1821–81): *Notes from the Underground* (1864), *Crime and Punishment* (1866), *The Idiot* (1869), *The Possessed* (1871–72), *The Brothers Karamazov* (1880)

*Doyle, Sir Arthur Conan (English, 1859–1930): *Study in Scarlet* (1887), *The Sign of the Four* (1890), *The Adventures of Sherlock Holmes* (1892), *The Valley of Fear* (1915), *The Case Book of Sherlock Holmes* (1927)

Dryden, John (English, 1631–1700): *All for Love* (1678), *Absalom and Achitophel* (1681), *The Medal* (1682), *MacFlecknoe* (1682)

*Dumas, Alexandre, père (French, 1802–70): *The Count of Monte-Cristo* (1844–45), *The Three Musketeers* (1844), *The Corsican Brothers* (1844)

Durrell, Lawrence (English, 1912–90): *The Alexandria Quartet* (1957–60)

*Eliot, George [Mary Ann Evans] (English, 1819–80): *Silas Marner* (1861), *Middlemarch* (1871–72)

Fielding, Henry (English, 1707–54): *The Tragedy of Tragedies; or, The Life and Death of Tom Thumb the Great* (1731), *Joseph Andrews* (1742), *Tom Jones* (1749)

Flaubert, Gustave (French, 1821–80): *Madame Bovary* (1857), *Sentimental Education* (1869)

Forster, E. M. (English, 1879–1970): *A Room with a View* (1908), *Howard's End* (1910), *A Passage to India* (1924)

García Lorca, Federico (Spanish, 1898–1936): *Canciones* (1927), *Ode to Walt Whitman* (1933), *Lament for the Death of Ignacio Sanchez Mejias* (1935), *Poet in New York* (1940)

Gide, André (French, 1869–1951)†: *The Immoralist* (1902), *Straight is the Gate* (1909), *The Pastoral Symphony* (1919), *The Counterfeiters* (1926)

Goethe, Johann Wolfgang von (German, 1749–1832): *Wilhelm Meister's Apprenticeship* (1795–96), *Faust*, Part I (1819), Part II (1821)

Gogol, Nikolai (Russian, 1809–52): *Arabesques* (1835), *Mirgorod* (1835), *The Inspector General* (1836), *Dead Souls* (1842), *Collected Works* (1842)

*Golding, William (English, 1911–   )†: *Lord of the Flies* (1954), *FreeFall* (1959), *Rites of Passage* (1980)

Gombrowicz, Witold (Polish, 1904–69): *Memoir from Adolescence* (1933), *Ferdydurke* (1937)

Gorky, Maxim (Russian, 1868–1936): *Foma Gordeyev* (1899), *Twenty-Six Men and a Girl and Other Stories* (1902), *The Lower Depths* (1902), *Mother* (1906)

Grass, Günter (German, 1927–   ): *The Tin Drum* (1959), *The Flounder* (1977)

*Grimm, Wilhelm (German, 1786–1859);
Grimm, Jakob (German, 1785–1863): *Grimm's Fairy Tales* (1812–15)

Hamsun, Knut (Norwegian, 1859–1952)†: *Hunger* (1890), *Mysteries* (1892), *The Growth of the Soil* (1917)

*Hardy, Thomas (English, 1840–1928): *Far from the Madding Crowd* (1874), *The Return of the Native* (1878), *Tess of the D'Urbervilles* (1891), *Jude the Obscure* (1896)

Hasek, Jaroslav (Czech, 1883–1923): *The Good Soldier Svejk and Other Strange Stories* (1912), *The Good Soldier Svejk and His Fortunes in the World War* (4 vols., 1921–23)

Hesse, Hermann (German, 1877–1962)†:

Demian (1919), *Siddhartha* (1922), *Steppenwolf* (1927)

*Homer (Greek, c. 700 B.C.): *The Iliad, The Odyssey*

Hopkins, Gerard Manley (English, 1844–89): *Poems* (1918)

*Hugo, Victor Marie (French, 1802–85): *The Hunchback of Notre-Dame* (1831), *Lucretia Borgia* (1833), *Les Misérables* (1862)

Johnson, Samuel (English, 1709–84): *A Dictionary of the English Language* (1755)

Joyce, James (Irish, 1882–1941): *Dubliners* (1914), *Portrait of the Artist as a Young Man* (1916), *Ulysses* (1922), *Finnegan's Wake* (1939)

Kafka, Franz (German, 1883–1924): *Metamorphosis* (1915), *The Judgment* (1916), *In the Penal Colony* (1919), *The Trial* (1925), *The Castle* (1926), *Amerika* (1927)

*Keats, John (English, 1795–1821): *The Poems of John Keats* (1817), *Endymion* (1818), *Lamia, Isabella, and The Eve of St. Agnes and Other Poems* (1820)

*Kipling, Rudyard (English, 1865–1936)†: *Plain Tales from the Hills* (1888), *The Phantom Rickshaw* (1889), *Barrack-Room Ballads* (1892), *The Jungle Book* (1894), *The Second Jungle Book* (1895), *Captains Courageous* (1897), *Kim* (1901), *Just So Stories* (1902)

Lawrence, D(avid) H(erbert) (English, 1885–1930): *Sons and Lovers* (1913), *Women in Love* (1920)

Lessing, Doris (British, 1919–   ): *The Grass Is Singing* (1950), *Martha Quest* (1952), *The Golden Notebook* (1962), *Briefing for a Descent into Hell* (1971), *The Good Terrorist* (1986), *African Laughter: Four Visits to Zimbabwe* (1992)

Lowry, Malcolm (English, 1909–57): *Ultramarine* (1933), *Under the Volcano* (1947), *Hear Us O Lord from Heaven Thy Dwelling Place* (1961)

*Malory, Sir Thomas (English,   ?–1471): *The Death of Arthur* (1485)

Malraux, André (French, 1901–76): *Man's Fate* (1933), *Man's Hope* (1937)

Mandelstam, Osip Emilevich (Russian, 1891–1938): *Kamen* (1913), *Tristia* (1922), *Journey to Armenia* (1933)

Mann, Thomas (German, 1875–1955)†: *Buddenbrooks* (1900), *Death in Venice* (1912), *The Magic Mountain* (1924)

Manzoni, Alessandro (Italian, 1785–1873): *The Betrothed* (1827)

Marvell, Andrew (English, 1621–78): *Miscellaneous Poems* (1681)

Maugham, William Somerset (English, 1874–1965): *Of Human Bondage* (1915), *Cakes and Ale* (1930), *The Summing Up* (1938), *The Razor's Edge* (1944)

Maupassant, Henri René Albert Guy de (French, 1850–93): *"Ball of Fat"* (1880), *The Tellier House* (1881), *Bel-Ami* (1885), *Peter and John* (1888), *Yvette* (1885)

Mauriac, François-Charles (French, 1885–1970)†: *The Family* (1923), *Thérèse* (1927), *The Desert of Love* (1929), *A Woman of the Pharisees* (1941)

Milton, John (English, 1608–74): *Paradise Lost* (1667), *Paradise Regained* (1671)

Montaigne, Michel de (French, 1533–92): *Essays* (1580)

Nabokov, Vladimir Vladimirovich (Russian, 1899–1977): *Lolita* (1955), *Invitation to a Beheading* (1959), *Pale Fire* (1962), *Speak, Memory* (1967)

*Orwell, George [Eric Blair] (English, 1903–50): *Animal Farm* (1945), *1984* (1949)

Ovid (Roman, 43 B.C.–A.D. 17): *Metamorphoses*

Pasternak, Boris Leonidovich (Russian, 1890–1960)†: *My Sister—Life* (1922), *Doctor Zhivago* (1957)

Petrarch (Italian, 1304–1374): *Collected Works* (1544)

Petronius (Roman, ?–66): *Satyricon* (c. 50)

Plutarch (Greek, c. 46–120): *Moralia, Parallel Lives*

Pope, Alexander (English, 1688–1744):

An Essay on Criticism (1711), *The Rape of the Lock* (1714)

Proust, Marcel (French, 1871–1922): *Remembrance of Things Past* (7 vols., 1913–27)

Pushkin, Alexander Sergeevich (Russian, 1789–1837): *Eugene Onegin* (1831)

Rabelais, François (French, 1494?–1553): *Gargantua and Pantagruel* (1532–64)

Rilke, Rainer Maria (German, 1875–1926): *Poems from the Book of Hours* (1905), *New Poems* (2 vols., 1907–08), *Duino Elegies* (1923), *Sonnets to Orpheus* (1923)

Rimbaud, Arthur (French, 1854–91): *A Season in Hell* (1873), *Illuminations* (1886)

*****Rostand, Edmond** (French, 1868–1918): *The Princess Faraway* (1895), *Cyrano de Bergerac* (1897)

*****Rushdie, Salman** (English, 1947–   ): *Midnight's Children* (1981), *Shame* (1983), *The Satanic Verses* (1988), **Haroun and the Sea of Stories* (1990)

Sand, George [Amandine-Aurore-Lucie Dupin] (French, 1804–76): *Indiana* (1832), *Lelia* (1833), *The Companion of the Tour of France* (1841), *Consuelo* (1842–43), *He and She* (1859), *The Marquis of Villemer* (1860–61)

Sappho (Greek, c. 612 B.C.–   ?): verse

Sartre, Jean-Paul (French, 1905–80)†: *Nausea* (1938), *The Flies* (1943), *Being and Nothingness* (1943), *No Exit* (1944), *The Condemned of Altona* (1959)

*****Scott, Sir Walter** (Scottish, 1771–1832): *The Heart of Midlothian* (1818), *The Bride of Lammermoor* (1819), *Ivanhoe* (1819), *Kenilworth* (1821)

*****Shelley, Mary Wollstonecraft** (English, 1797–1851): *Frankenstein, or the Modern Prometheus* (1818)

Shelley, Percy Bysshe (English, 1792–1822): *Prometheus Unbound* (1820), *Adonais* (1821)

Solzhenitsyn, Aleksandr I. (Russian, 1918–   )†: *One Day in the Life of Ivan Denisovich* (1962), *The Cancer Ward* (1968), *The Gulag Archipelago* (1973–76)

Spenser, Edmund (English, c. 1552–99): *The Faerie Queene* (1590)

Stendhal [Marie-Henri Beyle] (French, 1788–1842): *The Red and the Black* (1830), *The Charterhouse of Parma* (1839)

*****Stevenson, Robert Louis** (Scottish, 1850–94): *Treasure Island* (1883), *The Stange Case of Dr. Jekyll and Mr. Hyde* (1886)

*****Swift, Jonathan** (Irish, 1667–1745): *Gulliver's Travels* (1726)

Swinburne, Algernon Charles (English, 1837–1909): *Atalanta in Calydon* (1865), *Poems and Ballads: First Series* (1866), *Poems and Ballads: Second Series* (1878), *Astrophel* (1894), *A Tale of Balen* (1896)

Tennyson, Alfred (Lord) (English, 1809–92): *Poems, Chiefly Lyrical* (1830), *Poems* (1832), *Poems* (1842), *Locksley Hall* (1842), *In Memoriam* (1833–50), *Maud, and Other Poems* (1855), *Idylls of the King* (1859–85)

Thackeray, William Makepeace (English, 1811–63): *Barry Lyndon* (1844), *Vanity Fair* (1847–48)

*****Thomas, Dylan Marlais** (Welsh, 1914–53): *A Child's Christmas in Wales* (1952)

Tocqueville, Alexis de (1805–59): *Democracy in America* (2 vols., 1835; 2 supplementary vols., 1840), *The Old Regime and the Revolution* (1856)

Tolstoy, Leo [Count Lev Nikolaievich] (Russian, 1828–1910): *War and Peace* (1863–69), *Anna Karenina* (1875–77)

Trollope, Anthony (English, 1815–82): *The Warden* (1855), *Barchester Towers* (1857)

Turgenev, Ivan (Russian, 1818–83): *A Sportsman's Sketches* (1852), *A Month in the Country* (1855), *A Nest of Gentlefolk* (1859), *On the Eve* (1860), *Fathers and Sons* (1862), *Smoke* (1867)

Undset, Sigrid (Norwegian, 1882–1949)†: *Kristin Lavransdatter* (1920–22), *Olaf Andunsson* (1925–27)

Valéry, Paul (French, 1871–1945): *Charms* (1922)

*** Verne, Jules** (French, 1828–1905): *A Voyage to the Center of the Earth* (1864), *Twenty Thousand Leagues Under the Sea* (1870), *Around the World in Eighty Days* (1873)

Virgil [Publius Vergilius Maro] (Roman, 70–19 B.C.): *Aeneid* (30–19 B.C.)

Voltaire [François-Marie Arouet] (French, 1694–1778): *Candide* (1759)

*** Wilde, Oscar** (Irish, 1854–1900): *The Importance of Being Earnest* (1899), *The Happy Prince and Other Tales* (1888)

Woolf, Virginia (English, 1882–1941): *Mrs. Dalloway* (1925), *To the Lighthouse* (1927), *A Room of One's Own* (1929)

Wordsworth, William (English, 1770–1850): *Lyrical Ballads* (1798), *Poems Chiefly of Early and Late Years* (1842)

*** Yeats, William Butler** (Irish, 1865–1939)†: *The Wind Among the Reeds* (1899), *The Wild Swans at Coole* (1919), *The Winding Stair* (1929), *Collected Poems* (1933)

Zola, Émile (French, 1840–1902): *Thérèse Raquin* (1867), *Nana* (1880), *Germinal* (1885)

IMPORTANT ASIAN, AFRICAN, AND LATIN AMERICAN AUTHORS AND THEIR WORKS

Armah, Ayi Kweh (Ghanaian, 1939–   ): *The Beautiful Ones Are Not Yet Born* (1968), *Why Are We So Blest?* (1972)

*** Bashō [Matsuo Munefusa]** (Japanese, 1644–94): *The Narrow Road to the Deep North* (1689)

Beti, Mongo [Alexandre Biyidi] (Cameroonian, 1932–   ): *The Poor Christ of Bomba* (1956), *Mission ended* (1957), *Le roi miraculé* (*The Miraculously Cured King*) (1958)

Borges, Jorge Luis (Argentinian, 1899–1986): *A Universal History of Infamy* (1935), *Six Problems for Don Isidro Parodi* (1942), *Ficciones* (1934), *The Aleph and Other Stories* (1949), *Labyrinthe* (1960), *The Book of Sand* (1975)

Cesaire, Aimé (West Indian, 1913–   ): *Return to My Native Land* (1939), *State of the Union* (1946), *The Tragedy of King Christophe* (1963)

*** Chatterje, Bankim-Chandra** (Indian, 1838–94): *The Chieftain's Daughter* (1880), *Kopal-Kundala: A Tale of Bengali Life* (1885), *Krishna Kante's Will* (1895)

Confucius (Chinese, c. 551–479 B.C.): *The Analects of Confucius*

Fuentes, Carlos (Mexican, 1928–   ): *The Death of Artemio Cruz* (1962), *Distant Relations* (1981)

García Márquez, Gabriel (Colombian, 1928–   )†: *One Hundred Years of Solitude* (1967), *The Autumn of the Patriarch* (1975), *Love in the Time of Cholera* (1988), *The General in his Labyrinth* (1990)

Gordimer, Nadine (South African, 1923–   )†: *Occasion for Loving* (1963), *A Guest of Honor* (1970), *Burgher's Daughter* (1979), *Something Out There* (1984), *My Son's Story* (1991)

Guzmán, Martín Luis (Mexican, 1887–1976): *The Eagle and the Serpent* (1928), *Memorias de Pancho Villa* (4 vols., 1938–40)

Kawabata, Yasunari (Japanese, 1899–1972)†: *Snow Country* (1948), *Thousand Cranes* (1952), *Beauty and Sadness* (1965)

Lao-tzu (Chinese, c. 6th century B.C.): *Tao-te-ching*

Laye, Camara (Guinean, 1928–80): *The African Child* (1953), *The Radiance of the King* (1954), *The Guardian of the Word* (1978)

*** Li Po** (Chinese, 701–62): *Complete Works*

Machado de Assis, Joaquim Maria (Brazilian, 1839–1908): *The Posthumous Memoirs of Braz Cubas* (1881), *Philosopher or Dog?* (1891), *Dom Casmurro* (1899)

Mahfouz, Naguib (Egyptian, 1911–   )†: *Stories of the Neighborhood* (1982),

Search (1987), *Palace Walk* (1990), *Palace of Desire* (1991), *Sugar Street* (1992), (all are dates of English translations)

Márquez, Gabriel García *See* **García Márquez, Gabriel.**

Mishima, Yukio (Japanese, 1925–70): *Confessions of a Mask* (1949), *Forbidden Colors* (2 vols., 1951–53), *The Sailor Who Fell from Grace with the Sea* (1963), *The Sea of Fertility* (4 vols., 1969–71)

Mistral, Gabriela†: *Selected Poems* (trans. Langston Hughes, 1962), *Despair* (1922), *Tenderness* (1924), *Tula* (1938), *Wine Press* (1954)

Murasaki, Shikibu (Japanese, c. 978–1015): *The Tale of the Genji* (c. 1010)

Naipaul, V. S. (Trinidadian, 1932–   ): *The Mystic Masseur* (1957), *A House for Mr. Biswas* (1961), *The Middle Passage* (1962), *In a Free State* (1971)

Natsume Sōseki (Japanese, 1867–1916): *I Am a Cat* (1905–07), *The Three-Cornered World* (1907), *And Then* (1910)

Neruda, Pablo [Neftali Ricardo Reyes Basoalto] (Chilean, 1904–73)†: *Twenty Love Poems and a Story of Despair* (1924), *Canto General* (1950), *Elementary Odes* (3 vols., 1954–57), *We Are Many* (1967), *End of the World* (1969)

Omar Khayyam (Persian, 1048–1131): *Rubaiyat* (1859)

Paton, Alan Stewart (South African, 1903–88): *Cry the Beloved Country* (1948)

Paz, Octavio (Mexican, 1914–   )†: *The Labyrinth of Solitude* (1950), *Sun-Stone* (1957), *Salamandra 1958–1961* (1962), *Ladera esta 1962–1968* (1969), *Vuelta* (1976)

Sembene, Ousmane (Senegalese, 1923–   ): *The Black Docker* (1956), *The Money Order* (1965)

Senghor, Léopold Sédar (Senegalese, 1906–   ): *Shadow Chants d'ombre* (1945), *Nocturnes* (1961), *Liberté I. Negritude et Humanisme* (1964)

Soyinka, Wole (Nigerian 1934–   )†: *Three Plays* (1963), *The Road* (1965), *The Forest of a Thousand Daemons* (1968), *Aké* (1981)

*Tagore, Rabindranath (Indian, 1861–1941)†: *Gitanjali: Song Offering* (1912), *King of the Dark Chamber* (1914), *Gora* (1924)

Tanizaki Jun'chiro (Japanese, 1886–1965): *Tattoo* (1911), *The Secret History of the Lord Musashi* (1935), *The Key* (1956), *Seven Japanese Tales* (1963)

Ts'ao Hsueh-ch'in (Chinese, c. 1715–63): *The Dream of Red Chamber* (c. 1763)

Vargas Llosa, Mario (Peruvian, 1936–   ): *The Green House* (1966), *Conversations in the Cathedral* (1969), *The War of the End of the World* (1984), *The Real Life of Alejandro Mayta* (1986)

PLAYWRIGHTS AND THEIR BEST-KNOWN WORKS

An asterisk (*) before a play's title indicates a play that was awarded a Pulitzer Prize for drama. An asterisk before a playwright's name indicates that he or she has written a play or plays of particular interest to young people. A dagger (†) indicates that the playwright was awarded a Nobel Prize in Literature.

American

Albee, Edward (1928–   ): *Who's Afraid of Virginia Woolf* (1962), *The Zoo Story* (1959), *A Delicate Balance* (1966)

*Barry, Philip (1896–1949): *Holiday* (1929), *The Animal Kingdom* (1932), *The Philadelphia Story* (1939)

*Chayesfky, Paddy [Sidney] (1923–   ): *Marty* (1953), *The Tenth Man* (1959), *Network* (1976)

Eliot, T(homas) S(tearns) (1888–1965)†: *Murder In the Cathedral* (1935), *The Cocktail Party* (1949)

*Hellman, Lilian (1905–84): *The Children's Hour* (1934), *The Little Foxes* (1939), and *Watch on The Rhine* (1941)

Inge, William (1913–73): *Come Back, Lit-*

tle Sheba (1950), *Picnic* (1953), *Bus Stop* (1955), *The Dark at the Top of the Stairs* (1957)

Mamet, David (1947–   ): *American Buffalo* (1975)

Miller, Arthur (1915–   ): **Death of a Salesman* (1949), *The Crucible* (1953), *A View From The Bridge* (1955)

Odets, Clifford (1906–63): *Waiting For Lefty* (1935), *Awake and Sing* (1935), *Golden Boy* (1937), *The Big Knife* (1949), *The Country Girl* (1951)

O'Neill, Eugene (1888–1953)†: *The Iceman Cometh* (1939), *Long Day's Journey Into Night* (1941), *A Moon For the Misbegotten* (1943), *Anna Christie* (1920), *Desire Under the Elms* (1924), *Ah, Wilderness!* (1933)

Saroyan, William (1908–81): **The Time of Your Life* (1939)

Shepard, Sam (1943–   ): *Operation Sidewinder* (1970), *Buried Child* (1978), *Fool For Love* (1984)

Sherwood, Robert (1896–1955): *The Petrified Forest* (1935), *Idiot's Delight* (1936), *There Shall Be No Night* (1940)

*Wilder, Thornton (1897–1975): **Our Town* (1938), **The Skin of Our Teeth* (1942), *The Matchmaker* (1953)

Williams, Tennessee (1911–83): *The Glass Menagerie* (1945), **A Streetcar Named Desire* (1947), *Summer and Smoke* (1948), **Cat On a Hot Tin Roof* (1955), *Night of the Iguana* (1961)

British

Beaumont, Francis (c. 1584–1616): *The Knight of the Burning Pestle* (c. 1607)

*Coward, Noël (1899–1973): *Private Lives* (1930), *Design For Living* (1930), *Blithe Spirit* (1933)

Dekker, Thomas (c. 1572–1632): *The Shoemakers's Holiday* (1600), *Westward Ho!* (with John Webster, 1604)

Fletcher, John (1579–1625): *Wit Without Money* (c. 1614), *Rule a Wife and Have a Wife* (1624)

Goldsmith, Oliver (1728–74): *She Stoops To Conquer* (1773)

Jonson, Ben (1527–1637): *Volpone* (1605–06), *Epicoene* (1610), *The Alchemist* (1610), *Bartholomew Fair* (1614)

*Kyd, Thomas (1558–94): *The Spanish Tragedy* (1592)

*Marlowe, Christopher (1564–93): *Tamburlaine The Great:* Part I (c. 1586–87; Part II, 1587), *Dr. Faustus* (c. 1588), *The Jew of Malta* (c. 1589), *Edward II* (1591)

Middleton, Thomas (c. 1570–1627): *A Trick to Catch the Old One* (c. 1607), *A Chaste Maid in Cheapside* (1611), *The Changeling* (with William Rowley, 1622), *Women Beware Women* (c. 1625)

Osborne, John (1929–   ): *Look Back in Anger* (1956), *The Entertainer* (1957), *Luther* (1961), *Inadmissible Evidence* (1964)

Pinter, Harold (1930–   ): *The Birthday Party* (1958), *The Dumb Waiter* (1959), *The Homecoming* (1965), *Betrayal* (1978)

Rowley, William (1585?–1642?): *The Changeling* (with Thomas Middleton, 1622), *The Birth of Merlin* (c. 1608)

*Shakespeare, William (1564–1616): *Titus Andronicus* (1594), *Romeo and Juliet* (c. 1595–06), *Julius Caesar* (1599), *Hamlet* (1602), *Othello* (1602–03), *Timon of Athens* (1604–05), *King Lear* (1605–06), *Macbeth* (1605–06), *Antony and Cleopatra* (1606–07), *Coriolanus* (1607–10), *The Comedy of Errors* (1591–04), *The Taming of the Shrew* (1593–04), *The Two Gentlemen of Verona* (1594–05), *Love's Labour's Lost* (1593–95), *A Midsummer Night's Dream* (1595–06), *The Merchant of Venice* (1596–07), *Much Ado About Nothing* (1598–99), *The Merry Wives of Windsor* (1598–99), *As You Like It* (1599–1600), *Twelfth Night* (1599–1600), *Troilus and Cressida* (1601–02), *All's Well That Ends Well* (1602–03), *Measure For Measure* (1603–04), *Pericles* (1606–08), *Cymbeline* (1609–10), *The Winter's Tale* (1610–11),

The Tempest (1611), *Henry VI: Part I* (1589–91), *Henry VI: Part II* (1590–91), *Henry VI: Part III* (1590–91), *Richard III* (1593), *Richard II* (1595), *King John* (1596–07), *Henry IV: Part I* (1597–08), *Henry IV: Part II* (1597–08), *Henry V* (1598–09), *Henry VIII* (1612)

*Shaw, George Bernard (1856–1950)†: *Arms and the Man* (1894), *Man and Superman* (1905), *Major Barbara* (1905), *Pygmalion* (1912), *Heartbreak House* (1913–19), *Saint Joan* (1923)

*Sheridan, Richard Brinsley (1751–1816): *The Rivals* (1775), *The School For Scandal* (1777)

Stoppard, Tom (1937–   ): *Rosencrantz and Guildenstern Are Dead* (1967), *The Real Inspector Hound* (1968)

Tourneur, Cyril (1575–1626): *The Revenger's Tragedy* (1606–07), *The Atheists Tragedy* (1607–11)

Webster, John (c. 1580–1634): *The White Devil* (1609–12), *The Duchess of Malfi* (1613–14)

*Wilde, Oscar (1854–1900): *The Importance of Being Earnest* (1895)

French

Anouilh, Jean (1910–87): *Thieves' Carnival* (1932), *Antigone* (1944), *The Waltz of the Toreadors* (1952), *The Lark* (1953)

Corneille, Pierre (1606–84): *The Cid* (1637), *Horace* (1640), *Cinna* (1640–41), *Polyeuctes* (1641–42)

Genet, Jean (1919–86): *The Maids* (1947), *The Balcony* (1956), *The Blacks* (1959)

Giraudoux, Jean (1882–1944): *Tiger At The Gates* (1935), *The Madwoman of Chaillot* (1946)

Hugo, Victor-Marie (1802–85): *Hernani* (1830), *The King Amuses Himself* (1832—the source for Verdi's opera *Rigoletto*), *Ruy Blas* (1838), *The Burgraves* (1843)

Ionesco, Eugene (1912–   ): *The Bald Soprano* (1950), *The Lesson* (1951), *Rhinoceros* (1959)

*Molière (Jean-Baptiste-Poquelin) (1622–73): *The School For Wives* (1662), *Tartuffe* (1664), *The Misanthrope* (1666), *The Miser* (1668), *The Bourgeois Gentleman* (1670)

Racine, Jean (1639–99): *Andromache* (1667), *Bérénice* (1670), *Phèdre* (1676), *Athalie* (1691)

*Rostand, Edmund (1868–1918): *Cyrano de Bergerac* (1897)

Sartre, Jean-Paul (1905–80)†: *No Exit* (1944), *Dirty Hands* (1948)

German

Brecht, Bertolt (1895–1956): *In The Jungle of Cities* (1923), *The Threepenny Opera* (1928), *Galileo* (1938–39), *Mother Courage and Her Children* (1941), *The Good Woman of Setzuan* (1943)

Büchner, Georg (1813–37): *Danton's Death* (1835), *Woyzeck* (1836)

Greek

Aeschylus (525–456 B.C.): *Prometheus Bound* (466–59 B.C.), *The Oresteia, Trilogy* (458 B.C.)

Aristophanes (c. 445–c. 385 B.C.): *The Acharnians* (425 B.C.), *The Clouds* (423 B.C.), *The Wasps* (422 B.C.), *Peace* (422 B.C.), *The Birds* (414 B.C.), *Lysistrata* (411 B.C.), *The Frogs* (405 B.C.)

Euripides (480–06 B.C.): *Alcestis* (438 B.C.), *Medea* (431 B.C.), *The Trojan Women* (415 B.C.), *Electra* (413 B.C.), *Iphegenia in Tauris* (412 B.C.), *Orestes* (408 B.C.), *The Bacchae* (405 B.C.)

Sophocles (c. 496–06 B.C.): *Antigone* (c. 442–41 B.C.), *Oedipus Rex* (c. 430–26 B.C.), *Electra* (409 B.C.?), *Oedipus At Colonus* (c. 404–01 B.C.)

Irish

Beckett, Samuel (1906–89)†: *Waiting for Godot* (1952), *Endgame* (1957)

*O'Casey, Sean (1880–1964): *The Shadow

Pen Names of Famous Authors

Most of the authors in this list published under both their real names and pen names (pseudonyms).

Real Name	Pen Name or Pseudonym
Hans Christian Andersen	Villiam Christian Walter
Isaac Asimov	Dr. A., Paul French
L. Frank Baum	Edith Van Dyne
Robert Benchley	Guy Fawkes
Eric Arthur Blair	George Orwell
Anne Brontë	Acton Bell, Lady Geralda, Olivia Vernon, Alexandria Zenobia
Charlotte Brontë	C. B., Currer Bell, Marquis of Douro, Genius, Lord Charles Wellesley
Emily Jane Brontë	R. Alcon, Ellis Bell
Barbara Cartland	Barbara Hamilton McCorquodale
Agatha Christie	Agatha Christie Mallowen, Mary Westmacott
Samuel Langhorne Clemens	Mark Twain
Erle Stanley Gardner	A. A. Fair, Charles M. Green, Carleton Kendrake, Charles J. Kenny
Theodor Seuss Geisel	Theo Lesieg, Dr. Seuss
Edward St. John Gorey	Eduard Blutig, Mrs. Regera Dowdy, Redway Grode, O. Mude, Hyacinthe Phypps, Ogdred Weary, Dreary Wodge
Dashiell Hammett	Peter Collinson
Robert A. Heinlein	Anson MacDonald
Ford Madox Hueffer	Ford Madox Ford
Teodor Jozef Konrad Korzeniowski	Joseph Conrad
Louis LaMoore	Louis L'Amour, Tex Burns
Manfred Lee and Frederic Dannay	Ellery Queen, Barnaby Ross
Salvatore A. Lombine	Evan Hunter
Kenneth Millar	John Ross Macdonald, Ross Macdonald
Dorothy Parker	Constant Reader
William Sydney Porter	O. Henry
J. A. Wight	James Herriot

of a Gunman (1923), *Juno and the Paycock* (1924), *The Plough and the Stars* (1926)

***Synge, John Millington** (1871–1909): *In The Shadow of the Glen* (1903), *Riders To the Sea* (1904), *The Playboy of the Western World* (1907)

Italian

***Pirandello, Luigi** (1867–1936)†: *Right You Are—If You Think You Are* (1917), *Six Characters in Search of an Author* (1921), *The Man With the Flower in His Mouth* (1923)

Norwegian

*Ibsen, Henrik (1828–1906): *Peer Gynt* (1867), *A Doll's House* (1879), *Ghosts* (1881), *An Enemy of the People* (1883), *The Wild Duck* (1884), *Hedda Gabler* (1891)

Roman

Plautus (c. 251–c. 184 B.C.): *Pseudolus* (191 B.C.), *The Menaechmi* (date unknown)

*Seneca (4 B.C.–A.D. 65): *Agamemnon, Medea, Phaedre* (dates unknown)

Russian

*Chekhov, Anton Pavlovich (1860–1904): *The Seagull* (1896), *Uncle Vanya* (1899), *The Three Sisters* (1901), *The Cherry Orchard* (1904)

Gorky, Maxim [Alexei Maximovich Peshkov] (1868–1936): *The Lower Depths* (1902)

Spanish

*Calderón de la Barca, Pedro (1600–81): *The Phantom Lady* (1629), *Life Is a Dream* (1631–32), *Devotion To The Cross* (1633), *Secret Vengeance for Secret Insult* (1635), *The Mayor of Zalamea* (1640–44)

*García Lorca, Federico (1899–1936): *Blood Wedding* (1933), *Yerma* (1934), *The House of Bernarda Alba* (1936)

Molina, Tirso de [Gabriel Téllez] (c. 1571–1648): *The Trickster of Seville* (c. 1625)

*Vega Carpio, Lope de (1562–1635): *Fuenteovejuna* (1612), *The Peasant in His Nook* (1611–15), *The King's the Best Magistrate* (1620–23), *The Knight From Olmedo* (1620–25)

Swedish

Strindberg, Johan August (1849–1912): *The Father* (1887), *Miss Julie* (1889), *The Dance of Death* (Part I and Part II–1900), *A Dream Play* (1902)

LITERATURE FROM A TO Z

allegory A story that has a symbolic meaning. Characters in an allegory stand for certain qualities; for example, Spenser's Redcrosse Knight in *The Faerie Queen* stands for holiness. *The Pilgrim's Progress* (1678) by John Bunyan is a famous English allegory in which the pilgrim's journey stands for the journey of life itself.

alliteration The use of the same consonant, usually at the beginning of each word, in a line of a poem or in prose. An example is "The *f*at *f*rantic *f*rog *f*led the *f*ire."

anachronism A deliberate mistake in a story or poem that places a person, event, or object in an impossible historical setting. An example would be King Arthur driving a minivan to go to work at his court.

antagonist The major character opposing a hero or protagonist.

anthropomorphism The assigning of human characteristics and feelings to animals and nonhuman things.

anticlimax Something that undermines a climax, such as humor.

antihero A protagonist who lacks heroic qualities like courage, idealism, and honesty.

autobiography The story of a person's own life as written by that person.

ballad A poem, often meant to be sung, that tells a story.

belles-lettres Literature.

bibliography A reading list of books on a particular subject or by one author or group of authors.

biography The story of someone's life written by another person.

blank verse Unrhymed poetry.

climax The high point of a story or play

where it reaches its dramatic and emotional peak.

couplet Two successive lines of poetry, usually rhymed.

denouement The events following the climax of a story or play.

elegy A poetic lament.

epic A long narrative poem.

epistolary novel A novel written in the form of letters.

essay A short written work of nonfiction, usually on one topic.

fable A prose or poetic story that illustrates a moral.

fiction An invented work of prose, verse, or drama.

free verse A poem without regular meter or line length.

haiku A three-line poem that does not rhyme. The first line has five syllables, the second has seven, and the third, five. Haiku originated in Japan and expresses the strong sensations of a moment in sharp images.

hero A character, often the main character, who has courage, idealism, and honesty.

high comedy Comedy that is characterized by intellect or wit.

historical novel A narrative that places fictional characters or events in historically accurate surroundings.

iamb A metrical foot that contains one short or unstressed syllable before one long or stressed syllable.

iambic pentameter Poetry consisting of five parts per line, each part having one short or unstressed syllable and one long or stressed syllable.

imagery Language used to evoke particular mental pictures.

literature Novels, stories, poems, and plays of high standards that entertain, inform, stimulate, or provide artistic pleasure.

low comedy Humorous material that uses physical actions or jokes of poor taste.

metaphor A comparison between two unlike things, such as a lion and a man.

meter The pattern of stressed and unstressed syllables in poetry.

myth A legend, usually made up in part of historical events, that helps define the beliefs of a people. Myths often have developed to explain rituals and natural phenomena.

nonfiction Literature that is based on historical, scientific, or biographical fact and is not invented by the author.

novel A long work of fictional prose.

novella A short novel.

ode A poem marked by strong expressions of feeling and an elaborate style.

onomatopoeia Formation of a word by imitating the natural sound associated with the object or action involved, such as *moo*.

oxymoron A figure of speech that uses two contradictory terms.

parable A short story that illustrates a moral.

parody A humorous, often exaggerated, imitation of a serious literary work.

personification The assigning of human attributes to abstractions, objects, and other nonhuman things.

plot The organization of individual incidents in a narrative or play.

poem A rhythmic expression of feelings or ideas, often using metaphor, meter, and rhyme.

prologue An introductory speech or monologue, given by an actor or actress before a play, which helps to set the stage for what is to come.

prose Literary writing that varies in rhythm and is more like ordinary speech than poetry.

protagonist The main character of a play, novel, or story, usually the hero.

refrain A phrase or verse that is repeated throughout a poem or song.

rhyme The repetition of similar or identical sounds at the ends of lines of verse.

rhythm The pattern of stressed and unstressed syllables in a line of poetry or prose.

satire A work that makes fun of its characters.

short story A brief work of narrative prose.

simile A comparison of two unlike things, usually introduced by *like* or *as*, such as "built *like an ox*."

soliloquy A dramatic speech performed by one actor in a play or a character in a story. Hamlet's "To be or not to be . . ." is a famous soliloquy.

sonnet A poem of fourteen iambic pentameter lines with a rigidly prescribed rhyming scheme.

style An author's individual method and tone.

subplot A secondary plot in a story.

symbol In literature, something that stands for, or means, something else. For example, snow may stand for death in a poem.

theme The central idea of a work.

verse Lines of writing arranged in metrical patterns, or a single such line.

INFORMATION, PLEASE

Brewer, Ebenezer Cobham. *Brewer's Dictionary of Phrase and Fable*. 14th ed by Ivor H. Evans. Harper & Row, 1989.

Chute, Marchette B. *Stories from Shakespeare*. New American Library, 1976.

Deutsch, Babette. *Poetry Handbook: A Dictionary of Terms*. 4th ed. Harper & Row, 1982.

Gardner, Helen L. *The New Oxford Book of English Verse: 1250–1950*. Oxford University Press, 1972.

Hurd, Charles. *A Treasury of Great American Speeches*. New and rev. ed. by Andrew Bauer. Hawthorne Books, 1970.

Sixth Book of Junior Authors & Illustrators. Edited by Sally Holmes Holtze. Wilson, 1989.

Stevenson, Burton E. *The Home Book of Verse for Young Folks*. Rev. ed. Holt, Rinehart, and Winston, 1957.

17

LIBRARIES AND MUSEUMS

Libraries and museums are two of the main ways we obtain information about our culture and our world.

TYPES OF LIBRARIES

Here are the major types of libraries:

public Most communities sponsor public lending libraries that anyone may use. These contain general collections that appeal to a broad range of interests.

school Most school systems maintain three levels of libraries: elementary, middle school, and high school, each with collections geared to the appropriate age group.

college, university, and research The largest collections of scholarly books reside in these libraries. College and university libraries are open to their students and graduates, and to qualified scholars.

government The federal government maintains nearly 2,800 libraries, including two major libraries located in Washington, D.C.: the Library of Congress, which since 1870 has received two copies of every book published in the United States; and the National Archives, which houses the federal government's records.

Many other federal agencies and departments operate extensive libraries that are open to qualified researchers. Important libraries, for example, are the National Agricultural Library, second in size to the Library of Congress; the National Medical Library, one of the finest medical research facilities in the world; the National Institute of Standards and Technology library; and the Office of Management and Budget's library, all located in Washington, D.C.

industrial and professional Many industry groups and even individual businesses maintain reference libraries for their employees. There are specialized libraries for lawyers, bankers, editors, physicians, and scientists, to name but a few.

private Open to the public (sometimes by appointment), these libraries are often formed around private collections and run by foundations. Among the important private libraries in the United States are the Morgan Library in New York City, an extensive collection of rare manuscripts and books; the Folger Shakespeare Library in Washington,

---

Where the Books Are

- The largest library in the world is the Library of Congress in Washington, D.C. It houses over 15 million books, which occupy almost 600 miles of shelves.
- The next largest library is believed to be the Beijing Library in the People's Republic of China, with 14 million books.
- Running a close second to the Beijing Library is the New York Public Library, with 13.8 million books sitting on 180 miles of shelves.
- Harvard University Library, the first library in the United States (founded in 1638), houses 11 million books.
- The second-largest university library in the United States is Yale, with 8.8 million books.
- Other university libraries with unusually large collections include: University of Illinois at Urbana (7 million books); Stanford and Columbia University (5.4 million books each); University of Los Angeles (5.4 million); and the University of Chicago (4.6 million).

D.C.; the Huntington Library in San Marino, California, which houses extensive collections on Chaucer and Shakespeare; and the Newberry Library in Chicago, which houses an excellent collection of children's books.

HELP, SOMEBODY, PLEASE: SPECIAL LIBRARY SERVICES FOR CHILDREN AND YOUNG ADULTS

Libraries are interested in developing children and young adults as avid readers. To this end, most school and public libraries offer special services and programs for young readers. Here are some of the programs you can expect to find at your school or local library:

story hour Special readings and other programs for young people.

book clubs Many libraries sponsor reading groups for young persons.

exhibits Many public libraries sponsor exhibits of books, drawings, and photographs in their collections, and a few run exhibits of special interest to children and young adults, often on topics such as careers or sports.

special lending programs Lots of school and public libraries have special extended loans for the summer months.

library clubs Schools often sponsor these groups, which teach young adults about how a library operates and sometimes permit them to assist the librarians.

career centers High school and public libraries often maintain special career information centers.

special collections School and public libraries often form special collections of interest to youth. Popular subjects include dinosaurs, cars, sports, travel, trains, toys, and costumes.

GETTING THE MOST OUT OF A LIBRARY

Some people like to explore libraries by browsing through the shelves. On occasions when you are looking for a special book to read for pleasure, this is a good method. But when you have something specific to look up, you should probably enlist the aid of a librarian.

Librarians are specially trained workers who can help you find any information you need—even when it isn't in their libraries. Librarians will know what kind of materials are available to answer your questions. While the largest part of most libraries' collections are books, libraries also house audiovisual materials, journals and magazines, pamphlets, newspapers, and pictures and photographs, which are often kept in a special place called the vertical file.

If the book or magazine you need isn't available in the library, a librarian can sometimes arrange for it to be sent from another library. Because no one library can house every book—let alone every journal or magazine—libraries often cooperate with one another by sharing their collections. This means you can borrow books from other libraries.

The Library of Congress maintains two lists, or bibliographies, designed to help you locate materials in other libraries:

National Union Catalog This book lists published works in 1,000 U.S. and Canadian libraries.
Union List of Serials in the United States and Canada This book lists 100,000 magazines in many different libraries.

These books are available at the Library of Congress and in other large public and university libraries.

The Library of Congress also buys foreign books, some of which it keeps for its own collections, and some of which it distributes to libraries around the country.

When you want to borrow a book or other printed material from another library, the interlibrary loan program can help you. Once you have located the book you need, you file a written request, and either the original book or magazine or a photocopy of the material you need will be sent to you within seven or eight weeks.

When something is available in your library, it helps to know how to locate it. Libraries use one of two systems to store their materials: the Dewey Decimal System and the Library of Congress Classification System.

The Dewey Decimal System and How to Use It

Melvil Dewey (1851–1931) was a man who believed in organization. Even as a child he was busy devising a way to arrange his family's pantry to make it more efficient. Before his system of classifying library books was adopted, many libraries relied on systems that filed books by size or color—cumbersome and not very useful methods at best. While working as a librarian at Amherst College, Dewey developed a system that is used by most school and small public libraries today. Published anonymously in 1876, his classifications divide nonfiction books into ten broad categories:

000–099	General works (encyclopedias and similar reference works)
100–199	Philosophy (how people think and what they believe)
200–299	Religion (including mythology and religions of the world)
300–399	Social sciences (folklore and legends, government, manners and customs, vocations)
400–499	Language (dictionaries, grammars)
500–599	Pure science (mathematics, astronomy, chemistry, nature study)
600–699	Technology (applied sciences—aviation, building, engineering, homemaking)
700–799	Arts (photography, drawing, painting, music, sports)
800–899	Literature (plays, poetry)
900–999	History (ancient and modern, geography, travel)

Each of these sections is further divided for accuracy in classification. For example, the numbers 500–599 cover the pure sciences, such as astronomy, chemistry, mathematics, paleontology, and physics. Each of these areas has its own division and section number. All books on mathematics are assigned numbers in the 510 to 519 range; mathematics is then broken down into types, such as algebra, arithmetic, and geometry. Geometry's specific number is 513, which can be subdivided through the use of decimal points to provide ten basic categories. Additional digits can be added, creating an ever more precise categorization system.

Books are arranged alphabetically within each classification by the first letters of the author's last name. Therefore, a library that has several books on American history of the colonial period will assign the same basic number (973.2) to all the books and shelve them alphabetically.

Dewey's aim was to create a system that would be simple enough for even casual users to understand, but complex enough to meet a library's expanding needs. His system was developed to meet the needs of many libraries. A second popular system was created to fit the requirements of a specific library, the Library of Congress. This system, now in wide use, is even more detailed and has the advantage of being designed to accommodate growth of knowledge in unexpected areas.

The Library of Congress Classification System

The Library of Congress Classification System is used in most large public and university libraries today. A Library of Congress (LC) classification number contains three lines: a letter at the top, a number in the middle, and a letter-number combination at the bottom.

The Library of Congress went through several systems before devising its own method. Because the Library of Congress contains almost every book ever published in the United States, as well as valuable tapes and research materials, it needs a highly flexible system.

The Library of Congress Classification System contains 20 classes:

A: General works
B: Philosophy and religion
C: History—auxiliary sciences
D: History and topography (except America)
E–F: American history
G: Geography, anthropology, folklore, manners and customs, recreation
H: Social sciences
J: Political sciences
K: Law of the United States
L: Education
M: Music and books on music
N: Fine arts
P: Language and literature
Q: Science
R: Medicine
S: Agriculture and plant and animal industry
T: Technology
U: Military science
V: Naval science
Z: Bibliography and library science

Each of these classes can be divided into a subclass with the addition of a second letter. By adding numbers, the category becomes even more specific. The flexibility of the system becomes obvious when one sees that the alphabet permits 26 subdivisions of any one class. Each of the subdivisions can be broken down further by using the numbers 1 to 9999.

WRITING RESEARCH PAPERS: A HOW-TO GUIDE THAT HELPS YOU GET THE JOB DONE

Most students become acquainted with libraries when they are asked to write school reports that involve research. Here are some guidelines to help you write research papers.

Eleven Steps to Preparing an Excellent Research Paper

1. *Choose a topic.* Be sure the topic is acceptable to your teacher, which also means you must understand the assignment. It's important to choose a topic that is not too broad in scope. Most school papers are 2 to 20 pages long, and that length calls for a fairly narrow topic. Also, in selecting your topic, be sure there is enough research material to allow you to prepare the paper you are being asked to write. To find out whether there is, check the card catalog of your library, the *Reader's Guide to Periodical Literature,* and one or two other general books on your subject.

2. *Write down your ideas.* Once you have done a bit of preliminary reading, you should have some ideas about your subject. Write these down, along with any questions you want to answer.

3. *Formulate a thesis.* Write, in one sentence of twenty words or less, a topic sentence that describes what you plan to write about. If you can't do this, your subject is probably still too broad. This thesis will form the basis of your research.

4. *Survey your research sources.* Check card catalogs and other indexes for all the material under your topic. You may find yourself working with a variety of materials, including magazines, newspapers, journals, books, vertical files (folders of clippings), and audiovisual materials.

5. *Read your sources.* Once you have located your sources, begin to read them, taking notes as you go. Write one note card for each idea, thought, or fact, and one bibliography card for each source.

6. *Organize your note cards.* Once you have read all your source material and carefully noted all your sources on bibliography cards, it is time to organize the cards. In the course of organizing them, you will discover the best and most logical way to organize your paper. Here are some of the ways papers can be organized:

   - Chronologically—in the order in which events happened
   - Comparison/contrast—comparing and contrasting ideas about one or more topics
   - Topically—that is, by subject. This is the way many encyclopedias are organized. Write about the most important topics first, and if you have space, include the smaller ones as well.

7. *Write an outline.* It's almost impossible to write a paper of any length without first outlining it. This helps you organize your thoughts and ideas. Write down the main topics, then list each of the smaller topics under the appropriate larger topic.

8. *Write the first draft.* Your outline should serve as a model for the first draft. You will refer to your note cards for specific facts and figures.

9. *Edit your work.* No one's work is perfect the first time around, and even professional writers edit their work heavily and often write several drafts before they are happy with what they have written.

10. *Write footnotes and prepare the bibliography.* Footnotes are brief citations, or notes, about your sources. For example, if you quote someone or use a statistic from a research source, you would write a footnote for the source. Footnotes may appear at the bottom of the page or at the end of the paper as

The Stuff at the End of a Paper: Footnotes, Endnotes, and Bibliographies

Many students confuse footnotes and bibliographical notes, or aren't quite sure how to go about writing them.

Footnotes

These notes, found in books and research papers, give credit to the work and ideas of others. Each note is indicated in your paper with a raised number, and the footnote is written at the bottom of the same page. If your notes are written all together on a separate page at the end of the paper, they are called endnotes.

Examples of footnotes:

For a book:	[1] Henry James, *A London Life,* p. 32
For a newspaper article:	[2] Dele Olejede, *Newsday,* pp. 4–5.
For a magazine article:	[3] Jane Jones, "Better Late Than Never," *Young Woman Magazine,* pp. 31–36.
Repeat references:	[4] *Ibid.,* p. 4.
	[5] James, p. 45.

If you have just listed a source and plan to cite it again in the very next footnote, as in footnote 3, write *Ibid.,* an abbreviation of the word *ibidem,* which means "cited in the previously mentioned book."

If you listed a source elsewhere and want to mention it later on, write a short reference, as in footnote 4, that consists of the author's name and the page number.

Bibliography

This is a list of all the research sources you used to write your paper, gathered from your bibliography cards. The form of a bibliography card varies, depending upon whether your reference is a book, a magazine, or a newspaper article. Bibliographies are typed on a separate page at the end of the paper. Here are some examples of bibliography cards:

For a book:
James, Henry. *A London Life.* New York: Grove Press, 1979.
For a magazine article:
Jones, Sally. "Ten Ways to Get A's." *Student Weekly*, vol. 23, April 24, 1995, pp. 23–27.
For a newspaper article:
Olejede, Dele. "ANC Halts Talks." *Newsday,* 6/22/92, p. 4.

endnotes. In books, they sometimes appear at the end of each chapter.

A bibliography is a list of the reference works that you have found on the subject you are writing about. Footnotes and bibliographies often contain the same information, but it is arranged differently. Bibliographies appear at the end of the paper or at the end of a book. If you carefully prepared

Library Lore

World's Longest Overdue Book On December 7, 1968, Richard Dodd returned a book to the University of Cincinnati Medical Library (now renamed the Health Sciences Library) that his great-grandfather had checked out in 1823. In this case the fine of $2,264 was waived.

World's First University Library In the fourth century B.C. Aristotle established what may well have been the world's first university library at his school in the Athenian Lyceum in Athens. Like many other important ancient libraries, this one vanished without a trace—either sacked, according to legend, by a Roman general or sold to the Alexandrian Library, the world's largest library of ancient papyrus scrolls, which also inexplicably vanished.

World's First Public Library Julius Caesar planned the world's first public library, but it was probably built by Emperor Augustus around A.D. 37 in Rome. By A.D. 337 Rome could boast 28 public libraries. All of them disappeared, and only 1,800 scrolls, housed in the National Museum in Naples, have survived.

World's Biggest Library Endower American industrialist Andrew Carnegie helped to establish more than 2,800 public libraries in the United States during the late nineteenth century.

bibliography cards as you went along, writing a bibliography will be easy. Use the note cards and bibliography cards to guide you as you work.

11. *Type the final draft.* Once you have made all your changes, it is time to type the final draft, complete with footnotes and bibliography.

TYPES OF MUSEUMS

What libraries are to books, museums are to works of art and other interesting objects that are of special cultural interest to us.

Like libraries, museums can be divided into broad categories. Some museums are public, others private. Most private museums are open to the public, although a few, such as the Frick in New York City, do not admit children under a certain age. Here are the two major types of museums:

general General museums offer a broad array of work. A general art museum, such as the Metropolitan Museum of New York City, for example, shows art from ancient cultures, Asian and African art, as well as European and American art.

specialized Specialized museums may show only one collector's work, which is often limited to one period, or the work may be limited to a single artist, subject, or historical or geographical period. The Museum of Science and Industry in Chicago, for example, is a huge museum that specializes, as its name indicates, in science and industry, or technology. The Museum of Modern Art in New York City shows only art of the last 100 years.

VISITING A MUSEUM: WHAT'S EXPECTED OF YOU

Here are some guidelines to make your visit to a museum more pleasant and interesting:

- Unlike a library, a museum may charge you a general admission fee, but many have a day or an evening when the museum is free. Sometimes museums charge for special exhibits and require that visitors obtain tickets in advance.
- Expect to find your own way around. Most of the time, visitors to museums walk through the collections alone, sometimes aided by printed material or

audio guides. Guards posted in virtually every room can also give you directions.

- Many museums sponsor public lectures and gallery talks, to which the public is invited. They are often free, but sometimes there is a charge.
- Talk softly and move quietly through the collection, taking care not to distract fellow visitors.
- Don't touch the exhibits.
- Don't jump or run, even when a long hall looks inviting, because you could accidentally damage the objects on display.
- Take a sweater. Because museums are often temperature controlled to protect the works they preserve, you may want to take along a light sweater even on the hottest summer day.
- Plan to check your coat, any packages you are carrying, and umbrellas.
- If you need information, ask at the information desk at the front of the museum. Most museums maintain a desk where literature is available, including a map to the collections. Volunteers who work at these desks can direct you to specific exhibits.
- Plan a rest stop if the museum is large. Many museums have cafes, cafeterias, and even full-fledged restaurants. Public restrooms are also available.

THIRTEEN EXTRAORDINARY MUSEUMS FOR YOUNG PEOPLE

In addition to the exhibits listed below, many of these museums have special programs (which often change daily) for children. To learn about them, ask at the information desk when you arrive.

1. **Smithsonian Institution's National Air and Space Museum, Washington, D.C.** This is the world's most comprehensive museum of air and space exploration, with more than 23 exhibit galleries that depict early flight through manned and unmanned space exploration.

Favorite places to visit: Hands down, the winner is the awe-inspiring "Milestones of Flight" gallery, which holds, among other aircraft, the *Spirit of St. Louis*, the airplane in which Charles Lindbergh crossed the Atlantic; the Wright brothers' airplane; the *Belle X-1*, nicknamed "Glamorous Glennis," the plane in which Capt. Charles E. "Chuck" Yeager broke the sound barrier; *Voyager*, the aircraft that went around the world on a single tank of gas; *Friendship 7*, the spaceship in which John Glenn became the first American to orbit the earth; *Gemini 4*, the spaceship from which Americans took their first walk in space; and the *Apollo 11* command module that brought the Apollo astronauts back to Earth after they had landed on the moon.

2. **Field Museum of Natural History, Chicago, Illinois** The Field Museum is one of the country's largest, most comprehensive natural history museums.

Favorite places to visit: The Field Museum is best known to many generations of children for its dinosaurs, but they are being refurbished and won't be on display again until November 1994.

But don't miss the "Inside Ancient Egypt" exhibit, where you can go inside an actual Egyptian tomb, and the "Into the Wild" exhibit, where you go on a simulated nature walk that is so real that when you are in a swampland, you are standing on actual swampland soil. There are logs to roll over so you can "find" salamanders, and at one point, you turn a corner and find yourself nose-to-nose with a life-size model of a grizzly bear.

Small children love the "Place for Wonder," a room filled with touchable objects, such as animal skins and bones, and drawers that open to reveal starfish and other small artifacts.

3. **Henry Ford Museum and Greenfield**

Village, Dearborn, Michigan The museum is 12 acres of American history under one roof, plus Greenfield Village with 81 acres of exhibits on past American life.

Favorite places to visit: Re-creations of Thomas Edison's Menlo Park laboratory; the Wright brothers' home and bicycle shop; and the exhibit on "African-American Family Life and Culture," which has two former slave houses and a head slave's house from the Hermitage plantation, near Savannah, Georgia.

4. **American Museum of Natural History, New York City** Like the Field Museum, this is a large, fascinating, well-rounded natural history museum.

Favorite places to visit: The huge and well-displayed gem collection thrills everyone; as does the African and Asian collection, with its wonderful masks, costumes, and dioramas of life in those parts of the world; the "Whale's Lair," where a huge blue whale hangs from the ceiling, and, of course, the dinosaurs.

5. **Metropolitan Museum of Art, New York City** This is an encyclopedic art museum spanning all cultures and ages from 5000 B.C. to the present.

Favorite places to visit: The mummies and tombs in the Egyptian wing, and the permanent exhibits of medieval arms and armor, including the stunning displays of parade armor (this was your "best" suit of armor, which you wore only to victory parades), armor mounted on horses, and Asian armor.

6. **Brooklyn Museum, Brooklyn, New York** This is an encyclopedic museum with 1.5 million objects on everything from ancient Egyptian artifacts, decorative arts, and African-Oceanic-New World art to contemporary works of art.

Favorite places to visit: The large pieces of Egyptian art, the collection of Egyptian sarcophagi (tombs), and seven large and very impressive totem poles in the African-Oceanic-New World collection are especially popular.

7. **Museum of Science and Industry, Chicago, Illinois** The museum, which has more than 2,000 exhibits covering all aspects of science and industry, is an especially hands-on, participatory museum.

Favorite places to visit: Several generations of children have enjoyed touring the genuine World War II German submarine and the subterranean coal mine. Also popular is the Fairy Castle, a very large dollhouse donated by silent-screen star Colleen Moore. It has real plumbing, chandeliers studded with real diamonds, genuine Oriental rugs, and gold flatware on the dining room table. Another popular place is the 16-foot, walk-through replica of a human heart.

8. **Old Sturbridge Village, Sturbridge, Massachusetts** This living-history museum re-creates a New England town of the 1830s. The museum covers 200 acres, with more than 40 exhibit buildings, where people in historical dress demonstrate the life, work, and community celebrations of early nineteenth-century New Englanders.

Favorite places to visit: The farm, where you can see—and sometimes pet and hold—all kinds of farm animals. Don't miss a chance to join the nineteenth-century children's games on the common.

9. **Colonial Williamsburg, Williamsburg, Virginia** This 173-acre living-history museum re-creates 1770s Williamsburg, Virginia. There are more than 400 buildings, of which 30 or more are open for tours or demonstrations of eighteenth-century trades and crafts, such as silversmithing and wigmaking. Tour guides and craftspersons are in costume.

Favorite places to visit: The brick yard,

where, during the summer, children are invited to use their bare feet to help knead the clay and water to make bricks. In the fall, you can help build a kiln that is used to bake the bricks.

Another favorite activity is the military encampment, where platoons, including children, are recruited for the British army (don't forget: this is a *pre*-Revolutionary village). You will learn to shoulder a musket "stick," fire a cannon, and build a fortification.

10. **The Huntington Library, Art Gallery, and Botanical Garden, San Marino, California** This establishment has 150 acres of gardens; an art collection of British and American eighteenth- to twentieth-century artwork; and a library exhibit hall that displays more than 200 books, manuscripts, and maps, mainly related to Anglo-American history.
Favorite places to visit: Don't miss the 12-acre cactus garden, which contains some pretty bizarre specimens, or two very famous paintings of children: Thomas Gainsborough's *The Blue Boy* and Sir Lawrence Thomas's *Pinkie*. Older children love the library exhibit, where you can see Benjamin Franklin's autobiography—in his own handwriting.

11. **The Exploratorium, San Francisco, California** The first important science discovery center, this is the one that everyone else has tried to imitate. The hundreds of exhibits are constantly changing, but this is a place where you can explore the latest in computer technology or touch a column of fog and watch the air waves spin down.
Favorite places to visit: Hands down—literally—the star of this museum is the Tactile Dome, a totally dark crawl space you can explore only by using your hands. It's so popular, in fact, that there's an extra fee to enter the Dome, and you must make advance reservations.

12. **Los Angeles Children's Museum, Los Angeles, California** Here you can cut your own tape in a real recording studio, visit an animator's workshop (where you can create your own cartoon characters), and play doctor (or patient) in an emergency room.
Favorite places to visit: A real favorite is Sticky City, a collection of huge velcro-taped foam cushions that you can shape into tunnels, bridges, or even skyscrapers. But the most popular activity at this museum isn't even in the museum. It's the regularly scheduled tours of Los Angeles—to such places as a sneaker factory, a space simulation laboratory, and the Dodgers' dugout. (The tours are listed in the magazine *Inside L.A.*)

13. **The Computer Museum, Boston, Massachusetts** Here's everything you ever wanted to know about computers under one roof. The museum's 125 interactive exhibits will thrill adults and kids alike.
Favorite places to visit: The Giant Walk-Through Computer is a working model of a desktop personal computer that is fifty times larger than life—and you can explore every nook, cranny, and transistor. Children especially enjoy the exhibit called "Tools and Toys: The Amazing Personal Computer" because it lets you use a video camera to make your own commercial and also lets you explore "virtual reality" and pen-based writing (the computer responds to your handwriting).

INFORMATION, PLEASE

Alward, Edgar C. *Research Paper, Step-by-Step*. Rev. ed. (Orig. title: *Easing the Agony of the Research Paper.*) Pine Island Press, 1991.

Arwell, Nancie, intro. *Coming to Know: Writing to Learn in the Intermediate Grades*. Heinemann, 1990.

Baugh, L. Sue. *How To Write Term Papers and Reports*. VGM Career Horizons, 1992.

Dickson, Paul. *The Library in America: A Cele-bration in Words and Pictures*. Facts On File, 1986.

Everhart, Nancy. *So You Have to Write a Term Paper!* Watts, 1987.

Lauderdale, Leslie. *You Can Do It Guide to Great School Reports*. Willowsip Press, 1988.

Spaeth, Eloise. *American Art Museums: An Introduction to Looking*. 3rd ed. Harper & Row, 1975.

Strunk, William, Jr., and E. B. White. *The Elements of Style*. New York: Macmillan, 1972.

Terry, Patricia, and Carolyn Bogart. *Research Papers: A Complete Guide for High School Students*. Discovery Dix, 1991.

18

RELIGION

People worship in many different ways. Some worship one God, while others worship many. Some people's gods resemble humans, or were once humans who became gods upon their death. Other people's gods are animal spirits or other spirits from nature. Some people gather to worship together in a special building, while others worship at home or alone.

THE WORLD'S MAJOR RELIGIONS

Bahá'í Bahá'í developed out of Islam in the nineteenth century. It was founded by Baha'Ullah after he was banished from Persia (today Iran). Originally a strict religion much like Islam, Bahá'í became and still is a universalist religion, which means it seeks to include all

The World's Major Religions: How Big Are They?

Estimated Number of Followers of Each Religion

Roman Catholic	971,702,000
Protestant	422,429,000
Orthodox Eastern	163,623,000
Non-Christian	
Islam	924,612,000
Hinduism	689,205,000
Buddhism	311,438,000
Sikhism	17,735,000
Judaism	17,357,000
Confucianism	5,600,000
Bahá'í	4,500,000

faiths and works for sexual equality, worldwide education, and world peace.

Buddhism Buddhism was founded in the sixth and fifth centuries B.C. in India by Siddhartha Gautama, who became the first Buddha and was followed by a long line of Buddhas stretching to today. Buddhism, which is composed of many different groups, stresses the practice of meditation, as do many other Indian religions. Buddhists believe in reincarnation, a cycle in which one's soul is reborn in different forms, depending on one's behavior in life. Although Buddhism has no holy book or spiritual text, informal teachings encourage Buddhists to follow the rules for a right life. They are guided in this by the Four Noble Truths and the Eightfold Path.

Confucianism Confucianism was founded by Confucius, a Chinese philosopher, in the sixth and fifth centuries B.C. Confucius's sayings and dialogues, known as the *Analects,* were written down by his followers. Confucianism stresses ethical behavior between individuals, families, and society. Its followers believe in *li,* or proper behavior, and *jen,* or a sympathetic attitude toward one's fellow humans. A basic belief is that one is treated as well as one treats others. Confucianism was nearly destroyed by the state after the Communist takeover of China in 1949, but it survives in large part because its ethics are so much a part of Chinese culture.

Hinduism Hinduism developed around 1500 B.C. in India, where a majority of the people follow its ideas and beliefs. These beliefs include an attempt to break the cycle of reincarnation, or repeated lives and deaths, and a caste system that ranks people from birth as Brahmins, or priests; as rulers and warriors; as farmers and merchants; or as peasants and laborers. Hindus seek release from repeated lives by practicing spiritual yoga, by following the *Veda,* or Hindi holy scripture, and by devotion to a guru, or personal leader. Although there are many groups of Hindus, who worship many different gods, the three main gods of Hinduism are Brahma, the creator; Vishnu, the preserver; and Shiva, the destroyer.

Islam Islam was founded by a prophet named Muhammad about A.D. 610. Muhammad is said to have personally received the holy scriptures, the *Koran* of Islam, from God. Muhammad is believed to be the last in a long list of prophets that includes Adam, Abraham, Moses, and Jesus. Followers of Islam must study the *Koran,* pray five times a day, give to charity, and try to make a pilgrimage to Mecca, the holy city of Islam, at least once in their lifetime. Islam forbids its followers to eat pork or use alcohol, and has many rules for proper behavior, including ones that forbid usury (charging interest for loans), fraud, and slander of one's fellow humans. Today the most important divisions in Islam are the Sunni and the Shiites.

Judaism Judaism, founded around 2000 B.C. by a prophet called Abraham, introduced the idea of one God into Western religion. Moses is another key figure in Judaism because he is believed to have been given the *Torah,* or Hebrew Bible, personally by God. The followers of Judaism believe God will eventually send a messiah, who in turn will bring heaven on earth. They also believe in a God who judges peoples' actions and rewards and punishes them. Jewish worship takes place at home and in a synagogue or temple, where prayers are led by a rabbi, or specially ordained teacher and spiritual leader. The three main groups of Judaism are Orthodox, Conservative, and Reform.

Orthodox Eastern Church The Orthodox Eastern Church is the third-largest Christian community in the world. It arose from a split with the Roman Catholic Church begun in the fifth century and finalized in 1054. Followers of Eastern Orthodoxy reject the Pope as a spiritual leader and follow the teachings of both the Old Testament and the New Testament of the Bible. Like most Christians, followers believe in a three-part God, represented by the Father, the Son, and the Holy Ghost. Parish priests are permitted to marry, although bishops and monks are not. One of the most basic Orthodox Eastern beliefs is that God is essentially unknowable but is everywhere. The liturgy, or church service, is sung, and unlike the Roman Catholic Church, it is not celebrated daily. Many different groups exist within the Orthodox tradition, such as the churches of Cyprus, Russia, Bulgaria, Greece, and Serbia.

Protestantism Protestantism is the second major denomination of Christianity. It arose in the late 1400s in protest against the power of the Roman Catholic Church. Like adherents of the other two major Christian denominations, Protestants use the Bible as their holy book and strongly believe in a three-part God. Protestantism has fewer sacraments than either of the other Christian groups (most groups recognize only communion and baptism, and some branches do not recognize any sacraments) and is less ceremonial. It does not recognize the power of the Pope, and its priests and ministers may marry. Lay persons play a large and often powerful role in some Protestant denominations. Protestants represent a broad range of beliefs, ranging from fundamentalists, who interpret the Bible literally, to liberals, who view the writings of the Bible primarily as symbolic. Protestantism is strong in the United States, Great Britain, Scotland, Ireland, Germany, and the Scandinavian countries.

Roman Catholicism The Roman Catholic Church is the largest single denomination of Christianity. It is headed by the Pope. Compared to Protestantism and the Orthodox Eastern Church, Roman Catholicism is more sacramental and ceremonial. Its worship service, called Mass, centers on the sacrament of the Eucharist, or Holy Communion, which Catholics believe is the body of Christ. Roman Catholic priests and nuns may not marry. Roman Catholicism is the dominant religion in most of Western Europe and is strong in the United States and in Latin America.

Shinto Shinto is the ancient religion of Japan, established in the fifth century A.D., even before writing was introduced. The origins of the Shinto beliefs are unknown. Followers of Shinto believe in many gods, known as *kami,* who are honored at shrines and with special holidays. Believers also are expected to honor their ancestors. Beyond these beliefs, there are few others in Shinto, except to remain pure and sincere, and to enjoy life.

Taoism Taoism was founded in China by Lao-tzu, who is believed to have been born in 604 B.C. Its beliefs are based on the *Tao-te-ching* and other sacred texts. The *Tao-te-ching* teaches people to live simply, spontaneously, and in close touch with nature. Meditation is used to help followers get in touch with Tao values. Taoists believe in hundreds of spirits, who will control people's lives if they are not controlled through meditation or ritual. Some groups within Taoism have priests and maintain temples and monasteries. Although Taoism continues to flourish in Taiwan, it has been actively discouraged by the People's Republic of China, and no one knows how many Taoists practice their religion today.

RELIGION FROM A TO Z

See "The World's Major Religions" in this chapter for specific religions.

Abraham An important figure in Judaism and Islam. Jews believe Abraham made a covenant, or pact, with God, which they are responsible for keeping. In Islam, Abraham is an important figure, along with Moses. Both are mentioned frequently in the Koran.

Anglicanism The Church of England, which formed when Henry VIII broke with the Roman Church at the time of the Reformation. It combines aspects of Roman Catholicism and Protestantism.

apostle One of the original twelve disciples, or followers, of Jesus Christ. (Judas, the thirteenth apostle, is generally not included, since he betrayed Christ.)

baptism Christian practice of admitting a person in the church by dipping him or her in water (either full-body immersion or sprinkling water on one's head).

Bhagavad-Gita Poem written in Sanskrit that is part of the Indian epic tale known as the *Mahabharata*. It describes the Hindu path to spiritual wisdom and unity with God, which can be achieved through *karma* (action), *bhakti* (devotion), and *jnana* (knowledge). Written between 200 B.C. and A.D. 200.

Brahma One of the three important gods of Hinduism, the creator of the universe.

Buddha This name is used by Buddhists for Siddhartha Gautama, the religious leader who lived in India about 563–483 B.C. and founded Buddhism. It is also given as a title of respect to people who embody divine wisdom and virtue.

church House of worship for Christians.

communion A sacrament for Christians that consists of swallowing bread or bread and wine that has been blessed in memory of Christ.

Confucius Founder of Confucianism, a religion of China.

deity A god.

Eightfold Path In Buddhism, the fourth of the Four Noble Truths is the Eightfold Path, which, in turn, is the way to enlightenment. It consists of (1) right speech, (2) right resolve, (3) right action,

(4) right work, (5) right effort, (6) right mindfulness, (7) right bodily action, and (8) right concentration (meditation).

enlightenment A concept in many Indian religions; the highest level of spiritual understanding.

Five Classics The holy books of Confucianism. These five books, attributed to Confucius, are the *Spring and Autumn Annals,* a history of Confucius's homeland; the *I Ching,* a book that foretells the future; the *Book of Rites,* which outlines ceremonies and describes the ideal government; the *Book of History,* a collection of documents and speeches made by Chinese rulers; and the *Book of Songs,* a collection of poems and songs. The Five Classics were written sometime before the third century B.C.

Four Noble Truths In Buddhism, the four guiding principles, which are: (1) life is a state of suffering; (2) suffering comes from desire and a belief in one's own importance; (3) suffering stops when one reaches a state called Nirvana; and (4) Nirvana can be reached by living a morally "right" life.

fundamentalist A religious believer of any faith who believes in the complete and literal truth of the scriptures. Fundamentalism is popular today among some Christians, Jews, and Muslims.

guru A spiritual leader in Hinduism.

Jesus Christ Founder of Christianity, a religion that was begun in the first century A.D. by Jesus' followers. Christians stress love for their fellow humans, and believe that the poor, the weak, and the humble are most worthy of entering heaven. The Christian God is viewed as kind and forgiving.

jnana An important religious concept in Indian religion and culture, which teaches that spiritual truth is achieved by thinking about human nature in a certain way.

karma A religious concept in Indian religion and culture, which teaches that one's actions are rewarded if they have been good and not rewarded if they have not been good.

Koran The primary holy book of Islam. Made up of fourteen chapters, the Koran appeals passionately to the followers of Islam to believe in God, encourages them to live a good life, tells stories of what happens to those who do (as well as those who don't), and sets forth the rules of social and religious life for Muslims. Muslims believe the Koran contains the actual words of God as they were revealed to the prophet Muhammad. The Koran was written in part during Muhammad's lifetime, although the most widely accepted version of the scriptures was not written until after his death.

laity People of a religion who are not ordained clergy; the congregation.

liturgy The form of a religious service, as set forth by the rules of the religion.

Mass A type of religious service centered around communion; the service of Roman Catholics and some other faiths, most notably, Anglican, is called Mass.

Mecca The holiest city in Islam, located in Saudi Arabia. At the heart of the city is the Great Mosque, open only to Muslims. Followers of Islam are instructed to make at least one pilgrimage to this holy site in their lifetime.

meditation State of quiet contemplation; it is used by some faiths, especially those of India, to achieve a higher state of being.

messiah A savior. Christians believe Jesus Christ is the messiah, and Jews and Muslims believe the messiah is yet to come.

minister Religious leader in the Protestant faith. A minister may be ordained, usually after several years of advanced education, or may be a lay minister, a term used for unordained preachers.

Moses A central figure of Judaism, and an important Biblical figure in Christianity. Moses received the Ten Commandments from God. He also led the Jews out of slavery in Egypt and into the promised land of Canaan.

mosque House of worship for Muslims.

Muhammad The central figure in Islam. Like Jesus in Christianity and Moses in Judaism, Muhammad was chosen by God to convey his message to his followers.

Muslim A follower of Islam.

New Testament Holy book of Christianity that combines with the Old Testament to form the Christian Bible. The New Testament contains 27 books, which contain the words of Jesus, the story of his life and works, the story of his death and resurrection (which is celebrated as Easter), and the teachings and writings of the apostles, the early followers of Jesus. Written around A.D. 100.

Nirvana In Buddhism and other Indian religions, this is the highest possible state of happiness. A person who reaches Nirvana is without desires and in a state of extreme tranquility.

Old Testament The Hebrew Bible; the Christian name for the first part of the Christian Bible. In Judaism the Bible is made up of three parts: the *Torah* (or law), which describes the origins of the world, the agreement between God and Israel, and the Jews' exodus from Egypt into the promised land of Canaan; the *Prophets,* which describes the history of the Israelites and the stories of their kings and leaders; and the *Writings,* which has stories about the Israelites and contains poems and songs. Books of the Bible that are regarded as sacred by the Jews are not considered sacred by Christians. Protestants and Catholics disagree about some of the books of the Old Testament and their order in the Bible. The Old Testament was compiled between about 1000 B.C. and 100 B.C.

penance A sacrament in the Roman Catholic Church and in some Episcopalian churches, a plea for forgiveness for one's sins. Also known as confession.

prophet An important religious leader whose words are believed to be divinely inspired.

Pope Spiritual leader of the Roman Catholic Church.

priest A clergyperson in certain Christian faiths, such as Catholicism.

rabbi In Judaism, a religious leader of a congregation. A rabbi is considered a teacher and spiritual guide.

reincarnation An important belief, common in many Indian religions, that humans are reborn after death.

Reformation Movement begun by Martin Luther in the sixteenth century to reform the Roman Catholic Church. The Reformation eventually led to the formation of the Protestant faith.

resurrection An important belief in Christianity that Jesus Christ, who was crucified to save humanity from their sins, arose from the dead to experience an everlasting life in heaven with God, his father. See also **trinity.**

ritual A religious ceremony.

sacrament A religious act for Christians, believed to have been commanded by Jesus to show his symbolic presence on earth. Among Catholics, the sacraments are baptism, confirmation, communion, penance (or confession), sacrament of the sick, holy orders (priestly ordination), and marriage. Among Protestants, sacraments vary, but the most common ones are communion and baptism.

Shiva One of the three main gods of Hinduism, Shiva is the destroyer.

shrine A holy or sacred place; may be a temple, sanctuary, or memorial. The Great Mosque of Islam in Mecca, Saudi Arabia, for example, contains a shrine at its center.

Siddhartha Gautama Founder of Buddhism, and the first Buddha, who lived in India in the sixth to fifth century B.C.

synagogue A house of worship for Jews. Also called a temple.

Talmud A collection of Jewish oral laws and rabbinical teachings. The *Talmud* consists of two parts: the *Mishna,* which is the main oral law, and the *Gemara,* a commentary on the law. The *Talmud* is also divided into a legal section, called the *Halakhah,* and a section of stories and legends, called the *Aggada.*

Tao-te-ching The basic text of Taoism, made up of 81 chapters or poems that describe how to live a holy life according to Taoist philosophy. The book is believed to have been written by Lao-tzu, who lived at the same time as Confucius in the sixth to fifth century B.C., but parts of it were compiled as early as the third century B.C.

temple A house of worship for many faiths.

Ten Commandments The ten main laws of Judaism, Islam, and Christianity. The Ten Commandments are believed to have been given by God directly to Moses when he spent 40 days on Mt. Sinai.

Torah The first five books of the Hebrew Bible, which are Genesis, Exodus, Leviticus, Numbers, and Deuteronomy.

trinity Concept in Christianity that God, who is one unity, nevertheless reveals himself in three parts: the Father, the Son, and the Holy Spirit. Some Christians, most notably the Orthodox Eastern Catholics and the Unitarians, reject the idea of a trinity.

universalism Religious belief that all persons can be saved, regardless of their faith. In contrast, some religions, such as Islam, believe that only its followers can be saved.

Veda The holy books of Hinduism: the *Samhita,* a collection of prayers and hymns that reveal an eternal truth, written by poets who were said to be inspired by gods; The *Rig-Veda, Sama-Veda, and Yajur-Veda,* also books of hymns; the *Atharva-Veda,* a compilation of magic spells; and the final important section called the *Upanishads,* which describes the relationship between the Brahman, or universal soul, and the individual soul, and also contains information about the practice of spiritual yoga. These texts were compiled from about 1000 B.C. to 500 B.C., making them the oldest holy books in the world.

Vishnu One of the three main gods of Hinduism, Vishnu is the preserver.

The Ten Commandments

The Ten Commandments, believed to have been given to Moses by God on Mt. Sinai, are rules of grave importance in Judaism, Christianity, and Islam. Here are the Ten Commandments, in brief form:

I. You shall have no other gods before me.
II. You shall not worship any graven images.
III. You shall not take the name of the Lord in vain.
IV. Remember the Sabbath, to keep it holy.
V. Honor your father and mother.
VI. You shall not kill.
VII. You shall not commit adultery.
VIII. You shall not steal.
IX. You shall not bear false witness against your neighbor.
X. You shall not covet.

How Religion Began

Although scholars are still working on the question of how religious worship began, the theories of three scholars regarding the origins of religion have become widely accepted.

Tylor's theory Sir Edward Tylor, a British anthropologist who lived in the 1800s, believed that the first worship occurred when people prayed to animals and natural phenomena, such as the moon and the sun. They believed these phenomena were spirits that controlled many aspects of their lives. This kind of worship is known as animism.

Müller's theory Friedrich Max Müller, whom many consider the first historian of religion, also lived in the 1800s. Like Tylor, he believed that worship started with spirit worship, but he suggested that prehistoric humans quickly gave human traits to their gods. This meant that gods could be angry or peace-loving, kind or evil, concepts that are applied to gods even today.

Schmidt's theory Wilhelm Schmidt, an anthropologist who lived in the 1900s, believed that humans created religion when they came to believe that only one holy source was responsible for all life. For prehistoric peoples, the source might have been the sun, the moon, or even a river. This ancient belief in one source as the creator of the world led to the modern belief in one God.

SIGNIFICANT DATES IN THE HISTORY OF RELIGION

Date	Event
B.C.	
c. 2000?	Abraham, founder of Judaism, is alive
c. 1200	Moses, Hebrew lawgiver, is alive
c. 1000–500	*Veda,* holy book of the Hindus and believed to be the oldest such book in the world, is compiled
c. 563–483	Buddha, founder of Buddhism, is alive
551–479	Confucius, founder of Confucianism, is alive
c. 1000–100	Old Testament is compiled
600s–500s	*Tao-te-Ching,* holy book of Taoism, is compiled
c. 400	*Bhagavad Gita,* holy book of Hinduism, is written

c. 200	*Five Classics,* the holy books of Confucianism, are compiled by followers of Confucius
c. 6 or 4– **A.D. 33**	Jesus, founder of Christianity, is alive
A.D. **33?**	Crucifixion and death of Jesus
64?	Peter, Jesus' disciple who continued his teachings and is considered to have founded the Christian church, dies
c. 70–100	New Testament is written
354–430	Saint Augustine, considered the founder of Christian theology (teaching), is alive and writing *Confessions* and *City of God*
400s	Two important Buddhist sects, Zen and Pure Land (Amidism), are founded
c. 570–632	Mohammed is alive, and the *Koran,* the holy book of Islam, is written
622	Muhammad flees persecution in Mecca and goes to live in Yathrib (Medina); the first day of the lunar year in which this event takes place is known as the Hegira and marks the start of the Muslim era
1054	The split between the Orthodox Eastern and the Roman Catholic churches is complete
1095–1229	European Christians undertake the Crusades, a series of holy wars intended to recapture Jerusalem from Muslims
c. 1224–74	Saint Thomas Aquinas, a Roman Catholic and one of the world's great religious writers, is alive
1309–77	Great Schism, or split, in the Catholic church leads to two popes: one in Avignon, France, and another in Rome
1483–1546	Martin Luther begins his protests against the Roman Catholic Church that will eventually lead to Reformation and the founding of Protestantism
1491–1556	Ignatius Loyola, founder of the Jesuits, one of the great Roman Catholic priestly orders, is alive
1509–64	John Calvin, a major leader of the Protestant Reformation, is alive
1549	Christians, who believe in seeking converts, found first mission in Japan and begin attempt to Christianize Asia
1620	Plymouth colony is founded in North America by 102 religious-freedom seekers called Puritans
1624	George Fox, founder of the Society of Friends (Quakers), is alive
1703–91	John Wesley, founder of the Methodist church, is alive
1869–1948	Mohandas K. Gandhi, Indian spiritual and political leader who helped his country achieve independence from Britain and sought reconciliation between Hindus and Muslims, is alive
1933–45	The systematic persecution and

attempted extermination of European Jews, known as the Holocaust, led by Adolf Hitler's Nazi party, takes place

1948   The independent Jewish state of Israel is declared

1962–65   The second Roman Catholic Vatican Council, at which changes were made in the liturgy and greater participation in services by lay church members was encouraged, is convened by Pope John XXIII and concluded by Pope Paul VI

1980s   Rise of fundamentalist religious belief and practice throughout the world becomes the source of internal strife in many countries, especially the Middle East and Eastern Europe

MAJOR RELIGIOUS HOLIDAYS IN THE UNITED STATES

Since the earliest times, people have created special days for worship. Prehistoric peoples held worshipful celebrations when they brought in the harvest, or when the seasons changed. Some of our present-day religious holidays can be traced to ancient ones. Our word *holiday,* in fact, comes from "holy day."

Date	Holiday
January 6	*Feast of the Epiphany* (Christian) celebrates the arrival of the Three Wise Men who sought the newborn baby Jesus; marks the Twelfth Night, or end, of the Christmas season
February 2	*Candlemas* (Christian) celebrates the presentation of the Christ child in the temple and the purification of the Blessed Virgin Mary 40 days after she gave birth to Jesus; mostly observed in Roman Catholic, Orthodox Eastern, and Anglican churches
February 14	*St. Valentine's Day* (Roman Catholic) celebrates the feast day of the patron saint of lovers, engaged couples, and anyone wishing to marry; it has, by tradition, become a nonreligious holiday celebrating love and affection
February or March	*Purim* (Jewish), the Feast of Lots, memorializes Queen Esther's prevention of the annihilation of the Persian Jews, with a celebratory festival of food, entertainment, and costumes; held on the 14th day of the lunar month of Adar
	Shrove Tuesday (Christian), or Mardi Gras, is the last day before the beginning of Lent; it is celebrated by eating rich foods forbidden during Lent and by carnivals in such cities as New Orleans; Rio de Janeiro; and Nice, France

February, March, or April	*Lent* (Christian) is a 40-day period of fasting and penitence in preparation for Easter; Lent begins on Ash Wednesday in Western churches and on the Monday 42 days before Easter in the Orthodox Eastern Church
March 17	*St. Patrick's Day* (Roman Catholic) celebrates the feast day of the patron saint of Ireland; by tradition, it has become a day to celebrate the Irish and their contributions to our culture
March or April	*Passover* (Jewish), or Pesach, commemorates the time when Moses led the Jews out of Egypt; it is celebrated for 7 days by Reform and Israeli Jews and for 8 days by Orthodox and Conservative Jews, beginning the 14th day of the lunar month Nisan, and starting with a meal of remembrance called a seder
	Palm Sunday (Christian) celebrates Jesus's triumphal ride into Jerusalem and the start of Holy Week; it is observed the Sunday before Easter
	Maundy (or *Holy*) *Thursday* (Christian), the Thursday before Easter; marks the Last Supper, the Agony in the Garden, and the arrest of Jesus
	Good Friday (Christian), the Friday before Easter, commemorates Jesus' Crucifixion
	Holy Saturday (Christian), the Saturday before Easter, is observed primarily in Roman Catholic, Orthodox Eastern, and Anglican churches
	Easter Sunday (Christian) celebrates the day Jesus Christ rose from the dead
May or June	*Ascension Day* (Christian) celebrates Christ's ascent to Heaven; it occurs 40 days after Easter
	Shavuot (Jewish) the Feast of Weeks, celebrates the harvest of grain while also observing the receipt of the Ten Commandments by Israel; it is held for one day by Reform and Israeli Jews or for two days by Orthodox and Conservative Jews, starting the 6th day of the lunar month of Sivan
	Pentecost (Christian), or Whitsunday, marks the descent of the Holy Spirit on the Apostles; it is held on the seventh Sunday after Easter
August 15	*The Assumption of the Blessed Virgin Mary* (Roman Catholic and Orthodox Eastern) is the principal feast day in honor of Mary,

September or October

celebrating her assumption, body and soul, into Heaven after her death

Rosh Hashanah (Jewish) marks the start of the new year with solemn prayer and the blowing of the shofar, a ram's horn; it is observed for one day by Reform Jews or for two days by Israeli, Orthodox, and Conservative Jews, starting the first day of the lunar month of Tishri

Yom Kippur (Jewish), the Day of Atonement, is a day of fasting and repentance for the previous year's sins; it follows the 10 days of penitence that began on Rosh Hashanah; it is observed on the 10th day of the lunar month of Tishri

Sukkot (Jewish), the Feast of Tabernacles, is an autumn harvest festival that recalls the wandering of the Jews in the wilderness; it is celebrated for 8 days (7 in Israel) starting on the 15th day of the lunar month of Tishri

Sunday nearest October 31

Reformation Sunday (Protestant) celebrates the day Martin Luther nailed his "95 Theses" to a church door, starting the Protestant Reformation

November 1

All Saints' Day (Christian) is the feast day honoring all martyrs and the Virgin Mary; it is celebrated by Roman Catholic, Orthodox Eastern, and Anglican churches; it is also known as All Hallows' Day and is preceded by Halloween on October 31

Sunday nearest November 30 through Christmas Eve

Advent (Christian) is the period of repentance in preparation for the anniversary of the birth of Christ

December

Hanukkah (Jewish), the Festival of Lights, is marked by the lighting of 8 candles in a menorah; it commemorates the restoration of traditional worship and the rededication of the temple in Jerusalem as well as the rededication of the Jews to their religious ancestry; it is held for 8 days beginning on the 25th day of the lunar month of Kislev

December 8

Feast of the Immaculate Conception (Roman Catholic) honors the Virgin Mary's state of freedom from original sin from the time of her conception

December 9

Feast of the Conception of St. Anne (Orthodox Eastern) celebrates the conception of the Virgin Mary

December 25

Christmas Day (Christian) celebrates

the birth of Jesus Christ; in many Western countries it has become a major winter holiday

Ramadan (Muslim). A monthlong Islamic festival, in which adults fast during the day and celebrate during the evening. This holiday commemorates the date when the Koran was revealed by Allah to Muhammed. It falls in the ninth month of the Muslim year, but because of the lunar calendar, it falls in different seasons in different years

ANCIENT GODS AND GODDESSES

The names and personalities of many of the gods and goddesses revered in ancient times have come down to us today, and are part of our literature, folklore, and mythology. Among the most prominent are Greek, Roman, Germanic (Norse), and Celtic gods and goddesses. Ancient Greeks and Romans had many similar gods, even though their names were different, for the most part.

Greek Deities

Adonis	God who died each year and was reborn. Symbolizes the death of nature each autumn and its rebirth in the spring
Aeolus	God of the winds
Aesculapius	God of medicine
Aphrodite	Goddess of love and beauty
Apollo	God of beauty, youth, poetry, music, prophecy, and archery
Ares	God of war
Artemis	Goddess of the hunt, the moon, and nature
Athena	Goddess of wisdom
Chaos	God of the shapeless void that preceded the creation of the Earth
Chloris	Goddess of flowers
Cronus	Leader of the Titans who ruled the heavens after overthrowing his father, Uranus
Demeter	Goddess of the earth, grain, and harvests
Dionysus	God of wine
Eos	Goddess of dawn
Eris	Goddess of strife and discord
Eros	God of love
Gorgons	Three winged sisters—Euryale, Medusa, and Stheno—the sight of whom turned mortals to stone
Hades	God of the underworld
Hephaestus	God of fire
Hera	Queen of the goddesses; sister and wife of Zeus
Herakles	Son of Zeus; greatest of Greek heroes, who performed 12 labors and was eventually granted immortality

Hermaphroditus	Son of Hermes and Aphrodite who was joined forever to the nymph of the fountain of Salmacis, creating one body that was both male and female
Hermes	Messenger of the gods; patron of thieves
Hestia	Goddess of the hearth
Hygeia	Goddess of health
Hymen	God of marriage
Hypnus	God of sleep
Metis	First wife of Zeus, who helped him become king of the gods; known for her prudence
Morpheus	God of dreams
Muses	Goddesses of the arts and sciences: Clio (history), Euterpe (lyric poetry), Thalia (comedy), Melpomene (tragedy), Terpsichore (dance), Erato (love poetry), Polyhymnia (sacred poetry), Urania (astronomy), and Calliope (epic poetry, chief of the Muses); nine sisters, daughters of Zeus.
Nemesis	Goddess of vengeance
Nike	Goddess of victory
Nymphs	Nature spirits of water, trees, mountains, valleys, and particular locations
Nyx	Goddess of night
Pan	God of flocks and shepherds
Persephone	Goddess of the underworld; symbol of the death of nature each autumn and its rebirth each spring
Plutus	God of wealth
Poseidon	God of the oceans
Priapus	God of fertility
Rhea	Wife of Cronus; mother of the Olympian gods and goddesses Demeter, Hades, Hera, Hestia, Poseidon, and Zeus
Satyrs	Field and forest gods representing nature's bounty
Selene	Goddess of the moon
Sirens	Sea nymphs whose singing enchanted those who heard it
Thanatos	God of death
Titans	Sons and daughters of Uranus, who took power when Cronus overthrew their father: Atlas, Coeus, Crius, Dione, Epimetheus, Eurynome, Hyperion, Iapetus, Leto, Maia, Mnemosyne, Oceanus, Ophion, Pallas, Phoebe, Prometheus, Rhea, Tethys, Themis, and Thia

Tyche	Goddess of fortune or fate	Juno	Queen of the gods; wife of Jupiter
Uranus	God of heaven; father of the Titans	Jupiter (Jove)	The supreme god; ruler of heaven
Zeus	Chief god of Olympus; ruler of heaven, who wielded thunder and lightning	Juventas	Goddess of youth
		Lares	Spirits of ancestors who watched over homes and cities
		Lemures	Spirits of the dead, both good and bad

Roman Deities

		Liber	Another name for Bacchus
Aurora	Goddess of the dawn	Luna	Goddess of the moon
Apollo	God of beauty, youth, poetry, and music	Mars	God of war
		Mercury	Messenger of the gods
Bacchus	God of wine	Minerva	Goddess of wisdom
Cerberus	Guardian of the gates of hell	Mors	God of death
Ceres	Goddess of the earth, grain, and harvests	Neptune	God of the oceans
		Nox	Goddess of night
Coelus	God of heaven	Orcus	God of the underworld
Cupid	God of love	Picus	God who could foresee the future
Diana	Goddess of the hunt, the moon, and nature	Pluto	God of the underworld; another name for Dis
Dis	God of the underworld; another name for Pluto		
		Pomona	Goddess of fruit trees and gardens
Faunus	God of fields and shepherds	Proserpine	Goddess of the underworld
Flora	Goddess of flowers	Psyche	Goddess of the soul, who was united with Cupid
Graces	Three sisters— Aglaia, Euphrosyne, and Thalia—who were goddesses of banquets, dances, social enjoyments, and the arts		
		Salacia	Goddess of the oceans
		Saturn	Roman name for the Greek god Cronus
		Somnus	God of sleep
		Tartarus	God of the underworld
Hercules	Roman name for Herakles	Venus	Goddess of love and beauty
Janus	God of beginnings, responsible for the new year and the seasons	Vesta	Goddess of the hearth
		Victoria	Goddess of victory
		Vulcan	God of fire

Northern European Deities

Aesir — Ancient race of gods led by Odin

Asgard — Home of the gods

Baldur — God of beauty and light; favorite of the gods

Brunhild — Leader of the Valkyries

Fenrir — Vicious wolf, son of Loki; bit off hand of Tyr

Frey — God of fertility; a Vanir

Freya — Goddess of beauty and love; leader of the vanir; sister of Frey; later wife of Odin

Frigga — Principal wife of Odin; mother of the gods; protector of Baldur

Götterdämmerung — Another name for Ragnarok

Loki — Evil giant god who killed Baldur with a dart of mistletoe

Midgard — World of humans

Nanna — Goddess of the moon; wife of Baldur

Njord — God of ships and sailing; father of Frey and Freya

Norns — Three goddesses who determined humans' fate with their weaving and spinning

Odin — Chief god of the giants; ruler of the world; god of battle; also called Wotan, Woden

Ragnorok — Coming day of destruction for gods; twilight of the gods; also called Götterdämmerung

Thor — Chief god of war and thunder; son of Odin

Tyr — God of battles

Valhalla — Great hall in Asgard where souls of dead warriors lived on; Odin feasted with them every night.

Valkyries — Priestesses of Freya, woman warriors who rode out over battlefields each night and decided who would live and who would die; they brought dead warriors to Valhalla

Vanir — Ancient race of gods led by Freya; rivals of the Aesir

Wotan — Another name for Odin

Celtic Deities

Balor — Grandfather of Lug, whom Lug conquered in a fight

Belenus — God of war

Brigits — Goddesses, much like Greek

Muses, who presided over poetry, metalwork, and healing

Cormac MacAirt — Wise man and warrior of Irish legend who had a gold cup that shattered when three lies were said into it and re-formed when three truths were told into it; possessor of a magical branch that protected the sick and wounded

Cuchulainn — God of warriors; son of Lug; may have been model for Sir Gawain in the legend of King Arthur; both wore magical belts that protected them

Danann — Mother goddess of Ireland and goddess of the Tuatha

Diarmuid — Friend and nephew of Finn MacCool who fell in love with Grainne

Fenians — Band of warriors led by Finn MacCool; a legendary Irish people, who admitted to their number only those who were learned, wise, and brave, by means of several tests including fighting 9 warriors while standing in a waist-high hole without suffering any injuries.

Finn MacCool — Leader of Fenians, a legendary Irish people that admitted only those who were learned, wise, and brave; defender of his country against foreigners

Grainne — Daughter of an Irish king who was supposed to wed Finn MacCool but who instead eloped with Diarmuid, who was killed by Finn MacCool, after which Grainne fell in love with MacCool and became his wife

Lug — Chief god who was so wise he was permitted to join and rule the Tuatha

Oisin — Son of Finn MacCool, who aided him in battle

Tuatha — Legendary race of Irish wizards, originally the people of the goddess

Danann; later defeated, they reputedly lost everything but the right to control the underground, where they became the "Little People," or leprechauns of Ireland

Deities of North American Native Peoples

Agwe	Hawaiian sea god
Amotken	Creator god of the Selish, one of the oldest North American peoples
Asgaya Gigagei	Thunder god of the Cherokees
Atius Tirawa	Creator of the Pawnees
Awonawilona	Creator god of the Zuni Pueblo
Estsanatlehi	Most revered goddess of the Navajo; her name means "the woman who changes" because she grows old, then slips into youth again, and continues this process endlessly
Gluskap	Creator god of the Abnaki, an Algonquin tribe
Hahgwehdiyu	Creator god of the Iroquois
Hisakitaimisi	Creator god of the Creek peoples

Igaluk	Inuit Eskimo moon god
Iyatiku	Pueblo corn goddess
Kici Manitu	Supreme god of the Algonquin
Kwatee	Trickster god of Indians of the Puget Sound region of Washington
Masewi	Along with Oyoyewa, one of the twin gods of the Pueblo people, sent by the universal mother to arrange the sun in the sky and assign people to clans
Napi	Creator of the Blackfoot people
Nayenezgani	Slayer of alien gods; lord of light; along with Tobadzistsini, twin gods of the Navajos
Oyoyewa	Along with Masewi, a twin god of the Pueblos.
Pinga	Eskimo goddess; guardian of game and protector of the living
Sedna	Evil sea goddess of the Inuit Eskimos
Tobadzistsini	Child of water and the lord of darkness; protector of the Navajos from alien peoples; a

	twin god, along with Nayenexgani, both offspring of Estsanatlehi and Tsohanoai
Tsohanoai	Sun god of the Navajos
Wakonda	Great wise power and supreme hunter of the Plains Indians
Wonomi	Supreme god of the Maidu in California

Deities of Central and South American Peoples

Agwe	Haitian Vodou god of the sea, married to Erzulie
Ah Puch	Mayan god of death
Chac	Mayan rain god
Cintoetl	Aztec corn god
Coatlicue	Aztec earth goddess in form of a snake
Damballah	Powerful serpent god of Haitian Vodou; with his wife, Erzulie, forms a rainbow that shelters the earth
Erzulie	Haitian Vodou goddess of basic life forces, who was wife of Damballah, Agwe, and Ogoun
Ghede	Wise god of death in Haitian Vodou

Guinechen	Master god of the Auca tribe of Chile; opponent of the Incas
Huitzilopochtli	Aztec god of war
Hunab	Mayan creator god
Inti	Inca sun god
Itzamna	Mayan god; son of creator god Hunab; lord of heavens and day and night
Mictlantecuhtli	Aztec god of death
Ogoun	Warrior god of Haitian Vodou; married to Erzulie
Ometecuhtli	Aztec supreme deity
Pachamama	Earth goddess of the Incas
Quetzalcoatl	Plumed serpent god of Central America; creator; sun god
Simbi	Haitian Vodou god; patron of spring and rains
Tlaloc	Rain god of the Toltec and Aztec peoples

Deities of African Peoples

Anansi	Trickster god of West African legend; creator god in form of a spider
Asa	Father god of Ahamba people of Kenya
Chiuta	Supreme deity of the Timbuktu people in Malawi

The Search for the Holy Grail: British Legend

Although Arthur and the Knights of the Round Table were not gods, the legends surrounding these mythic figures have religious overtones and are an important part of Northern European mythology.

Arthur Famous king of British legend; leader of the Knights of the Round Table.

Gawain Member of the Knights of the Round Table; the perfect knight.

Guinevere Wife of Arthur, who loved Lancelot.

Holy Grail Mythic cup believed to have been cup used at Christ's Last Supper and also the cup that held the blood from his wounds when he was crucified. The Holy Grail was brought to England, then lost. The Knights of the Round Table spent their lives searching for it.

Lancelot Knight loved by Guinevere, Arthur's wife.

Merlin Magician and counselor of Arthur, whom he raised. Merlin was born of a human mother and an Incubus father. (The Incubus were a race that were good, but also had overtones of evil and special powers.)

Round Table Gathering of the greatest knights of the land; bound by special oaths to defend one another, to protect the weak, and to follow other customs that became known as the rules of chivalry.

Fascinating Facts

world's largest religious gathering On February 6, 1989, 15 million people gathered at Kumbh mela, a Hindu festival, held in India.

first house of worship Archaeologists believe that many of the prehistoric caves (30,000–10,000 B.C.) in Europe were among the world's first places of worship.

oldest U.S. church St. Luke's, a Protestant church built in 1637 in Isle Wright County, Virginia, is the oldest U.S. church building still in existence.

oldest U.S. synagogue Touro Synagogue, built in 1763 in Newport, Rhode Island, is the oldest synagogue building in the United States.

world's largest gothic cathedral St. John the Divine, an Episcopalian church in New York City, is the largest gothic cathedral in the world. Begun in 1892, construction of the cathedral was halted during World War II and resumed in 1979. The workers who are carving the facade will spend the rest of their lives completing the church.

world's largest religious structure Angkor Wat, in Cambodia, built in the first half of the twelfth century and dedicated to the Hindu god Vishnu, is the world's largest religious structure, covering 402 acres.

world's oldest burial ground The Shanidar cave, dating back to 60,000 B.C., in northern Iraq contains the oldest human relics that are believed to have been buried in a religious ritual.

most priceless sacred object The world's most priceless sacred object is believed to be a fifteenth-century gold Buddha in the Wat Trimitr Temple in Bangkok. Standing 10 feet tall and weighing an estimated 6.06 tons, it is valued at approximately $35 million, based on the current price of gold.

Sabbath Day

Most of the religions practiced in the United States set aside one day a week for worship. It is called the sabbath, a word that comes from the Hebrew *shabat,* and means "day of rest."

Religion	Sabbath
Christians	Sunday
Jews	Sunset Friday through sunset Saturday
Muslims	Friday

Chuku — Great creator spirit of the Ibo people of Eastern Nigeria

En-kai — Rain god of the Maasai people of East Africa

Hai-uri — Monster god, much feared, of the Hottentot people

Heitsi-eibib — Heroic god of the Hottentot

Holawaka — Mythical bird sent by God to tell Ethiopians they would live forever

Imana — Supreme god of the Banyarwanda people of Rwanda

Kaang — Creator god of the Bushmen of South Africa

Kalumba — Creator god of the Luba people in Zaire

Katonda — Creator god of the Ganda people in East Africa

Le-eyo — Great ancestor of the Maasai people

Mwambu — Along with Sela, the ancestor god of the Abaluyia people of Kenya

Njambi — Creator god of the Lele people

Nommo — Creator god of the Dogon people

Nyame — Creator god of the Ashanti people; leader of the gods

Ogun — Yoruban people's god of iron and war

Olorun — Chief of the 1,700 deities of the Yoruban people

Sela — Along with Mwambu, the ancestor god of the Abaluyia people of Kenya

Tilo — God of the Tonga people of Zambia and Malawi

Unkulunkulu — Chief creator and war god of the Zulu people

Utixo — Good god of the Hottentot people who sends rain for the crops; Utixo's voice is thunder

Wele — Supreme deity of the Abaluyian people, a Bantu group of Kenya

Interesting Words for Interesting Ideas:

Not everyone believes in god in the same way. Different words describe different views of god.

theist Someone who believes in a god or gods. Most religions are theist.

monotheist One who believes in only one God. Christianity, Judaism, and Islam are monotheistic religions.

polytheist Someone who believes in more than one god. The ancient Greeks and Romans had many gods. Today, Hindus and many people in Africa and the South Pacific Islands worship many gods and goddesses.

atheist One who does not believe in god. Atheists are not necessarily opposed to religion, as is commonly believed. For example, Confucianism and some forms of Buddhism are considered atheistic religions because they follow a system of beliefs that is not centered around the existence of a god. Similarly, followers of Ethical Culture believe in ethics and morality, but do not follow any specific religious beliefs.

agnostic Someone who does not believe the existence of god can be proved or disproved.

INFORMATION, PLEASE

Alexander, Pat, et al., eds. *The Lion Encyclopedia of the Bible*. Lion Publishing, 1986.

Barber, Richard. *A Companion to World Mythology*. Delacorte, 1979.

Bulfinch's Mythology. Spring Books. 1964.

Burland, Cottie Arthur. *Mythology of the Americas*. Hamlyn, 1970.

Ickis, Marguerite. *The Book of Religious Holidays and Celebrations*. Dodd, Mead, 1966.

Makhlouf, Georgia. *The Rise of Major Religions*. Silver, 1988.

Ward, Hiley H. *Friends' Beliefs: A Young Reader's Guide to World Religion*. Walker, 1988.

19

ETIQUETTE

Good manners, also called etiquette, provide us with two important elements in our lives:

1. They give us the ceremonies and rit-

uals that add special meaning to our lives.
2. They serve as guidelines for treating one another with respect.

Everyday Manners: Five Magic Rules

Although we often think of manners as something we put on for company or special occasions, their real purpose is to help us get along with one another on a daily basis. That's why the most important manners are the ones you use with your family, friends, and schoolmates. Although etiquette books are filled with detailed information about all aspects of manners, five simple guidelines will get you through most occasions and help to keep you popular with your friends and family.

The Five Magic Rules

1. Say "please" and "thank you." They can work wonders.
2. Be prompt. Showing up on time is a sign of respect for others. It says, "I understand your time is important."
3. Listen to others. When someone speaks to you, really pay attention to what he or she has to say. Do not interrupt others.
4. Respect others' privacy. This may seem like a funny rule of etiquette, but it is an important key to getting along with people. Do not use others' belongings without their permission. Do not snoop into others' personal objects or papers. Do not listen in on others' conversations.
5. Be neat. This, too, probably seems like a funny rule to help you get along with others, but neatness—at home, at school, and at work—goes a long way toward making the environment pleasant for others. It is one of the most important ways we can show others that we respect them.

THE IMPORTANT MOMENTS: CEREMONIES

Christian Birth Ceremonies

Virtually every religion has some ceremony to recognize the arrival of a new baby. In Christianity, the birth ceremony is called christening or baptism.

Most Christians are christened, or baptized, as small babies, too young to remember the experience. In some churches, though, children are not christened until they are old enough to know what is happening. They also may be present when younger sisters and brothers are christened.

On its christening day, an infant is dressed in white, often in a long white dress that has been handed down in the family. Older girls wear a white or pastel dress, and boys wear a navy blazer and gray pants or a suit. Most christenings take place in church, but some Protestants christen their children in home ceremonies.

A party is usually held afterward, where a special white cake is served and people offer toasts to the new baby.

Jewish Birth Ceremonies

A *brit* is a circumcision ceremony for a Jewish boy. It is held in the parents' home on the eighth day of the baby's life. A Jewish official called a moyel presides over the ceremony. After the religious ceremony, there is a special party to honor the newborn, who is by this time usually fast asleep in his bed.

The birth of a girl is celebrated at a naming ceremony held in the synagogue and followed by a party at home afterward. This ceremony is held on one of the first Sabbaths after the girl's birth.

First Communion

Roman Catholic children celebrate First Communion when they are six or seven years old. The ceremony, a Mass, in which the children receive the sacrament of the Eucharist for the first time, is held in church. The ceremony is usually followed by a reception at the church and sometimes another family party at home.

Boys wear white shirts, dark pants, or a suit. What a girl wears depends upon the custom in her community. In some communities, girls wear short, white dresses, while in others they wear elaborate, long, white ones that resemble wedding dresses. On her head, a girl may wear a small piece of lace or an elaborate veil.

Confirmation

Protestants take their first communion (and become members of the church) between the ages of eleven and fifteen and Roman Catholics between eleven and twelve, after several months of study. This coming-of-age ceremony takes place at church and is sometimes followed by a family celebration.

Boys wear suits or a white shirt and pants, and girls wear modest, pastel dresses. Bright colors or black are not appropriate on this occasion.

Bar/Bat Mitzvah

When they are thirteen, Jewish children celebrate their Bar Mitzvah (for boys) or Bat Mitzvah (for girls). After months of preparation, the young person is called to read from the Torah for the first time. The Torah is a scroll written in Hebrew that contains part of the Jewish Bible.

The ceremony is held in a synagogue. Afterward, the entire congregation celebrates with a reception called a kiddish. There may also be a special party for family and friends on Saturday night or Sunday. Often many people are invited to the party, lunch or dinner is served, and there is music and dancing.

Girls wear pretty dresses, and boys usually wear suits.

Graduation

Graduations are family celebrations, and naturally, every family has its own customs and traditions to follow. Although some schools hold graduation ceremonies for the lower grades, the big graduations in your life will be high school and college. There is a school ceremony, which your family will attend (although tickets are often limited), followed by a party, usually held at home or in a restaurant and attended by your family and friends.

Weddings

Marriage is one of the biggest steps in anyone's life, and people celebrate this occasion in many different ways. Some people get married in a house of worship, and then have a party, called a reception. Others prefer to keep the occasion small and private. These people may marry in a chapel, the clergyperson's study, or at City Hall.

A marriage is a legal ceremony. The county or city in which you live will request certain information from those who wish to marry, and also may require a blood test before it will issue a marriage license.

By tradition, a bride wears white—often an elaborate white dress with a veil. If the wedding is large, the couple will ask their close friends and relatives to be part of their wedding party, as bridesmaids and ushers.

Some special roles in the wedding party are reserved for young persons. The flower girl and ring bearer are children aged four to six or seven. Junior bridesmaids and ushers are children aged eight to twelve. Junior attendants dress similarly to the rest of the wedding party.

Funerals

The most somber moments in our lives are when we must say good-bye to a relative or dear friend, and much ceremony surrounds this event. The death of a person is usually marked by a funeral service, which may be held in a house of worship or at a funeral home. Sometimes a memorial service is held instead of a funeral service.

Every religion has its own practices regarding the end of a person's life. A person's body may be either buried or cremated, for example, depending upon his or her religious beliefs. In another example, it is customary to send flowers to a Christian funeral (although increasingly often these days, donations to charities are requested instead) but not to a Jewish funeral. Children typically do not attend funerals until they are six or seven.

CELEBRATIONS: ALL ABOUT PARTIES

Etiquette books help show us how to entertain our friends. Parties, for instance, are wonderful ways to spend time with friends and family. They are often organized around special occasions such as birthdays, confirmations, and graduations. Some parties will include your extended family and even your parents' friends, and other parties, especially as you enter your teens, will be exclusively with your own friends.

Birthday Party

Most children love birthday parties, and most families plan some sort of celebration—either a small family party or a larger party that includes friends—to honor the occasion. Your parents may give you a birthday party every year, or you may have one every few years. On the years you do not have a party, the family will still celebrate with cake and candles, and you will receive presents.

Birthday parties are sometimes organized around themes, or your parents may take you and several friends somewhere special, such as an amusement park, athletic event, or a play or musical performance. Obviously, what you wear depends on what you are doing.

Your parents will plan the party, usually

asking you about the plans as they do so. As the guest of honor, you will make the biggest contribution by helping to decide whom to invite. If the entertainment is expensive, you may be able to invite only your closest friends. If you are able to invite your entire class, it is good manners to make sure that no one is excluded.

Sweet Sixteen Party

The sixteenth birthday marks a young person's passage into almost-adulthood, and many girls like to celebrate with a special party. For many years, a traditional Sweet Sixteen party was a dinner dance with sophisticated pink decorations. But there is no reason that this special occasion could not be marked with some other kind of social event—a swimming or skiing party, for example—any more than there is a reason to limit this rite of passage exclusively to girls.

Teen Party

It goes along with being a teenager that you will want to entertain your friends at parties. Teens who are old enough to give parties for their friends are also old enough—and usually quite willing—to help with the planning as well. The main entertainment at teen parties is music, and there is usually dancing.

The number of people you can invite will depend on the size of your home (or backyard), and your parents' patience. Even though you will plan most of the party (and take responsibility for the cleanup), teen parties should not be given without your parents' permission and supervision.

Graduation Party

When you graduate from high school and possibly college, your parents may want to plan a party for you. Graduation parties are often held the day of the ceremony or within a few weeks afterward.

Formal printed announcements are sent inviting family and close friends. Most of your friends will not be able to attend your high school graduation party because they will be celebrating with their own families, but since college graduations are held at different times, your friends can probably join you to celebrate that graduation.

As the guest of honor, you are expected to mingle and talk for at least a few minutes with every guest—and yes, that includes your cousin Sam, whom you cannot stand. The flip side of this obligation (and this will help you get away from the Cousin Sams of the world whom you don't want to talk to) is that since you are the guest of honor, you must mix with everyone and cannot talk too long to any one person. Although at other parties the guest of honor usually leaves first, on this occasion, you are expected to stay until the last guest departs.

What you wear will depend on how dressy the party is. You may still be wearing the suit or dress you wore to the graduation ceremony, or you may change into a less formal outfit. Ask your parents what they would like you to wear if you aren't sure.

DATING DAYS

The age at which you begin dating depends on you and, often your parents. Usually interest in the opposite sex is sparked during the preteen or teenage years.

The first organized boy-girl social events may be parties or other outings. Everyone goes in a group, and there is little pairing off at this stage.

As you enter your later teens, though, you may begin to date one special person. The two of you may even decide to date one another exclusively for a time.

Someone has to initiate a date. For this to happen, one of you—either the boy or the girl—will ask her or him. If the other person accepts, it's a date. The person who did the asking then plans the activities of the date, although it's polite to ask the other person what he or she would like to do.

Sometimes the person who does the asking pays for everything; sometimes, especially for a big dance or a prom, expenses are shared. Once a couple have been dating for a while, they usually share expenses.

Eight Popular Things for Teens to Do on Dates

Go to the movies

Play miniature golf

Go to a school sports event

Go to a school (or some other sponsor's) dance

Play a sport together—tennis or biking, anyone?

Go to a concert

Go to a school or community event, such as a play

Go to a party

GIVING AND RECEIVING: BEING GRACIOUS ABOUT GIFTS

There is an old saying that " 'Tis better to give than to receive," but what the saying doesn't tell us is how difficult it sometimes is to be the gracious recipient of a gift. As you grow up, you will need to master the art of both giving and receiving.

When you are very young, your parents will help you pick out gifts, but as you get older, you will want to become more involved in making the choices. Here are some of the occasions when young people give gifts to family and friends:

Birthday of parents, siblings, and friends

Bar and Bat Mitzvah

Confirmation

Parents' wedding anniversary

Mother's Day

Father's Day

Christmas or Hanukkah

Graduation

Choosing Gifts People Will Like

Try to give people gifts they want, rather than what you want to give them. To find out what people want, watch to see what their interests are, what books they read or hobbies they follow, how they dress, what colors they wear. All these are clues that will help you choose presents that will please others.

Gifts are usually wrapped with special paper and ribbon. Until you learn to wrap your own, ask a parent or some other adult to help you.

Anniversary Gifts

The following list shows traditional gifts for wedding anniversaries. It will help you select presents for your parents. You may also want to refer to the list of birthstones (see page 26) when choosing birthday gifts for special friends.

Year	Gift
1	Paper or plastics
2	Cotton or calico
3	Leather
4	Linen, silk, or synthetics (rayon, nylon)
5	Wood
6	Iron
7	Copper, wool, or brass
8	Bronze or electrical appliances
9	Pottery
10	Tin or aluminum
11	Steel
12	Silk or linen
13	Lace
14	Ivory
15	Crystal or glass
20	China
25	Silver
30	Pearls
35	Coral or jade
40	Rubies or garnets
45	Sapphires or tourmalines
50	Gold
55	Emeralds or turquoise
60	Diamonds or gold
75	Diamonds or gold

Receiving Gifts

When one person gives you a gift, you can usually open it on the spot. When you are given several gifts at the same time, as at a birthday or graduation party, it is polite to wait until later in the party and then open the gifts all at once with your guests gathered around.

To open any gift, begin with the card. Open and read it carefully, announcing to everyone present who the gift is from. Then you can open the gift, and again, the key word is carefully. If the wrapping paper and bow are especially beautiful, take a moment to show them off rather than just ripping the gift open.

When you finally see the gift, it is good manners to act pleased and excited about it and to thank the person who gave it to you. Do this even if you already have five other versions of the gift, and even if you do not like it. To behave otherwise would hurt the giver's feelings, and no matter how wrong the gift may be for you, the giver has taken time and spent money to get it.

Even when you don't like a gift, try to find something to praise about it anyway. Let's say your great-aunt Josephine has just given you a sweater you wouldn't be caught dead wearing. You would probably sound insincere saying you love it, but you can bring yourself to say that you love the color or the buttons.

The important thing to remember is that your great-aunt went to considerable time and trouble to buy you a gift, and even if she totally missed, it is her good thoughts toward you that count.

When your guests leave, thank each of them again for his or her gift.

On the Receiving End: Thank-You Notes You Have to Write

When someone has taken the time and trouble to buy you a present, you must send a written thank-you note. Your parents may order special stationery with your name im-printed on it (these are called informals) for you to use, or you may buy some pretty writing paper at a local store for this purpose.

Thank-you notes can be short, but they must mention the gift and something you especially like about it. Here is a sample thank-you note:

Dear Aunt Josephine,

Thank you so much for the pink mohair sweater you gave me for my birthday. I especially love the pink duck buttons.

I'm so glad you were able to be with me on my birthday. It made turning sixteen much more special. Thanks again for the lovely present and for coming to my party.

Love,
Susie

GETTING ALONG AT HOME

We don't usually think of manners as something we have to use at home, and it's true that this is someplace where you can relax and be yourself. But just consider how much more smoothly your life will go if you treat those who are closest to you with consideration and respect.

Telephone Talk

Most young people like to talk on the telephone—often for hours at a time. This often causes conflicts within families. Here are a few guidelines to help you stay in touch with your friends and also stay on speaking terms with your family:

- *If you are going to tie up the phone for more than a few minutes, ask the other members of your family whether they are expecting an important call.* If someone is, then delay your phone call until that call has been received.
- *Don't tie up the phone for hours on end.* Check your watch and use a self-imposed limit on your calls—say, 20 or 30 minutes. Remember, you can always call someone back if you need to.

Watching Your Ps & Qs: Special Rules That Children Used To Have to Follow

Manners used to make children's lives far more rigid and unpleasant than they do today. Children are still expected to show respect for their elders, but the demands have eased up on them considerably from what they were hundreds of years ago.

- In the Middle Ages, knowing how to serve a formal dinner was considered part of one's education, and young persons were often sent to live with—and wait on—another family for several years so they could learn how to do this.
- During the Renaissance, children were expected to stand continuously in the presence of their parents—unless they were given the high honor of kneeling. For many years, children were also taught to kneel in the presence of their teachers.
- In the seventeenth and eighteenth centuries, a young man could not speak to a young woman unless they had first been properly introduced. Once they were introduced, he still could not say hello to her unless she acknowledged him first.
- A hundred years ago, children were often not permitted to speak unless spoken to.
- Until about fifty years ago, boys were expected to bow and girls were expected to curtsy when introduced to anyone.
- In colonial times, children usually bowed before leaving their parents' table after dinner.

- *When someone else wants or needs to use the family phone, relinquish it graciously—and quickly.*
- *Answer the phone correctly.* Your parents will tell you how they want you to do this. Perhaps they want you to say "Jones residence" or simply "Hello." Follow these instructions because they may involve security and safety as well as good manners.
- *When you answer the phone and it's for someone else, be polite.* Don't ask who it is if the person doesn't offer that information or your parents haven't asked you to get it. If the family member isn't home or can't come to the phone, offer to take a message. Be sure to write down the message. It's a good idea to read it back to the caller so you're sure you got it right.
- *When you call someone else, use your good manners to impress the person who answers the phone.* Don't say, "Is Julie there?" but say, "Hello, Mrs. Simpson.

This is Hillary. May I please speak with Julie?"
- *Except when calling your closest relatives and maybe your closest friends, don't expect people to know your voice on the phone.* Identify yourself immediately.

Showing Responsibility: What Kids Can Do to Help at Home

Every family has moments when they are less helpful or kind to one another than they should or could be. A few simple hints will help family life go more smoothly:

- *Clean the bathroom after you use it.* Hang up your towels and clean the bathtub and sink. Pick up your dirty clothes.
- *If you make a mess in a shared space, such as the living or family room, clean it up as soon as you can.*
- *Clean up after yourself in the kitchen.* For

You Bow, I Kiss: Customs Around the World

Manners are not the same around the world. While certain basic courtesies will serve you well anywhere in the world, many local customs vary from country to country or even city to city. Some examples:

- The Japanese bow to one another in greeting. The person of lower rank is expected to bow lower than his or her superior.
- In certain Buddhist countries, people greet one another with a brief prayerful pose, hands together.
- In the United States, a host goes through doors last as a sign of courtesy to a guest or higher-ranking person. In Arab countries, the host goes through doors first as a gesture of protection toward the guest.
- In some cultures (for example, much of the Arab world), women are expected to look away in the presence of men. In the United States and most of Europe, men and women make direct eye contact when they converse.
- In South America, it would be rude not to ask a man about his wife and children. In Arab countries, it would be rude to do so.
- Even within countries, customs may vary. Consider, for example, greeting customs in various regions of the United States. New Yorkers often kiss one another when they greet, and they may even greet persons whom they do not know well this way. In much of the rest of the country, a greeting kiss is reserved for close friends and family—and only after you haven't seen them for a while.
- Among those who kiss as a greeting, customs vary widely. Americans kiss briefly on one cheek. The French kiss on both cheeks. In the United States, men rarely kiss in greeting, but in much of the rest of the world—the Arab countries, for example—men kiss one another on both cheeks in greeting.
- Time changes some customs. In the eighteenth century, for example, Americans shook hands at eye level.

example, if you have a glass of milk, wash the glass.

- *Pitch in and help out when your entire family is involved in a cleaning project.* If everyone is raking leaves or helping to clean out the garage, join them.
- *Try to do whatever your parents ask you to do helpfully and with no complaints.* If you aren't sure what your parents would like you to do, ask them. Remember, they took care of you and picked up after you for many years when you were too little to do it for yourself.

GETTING ALONG IN PUBLIC

Here are some hints to help you get along in public.

Introductions

Introductions are easy if you know how to do them. The cardinal rule of introductions is this: *Always introduce the younger or less important person to the older or more honored person.* Here are some examples:

- Introduce your friends to your parents and other adults:

    Mom, I'd like you to meet Andrea. She's my new friend.

- Introduce younger, less important persons to teachers, clergypersons, and public officials:

    Reverend Wells, I'd like you to meet my mother, Alice Wilder.

    Mr. Mayor, I'd like you to meet my mother.

- Introduce anyone who comes to your home to your parents, who are honored because they are the hosts:

    Mom and Dad, I'd like you to meet Mrs. Perry, my teacher.

- Introduce children and young people to adults:

    Aunt Mary, I'd like you to meet my school friend Josie.

And now that you know the rules, don't worry if you break them. The important thing is to make sure people meet each other. Say everyone's name clearly when making an introduction. When you are introduced to someone, say "How do you do" or "Nice to meet you." Even a simple "Hello" will be fine.

When young people meet these days, there is a tendency to introduce each other using only first names. If you really want someone to know who you are, and you want to know others, it's a good idea to use last names as well. For example: Sally, this is my friend Jodie Stewart. Jodie, this is Sally Gold.

Behavior in Public Places

Few young persons realize how rowdy and noisy they can be when they fill up a sidewalk, a bus, or a mall walkway. When out in public, follow a few simple rules:

- *Keep your voice down.* Don't yell at your friends or call to them. When you want to talk to them, walk over and do so in a normal voice. This means if one friend is at the back of the bus, and you're at the front, wait until you get off to talk, or walk back to talk quietly with your friend.
- *Don't monopolize public spaces.* Never walk more than two or three abreast on public sidewalks or at malls. Break into smaller, less intimidating groups when

---

Men and Women and Manners

Perhaps in no other area have manners changed so much or so fast, especially in recent years, as they have between the sexes. Starting in eleventh-century France, when chivalry—or devotion to women—was one of the most important things that young knights were taught, men began to use manners to show respect for women, who were considered the weaker sex.

Over the centuries the code of behavior between men and women became simpler, but many remnants of the old rules of chivalry continued to exist—until the 1960s. That was when women, in large part due to the women's movement, decided they could do with a little less respect and a lot more equality. Here are some of the things men (and boys) were until only recently expected to do for women:

- Tip their hats when greeting them and remove them in their presence
- Hold a woman's coat for her and help her put it on
- Hold a woman's arm when a couple walked together
- If seated, stand up when a woman arrived
- Ask her for dates (she could never ask) and pay for everything

you get on buses and other forms of public transportation.

- *Show respect for those around you.* Offer your seat to someone older or a parent with a young child. Apologize if you accidentally step on someone or bump into him or her.
- *Show respect to those who serve you in public.* This includes waiters, bus drivers, and clerks in stores. Say "please" and "thank you" when someone provides you with even the smallest service, such as handing you a bus transfer.

GETTING ALONG WITH OLDER PEOPLE

In our society, young people are expected to show some forms of respect to older persons. Here are some guidelines to help you:

- *Say "hello" and call adults by their names when greeting them.*
- *Do not call an adult by his or her first name unless you have been asked to do so by the adult.*
- *Stand to greet your parents' friends or any other adults.* Remain standing until the adult tells you or motions you to sit down, or turns his or her attention elsewhere.
- *Be helpful whenever you can.* Open doors, offer a chair, offer to carry packages, or do anything else an older person may need.

TABLE MANNERS

Table manners have a purpose: They make eating more pleasant. None of us, for example, really wants to watch another person chew food with his or her mouth open. So without spending a lot of time on the finer points of table manners (such as which fork you need to eat oysters), here are a few easy rules to get you through any meal without offending your table mates.

Some Simple Rules for All Those Forks

This place setting shows what you are likely to encounter when you sit down for a formal meal. When you are dining at home, your family probably uses far fewer dishes and utensils, but it never hurts to be prepared.

When you do encounter something unfamiliar or totally unexpected, two simple rules can get you through any meal no matter how formal or unusual the food:

- *Watch your host or hostess.* He or she is supposed to take the first bite. So if there is a food you don't know how to eat, watch what he or she does—and do the same.
- *When you have to decide which fork or spoon to use, start on the outside and work your way in.* If a soup is the first course, a soup spoon will be the outermost spoon. Similarly, if shrimp cocktail is served first, a small seafood fork will be on the outside, or sometimes it will be brought on a plate under the shrimp cocktail.

10 Rules to Get You Through Any Meal

1. Put your napkin in your lap as soon as you sit down and leave it beside your plate when you have finished eating.
2. Sit up straight. It will help you digest your food, and it's polite. You need not sit rigidly, and if you don't slouch, you can place your elbow on the table occasionally.
3. When you are a guest, take a small portion of everything that is served. Your parents may not expect you to eat something you don't like, but others will expect you to take a small portion. No one will say anything if you don't finish it.
4. Use your napkin on your mouth after eating solid food and before drinking liquids.
5. Say "Please" and "Thank you" when

Place Setting

a) oyster or shellfish fork
b) soup spoon
c) fork and knife for fish
d) fork and knife for meat
e) fork and knife for salad and cheese
f) water goblet
g)wine glass

asking someone to pass you something. Pass food promptly to others.

6. Don't chew food with your mouth open. This also means don't talk with your mouth full.

7. Don't announce that you hate a certain food. Someone worked hard to prepare it and won't appreciate hearing this.

8. Don't wave your eating utensils around. When you are done eating or are resting between bites, put them on your plate.

9. Cut food into small, bite-size pieces one piece at a time. Only babies have their food cut up all at once—and their parents only do that to save time.

10. Ask to be excused when you are ready to leave the table.

The Golden Rule of Eating (Or How to Get Invited Back)

Thank the hostess or host for preparing the meal for you. Think about doing this even when the hostess is your own parent, and it's the same meal you see every Thursday night. You'll get a lot of mileage out of this kind of gesture.

AWKWARD MOMENTS: HOW TO HANDLE THEM

Occasionally, we need to share sad or troubling information with a friend, or a situation arises that is touchy to handle. For example, if a school friend does not know that your parents are divorced, he or she may accidentally say something that will hurt your feelings.

Although these moments of sharing difficult information can be trying, the best strategy is to get them over with as quickly and easily as possible. It is better to announce these facts when you are becoming friends with someone, rather than waiting for an awkward moment to come along and then being forced to deal with it when you are least prepared to do so.

Telling People You Are Adopted

If you are adopted, your parents probably told you when you were old enough to understand. But it will probably be up to you to tell your friends. Simply say to a friend, "Did you know that I'm adopted?" After this, it is up to you to share as little or as much about this part of your life as you wish.

Dealing with Your Parents' Divorce or Separation

The fact that your parents are separated or divorced is also painful. It's better if your friends know this so they can avoid saying anything that might hurt your feelings. When you are talking with your friends about your home life or your parents, you can just calmly mention that your parents are divorced. Again, you can talk as little or as much as you like about this deeply personal topic.

When One Person Says Something Bad About Another Person

Most of us learn early that it is extremely unkind to make derogatory comments about a person's race or religion. It isn't even polite to ask people what religion or nationality they are, although if you become good friends, you will undoubtedly talk about these things.

Sadly, a few of us don't learn or don't care about hurting others. And you may be present someday when a friend says something hurtful to another friend. What can you do? You can refuse to join in, even if the other person says he's only teasing. You can speak up and say that you don't like to hear such hurtful things. Finally, you can show your sympathy to the friend who was hurt. This may mean doing something as simple as walking him or her home or telling the friend that you dislike talk like that and are sorry it happened.

Dealing with the Death of a Parent or Close Relative

Most children and young adults are fortunate in that they rarely have to deal with death. Not all of us are so lucky, though. You may already have lost a close family member, or someone else may have died and you aren't sure what behavior is expected of you.

If your relative died some time ago and you are making new friends, you may want to mention your loss when you talk with a friend or group of friends. Simply say, "My grandmother died last year." Your friends will probably say they are sorry to hear that. You can say, "Thank you."

When someone in your family dies, it helps to know what is going to happen. There will probably be a funeral, and your relatives and the family's friends will come to it. Depending upon how old you are, your parents may discuss with you whether you want to attend a funeral or if you want to speak at the funeral about your memories of the person. This choice will probably be left up to you.

If you are Christian, before the funeral your family will gather at the funeral home for one or more days to receive calls from friends. If you are Jewish, this period of mourning, called shiva, will be held after the funeral in some family member's home.

During this period, many people will approach you to tell you how sad they feel about your loss. All you have to say is "Thank you."

Occasionally, you may attend a funeral because someone you know has died. You usually say "hello" after the service to the family of the person who died. Don't worry about what to say; "I'm sorry" is all that is expected.

WRITING AND GREETING OFFICIALS THE RIGHT WAY

There is a set of rules to help you deal with important persons and officials; this is called *protocol*. Protocol is used by government employees, who need to know how to show respect to high-ranking officials as well as foreign diplomats. Protocol also shows you how to speak to clergy, who are accorded special respect because of their positions. The following chart shows how to greet and address letters to dignitaries.

Person	Letter Address	Letter Greeting	Spoken Greeting	Formal Introduction
President of the United States	The President The White House Washington, DC 20500	Dear Mr. President	Mr. President	The President or the President of the United States
former President	The Honorable John J. Jones Address	Dear Mr. Jones	Mr. Jones	The Honorable John J. Jones
Vice President	The Vice President Executive Office Building Washington, DC 20501	Dear Mr. Vice President	Mr. Vice President	The Vice President or the Vice President of the United States
Cabinet members	The Honorable John (or Jane) Jones The Secretary of _____ or the Postmaster General or the Attorney General Washington, DC	Dear Mr. (or Madam) Secretary	Mr. (or Madam) Secretary	The Secretary of _____
Chief Justice	The Chief Justice The Supreme Court Washington, DC 20543	Dear Mr. Justice or Dear Mr. Chief Justice	Mr. Chief Justice	The Chief Justice
Associate Justice	Mr. Justice Jones or Madam Justice Jones The Supreme Court Washington, DC 20543	Dear Mr. (or Madam) Justice	Mr. Justice or Mr. Justice Jones; Madam Justice or Madam Justice Jones	Mr. Justice Jones; Madam Justice Jones
United States Senator	The Honorable John (or Jane) Jones United States Senate Washington, DC 20001	Dear Senator Jones	Senator Jones	Senator Jones from Montana

(continued)

Person	Letter Address	Letter Greeting	Spoken Greeting	Formal Introduction
Speaker of the House	The Honorable John (or Jane) Jones Speaker of the House of Representatives United States Capitol Washington, DC 20001	Dear Mr. (or Madam) Speaker	Mr. Speaker; Madam Speaker	The Speaker of the House of Representatives
United States Representative	The Honorable John (or Jane) Jones United States House of Representatives Washington, DC 20001	Dear Mr. (or Mrs., Ms.) Jones	Mr. (or Mrs., Ms.) Jones	Representative Jones from New Jersey
United Nations Representative	The Honorable John (or Jane) Jones U.S. Representative to the United Nations United Nations Plaza New York, NY 10017	Dear Mr. (or Madam) Ambassador	Mr. (or Madam) Ambassador	The United States Representative to the United Nations
Ambassador	The Honorable John (or Jane) Jones Ambassador of the United States American Embassy Address	Dear Mr. (or Madam) Ambassador	Mr. (or Madam) Ambassador	The American Ambassador
Consul-General	The Honorable John (or Jane) Jones American Consul General Address	Dear Mr. (or Mrs., Ms.) Jones	Mr. (or Mrs., Ms.) Jones	Mr. (or Mrs., Ms.) Jones

Person	Letter Address	Letter Greeting	Spoken Greeting	Formal Introduction
Foreign Ambassador	His (or Her) Excellency John (or Jean) Johnson The Ambassador of _____ Address	Excellency or Dear Mr. (or Madam) Ambassador	Excellency; or Mr. (or Madam) Ambassador	The Ambassador of _____
Secretary-General of the United Nations	His (or Her) Excellency Milo (or Mara) Jones Secretary-General of the United Nations United Nations Plaza New York, NY 10017	Dear Mr. (or Madam) Secretary-General	Mr. (or Madam) Secretary-General	The Secretary-General of the United Nations
Governor	The Honorable John (or Jane) Jones Governor of _____ State Capitol Address	Dear Governor Jones	Governor or Governor Jones	The Governor of Maine; Governor Jones of Maine
State legislators	The Honorable John (or Jane) Jones Address	Dear Mr. (or Mrs., Ms.) Jones	Mr. (or Mrs., Ms.) Jones	Mr. (or Mrs., Ms.) Jones
Judges	The Honorable John J. Jones Justice, Appellate Division Supreme Court of the State of _____ Address	Dear Judge Jones	Mrs. Justice or Judge Jones; Madam Justice or Judge Jones	The Honorable John (or Jane) Jones; Mr. Justice Jones or Judge Jones; Madam Justice Jones or Judge Jones
Mayor	The Honorable John (or Jane) Jones;	Dear Mayor Jones	Mayor Jones; Mr. (or Madam) Mayor; Your Honor	Mayor Jones; The Mayor

(continued)

Person	Letter Address	Letter Greeting	Spoken Greeting	Formal Introduction
	His (or Her) Honor the Mayor City Hall Address			
The Pope	His Holiness, the Pope or His Holiness, Pope John XII Vatican City Rome, Italy	Your Holiness or Most Holy Father	Your Holiness or Most Holy Father	His Holiness, the Holy Father; the Pope; the Pontiff
Cardinals	His Eminence, John Cardinal Jones, Archbishop of _____ Address	Your Eminence or Dear Cardinal Jones	Your Eminence or Cardinal Jones	His Eminence, Cardinal Jones
Bishops	The Most Reverend John Jones, Bishop (or Archbishop) of _____ Address	Your Excellency or Dear Bishop (Archbishop) Jones	Your Excellency or Bishop (Archbishop) Jones	His Excellency or Bishop (Archbishop) Jones
Monsignor	The Right Reverend Monsignor Harding Address	Right Reverend Monsignor or Dear Monsignor Harding	Monsignor Harding or Monsignor	Monsignor Harding
Priest	The Reverend John Jones Address	Reverend Father or Dear Father Jones	Father or Father Jones	Father Jones
Brother	Brother John or Brother John Jones Address	Dear Brother John or Dear Brother	Brother John or Brother	Brother John
Sister	Sister Mary Luke Address	Dear Sister Mary Luke or Dear Sister	Sister Mary Luke or Sister	Sister Mary Luke
Protestant Clergy	The Reverend John (or Jane) Jones	Dear Dr. (or Mr., Ms.) Jones	Dr. (or Mr., Ms.) Jones	The Reverend (or Dr.) John Jones

Person	Letter Address	Letter Greeting	Spoken Greeting	Formal Introduction
Bishop (Episcopal)	The Right Reverend John Jones Bishop of _____ Address	Dear Bishop Jones	Bishop Jones	The Right Reverend John Jones, Bishop of Detroit
Rabbi	Rabbi Arthur (or Anne) Milgrom Address	Dear Rabbi (or Dr.) Milgrom	Rabbi Milgrom or Dr. Milgrom or Rabbi	Rabbi (or Dr.) Arthur Milgrom
King or Queen	His (Her) Majesty King (Queen) _____ Address (letters traditionally are sent to reigning monarchs not directly but via the private secretary)		Your Majesty; Sir or Madam	Varies depending on titles, holdings, etc.
Other royalty	His (Her) Royal Highness, The Prince (Princess) of _____ Address	Your Royal Highness	Your Royal Highness; Sir or Madam	His (Her) Royal Highness, the Duke (Duchess) of Gloucester
Duke/Duchess	His/Her Grace, the D__ of _____	My Lord Duke/ Madam or Dear Duke of _____/Dear Duchess	Your Grace or Duke/Duchess	His/Her Grace, the Duke/ Duchess of Bridgeport
Marquess/ Marchioness	The Most Honorable the M__ of Bridgeport	My Lord/Madam or Dear Lord/ Lady Bridgeport	Lord/Lady Bridgeport	Lord/Lady Bridgeport
Earl	The Right Honorable the Earl of Franklin	My Lord or Dear Lord Franklin	Lord Franklin	Lord Franklin
Countess (wife of an earl)	The Right Honorable the Countess of Franklin	Madam or Dear Lady Franklin	Lady Franklin	Lady Franklin

(continued)

Person	Letter Address	Letter Greeting	Spoken Greeting	Formal Introduction
Viscount/ Viscountess	The Right Honorable the V ___ Tyburn	My Lord/Madam or Dear Lord/ Lady Tyburn	Lord/Lady Tyburn	Lord/Lady Tyburn
Baron/Baroness	The Right Honorable Lord/ Lady Austin	My Lord/Madam or Dear Lord/ Lady Austin	Lord/Lady Austin	Lord/Lady Austin
Baronet	Sir John Jones, Bt.	Dear Sir or Dear Sir John	Sir John	Sir John Jones
Wife of baronet	Lady Jones	Dear Madam or Dear Lady Jones	Lady Jones	Lady Jones
Knight	Sir John Jones	Dear Sir or Dear Sir John	Sir John	Sir John Jones
Wife of knight	Lady Jones	Dear Madam or Dear Lady Jones	Lady Jones	Lady Jones

---

The Ticket to Social Success: The Origins of "Etiquette"

The word *etiquette* is believed to have originated in the seventeenth century, at the court of French King Louis XIV. Courtiers seeking admission to the court were given a ticket, or "etiquette." With time, this ticket grew longer and longer as it became an excessively elaborate list of all the minute rules that were to be followed at court. Both doors of a set of French doors, for example, were to be thrown open for a granddaughter of France (a member of the royal family), while only one door was opened for a lower-ranking princess.

Occasionally, court etiquette was charming. When Louis XIII of France paid a visit to the ailing Cardinal Richelieu, he found the cardinal too ill to rise, even though court etiquette prescribed that no one could sit while the king stood, nor lie down while the king sat. The king's solution when he wanted to continue the visit with his friend: He lay down beside the cardinal for the duration of the visit.

And sometimes manners were painful, as was the case when the queen of Spain fell partway off her horse and was trapped, upside down, by her stirrup. The queen's courtiers stood by helpless, unable to touch her because of their lower rank. The servant whose only job was to help her on and off her horse was not present. A passerby did stop to help. He was given a generous reward—and promptly banished for his impudence.

INFORMATION, PLEASE

Hoving, Walter. *Tiffany's Table Manners for Teenagers*. Random House, 1989.

Martin, Judith. *Miss Manners' Guide to Excruciatingly Correct Behavior*. Warner Books, 1982.

Young, Debby. *Don't Do That: A Child's Guide to Bad Manners, Ridiculous Rules & Inadequate Etiquette*. Rainbow Morn, 1989.

Young, Marjabelle, and Ann Buchwald. *White Gloves & Party Manners*. Luce, 1988.

Stewart, Marjabelle. *The New Etiquette: An A to Z Guide to Today's Practical and Gracious Manners*. St. Martin's Press, 1987.

20

OUR LEGAL SYSTEM

Young people usually become involved with the legal system when they are the subject of a custody hearing if their parents divorce, when they commit a crime or are in need of supervision, or when they are abused or neglected.

When young people do become involved with the courts, they are usually treated differently from adults. Some laws, for example, such as those about child abuse and child labor, apply only to children. When children are charged with crimes, they are often, but not always, treated differently from adult defendants.

SPECIAL TREATMENT: CHILDREN'S LEGAL RIGHTS

Years ago, children had virtually no legal rights. A parent could refuse to support a child, meet his or her medical needs, or provide an education. A parent could force a child to drop out of school to go to work. Adult criminals had more rights than juvenile offenders.

During the nineteenth century, advocates of children's rights began to push for better treatment of children. They wanted to offer them the same—and sometimes more—protection than adults received. They

worked, for example, to pass child labor laws and laws that required children to attend school until a certain age. Above all, they pushed for a special juvenile court that would handle the problems of youth.

Growing Up: From Minority to Majority

The idea that children's rights are different from those of adults is based in part on the concepts of majority and minority. Children are considered minors until they reach what is called the age of consent. Once a child reaches the age of majority—usually 18 but sometimes 21, depending on the state—he or she is presumed to be responsible for his or her own actions. Prior to that, a child's parents or the state is responsible for him or her and must provide for the child's basic needs, including education. When the parents cannot take care of a child or when they refuse to do so, the state steps in as the child's protector.

Emancipated Minors

Minors who are not under the control of their parents or the state are considered emancipated, or free, minors. Emancipation grants minors the rights of adults. An emancipated minor, for example, handles his or her own money, supports himself, and often lives on his own. The most common example of an emancipated minor is a young person who operates his or her own business. An emancipated minor's parents are no longer responsible for him or for his debts or legal obligations.

Parents must emancipate a minor, either orally, in writing, or by implication. A minor cannot emancipate himself or herself. Neglect and desertion are not the same as emancipation. In those cases, the parents are in violation of the law. If an emancipated minor no longer wishes to be so or is incapable of supporting himself, his parents must take him back and assume responsibility for him.

Two specific actions also emancipate a minor:

- Marrying while still a minor
- Joining the military

JUVENILE COURT

Special courts, called juvenile or family courts, are set up to handle legal situations involving youth. Juvenile courts typically handle three kinds of cases:

1. Criminal matters involving youth
2. Neglect or abuse of youth
3. Youth in need of supervision (young persons whose families can no longer control them or who fail to properly supervise them)

Juvenile courts do not handle some cases. For example, minors go to adult court for the following:

- traffic violations
- civil suits (where you sue someone or someone sues you)

Juvenile courts operate on the principle that youths are entitled to greater protection than are adults. Therefore, juvenile courts operate differently in some ways than adult courts.

- *Juvenile proceedings are called hearings rather than trials.* This is designed, as are many other procedures in juvenile court, to prevent a youth from being publicly labeled a criminal. A hearing can also be conducted less formally than a trial.
- *Juvenile hearings are heard by a judge rather than by a jury.* Only a few states permit a jury trial in juvenile court. A trial with a judge is considered more private. However, a juvenile can ask to have his or her case heard in adult court by a jury.
- *Juvenile trials are closed to the public.* Again, juveniles are entitled to greater privacy.
- *The records for a juvenile proceeding are sealed.* They are available only to the judge and parties involved in the case. In some states, the press can have access to the records but cannot use the juvenile's name.
- *Juveniles are not subject to the same punishments as adults.* Rather, the judge is asked to dispose of, or resolve, the case in a way that best promotes the youth's welfare. In many states, however, if the crime is serious enough, an older child may be treated as an adult and subject to the same punishment.
- *The records of juvenile proceedings are often expunged, or erased, after a specified period of time.* A growing trend exists for juvenile courts to erase a juvenile offender record under certain conditions, namely, that the juvenile has not been involved in any criminal acts and that he or she shows signs of having been rehabilitated. The usual time limit is two years. A youth must petition the court to have his or her records erased.

Resolving Juvenile Cases

Juvenile welfare cases are resolved in one of five ways:

1. The case is dismissed, or discharged.
2. The youth is put on probation, subject to certain conditions imposed by the court.
3. The youth is placed in a foster home.
4. The youth is committed to either a charitable or religious institution or a training school.
5. The youth is sentenced to serve time in a juvenile facility. Even after sentencing, the sentence may be suspended (in which case the youth goes free) or the execution of the judgment may be temporarily suspended, pending any further misbehavior by the youth.

Making Exceptions: Age Limits and Juvenile Crime

- *By custom, children under the age of seven are not prosecuted for breaking either federal or state laws.*
- *By law, a youth who breaks a federal law is treated as a minor until the age of 18; in some circumstances, until age 21.*
- *Each state has its own regulations regarding when a youth is still considered a juvenile. Somewhere between ages 16 and 21, with 18 being the most common age, youths lose their right to have their cases heard in juvenile court.*
- *For serious crimes, those involving a sentence of more than 10 years or a death sentence, a juvenile as young as 14 can be tried as an adult.*

Children's Rights in a Legal Proceeding

Before juvenile courts were established to protect children, for many years children did not have the same protections as adults in a courtroom. Gradually, legal experts recognized that this sometimes harmed children rather than helping them, and some special rights of children were recognized. These are:

- The right to have one's family notified of any charges against a minor or of any proceedings
- The right to be represented by a lawyer
- The right to have written records of proceedings involving minors
- The right to confront one's accusers
- The right to examine witnesses

THE LAW AND THE FAMILY

Family law is an important area where children have contact with the legal system. Although you may not be present for them, legal proceedings involving you will be held if your parents divorce and there is a custody or visitation hearing, if you are subject to abuse, or if you are adopted.

Custody

Custody establishes which parent you will live with if your parents separate or divorce. The parent who has custody makes the important decisions about your life. Either your parents will share custody of you or, as is most common, one parent will have sole custody.

Sometimes your parents will work out custody arrangements between themselves, but fairly often this is decided by a court. In deciding custody, the court will take into account several issues involving your welfare:

- *Your age, physical condition, and health* If you are very young, you may be more likely to stay with your mother. If you have a medical condition that one parent has cared for more than the other, you will likely stay with that parent.
- *Your siblings* The court will try not to separate you from your sisters and brothers.

- *Your education and living arrangements* The court prefers that you continue living where you have been, and also is concerned that you not have to change schools.
- *Your preference* The court will be interested to know if you have a preference about which parent to live with. The older you are, the greater weight your opinion will carry.

Several issues are considered irrelevant to your welfare, among them:

- *Difference in parents' financial means* The wealthier parent should contribute to your expenses even if you live with the other parent.
- *Difference in parents' educational levels* Plans for your education do count heavily, but your parents' education is irrelevant since that has little to do with their ability to take care of you.

Telling the Court What You Want

Most children rightfully dread the moment when they might be called on to choose between their parents in a court of law. Usually, this does not happen. What may happen is that the judge will decide to talk with you *in camera,* a legal expression for a private meeting in the judge's chambers or some other private room.

A court stenographer may or may not be present at this meeting, which is strictly between you and the judge, who will want to hear what will make you most comfortable. Records of the meeting will be sealed, and they can never be read by anyone but the judge. No one, including your parents, ever knows what you say in this meeting, and the decision is still up to the judge.

Visitation

Visitation refers to when and how the parent who does not have custody is allowed to visit with you. Sometimes that parent can see you whenever he or she wants to. More often,

though, a schedule is established so that your school and regular activities are not interrupted.

Your visiting parent usually gets to see you even if he or she is behind on child-support payments, but sometimes the court takes away visiting rights until the parent catches up on the payments.

When you become a teenager, you may refuse visitation if you want.

Children's Bill of Rights During Divorce

Children are recognized as having some rights in a divorce. A children's bill of rights originated in the Wisconsin courts and is now widely recognized by most state courts. Here is what it says:

1. You are entitled to be treated as an interested party who will be affected by the divorce.
2. You are entitled to grow up in the home environment that will give you the best chance to develop into a responsible, mature citizen.
3. You are entitled to daily love, care, discipline, and protection from your custodial parent.
4. You are entitled to know your noncustodial parent and to visit with him or her.
5. You have a right to a good relationship with both parents, and neither parent should belittle the other or undermine this relationship.
6. You have a right to moral and ethical values, which should be taught to you by your parents, and to have limits set on your behavior so you can develop self-discipline.
7. You have a right to the most adequate level of economic support that your parents can provide.
8. You have a right to the same opportunities for education that you would have had if your parents had not divorced.

9. You have a right to periodic review of your custody arrangements and child support.
10. You have a right to recognition that you are a disadvantaged party for whom the court must take affirmative steps to protect your welfare.

The court may appoint a special lawyer, called a *guardian ad litem*, to represent your interests during the divorce. This lawyer is not on either your mother's or your father's side. Your best interests are his or her only concern.

Adoption

Adoption is another legal process that involves children. You may not be present in court during your adoption proceedings (especially if you are an infant), but most children are interested in what adoption involves.

Adoption is a legal arrangement whereby biological parents relinquish their legal obligations to a child, and the adoptive parents assume all legal obligations. An adopted child has all the rights, duties, and privileges of a biological child.

How Are Adoptions Arranged?

There are basically three kinds of adoptions:

- *Agency adoptions* These are arranged through a social service agency, and are the most common kind of adoption. The agency conducts an extensive investigation of the adoptive parents' background, and also ensures that the biological mother understands the decision she is making and is making it willingly.
- *Independent adoptions* These are arranged through lawyers, with no agency involved. Typically, no background investigation is conducted on the adoptive parents.
- *Foreign adoption* In recent years, with the scarcity of U.S. babies, many couples have turned to foreign adoptions. These

may be arranged through agencies or independently, and usually involve much more paperwork and government regulations than a U.S. adoption. Each country has its own requirements. Usually the adoptive parent must spend several weeks or even months in the country where he or she hopes to adopt.

What's Involved in a Typical Adoption Proceeding?

An adoption usually involves the following steps:

1. *Placement* A child is placed in the adoptive home.
2. *Surrender* The biological parents formally surrender their rights, but there is a period when they can still change their minds.
3. *Termination* The biological parents make a final surrender of their rights. After this, they cannot change their minds.
4. *Waiting period* Some time, usually several months, must pass before the adoption is legally finalized. During this period, the social worker visits the adoptive parents and the child to be sure they are doing well.
5. *Preparation for the hearing* Prior to finalizing the adoption, the adoptive parents must submit several important papers to the court, such as the petition for adoption, adoption agreements, and the financial arrangements connected to the adoption. (It is illegal to sell a child, but adoptive parents may pay the biological mother's medical or living expenses during her pregnancy.) One document seals the papers identifying the child's biological parents. A new birth certificate is issued for the child in his or her adoptive parents' names.
6. *Finalization* A private court hearing is held, often in the judge's chambers, and the old birth records are sealed. The adoption is completed.

Consent of the Biological Parent

Here are some facts about the biological parent's rights in an adoption:

- *The consent of the biological parent is required most of the time for an adoption to take place.*
- *If the biological parent has abandoned or deserted a child or lost custody, his or her consent is not required for an adoption.*
- *When biological parents are divorced or separated, the rules vary.* Sometimes both must consent to an adoption; sometimes only one parent must give permission.
- *The Supreme Court has ruled that a biological father who has never been married to a child's mother can contest an adoption.* His approval, though, is not required to arrange for the adoption.

Child Abuse: What Is It?

It is illegal in all 50 states to abuse a child. According to the Federal Child Abuse Act, child abuse is defined as any of the following:

> physical injury
> mental injury
> sexual abuse
> negligent treatment (failing to provide a
>   child's basic needs)
> maltreatment

Child abuse is considered either minor or severe. Minor abuse is:

> throwing something
> pushing, grabbing, or shoving
> slapping or spanking

Severe abuse is:

> kicking, hitting, hitting with fist
> beating
> threatening with a gun or a knife
> using a gun or a knife

If you are thinking that one of your parents grabbed or shoved you recently, and you didn't feel abused, you may be right. In instances of minor abuse, juvenile and family courts look for a pattern of abuse rather than isolated incidents.

How Many Children Are Abused?

Although several agencies monitor child abuse in the United States, no one agrees on how many children are abused each year. This is because every state has different reporting procedures, and because many instances of child abuse go unreported.

There is a long tradition in the United States of not interfering with a family's privacy, if possible. Sometimes this custom has protected parents who were not abusing their children, but often it has protected parents who were doing so. In recent years, Americans have learned more about child abuse, and it is now reported in greater numbers.

According to the best estimates, between 1.5 million and 4 million children are abused each year, and 4,000 children die every year because of child abuse.

What Is Mandatory Reporting?

All 50 states now have mandatory reporting. This means that certain adults who observe a child being abused or who see signs that a child may have been abused must report this to the proper authorities. Mandatory reporters include the following:

> physicians
> nurses
> teachers
> social workers
> police (in 35 states)

Domestic Violence

Domestic violence refers to abuse of women and children or of women alone. (And to be fair, while the overwhelming percentage of domestic violence is directed at women and children, occasionally women abuse men.

The law offers them the same protection it offers women.)

A mother is not legally obligated to report her abuse, but if she permits a child's abuse, or does nothing to stop it, she can be charged with child abuse or neglect, and even if she is also abused, she may lose custody of the child.

Getting Help for Abuse

If you have been abused:

1. Talk to a trusted adult—your clergyman or physician, or a teacher or counselor. Remember, though, that if you talk to a mandated reporter, he or she is legally obligated to report your abuse, and this may result in your being removed from your home and your parents' supervision.

2. Call a hotline. This is a good and anonymous way to begin talking about your abuse. Several hotline numbers exist for you to report your own, a parent's, or a sibling's abuse. The persons who answer the telephone at a hotline are there to talk to you about your problem and help you decide what to do about it. These counselors are not mandatory reporters, plus you will probably not tell them your name in any event. They will help you get additional help, by referring you either to an agency that will start legal action to help you or to a counselor who can talk to you more. Hotlines encourage callers to report their abuse, though, and will even help you do this if necessary.

THE LAW AND SCHOOL

In the United States, education is compulsory. This means that, by law, children must attend school a required number of years.

The number of years and grade level you must achieve vary from state to state. Most states require that children attend school between the ages of 7 and 16. Some set the starting date at 6 or 8, and a few require school attendance through age 17 or 18.

Required attendance must be reasonable. A child who is too ill, for example, cannot be forced to attend regular classes, but the state may have to provide alternative education.

Most states' laws permit children to be tutored at home, but some school systems rarely grant permission for home education. If it is granted, and if parents say they will educate their children at home, they must do so. They cannot be deceitful about home education, saying they will educate their children when they have no intention of doing so.

Children who do not attend school are considered truants. Truant officers investigate students' absences from school.

The School and You

Not only are you required to attend school, but schools also wield a great deal of power over you. Some Americans believe that schools' powers infringe on individual civil rights, and there are many instances where citizens have tested the power of schools in court. In fact, if you do not like something the school system requires of you, your only course of action is to sue. Following are the results of some of the more important lawsuits between public school systems and individuals.

Behave or Else: The School's General Authority Over You

The general guideline that has emerged from many court rulings over the years is this: Schools have a right to regulate your actions (including behavior, dress, and even hair length) to ensure that they are not disruptive to other students or to the general atmosphere at school. Any restrictions must be reasonable. A school also has the power to punish you if you disobey school regulations and rules.

Spare the Rod But Don't Spoil the Child: Punishment in Schools

Years ago, experts believed that corporal, or bodily, punishment was an excellent way to control a child's behavior. Gradually, our thinking about this has changed, and so have the rules about corporal punishment.

Today many states regulate the kinds of physical punishment that a school can hand out. Most school systems do have the power to strike a child, but many states require that physical punishment be carried out only in the presence of the principal or that the principal must carry it out. Physical punishment is restricted to a few serious offenses. And it must be reasonable. The school is expected to use the same restraint that the law requires of parents. Even though they have a legal right to use physical punishment, very few schools actually use it these days. If you are subjected to physical punishment at school, you should discuss this with your parents or another adult.

Schools generally punish students for three offenses:

> poor grades
> misbehavior
> failure to do assigned work

Schools have the legal right to discipline you in the following ways:

- *Restrict your club memberships.* This is often done to students with poor grades.
- *Restrict your participation in athletic activities.* This is often done to students with poor grades.
- *Require that you stay after school or inside at recess or other breaks.* This is called detention.
- *Suspend you.* Suspension means you are temporarily barred from school, although you must make up the time you miss.
- *Expel you.* Expulsion, the most serious offense, means that you are permanently barred from school.

The Ultimate Punishments: Suspension and Expulsion

There are, in most states, six grounds for suspending or expelling a student:

1. Truancy
2. Drunkenness
3. Damage or destruction of school property
4. Refusal to do schoolwork
5. Refusal to follow regulations and instructions
6. Refusal to give names of fellow students who are guilty of breaking the rules

In some states, if you are suspended or expelled, you are entitled to a hearing before school officials. Sometimes you are permitted to have an attorney present for the hearing. In other states, your parents must be informed in advance of your expulsion or suspension.

Walking a Fine Line: The Limits of a School's Authority Over You

Schools cannot punish you for actions at home or when you are under your parent's supervision. They can, however, punish you for actions that occur when you are going to or from classes.

If, for example, you talk to a group of fellow students on the way home from school and encourage them to skip school with you the next day, the school could punish you for this. Or if you were to destroy property on the way home from school, the school might have authority over you in this instance as well.

The Long and Short of It: Hair and Dress Codes

In the 1960s, students rebelled in ways that led to several important lawsuits concerning students' rights. The biggest topic was hair length: Students wore their hair long as a sign of social protest. In other eras, young persons had worn long hair, but it was not seen as a sign of rebellion. Schools began to establish dress codes on the grounds that long hair was disruptive, and the issue was settled in courtrooms across America.

The courts found that the schools do have a right to impose dress codes, but the codes must be reasonable. They cannot be imposed for behavior that is not disruptive, and they cannot be imposed in anticipation of disruptive behavior. Indeed, now that most students' modes of dress and hair length are no longer viewed as forms of social and political rebellion, schools have become looser about dress codes.

Invading Your Privacy: Your Locker and Your School Records

The courts have largely been unable to resolve the issue of whether a school has a right to search a student's locker without his or her permission. Illegal searches are an invasion of your rights under the Fourth Amendment of the Constitution. Yet some courts have found that it is unclear who owns school lockers—the student or the school. If the school owns the lockers, they can be searched by the school and by other authorities, with the school's permission. If the students own the lockers, they cannot be searched without the students' permission.

A few guidelines have been established:

- *A school can search your locker without your permission when public safety is at stake—when there is a bomb scare, for example.*
- *The police can search with a warrant.* And it is rare that a school will deny them access to your locker if they show up with one.

  On the subject of your school records and who has access to them, the courts have been clearer:
- *You are entitled to view your school records.* Under the Freedom of Information Act, you have access to your school records. So do your parents. School officials also have access to your records.

Married and Pregnant Students

Most, but not all, states permit married students to attend school. The attendance of pregnant students, which is believed by many schools to be disruptive, is left to the individual school district. Some school systems refuse to let them attend classes, while others organize special schools for them or permit them to attend their regular classes.

Two things are important to know:

- *No one can restrict a girl from attending school after the baby is born.*
- *These rules have been applied only to girls.* No one has attempted to regulate school attendance of fathers.

Obscenity

Where obscene speech is concerned, the courts have tried to give students some leeway to practice their First Amendment right to free speech, while acknowledging the responsibility of the state to educate its citizens. In the process, they have determined that the right to free speech is not without some limits.

One of the more interesting cases in this area involved a student who printed material that contained obscene language. The same words, however, were found in books and magazines in the school library. The court supported the student's right, in this particular instance, to print the obscene words, but it also said that the school system had a right to limit free speech that disrupted other students.

Political Activities

Most of the court decisions about political activity arose during the Vietnam era, when students spearheaded the opposition to U.S. involvement in the war. The results were mixed, but here is a rundown of your legal rights to engage in political activism at school:

- *The school can bar speakers it deems radical or potentially disruptive.*
- *The school can bar the distribution of pamphlets or other materials it considers disruptive.*
- *The school cannot bar you from wearing political buttons or armbands.* This right grew out of a 1969 court decision regarding students who protested the war by wearing black armbands. The decision will probably be used to extend, rather than restrict, students' rights in the future.
- *The school cannot restrict students' right to demonstrate.* This is a Fourteenth Amendment right. Students do not need prior approval from the administration, but there are restrictions on demonstrating students:

1. You cannot use obscene signs that threaten to disrupt the school.
2. You cannot block access to the school.
3. You cannot participate in a sit-in on school property or otherwise occupy it.

Religion

Because schools in the past often taught from the Bible or required Bible readings, religion has long been an issue of controversy in public schools. The Constitution requires the separation of church and state. This has been interpreted to mean that parochial and private schools may teach religion, while public schools may not. A related issue is whether a student can be forced to pledge allegiance to the flag if this is forbidden by the student's religion. Based on several court cases, here are your rights regarding the practice of religion in public schools:

- *Students cannot be forced to read the Bible at school.*
- *Students cannot be forced to observe religious holidays at school, or even to witness them.* This means symbols such as Christmas trees are banned in some schools, as are Christmas carols. Some schools satisfy this ruling with ecumenical, or universal, school programs that celebrate the religious holidays of all their students.
- *Students cannot be forced to participate in school prayers, nor do they have to witness them.*
- *Students cannot be forced to pledge allegiance to the flag, nor to witness this.*

CHILDREN AND WORK

Work performed by children is regulated by the Federal Fair Labors Standards Act and a network of state laws. Federal and state laws, which are similar to one another, serve to:

- regulate the age at which a child may work.
- make sure work does not interfere with a child's education.
- set the number of hours a child may work during school or at night.
- prohibit minors from doing dangerous work.

Dangerous work is generally defined as:

- operation of cranes or elevators
- demolition, mining, excavating, construction or working in quarries or around dangerous chemicals, including in some states, gasoline and oil
- operation of dangerous machines, such as metal-shaping, bakery, or hoisting equipment
- driving a vehicle on highways (as opposed to local roads)

Work Permits

Some states require work permits before a minor under 16 or 18 can work. Here is what you need to know about these:

- Apply for them at school.

The Answers to the Four Questions Most Often Asked about Kids Working

- Yes, you need a Social Security card. Apply for one at your local Social Security office.
- Yes, you are entitled to be paid the minimum wage under certain conditions, such as when the product you are making will be used in interstate commerce.
- Yes, you are entitled to overtime, just as adult workers are.
- Yes, you must pay any Social Security, federal, and state taxes.

- You may have to have a job in order to get one.
- A letter from a prospective employer describing the nature of the work may be required.
- You may be required to submit proof of your age, take a physical examination, and get your parents' permission.

YOUR BUYING RIGHTS: MINORS AND CONTRACTS

Contracts are legal agreements that obligate each party to do something for the other. The most common kind of contract is for products bought on credit. The buyer agrees to pay for the item over a specified period, and the seller agrees to provide the product. Here are some things you need to know about minors' ability to form contracts:

- *Minors can form some kinds of contracts.* Their ability to do so depends on finding someone willing to sell them something on credit.
- *Minors cannot buy or sell real property (land) without having an adult cosign the contract.*
- *Minors have the right to disavow, or deny, a contract.* This is a right adults do not have, and it is the reason that most merchants will not sell major items to minors on credit, or even for cash: Even cash goods can be returned for no reason. Mi-

nors lose the right to disavow a contract when they reach 21 or their majority.
- *Minors cannot disavow contracts made to purchase necessities.* Necessities have been interpreted to mean food, clothing, and shelter. Education and cars have not been deemed necessities.

DRIVING LAWS

Anyone, of whatever age; who uses a motorized vehicle is subject to certain laws and regulations. These are called traffic laws. Persons who drive motorized vehicles are licensed by the individual states.

Licensing is done for several reasons:

- to protect public safety
- to regulate traffic
- to ensure competency of vehicle operators

The qualifications for licensing drivers cannot be capricious. In all the states, they are based on four standards:

- age
- physical and mental limitations
- ability to drive
- comprehension of traffic laws

To prove that you are qualified, most states require that you take three tests before you will be issued a driver's license for the first time:

1. a written examination about traffic rules and regulations
2. an eye examination
3. a driving test

The process of obtaining a driver's license usually consists of two stages:

- a learner's permit, which allows a new driver to drive only with another licensed driver in the vehicle
- the examinations

After the new driver has completed these two stages, a driver's license is issued.

A driver's license is a privilege. As such it can be revoked (permanently withdrawn) or suspended (temporarily withdrawn). This happens for the following reasons:

- violation of the traffic laws
- involvement in a fatal accident
- failure to pay traffic fines
- driving while intoxicated by alcohol or drugs

Your First Driver's License

Most states permit youth to obtain a driver's license somewhere between the age of 16 and 18.

Some states issue special licenses to operators of mopeds, motorscooters, and motorcycles. The age limit may be reduced to 15, or you may be permitted to drive one of these vehicles by yourself with a learner's permit.

No permit or license is required for nonmotorized vehicles (such as bicycles) or nonroad vehicles (such as minibikes).

CHILDREN AND CRIME

The experts who keep records of juvenile crime divide child criminals into two age groups:

- younger teens, aged 12–15
- older teens, aged 16–19

For purposes of keeping statistics, crimes are divided into two categories:

- violent (rape, robbery, and assault)
- nonviolent (theft and other property crimes, such as vandalism)

Things to Think About: Seven Facts About Crimes *Against* Children

1. The same crimes that are committed against adults are committed against children—rape, robbery, and assault, in addition to theft and other nonviolent crimes.
2. Younger teens experience violent crime most often during the day, when they are at school, on the streets after school, and in parks.
3. The single most common crime toward young teens is assault at school.
4. Older teens are more likely than younger teens to be the victims of crimes involving weapons.
5. Teens are more likely than adults to be attacked during a crime.
6. Teens are less likely than adults to report a crime. They tend to view most crime as personal and private, something they can handle themselves.
7. Teens are more likely than adults to report rape.

More Things to Think About: Six Facts About Crimes Committed *by* Children

1. The age of criminal offenders keeps getting younger. In New York state, for example, two-thirds of juvenile offenders are 14 and 15.
2. There are few juvenile offenders under the age of 10.
3. Juvenile crime is growing fastest among young teens, many of whose crimes are related to drugs. Drugs used to be found

regularly in high schools; they are now a regular presence in elementary schools as well.

4. The majority of teens who commit crimes are from poor, urban backgrounds, but a significant number of middle-class, suburban teens are also involved in crime.
5. Children commit relatively few serious crimes: about 5 percent of all murders and 10 percent of all rapes.
6. The serious crimes that children are involved in include selling drugs, theft, assault, and criminal mischief.

What Can Children Be Arrested For?

Children can be arrested for the same crimes for which adults can be arrested.

What Happens When a Child Is Arrested?

An arrest refers to the taking of a suspect into custody. When you are arrested, you are deprived of your liberty.

Who Can Arrest You?

- The police can make arrests for any crime.
- FBI agents can arrest you for some crimes.
- Private citizens can make a citizen's arrest if a serious crime is committed in their presence. A citizen's arrest cannot be made for a minor crime, such as a traffic violation.

When Can You Be Arrested?

You can be arrested under these conditions:

- If you are observed committing a crime by a police officer.
- When you are accused of a serious crime, such as murder or theft.
- When a warrant is issued.

What's a Warrant?

A warrant is a written court document ordering that someone be arrested, or taken into custody.

- A judge can issue a bench warrant to order someone to appear before a court.
- A judge can issue a warrant to compel someone to pay a court-ordered judgment.
- A judge can issue a search warrant when someone is suspected of a serious crime. Police officers use a search warrant to look for evidence, and if they find it, they arrest the person suspected of the crime.

What Happens After You Are Arrested?

You will be held in custody for questioning about the crime. After your arrest you are entitled to certain rights that were established by a Supreme Court ruling called *Miranda v. Arizona*.

Your *Miranda* rights are:

- The right to remain silent so you do not incriminate yourself.
- The right to have an attorney present when you are questioned. (If you cannot afford an attorney, one will be appointed for you.)
- The right to know that any statement you make can and will be used against you in a court of law.

You have certain other rights:

- You are entitled to make one phone call.
- As a child, you are entitled to have your family informed of your arrest.
- You are entitled to a court hearing as soon as possible. This means that you must be either charged with a crime at the hearing or set free. It is illegal to old someone in jail for an unreasonably long period without a hearing, although

the Constitution does not specify what amount of time is unreasonable.

If you are charged with a crime, one of three things will happen:

- *You will stay in jail if the crime is serious enough.*
- *You will be set free on bail, pending trial.* Bail refers to a monetary payment established by a judge that a defendant or his representative (sometimes a professional bail bondsman) makes to the court to ensure that the defendant will show up in court at the appointed times. In order to make bail, a defendant must pay 10 percent up front. If the defendant does not show up (this is called "skipping bail"), then the rest of the bail money must be paid to the court. Sometimes a judge will refuse to allow bail because he or she believes the suspect still may not show up for court dates. Some states do not permit bail for persons accused of serious crimes, such as murder or espionage (spying for a foreign country).
- *You will be freed on your own recognizance.* This means you will not have to pay bail, but you must show up for court appearances.

THE COURT SYSTEM: HOW IT WORKS

What's a Lawsuit?

A dispute that is settled by our legal system is called a lawsuit. A dispute between two citizens is a civil suit, whereas a suit that involves a crime is called a criminal suit. Even though a crime harms a victim, it is considered an offense against the state, and the state sues the alleged criminal on behalf of the injured party.

When a lawsuit has been filed, one of several things will happen to it. There may be a trial involving either a judge or a jury, or the case may be settled before it goes to trial.

Fewer than 10 percent of all lawsuits are settled by a trial. More often, civil suits are resolved with an out-of-court settlement. The lawyers for both parties negotiate an agreement that satisfies both sides.

A criminal suit is resolved with another kind of settlement called a plea bargain. A prosecutor offers an alleged criminal the right to plead guilty to a lesser charge and receive a lighter sentence than he or she would receive if the case went to trial and he or she were convicted.

People named in civil and criminal suits are often eager to avoid a trial because of the time and expense involved, and even more important, because no one can predict the outcome of a trial.

The U.S. Court System

The U.S. has a two-tier court system consisting of federal courts and state and local courts (see following page).

Whose Turf Is This? Jurisdiction in the Courts

A court must have jurisdiction, or power, in order to hear a case. To begin with, the Constitution requires that a trial be held in the community where a crime was committed.

Local and state courts handle domestic cases, such as those involving juvenile crimes, custody, and abuse and neglect; minor criminal cases and traffic lawsuits; and some civil suits where two citizens are suing one another.

Federal courts handle criminal and civil cases involving federal law, tax cases, maritime cases (those involving the laws at sea), bankruptcy, patent and copyright cases, and lawsuits in which two states or groups of citizens from different states are suing one another.

In addition to having the original jurisdiction because a case began in its geographic region, courts have either limited or general

The Supreme Court
|
U.S. courts of appeals
|
U.S. district courts

State supreme courts
|
State appellate courts
|
General jurisdiction courts
|
Limited jurisdiction courts

U.S. special courts:

Tax Court

Claims Court

Court of Military Appeals

Court of International
Trade

jurisdiction, often over either civil or criminal cases.

- *Limited jurisdiction courts* Examples of these are juvenile courts, which deal only with minors, and traffic courts, which handle only traffic violations.
- *General jurisdiction courts* These handle a wide array of cases. The major trial court of most cities or states is a general jurisdiction court.
- *Civil courts* Civil courts handle lawsuits brought by one citizen against another, and usually involve contract disputes, divorces, and personal injury.
- *Criminal courts* Criminal courts handle suits involving crimes against society, such as murder, robbery, or assault.

Where Cases Begin: State and Local Courts

The lowest tier in the state and local court system—and the place where most lawsuits originate—is the limited jurisdiction courts. These typically include the following:

- *Police courts* These try persons accused of state and local crimes.
- *County courts* These settle issues of state and local law.
- *Small claims courts* These settle disputes involving small financial claims, usually under a specified amount.

- *Probate and surrogate courts* These dispose of wills.
- *Traffic courts* These handle traffic offenses.
- *Family courts* These handle cases involving juveniles, child custody, and divorce.

Where Cases End: General Jurisdiction Courts

Every state has one or more general jurisdiction courts. These are usually called:

- *Circuit courts*
- *Superior courts*
- *Courts of common pleas*

Half of all states also have an intermediate appeals court, which permits a defendant or party to a lawsuit to get another opinion from a higher court. All states have a state supreme court, although it may not go by that name. This is the highest court, and the court of last appeal.

Federal Courts

The federal court system has four levels:

1. *Specialized courts* To expedite cases, the federal court system has a number of specialized courts, each of which han-

dles only certain kinds of cases. Some examples:

- *Tax court* Handles only tax cases.
- *Claims court* Handles claims against the federal government.
- *Military court* Handles offenses by members of the U.S. armed forces.
- *Court of International Trade* Handles only disputes over imports.

2. *District courts* These are the courts of original jurisdiction for most cases involving federal laws.
3. *Appeals courts* The country is divided into 12 circuits, each with an appeals court, plus one appellate court with nationwide jurisdiction, the U.S. Court of Appeals for the Federal Circuit. These courts hear appeals from district courts, as well as cases involving some federal agencies.
4. *Supreme Court* The court of last resort, from which there is no appeal, this is the highest court in the land. Nine justices, who are appointed for life, sit on the Supreme Court. The Supreme Court has original jurisdiction in cases involving two or more states as well as foreign countries.

Supreme Court Justices

Here is a list of the men and one woman who have served on the U.S. Supreme Court:

Justice	Term
*John Jay	1789–95
John Blair	1789–96
William Cushing	1789–1810
Robert H. Harrison	1789–90
John Rutledge	1789–91
James Wilson	1789–98
James Iredell	1790–99
Thomas Johnson	1791–93
William Paterson	1793–1806
*John Rutledge (Congress rejected his appointment as chief justice)	1795
*Oliver Ellsworth	1796–99
Samuel Chase	1796–1811
Bushrod Washington	1798–1829
Alfred Moore	1799–1804
*John Marshall	1801–35
William Johnson	1804–34
Brockolst Livingston	1806–23
Thomas Todd	1807–26
Joseph Story	1811–45
Gabriel Duval	1812–35
Smith Thompson	1823–43
Robert Trimble	1826–28
John McLean	1829–61
Henry Baldwin	1830–44
James M. Wayne	1835–67
*Roger B. Taney	1836–64
Philip P. Barbour	1836–41
John Catron	1837–65
John McKinley	1837–52
Peter V. Daniel	1841–60
Samuel Nelson	1845–72
Levi Woodbury	1845–51
Robert C. Grier	1846–70
Benjamin R. Curtis	1851–57
John A. Campbell	1853–61
Nathan Clifford	1858–81
David Davis	1862–77
Samuel F. Miller	1862–90
Noah H. Swayne	1862–81
Stephen J. Field	1863–97
*Salmon P. Chase	1864–73
Joseph P. Bradley	1870–92
William Strong	1870–80
Ward Hunt	1873–82
*Morrison R. Waite	1874–88
John M. Harlan	1877–1911
Stanley Matthews	1881–89
William B. Woods	1881–87
Samuel Blatchford	1882–1903
Horace Gray	1882–1902
*Melville W. Fuller	1888–1910
Lucius Q. C. Lamar	1888–93
David J. Brewer	1890–1910
Henry B. Brown	1891–1906
George Shiras, Jr.	1892–1903
Howell E. Jackson	1893–95
Edward D. White	1894–1910
Rufus W. Peckham	1896–1909

(*continued*)

Justice	Term
Joseph McKenna	1898–1925
Oliver W. Holmes	1902–32
William R. Day	1903–22
William H. Moody	1906–10
*Edward D. White	1910–21
**Charles E. Hughes	1910–16*
Horace H. Lurton	1910–14
Joseph R. Lamar	1911–16
Willis Van Devanter	1911–37
Mahlon Pitney	1912–22
James C. McReynolds	1914–41
Louis D. Brandeis	1916–39
John H. Clarke	1916–22
*William H. Taft	1921–30
Pierce Butler	1922–39
George Sutherland	1922–38
Edward T. Sanford	1923–30
Harlan F. Stone	1925–41
*Charles E. Hughes	1930–41
Owen J. Roberts	1930–45
Benjamin N. Cardozo	1932–38
Hugo L. Black	1937–71
Stanley F. Reed	1938–57
William O. Douglas	1939–75
Felix Frankfurter	1939–62
Frank Murphy	1940–49
*Harlan F. Stone	1941–46
James F. Byrnes	1941–42
Robert H. Jackson	1941–54
Wiley B. Rutledge	1943–49
Harold H. Burton	1945–58
*Fred M. Vinson	1946–53
Tom C. Clark	1949–67
Sherman Minton	1949–56
*Earl Warren	1953–69
John Marshall Harlan	1955–71
William H. Brennan, Jr.	1956–90
Charles E. Whittaker	1957–62
Potter Stewart	1958–81
Arthur J. Goldberg	1962–65
Byron R. White	1962–93
Abe Fortas	1965–69
Thurgood Marshall	1967–91
*Warren E. Burger	1969–86
Harry A. Blackmun	1970–
Lewis F. Powell, Jr.	1972–87
*William H. Renquist	1972–

John Paul Stevens, III	1975–
Sandra Day O'Connor	1981–
Antonin Scalia	1986–
Anthony Kennedy	1988–
David H. Souter	1990–
Clarence Thomas	1991–
Ruth Bader-Ginsburg	1993–

* chief justice
** served on court at two different times

Important Supreme Court Cases

The Supreme Court is often asked to decide important legal issues, such as whether black and white children should attend school together (Brown v. Board of Education) or whether a woman has a right to obtain an abortion (Roe v. Wade). Following are some of the most important cases the Supreme Court has settled.

1803 *Marbury v. Madison* For the first time, the Supreme Court ruled an act of Congress unconstitutional, establishing the principle of judicial review.

1819 *McCullock v. Maryland* The Court's ruling upheld the constitutionality of the creation of the Bank of the United States and denied to the states the power to tax such an institution because, as Justice John Marshall put it, "the power to tax is the power to destroy."

1819 *Trustees of Dartmouth College v. Woodward* The Court ruled that a state could not arbitrarily alter the terms of a contract. Although this case applied to a college, its implications widened in later years when the same principle was used to limit states' ability to interfere with business contracts.

1857 *Dred Scott v. Sanford* The Missouri Compromise was declared unconstitutional because it deprived a person of his property (a slave) without due process of law. This was only the second time that the Court had asserted the power of judicial review. The decision also stated that slaves are not citizens of any state or of the United States.

1877 *Munn v. Illinois* States were allowed to regulate businesses when "a public interest" was involved. This principle was weakened by rulings in other cases in the late nineteenth century.

1895 *U.S. v. E. C. Knight Co.* In stating that manufacturing and commerce are not connected, and that the Sherman Anti-Trust Act could not be applied to manufacturers, the Court seriously impaired the government's ability to regulate monopolies.

1896 *Plessy v. Ferguson* The Supreme Court ruled that state laws enforcing segregation by race are constitutional if accommodations are equal as well as separate. Subsequently overturned by Brown v. Board of Education of Topeka (1954).

1904 *Northern Securities Co. v. U.S.* The High Court backed government action against big businesses that restrained trade, in effect putting teeth in the Sherman Anti-Trust Act.

1908 *Muller v. Oregon* The Court ruled that a state could legislate maximum working hours, based on evidence compiled by attorney Louis Brandeis.

1911 *Standard Oil Co. of New Jersey Et Al. v. U.S.* The Court dissolved the Standard Oil Trust not because of its size but because of its unreasonable restraint of trade. The principle involved is called "the rule of reason."

1919 *Schenck v. U.S.* The Court upheld the World War I Espionage Act. In a landmark decision dealing with free speech, Justice Oliver W. Holmes said that a person who encourages draft resistance during a war is a "clear and present danger."

1935 *Schechter v. U.S.* Invalidating the National Industrial Recovery Act of the New Deal, the Court declared that Congress could not delegate its powers to the President.

1951 *Dennis Et Al. v. U.S.* The Supreme Court ruled the 1946 Smith Act constitutional; the act made it a crime to advocate the overthrow of the government by force.

1954 *Brown v. Board of Education of Topeka* The Court held unconstitutional laws enforcing segregated schools; it called for desegregation of schools "with all deliberate speed."

1957 *Roth v. U.S.* The ruling based obscenity decisions on whether a publication appeals to "prurient interests." The Court also said that obscene material is that which lacks any "redeeming social importance."

1961 *Mapp v. Ohio* The High Court extended the federal exclusionary rule to the states; this rule prevented prosecutors from using illegally obtained evidence in a criminal trial.

1962 *Baker v. Carr* The Court held that state legislatures must be apportioned to provide equal protection under the law (Fourteenth Amendment). A follow-up decision applied the same principle to the size of congressional districts, insisting that they be approximately equal in population.

1966 *Miranda v. Arizona* The case declared that before questioning suspects, police must inform them of their right to remain silent, that any statements they make can be used against them, and that they have the right to remain silent until they have an attorney, which the state will provide if they cannot afford to pay.

1972 *Furman v. Georgia* The Court found unconstitutional all death penalty statutes then in force in the states, but held out the possibility that if they were rewritten so as to be less subjective and randomly imposed, they might be constitutional (as the Court has subsequently held in many instances).

1973 *Roe v. Wade* The Court ruled state anti-abortion laws unconstitutional, except as they apply to the last trimester of pregnancy.

1978 *University of California v. Bakke* The ruling allowed a university to admit students on the basis of race if the school's aim is to combat discrimination. Subsequent decisions of the Court have filled in the details of how government and business may use quotas to make up for past racism.

1986 *Bowers v. Hardwick* The Court ruled that states have the power to regulate sexual relations in private between consenting adults.

Criminal Versus Civil: Court Procedures

Courts follow different procedures depending on their status as criminal or civil courts.

What Happens in Civil Court?

Here are the stages of a lawsuit in a civil court:

1. **Complaint** The plaintiff, or person who is suing, files a complaint describing his case and asking for a specified amount of damages, usually money.

2. **Answer** The defendant, or person being sued, files an answer. This is a report describing his or her version of events. He or she also may file a counterclaim, or parallel lawsuit requesting damages.

3. **Settlement** This can occur at any time after the complaint and answer have been filed. Most cases are settled at this stage without going to trial.

4. **Discovery** If the plaintiff and the defendant cannot settle the case themselves, the process of discovery begins. It is a preparation for going to trial. During discovery, each side must reveal to the other the facts that it will use during the trial.

5. **Trial** If the case is still in dispute after discovery, it proceeds to trial, and a judge or a jury renders a decision. The plaintiff is awarded money in the amount he asked for or a lesser amount, whichever the judge or jury decides.

What Happens in Criminal Court?

Here are the stages in a criminal case:

1. **Questioning** The person suspected of committing a crime is arrested and brought to the police station for questioning.

2. **Preliminary hearing** The suspect is charged during a preliminary hearing. A judge listens to the state's evidence, which is presented by a prosecuting attorney (an employee of the state) before deciding whether to charge the suspect with the crime.

3. **Arraignment** In this hearing, the defendant is formally charged with a crime and given an opportunity to respond to the charges. He or she can respond in one of three ways:

   - Plead guilty and be sentenced.
   - Plea bargain, which usually involves reduced charges and a lesser sentence.
   - Plead innocent, in which case the case goes to trial, and a jury decides what happens to the suspect.

4. **Trial** During a trial, the court is called upon to do two things:

   - Examine the evidence.
   - Apply the appropriate law to bring about a resolution and, if found guilty, sentence the person to pay for his or her crime, usually with a jail sentence.

How Are Jurors Chosen, and What Happens When You Are Called for Jury Duty?

Potential jurors are chosen from polling lists, tax lists, and the telephone directory. Jurors must be 18 years of age.

The Constitution requires that jurors:

- be neutral regarding the facts of the case.
- be from the community where the crime occurred.

What Happens When You are Summoned for Jury Duty?

You will receive a summons, or letter, telling you to report for jury duty on a specific day and hour.

Jury duty is considered your civic duty, and there are few exceptions about who may serve. If you have an illness that would make it difficult for you to serve, you may be excused. Parents with primary care of young children are excused. Lawyers used to be exempt from jury duty, but states now often let them serve.

When you report, you will join a large pool of other potential jurors. At some point, you will participate in the legal process known as *voir dire,* which refers to the questioning of potential jurors by lawyers on both sides of a specific case.

After you are questioned, you will be either accepted or rejected for duty on that particular jury. A potential juror can be dismissed in one of two ways:

- *For cause* One of the lawyers gives the court a reason for dismissing a juror. A potential juror might be dismissed because he or she knows someone connected to the case, for example.
- *Peremptory challenge* Each side is allowed a certain number of dismissals for no reason that needs to be declared to the court. A juror cannot be dismissed because of his or her race, however.

If you are chosen to serve on a jury, you will hear the case. Most juries meet for a week or less. Once you have served on jury duty, you will probably not be called again for about two years.

Statutes of Limitation

Almost every civil or criminal legal action has a mandatory time limit. After that limit has passed, the plaintiff cannot bring charges against the accused for the injury or offense.

Federal Statute of Limitations

- *Capital offenses* There is no statute of limitation on cases punishable by death, or for murder, even when a state does not have the death penalty.
- *Noncapital offenses* Unless Congress has made a specific exception, the statute of limitations is 5 years.

State Statute of Limitations

The statutes of limitation vary from crime to crime and from state to state.

The Death Penalty

States That Have Capital Punishment		States That Do Not Have Capital Punishment
Alabama	Nevada	Alaska
Arizona	New Hampshire	Hawaii
Arkansas	New Jersey	Iowa
California	New Mexico	Kansas
Colorado	North Carolina	Maine
Connecticut	Ohio	Massachusetts
Delaware	Oklahoma	Michigan
Florida	Oregon	Minnesota
Georgia	Pennsylvania	New York
Idaho	South Carolina	North Dakota
Illinois	South Dakota	Rhode Island
Indiana	Tennessee	Washington, D.C.
Kentucky	Texas	West Virginia
Louisiana	Utah	Wisconsin
Maryland	Vermont	
Mississippi	Virginia	
Missouri	Washington	
Montana	Wyoming	
Nebraska		

Where the Power Is: Judge and Jury

The judge is the central figure at a trial. He or she presides over it, and sometimes renders the decision himself or herself. Every person charged with a crime can decide whether to have his or her case heard by a judge or by a jury.

If the trial is heard by a jury, they become the most important persons in the courtroom because they are the ones who decide whether the defendant is guilty or innocent. A jury consists of 6 to 12 men and women (the total number depends on state and local requirements) who hear the evidence and render a decision.

At a jury trial, the judge interprets the law for the jury, but it is the jury's job to reach a verdict. It can find the defendant guilty or not guilty. Usually a jury's verdict must be unanimous, but some states set the number of jurors who must agree in order for a verdict to be reached. Occasionally, a jury is unable to agree on a verdict. It is called a "hung jury," and usually a new trial is ordered for the defendant.

The Right of Appeal

A person who is unhappy with either a civil or a criminal verdict can sometimes appeal to a higher court. The appellate court, as higher courts are called, can only decide whether the law was correctly applied. It cannot rehear the entire case. Once a case has been appealed to the highest court in a state or to the Supreme Court, there is no further course of action. It is settled once and for all.

State Courts

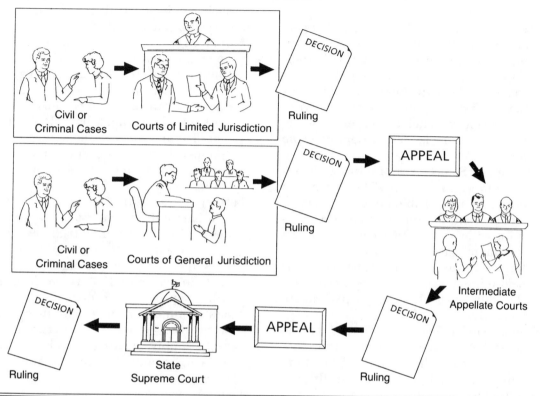

Civil or Criminal Cases → Courts of Limited Jurisdiction → DECISION Ruling

Civil or Criminal Cases → Courts of General Jurisdiction → DECISION Ruling → APPEAL → Intermediate Appellate Courts

DECISION Ruling → APPEAL → State Supreme Court → DECISION Ruling

---

Skip That Skunk Hunt: Ten Crazy Laws

All states have a few crazy laws on their books—laws that maybe made sense a hundred years ago but mostly amuse us today. Most of these laws have long since been forgotten, but they *are* still on the books, and not a small number of them affect kids' lives. For example:

1. In Lexington, Kentucky, it is illegal to carry an ice-cream cone in your pocket.
2. In Hartford, Connecticut, you can't cross a street while walking on your hands.
3. In New York City, beanshooters are illegal weapons for children.
4. In Denver, Colorado, you can't bicycle with your feet higher than the front of your bike.
5. In Baldwin Park, California, you cannot ride your bike into a swimming pool.
6. In several cities, you cannot eat ice cream on Sunday because it's the Christian Sabbath—and in some cities, children can't be bathed on Sunday.
7. In Portland, Oregon, you cannot roller-skate into a public restroom.
8. Kids are banned from flying kites in many communities—and in some, you are required to get a permit.
9. In Winnetka, Illinois, you can be arrested if you take off your shoes in a movie theater—and your feet stink.
10. In no small number of towns and states, teasing or otherwise annoying skunks is strictly forbidden. And in Alabama, you can't even call someone a skunk without risking arrest.

THE LAW FROM A TO Z

accessory Someone who helps another person commit or try to commit a crime, but who is not present when it is committed. An *accessory during the fact* is someone who witnesses a crime but does not do what he or she could do to prevent it; someone who helps another avoid arrest for a crime is an *accessory after the fact*.

accomplice Someone who joins with another to commit a crime. The accomplice is equally responsible under the law.

age of consent The minimum age for marrying without parental consent; also, the minimum age for consenting sexual relations. Sexual intercourse with a minor before the age of consent is a crime for the adult, even if both people participate willingly.

amicus curiae Latin for "friend of the court." A person or organization not party to a case who submits information. Amicus curiae briefs are generally submitted when a suit involves matters of wide public interest.

appeal A request to a higher court to reverse the decision of a lower court or government agency, or to grant a new trial.

appellate court A court whose only job is to review the decisions of lower courts.

arraignment A court procedure in which formal charges are brought against a defendant, who is advised of his or her constitutional rights and may have the opportunity to offer a plea; hearing.

assault A threatened or attempted physical attack in which the attacker appears to have the ability to bring about bodily harm if not stopped; *aggravated assault* involves an attack perpetrated with recklessness and intent to injure seriously, or an assault with a deadly weapon. *Battery* is an assault in which the assailant makes contact.

bail Money or property pledged to make sure that the defendant in a court case shows up in court when he or she is supposed to. A judge sets a specified amount of money, and the defendant or someone he or she knows must pay 10 percent of that money so the defendant can go free until the case has been decided. Defendants who raise the 10 percent security are said to have "made bail." Defendants who flee and give up the security have "jumped bail." The document that ensures a defendant's release on bail is called a *bail bond*.

battery *See* **assault**

bill of particulars The list of events to be dealt with in a criminal trial, presented to the defendant so that he or she may effectively prepare a defense.

breach of contract Failure to do something required in a contract.

breaking and entering The illegal entrance into premises with criminal intent. Simply pushing a door open and walking in may constitute breaking and entering.

brief A document in which a lawyer makes his or her client's case by explaining legal points.

burglary Unlawful presence in a building with the aim of committing a felony or taking something of value. *See also* **robbery**.

capacity The ability to understand the facts and significance of one's behavior. A defendant cannot be convicted of a crime in which he or she did not have the legal capacity to comprehend it.

character witness *See* **witness**

circumstantial evidence Evidence based not on direct observation or knowledge but rather implied from things already known.

complaint The first statement of facts (in a civil proceeding) or accusation (in a criminal case); the statement that starts a lawsuit.

conspiracy The plotting by two or more people to break the law.

contempt of court Anything done to hinder the work of the court. An outburst in a courtroom might be viewed as contempt of court.

contract An agreement between two or more parties, enforceable by law.

corpus delicti The object upon which a crime has been committed. The term does not necessarily refer to a body, although a corpse with a knife in its back would be an example in an alleged homicide.

corroborating evidence Additional evidence that backs up proof already offered in a proceeding.

criminal negligence *See* **negligence**

cross-examination The questioning of a witness to discredit what he or she has already said.

custody In a divorce case, the right to house, care for, and discipline a child.

damages A court-ordered award, usually money, to someone who has been hurt by another.

decree A court's decision in a case; its judgment.

defamation The damaging of another person's reputation through writing (libel) or speaking (slander) about him or her.

defendant A person or institution in a legal proceeding who is accused of a crime or sued for a civil wrong.

deposition A pretrial interrogation of a witness, usually in a lawyer's office.

discovery A pretrial process that lets one side in a lawsuit gather information from the other side about facts in the case.

disorderly conduct An offense, such as drunkenness or fighting, that disturbs the public peace.

district attorney *See* **prosecutor**

docket A list of cases to be tried by a court; its calendar.

emancipation The giving up by a parent of control over and responsibility for a minor.

evidence Testimony, documents, and objects used to prove matters of fact at a trial.

exclusionary rule A rule preventing introduction at a criminal trial of evidence obtained in violation of the Constitution's prohibition against unreasonable searches and seizures, even if that evidence would otherwise be admissable. *See also* **search and seizure**.

executor A person appointed to handle a will.

eyewitness One who can swear in court as to what happened because he or she was there when it happened and saw it.

false imprisonment *See* **kidnapping**

felony A serious crime, as opposed to a *misdemeanor*, or minor crime. Felonies are punishable by a certain minimum prison term—under federal law, a year.

felony murder Homicide committed in the course of another crime, such as a burglary.

fiduciary A person in a position of trust who acts for the benefit of another person; examples are executors, corporate directors, and children's guardians. A person who has a fiduciary relationship to some other person or group must take extra care to protect the interests of the persons whom he is protecting.

fraud The injury of a person or group of persons through deceit.

grand jury A jury of from 12 to 23 people who look into possible criminal activity in an area, report on it, and indict individuals when it finds evidence that they have committed crimes.

guardian A person who looks out for the interests of a minor or an incompetent person.

hearsay evidence Statements made outside of court attesting to some fact by a person who may not be cross-examined. For example, if A testifies in court that he or she heard B say something, in most cases, B's statement will not be admitted as evidence.

homicide An act in which one person

causes the death of another. *See also* **manslaughter; murder**.

hung jury A jury that is unable to reach a verdict.

immunity from prosecution Agreement by a court to permit a witness in a lawsuit to testify without fear of prosecution. A person seeks immunity from prosecution when he or she might have done something wrong.

in camera Literally "in the judge's chambers" (private office). A meeting between a judge and one or more persons involved in a lawsuit. For example, in a custody suit, a judge might see a child in camera to ask which parent he or she would be most comfortable living with.

infant Any person who has not reached the age of majority (usually 18), at which he or she enjoys the full rights of citizenship and is legally responsible for his or her acts.

injunction A court order preventing someone from doing a specific act.

injury The violation of a person's rights to the point where he or she suffers any kind of damage, including financial.

in loco parentis A person or institution acting toward a minor "in place of parents" without a formal adoption procedure; for example, the relationship between a school and a student is considered parental.

insanity A legal mental state in which one lacks legal responsibility.

judgment A court's final decision in a case.

jury A representative group of people who hear evidence and decide whether a defendant is guilty or innocent. The Constitution guarantees the right to trial by jury for all crimes punishable by imprisonment for more than six months. In civil trials, juries range in number from 6 to 12 people. State trial juries do not need a unanimous vote to convict (with the exception of 6-person juries), but federal juries do.

kidnapping The illegal seizure of a person without his or her consent. *False imprisonment* involves illegally confining a person against his or her will without moving that person to another place.

larceny Stealing or otherwise getting someone else's property through an overtly illegal act, as in stealing a car. *Grand larceny* involves the theft of an object worth more than a specified amount. *See also* **robbery**.

magistrate An official, such as a justice of the peace, who performs low-level judicial functions.

majority, age of *See* **infant**

manslaughter Homicide without advance planning or spiteful intentions. A *voluntary homicide* might occur when one person kills another in a fight. *Involuntary homicide* might occur when a drunken driver kills someone in an accident. In neither instance did the person intend to kill someone, yet in each instance a crime was committed.

material witness *See* **witness**

Miranda rule The right of a person to be warned about certain civil rights accorded to those suspected or accused of a crime. For example, a person has a right to be represented by an attorney, to have the attorney present during questioning, and to be informed that anything he or she says can be used as evidence in a court of law.

misdemeanor A minor crime, typically punished by less than a year in prison. *See* **felony**.

mistrial The ending of a trial before a verdict is reached. One common cause is a hung jury.

murder Homicide with preplanning, or premeditation. Murder in the second degree generally involves less premeditation than the same crime in the first degree.

negligence Carelessness, acting without reasonable caution, putting another person at risk of injury. In *criminal negli-*

gence there is the added element of recklessness.

open court Judicial proceedings open to the public.

pardon An act by which a governor or the president can excuse a person from punishment and restore his or her civil rights; however, a pardon usually does not wipe a conviction from a person's record.

parole The release of a person from prison under controlled conditions. The parolee must fulfill certain requirements, such as reporting regularly to a parole officer.

plaintiff The person who initiates a lawsuit.

plea A defendant's answer to a complaint.

plea bargaining A deal between prosecutor and accused, in which the accused pleads guilty in return for lesser punishment than might be received at the end of a trial.

polling the jury A proceeding in which the judge asks each juror, after the verdict has been rendered, to restate his or her decision in the case.

power of attorney A document in which one person authorizes another to act as an agent on his or her behalf.

preliminary hearing A court meeting held after an arrest but before an indictment to see whether there is enough evidence to continue holding the prisoner and proceed with a case.

premeditation Degree of preplanning, often a factor in determining the degree of guilt in a murder case.

preventive detention The holding of a prisoner without bail; also accomplished by setting bail so high that the prisoner cannot meet it.

probable cause The rule under which police need to have a reasonable belief that someone has committed a crime before making an arrest, or that the object for which they are searching in connection with a crime is at a specific location be-

fore they search for and seize it. *See also* **search and seizure.**

probation The procedure under which a court, rather than imprisoning a person convicted of a crime, leaves that individual at liberty but under court supervision.

pro bono Designating the taking of a case by an attorney without a fee. Pro bono cases are often defended on behalf of groups backing important causes.

process An order requiring that a person appear in court.

prosecutor The government official, typically a lawyer, who is responsible for bringing a lawsuit against a person accused of a crime. Citizens can sue one another, but the state can also prosecute, or sue, someone. Generally, citizens sue one another over civil wrongs, but the state sues when a crime has been committed.

protective custody The protection of a person by the state when the person has witnessed a crime or is otherwise involved in a lawsuit.

public defender A lawyer provided by the state to an accused person who cannot afford or who refuses counsel.

reasonable doubt The criteria against which jurors are told to weigh the evidence in a criminal case. The jurors must find the prosecution's case proven beyond the point at which a reasonable, average, prudent person would be convinced before returning a verdict of guilty.

release on one's own recognizance Release of the accused on a promise to appear in court, rather than on bail.

restraining order A temporary order granted to prevent some action until a hearing can be held on that action.

robbery The use of violence or intimidation to seize another person's property. *See also* **burglary.**

search and seizure A law enforcement procedure involving the search of a person or premises when police have probable cause to suspect they will find and be able to seize criminal evidence. *See also* **probable cause; search warrant.**

search warrant A court order authorizing law enforcement officials to look for objects or people involved in the commission of a crime and to produce them in court; the order names the places that the officials may search.

self-defense A plea by which a person may justify the use of force to ward off an attack if the attack was unprovoked, retreat was impossible, and the threat of harm seemed highly likely.

self-incrimination An act in a legal proceeding by which a person says something that incriminates himself or herself; under the Fifth Amendment, a person cannot be forced to make such a statement.

statute of limitations The time limitation for bringing a legal action.

statutory rape A criminal offense involving sex with a girl under the age of consent; the age of consent differs in various states.

stop and frisk A procedure in which police who believe a suspect may be carrying a weapon with intent to use it can stop that person and search the suspect's outer layer of clothing for a weapon.

subpoena A written court order requiring a person to appear to testify at a judicial proceeding at a specific time and place under penalty of law.

summons A notice to appear in court as a defendant in a suit.

verdict A judge or jury's decision, or finding of fact. The judgment, not the verdict, is the final determination in a case; for example, a judge can declare a jury's verdict "false"—that is, invalid because it is not based on the evidence.

voir dire examination A term usually applied to the interrogation of people to see whether they qualify as jurors. The term, which is French for "speak the truth," also describes a trial hearing without the jury present to determine a matter of fact or law, such as the validity of a confession.

waiver The willing surrender of a legal right.

warrant A court order directing a public employee to do something, for example, to make an arrest.

witness A person who testifies in court under oath. A *material witness* is one whose testimony is central to a case; a *character witness* testifies to the character of an individual.

youthful offender One who, at a judge's discretion, may be sentenced with special consideration given to his or her age. The category applies to defendants older than juveniles (no longer minors) but not yet, in the opinion of the judge, adults.

INFORMATION, PLEASE

Beaudry, Jo, and Lynne Ketchum. *Carla Goes to Court.* Human Sciences, 1983.

Dolan, Edward, Jr. *Protect Your Legal Rights: A Handbook for Teenagers.* Messner, 1983.

Findlay, Bruce. *Your Rugged Constitution: How America's House of Freedom Is Planned and Built.* 2d rev. ed. Stanford University Press, 1974.

Fritz, Jean. *Shh! We're Writing the Constitution.* Putnam, 1987.

Greene, Carol. *The Supreme Court.* Childrens, 1985.

Johnson, Joan. *Justice.* Watts, 1985.

Lawson, Don. *Landmark Supreme Court Cases.* Enslow, 1987.

Manetti, Lisa. *Equality.* Watts, 1985.

21

SPORTS, GAMES, AND FUN

All sports and games share these things in common: rules to play by, a special area where the game takes place, some method by which to judge who wins, and, most important, a sense of fair competition. The old saying is really true. It's not whether you win or lose, but how you play the game.

In general, sports are organized at both amateur and professional levels.

- *Amateur* sports are carried on as recreation or for an educational purpose. The sports played on your local playground and by school teams are amateur sports.
- In *professional* sports, participants are paid money. Tennis players who play in tournaments for prize money, for example, are professional athletes.

Any one particular sport can be both amateur and professional. Baseball, for example, is amateur when played by Little Leaguers, but professional in the Major Leagues.

The terms *amateur* and *professional* tell very little about the quality or caliber of competition. These days those two categories are often blurred, as in the Olympics. Athletes qualifying for the Olympic games used to be called amateur. Now, however, each Olym-

pic sport is governed by a federation, and that group decides which athletes are allowed. Tennis and basketball, for example, are open to all amateurs and professionals, whereas ice skating is open to amateurs only. Many Olympic athletes also now receive financial support from their sport's governing body. Thus, today, the criteria for amateur and professional are confusing for everybody.

Some nonathletic games, such as bridge and chess, are also played at amateur and professional levels. The *games* discussed in this chapter are played only for recreation. However, most *sports* discussed here are organized at both amateur and professional levels.

BASEBALL

Baseball is an outdoor game of skill and strategy with two teams of nine players each. The playing area consists of the infield and the outfield. The dirt *infield* is laid out in the shape of a diamond, with three bases (first, second, and third) and home plate. The broad arc of grass or turf extending behind the bases is called the *outfield*. The object is to

Girls and Women in Sports

Today girls and women are encouraged to play sports. But until recently, schools rarely offered sports teams for girls.

Then, in 1972, Congress passed a law called Title IX of the Education Amendments of 1972. This federal law ordered that females be given equal opportunity in school sports. The law says: "No person in the United States shall, on the basis of sex, be excluded from participation in, be denied the benefits of, or be subjected to discrimination under any education program or activity receiving federal financial assistance."

After Title IX, high schools and colleges began funding athletic programs for girls and women where there had been none before. These programs grew at a fast pace. Women began breaking the barriers in all sports—Olympic, professional, and scholastic:

- In 1976, Janet Guthrie became the first woman to race the Indianapolis 500.
- Kathrine Switzer proved that women could run marathons. In 1972, she became the first woman to run the Boston Marathon (by entering disguised as a man).
- Diana Nyad became the greatest long-distance swimmer ever known by swimming farther (89 miles) than any man or woman ever had. In 1979, she swam from the Bahamas to Florida in 27 hours, 38 minutes.

Now there are many national championships for women, and women athletes are role models for young girls, symbols of their unrestricted future.

---

score more runs than the opposing team over the course of nine innings. One run is scored each time a player is able to round the bases and touch home plate.

The game starts when a player (the pitcher) throws a small cowhide-covered ball over home plate. A player of the opposing team (the batter) tries to hit the ball with a wooden or metal bat. If the batter hits the ball, he runs toward first base, while the defending team tries to field the ball and throw it to first base.

If the batter gets there before the ball does, that is a single base hit. He stays on first base until the next batter can move him around the other bases. If the fielded ball is caught by the first baseman before the batter reaches the base, he is out and he leaves the field. The batter is also out if the ball is caught before it hits the ground. If the pitcher throws three pitches across a specified zone above home plate (the strike zone), none of which is hit, the batter is out. Each of these pitches is called a strike. If the pitcher throws four pitches out of the strike zone, the batter walks to first base. Each of these pitches is called a ball.

Three outs and the batting team takes the field, switching places with the fielding team. After each team takes its turn in the field and at bat, the inning is over. Then they repeat the cycle in the next inning.

If the batter can make it to second base on one hit, it's called a double. If he runs to third base without being tagged out, it's called a triple. A home run is hit when the ball flies over the outfield fence, or is hit so well that none of the three outfielders can reach it and throw to the catcher in time to beat the base-runner to home plate.

Baseball Field

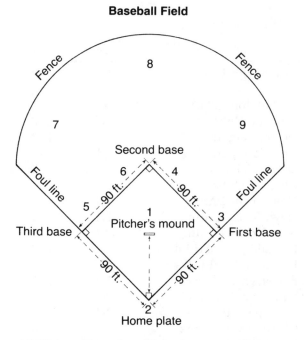

(1) Pitcher; (2) catcher; (3) first baseman; (4) second baseman; (5) third baseman; (6) shortstop; (7)left fielder; (8) center fielder; (9) right fielder.

Baseball has been the most popular sport of the twentieth century. Before baseball was racially integrated in 1947, there were separate Negro Leagues of black men who competed across the United States. From 1943 to 1952, women formed the only professional baseball league competing during World War II. In the 1970s, girls won the right to join formerly all-boy Little League teams. Girls and young women play a similar sport, softball, in high school and college. But today only men compete in baseball on the professional level.

Professional baseball is comprised of two major leagues: the American League and the National League. The season runs from early April to October, and consists of 162 games for each team. Every year since 1903, the championship teams from each league have competed against each other in the World Series. The winner is considered the best team in baseball.

U.S. and Canadian Major League Baseball (MLB)

American League (AL)

Eastern Division	*Western Division*
Baltimore Orioles	California Angels
Boston Red Sox	Chicago White Sox
Cleveland Indians	Kansas City Royals
Detroit Tigers	Minnesota Twins
Milwaukee Brewers	Oakland Athletics
New York Yankees	Seattle Mariners
Toronto Blue Jays	Texas Rangers

National League (NL)

Eastern Division	*Western Division*
Chicago Cubs	Atlanta Braves
Florida Marlins*	Cincinnati Reds
Montreal Expos	Colorado Rockies*
New York Mets	Houston Astros
Philadelphia Phillies	Los Angeles Dodgers
Pittsburgh Pirates	San Diego Padres
St. Louis Cardinals	San Francisco Giants

*First season: 1993

World Series Champions

Year	Winner	League	Loser	League	Games
1903	Boston Red Sox	AL	Pittsburgh Pirates	NL	5–3
1904	No series				
1905	New York Giants	NL	Philadelphia Athletics	AL	4–1
1906	Chicago White Sox	AL	Chicago Cubs	NL	4–2
1907	Chicago Cubs	NL	Detroit Tigers	AL	4–0
1908	Chicago Cubs	NL	Detroit Tigers	AL	4–1
1909	Pittsburgh Pirates	NL	Detroit Tigers	AL	4–3
1910	Philadelphia Athletics	AL	Chicago Cubs	NL	4–1
1911	Philadelphia Athletics	AL	New York Giants	NL	4–2
1912	Boston Red Sox	AL	New York Giants	NL	4–3
1913	Philadelphia Athletics	AL	New York Giants	NL	4–1
1914	Boston Braves	NL	Philadelphia Athletics	AL	4–0
1915	Boston Red Sox	AL	Philadelphia Phillies	NL	4–1
1916	Boston Red Sox	AL	Brooklyn Dodgers	NL	4–1
1917	Chicago White Sox	AL	New York Giants	NL	4–2
1918	Boston Red Sox	AL	Chicago Cubs	NL	4–2
1919	Cincinnati Reds	NL	Chicago White Sox	AL	5–3
1920	Cleveland Indians	AL	Brooklyn Dodgers	NL	5–2
1921	New York Giants	NL	New York Yankees	AL	5–3
1922	New York Giants	NL	New York Yankees	AL	4–0
1923	New York Yankees	AL	New York Giants	NL	4–2
1924	Washington Senators	AL	New York Giants	NL	4–3
1925	Pittsburgh Pirates	NL	Washington Senators	AL	4–3
1926	St. Louis Cardinals	NL	New York Yankees	AL	4–3
1927	New York Yankees	AL	Pittsburgh Pirates	NL	4–0
1928	New York Yankees	AL	St. Louis Cardinals	NL	4–0
1929	Philadelphia Athletics	AL	Chicago Cubs	NL	4–1
1930	Philadelphia Athletics	AL	St. Louis Cardinals	NL	4–2
1931	St. Louis Cardinals	NL	Philadelphia Athletics	AL	4–3
1932	New York Yankees	AL	Chicago Cubs	NL	4–0
1933	New York Giants	NL	Washington Senators	AL	4–1
1934	St. Louis Cardinals	NL	Detroit Tigers	AL	4–3
1935	Detroit Tigers	AL	Chicago Cubs	NL	4–2
1936	New York Yankees	AL	New York Giants	NL	4–2
1937	New York Yankees	AL	New York Giants	NL	4–1
1938	New York Yankees	AL	Chicago Cubs	NL	4–0
1939	New York Yankees	AL	Cincinnati Reds	NL	4–0
1940	Cincinnati Reds	NL	Detroit Tigers	AL	4–3
1941	New York Yankees	AL	Brooklyn Dodgers	NL	4–1
1942	St. Louis Cardinals	NL	New York Yankees	AL	4–1
1943	New York Yankees	AL	St. Louis Cardinals	NL	4–1
1944	St. Louis Cardinals	NL	St. Louis Browns	AL	4–2
1945	Detroit Tigers	AL	Chicago Cubs	NL	4–3
1946	St. Louis Cardinals	NL	Boston Red Sox	AL	4–3

Year	Winner	League	Loser	League	Games
1947	New York Yankees	AL	Brooklyn Dodgers	NL	4–3
1948	Cleveland Indians	AL	Boston Braves	NL	4–2
1949	New York Yankees	AL	Brooklyn Dodgers	NL	4–1
1950	New York Yankees	AL	Philadelphia Phillies	NL	4–0
1951	New York Yankees	AL	New York Giants	NL	4–2
1952	New York Yankees	AL	Brooklyn Dodgers	NL	4–3
1953	New York Yankees	AL	Brooklyn Dodgers	NL	4–2
1954	New York Giants	NL	Cleveland Indians	AL	4–0
1955	Brooklyn Dodgers	NL	New York Yankees	AL	4–3
1956	New York Yankees	AL	Brooklyn Dodgers	NL	4–3
1957	Milwaukee Braves	NL	New York Yankees	AL	4–3
1958	New York Yankees	AL	Milwaukee Braves	NL	4–3
1959	Los Angeles Dodgers	NL	Chicago White Sox	AL	4–2
1960	Pittsburgh Pirates	NL	New York Yankees	AL	4–3
1961	New York Yankees	AL	Cincinnati Reds	NL	4–1
1962	New York Yankees	AL	San Francisco Giants	NL	4–3
1963	Los Angeles Dodgers	NL	New York Yankees	AL	4–0
1964	St. Louis Cardinals	NL	New York Yankees	AL	4–3
1965	Los Angeles Dodgers	NL	Minnesota Twins	AL	4–3
1966	Baltimore Orioles	AL	Los Angeles Dodgers	NL	4–0
1967	St. Louis Cardinals	NL	Boston Red Sox	AL	4–3
1968	Detroit Tigers	AL	St. Louis Cardinals	NL	4–3
1969	New York Mets	NL	Baltimore Orioles	AL	4–1
1970	Baltimore Orioles	AL	Cincinnati Reds	NL	4–1
1971	Pittsburgh Pirates	NL	Baltimore Orioles	AL	4–3
1972	Oakland Athletics	AL	Cincinnati Reds	NL	4–3
1973	Oakland Athletics	AL	New York Mets	NL	4–3
1974	Oakland Athletics	AL	Los Angeles Dodgers	NL	4–1
1975	Cincinnati Reds	NL	Boston Red Sox	AL	4–3
1976	Cincinnati Reds	NL	New York Yankees	AL	4–0
1977	New York Yankees	AL	Los Angeles Dodgers	NL	4–2
1978	New York Yankees	AL	Los Angeles Dodgers	NL	4–2
1979	Pittsburgh Pirates	NL	Baltimore Orioles	AL	4–3
1980	Philadelphia Phillies	NL	Kansas City Royals	AL	4–2
1981	Los Angeles Dodgers	NL	New York Yankees	AL	4–2
1982	St. Louis Cardinals	NL	Milwaukee Brewers	AL	4–3
1983	Baltimore Orioles	AL	Philadelphia Phillies	NL	4–1
1984	Detroit Tigers	AL	San Diego Padres	NL	4–3
1985	Kansas City Royals	AL	St. Louis Cardinals	NL	4–3
1986	New York Mets	NL	Boston Red Sox	AL	4–1
1987	Minnesota Twins	AL	St. Louis Cardinals	NL	4–0
1988	Los Angeles Dodgers	NL	Oakland Athletics	AL	4–0
1989	Oakland Athletics	AL	San Francisco Giants	NL	4–3
1990	Cincinnati Reds	NL	Oakland Athletics	AL	4–0
1991	Minnesota Twins	AL	Atlanta Braves	NL	4–3
1992	Toronto Blue Jays	AL	Atlanta Braves	NL	4–2

Baseball Record Holders*

Major League Leaders

Games		At Bats		Runs Scored		Hits	
Pete Rose	3,562	Pete Rose	14,043	Ty Cobb	2,245	Pete Rose	4,256
Carl Yastrzemski	3,308	Hank Aaron	12,364	Hank Aaron	2,174	Ty Cobb	4,191
Hank Aaron	3,298	Carl Yastrzemski	11,988	Babe Ruth	2,174	Hank Aaron	3,771
Ty Cobb	3,033	Ty Cobb	11,429	Pete Rose	2,165	Stan Musial	3,630
Stan Musial	3,026	Stan Musial	10,972	Willie Mays	2,062	Tris Speaker	3,515
Willie Mays	2,992	Willie Mays	10,881	Stan Musial	1,949	Honus Wagner	3,430
Rusty Staub	2,951	Brooks Robinson	10,654	Lou Gehrig	1,888	Carl Yastrzemski	3,419
Brooks Robinson	2,896	Robin Yount	10,554	Tris Speaker	1,881	Eddie Collins	3,309
Al Kaline	2,834	Honus Wagner	10,427	Mel Ott	1,859	Willie Mays	3,283
Eddie Collins	2,826	Lou Brock	10,332	Frank Robinson	1,829	Nap Lajoie	3,252

Runs Batted In		Stolen Bases Since 1898		Shutouts		Strikeouts	
Hank Aaron	2,297	Rickey Henderson	1,042	Walter Johnson	110	Nolan Ryan	5,668
Babe Ruth	2,204	Lou Brock	938	Grover C. Alexander	90	Steve Carlton	4,136
Lou Gehrig	1,990	Ty Cobb	892	Christy Mathewson	83	Bert Blyleven	3,701
Ty Cobb	1,961	Eddie Collins	742	Cy Young	77	Tom Seaver	3,640
Stan Musial	1,951	Max Carey	736	Eddie Plank	69	Don Sutton	3,574
Jimmie Foxx	1,922	Tim Raines	730	Warren Spahn	63	Gaylord Perry	3,534
Willie Mays	1,903	Honus Wagner	703	Mordecai Brown	63	Walter Johnson	3,508
Mel Ott	1,860	Joe Morgan	689	Tom Seaver	61	Phil Niekro	3,340
Carl Yastrzemski	1,844	Willie Wilson	660	Nolan Ryan	61	Ferguson Jenkins	3,192
Ted Williams	1,839	Bert Campaneris	649	Bert Blyleven	60	Bob Gibson	3,117

Top Home Run Hitters

Player	HR	Player	HR	Player	HR	Player	HR
Hank Aaron	755	Ted Williams	521	Dave Kingman	442	Dale Murphy	398
Babe Ruth	714	Willie McCovey	521	Dave Winfield	432	Graig Nettles	390
Willie Mays	660	Ed Mathews	512	Billy Williams	426	Johnny Bench	389
Frank Robinson	586	Ernie Banks	512	Eddie Murray	414	Dwight Evans	385
Harmon Killebrew	573	Mel Ott	511	Darrell Evans	414	Frank Howard	382
Reggie Jackson	563	Lou Gehrig	493	Duke Snider	407	Jim Rice	382
Mike Schmidt	548	Stan Musial	475	Al Kaline	399	Orlando Capoda	379
Mickey Mantle	536	Willie Stargell	475	Andre Dawson	399	Tony Perez	379
Jimmy Foxx	534	Carl Yastrzemski	452				

Players With 3,000 Major League Hits

Player	Hits	Player	Hits	Player	Hits	Player	Hits
Pete Rose	4,256	Honus Wagner	3,430	Paul Waner	3,152	Al Kaline	3,007
Ty Cobb	4,191	Carl Yastrzemski	3,419	Cap Anson	3,081	George Brett	3,005
Hank Aaron	3,771	Eddie Collins	3,309	Rod Carew	3,053	Roberto Clemente	3,000
Stan Musial	3,630	Willie Mays	3,283	Robin Yount	3,025	Robin Yount	3,000
Tris Speaker	3,515	Nap Lajoie	3,252	Lou Brock	3,023	George Brett	3,000

*As of 1992

BASKETBALL

Two teams of five members each play this winter sport indoors on a rectangular wooden court. A rim is attached to a backboard at each end of the court. Around the rim a net hangs ten feet above the floor. This net is called the basket, or the goal. The object of the game is to score points by shooting or sinking a large rubber, leather-covered ball through the basket.

The game starts with a jump ball. At a center circle, an official throws the ball into the air, and two opponents try to tip the ball to their teammates. The team gaining possession of the ball tries to get close enough to shoot while the other team defends the goal. The player with the ball must dribble (bounce) the ball as he walks or runs, or pass it to a teammate. The defending team tries to block shots, intercept passes, and gain possession of the ball.

Basketball Record Holders

NBA Top Scorers

Year	Scoring Champion	Points	Year	Scoring Champion	Points
1947	Joe Fulks, Philadelphia	1,389	1968	Dave Bing, Detroit	2,142
1948	Max Zaslofsky, Chicago	1,007	1969	Elvin Hayes, San Diego	2,327
1949	George Mikan, Minneapolis	1,698	1970	Jerry West, Los Angeles	2,309
1950	George Mikan, Minneapolis	1,865	1971	Lew Alcindor, Milwaukee	2,596
1951	George Mikan, Minneapolis	1,932	1972	Kareem Abdul-Jabbar (Alcindor), Milwaukee	2,822
1952	Paul Arizin, Philadelphia	1,674			
1953	Neil Johnston, Philadelphia	1,564	1973	Nate Archibald, Kansas City-Omaha	2,719
1954	Neil Johnston, Philadelphia	1,759			
1955	Neil Johnston, Philadelphia	1,631	1974	Bob McAdoo, Buffalo	2,261
1956	Bob Pettit, St. Louis	1,849	1975	Bob McAdoo, Buffalo	2,831
1957	Paul Arizin, Philadelphia	1,817	1976	Bob McAdoo, Buffalo	2,427
1958	George Yardley, Detroit	2,001	1977	Pete Maravich, New Orleans	2,273
1959	Bob Pettit, St. Louis	2,105	1978	George Gervin, San Antonio	2,232
1960	Wilt Chamberlain, Philadelphia	2,707	1979	George Gervin, San Antonio	2,365
			1980	George Gervin, San Antonio	2,585
1961	Wilt Chamberlain, Philadelphia	3,033	1981	Adrian Dantley, Utah	2,452
			1982	George Gervin, San Antonio	2,551
1962	Wilt Chamberlain, Philadelphia	4,029	1983	Alex English, Denver	2,326
			1984	Adrian Dantley, Utah	2,418
1963	Wilt Chamberlain, San Francisco	3,586	1985	Bernard King, New York	1,809
			1986	Dominique Wilkins, Atlanta	2,366
1964	Wilt Chamberlain, San Francisco	2,948	1987	Michael Jordan, Chicago	3,041
			1988	Michael Jordan, Chicago	2,868
1965	Wilt Chamberlain, San Fran., Phila.	2,534	1989	Michael Jordan, Chicago	2,633
			1990	Michael Jordan, Chicago	2,753
1966	Wilt Chamberlain, Philadelphia	2,649	1991	Michael Jordan, Chicago	2,580
			1992	Michael Jordan, Chicago	2,404
1967	Rick Barry, San Francisco	2,775			

If a shot is successful, the team on offense gains two points and turns over the ball to its opponents, who run back toward their goal. (Three points are scored if a player sinks the basket from a distance of more than 23 feet.) After a missed shot, any player may catch the ball on the rebound, usually when it bounces off the rim or backboard. Then the shooting team may try again or, if the defenders gain possession, they go directly on offense.

All players try to use their arms and bodies to make it difficult for opponents to move freely. When body contact becomes too rough, officials call a foul and award a foul shot or a free throw to the other team. Then a player may shoot from 15 feet away without being blocked. Such a basket scores one point.

Basketball is a popular interscholastic and intercollegiate sport for both women and men. Excellent high school players can earn athletic scholarships to play the sport in college. After the completion of their education, the best male players may be invited into the professional ranks. In the United States there is no longer a professional league for women. Some women do go on to compete in professional women's basketball leagues in Europe, however.

Professional men's basketball games consist of four 12-minute quarters. The teams in the National Basketball Association (NBA) are divided into two conferences and four divisions. Champions of the Eastern Conference meet those of the Western Conference every spring. That series of seven games decides the NBA championship.

Basketball Court

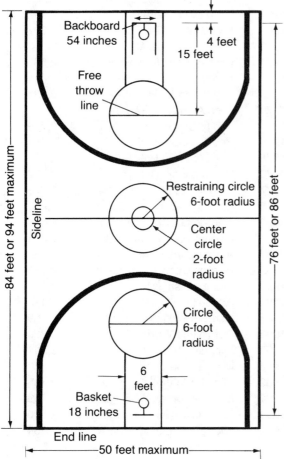

National Basketball Association (NBA)

Eastern Conference

Atlantic Division	*Central Division*
Boston Celtics	Atlanta Hawks
Charlotte Hornets	Chicago Bulls
New Jersey Nets	Cleveland Cavaliers
New York Knickerbockers	Detroit Pistons
Philadelphia 76ers	Indiana Pacers
Washington Bullets	Milwaukee Bucks

Western Conference

Midwest Division	*Pacific Division*
Dallas Mavericks	Golden State Warriors
Denver Nuggets	Los Angeles Clippers
Houston Rockets	Los Angeles Lakers
Miami Heat	Phoenix Suns
San Antonio Spurs	Portland Trailblazers
Utah Jazz	Seattle Supersonics

National Basketball Association Champions

Year	Winners	Conference	Losers	Conference
1947	Philadelphia Warriors	E	Chicago Stags	W
1948	Baltimore Bullets	W	Philadelphia Warriors	E
1949	Minneapolis Lakers	W	Washington Capitols	E
1950	Minneapolis Lakers	W	Syracuse Nationals	E
1951	Rochester Royals	W	New York Knickerbockers	E
1952	Minneapolis Lakers	W	New York Knickerbockers	E
1953	Minneapolis Lakers	W	New York Knickerbockers	E
1954	Minneapolis Lakers	W	Syracuse Nationals	E
1955	Syracuse Nationals	E	Fort Wayne Pistons	W
1956	Philadelphia Warriors	E	Fort Wayne Pistons	W
1957	Boston Celtics	E	St. Louis Hawks	W
1958	St. Louis Hawks	W	Boston Celtics	E
1959	Boston Celtics	E	Minneapolis Lakers	W
1960	Boston Celtics	E	St. Louis Hawks	W
1961	Boston Celtics	E	St. Louis Hawks	W
1962	Boston Celtics	E	Los Angeles Lakers	W
1963	Boston Celtics	E	Los Angeles Lakers	W
1964	Boston Celtics	E	San Francisco Warriors	W
1965	Boston Celtics	E	Los Angeles Lakers	W
1966	Boston Celtics	E	Los Angeles Lakers	W
1967	Philadelphia 76ers	E	San Francisco Warriors	W
1968	Boston Celtics	E	Los Angeles Lakers	W
1969	Boston Celtics	E	Los Angeles Lakers	W
1970	New York Knickerbockers	E	Los Angeles Lakers	W
1971	Milwaukee Bucks	W	Baltimore Bullets	E
1972	Los Angeles Lakers	W	New York Knickerbockers	E
1973	New York Knickerbockers	E	Los Angeles Lakers	W
1974	Boston Celtics	E	Milwaukee Bucks	W
1975	Golden State Warriors	W	Washington Bullets	E
1976	Boston Celtics	E	Phoenix Suns	W
1977	Portland Trailblazers	W	Philadelphia 76ers	E
1978	Washington Bullets	E	Seattle Supersonics	W
1979	Seattle Supersonics	W	Washington Bullets	E
1980	Los Angeles Lakers	W	Philadelphia 76ers	E
1981	Boston Celtics	E	Houston Rockets	W
1982	Los Angeles Lakers	W	Philadelphia 76ers	E
1983	Philadelphia 76ers	E	Los Angeles Lakers	W
1984	Boston Celtics	E	Los Angeles Lakers	W
1985	Los Angeles Lakers	W	Boston Celtics	E
1986	Boston Celtics	E	Houston Rockets	W
1987	Los Angeles Lakers	W	Boston Celtics	E
1988	Los Angeles Lakers	W	Detroit Pistons	E
1989	Detroit Pistons	E	Los Angeles Lakers	W
1990	Detroit Pistons	E	Portland Trailblazers	W
1991	Chicago Bulls	E	Los Angeles Lakers	W
1992	Chicago Bulls	E	Portland Trailblazers	W
1993	Chicago Bulls	E	Phoenix Suns	W

Bowling Alley

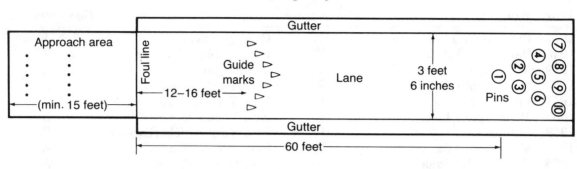

BOWLING

Bowling is an all-season, indoor sport that attracts more amateur participants than any other sport. It is also played by professionals. The nickname for bowling is tenpins, because the object of the game is to knock down ten wooden pins with a ball.

The ball weighs about 16 pounds and has three holes so you can grip it with your fingers. The pins, which are shaped like a bottle, are set up in a triangle at the end of a wooden lane, or alley.

A player gets two tries each turn to roll the ball down the alley. Each turn is called a frame, and there are ten frames to a game. The player with the highest score (the most pins knocked down after ten frames) wins.

In every frame, the goal is to knock down all ten pins at once for a strike. If any pins are left standing, a player can achieve the second-best goal, a spare, by leveling them all with the next roll of the ball. After a strike, the score for that frame is determined by adding 10 plus the number of pins knocked over with the next two balls in the following frame. After a spare, you add 10 plus the number knocked over by only the first ball of the next frame. If neither a strike nor a spare is rolled, the number of downed pins is counted after each frame.

Following a strike, the second ball of that frame is not played, except in the tenth and last frame. Then, if a strike is rolled, the player gets to roll two more balls. The high-est score possible is 300, which comes from rolling a perfect game of 12 strikes in a row.

FOOTBALL

A rectangular field 100 yards long is the setting for American football, a rough-and-tumble game with eleven players on a side. At both ends of the field is a 10-yard end zone, with the goal line in front and an H-shaped goalpost at the back. The object of the game is to move the ball down the field and across the goal line into the opponent's end zone.

The game begins with the kickoff, when one team kicks the oblong leather or pigskin ball to the other, who tries to run the ball as far as possible toward the opponent's goal. Wherever the ball is stopped is the receiving team's first down. Players in possession of the ball gather together (huddle) to decide their strategy. Then, before every play, the teams line up in either offensive or defensive positions with the ball between them. The ball is said to lie on the line of scrimmage.

When a team has the ball, it runs, passes, and kicks on the offense. Meanwhile, the defending team tries to prevent the ball's progress by blocking or intercepting passes and by tackling the ball carrier. (Football players wear protective helmets and padding because of this rough physical contact.) Because of its oblong shape, the ball is good for throwing, kicking, and clutching in the crook of the arm while running.

Each person on a team plays a specific role in offense or defense. The team on offense (in possession of the ball) hikes the ball to its quarterback. He hands it off or passes it to a teammate, or runs with it himself.

If a team can't move the ball forward 10 yards in four tries (called downs), it must turn the ball over to the opponents and go on the defensive. Every time 10 yards are more are gained, a first down is achieved and the offensive team earns another four downs.

After the third down, if it seems unlikely that by the end of the fourth down the necessary yardage will be gained, a team may decide to give up the ball by punting—trying to kick it deep into the opponents' territory. Then the defensive players go on the offense, while the attacking team switches to defensive tactics.

Another way for the defensive team to gain the ball is by catching a pass intended for the other team (interception). Also, when an offensive player drops the ball (fumbles), a defensive player may recover it; then his team's offense immediately takes over. (If the offensive player's teammate recovers the fumble, his team resumes offensive action.)

The team that scores the most points, within four 15-minute periods, wins. Crossing the goal line carrying the football, or catching it in the end zone, is called a touchdown and scores 6 points. One more point (called the point after) can be added by kicking the ball through the goalposts or running or passing it into the end zone after a touchdown. Other times, kicking the ball through the goalposts scores 3 points (a field goal). Two points can be scored by tackling an offensive player who is carrying the ball in his own end zone (a safety).

The sport's professional season starts in the fall. In January of the following year, winners of the National and American Conferences of the National Football League face off in the Super Bowl for the NFL championship.

Football Field

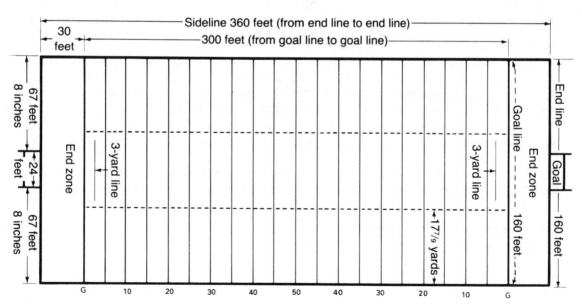

Football Record Holders

NFL and AFL* Top Lifetime Rushers

In football, rushers are offensive players who run with the ball. Rushes are the distance a player runs with the ball toward the other team's goal. Rushes are measured in yards.

Player	League	Yrs	Attempts	Yards	Avg
Walter Payton	NFL	13	3,838	16,726	4.4
Tony Dorsett	NFL	12	2,936	12,739	4.3
Eric Dickerson	NFL	9	2,783	12,439	4.5
Jim Brown	NFL	9	2,359	12,312	5.2
Franco Harris	NFL	13	2,949	12,120	4.1
John Riggins	NFL	14	2,916	11,352	3.9
O. J. Simpson	AFL-NFL	11	2,404	11,236	4.7
Ottis Anderson	NFL	13	2,552	10,242	4.0
Earl Campbell	NFL	8	2,187	9,407	4.3
Jim Taylor	NFL	10	1,941	8,597	4.4
Joe Perry	NFL	14	1,737	8,378	4.8
Marcus Allen	NFL	10	2,023	8,244	4.1
Gerald Riggs	NFL	10	1,989	8,188	4.1
Larry Csonka	AFL-NFL	11	1,891	8,081	4.3
James Brooks	NFL	11	1,667	7,918	4.7
Freeman McNeil	NFL	11	1,755	7,904	4.5
Roger Craig	NFL	9	1,848	7,654	4.1
Mike Pruitt	NFL	11	1,844	7,378	4.0
Leroy Kelly	NFL	10	1,727	7,274	4.2
George Rogers	NFL	7	1,692	7,176	4.2

Most Yards Gained, Season—2,105, Eric Dickerson, Los Angeles Rams, 1984.
Most Yards Gained, Game—275, Walter Payton, Chicago Bears vs. Minnesota Vikings, Nov. 20, 1977.
Most Games, 100 Yards or more, Season—12, Eric Dickerson, Los Angeles Rams, 1984.
Most Games, 100 Yards or more, Career–77, Walter Payton, Chicago Bears, 1975–87.
Most Touchdowns Rushing, Career—110, Walter Payton, Chicago Bears, 1975–87.
Most Touchdowns Rushing, Season—24, John Riggins, Washington Redskins, 1983.
Most Touchdowns Rushing, Game—6, Ernie Nevers, Chicago Cardinals vs. Chicago Bears, Nov. 8, 1929.
Most Rushing Attempts, Season—407, James Wilder, Tampa Bay Buccaneers, 1984.
Most Rushing Attempts, Game—45, Jamie Morris, Washington Redskins vs. Cincinnati Bengals, Dec. 17, 1988.

* American Football League, before it merged with the NFL.

National Football League (NFL)

National Conference

Eastern Division	Central Division	Western Division
Dallas Cowboys	Chicago Bears	Atlanta Falcons
New York Giants	Detroit Lions	New Orleans Saints
Philadelphia Eagles	Green Bay Packers	Los Angeles Rams
Phoenix Cardinals	Minnesota Vikings	San Francisco 49ers
Washington Redskins	Tampa Bay Buccaneers	

American Conference

Eastern Division	Central Division	Western Division
Buffalo Bills	Cincinnati Bengals	Denver Broncos
Indianapolis Colts	Cleveland Browns	Kansas City Chiefs
Miami Dolphins	Houston Oilers	Los Angeles Raiders
New England Patriots	Pittsburgh Steelers	San Diego Chargers
New York Jets		Seattle Seahawks

The Super Bowl Champions

The Super Bowl, played in January, marks the end of the professional football season that began the previous fall. The first four Super Bowls were played between the champions of the National Football League and those of the American Football League. The two leagues then merged; the game has since been played between the National Football Conference champions and the American Football Conference champions. The winners and losers follow:

No.	Year	Winners	League/ Conference	Losers	League/ Conference	Score
I	1967	Green Bay Packers	NFL	Kansas City Chiefs	AFL	35–10
II	1968	Green Bay Packers	NFL	Oakland Raiders	AFL	33–14
III	1969	New York Jets	AFL	Baltimore Colts	NFL	16–7
IV	1970	Kansas City Chiefs	AFL	Minnesota Vikings	NFL	23–7
V	1971	Baltimore Colts	AFC	Dallas Cowboys	NFC	16–13
VI	1972	Dallas Cowboys	NFC	Miami Dolphins	AFC	24–3
VII	1973	Miami Dolphins	AFC	Washington Redskins	NFC	14–7
VIII	1974	Miami Dolphins	AFC	Minnesota Vikings	NFC	24–7
IX	1975	Pittsburgh Steelers	AFC	Minnesota Vikings	NFC	16–6
X	1976	Pittsburgh Steelers	AFC	Dallas Cowboys	NFC	21–17
XI	1977	Oakland Raiders	AFC	Minnesota Vikings	NFC	32–14
XII	1978	Dallas Cowboys	NFC	Denver Broncos	AFC	27–10
XIII	1979	Pittsburgh Steelers	AFC	Dallas Cowboys	NFC	35–31
XIV	1980	Pittsburgh Steelers	AFC	Los Angeles Rams	NFC	31–19
XV	1981	Oakland Raiders	AFC	Philadelphia Eagles	NFC	27–10
XVI	1982	San Francisco 49ers	NFC	Cincinnati Bengals	AFC	26–21
XVII	1983	Washington Redskins	NFC	Miami Dolphins	AFC	27–17

(continued)

The Super Bowl Champions (*continued*)

No.	Year	Winners	League/Conference	Losers	League/Conference	Score
XVIII	1984	Los Angeles Raiders	AFC	Washington Redskins	NFC	38–9
XIX	1985	San Francisco 49ers	NFC	Miami Dolphins	AFC	38–16
XX	1986	Chicago Bears	NFC	New England Patriots	AFC	46–10
XXI	1987	New York Giants	NFC	Denver Broncos	AFC	39–20
XXII	1988	Washington Redskins	NFC	Denver Broncos	AFC	42–10
XXIII	1989	San Francisco 49ers	NFC	Cincinnati Bengals	AFC	20–16
XXIV	1990	San Francisco 49ers	NFC	Denver Broncos	AFC	55–10
XXV	1991	New York Giants	NFC	Buffalo Bills	AFC	20–19
XXVI	1992	Washington Redskins	NFC	Buffalo Bills	AFC	37–24
XXVII	1993	Dallas Cowboys	NFC	Buffalo Bills	AFC	52–17

ICE HOCKEY

Ice hockey is an action-packed team sport played in an ice rink. Each team is made up of six players and all the players wear ice skates. They streak with lightning speed up and down the rink, slamming a hard rubber disk called a puck along the ice with long sticks. Sometimes the puck reaches speeds of 100 miles per hour (160 kilometers per hour) as it flies across the ice. The players try to score points by hitting the puck into a goal cage or net. The side that scores the most goals wins the game.

A goalkeeper on each team defends the team's net. Goalkeepers must often slide across the front of the net on their stomachs, knees, or back to block the puck.

To keep the action fast, hockey allows players to be substituted while play is in progress. Fights often break out during the game, although fighting is against the rules.

The National Hockey League (NHL) is the one major professional league in the United States and Canada. The regular hockey season lasts from October to April. The top four teams in each division qualify for post-season playoffs, which may last as late as June. The finalists play for the Stanley Cup.

Hockey Rink

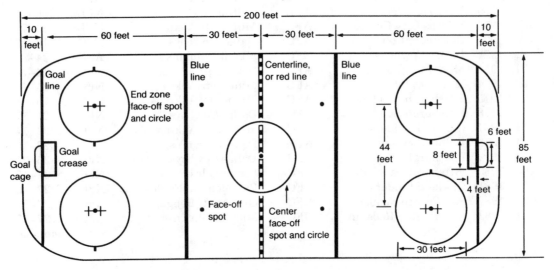

National Hockey League (NHL)

Western Conference

Pacific Division	Central Division
Anaheim Mighty Ducks	Chicago Blackhawks
Calgary Flames	Dallas Stars
Edmonton Oilers	Detroit Red Wings
Los Angeles Kings	St. Louis Blues
San Jose Sharks	Toronto Maple Leafs
Vancouver Canucks	Winnipeg Jets

Eastern Conference

Northeast Division	Atlantic Division
Boston Bruins	New Jersey Devils
Buffalo Sabres	New York Islanders
Hartford Whalers	New York Rangers
Montreal Canadiens	Philadelphia Flyers
Ottawa Senators	Florida Panthers
Pittsburgh Penguins	Tampa Bay Lightning
Quebec Nordiques	Washington Capitals

Stanley Cup Champions

Season	Winner	Loser	Games won-lost
1917–1918	Toronto Arenas	Vancouver Millionaires	3–2
1918–1919	No winner*		
1919–1920	Ottawa Senators	Seattle Metropolitans	3–2
1920–1921	Ottawa Senators	Vancouver Millionaires	3–2
1921–1922	Toronto St. Pats	Vancouver Millionaires	3–2
1922–1923	Ottawa Senators	Edmonton Eskimos	2–0
1923–1924	Montreal Canadiens	Calgary Tigers	2–0
1924–1925	Victoria Cougars†	Montreal Canadiens	3–1
1925–1926	Montreal Maroons	Victoria Cougars	3–1
1926–1927	Ottawa Senators	Boston Bruins	2–0
1927–1928	New York Rangers	Montreal Maroons	3–2
1928–1929	Boston Bruins	New York Rangers	2–0
1929–1930	Montreal Canadiens	Boston Bruins	2–0
1930–1931	Montreal Canadiens	Chicago Black Hawks	3–2
1931–1932	Toronto Maple Leafs	New York Rangers	3–0
1932–1933	New York Rangers	Toronto Maple Leafs	3–1
1933–1934	Chicago Black Hawks	Detroit Red Wings	3–1
1934–1935	Montreal Maroons	Toronto Maple Leafs	3–0
1935–1936	Detroit Red Wings	Toronto Maple Leafs	3–1

(*continued*)

Stanley Cup Champions (*continued*)

Season	Winner	Loser	Games won-lost
1936–1937	Detroit Red Wings	New York Rangers	3–2
1937–1938	Chicago Black Hawks	Toronto Maple Leafs	3–1
1938–1939	Boston Bruins	Toronto Maple Leafs	4–1
1939–1940	New York Rangers	Toronto Maple Leafs	4–2
1940–1941	Boston Bruins	Detroit Red Wings	4–0
1941–1942	Toronto Maple Leafs	Detroit Red Wings	4–3
1942–1943	Detroit Red Wings	Boston Bruins	4–0
1943–1944	Montreal Canadiens	Chicago Black Hawks	4–0
1944–1945	Toronto Maple Leafs	Detroit Red Wings	4–3
1945–1946	Montreal Canadiens	Boston Bruins	4–1
1946–1947	Toronto Maple Leafs	Montreal Canadiens	4–2
1947–1948	Toronto Maple Leafs	Detroit Red Wings	4–0
1948–1949	Toronto Maple Leafs	Detroit Red Wings	4–0
1949–1950	Detroit Red Wings	New York Rangers	4–3
1950–1951	Toronto Maple Leafs	Montreal Canadiens	4–1
1951–1952	Detroit Red Wings	Montreal Canadiens	4–0
1952–1953	Montreal Canadiens	Boston Bruins	4–1
1953–1954	Detroit Red Wings	Montreal Canadiens	4–3
1954–1955	Detroit Red Wings	Montreal Canadiens	4–3
1955–1956	Montreal Canadians	Detroit Red Wings	4–1
1956–1957	Montreal Canadiens	Boston Bruins	4–1
1957–1958	Montreal Canadiens	Boston Bruins	4–2
1958–1959	Montreal Canadiens	Toronto Maple Leafs	4–1
1959–1960	Montreal Canadiens	Toronto Maple Leafs	4–0
1960–1961	Chicago Black Hawks	Detroit Red Wings	4–2
1961–1962	Toronto Maple Leafs	Chicago Black Hawks	4–2
1962–1963	Toronto Maple Leafs	Detroit Red Wings	4–1
1963–1964	Toronto Maple Leafs	Detroit Red Wings	4–3
1964–1965	Montreal Canadiens	Chicago Black Hawks	4–3
1965–1966	Montreal Canadiens	Detroit Red Wings	4–2
1966–1967	Toronto Maple Leafs	Montreal Canadiens	4–2
1967–1968	Montreal Canadiens	St. Louis Blues	4–0
1968–1969	Montreal Canadiens	St. Louis Blues	4–0
1969–1970	Boston Bruins	St. Louis Blues	4–0
1970–1971	Montreal Canadiens	Chicago Black Hawks	4–3
1971–1972	Boston Bruins	New York Rangers	4–2
1972–1973	Montreal Canadiens	Chicago Black Hawks	4–2
1973–1974	Philadelphia Flyers	Boston Bruins	4–2
1974–1975	Philadelphia Flyers	Buffalo Sabres	4–2
1975–1976	Montreal Canadiens	Philadelphia Flyers	4–0
1976–1977	Montreal Canadiens	Boston Bruins	4–0
1977–1978	Montreal Canadiens	Boston Bruins	4–2
1978–1979	Montreal Canadiens	New York Rangers	4–1
1979–1980	New York Islanders	Philadelphia Flyers	4–2

Season	Winner	Loser	Games won-lost
1980–1981	New York Islanders	Minnesota North Stars	4–1
1981–1982	New York Islanders	Vancouver Canucks	4–0
1982–1983	New York Islanders	Edmonton Oilers	4–0
1983–1984	Edmonton Oilers	New York Islanders	4–1
1984–1985	Edmonton Oilers	Philadelphia Flyers	4–1
1985–1986	Montreal Canadiens	Calgary Flames	4–1
1986–1987	Edmonton Oilers	Philadelphia Flyers	4–3
1987–1988	Edmonton Oilers	Boston Bruins	4–0
1988–1989	Calgary Flames	Montreal Canadiens	4–2
1989–1990	Edmonton Oilers	Boston Bruins	4–1
1990–1991	Pittsburgh Penguins	Minnesota North Stars	4–2
1991–1992	Pittsburgh Penguins	Chicago Black Hawks	4–0
1992–1993	Montreal Canadians	Los Angeles Kings	4–1

* Playoff between Montreal Canadiens and Seattle Metropolitans not finished because of influenza epidemic in Seattle.
† Member, Pacific Coast League.

Hockey Record Holders

Most NHL Goals in One Season

Player	Team	Season	Goals	Player	Team	Season	Goals
Wayne Gretzky	Edmonton	1981–82	92	Jari Kurri	Edmonton	1985–86	68
Wayne Gretzky	Edmonton	1983–84	87	Phil Esposito	Boston	1971–72	66
Brett Hull	St. Louis	1990–91	86	Lanny McDonald	Calgary	1982–83	66
Mario Lemieux	Pittsburgh	1988–89	85	Steve Yzerman	Detroit	1988–89	65
Phil Esposito	Boston	1970–71	76	Mike Bossy	N.Y. Islanders	1981–82	64
Wayne Gretzky	Edmonton	1984–85	73	Wayne Gretzky	Edmonton	1986–87	62
Brett Hull	St. Louis	1989–90	72	Steve Yzerman	Detroit	1989–90	62
Wayne Gretzky	Edmonton	1982–83	71	Mike Bossy	N.Y. Islanders	1985–86	61
Jari Kurri	Edmonton	1984–85	71	Phil Esposito	Boston	1974–75	61
Mario Lemieux	Pittsburgh	1987–88	70	Reggie Leach	Philadelphia	1975–76	61
Bernie Nicholis	Los Angeles	1988–89	70	Mike Bossy	N.Y. Islanders	1982–83	60
Bret Hull	St. Louis	1991–92	70	Guy Lafleur	Montreal	1977–78	60
Mike Bossy	N.Y. Islanders	1978–79	69	Steve Shutt	Montreal	1976–77	60
Phil Esposito	Boston	1973–74	68	Dennis Maruk	Washington	1981–82	60
Mike Bossy	N.Y. Islanders	1980–81	68				

TENNIS

An all-season sport, tennis is played indoors and outdoors. The tennis court is rectangular with a clay, grass, or synthetic surface. A net stretches across the middle, three feet high.

A player uses a racquet to hit a ball over the net to his or her opponent's side of the court. The racquet is made of wood or metal with a tightly strung face. The rubber ball is small and covered with felt. Two sets of lines border the sides of the court. In a singles game (one person on each side of the court), players must keep the ball within the inside boundary. In a doubles game, the two-person teams use the space to the wider outside border.

The object of the game is to score points by hitting the ball so that the opponent can't return it. When a player can't return the ball, the opponent scores the point.

Each game begins with a player serving the ball diagonally across to the service area (a small box on the other side of the court). The server gets two tries. If the ball doesn't reach the service area after the second try, the server's opponent scores a point. A point is also scored after a player misses the ball or hits it into the net or outside the court boundaries. Points are scored no matter

who is serving. The service alternates after each game. Players switch sides after odd-numbered games.

Four points wins a game, scored 15, 30, 40, and game. Deuce is the term for a 40–40 tie. At deuce, a game is played out until one player is at least two points ahead. Whoever wins six games first wins the set, as long as she or he is ahead by two. For example, a player who wins six games to the opponent's four (6–4) wins the set. If they are tied 5–5, however, the set will be won by the player who goes two games ahead (7–5), and if the games are tied at 6 games apiece, a tie-breaker determines the outcome of the set. The overall winner of the match is the team or player who wins two out of three sets in women's play and the best three out of five in men's play.

Tennis has organized competition for both the young (Juniors) and the old (Masters). Four major professional championships make up the Grand Slam: the French Open. Australian Open, U.S. Open, and Wimbledon (England). Of these, Wimbledon is the oldest and has the most prestige. Following is a list of U.S. Open Singles Winners since 1881 and Wimbledon singles champions since 1950.

Tennis Court

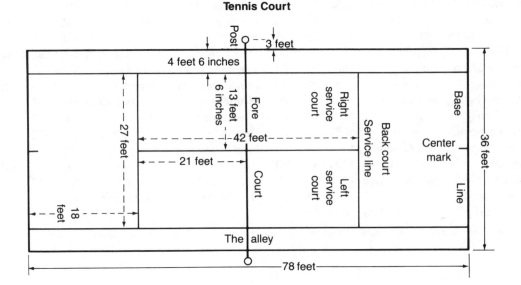

U.S. Open Winners

Men's Singles

McLoughlin

Year	Winner
1881	Richard D. Sears
1882	Richard D. Sears
1883	Richard D. Sears
1884	Richard D. Sears
1885	Richard D. Sears
1886	Richard D. Sears
1887	Richard D. Sears
1888	H. W. Slocum, Jr.
1889	H. W. Slocum, Jr.
1890	Oliver S. Campbell
1891	Oliver S. Campbell
1892	Oliver S. Campbell
1893	Robert D. Wrenn
1894	Robert D. Wrenn
1895	Frederick H. Hovey
1896	Robert D. Wrenn
1897	Robert D. Wrenn
1898	Malcolm D. Whitman
1899	Malcolm D. Whitman
1900	Malcolm D. Whitman
1901	William A. Larned
1902	William A. Larned
1903	H. Laurie Doherty
1904	Holcombe Ward
1905	Beals C. Wright
1906	William J. Clothier
1907	William A. Larned
1908	William A. Larned
1909	William A. Larned
1910	William A. Larned
1911	William A. Larned
1912	Maurice E. McLoughlin
1913	Maurice E. McLoughlin
1914	Richard N. Williams
1915	Bill Johnston
1916	Richard N. Williams
1917	R. L. Murray
1918	R. L. Murray

Year	Winner
1919	Bill Johnston
1920	Bill Tilden
1921	Bill Tilden
1922	Bill Tilden
1923	Bill Tilden
1924	Bill Tilden
1925	Bill Tilden
1926	Rene Lacoste
1927	Rene Lacoste
1928	Henri Cochet
1929	Bill Tilden
1930	John H. Doeg
1931	Ellsworth Vines
1932	Ellsworth Vines
1933	Fred Perry
1934	Fred Perry
1935	Wilmer L. Allison
1936	Fred Perry
1937	Don Budge
1938	Don Budge
1939	Bobby Riggs
1940	Don McNeill
1941	Bobby Riggs
1942	Ted Schroeder
1943	Joseph R. Hunt
1944	Frank Parker
1945	Frank Parker
1946	Jack Kramer
1947	Jack Kramer
1948	Pancho Gonzales
1949	Pancho Gonzales
1950	Arthur Larsen
1951	Frank Sedgman
1952	Frank Sedgman
1953	Tony Trabert
1954	Vic Seixas
1955	Tony Trabert
1956	Ken Rosewall

Year	Winner
1957	Mal Anderson
1958	Ashley J. Cooper
1959	Neale Fraser
1960	Neale Fraser
1961	Roy Emerson
1962	Rod Laver
1963	Rafael Osuna
1964	Roy Emerson
1965	Manuel Santana
1966	Fred Stolle
1967	John Newcombe
1968	Arthur Ashe
1968	Arthur Ashe
1969	Stan Smith
1969	Rod Laver
1970	Ken Rosewall
1971	Stan Smith
1972	Ilie Nastase
1973	John Newcombe
1974	Jimmy Connors
1975	Manuel Orantes
1976	Jimmy Connors
1977	Guillermo Vilas
1978	Jimmy Connors
1979	John McEnroe
1980	John McEnroe
1981	John McEnroe
1982	Jimmy Connors
1983	Jimmy Connors
1984	John McEnroe
1985	Ivan Lendl
1986	Ivan Lendl
1987	Ivan Lendl
1988	Mats Wilander
1989	Boris Becker
1990	Pete Sampras
1991	Stefan Edberg
1992	Stefan Edberg

Women's Singles

Year	Winner	Year	Winner	Year	Winner
1887	Ellen Hansell	1923	Helen Wills	1957	Althea Gibson
1888	Bertha L. Townsend	1924	Helen Wills	1958	Althea Gibson
1889	Bertha L. Townsend	1925	Helen Wills	1959	Maria Bueno
1890	Ellen C. Roosevelt	1926	Molla Bjurstedt	1960	Darlene Hard
1891	Mabel Cahill		Mallory	1961	Darlene Hard
1892	Mabel Cahill	1927	Helen Wills	1962	Margaret Smith
1893	Aline Terry	1928	Helen Wills	1963	Maria Bueno
1894	Helen Hellwig	1929	Helen Wills	1964	Maria Bueno
1895	Juliette Atkinson	1930	Betty Nuthall	1965	Margaret Smith
1896	Elisabeth Moore	1931	Helen Wills Moody	1966	Maria Bueno
1897	Juliette Atkinson	1932	Helen Jacobs	1967	Billie Jean King
1898	Juliette Atkinson	1933	Helen Jacobs	1968	Virginia Wade
1899	Marion Jones	1934	Helen Jacobs	1968	Margaret Smith Court
1900	Myrtle McAteer	1935	Helen Jacobs	1969	Margaret Smith Court
1901	Elisabeth Moore	1936	Alice Marble	1969	Margaret Smith Court
1902	Marion Jones	1937	Anita Lizane	1970	Margaret Smith Court
1903	Elisabeth Moore	1938	Alice Marble	1971	Billie Jean King
1904	May Sutton	1939	Alice Marble	1972	Billie Jean King
1905	Elisabeth Moore	1940	Alice Marble	1973	Margaret Smith Court
1906	Helen Homans	1941	Sarah Palfrey Cooke	1974	Billie Jean King
1907	Evelyn Sears	1942	Pauline Betz	1975	Chris Evert
1908	Maud Barger-Wallach	1943	Pauline Betz	1976	Chris Evert
1909	Hazel Hotchkiss	1944	Pauline Betz	1977	Chris Evert
1910	Hazel Hotchkiss	1945	Sarah Palfrey Cooke	1978	Chris Evert
1911	Hazel Hotchkiss	1946	Pauline Betz	1979	Tracy Austin
1912	Mary K. Browne	1947	Louise Brough	1980	Chris Evert Lloyd
1913	Mary K. Browne	1948	Margaret Osborne	1981	Tracy Austin
1914	Mary K. Browne		duPont	1982	Chris Evert Lloyd
1915	Molla Bjurstedt	1949	Margaret Osborne	1983	Martina Navratilova
1916	Molla Bjurstedt		duPont	1984	Martina Navratilova
1917	Molla Bjurstedt	1950	Margaret Osborne	1985	Hana Mandlikova
1918	Molla Bjurstedt		duPont	1986	Martina Navratilova
1919	Hazel Hotchkiss	1951	Maureen Connolly	1987	Martina Navratilova
	Wightman	1952	Maureen Connolly	1988	Steffi Graf
1920	Molla Bjurstedt	1953	Maureen Connolly	1989	Steffi Graf
	Mallory	1954	Doris Hart	1990	Gabriela Sabatini
1921	Molla Bjurstedt	1955	Doris Hart	1991	Monica Seles
	Mallory	1956	Shirley Fry	1992	Monica Seles
1922	Molla Bjurstedt				
	Mallory				

Wimbledon Champions

Year	Women	Men
1950	A. Louise Brough	Budge Patty
1951	Doris Hart	Dick Savitt
1952	Maureen Connolly	Frank Sedgman
1953	Maureen Connolly	Vic Seixas
1954	Maureen Connolly	Jaroslav Drobny
1955	A. Louise Brough	Tony Trabert
1956	Shirley Fry	Lew Hoad
1957	Althea Gibson	Lew Hoad
1958	Althea Gibson	Ashley Cooper
1959	Maria Bueno	Alex Olmedo
1960	Maria Bueno	Neale Fraser
1961	Angela Mortimer	Rod Laver
1962	Karen Susman	Rod Laver
1963	Margaret Smith	Chuck McKinley
1964	Maria Bueno	Roy Emerson
1965	Margaret Smith	Roy Emerson
1966	Billie Jean King	Manuel Santana
1967	Billie Jean King	John Newcombe
1968	Billie Jean King	Rod Laver
1969	Ann Jones	Rod Laver
1970	Margaret Smith Court	John Newcombe
1971	Evonne Goolagong	John Newcombe
1972	Billie Jean King	Stan Smith
1973	Billie Jean King	Jan Kodes
1974	Chris Evert	Jimmy Connors
1975	Billie Jean King	Arthur Ashe
1976	Chris Evert	Bjorn Borg
1977	Virginia Wade	Bjorn Borg
1978	Martina Navratilova	Bjorn Borg
1979	Martina Navratilova	Bjorn Borg
1980	Evonne Goolagong	Bjorn Borg
1981	Chris Evert Lloyd	John McEnroe
1982	Martina Navratilova	Jimmy Connors
1983	Martina Navratilova	John McEnroe
1984	Martina Navratilova	John McEnroe
1985	Martina Navratilova	Boris Becker
1986	Martina Navratilova	Boris Becker
1987	Martina Navratilova	Pat Cash
1988	Steffi Graf	Stefan Edberg
1989	Steffi Graf	Boris Becker
1990	Martina Navratilova	Stefan Edberg
1991	Steffi Graf	Michael Stich
1992	Steffi Graf	Andre Agassi
1993	Steffi Graf	Pete Sampras

Soccer Field

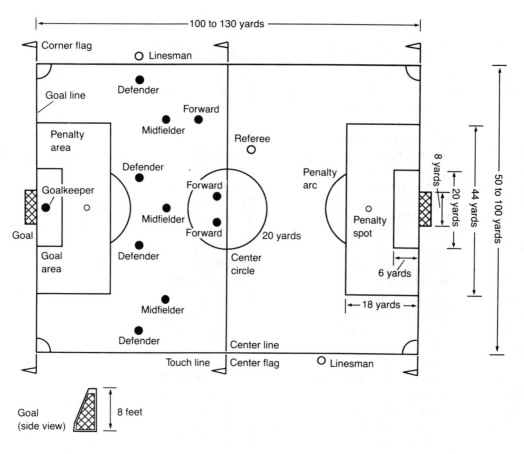

SOCCER

Soccer is one of the most popular sports in the world. Millions of people in 140 nations play soccer. It is the national pastime of many European and Latin American countries and is growing in popularity in the United States.

In soccer, two teams of eleven players each try to put the ball into each other's goal. Whichever team scores the most goals wins. Players can use their heads, feet, thighs, or chest to control, stop, or pass the ball—but never their hands. Only the goalkeepers may use their hands or arms to play the ball.

A soccer game is generally played for two 45-minute periods. It begins with a kick-off in the center of the field on the halfway line. Once the ball is in play, the attacking team tries to move the ball into the other team's territory. The defending players shift their positions to break up attacks. Hard body contact is permitted only when it results from an attempt to kick the ball or hit it with the head. Although soccer is called football in Great Britain and in some other countries, it is not a contact sport like American football. However, like American football, it is a fast-paced game full of excitement.

Most countries in Europe and Latin America have professional soccer leagues that are made up of a number of divisions. The winner of the top division is the country's national champion. Every four years national all-star teams compete for the World Cup. All member nations of the Fédération Internationale de Football Association (FIFA)

compete in qualifying rounds held two years before the championship. These rounds determine which 22 teams will join the host nation and the previous champion in the final tournament.

Soccer is also an event of the summer Olympic games.

World Cup Champions

Year	Winner	Runner-Up	Site
1930	Uruguay	Argentina	Uruguay
1934	Italy	Czechoslovakia	Italy
1938	Italy	Hungary	France
1950	Uruguay	Brazil	Brazil
1954	W. Germany	Hungary	Switzerland
1958	Brazil	Sweden	Sweden
1962	Brazil	Czechoslovakia	Chile
1966	England	W. Germany	England
1970	Brazil	Italy	Mexico
1974	W. Germany	Netherlands	W. Germany
1978	Argentina	Netherlands	Argentina
1982	Italy	W. Germany	Spain
1986	Argentina	W. Germany	Mexico
1990	Germany	Argentina	Italy

VOLLEYBALL

Volleyball is played indoors or outdoors on a rectangular court divided by a net eight feet high. With six players on a side, each team tries to hit a ball over the net before it touches the court floor. The ball may be volleyed three times on a side, but by the third hit the ball must be sent over the net.

Players are arranged to cover the area on their side. This arrangement of teammates rotates to give every player a chance to serve. After the ball is in motion, players may move anywhere on their side of the court.

The ball is put into play with the service. Players take turns serving from behind the far right corner line. After the ball is served, with the hand or fist, it can be hit by any part of the body. (Holding or catching the ball is not allowed.) The server continues serving

until his or her side fails to return the ball. Then the other team serves. Only the team serving can score: one point whenever its opponents let the ball touch the floor or hit it out of bounds or into the net. The first team to reach fifteen points, with a two-point lead, wins the game. In championship play, three out of five games wins the match.

THE OLYMPICS

The ancient Greeks probably started the Olympic games before 1400 B.C., as part of festivals honoring the gods. Around 776 B.C. the first games were played in the Stadium of Olympia in Greece. Afterward the games were held every four years, until an earthquake destroyed to stadium in A.D. 500.

The first modern Olympics were held in Athens, Greece, in 1896. Since then, the

Volleyball Court

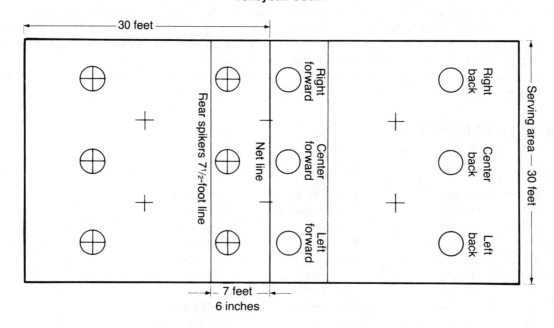

Olympics usually have occurred every four years. The games are divided into the summer games and the winter games. The Olympic Committee chooses the site of both games, and all expenses for the events are paid for by the host country. The summer Olympic games last a total of 16 days but are spread out over various months. Winter events are played in January or February and last about 16 days.

Until recently, the summer and winter games were held in the same year. After 1992, however, the games are to be staggered, so that there will be two years between the summer and winter Olympics. For example, the winter games are scheduled for 1994, and the summer Olympics for 1996.

Both the summer and winter Olympics have an opening ceremony. During the ceremony the Greek competitors march into the stadium first. All the other competing athletes follow them in alphabetical order according to their nation's name, except for the host country, which is last. The most moving part of the ceremony occurs when the Olympic torch is carried into the stadium by a runner, who lights the flame that will burn until the end of the games.

During 1992, athletes from 63 countries competed in the winter games. In the summer games, athletes from more than 100 countries competed. Men and women compete separately in both the summer and winter games. A few sports such as boxing and ice hockey are for men only. Both men and women athletes are chosen by the national Olympic committee of their country, often after selection trials. To qualify, athletes have to be citizens of the country they will represent. Until 1988, every Olympic athlete also had to be an amateur. But now paid professionals in sports such as soccer, tennis, and basketball may qualify.

For most individual events, up to three athletes from one nation can be part of any give competition. For team events, each country can be represented by only one team.

Different events are judged differently. In such sports as diving and gymnastics, judges assign points to each competitor's performance. The performer with the highest average wins. In boxing, each man competes

Olympic Games

Summer Games		*Winter Games*	
Year	Location	Year	Location
1896	Athens, Greece	1924	Chamonix, France
1900	Paris, France	1928	St. Moritz, Switzerland
1904	St. Louis, Missouri	1932	Lake Placid, New York
1908	London, England	1936	Garmisch-Partenkirchen
1912	Stockholm, Sweden	1948	St. Moritz, Switzerland
1920	Antwerp, Belgium	1952	Oslo, Norway
1924	Paris, France	1956	Cortina, Italy
1928	Amsterdam, The Netherlands	1960	Squaw Valley, California
1932	Los Angeles, California	1964	Innsbruck, Austria
1936	Berlin, Germany	1968	Grenoble, France
1948	London, England	1972	Sapporo, Japan
1952	Helsinki, Finland	1976	Innsbruck, Austria
1956	Melbourne, Australia	1980	Lake Placid, New York
1960	Rome, Italy	1984	Sarajevo, Yugoslavia
1964	Tokyo, Japan	1988	Calgary, Canada
1968	Mexico City, Mexico	1992	Albertville, France
1972	Munich, West Germany		
1976	Montreal, Canada		
1980	Moscow, USSR		
1984	Los Angeles, California		
1988	Seoul, South Korea		
1992	Barcelona, Spain		

1992 Olympic Events

Summer Games

Men	Men's Swimming	Men's Track and Field	
Boxing	50 m, 100 m, 200 m,	100 m, 200 m, 400 m	Long jump
Judo	400 m, 1500 m freestyle	dash	Triple jump
Canoeing	100 m, 200 m backstroke	800 m, 1500 m, 5000 m,	Pole vault
Soccer (team)	100 m, 200 m breast	10,000 m run	Shot put
Water polo	stroke	Marathon	Discus
(team)	100 m, 200 m butterfly	110 m, 400 m hurdles	throw
Weightlifting	200 m, 400 m individual	3000 m steeplechase	Javelin
Wrestling	medley	20 m, 50 m walk	throw
Freestyle	400 m, 800 m freestyle	400 m relay (4 × 100)	Hammer
Greco-Roman	relay	1600 m relay (4 × 400)	throw
	400 m medley relay	High jump	Decathlon
	Springboard dive		
	Platform dive		

Men and Women	Women's Swimming	Women's Track and Field
Archery	50 m, 100 m, 200 m, 400 m, 800 m	100 m, 200 m, 400 m
Basketball (team)	freestyle	dash
Cycling	100 m, 200 m backstroke	800 m, 1500 m, 3000 m
Equestrian*	100 m, 200 m breaststroke	run
Fencing	100 m, 200 m butterfly	100 m, 400 m hurdles
Field hockey	200 m, 400 m individual medley	400 m relay (4 × 100)
Gymnastics	400 m freestyle relay	1600 m relay (4 × 400)
Handball (team)	400 m medley relay	Marathon
Kayaking	Springboard dive	High jump
Rowing	Platform dive	Long jump
Shooting	Synchronized swimming	Shot put
Table tennis		Discus throw
Tennis		Javelin throw
Volleyball (team)		Heptathlon
Yachting		Modern pentathlon

* In equestrian sports, men and women compete against one another.

Winter Games

Except for biathlon, bobsledding, and ice hockey, all winter sports at the 1984, 1988, and 1992 games were divided into two classes, one for men and the other for women. Biathlon, bobsledding, and ice hockey were played by men only. In paired figure and ice dancing, men and women performed together.

10 K biathlon	Nordic skiing
20 K biathlon	Men's cross country
30 K biathlon relay	15 K, 30 K, 50 K
4-man bobsledding	40 K relay
2-man bobsledding	combined cross country and jumping
Figure skating	ski jumping: 90 m, 70 m
Ice dancing	Women's cross country
Ice hockey	5 K, 10 K, 20 K
Luge	20 K relay
Alpine skiing	Speed skating
Downhill	Men: 500 m, 100 m, 1500 m, 5 K, 10 K
Slalom	Women: 500 m, 100 m, 1500 m, 3 K, 5 K
Giant slalom	
Super giant slalom	
Freestyle skiing	

until he loses a bout. In speed skating and skiing, competitors are timed; the winner has the lowest average time in the event.

In individual events, the top three performers win a medal: gold for first place, silver for second, and bronze for third. All members of a winning team get a gold medal. Medals are awarded in a ceremony after each competition. During the ceremony the national flag of the gold-medal winner is raised and its national anthem is played.

BOARD GAMES

Checkers

Checkers is played by two players on a board with 64 squares alternating red and black. Only the black squares of the board are used. The board is eight squares wide and eight squares long. Each player uses 12 disks called checkers, usually red for one player and black for the other. The pieces are set up on the black squares of the first three ranks, four in each rank.

Players alternate turns by moving one checker forward diagonally toward the opposing player's checkers. The object is to jump over the opponent's pieces, which are then removed from play.

If a player manages to advance a piece to the last rank on the opposite end of the board, that piece becomes a king. A king acquires the ability to move backward as well as forward.

A player wins when all the opponent's pieces have been removed.

Chess

Chess is a game in which two players move pieces on a board divided into 64 squares. The chessboard is arranged in eight rows of eight squares each. Squares are alternately light and dark in color. Players sit at opposite ends of the board, each with a light-colored square at the right-hand corner.

Each player uses 16 pieces. One player's set is usually light-colored and the other's set dark-colored. The player who uses the light-colored set is called "White." The player with the dark-colored set is "Black." Each player's set includes identical pieces called pawns. The other eight pieces consist of a king, a queen, two rooks, or castles, two bishops, and two knights.

To begin the game, White moves first. Then the moves alternate between Black and White. The object of the game is to capture the enemy king, although the king is never

Checkers

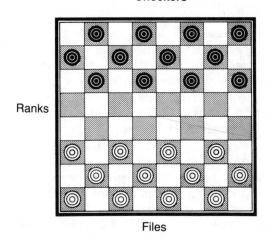

Ranks

Files

Chess

Chess Starting Position

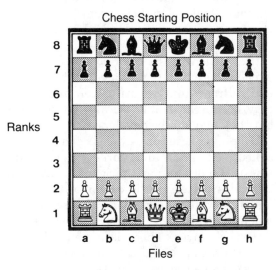

Files

actually removed from the board. When a move threatens the king, it is a check. The attack must immediately be defended against. The king can be moved, the player can capture the attacking piece, or the player can put a piece between the king and the threatening piece. When none of these defenses is possible, the king is checkmated, and the game is over. Many games end before checkmate, one player giving up because he sees he will eventually lose.

Monopoly®

Monopoly is a game for two to eight players who use a board with 40 spaces around the perimeter. Most of the spaces represent property up for sale. The object of the game is to drive opponents into bankruptcy by buying properties and charging rent for them.

Starting with a certain amount of money, each player rolls the dice in turn. The players advance their tokens around the board a number of spaces indicated on the dice. Landing on a property, the player may buy it by paying the stated price. The money goes into the bank, and the player receives the deed. Whenever an opponent lands on that property, he or she must pay rent to the owner.

Properties are grouped by colors, with two or three to a group. By buying all the properties within a single color group, a player has the right to develop those properties by purchasing houses and hotels which increase the rent dramatically.

In addition to the color-coded properties, which are given street names, there are also four railroads and two utility companies that may be purchased. These also carry rents, but they may not be developed.

If a player lands on any of six spaces, three called "Chance" and three "Community Chest," he or she must pick up a card from two piles placed in the center of the board and follow its instructions. These involve monetary transactions that either help or hurt the player. There is a neutral space called "Free Parking," a "Jail" space, two tax spaces, and a space called "Go."

Play begins on the Go space and the players collect $200 each time they circle the board and pass it. Players sometimes negotiate and trade properties among themselves. The game ends when everyone goes bankrupt except one player: the winner.

The Most Landed-On Spaces on the Monopoly® Game Board

According to Irvin R. Hertzel of Iowa State University, ten spaces on the Monopoly game® game board are landed on more than the others. Using a computer, the mathematician was able to figure out the overall probability of landing on each square. The following are the spaces you can count on landing on most often:

1. Illinois Avenue
2. Go
3. B.&O. Railroad
4. Free Parking
5. Tennessee Avenue
6. New York Avenue
7. Reading Railroad
8. St. James Place
9. Water Works
10. Pennsylvania Railroad

Scrabble®

Scrabble® is a word game for two to four players who use a Scrabble board with 225 spaces, 100 lettered tiles, and tile racks. Starting with seven letters, each player attempts to form words on the board using letters from his or her own hand in combination with words on the board.

Words may read from left to right or from top to bottom. Except for the first word that begins the game, every new word uses at least one letter from a word already on the board. Usually it interlocks at right angles, as in a crossword puzzle. Letters may also be added to an existing word to form a new one.

Each player—after using some or all of his or her tiles to form a word on the board—

replenishes the playing hand by drawing from the pool of remaining tiles, which are face down. Thus each player always has seven tiles with which to form words, except toward the end of the game when the pool runs out.

Each letter counts for a certain number of points. This numerical value is marked on the tile. Players score for each word formed, based on the value of each letter in the word. Scores are recorded on paper. Some special spaces on the board can double or triple the values of single letters or complete words.

When no player is able to form any more words, players conclude the game by adding up their scores. Values of unplayed letters stil held by each player are subtracted. The player with the highest score wins the game.

CARD GAMES
Animals

Three to six players use a regular 52-card deck to play Animals. Before the deal, each player picks an animal he wants to be, then makes the sound of that animal. Later, each player will be able to call the others by using that sound. Players try to be the first to make the animal sound of another player at the right time. The object of the game is to win all the cards in this way.

Starting to his left, the dealer deals the entire deck one card at a time to each player. The deal does not have to come out even. Players stack their cards face down in a pile in front of them. They take turns, starting from the left of the dealer, going clockwise.

The player turns over the top card and places it face up in front of his pile, starting a pack. If the card matches an upturned card of another player, both players try to call each other using the animal sound. The first to make the proper call of the other's animal identity wins that round. The winner takes the other player's upturned cards and places them below his own upturned pack. If both calls are correct, the one who called out first

wins. The loser of the calling contest leads the next round.

A player who gives the wrong call or calls at the wrong time must give the top card of his face-down pile (or of the pack if there is no pile) to the other player. After a pile of cards has been played out in an upturned pack, it is turned over and becomes a face-down pile as at the start of the game, and play continues. The winner of all the cards is the winner of the game.

Concentration

Concentration is a test of memory, for two to six players. Shuffle a standard 52-card deck and deal all the cards face down into any number of rows. To start, each player turns one card face up. The player with the highest-value card gets to go first. Before play the upturned cards are turned face down again in the same position.

The first player turns up two cards. If they form a pair (two cards of the same denomination), they are called a set. The person then places the set in front of him face down, and takes another turn. If they are not a matching pair, the player puts the cards back into the same position face down again. Next, the player on the left takes his turn.

Players try to make as many sets or pairs as possible. They do this by remembering where the match might be for the first card they pick each turn. The object of the game is to have the most sets, after all the cards have been paired and collected.

Dig

A game for two to five players, Dig uses a standard 52-card deck. Shuffle and deal seven cards to each player, one card at a time. Put the rest of the cards in the center, then turn the top card face up. The object of the game is to get rid of all the cards in your hand.

To start, the player on the dealer's left tries to match a card in her hand with the card turned up beside the deck. The match can be made by suit (any cards with the same symbol, such as his *one* of hearts and her *two* of hearts) or rank (any cards 1, 2, 3, 4 etc., such as his *three* of spades and her *three* of hearts) of card. If the card can match the upcard, she places it face up on top of the upcard. If she has no card that matches, she must pick (or dig) from the deck, taking the top card into his hand. She continues to dig until a card matches the upcard.

Eights are wild and may be matched on the upcard at any time. This changes the upcard to any suit or rank the player names. The winner is the first player to get rid of all the cards in her hand.

Donkey

Three to 13 players use a standard 52-card deck and a set of chips to play Donkey. First, the deck is stripped so that there is only a complete set of four cards of the same rank (four queens, four 4s, etc.) for each player in the game. For example, if there were eight players, the deck would consist of 32 cards. (It doesn't make any difference which sets are chosen.)

Place one chip in the center of the table for each player, minus one. For example, seven chips would be placed on the table if eight were playing.

Shuffle the pack and deal four cards, one at a time, to each player. Then say, "Go." At Go, each player passes a card to the player on his left at the same moment. All players continue passing until one player makes a match of four cards. Then he tries to grab a chip from the table's center without anyone noticing. As soon as he's observed, everyone tries to grab a chip. The player left without a chip is the "donkey" for that hand. The first player who took a chip must show his hand to prove his four cards match, otherwise he becomes the donkey. Then the chips are returned to the center of the table.

The object of the game is to make sets of four cards, while avoiding being the last to notice when someone else makes a set.

Each time a player loses a round, he earns a letter of the word *donkey* and has to write it on a piece of paper. The first player to spell D-O-N-K-E-Y loses. As each player is eliminated, a chip is removed from the center. Play continues until all the players but one are donkeys; the remaining player is the winner.

Frogs in the Pond

Also called Frogpond, this game can be played by two to five players, but the best matchup is with partners, two against two.

The object of the game is to win certain cards and to be the first to score 100 points. Scoring cards count as follows:

Cards	Points
Ten	10
Five	5
Ace	4
King	3
Queen	2
Jack	1

Deal a standard 52-card deck two at a time until each player has ten cards. The next ten cards are dealt face down to make a pile in the center. This pile represents the "Frogs in the Pond." Each player must always have the same number of cards as the number of Frogs in the Pond. (Deuces may be removed from the deck to make the number come out even, depending upon how many play. For example, if there are 3 players, deal all the cards, giving 13 cards to each player and 13 cards to the Frogs pile. When there are five players, remove the four deuces and deal 8 cards to each player and 8 to the frogs pile, etc.)

The player to the left of the dealer starts the game by "leading" a card: She picks a card from her hand and places it face up in the center of the table. The other players try to win the "trick" by putting down a higher scoring card of the same suit. Cards are ten (high), all the way down to two (low). If a player cannot follow suit, she plays any card. Whenever a player "revokes," or fails to follow suit when she can, she loses 10 points from her score.

Each time a player wins a trick, she takes the top card from the frog pile. Without letting anyone else see the card, she places it face down on the pile of cards she just won. If it is a scoring card, it counts with the rest in building her overall score at the end of the game. After picking from the frog pile, she leads again for the next trick.

When playing partners, the best strategy is to lead with an ace. Then, if your partner has a scoring card of the same suit, she can put it on the ace, and both cards will count for your team in the scoring.

After all the cards have been played, scores are added up and written down. Then the new dealer (the player to the left of the previous dealer) shuffles the cards and deals. The side or player to score 100 points first is the winner.

Go Fish

Two to five can play Go Fish with a regular 52-card deck. Deal the cards one at a time. For two players, each gets seven cards. For more than two, deal five cards to each player. Place the rest in the middle for the stock of cards.

In turn, each player asks any other player for a particular rank of card. For example, "Give me all your eights." The other player must then give the asker all the eights he has. The person requesting must have at least one of the cards he is asking for in his hand. His turn continues as long as he succeeds in getting the cards he's searching for. When a player does not have the requested card, he says, "Go fish." Then the asker takes the top card from the stock, and the turn moves to the left.

Four cards of the same rank make a book.

Whenever a player gets a book, he must show it by laying down the four matching cards. If a player matches up all his cards, with none left in his hand, he wins. Play can continue until the stock is used up. At that point, whoever has the most books wins.

Old Maid

Two to five players use the standard 52-card deck, minus one queen, to play Old Maid. All 51 remaining cards are dealt out one at a time. (It doesn't matter if the deal doesn't come out evenly.)

Spreading his cards face up, each player finds pairs that match up and discards them face up in the middle of the table. Players then shuffle their hands out of sight, usually behind their backs. If no queens have been paired and discarded, that means three queens remain in play. Then the player on the dealer's left draws one card from the dealer's hand. Or, if only one queen remains in play, the person holding it offers his hand for the first draw, with the cards facing away from the player drawing.

Drawing continues in rotation. If the card drawn matches one in the player's hand, he discards the pair into the center. Whether he makes a pair or not, he then shuffles his hand and allows the person on his left to draw.

The hand continues until all possible cards have been paired. The person stuck with the odd queen loses that hand. Play goes on until one person has been left holding the odd queen a set number of times. The player stuck with her the fewest times wins the game, and the player stuck with her the most times is the Old Maid.

Rummy

Rummy uses a regular deck of 52 cards. The cards rank king (high), down to ace (low). Deal the cards one at a time, clockwise, starting at the dealer's left. The number of cards dealt to each player depends on the number of players in the game: with two players, ten cards each; with three or four players, seven cards each; with five or six players, six cards each.

The undealt remainder of the deck is placed face down, forming the stock. Its top card is turned up next to the stock, forming the discard pile. The object is to form groups (three or more cards of the same rank) or sequences (three or more cards of the same suit in sequence of rank—ace, two, three, for example). This is called melding.

One at a time and proceeding clockwise, players draw one card from the top of the stack or the top of the discard pile. If melding is possible, groups or sequences are placed face up in front of the player. A player may also lay off, which means to add to his or her own or an opponent's melds. A player's turn ends by placing one card face up on the discard pile.

When one player melds all the cards remaining in a hand, that player goes out. This ends that deal, which is then scored. The player going out scores his or her own melds plus the points left in the opponents' hands. The other players score just their own melds. Aces count as one. All picture cards count as 10. The rest of the cards count as their face number. High score wins.

Except when going out, a player must discard one card after each play, whether or not that player has melded or laid off.

Slap Jack

Three to eight players use a standard 52-card deck. The winner is the player who wins all the cards by being the first to slap each jack as it comes to the center.

One at a time, cards are dealt to all the players in a clockwise rotation. The deal does not have to come out even. Players do not look at their cards. Instead, they stack their cards, face down, into a neat pile in front of them.

Play starts when the player to the dealer's left turns one of his cards over to begin a pile in the center of the table. Cards must be lifted away from the player, so that everyone has an equal chance to see it at the same time. Cards are placed in the center pile one by one by each player in turn, until the card is a jack. Then the first person to slap his hand down on it takes the pile. When more than one player slaps at the same time, the hand nearest the jack wins the pile.

The winner of each pile shuffles it along with her remaining cards to form her new hand. Play continues until one player wins all the cards.

Solitaire

One person plays Solitaire. Using a regular 52-card deck, deal seven piles of cards in front of you: one card in the far left pile, two cards in the next, increasing by one card each pile until the last one has seven cards. All cards are dealt face down except the top card on each pile, which is face up.

Using the cards left in your hand (the stock), build sequences on each pile of the layout. Sequences are built in descending order of card rank and in alternating colors (black and red). Turn over the first card in your stock pile (or use every third card) and look over the layout to see where it could go. If you turn over a red eight, for example, and one of the piles has a black nine exposed on top, you can place the eight on the nine. Then move on to the next card in your stock.

Whole lines of cards can be moved from one pile to another if an opportunity opens. For example, if one pile is topped by a red ten, you can move the line of cards beginning with the black nine onto it. Then you turn face up the next down card on the pile, and play it from there. If you can play a black jack, for example, you can move the entire line of cards beginning with the red ten onto it. This releases that pile for further play. If you turn up a king, use it to start a new sequence in one of the seven spaces where another pile has been used up.

Turn over the next card. If it is an ace, place it above the layout of cards. The goal is to set up four aces to form the foundations for winning the game.

The object of the game is to create entire sequences of the four suits from the foundation (ace) up to the king. You can use any suitable card that turns up to build the foundation: the next card in your stock, the next card turned up on a pile, or the last card at the bottom of a pile sequence.

The game is won if you can place the entire deck on the foundations after running through the stock once. Since this rarely happens, you may go through the stock over and over again until you can't make a play or until you succeed.

War

Also known as "Beggar-Your-Neighbor," this card game is for two players using a regular 52-card deck. The object is to capture all the cards.

Shuffle, then deal out all the cards alternately, each player ending up with 26 cards face down. Each player turns over his or her card at the same time, and places it face up in front of his pile. The highest-ranking card wins the other's card. Cards are ranked king (high) all the way down to ace (low).

At the point where the two cards are of the same rank, war begins. These two cards are placed into the center along with one more card from the top of each player's pile. Then, the higher of the next two following cards wins all six cards. If those two cards match in

rank, they are also placed in the center, and two more cards are added. The higher of the two cards following after that wins the whole group.

Play continues until all the cards are captured or, since this rarely happens, the game is won by the first player to win three wars.

INFORMATION, PLEASE

Bragonier, Reginald. *What's What in Sports: The Visual Glossary of the Sports World.* Hammond, 1984.

Brown, Michael. *Soccer Rules in Pictures.* Putnam, 1986.

Diagram Group. *Rules of the Game: The Complete Illustrated Encyclopedia of All the Sports in the World.* St. Martin's, 1990.

Fischler, Stan and Shirley. *The Hockey Encyclopedia: The Complete Record of Professional Ice Hockey.* Macmillan, 1983.

Hammon, Tim. *Sports.* Knopf, 1988.

Hollander, Zander. *The Complete Handbook of Pro Basketball.* New American Library, annual.

Morehead, Albert H., Richard L. Frey, and Geoffrey Mott-Smith. *The New Complete Hoyle.* Rev. by Richard L. Frey, Tom Smith, Philip Adler, and Matt Kearn. Doubleday, 1991.

Neft, David S., and Richard M. Cohen. *Sports Encyclopedia: Baseball.* 7th ed. St. Martins, 1987.

Neft, David S., et al. *Sports Encyclopedia: Pro Football, The Modern Era: 1960–The Present.* St. Martins, 1987.

22

HEALTH AND FITNESS

UP AND RUNNING: YOUR BODY'S SYSTEMS AND HOW THEY WORK

The human body is composed of several different systems. One, for example, controls the alimentary, or digestive, functions. Another is made up of your bones, and still another of your muscles. Here are the body's major systems:

The Skeleton

The 206 bones of the human body hold it up and support its internal organs. The bones are alive and are changing all the time. Inside some bones is marrow, which makes red blood cells. The bones are also the location of the body's minerals, including the all-important one for bone growth, calcium.

The joints, such as the knee and the elbow, are the parts of the skeletal system that hold the bones together. Joints are held in place by tough bands of tissue called ligaments.

The Muscles

Muscles, which are composed of elastic fibers, help the human body move, and like the bones, they protect internal organs. In fact,

in order to do this efficiently, many of the muscles are paired. One set performs a motion, and the other set performs the opposite motion. For example, muscles called the biceps are used to bend your arms, while muscles called the triceps are used to straighten your arms.

There are 650 muscles in the human body. Muscles need to be worked by exercise in order to stay strong.

The Digestive System

The digestive, or alimentary system, moves food through your body. It does this by transforming some of the food into substances that enter the bloodstream and help to maintain the body. The remaining food is changed into waste and eliminated. The work of the digestive tract is involuntary, which means it happens automatically without your consciously doing anything to make it happen. Muscular contractions move the food through the digestive tract.

The main parts of the digestive system are the esophagus, stomach, and large and small intestines, the liver, the pancreas, and the gallbladder.

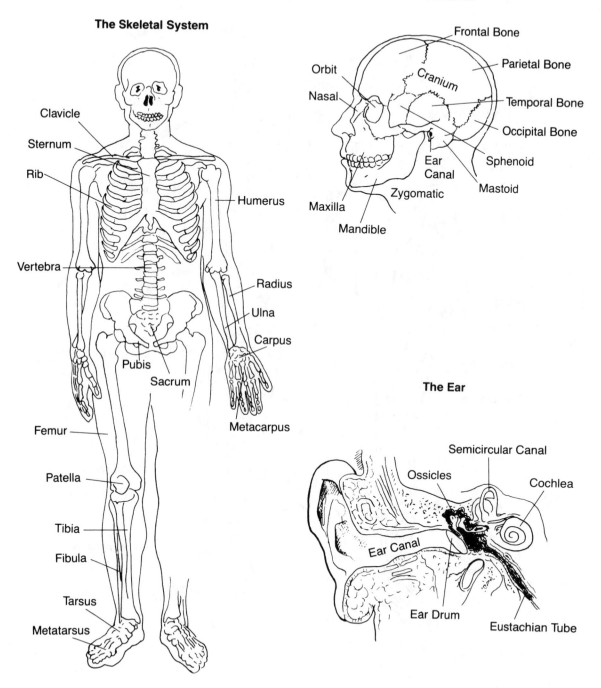

The Skeletal System

Clavicle

Sternum

Rib

Vertebra

Femur

Patella

Tibia

Fibula

Tarsus

Metatarsus

Humerus

Radius

Ulna

Carpus

Pubis

Sacrum

Metacarpus

The Skull

Frontal Bone

Parietal Bone

Orbit

Nasal

Cranium

Temporal Bone

Occipital Bone

Sphenoid

Ear
Canal

Mastoid

Maxilla

Zygomatic

Mandible

The Ear

Semicircular Canal

Ossicles

Cochlea

Ear Canal

Ear Drum

Eustachian Tube

The Muscles

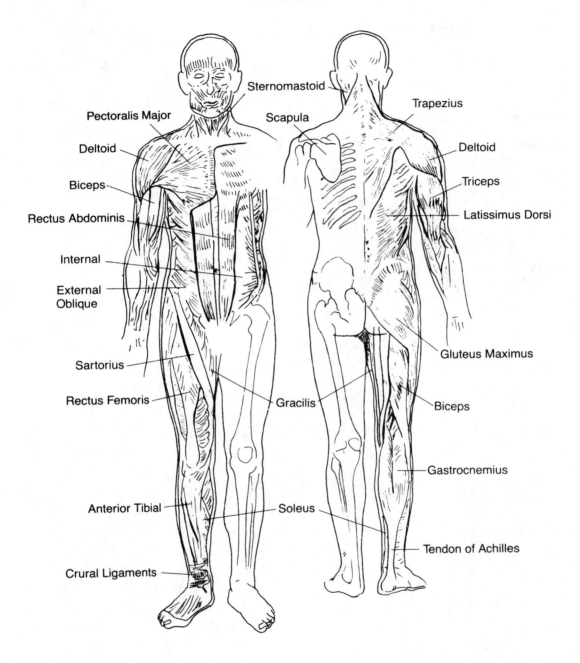

Sternomastoid

Pectoralis Major

Scapula

Deltoid

Trapezius

Biceps

Deltoid

Rectus Abdominis

Triceps

Internal

Latissimus Dorsi

External
Oblique

Sartorius

Gluteus Maximus

Rectus Femoris

Gracilis

Biceps

Gastrocnemius

Anterior Tibial

Soleus

Tendon of Achilles

Crural Ligaments

The Alimentary System

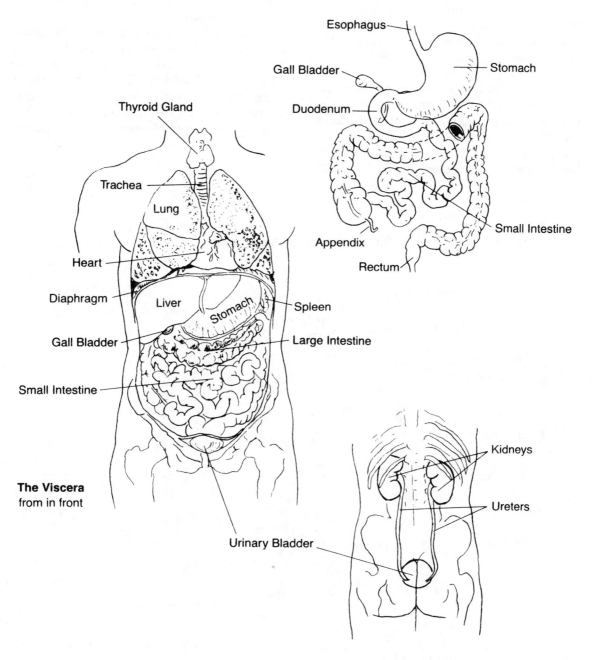

Esophagus

Gall Bladder

Duodenum

Stomach

Small Intestine

Appendix

Rectum

Thyroid Gland

Trachea

Lung

Heart

Diaphragm

Liver

Stomach

Spleen

Gall Bladder

Large Intestine

Small Intestine

The Viscera
from in front

Urinary Bladder

Kidneys

Ureters

The Urinary Tract

The Circulatory System

Blood is pumped through the body by your circulatory system, which is composed of your heart and the veins and arteries. This system supplies your tissues with oxygen and necessary nutrients.

The center of this system, your heart, is a pump, or to be more accurate, two pumps. One pump moves the blood out of the heart and throughout the body, and the second pump moves the blood back through the heart again. The heart, which typically weighs less than a pound, beats about 100,000 times per day and pumps 2,000 gallons of blood daily.

Veins and arteries transport the blood throughout the body. The arteries carry blood from the heart to the tissues, and the veins bring it back to the heart to be recycled.

The next time you go to the doctor, ask him or her to let you listen through the stethoscope to the sound of your own heart pumping.

The Heart and Major Blood Vessels

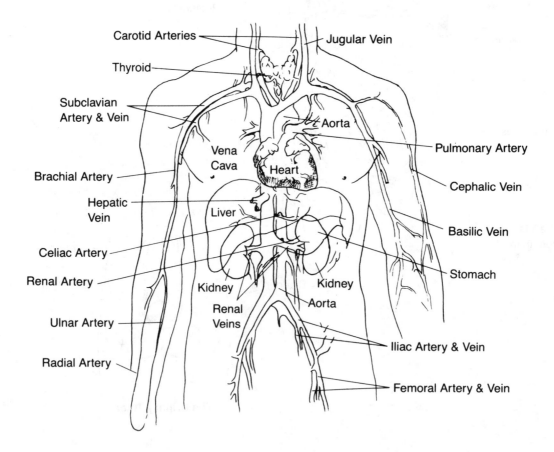

The Heart

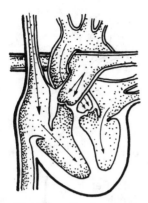

Blood in. When the heart relaxes, blood flows into all four chambers.

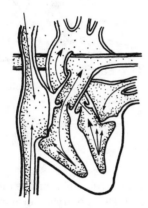

Blood out. When the heart contracts, blood is forced through arteries.

The Nervous System

The neurological system is composed of your brain, spinal cord, and billions of tiny nerve cells called neurons. It directs your learning, memory, movement, thought, and emotions. It also processes information from the outside world and lets you make sense of it.

The brain, made up of over 100 billion neurons, is the center of all this activity, although the spinal cord controls such vital functions as breathing, circulation, muscular movement, and blood circulation. The brain is composed of two main parts, the cerebrum and the cerebellum. The cerebrum controls conscious functions such as memory, learning, speech, and vision, while the cerebellum coordinates the unconscious functions, such as motion and balance.

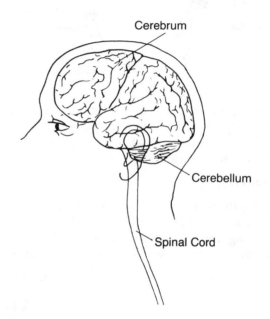

The Five Senses

Our senses are our contacts with the external world. Humans have five main senses: sight, hearing, smell, taste, and touch.

Without our senses, life would be dramatically different, both far more dangerous and far less pleasurable. Without your sense of touch, for example, what would stop you from picking up a hot skillet without a potholder or putting your hand in scalding water? Imagine not being able to hear your favorite music. Your senses make these sensations possible.

Sight

What you see of the world comes through your eyes. Rays of light enter the eye through the cornea, pupil, and lens and are sent to the retina. Special cells in the retina called rods and cones turn the light into electrical im-

The Eye

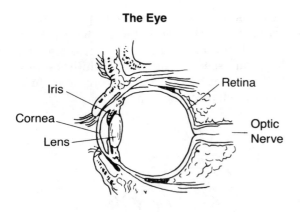

The Ear

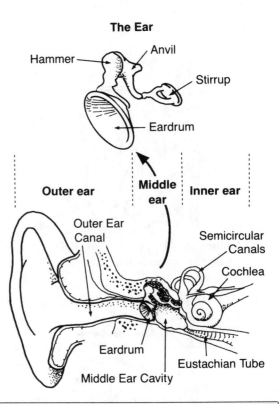

pulses, which are transmitted to the brain, where they are deciphered.

Your eyes move thousands of times a day to take in countless images.

Hearing

Everything you hear passes through your ears. Sound waves enter through your ear, passing into the eardrum, whose job is to deliver the sound waves to the inner ear. In

---

Noise: A Health Hazard?

Have you ever considered that loud noises are harmful to your health? It's true. Although we rarely think of noise as pollution, loud noises harm our hearing. The damage can be temporary or permanent. The very loud volume at a rock concert, for example, leaves your ears less sensitive for a few hours or a day, but then your hearing returns to normal. Constant exposure—such as that received by professional rock musicians—damages the hearing permanently.

To some extent, we are protected from loud noises by small bones in our ears that move, turning down the volume of the sound waves before they reach the cochlea. Continuous loud noise eventually breaks down this defense, however.

Noise is measured in decibels. Every three decibels represents a doubling in the volume of a noise. The chart that follows shows the decibel levels of sounds to which we are frequently exposed.

Noise Levels

Decibels	Source
130	Jet engine at 100 feet
110	Jackhammer
80	Diesel truck
40	Dog barking
10–20	Whispering

Skin Color: How Do We Get It?

The color of our skin is determined by the amount of melanin it contains. No one except an albino has what could be called truly white skin, and no one has truly black skin. Human beings come in many shades, ranging from ivory to ebony.

Melanin is produced by cells called melanocytes, which reside in the epidermis, the outer layer of skin. If these cells produce little melanin, our skin is a lighter color. If they produce a lot of melanin, our skin will be dark brown.

The purpose of melanin is to protect our skin from the sun. Africans' dark skins help them ward off the sun's strong rays. In contrast, people from the Northern Hemisphere, where there is far less sun, are lighter-skinned because they do not need the same protection from the sun's damaging rays.

the inner ear is the cochlea. Shell-shaped and filled with liquid, the cochlea converts the sound waves into electrical impulses, which are then transmitted to the brain, where they are interpreted.

Smell

The scent of a favorite flower or your favorite cookie just out of the oven is processed by your nose. Smell originates in your olfactory nerve, located in the back of your nose and made up very fine, sensitive hairs. An odor passes through the olfactory tract to the olfactory bulb, located in the front of your brain.

The Nose

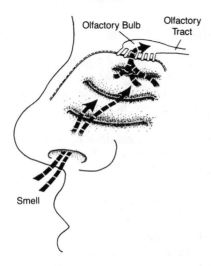

Taste

Have you ever noticed that you can't taste much when your nose is stuffed up? That's because your sense of taste works in conjunction with your sense of smell. Without your nose, your sense of taste is greatly diminished.

Taste begins in the tongue, which contains taste buds that enable you to sense sweet, salty, bitter, and sour tastes. The olfactory nerve also plays a role in transmitting taste.

The Tongue

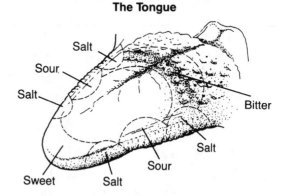

Touch

Specialized nerve endings just below the surface of the skin make up your sense of touch. These nerve endings send messages to the brain that interpret what you have touched as hot, cold, sharp, dull, or some other sensation.

The Reproductive System

The three main external parts of the male reproductive system are the testicles, the glands that make sperm; the scrotum, which is a sack that protects the testicles; and the penis. The sperm travel through tubes from the scrotum and leaves the man's body through the penis.

The Reproductive System

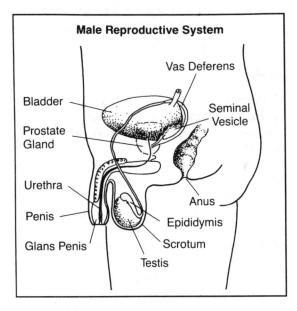

Male Reproductive System

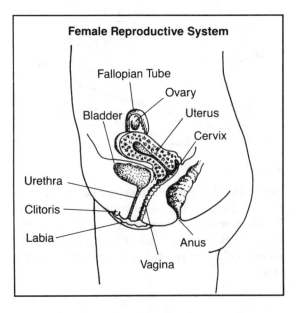

Female Reproductive System

The main female reproductive organs are two ovaries, which contain eggs; two fallopian tubes; the uterus; and the vagina, which extends to the outside of a woman's body. About once a month an egg is released from an ovary and travels down a fallopian tube, where it becomes ripe and can be fertilized. If the egg is not fertilized by sperm, it leaves the body about two weeks later in menstrual flow.

During sexual intercourse between a man and a woman, sperm travel through the penis into the woman's vagina. The sperm swim through the vagina, through the uterus, and into the fallopian tube, where one of them can fertilize an egg if it happens to be there.

The fertilized egg moves into the uterus, where it begins to divide and develop into a baby. About nine months later the baby will be born.

THE BASIC FOUR: YOUR GUIDE TO GOOD NUTRITION

One of the most important steps you can take toward good health is to eat a well-balanced diet. Such a diet includes an appropriate number of servings from the four basic food groups described below.

Grains

The first group, made up of breads, rice, wheat, corn, and oats, provides carbohydrates for energy as well as valuable vitamins and minerals.

Recommended number of servings per day

4–5

Size of typical serving

1 slice bread
1 cup uncooked cereal
½ cup cooked cereal, pasta, or rice

How Tall will You Grow?

Most young people want to know how tall they will grow. Here are a few guidelines that might help you predict your adult height.

First, look at your parents. Height, like hair and eye color, is hereditary. Since your parents' genes combined to make you, they will play a role in how tall you will be. If one parent is tall, and the other is short, you will probably grow to a height somewhere in between. If both parents are very tall, you will probably be tall, but shorter than they are; if both are very short, you will probably be short, but taller than they are.

Diet also plays a role in how tall people grow. Undernourished children do not grow as tall as well-fed ones.

Finally, you can play the law of averages. The following chart shows average heights for children, ages 1 through 18. If you are above or below average (or just average) now, you will probably be either above or below average (or just average) as an adult.

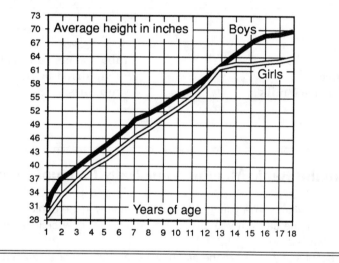

Fruits and Vegetables

The second group provides you with carbohydrates, fiber, and many different kinds of vitamins and minerals, all of which give you energy and maintain your body's systems.

Fruits are apples, oranges, grapefruits, melons, peaches, pears, plums, and similar foods.

Vegetables include broccoli, carrots, celery, spinach, cauliflower, green beans, lettuces, and similar foods.

Variety is the key to eating fruits and vegetables. Eat as many different kinds of foods in this group as you can.

Recommended number of servings per day

4–5

Size of typical serving

$\frac{1}{2}$ cup juice
1 cup raw vegetables
1 medium-size piece of fruit;
$\frac{1}{2}$ cantaloupe or grapefruit

Dairy Products

Young people need more products from the third group than adults do, because these are the bone builders. Dairy products include milk, yogurt, cheese, ice cream, and ice milk. (Butter and cream are also dairy products, but they are very high in fat and are not recommended as part of your regular, everyday diet.)

Recommended number of servings per day:

2–3 for ages 1–10; 4 for ages 10–24

Size of typical serving

1 cup milk
1 cup yogurt
1½ ounce cheese
2 cups cottage cheese
1¾ cup ice cream or ice milk

Protein

The fourth and last major food group is composed of meat, poultry, fish, dried beans, eggs, nuts, and peanut butter. Protein foods are needed to maintain the body's systems, as well as for energy. A few years ago, Americans built their diets around several daily servings of protein, but now dieticians recommend eating far less of these foods.

Recommended number of servings per day:

2

Size of typical serving

2–3 ounces of cooked lean meat, poultry, or fish
4 tablespoons peanut butter
1½ cup dried beans
½ cup nuts

Money in the Bank: Meeting Your Daily Calcium Requirement

Eating enough calcium when you're young is like putting money in the bank. Fifty years later, you can collect interest on it. All the calcium you ate as a child, experts now believe, will help you maintain strong bones when you are 80.

According to a recent study, here are the amounts of calcium you need each day while you are still growing:

Ages 1–11	800 milligrams daily
Ages 11–24	1200 milligrams daily

And here is where you can get your daily dose of calcium:

1 cup low-fat or skim milk	300 milligrams
1 cup low-fat yogurt	452 milligrams
1 ounce skim-milk cheeses such as ricotta and mozzarella	180–200 milligrams
½ cup broccoli	89 milligrams
¼ cup almonds	94 milligrams
½ cup ice cream	88 milligrams
½ cup cottage cheese	77 milligrams

Fats and Sweets

These make up another category of foods. Our body does require a very small amount of fat, and we often crave sugar. You can eat these foods, but it's important not to overdo them because they don't offer the nutritional benefits of other foods. A good plan is to eat all the servings you're supposed to eat of the four main food groups, and then, if you are still hungry, treat yourself to a small portion of the foods made up of fat and sugar.

Fats include salad dressing, mayonnaise, butter, cream, and oil, which are used to cook many of the foods in the other food groups. Sweets include candy bars, hard candies, cakes and pies, and jellies and jams.

Size of typical serving

1 tablespoon mayonnaise or salad dressing
1 teaspoon butter or margarine
1 teaspoon sugar
1 teaspoon jelly or jam

Water

Although rarely listed as a food, water is necessary for survival. It usually contains fluoride (or fluoride is added), which promotes strong, healthy teeth, along with other nutrients.

Every part of your body uses water, but your body stores it only in limited amounts. That's why it is important to get enough water every day. You get some water in the foods you eat, but you should still drink several glasses a day.

Recommended number of servings per day

6–8

Size of typical serving

8-ounce glass

THE BODY'S BUILDING BLOCKS: VITAMINS AND MINERALS

Vitamins and minerals are substances found in foods—but not in sugar or fat—that help to keep your body in optimal shape.

Vitamins

Although only small amounts of vitamins are needed, they play an important role in your body, such as keeping your nervous system running smoothly, helping to build blood cells, and creating hormones. The chart on the following page shows how vitamins help you grow.

Minerals

Minerals play an important role in keeping your body healthy. Calcium, for example, is necessary for bone growth. Potassium fuels muscle contractions. Sodium helps to regulate fluids in your body.

Nutritionists divide minerals into macrominerals and microminerals. You need large amounts of macrominerals, and only traces of microminerals. The best way to be sure you are getting enough minerals is to eat as wide a variety of foods as possible, especially fruits and vegetables.

As with vitamins, getting too few minerals can spell trouble. A lack of iron, for example, causes anemia, an abnormal blood condition that makes one tire easily. A lack of iodine can result in an enlarged thyroid gland.

Nutritionists are still figuring out how many and which minerals humans need, but the following have been established as necessary to any healthy diet.

Macrominerals	*Microminerals*
Calcium	Iron
Magnesium	Iodine
Phosphorus	Zinc
Potassium	Copper
Sodium	Fluoride
Sulfur	Selenium
	Manganese

Vitamins: Where You Get Them and What They Do

Vitamin	Best Sources	Main Roles	U.S. Government Recommended Doses
A	Liver, eggs, cheese, butter, margarine and milk, yellow, orange, and dark-green vegetables and fruits (such as carrots, broccoli, spinach, cantaloupe).	Helps to form and maintain healthy skin, hair; aids people to see in dim light (night vision); needed for bone growth, teeth development.	5,000 International Units (amount agreed on as an international standard)
B$_1$ (Thiamin)	Pork (especially ham), liver, oysters, whole-grain and enriched cereals, pasta, and bread, wheat germ, oatmeal, peas, lima beans.	Helps the body release energy from carbohydrates.	1.4–1.5 mg
B$_2$ (Riboflavin)	Liver, milk, meat, dark-green vegetables, eggs, whole-grain and enriched cereals, pasta, and bread, mushrooms, dried beans and peas.	Helps the body release energy from carbohydrates, proteins, and fats.	1.7 mg
B$_3$ (Niacin)	Liver, poultry, meat, tuna, eggs, whole-grain and enriched cereals, pasta, and bread, nuts, dried peas and beans.	Helps cells in the body produce energy.	20 mg
B$_6$	Whole-grain (but not enriched) cereals and bread, liver, avocados, spinach, green beans, bananas, fish, poultry, meats, nuts, potatoes, green leafy vegetables.	Helps the body take in and produce proteins, helps the body use fats, helps the body form red blood cells.	2.0 mg

B_{12}	Only in animal foods, liver, kidneys, meat, fish, eggs, milk, oysters.	Helps the body form red blood cells, helps the body to build genetic material, helps the nervous system to work well.	6 micrograms
Folacin	Liver, kidneys, dark-green leafy vegetables, wheat germ, dried beans and peas. Stored in the body, so it is not necessary to take it daily.	Acts with B_{12} in making genetic material, helps the body to form a key protein in red blood cells.	0.4 mg
C	Citrus fruits, tomatoes, strawberries, melon, green peppers, potatoes, dark-green vegetables.	Helps the body maintain capillaries, bones, and teeth, stops the body from burning up other vitamins, may stop development of cancer.	60 mg
D	Milk, egg yolk, liver, tuna, salmon, cod liver oil. Made on skin in sunlight	Helps to form and maintain bones and teeth; helps the body to take in and use of the minerals, calcium and phosphorus.	400 International Units
E	Vegetable oils, margarine, wheat germ, whole-grain cereals and bread, liver, dried beans, green leafy vegetables.	Helps in forming red blood cells, muscles, and other tissues.	30 International Units
K	Green leafy vegetables, cabbage, cauliflower, peas, potatoes, liver, cereals. Made by bacteria in human intestine.	Helps the body to make substances needed for the blood to clot; helps the body maintain normal bone production and growth.	—

Ideal Weights in Pounds for Boys and Girls 5 to 18 Years Old

Boys

Height (in inches)	Age 5	6	7	8	9	10	11	12	13	14	15	16	17	18
38	34	34												
39	35	35												
40	36	36												
41	38	38	38											
42	39	39	39	39										
43	41	41	41	41										
44	44	44	44	44										
45	46	46	46	46	46									
46	47	48	48	48	48									
47	49	50	50	50	50	50								
48		52	53	53	53	53								
49		55	55	55	55	55	55							
50		57	58	58	58	58	58	58						
51			61	61	61	61	61	61	61					
52			63	64	64	64	64	64	64					
53			66	67	67	67	67	68	68					
54				70	70	70	70	71	71	72				
55				72	72	73	73	74	74	74				
56				75	76	77	77	77	78	78	80			
57					79	80	81	81	82	83	83			
58					83	84	84	85	85	86	87			
59						87	88	89	89	90	90	90		
60						91	92	92	93	94	95	96		
61							95	96	97	99	100	103	106	
62							100	101	102	103	104	107	111	116
63							105	106	107	108	110	113	118	123
64								109	111	113	115	117	121	126
65								114	117	118	120	122	127	131
66									119	122	125	128	132	136
67									124	128	130	134	136	139
68										134	134	137	141	143
69										137	139	143	146	149
70										143	144	145	148	151
71										148	150	151	152	154
72											153	155	156	158
73											157	160	162	164
74											160	164	168	170

Girls

Height (in inches)	5	6	7	8	9	10	11	12	13	14	15	16	17	18
38	33	33												
39	34	34												
40	36	36	36											
41	37	37	37											
42	39	39	39											
43	41	41	41	41										
44	42	42	42	42										
45	45	45	45	45	45									
46	47	47	47	48	48									
47	49	50	50	50	50	50								
48		52	52	52	52	53	53							
49			54	55	55	56	56							
50			56	57	58	59	61	62						
51			59	60	61	61	63	65						
52			63	64	64	64	65	67						
53			66	67	67	68	68	69	71					
54				69	70	70	71	71	73					
55				72	74	74	74	75	77	78				
56					76	78	78	79	81	83				
57					80	82	82	82	84	88	92			
58						84	86	86	88	93	96	101		
59						87	90	90	92	96	100	103	104	
60						91	95	95	97	101	105	108	109	111
61							99	100	101	105	108	112	113	116
62							104	105	106	109	113	115	117	118
63								110	110	112	116	117	119	120
64								114	115	117	119	120	122	123
65								118	120	121	122	123	125	126
66									124	124	125	128	129	130
67									128	130	131	133	133	135
68									131	133	135	136	138	138
69										135	137	138	140	142
70										136	138	140	142	144
71										138	140	142	144	145

MAINTAINING A HEALTHY WEIGHT

Whatever your height, it is important to maintain a healthy weight. Although doctors haven't settled the question once and for all, many experts believe that weight, like height, is hereditary to some extent. Adopted children, for example, tend to gain weight like their biological parents, rather than their adoptive ones.

Weight is measured against height—that is, when you are a certain height, you should weigh a certain amount (give or take a few pounds). Whenever you grow taller, your weight will increase. And during adolescence, your weight will increase.

Remember, the weights shown on the charts are only approximate. It is still perfectly normal to weigh a few pounds more or less than the number shown on the charts.

Counting Calories

Calories are used to measure the energy we get from food. A calorie is the amount of heat required to raise the temperature of one gram of water 1 degree centigrade (1.8 degrees Fahrenheit).

Most experts believe the best way to lose weight is to change one's eating habits by reducing the fats and sugars consumed and adding more grains, fruits, and vegetables to the diet. Most young people, however, have the opposite problem: You need to consume enough calories every day to ensure strong, regular growth.

Recommended Daily Dietary Allowances (RDAs) of Calories for Young People

	Age	Calories
	1–3	1300
	4–6	1700
	7–10	2400
Male	11–14	2800
	15–18	3000
	19–22	3000
Female	11–14	2400
	15–19	2100
	19–22	2100

TEN GUIDELINES TO GOOD EATING FOR YOUNG PEOPLE

1. Get about half your calories from complex carbohydrates: grains, fruits, and vegetables.
2. Keep fat intake to a minimum.
3. Eat only a small amount—about the size of a deck of cards—of animal protein each day.
4. Drink at least four glasses of milk a day until you are an adult, when you will need less.
5. Use sweets for treats. Eat them only on special occasions.
6. Go easy on salt. Americans eat too much salt, which may cause high blood pressure later in life. It's best to train yourself to eat less of it when you're young.
7. Make sure you get fluoride in your daily diet. Usually this important toothbuilder is in your drinking water.
8. Get at least an hour's worth of exercise four or more times a week.
9. If you are trying to lose weight, the first step is to visit your doctor. He or she will check the weight charts to see if you are truly overweight (10 percent more than the top recommended weight). Then get more exercise.
10. Eat a wide variety of foods, especially fruits and vegetables. If you do, you probably won't need to take vitamin pills.

Grab Right: Choosing Healthy Snacks

Instead of	Choose
potato chips	pretzels
cookies	graham crackers, fig bars
salted peanuts	popcorn
a soft drink	milk, water
candy bar	banana
a hamburger	a chunk of hard cheese
hard candies	grapes
ice cream	ice milk
cake	lowfat muffin

COOKING FOR YOURSELF

Lots of young people cook for themselves, preparing everything from after-school snacks to dinner for the entire family. Here are twelve books to help you cook:

Better Homes and Gardens After-School Cooking. Better Homes and Gardens, 1987.

Better Homes and Gardens Step-by-Step Kids' Cookbook. Better Homes and Gardens, 1984.

Betty Crocker's New Boys' and Girls' Cookbook New York: Prentice Hall, 1990.

Betty Crocker's Boys' and Girls' Microwave Cookbook New York: Prentice Hall, 1992.

Coyle, Rena. *My First Baking Book*. Workman, 1988.

————. *My First Cookbook*. Workman, 1985.

Krementz, Jill. *The Fun of Cooking*. Knopf, 1985.

Meyer, Carolyn. *The Bread Book: All About Bread and How To Make It*. Harcourt, 1971.

Scherie, Strom. *Stuffin' Muffin: Muffin Pan Cooking for Kids*. Young People Press, 1982.

Van der Linde, Polly, and Tasha Van der Linde. *Around the World in Eighty Dishes*. Lerner, 1971.

Walker, Barbara M. *The Little House Cookbook*. Harper & Row, 1979.

Wishik, Cindy S. *Kids Dish It Up . . . Sugar-Free: A Teaching Tool for Beginning Cooks*. Peninsula, 1982.

Staying Substance Free

Even though there is no safe level of consumption for youths, more than 92 percent of all high school seniors have tried alcohol, and two-thirds have tried drugs. The average age for first contact with alcohol has now dropped to 12 or 13. While drug use has been steadily declining among young people for the past few years, alcohol use has remained steady.

For both drugs and alcohol, male users outnumber females, although the number of young women using alcohol has steadily increased since the 1970s.

The largest number of teen drinkers (54 percent) live in the Midwest, while the smallest number live in the East (21 percent). Illegal drug use is higher among U.S. teens than those of any other industrialized country. College-bound youth use fewer drugs than noncollege-bound youth.

Although young adults are only 10 percent of all licensed drivers, they are involved in 21 percent of alcohol-related accidents where someone is killed.

Asked why they used drugs, high-school students gave the following answers, in order of descending importance:

- To get high
- To have a good time with friends
- To get away from problems
- To get through the day
- To relax and relieve tension

Those who are least likely to use drugs or alcohol share these traits:

- They come from a close family.
- They have strong religious beliefs.
- They are independent thinkers.
- They feel fairly secure about themselves.
- They take friends home to meet their parents.
- Their parents use alcohol only moderately, take no drugs, and are comfortable discussing drinking and drugs.
- They have many interests.

EXERCISING RIGHT

The early years are the best time to develop a habit of getting regular exercise. Exercise is especially important for young people because it builds strong bones and muscles. It helps people digest their food and is a key factor in losing weight.

Many children get exercise through organized sports at school or in after-school programs. While such rigorous activity often burns 350 or more calories an hour, even walking or raking leaves qualifies as exercise. Children need at least an hour's worth of exercise four or more times a week.

Burning Calories

When your body works, it burns calories. Even at rest, a body is burning calories, but it burns them faster and more efficiently when you exercise.

The chart that follows shows roughly how many calories a body burns each hour during various activities. These figures are only approximate because many factors enter into how efficiently your body burns calories, among them your weight, your level of fitness, and how efficiently you perform any activity.

Type of Activity	Calories Burned per Hour
Rest and light activity	*50–200*
Lying down or sleeping	80
Sitting	100
Typing	110
Driving	120
Standing	140
Housework	180
Shining shoes	185
Moderate activity	*200–350*
Aerobics	300
Bicycling (5½ mph)	210
Walking (2½ mph)	210
Canoeing (2½ mph)	230

Golf (foursome)	250
Lawn mowing (power mower)	250
Fencing	300
Rowing a boat (2½ mph)	300
Swimming (¼ mph)	300
Calisthenics	300
Walking (3¼ mph)	300
Badminton	350
Horseback riding (trotting)	350
Square dancing	350
Volleyball	350
Roller skating	350
Stacking heavy objects (boxes, logs)	350
Vigorous activity	*350+*
Baseball pitching	360
Ditch digging (hand shovel)	400
Ice skating (10 mph)	400
Chopping or sawing wood	400
Bowling (continuous)	400
Tennis	420
Waterskiing	480
Hill climbing (100 feet per hour)	490
Basketball	500
Football	500
Skiing (10 mph)	600
Squash and handball	600
Bicycling (13 mph)	660
Rowing (machine)	720
Scull rowing (race)	840
Running (10 mph)	900

COMMON HEALTH PROBLEMS OF YOUNG PEOPLE

Allergies

Young people tend to suffer from allergies more than adults do, and one thing you might look forward to as you older is outgrowing at least some of your allergies. Allergy is the immune system's response to foreign substances. The most common allergens, as these substances are called, come

Youth Suicide

Suicide is the third leading cause of death among young persons. An estimated 500,000 teenagers attempt suicide every year, and between 5,000 and 6,000 teens actually commit suicide each year. Here are the breakdowns of suicide rates by sex and racial background:

Group	Per 100,000
White males	15.1
Black males	3.5
White females	6.5
Black females	1.7

Suicidal teens share three traits:

1. They tend to have unrealistically high expectations for themselves and/or for others.
2. They have difficulty coping with failure and loss.
3. They tend to form very intense relationships.

The teenage years are difficult ones for almost everyone, but some of us find it harder to cope with problems than others. We have trouble imagining that we will grow up to have successful careers and relationships, and that our intense feelings and stormy moods will gradually improve. If you feel you need help, first try to talk to one of your parents, a teacher, a counselor, or some other adult friend about your worries. If you cannot do this, you can call a hotline. Your call will be taken anonymously, if you like, but you will get help from someone who's been where you are and knows how it feels.

---

from animals (their dander), plants (their pollen), house dust, medications, and insects.

Allergic reactions can be caused by touching a foreign substance, but more often they are caused by breathing in an allergen. Most allergies are not serious, and rarely cause any more discomfort than a cold or runny nose. But some allergies are very serious. Highly sensitive persons can suffer serious trauma and even life-threatening shock from bee stings, an injection of penicillin, or even eating certain foods. These instances are rare, but such persons need to receive emergency medical care right away.

Symptoms: Runny nose, itching, teary eyes, and coughing or sneezing.

Treatment: If you allergies are minor, your family doctor will probably treat them. If they are serious, you may see an allergist who will take some tests to determine the cause of your allergy. The tests often consist of injecting small amounts of suspected allergens under your skin and waiting to see if you react to them. Allergies can be treated by avoiding the allergens and with medication.

Asthma

Asthma is a leading cause of chronic illness in children. It is twice as common in boys as in girls, but many young asthma patients outgrow their illness. Some experts think asthma is inherited.

Symptoms: Difficult breathing, wheezing, coughing, and a tight feeling in the chest. Attacks last from a few minutes to up to a week, and are triggered by exposure to allergens.

Treatment: As with allergies, you may be given skin tests to determine which allergens irritate you. Avoiding the allergens is the next step, and there are medicines that can help to prevent and control asthma.

Bed-wetting

Bed-wetting after the age of five is more of a problem for boys than for girls. Sometimes it is related to stress (such as a new sister or brother), a move, or a divorce, but at other times, no particular cause can be pinpointed.

Treatment: One of the first things most bed wetters do is limit their intake of water before bedtime. Another help is to have one of your parents or some other adult wake you up after you've been sleeping for a couple of hours and remind you to go to the bathroom. (Most bed-wetting occurs during the first third of the night.) Sometimes medication is given.

Braces

Few of us are blessed with perfect teeth, and that's why so many of us end up wearing braces at some point while we're growing up.

Symptoms: Braces are necessary when our jaw and teeth or not in alignment, producing what dentists called "overbite" or "under-

bite." A poorly aligned bite makes it difficult to chew food properly; it may also be unattractive.

Treatment: The solution is to wear braces, usually made of metal or sometimes ceramic, that gradually move the teeth into better alignment with the jaw. A special dentist called an orthodontist fits people with braces, which are typically worn for six months to two years. After the braces are removed, a retainer may be used for several years to help keep the teeth aligned.

Braces can be worn as soon as some adult teeth come in. Your regular dentist may refer you to an orthodontist when you are six or seven years old.

Your teeth will require some extra care, such as careful brushing, when you are wearing braces. Your orthodontist will teach you what to do.

Cancer

Cancer is an unusual growth of cells in a person's body. It is not contagious. Cancer is relatively rare in children, and the chances of a cure are better than with many adult cancers. The most common cancer in children is leukemia, a cancer of the blood system, followed by brain, kidney, and bone cancers.

Children with cancer are treated by a team of doctors, nurses, and social workers, usu-

Bites

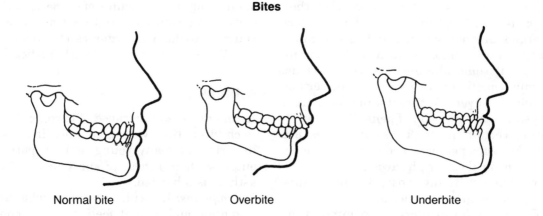

Normal bite   Overbite   Underbite

ally in a cancer center, children's hospital, or large hospital associated with a medical school.

Symptoms: These depend on the kind of cancer.

Treatment: Surgery; chemotherapy, which is treatment with strong chemicals that kill the cancer cells; or radiation, which is the use of radioactive material to kill the cancer cells.

Eating Disorders

The two major eating disorders, anorexia nervosa and bulimia, occur almost exclusively among teenage girls.

Symptoms of anorexia nervosa: Unrealistic fear of getting fat, excessive dieting and exercising, major weight loss, preoccupation with dieting and food.

Treatment: Talking with a counselor is an important first step in conquering this eating ailment, as is diet counseling to learn how to eat a healthy, well-balanced diet. If these fail to help, and the girl's weight continues to drop, hospitalization may be necessary.

Symptoms of bulimia: Eating huge amounts of food at one sitting (called binge eating); self-induced vomiting after eating; an excessive fear of being fat in a normal-weight person.

Treatment: Talking with a counselor is an important first step, followed by behavior modification therapy designed to change the patient's eating habits. If the problem is severe enough, hospitalization will be required.

Learning Disabilities

These occur when children with normal intelligence have trouble learning to speak, write, spell, or do math. In other words, they have trouble learning. A learning disability may be specific or general. An example of a specific learning disability, is dyslexia (difficulty in reading). If you have dyslexia, you may see the letters of words in the wrong order, such as *uoy* for *you*. An example of a general learning disability is hyperactivity (difficulty in focusing your attention on any one thing).

Doctors are not sure why people experience learning disabilities, but they believe some may be hereditary. Five to twenty percent of all students are estimated to have some form of learning disability.

Symptoms: Inability to learn no matter how hard you try, restlessness, being easily distracted from your schoolwork, poor memory.

Treatment: People with learning disabilities usually attend special education classes, which are designed to give them special skills for learning. Sometimes they also meet with a counselor to discuss their feelings and problems.

Speech Disorders

Stuttering is usually the first speech disorder that comes to mind, but children also mix up the words in a sentence and have trouble pronouncing certain sounds, among other symptoms.

Treatment: Special tests can be performed at your doctor's office or perhaps at a speech clinic to determine if you have a speech disorder. If you do, you will receive speech therapy one or two times a week. A therapist will help you practice speaking better. He or she will also show you how to practice at home.

WHAT ARE INFECTIOUS DISEASES, AND HOW DO PEOPLE GET THEM?

Infectious diseases are spread by microscopic organisms that enter the body and cause illness. There are five general kinds of infectious agents:

bacteria These one-celled organisms invade body cells and produce chemicals called toxins, which make you sick. Illnesses caused by bacteria include botul-

Infectious Agents

Bacterium

Helminth

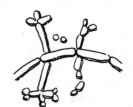

Fungus

Protozoan

Virus

ism, Lyme disease, and whooping cough (pertussis).

viruses These organisms enter your cells and change them in a way that make you ill. Gradually, the virus takes over the cell it enters and uses it to create more viral material. Illnesses caused by viruses include: mumps, AIDS, and measles.

fungi Mushrooms, molds, and yeasts are all fungi, although only the latter two cause infections. Many fungi, such as the yeast that causes bread to rise, are helpful, but about 1 in 100 is harmful to humans. Illnesses caused by fungi include histoplasmosis and blastomycosis.

protozoa These single-celled organisms usually live outside humans, but occasionally they enter a human body and cause disease. Illnesses caused by protozoa include malaria and toxoplasmosis.

helminths These larger parasites can be seen with the naked eye. They are multi-celled animals, usually worms, that invade the body's systems. They live on the same food you do. Illnesses caused by helminths include hookworm and tapeworm.

Here is a list of some of the more common infectious diseases and how they are transmitted:

Disease	Agent	Transmission
AIDS (acquired immune deficiency syndrome)	Virus	Contact of body fluid (semen, blood, vaginal secretions) with that of an infected person. Sexual contact and sharing of unclean paraphernalia for intravenous drugs are the most common means of transmission.
Blastomycosis	Fungus	Inhaling contaminated dust
Botulism	Bacteria	Consuming contaminated food
Chicken pox	Virus	Direct or indirect contact with infected person

Disease	Agent	Transmission
Common cold	Virus	Direct or indirect contact with infected person
Diphtheria	Bacteria	Direct contact with infected person
Encephalitis	Virus	Mosquito bite
Gonorrhea	Bacteria	Sexual contact
Hepatitis	Virus	Direct or indirect contact with infected person
Herpes simplex	Virus	Direct contact with infected person
Histoplasmosis	Fungus	Inhaling contaminated dust
Hookworm	Helminth	Contact with contaminated soil
Infectious mononucleosis	Virus	Direct or indirect contact with infected person
Influenza	Virus	Direct or indirect contact with infected person
Lyme disease	Bacteria	Deer tick bite
Malaria	Protozoa	Mosquito bite
Measles	Virus	Direct or indirect contact with infected person
Mumps	Virus	Direct or indirect contact with infected person
Pertussis (whooping cough)	Bacteria	Direct or indirect contact with infected person
Poliomyelitis	Virus	Direct contact with infected person
Rubella (German measles)	Virus	Direct or indirect contact with infected person
Scarlet fever	Bacteria	Direct or indirect contact with infected person
Spotted fever	Rickettsia	Tick bite
Syphilis	Bacteria	Sexual contact
Tapeworm	Helminth	Consuming infected meat or fish
Toxoplasmosis	Protozoa	Consuming raw meat; contact with contaminated soil
Trichomoniasis	Protozoa	Sexual contact
Typhus	Rickettsia	Lice, flea, tick bite
Yellow fever	Virus	Mosquito bite

HELP IN STAYING HEALTHY: VACCINES

Fortunately, many of the world's most dangerous diseases can be controlled—and sometimes eradicated—through the use of vaccines. A vaccine is a substance, usually given by injection, that leaves you immune, or resistant, to a specific disease.

Vaccines work by briefly fooling the body into thinking that it is sick when it isn't. The body's immune system rallies to fight off the disease by forming substances that leave the body resistant to it afterward.

Vaccines are made of dead, weakened, or related germs of the disease. The germs are killed by heat, ultraviolet light, or chemicals. Vaccines for whooping cough and typhoid fever are made from dead bacteria, for example. Occasionally a vaccine, such as the oral polio vaccine, will not work if the viruses have been killed, so those viruses are the weakened type. And vaccines for diseases such as smallpox and tuberculosis are made from related forms of the disease: Tuberculosis vaccine, for example, is made from cowpox virus, a lesser form that causes a skin disease in cattle but makes humans immune to TB.

AIDS: Facts and Myths

AIDS is a viral disease that destroys the body's natural immune system—the body's "Department of Defense" that fights off disease. Once the infected person's immune system starts breaking down, he or she becomes very sick.

Throughout the world, including the United States, AIDS is a major health problem. At present, there is no cure for AIDS, but through intensive medical research and wider experience in treating the symptoms of this serious disease, doctors are able to help AIDS victims enjoy longer, healthier, and more productive lives than was possible even a few years ago.

A person's best defense against AIDS is knowing the facts about it and how it is spread. Separating the facts from the myths about AIDS can help you understand the disease and protect yourself against it.

The AIDS virus is transmitted through bodily fluids, mainly blood, semen, and vaginal secretions. There are three ways AIDS can be passed from one person's bodily fluids to to another's.

1. *Sexual activity,* particularly when a person has many sexual partners and therefore faces a greater chance of meeting someone who already has the AIDS virus. Protected sex, where a man uses a condom, is one of the chief defensive weapons to prevent the spread of the disease. People who are not sexually active generally will not contract this disease unless they are drug users or receive contaminated blood transfusions. A baby whose mother was infected with the AIDS virus when he or she was born may also be infected.
2. *Intravenous drug use,* where people addicted to drugs share needles. The needle becomes contaminated with blood from an infected individual, and the next person who uses the needle may also become infected with the virus. The best defense against this kind of transmission is never to use drugs.
3. *Transfusions of contaminated blood.* All blood that is gathered by reputable blood banks in this country is now tested for the AIDS virus. In general, our blood supply is safe. Very rarely the virus escapes detection; in this case, people who require regular transfusions, such as hemophiliacs who were born with a serious blood disease, are at risk of contracting the AIDS virus.

The biggest myth about AIDS is that it can be spread by what doctors call casual contact: shaking hands with an infected person, eating in a restaurant where a waiter might have the virus, or visiting an AIDS patient in the hospital. It is not spread by sneezing or living in the same household with someone with AIDS. Not one case of the disease has ever been traced to such contact. Thus, people with AIDS should not be avoided, should not be isolated from noninfected people, and should be allowed to live as normal a life as the disease will permit.

Some people believe that AIDS is a solely gay person's disease, but this is not true. AIDS is passed through sexual contact between a man and a woman as well. While the disease originated in the United States in the homosexual community, today the fastest-growing group of AIDS victims in this country are young women, aged 18 to 21. In Africa, men and women get AIDS in approximately equal numbers. Many young African children are victims of AIDS. When women get AIDS, there is always a concern that they will pass the disease on to their children.

Researchers are working very hard to discover a vaccine that will prevent the disease and to develop medical treatments that will strengthen the immune system and ultimately cure AIDS patients.

By age 6, you will have received most of the vaccines you need. Some schools will not permit you to attend if you cannot prove you have been vaccinated. Here is a list of the vaccinations that most people living in the United States receive:

Vaccine	*Immunization Period*
Combination (diphtheria, tetanus toxoids, and whooping cough)	5–10 years
Diphtheria (antitoxin)	2–3 months
Diphtheria (toxoid)	5–20 years
Measles (attenuated virus)	Over 10 years
Measles (immune blood serum, gamma globulin, or placental extract)	A few weeks
Mumps (attenuated virus)	Probably life
Poliomyelitis (dead or attenuated virus)	Unknown
Rabies (attenuated virus)	Unknown
Rubella (attenuated virus)	Unknown
Tetanus (antitoxin)	A few weeks
Tetanus (toxoid)	5–10 years
Typhoid (dead germs)	2–3 years
Whooping cough (dead germs)	2–5 years

WHO HELPS WHEN YOU'RE SICK?

Fifty years ago, if you were sick, you would have gone to a general practitioner, and so would the rest of your family—including the new baby and grandma. Today, grandma goes to her own physician, called a **geriatric specialist**, and more than nine subspecialties exist just to treat children.

Here are other specialists that provide most of the general health care for families:

Allergist Treats allergies

Cardiologist Treats diseases and conditions involving the heart

Dermatologist Treats diseases of the skin

Emergency medicine physician Treats emergencies, usually in the emergency room of a hospital

Family practitioner Treats general illness, often referring patients to other specialists

Immunologist Treats diseases of the immune system, such as AIDS

Internist Treats the body's internal systems; often functions as a family practitioner

Neurologist Treats diseases of the nervous system

Obstetrician/Gynecologist Treats women's reproductive systems and cares for pregnant women

Oncologist Treats cancer and noncancerous tumors

Ophthalmologist Treats the eyes

Orthopedic surgeon Treats conditions and injuries of the bones, especially those requiring surgery

Otolaryngolist Treats ears, noses, and throats

Pediatrician Treats general illnesses of children and provides well-care, such as checkups and vaccinations

Physical medicine and rehabilitationist Treats sports injuries

Psychiatrist Treats mental illness

Radiologist Helps to diagnose illness through the use of X-rays, CAT scans, and magnetic resonance imaging; treats cancer patients by administering radiation

Surgeon Performs surgery

Urologist Treats diseases of the urinary tract

Here are the specialists that treat children:

Child psychiatrist Counsels about emotional or mental problems

Neonatologist/Perinatologist Treats fetuses in the womb and newborns with special problems

Pediatric critical care specialist Manages care of very ill children

Pediatric endocrinologist Treats serious diseases and problems of the endocrine system

Pediatric hematologist Treats serious diseases of the blood

Pediatric oncologist Treats cancer in children

Pediatric pulmonary specialist Treats serious diseases of the pulmonary system

Pediatric surgeon Specialist in surgery on children

A HEALTHY MOUTH: DENTAL HYGIENE

What Are Your Teeth Made Of?

The outermost part of a tooth—what you see when you look inside your mouth—isn't the whole story by any means. Teeth are made of several layers, located above and below your gum.

The Tooth

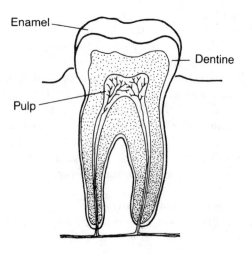

Enamel The white, outermost layer that you see. The enamel on your teeth is the hardest substance in your body.

Dentine This is another hard layer, though not so hard as the enamel. Its purpose is to absorb bumps and blows to your mouth.

Pulp This innermost section of your teeth contains the blood vessels that keep the tooth alive. The roots of the teeth, which contain nerve endings, are also in the pulp.

Taking Care of Your Teeth: A Complete Program

You probably were handed your first toothbrush when you were still a toddler. Years ago, dentists did not believe it was necessary to take care of baby teeth, but now it is known that the earlier dental care starts, the better.

Dental checkups begin at around age 3. You should have your teeth checked and cleaned by a dentist every 6 months.

Taking care of your mouth is simpler than you probably think. Here are a few guidelines:

1. Eat a sensible diet. Avoid sweet and sticky foods, and brush carefully after eating carbohydrates (starchy and sweet foods). These are the foods that most readily cause decay.
2. Get regular dental checkups.
3. Brush regularly—at least twice a day—but even better, after every meal.
4. Floss between teeth regularly.

Toothbrush Tactics

- Choose a soft, round-bristled toothbrush.
- Use a toothbrush the proper size for your mouth.
- Buy a new toothbrush every three or four months, as soon as the bristles on your old one start to spread.

Why Do We Have Baby Teeth and What Are Wisdom Teeth?

We have two sets of teeth during our lifetimes. One, our baby teeth (also called "milk teeth"), began to form below the gums several months before birth; the other, adult, set of teeth begin to come in at around age six, as we loose our baby teeth.

We need our baby teeth because when we are little, our mouths are too small to accommodate adult teeth—and when we are grown, our mouths are too big for our baby teeth to do the job.

A baby cuts his or her first tooth somewhere between five and nine months. He or she has six to eight teeth by the time he or she is a year old.

Wisdom teeth appear at the back of each side of the jaw, both top and bottom. You usually get your last teeth—your wisdom teeth—somewhere between the age of 15 and 25, about the time you stop growing, although not everyone gets wisdom teeth.

Humans have 20 baby teeth and 32 adult teeth.

Cleaning Your Teeth

- Begin by cleaning the outer surfaces of all your teeth and the inner surfaces of your back teeth.
- Use a vertical motion to clean the inner surfaces.
- Clean your gums by brushing them lightly.
- Floss between your teeth at least once a day. Use an 18-inch length of floss, wrapped around your middle fingers and held by your index finger. Gently work it up and down several times between all of your teeth.

What's a Cavity?

Sometimes, despite all your best efforts, you may still get a cavity. Cavities are caused when bacteria grow in food particles left on or between your teeth. The bacteria form an acid that eats away enamel and then spreads throughout the tooth.

Regular dental checkups will catch dental decay at an early stage. The dentist examines your teeth and sometimes x-rays them to find cavities, then repairs decay by drilling out the bad part of the tooth and filling in the hole with plastic or metal.

Signs That Something Is Wrong

Any of these symptoms would be a reason to see your dentist:

- Bad breath
- Bleeding gums
- Soft gums
- Painful gums
- Loose teeth (other than your baby teeth)
- Pus around a tooth

INFORMATION, PLEASE

American Medical Association Family Medical Guide. Rev. and updated. Random House, 1987.

Bruun, Ruth, M.D., and Bertel Bruun, M.D. *The Human Body.* Random House, 1982.

Gilmour, Ann and James. *Understanding Your Senses.* Warne, 1963.

Long, Lynette. *On My Own: The Kids' Self-Care Book.* Acropolis, 1984.

Whitfield, Dr. Philip, and Dr. Ruth Whitfield. *Why Do Our Bodies Stop Growing?* Viking, 1988.

23

THE UNITED STATES

GREAT EVENTS THAT SHAPED THE UNITED STATES

Certain events have proven to be turning points in American history. The list that follows describes some of the great achievements in American history:

Date	Event
1492	Columbus sails to Caribbean Islands. Europeans honor him as the discoverer of America.
1497	John Cabot explores North America from Canada to Delaware.
1513	Juan Ponce de León explores Florida, seeking the Fountain of Youth.
1524	Giovanni da Verrazano leads French expedition along the coast from Carolina to Nova Scotia, entering New York harbor.
1565	St. Augustine, Florida, is founded by Spaniards.
1579	Francis Drake claims California for Britain.
1586	St. Augustine is destroyed by Francis Drake.
1587	Virginia Dare is the first baby born in America to English parents.

Date	Event
1607	The first permanent British settlement in America is established at Jamestown, Virginia.
1609	Henry Hudson explores New York harbor and the Hudson River to Albany; Samuel de Champlain explores Lake Champlain in upstate New York: Spaniards settle Santa Fe, New Mexico.
1619	The first black slaves are brought to Jamestown, Virginia; the House of Burgesses, the first representative assembly in America, is established in Virginia.
1620	Pilgrims land at Plymouth, Massachusetts; the Mayflower Compact is drafted and signed.
1623	The Dutch found New Netherland (later New York).
1626	Peter Minuit buys Manhattan Island from Native Americans.
1630	The Massachusetts Bay Colony is founded.
1634	Maryland is founded as a Catholic colony.
1635	New Hampshire is founded by Captain John Mason; the first public school, the Boston Latin School, is established.

1636 Harvard, the first college in America, is founded.

1639 The first constitution in America, the Fundamental Orders of Connecticut, is written.

1647 Margaret Brent is the first woman to claim the right to vote. Massachusetts establishes the first colonial public school system.

1648 The first labor organization in the United States is authorized in the Massachusetts Bay Colony.

1649 Maryland passes the first religious toleration act in North America.

1654 The first Jews arrive in New Amsterdam (later New York City).

1663 The Colony of New Jersey is founded by Sir William Berkeley and Sir George Carteret; the Carolinas are founded.

1664 The English capture New Netherland.

1682 Pennsylvania is founded.

1688 The first formal protest against slavery is made, by Pennsylvania Quakers.

1692 Nineteen persons (mostly women) are executed for "witchcraft" in Salem, Massachusetts.

1712 A slave revolt in New York leads to the execution of 21 blacks; six commit suicide.

1731 The first circulating library is founded, in Philadelphia.

1732 Georgia is founded by James Oglethorpe and others; Benjamin Franklin publishes the first *Poor Richard's Almanac.*

1741 The second slave uprising takes place in New York; 13 are hanged, 13 burned, and 71 deported.

1749 Black slavery is legalized in Georgia.

1754 The French and Indian War begins (called the Seven Years' War in Europe).

c. 1757 The first streetlights in the colonies are installed in Philadelphia.

1758 The first Indian reservation is established.

1763 Britain defeats France in the French and Indian War and now controls eastern North America.

1764 The British Parliament passes the Sugar Act, placing duties on lumber, foodstuffs, molasses, and rum in the colonies.

1765 Passage of the Stamp Act by Britain leads to the Declaration of Rights, signed by nine colonies opposed to taxation without representation.

1766 Britain repeals the Stamp Act.

1767 The Townshend Acts tax glass, painter's lead, paper, and tea in the colonies.

1770 Five colonists are killed by British troops in the Boston Massacre.

1773 The Boston Tea Party takes place, in which colonists dump British tea into Boston Harbor.

1774 The Intolerable Acts passed by Parliament limit Massachusetts's self-rule and close Boston Harbor.

1775 The American Revolution begins in Massachusetts, with the battles of Lexington and Concord.

1776 France and Spain each donate arms to Americans; the Declaration of Independence is drafted and signed; Nathan Hale is executed by the British as a spy; the first American fraternity, Phi Beta Kappa, is founded at the College of William and Mary; the Journeymen Printers' Strike is the first in the United States.

1777 The Continental Congress adopts a flag with stars and stripes; Washington defeats Lord Cornwallis at the battle of Princeton; Major General John Burgoyne captures Fort Ticonderoga, but Americans defeat him at Saratoga, New York.

1778 France agrees to assist the United States and sends a fleet; the British evacuate Philadelphia.

1779 George Washington orders a military campaign against the Iroquois.

1780 American general Benedict Arnold is discovered to be a traitor and escapes to the British.

1781 Colonial and French armies defeat the British at Yorktown, the last major battle of the Revolutionary War.

1783 The Revolutionary War ends with a treaty.

1784 The first daily newspaper, *Pennsylvania Packet and General Advertiser,* is published in Philadelphia.

1787 The Constitutional Convention begins in Philadelphia, and the Constitution is written.

1788 New Hampshire ratifies the Constitution, putting it into effect.

1789 George Washington is chosen the first President; John Adams, Vice President; Thomas Jefferson, secretary of state; and Alexander Hamilton, secretary of the treasury.

1790s The first U.S. political parties develop.

1790 Congress meets in Philadelphia, the temporary capital, and votes to found a new capital on the Potomac River; the United States signs the first treaty with the Iroquois.

1791 The Bill of Rights goes into effect; Vermont is the first state to enter the Union after the original 13 colonies.

1793 The invention of the cotton gin, which spins cotton, revives slavery in the South.

1794 Suppression by the U.S. militia of the Whiskey Rebellion, in which farmers protest the liquor tax of 1791, establishes the authority of the new federal government.

1801 Tripoli declares war on the United States.

1803 The Supreme Court declares an act of Congress unconstitional in Marbury v. Madison; the United States buys the Louisiana Territory from France, nearly doubling its land holdings. (The Purchase included most of the land between the Mississippi River and the Rocky Mountains.)

1804 President Jefferson orders the Lewis and Clark expedition to explore the northwest; Vice President Aaron Burr and Alexander Hamilton duel; Hamilton dies the next day.

1805 War with Tripoli ends.

1808 The importation of slaves is outlawed (about 250,000 slaves are illegally imported between 1808 and 1860).

1812 The War of 1812 between the U.S. and Great Britain begins.

1814 The War of 1812 ends with the Treaty of Ghent. Neither side wins.

1815 Florida is granted to the United States by Spain.

1816 The first savings bank, the Provident Institute for Savings, is established in Boston.

1821 Missouri is admitted to the Union as a slave state; Troy Female Seminary, the first women's college in the United States, is founded.

1825 The Erie Canal is opened, cutting travel time from New York City to Buffalo and the Great Lakes by one-third.

1827 *Freedom's Journal,* the first black U.S. newspaper, is published.

1828 The first Native American newspaper, *Cherokee Phoenix,* begins publication.

1829 The first school for the blind is incorporated in the United States.

1830 President Jackson signs the Indian Removal Act.

1831 Nat Turner leads an unsuccessful slave rebellion in Virginia.

1832 The first meeting of the New England Anti-Slavery Society is held; Oberlin College, Ohio, becomes the first college to establish coeducation.

1836 Texas declares independence from Mexico.

1837 The panic of 1837 begins a seven-year depression.

1838 Cherokees start on the Trail of Tears, their 1,200-mile forced march from the Southeast to Oklahoma.

1841 Oberlin College, Ohio, becomes the first college to give degrees to women; the first wagon train leaves from Independence, Missouri, for California.

1843 Sojourner Truth, former slave, begins an abolitionist lecture tour.

1844 The first telegraph message is sent from Washington to Baltimore.

1845 U.S. makes Mexico part of the country.

1846 The United States declares war on Mexico; a treaty with Great Britain gives the United States the Oregon Territory to the 49th parallel; Henry David Thoreau is jailed for refusing to pay taxes.

1847 The first postage stamp is issued; Michigan becomes the first state to abolish capital punishment.

1848 The United States signs the Treaty of Guadalupe Hidalgo with Mexico, ending the Mexican War and giving the U.S. much of the present-day American Southwest, including California; the first women's rights convention is held in Seneca Falls, New York; gold is discovered in California.

1849 Eighty thousand gold prospectors flood California.

1850 Senator Henry Clay's Compromise of 1850 admits California to the Union as a nonslave state, while Utah and New Mexico also enter the union with no decision on slavery.

1852 The antislavery novel *Uncle Tom's Cabin,* by Harriet Beecher Stowe, is published.

1853 The American Labor Union is founded; the U.S. buys New Mexico from Mexico.

1854 The Republican party is formed in opposition to the Kansas-Nebraska Act, which left the issue of slavery to a vote by settlers.

1857 The Dred Scott decision by the Supreme Court says that blacks are not citizens.

1858 The Lincoln-Douglas debates are held in Illinois.

1860 A nationwide shoemakers' strike wins workers higher wages; the National Labor Union is founded.

1861 The American Miners Association, the first national coal miners' union, is founded; the Civil War between the North and the South begins when Southerners (Confederates) fire on Fort Sumter, South Carolina.

1862 Slavery is abolished in Washington, D.C.; the Homestead Act grants land to settlers.

1863 President Lincoln delivers the Gettysburg Address and issues the Emancipation Proclamation; draft riots in New York City kill approximately a thousand, including blacks who are hanged by a mob.

1864 Black prisoners of war are massacred by Confederate soldiers at Fort Pillow, Tennessee; General Sherman marches through Georgia, capturing Atlanta for the Northern side; the *New Orleans Tribune,* a black-run daily newspaper, begins publication; 133 Cheyenne and Arapahoe are killed by Colorado cavalry volunteers at Sand Creek, Colorado.

1865 The Confederacy surrenders at Appomattox, Virginia, ending the Civil War; the first state civil rights law is passed, in Massachusetts; the Thirteenth Amendment abolishes slavery; the Ku Klux Klan is formed in Pulaski, Tennessee; President Lincoln is assassinated.

1868 Impeachment proceedings begin against President Andrew Johnson; the Fourteenth Amendment is ratified, guaranteeing legal protection to all but Native Americans; a U.S.–Sioux treaty is signed at Fort Laramie, Wyoming.

1869 The first national black labor group, the Colored National Labor Convention, meets in Washington, D.C.: the Central Pacific and Union Pacific railroads are joined together at Promontory, Utah, forming the first transcontinental railroad; Wyoming territory is the first to grant women the right to vote.

1870 The first woman candidate for U.S. President, Victoria Claflin Woodhull, announces she will run; the first sorority, Kappa Alpha Theta, is established at De Pauw University; Ada H. Kepley, the first American woman graduate of a law school, receives degree from Union College of Law, Chicago.

1872 The Amnesty Act restores rights to Southern citizens except for 500 Confederate leaders; Yellowstone, the first U.S. national park, opens in Wyoming.

1873 The first illustrated daily newspaper, *New York Daily Graphic,* is established.

1875 The Civil Rights Act gives equal rights to blacks in public accommodations and jury duty.

1876 General Custer is defeated by Sioux warriors led by Crazy Horse at the battle of the Little Bighorn.

1877 The United States violates its treaty with the Dakota Sioux by seizing the Black Hills; Chief Joseph surrenders with starving survivors of the Nez-Percé people.

1881 Chief Sitting Bull of the Sioux surrenders; President Garfield is shot and killed; Booker T. Washington founds Tuskegee Institute for blacks.

1883 The Supreme Court rules that Native Americans are aliens; the Supreme Court rules that the Civil Rights Act of 1875 is illegal.

1885 The first skyscraper is built in Chicago.

1886 The Haymarket Square massacre occurs in Chicago as a bomb explodes and protestors demanding an eight-hour workday are arrested; Geronimo surrenders to Arizona Territory leaders; the American Federation of Labor (AFL) is founded.

1887 Crazy Horse is assassinated while in custody.

1890 The United Mine Workers is formed; Sitting Bull is killed by police at Standing Rock Reservation, South Dakota; 200 Sioux are massacred by troops at Wounded Knee, South Dakota; William Kemmler is the first criminal to be executed by electrocution, at Auburn Prison, New York; Ellis Island becomes a port of entry for immigrants.

1893 Financial panic lasting for four years begins.

1896 The Supreme Court's Plessy v. Ferguson decision says that segregation is legal if blacks and whites have "separate but equal" schools, hospitals, and so forth.

1898 The United States declares war on Spain; U.S. troops invade Puerto Rico to liberate it from Spain; Admiral Dewey captures Manila Harbor, destroying all Spanish ships there.

1899 Philippine rebellion against U.S. rule begins; the Open Door Policy makes China an international market and preserves its integrity as a nation.

1900 The International Ladies Garment Workers Union is founded; Carry Nation leads the first liquor bottle–smashing raid, in Wichita, Kansas.

1901 President McKinley is assassinated.

1902 The last Philippine resistance to U.S. intervention ends.

1903 Panama declares its independence from Colombia, with U.S. support, and signs the Panama Canal Treaty; Orville and Wilbur Wright make the first flights in a mechanically propelled plane.

1905 The Niagara Movement, later to become the NAACP, is founded.

1906 The San Francisco earthquake and fire occur.

1907 Charles Curtis of Kansas becomes the first Native American U.S. senator.

1908 The United States stops Japanese immigration; women demonstrate in New York City, demanding an end to sweatshops and child labor; the Federal Bureau of Investigation (FBI) is established.

1909 The National Association for the Advancement of Colored People (NAACP) is founded; Native American leader Geronimo dies.

1911 The Triangle Shirt Waist Company fire in New York City kills 146 sweatshop workers, mostly women, and leads to demands for better working conditions.

1912 The "Bread and Roses" strike by 10,000 textile workers begins in Lawrence, Massachusetts.

1913 The Sixteenth Amendment permits the income tax; the first important U.S. exhibition of modern art is held at the New York City Armory.

1914 The Colorado National Guard burns a striking miners' camp and kills 13 children and seven adults in the Ludlow Massacre.

1915 The Women's International League for Peace and Freedom is founded; 25,000 women march in New York City demanding the right to vote; Haiti becomes a U.S. protectorate after U.S. troops land there.

1916 The National Women's Party is founded; the first public birth control clinic opens, in Brooklyn, New York; Jeannette Rankin of Montana becomes the first woman elected to the House of Representatives; Margaret Sanger is arrested for operating a birth control clinic; the United States buys the Virgin Islands from Denmark; a military government is established in the Dominican Republic as the country is occupied by U.S. Marines.

1917 Women picket in front of the White House, demanding the right to vote; Puerto Rico becomes a U.S. territory; the United States declares war on Germany, entering World War I; a wartime draft is enacted.

1918 World War I ends.

1919 The Supreme Court holds that freedom of speech does not apply to draft resistance; a women's suffrage (right to vote) bill passes the House of Representatives; the Communist party of America is founded.

1920 The sale of alcoholic beverages is banned (Prohibition) under the Eighteenth Amendment; women win the right to vote with ratification of the Nineteenth Amendment; the League of Women Voters is founded; the first transcontinental airmail route is established between New York City and San Francisco.

1921 Immigration is limited by quotas set by Congress; the Ku Klux Klan revives violence against blacks in the North, South, and Midwest.

1922 Rebecca L. Felton, from Georgia, is appointed the first woman U.S. senator.

1924 Native Americans are declared citizens by Congress; the first U.S. gay rights organization, the Society for Human Rights, is founded in Chicago.

1925 Nellie Taylor Ross, the first woman governor in the United States, is sworn in, in Wyoming; John T.

Scopes is convicted of teaching the theory of evolution; Tennessee bans the teaching of evolution.

1927 American aviator Charles Lindbergh makes the first intercontinental flight.

1929 The stock market crashes, beginning the Great Depression.

1932 Hattie Caraway, of Tennessee, is the first woman elected to the U.S. Senate.

1933 President Franklin Roosevelt closes all U.S. banks; during a special session of Congress, called the "100 days," important New Deal legislation is passed, including the establishment of the National Recovery Administration and the Tennessee Valley Authority (TVA); Frances Perkins, Secretary of Labor, becomes the first woman Cabinet member; the Twenty-first Amendment, ending Prohibition, is passed.

1935 The Works Projects Administration (WPA) is established; the National Labor Relations Act, recognizing workers' right to organize and bargain collectively, passes; President Roosevelt signs the Social Security Act.

1937 American aviator Amelia Earhart and her copilot disappear over the Pacific.

1938 A national minimum-wage bill is passed; the "War of the Worlds," a fictional broadcast by Orson Wells, causes nationwide fear that Martians have invaded Earth.

1939 Sit-down strikes are outlawed by the Supreme Court; World War II begins with the German invasion of Poland.

1940 Congress approves the first peacetime draft.

1941 The Ford Motor Company signs its first contract with the United Auto Workers Union; the Japanese attack Pearl Harbor, causing the United States to enter World War II.

1942 President Roosevelt orders the imprisonment of 120,000 Japanese-Americans on the West Coast; the Manhattan Project led by scientists begins developing the atomic bomb.

1943 President Roosevelt bars all war manufacturers from racial discrimination in the hiring of workers.

1944 Allies invade Normandy; Congress passes the G.I. Bill of Rights, providing veterans' benefits.

1945 The Yalta conference, attended by Roosevelt, Churchill, and Stalin, brings Russia into World War II against Japan; Roosevelt dies; Truman becomes President; Nazi Germany and Japan are defeated, ending World War II in Europe and the Pacific; U.S. troops liberate the concentration camp at Dachau; the first atomic bomb is exploded, at Alamagordo, New Mexico; the United States drops atomic bombs on the Japanese cities of Hiroshima and Nagasaki; the United Nations Charter is adopted.

1946 The Atomic Energy Commission is formed; the U.S. gives the Philippines its independence.

1947 The first draft-card burning takes place: the cold war between the U.S. and the U.S.S.R. begins; the U.S. gives aid to Greece and Turkey under the Truman Doctrine; Jackie Robinson, the first black major league baseball player, appears in his first game with the Brooklyn Dodgers; the Marshall Plan for European recovery is announced; the Department of Defense is created; the Central Intelligence Agency (CIA) and the National Security Council are established under the National Security Act.

1948 Twelve Communist party leaders are indicted by the United States, which says that they advocated the overthrow of the government.

1949 The North Atlantic Treaty Organization (NATO) is formed by the United States, Canada, and 10 European nations.

1950 President Truman orders the development of the hydrogen bomb; Senator Joseph McCarthy accuses State Department employees of being members of the Communist party; the Korean War between North and South Korea, with the United Nations aiding South Korea, begins; the United States sends 35 military advisers and agrees to give military and economic aid to South Vietnam.

1951 The Americans Julius and Ethel Rosenberg and Morton Sobel are convicted of spying for the Soviets; the Mattachine Society, an early gay rights organization, is formed in California; atomic energy is first used to generate electricity in the United States; Korean cease-fire talks begin.

1952 The United States explodes the world's first hydrogen bomb; the Immigration and Naturalization Act is passed, ending the last racial and ethnic barriers to U.S. citizenship.

1953 President Truman announces development of the hydrogen bomb; Julius and Ethel Rosenberg are executed; the Korean conflict ends.

1954 Seven thousand square miles of the Pacific are irradiated by a Bikini Island hydrogen bomb test, which contaminates Japanese fishermen; the U.S. Air Force begins flying French reinforcements to Indochina: in Brown v. Board of Education, the Supreme Court outlaws segregation in public schools; the Southeast Asia Treaty Organization (SEATO) is formed, comprising the United States, Great Britain, France, Australia, New Zealand, the Philippines, Pakistan, and Thailand.

1955 A black woman, Rosa Parks, refuses to give up her bus seat to a white person and begins the Montgomery, Alabama, bus boycott by blacks; the AFL and CIO become one labor union; the United States agrees to help train the South Vietnamese army.

1956 Passage of the Federal Highway Aid Act begins the first interstate highway system.

1957 In Alabama, Elizabeth Eckford is blocked from becoming the first black student at Little Rock Central High School; nine black students enroll at Little Rock High School with the help of federal troops; Congress approves the first bill protecting blacks' right to vote since the 1870s.

1958 The United States launches its first satellite into orbit.

1959 Alaska and Hawaii become the forty-ninth and fiftieth states, respectively.

1960 More than 70,000 black and white students participate in sit-ins to protest a Greensboro, North Carolina, incident in which four blacks were denied service at a lunch counter.

1961 The United States breaks diplomatic ties with Cuba; the Bay of Pigs invasion of Cuba by the U.S. fails: "freedom riders" test segregation laws in the Deep South; the Student Non-Violent Coordinating Committee (SNCC) drive to register black voters begins in the South; Alan B. Shepard, Jr., travels on the first U.S. manned space flight.

1962 The United States announces it will resume atmospheric nuclear testing after test-ban negotiations fail; James Meredith becomes the first black to enroll at the University of Mississippi; President Kennedy orders a blockade of Cuba, which begins the Cuban Missile Crisis.

1963   The Supreme Court rules that states must provide free legal counsel for people who cannot afford lawyers; blacks in Birmingham, Alabama, begin mass demonstrations for civil rights; the Supreme Court bars Bible readings in public schools; Martin Luther King, Jr., leads a civil rights march on Washington, D.C.; President Kennedy is assassinated; Congress passes the first Clean Air Act.

1964   A Civil Rights Act is passed by Congress; Congress passes the Gulf of Tonkin Resolution, giving President Lyndon Johnson power to wage war in Indochina; Martin Luther King, Jr., receives the Nobel Peace Prize; Panama breaks off relations with the United States, which offers to negotiate a new Canal treaty.

1965   Malcolm X, black leader, is assassinated; in Selma, Alabama, Martin Luther King, Jr., leads a march to force the state to allow blacks to register to vote.

1966   Federal courts outlaw the last poll, or voting, tax; the National Organization for Women (NOW) is founded; Medicare begins to pay the health-care expenses of the U.S. citizens aged 65 and older.

1967   Two hundred thousand people march against the Vietnam War in New York City; six days of racial rioting in Newark, New Jersey, leave 23 dead; week-long racial rioting in Detroit leaves 43 dead; J. Edgar Hoover, director of the FBI, authorizes activities against black nationalist groups.

1968   Four black student demonstrators are killed by police in Orangeburg, South Carolina; 500 unarmed Vietnamese are killed by U.S. troops in the My Lai massacre; Martin Luther King, Jr., is assassinated; Robert F. Kennedy is assassinated hours after his California primary victory; the American Indian Movement is founded; a coalition of women's groups interrupts the Miss America Pageant in the first mass demonstration of the modern women's movement; the United States ends the bombing of North Vietnam; Representative Shirley Chisholm, from New York, becomes the first black woman elected to Congress.

1969   The Stonewall rebellion, at a bar in New York City, starts the modern gay rights movement; the Woodstock festival in upstate New York draws 300,000 for "three days of peace and music"; the Chicago Seven conspiracy trial begins, in which seven defendants are accused of having encouraged a riot at the 1968 Democratic National Convention; 2 million people nationwide demonstrate against U.S. involvement in Vietnam; 78 Native Americans seize Alcatraz Island, demanding it be made into a cultural center; Fred Hampton and Mark Clark, members of a militant group called the Black Panthers, are murdered by Chicago police; the United States begins peace talks with Vietnam, as troop withdrawal starts; Neil Armstrong becomes the first man to walk on the moon.

1970   Chicano activists gather in Crystal City, Texas, to found La Raza Unida Party; the Ohio National Guard kills four students during a Vietnam War protest at Kent State University; Mississippi police kill two black students at Jackson State University; President Nixon signs a law giving 18-year-olds the right to vote; the Environmental Protection Agency (EPA) is established; Congress passes the Occupational Safety and Health Act (OSHA); the Chicago Seven are found not guilty, though five are convicted of crossing state lines with intent to encourage riots; the first two U.S. women generals are named by President Nixon.

1971 Five hundred thousand people demonstrate in Washington, D.C., against the Vietnam War and 14,000 are arrested.

1972 The Watergate break-in, which leads to the resignation of President Nixon, takes place; Nixon visits China, leading the U.S. to recognize the Communist Chinese government as the official government of China; the Senate approves a constitutional amendment banning discrimination against women because of their sex and sends the measure to the states to ratify.

1973 A peace treaty is signed between North and South Vietnam, ending U.S. participation in that war; President Nixon signs the Endangered Species Act; Oglala Sioux occupy Wounded Knee, South Dakota, and declare an independent Oglala Sioux nation; Spiro T. Agnew resigns as Vice President, and Gerald Ford becomes the first appointed Vice President; five of seven defendants in the Watergate trial plead guilty, and two are convicted; in *Roe v. Wade*, the Supreme Court rules that a state may not prevent a woman from having an abortion during the first six months of pregnancy.

1974 The House Judiciary Committee votes to support the impeachment of President Nixon, and Nixon resigns; President Ford pardons former President Nixon.

1975 North Vietnamese troops enter Saigon; the Mohawk tribe reclaims part of its homeland in New York State; former Attorney General John N. Mitchell and ex-presidential advisers H. R. Haldeman and John D. Ehrlichman are found guilty in the Watergate trial.

1976 The Supreme Court supports the death penalty. The nation celebrates its Bicentennial (200 years of existence).

1977 President Carter pardons 10,000 Vietnam draft resisters; the Department of Energy is established.

1978 The "longest walk," by 300 Native Americans, begins, to protect treaty rights; the Senate votes to give the Panama Canal to Panama. The Middle East "Framework for Peace" is signed by Egypt and Israel after a Camp David conference led by President Carter.

1979 The Three-Mile Island nuclear power plant has a near meltdown; 110,000 demonstrate in Washington, D.C., against nuclear power; Iranian students seize the U.S. embassy in Teheran.

1980 Fifty thousand people march in Chicago for passage of the Equal Rights Amendment (ERA); President Carter announces an embargo on the sale of grain and high technology to the Soviet Union because of its invasion of Afghanistan; the U.S. Olympic Committee votes not to participate in the Olympic Games in Moscow.

1981 Iran releases 52 American hostages held 444 days; Sandra Day O'Connor is appointed the first woman Supreme Court justice; the first reusable spacecraft, the shuttle *Columbia*, completes its two-day mission in space.

1982 The ERA fails to be ratified by enough states to become federal law.

1983 Five thousand U.S. Marines and

Army Rangers invade the Caribbean island of Grenada; Congress demands that troops leave Grenada; the Supreme Court rules that the Internal Revenue Service can deny tax exemptions to private schools that practice racial discrimination.

1984 The Senate votes to impose economic sanctions on South Africa to protest apartheid; Palestinian Liberation Organization (PLO) hijackers seize an Italian cruise ship with Americans abroad, killing one American.

1985 The United States and the Soviet Union agree to resume negotiations on reducing nuclear arms and the space weapons race; Soviet leader Chernenko dies and is succeeded by Mikhail Gorbachev; a summit meeting agreement is reached by Reagan and Gorbachev on stepping up arms control talks and cultural ties.

1986 The first official observance of the birthday of Martin Luther King, Jr., occurs; the space shuttle *Challenger* explodes moments after liftoff, killing all crew members, including a civilian, Christa McAuliffe; the United States bombs Tripoli and Benghazi, Libya, in retaliation against terrorist attacks; U.S. officials announce that AIDS cases and deaths will increase tenfold in the next five years; President Reagan walks out on arms talks with Soviet leader Mikhail Gorbachev in Iceland.

1987 The Iran-contra affair dominates public attention when it is revealed that the U.S. traded arms to Iran to free the hostages held by Iran and used money to finance the contras in Nicaragua; the United States imposes taxes on Japanese imports to reduce the trade deficit; the drug AZT is approved for fighting AIDS;

on "Black Monday," the Wall Street stock market experiences its three biggest one-day losses ever.

1988 The space shuttle *Discovery* is launched successfully after delays caused by the 1986 *Challenger* tragedy; the U.S. agrees to meet with the Palestine Liberation Organization.

1990 President George Bush sends the largest military force since the Vietnam War to Saudi Arabia to defend that country after the invasion of Kuwait by neighboring Iraq.

1993 President Bush and Russian President Boris Yeltsin sign the second Strategic Arms Reduction Treaty (S.T.A.R.T. II). The treaty eliminates multiple warhead missiles and reduces total missiles by two-thirds.

FAMOUS PEOPLE WHO SHAPED THE UNITED STATES

There have been many Americans who have made significant contributions to their country that have changed it forever. The list that follows describes some of the people who have helped change America. They are listed chronologically. For a chronology of U.S. History, see the "Great Events That Have Shaped Our World" at the beginning of Chapter 24.

1607 John Smith founds English colony at Jamestown, Virginia.

1636 Roger Williams, pioneer of religious tolerance, founds Rhode Island.

1681 William Penn founds Pennsylvania.

1752 Benjamin Franklin flies a homemade kite during a storm to prove that lightning is a form of electricity. As inventor, practical philosopher, and politician, Franklin symbolizes the early eighteenth-century American.

1775 Thomas Paine publishes *Common*

Sense, a pamphlet arguing that Americans must declare themselves free from England.

1776 Thomas Jefferson writes the Declaration of Independence.

1790 Samuel Slater builds America's first successful water-powered machines for spinning cotton, and the first American factory begins production.

1793 Eli Whitney invents the cotton gin, a machine that separates cotton fiber from the seeds as fast as 50 people can by hand.

1801– 35 John Marshall serves as the first Chief Justice of the Supreme Court.

1804– 06 Meriwether Lewis and William Clark begin exploration of the American Northwest, traveling all the way to the Pacific Ocean.

1812 James Madison, 4th President, requests Congress to declare war on Britain, beginning the War of 1812.

1823 James Monroe, 5th President, issues the Monroe Doctrine, warning European nations not to interfere in the Western Hemisphere.

1828 Andrew Jackson, 7th President, takes steps to reduce the power of wealthy Easterners and to aid the "common man."

1831 William Lloyd Garrison, abolitionist (one who supports an end to slavery), founds the *Liberator*, an important abolitionist journal.

1834 Cyrus McCormick patents the mechanical reaper, allowing farmers to harvest grain much more quickly than previously.

1836 Sam Houston, former governor of Tennessee, directs Texas troops to a victory over the Mexican army, leading to the annexation of Texas by the United States.

1839 John Deere manufactures steel plows.

1844 Samuel F. B. Morse demonstrates his invention, the electric telegraph.

1845 Frederick Douglass, ex-slave, writes his *Narrative of the Life of Frederick Douglass*.

1846 Elias Howe patents the sewing machine.

1846 James K. Polk, 11th President, requests Congress to declare war on Mexico, leading to the U.S. gain of a vast stretch of land from Texas west to the Pacific and north to Oregon.

1848 Lucretia Mott and Elizabeth Cady Stanton organize a Women's Rights Convention in Seneca Falls, New York.

1851 Herman Melville publishes his novel *Moby Dick*.

1851– 52 Harriet Beecher Stowe's antislavery novel *Uncle Tom's Cabin* becomes one of the most widely read books in America.

1854 Henry David Thoreau publishes *Walden*, a book of essays.

1855 Walt Whitman, poet, publishes *Leaves of Grass*.

1859 John Brown, abolitionist, seizes the federal arsenal at Harper's Ferry, Virginia, in an attempt to start a slave rebellion; he is captured and executed.

1863 Abraham Lincoln announces the Emancipation Proclamation, declaring the end to slavery in the Confederate states.

1863 Harriet Tubman, a leader of the Underground Railroad bringing slaves to safety, frees 750 slaves in a raid.

1864 William Tecumseh Sherman, Union general, marches through Georgia, burning Atlanta.

1865 Robert E. Lee surrenders to Ulysses S. Grant, Union general, at Appomattox Courthouse, Virginia, virtually ending the Civil War.

1865 John Wilkes Booth, actor, assassinates President Lincoln.

1865 Vassar College in Poughkeepsie, New York, becomes the first college for women in the United States.

1872   Susan B. Anthony is arrested for voting.

1874   Joseph F. Gidden invents barbed wire.

1876   Alexander Graham Bell invents the telephone.

1877   Thomas Alva Edison invents the phonograph and, three years later, the electric light.

1881   Samuel Gompers founds the American Federal of Labor.

1984   Mark Twain publishes the novel *The Adventures of Huckleberry Finn*.

1889   Jane Addams founds Hull House in Chicago, to help the urban poor.

1895   Stephen Crane publishes the novel *The Red Badge of Courage* about the Civil War.

1896   Democratic presidential candidate William Jennings Bryan delivers his famous "Cross of Gold" speech.

1901   J. P. Morgan announces formation of U.S. Steel Corporation, the nation's first billion-dollar company.

1903   Orville and Wilbur Wright make the first successful airplane flight at Kitty Hawk, North Carolina.

1906   Upton Sinclair publishes *The Jungle*, a novel about unsanitary conditions in the meat-packing industry.

1911   Frederick Winslow Taylor, industrial engineer, publishes *The Principles of Scientific Management*, a book that will profoundly affect American management techniques.

1918   Woodrow Wilson, 28th President, outlines Fourteen Points designed to make the world "fit and safe to live in."

1920   Sinclair Lewis, novelist, publishes *Main Street*, an attack on middle-American values.

1925   F. Scott Fitzgerald publishes *The Great Gatsby*, a novel about the emptiness of American values.

1927   Charles Lindbergh completes the first nonstop transatlantic flight from New York to Paris.

1932   William Faulkner publishes his novel *Light in August* about the clash between the old and the new South.

1932   Franklin Delano Roosevelt, 32nd President, starts the New Deal, a program for reform and recovery from the Great Depression.

1939   John Steinbeck publishes his novel *The Grapes of Wrath* about a family during the Great Depression.

1945   Harry S. Truman, 33d President, orders the atom bomb to be dropped on the Japanese cities of Hiroshima and Nagasaki, effectively ending World War II.

1947   Secretary of State George C. Marshall suggests a program to help rebuild war-devasted Europe with United States aid. The program becomes known as the Marshall Plan.

1950   Joseph R. McCarthy, U.S. senator, gains national fame by charging that communists have infiltrated the federal government.

1952   Edward Teller, physicist, develops hydrogen bomb.

1955   Martin Luther King, Jr., begins organizing a movement to protest discrimination against blacks.

1957   Albert Sabin develops a live-virus polio vaccine.

1960   John F. Kennedy becomes the youngest person elected President.

1961   Alan B. Shepard, Jr., becomes the first American in space.

1962   James Meredith becomes the first black to enroll at the University of Mississippi.

1962   Rachel Carson publishes *Silent Spring*, starting the environmental movement.

1962   John Glenn, Jr., becomes the first American to orbit the earth.

1963   Betty Friedan publishes *The Feminine Mystique*, setting into motion the woman's rights movement.

1964   Lyndon B. Johnson, 36th President, declares "War on Poverty."

1967   Thurgood Marshall becomes the first black Supreme Court Justice.

1969 Neil Armstrong becomes the first person to walk on the moon.

1972 Bob Woodward and Carl Bernstein write about a robbery attempt in a Washington apartment complex called Watergate. According to the two *Washington Post* reporters, the crime is linked to the Committee for the Re-election of the President, Richard M. Nixon.

1972 Gloria Steinem becomes editor of a new women's magazine, *Ms.*

1973 Bobby Fischer becomes the first American to win the World Chess title.

1973 Philip H. Knight founds Nike, Inc.

1974 President Nixon resigns in disgrace after having been accused of trying to cover up his role in the Watergate break-in. He is the first president to quit while in office.

1974 Henry Jay Heimlich, a surgeon, describes a way to save people from choking to death on food. The Heimlich Maneuver is subsequently used successfully around the world.

1975 William Henry Gates III and Paul Gardner Allen found Microsoft, which becomes the biggest seller of computer software.

1976 Steven Jobs and Stephen G. Wozniak found Apple Computer.

1976 Alex Haley publishes *Roots*, a story based on his African-American heritage. In 1977, the story becomes a seven-part television miniseries that is watched by millions of Americans.

1981 Sandra Day O'Connor becomes the first woman justice on the Supreme Court.

1983 Dr. Sally K. Ride becomes the first American woman astronaut to travel in space.

1984 Dr. Kathryn D. Sullivan becomes the first woman astronaut to walk in space; Geraldine A. Ferraro is the first woman candidate on a major party ticket to run for Vice President.

1991 Earvin "Magic" Johnson, star of the Los Angeles Lakers, retires from basketball after announcing that he has the AIDs virus.

1993 Janet Reno becomes the first woman Attorney General of the United States.

WARS FOUGHT BY THE UNITED STATES

War of Independence	1775–1783	U.S. (and later France) v. Great Britain
War of 1812	1812–1814	U.S. v. Great Britain
Mexican-American War	1846–1848	U.S. v. Mexico
Civil War	1861–1865	Union (23 northern states) v. Confederacy (11 southern states)
Spanish-American War	1898	U.S. v. Spain
World War I	1914–1918	U.S. v. Germany, Austria-Hungary, Bulgaria, Ottoman Empire
World War II	1939–1945	Allied forces (including U.S.) v. Axis forces (Germany, Italy, and Japan)
Korean War	1950–1953	U.N. (including the U.S.) and South Korea v. North Korea and China

| Vietnam War | 1954–1975 (U.S. sent first combat troops in 1964) | Republic of Vietnam (South Vietnam), and their allies, including the U.S. v. Communist Democratic Republic of Vietnam (North Vietnam) |
| Persian Gulf Conflict | 1991 (January–February) | U.S. (part of UN forces) v. Iraq |

HOW THE FEDERAL GOVERNMENT IS ORGANIZED

The Constitution established a federal government with three branches: the legislative, executive, and judicial. Each branch has the power to check and balance the other two branches so that no branch will become too powerful.

The legislative branch—both houses of Congress—proposes and makes laws. The executive branch is headed by the President, who has the ultimate power to enforce the law and administer the government. The executive branch is divided into departments that report to the President. Besides these departments, there are many agencies, commissions, and administrations that keep the government running.

The judicial branch explains the law by ruling whether laws are constitutional. Another function of the judiciary is to try cases. At the top of the judicial branch is the Supreme Court, whose nine members are appointed for life by the President (subject to confirmation by the Senate). Below this court are various federal courts.

The following chart shows the structure of the U.S. government:

HOW A BILL BECOMES LAW

First Reading

To become law, a bill is introduced by a senator or representative in the Senate or Congress. Next the bill is assigned a number or title by the clerk of the House. Then the bill is assigned to the committee of the Senate or House of Representatives that is responsible for the particular area to which the bill relates. For example, a bill providing aid to farmers goes to the Committee on Agriculture. The committee debates the bill, listens to the opinions of interested people and members of the Congress, and sometimes offers amendments or additions to the bill. The bill is then voted on by the committee. If it is passed, the bill is sent back to the clerk of the House of Representatives. If the bill is unacceptable to the committee when they receive it, they may table it, stopping consideration of the bill. This process is called the first reading of the bill.

Second and Third Readings

In the second reading, the clerk of the House of Representatives reads the bill to the House. Then the House debates it and suggests amendments. At the third reading, after the bill is debated, a vote is called for and the title of the bill is read before the vote.

Passage

If the bill passes in the Senate, it is sent to the House of Representatives. There it is again debated, amendments are added, and members vote for or against it. If the bill passes with amendments, a joint congressional committee (composed of members of both the House and Senate) tries to reach a compromise between the two versions of the bill. If the bill is not passed by the second house, it dies.

Government Structure

The chart below shows the structure of the U.S. Government and its departments and agencies as of July 1, 1985. As the chart shows, the Constitution established the organization of the government, which operates on a system of checks and balances. The three branches of government, the legislative, executive, and judicial, each have the power to check the other. The legislative branch, the Congress, has the power to propose and make laws. The executive branch contains the office of the President. The president has the ultimate power to enforce the law and oversee the government. The judicial branch rules on the constitutionality of laws and tries cases.

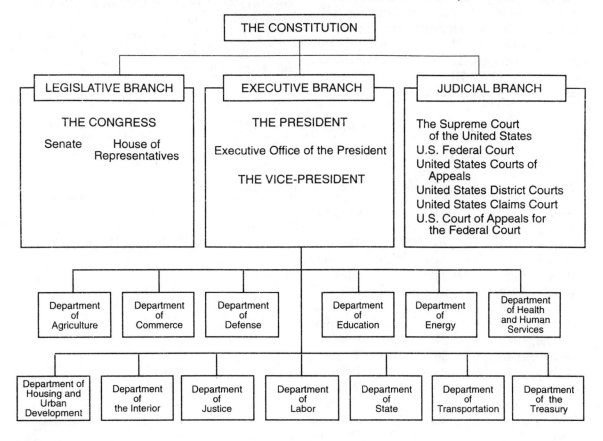

Veto Power

After the bill is passed, it is sent to the President, who has the power to veto it. He may send the bill back to the house that originally produced it, offering his suggestions for change. If the President signs the bill, it becomes a law.

Once it is back in the house, the bill is debated again in relation to the President's comments. Then a roll-call vote is taken. To remain active, the bill must receive at least a two-thirds vote of support from that house. If it does not, the bill is defeated. If the bill is supported by two-thirds of that house, it is sent to the other house. There it again must receive a vote of two-thirds to override a presidential veto.

The bill is returned to the President. If the President holds on to the bill for 10 days (not including Sunday), it automatically becomes law without his signature. The President may still kill the bill through a *pocket veto* if Congress has adjourned within those 10 days.

THE UNITED STATES FLAG

The Italian sea captain John Cabot, sailing for England, raised the first flag over what is now the United States, in 1497. By 1707, each colony had its own flag. The first flag for all the colonies was probably raised in Boston at the Battle of Bunker Hill (1775) during the American Revolution. This flag had the cross of the British flag in the upper left corner and 13 red and white horizontal and alternating stripes. At the Second Continental Congress (1775–76), delegates decided to add thirteen white stars on a field of blue.

In 1794, Congress voted to add two stripes and two stars to represent the new states of Vermont and Kentucky. By 1818 five more states had joined. That same year Congress voted to keep the number of stripes at 13, in honor of the original 13 colonies, but to add a star for every new state. This star is added on the July 4th following the admission of the state to the Union.

The following chart shows the order in which states joined the Union after the original 13 colonies:

The U.S. Flag: 1777–1960

Date	Number of Stars	States Represented
June 14, 1777	13	Original 13 colonies
May 1, 1795	15	Vermont, Kentucky
July 4, 1818	20	Tennessee, Ohio, Louisiana, Indiana, Mississippi
July 4, 1819	21	Illinois
July 4, 1820	23	Alabama, Maine
July 4, 1822	24	Missouri
July 4, 1836	25	Arkansas
July 4, 1837	26	Michigan
July 4, 1845	27	Florida
July 4, 1846	28	Texas
July 4, 1847	29	Iowa
July 4, 1848	30	Wisconsin
July 4, 1851	31	California
July 4, 1858	32	Minnesota
July 4, 1859	33	Oregon
July 4, 1861	34	Kansas
July 4, 1863	35	West Virginia
July 4, 1865	36	Nevada
July 4, 1867	37	Nebraska
July 4, 1877	38	Colorado
July 4, 1890	43	North Dakota, South Dakota, Montana, Washington, Idaho
July 4, 1891	44	Wyoming
July 4, 1986	45	Utah
July 4, 1908	46	Oklahoma
July 4, 1912	48	New Mexico, Arizona
July 4, 1959	49	Alaska
July 4, 1960	50	Hawaii

How to Fly the Flag

The main requirement for flying the U.S. flag is to treat it with respect. Here are some ways to show this respect:

- Fly the flag only in good weather.
- Fly it on all holidays and special occasions.
- Fly it at noon on Memorial Day.
- Never let the flag touch the ground.
- Raise the flag quickly and lower it slowly.

- Salute the flag when it passes in a parade or review, when it is being raised or lowered, during the playing of the national anthem, and while reciting the Pledge of Allegiance. The proper way to salute is to stand at attention and place your hand over your heart.

UNITED STATES PRESIDENTS AND VICE PRESIDENTS

Here is a list of American presidents and the vice presidents who have served with them:

President	Term	Years of Birth and Death	Party*	Vice President	Congresses
1. George Washington	4/30/1789–3/3/1797	1732–1799	F	John Adams	1, 2, 3, 4
2. John Adams	3/4/1797–3/3/1801	1735–1826	F	Thomas Jefferson	5, 6
3. Thomas Jefferson	3/4/1801–3/3/1805	1743–1826	D-R	Aaron Burr	7, 8
	3/4/1805–3/3/1809			George Clinton	9, 10
4. James Madison	3/4/1809–3/3/1813	1751–1836	D-R	George Clinton	11, 12
	3/4/1813–3/3/1817			Elbridge Gerry	13, 14
5. James Monroe	3/4/1817–3/3/1821	1758–1831	D-R	Daniel D. Tompkins	15, 16, 17, 18
	3/4/1821–3/3/1825				
6. John Quincy Adams	3/4/1825–3/3/1829	1767–1848	D-R	John C. Calhoun	19, 20
7. Andrew Jackson	3/4/1829–3/3/1833	1767–1845	D-R	John C. Calhoun	21, 22
	3/4/1833–3/3/1837			Martin Van Buren	23, 24
8. Martin Van Buren	3/4/1837–3/3/1841	1782–1862	D	Richard M. Johnson	25, 26
9. William Henry Harrison	3/4/1841–4/4/1841	1773–1841	W	John Tyler	27
10. John Tyler	4/6/1841–3/3/1845	1790–1862	W	—	27, 28
11. James K. Polk	3/4/1845–3/3/1849	1795–1849	D	George M. Dallas	29, 30
12. Zachary Taylor	3/4/1850–7/9/1850	1784–1850	W	Millard Fillmore	31
13. Millard Fillmore	7/10/1850–	1800–1874	W	—	31, 32

(*continued*)

President	Term	Years of Birth and Death	Party*	Vice President	Congresses
14. Franklin Pierce	3/3/1853 3/4/1853– 3/3/1857	1804–1869	D	William R. King	33, 34
15. James Buchanan	3/4/1857– 3/3/1861	1791–1868	D	John C. Breckinridge	35, 36
16. Abraham Lincoln	3/4/1861– 3/3/1865	1809–1865	R	Hannibal Hamlin	37, 38
	3/4/1865– 4/15/1865			Andrew Johnson	39
17. Andrew Johnson	4/15/1865– 3/3/1869	1808–1875	NU	—	39, 40
18. Ulysses S. Grant	3/4/1869– 3/3/1873	1822–1885	R	Schuyler Colfax	41, 42
	3/4/1873– 3/3/1877			Henry Wilson	43, 44
19. Rutherford B. Hayes	3/4/1877– 3/3/1881	1822–1893	R	William A. Wheeler	45, 46
20. James Garfield	3/4/1881– 9/19/1881	1831–1881	R	Chester A. Arthur	47
21. Chester A. Arthur	9/20/1881– 3/3/1885	1829–1886	R	—	47, 48
22. Grover Cleveland	3/4/1885– 3/3/1889	1837–1908	D	Thomas A. Hendricks	49, 50
23. Benjamin Harrison	3/4/1889– 3/3/1893	1833–1901	R	Levi P. Morton	51, 52
24. Grover Cleveland	3/4/1893– 3/3/1897	1837–1908	D	Adlai E. Stevenson	53, 54
25. William McKinley	3/4/1897– 3/3/1901	1843–1901	R	Garret A. Hobart	55, 56
	3/4/1901– 9/14/1901			Theodore Roosevelt	57
26. Theodore Roosevelt	9/14/1901– 3/3/1905	1858–1919	R	—	57, 58
	3/4/1905– 3/3/1909			Charles W. Fairbanks	59, 60
27. William H. Taft	3/4/1909– 3/3/1913	1857–1930	R	James S. Sherman	61, 62
28. Woodrow Wilson	3/4/1913– 3/3/1917 3/14/1917– 3/3/1921	1856–1924	D	Thomas R. Marshall	63, 64, 65, 66
29. Warren G. Harding	3/4/1921– 8/2/1923	1865–1923	R	Calvin Coolidge	67
30. Calvin Coolidge	8/3/1923– 3/3/1925	1872–1933	R	—	68
	3/4/1925– 3/3/1929			Charles G. Dawes	69, 70
31. Herbert C. Hoover	3/4/1929– 3/3/1933	1874–1964	R	Charles Curtis	71, 72

President	Term	Years of Birth and Death	Party*	Vice President	Congresses
32. Franklin D. Roosevelt	3/4/1933– 1/20/1941	1882–1845	D	John N. Garner	73, 74, 75, 76
	1/20/1941– 1/20/1945			Henry A. Wallace	77, 78
	1/20/1945– 4/12/1945			Harry S Truman	79
33. Harry S Truman	4/12/1945– 1/20/1949	1844–1972	D	—	79, 80
	1/20/1949– 1/20/1953			Alben W. Barkley	81, 82
34. Dwight D. Eisenhower	1/20/1953– 1/20/1961	1890–1969	R	Richard M. Nixon	83, 84, 85, 86
35. John F. Kennedy	1/20/1961– 11/22/1963	1917–1963	D	Lyndon B. Johnson	87, 88
36. Lyndon B. Johnson	11/22/1963– 1/20/1965	1908–1973	D	—	88
	1/20/1965– 1/20/1969			Hubert H. Humphrey	89, 90
37. Richard M. Nixon	1/20/1969– 1/20/1973	1913–	R	Spiro T. Agnew	91, 92, 93
	1/20/1973– 8/9/1974			Gerald R. Ford	93
38. Gerald R. Ford	8/9/1974– 1/20/1977	1913–	R	Nelson A. Rockefeller	93, 94
39. James Carter	1/20/1977– 1/20/81	1924–	D	Walter F. Mondale	95, 96
40. Ronald Reagan	1/20/1981– 1/20/1985 1/20/1985– 1/20/1989	1911–	R	George Bush	97, 98
41. George Bush	1/20/1989– 1/20/1993	1924–	R	J. Danforth Quayle	101, 102
42. William Clinton	1/20/1993– 1/20/1997	1946–	D	Albert Gore, Jr.	103

* F = Federalist; D-R = Democratic-Republican; D = Democrat; W = Whig; R = Republican; NU = National Union Party, a coalition of Republicans and War Democrats (Andrew Johnson was a Democrat).

Who Becomes President If the President Dies or Is Impeached?

The law provides for an orderly succession to the office of President of the United States. Any successor must meet the requirements for the office as established in the Constitution.

The Sequence of Presidential Succession
1. Vice President
2. Speaker of the House
3. President Pro Tempore of the Senate
4. Secretary of State
5. Secretary of the Treasury
6. Secretary of Defense
7. Attorney General

8. Secretary of the Interior
9. Secretary of Agriculture
10. Secretary of Commerce
11. Secretary of Labor
12. Secretary of Health and Human Services
13. Secretary of Housing and Urban Development
14. Secretary of Transportation
15. Secretary of Energy
16. Secretary of Education

POPULATION

For much of its history, the United States has been a nation with a broadly mixed population. For this reason, historians began calling America a nation of immigrants or a melting pot. This description is even more true today than it was before.

The last counting of the American people was conducted by the Department of Commerce, Bureau of the Census, in 1990. The following tables show that the United States has a racially and ethnically mixed population. According to the 1990 census, the population has risen 9.8 percent, from 226.5 million to 248.7 million since the previous census taken in 1980. The following tables were drawn primarily from the Bureau of the Census, and show the most accurate data available of the population by race, sex, age, and region.

Total U.S. Population by Age, Sex, and Race

(Numbers in Thousands)

	Birth to 14	15 to 29	30 to 44	45 to 59	60 to 79	80 and over	All ages
WHITE							
Male	21,548	25,638	23,018	14,406	13,403	1,795	99,808
Female	20,444	25,012	23,000	15,198	16,949	3,890	104,493
BLACK							
Male	4,048	4,084	2,756	1,596	1,254	173	13,892
Female	3,937	4,278	3,234	1,950	1,685	299	15,414
SPANISH ORIGIN							
Male	2,843	2,909	1,978	965	468*	NA	9,294
Female	2,733	1,950	1,951	1,052	578*	NA	9,208
OTHER RACES							
Male	1,017	1,018	878	434	280	34	3,661
Female	990	977	957	498	344	49	3,811
ALL PERSONS							
Male	26,612	30,741	26,653	16,436	14,939	1,981	117,360
Female	25,371	30,297	27,190	16,646	18,978	4,237	123,718

* Indicates that some figures are not available within this age group.
NA = Not available.

Population of States

State	1990 Population	Percent Change 1980–90	Minority Population 1990	Minority Percent Change 1980–90
United States	248,709,873	9.8%	60,581,577	30.9%
California	29,760,021	25.7	12,730,895	61.1
New York	17,990,455	2.5	5,530,266	25.9
Texas	16,986,510	19.4	6,694,830	37.2
Florida	12,937,926	32.7	3,462,600	52.3
Pennsylvania	11,881,643	0.1	1,459,585	13.3
Illinois	11,430,602	0.0	2,880,394	14.5
Ohio	10,847,115	0.5	1,402,493	10.4
Michigan	9,295,297	0.4	1,645,346	11.4
New Jersey	7,730,188	5.0	2,011,222	30.7
North Carolina	6,628,637	12.7	1,657,510	14.1
Georgia	6,478,216	18.6	1,934,791	24.9
Virginia	6,187,358	15.7	1,485,708	27.3
Massachusetts	6,016,425	4.9	736,133	66.2
Indiana	5,544,159	1.0	578,917	7.9
Missouri	5,117,073	4.1	668,608	10.5
Wisconsin	4,891,769	4.0	427,092	42.3
Tennessee	4,877,185	6.2	849,554	9.2
Washington	4,866,692	17.8	645,070	58.8
Maryland	4,781,468	13.4	1,455,359	32.2
Minnesota	4,375,099	7.3	273,833	71.7
Louisiana	4,219,973	0.3	1,443,951	5.8
Alabama	4,040,587	3.8	1,080,420	4.1
Kentucky	3,685,296	0.7	307,274	1.7
Arizona	3,665,228	34.8	1,039,043	50.2
South Carolina	3,486,703	11.7	1,096,647	10.8
Colorado	3,294,394	14.0	635,449	27.2
Connecticut	3,287,116	5.8	532,932	43.2
Oklahoma	3,145,585	4.0	597,997	31.6
Oregon	2,842,321	7.9	262,589	48.3
Iowa	2,776,755	−4.7	112,915	24.8
Mississippi	2,573,216	2.1	949,018	3.5
Kansas	2,477,574	4.8	287,050	27.5
Arkansas	2,350,725	2.8	417,643	2.7
West Virginia	1,793,477	−8.0	74,581	−13.3
Utah	1,722,850	17.9	151,596	37.1
Nebraska	1,578,385	0.5	118,290	25.2
New Mexico	1,515,069	16.3	750,905	21.7
Maine	1,227,928	9.2	24,571	30.7
Nevada	1,201,833	50.1	255,476	90.5
New Hampshire	1,109,252	20.5	29,768	97.1

(*continued*)

Population of States (*continued*)

State	1990 Population	Percent Change 1980–90	Minority Population 1990	Minority Percent Change 1980–90
Hawaii	1,108,229	14.9	760,585	14.4
Idaho	1,006,749	6.7	78,088	35.2
Rhode Island	1,003,464	5.9	107,355	71.8
Montana	799,065	1.6	65,187	24.7
South Dakota	696,004	0.8	61,216	14.9
Delaware	666,168	12.1	138,076	24.2
North Dakota	638,800	−2.1	37,208	26.1
District of Columbia	606,900	−4.9	440,769	−7.0
Vermont	562,758	10.0	10,574	39.4
Alaska	550,043	36.9	143,321	47.4
Wyoming	453,588	−3.4	40,877	8.7

* Note: "Minority" includes African-Americans, Asians, Hispanics, and other races.

STATE GOVERNMENTS

Just like the federal government, all states have legislative, judicial, and executive branches. In each state, the legislature makes state laws; the judiciary, or court system, enforces and interprets these laws; and the executive, headed by the Governor, administers them.

In most states, the lawmaking body is divided into two houses. The upper house is generally called the senate, and the lower house the house of representatives. The one exception is Nebraska, where there is only one house and officials are called senators. State senators are elected every four years. Representatives, or assembly members, are elected every two years. The following table shows the name of each of the 50 states, the year it became a state, the official U.S. Postal Service abbreviation, the state capital, and the name of the lawmaking body.

State Facts

State	Date Entered Union	Postal Abbreviation	Capital	Name of Lawmaking Body
Alabama	1819	AL	Montgomery	Legislature
Alaska	1959	AK	Juneau	Legislature
Arizona	1912	AZ	Phoenix	Legislature
Arkansas	1836	AR	Little Rock	General Assembly
California	1850	CA	Sacramento	Legislature[1]
Colorado	1876	CO	Denver	General Assembly
Connecticut	1788	CT	Hartford	General Assembly
Delaware	1787	DE	Dover	General Assembly
Florida	1845	FL	Tallahassee	Legislature
Georgia	1788	GA	Atlanta	General Assembly

State	Date Entered Union	Postal Abbreviation	Capital	Name of Lawmaking Body
Hawaii	1959	HI	Honolulu	Legislature
Idaho	1890	ID	Boise	Legislature
Illinois	1818	IL	Springfield	General Assembly
Indiana	1816	IN	Indianapolis	General Assembly
Iowa	1846	IA	Des Moines	General Assembly
Kansas	1861	KS	Topeka	Legislature
Kentucky	1792	KY	Frankfort	General Assembly
Louisiana	1812	LA	Baton Rouge	Legislature
Maine	1820	ME	Augusta	Legislature
Maryland	1788	MD	Annapolis	General Assembly[2]
Massachusetts	1788	MA	Boston	General Court
Michigan	1837	MI	Lansing	Legislature
Minnesota	1858	MN	St. Paul	Legislature
Mississippi	1817	MS	Jackson	Legislature
Missouri	1821	MO	Jefferson City	General Assembly
Montana	1889	MT	Helena	Legislative Assembly
Nebraska	1867	NE	Lincoln	Legislature
Nevada	1864	NV	Carson City	Legislature[1]
New Hampshire	1788	NH	Concord	General Court
New Jersey	1787	NJ	Trenton	Legislature[3]
New Mexico	1912	NM	Santa Fe	Legislature
New York	1788	NY	Albany	Legislature[1]
North Carolina	1789	NC	Raleigh	General Assembly
North Dakota	1889	ND	Bismarck	Legislative Assembly
Ohio	1803	OH	Columbus	General Assembly
Oklahoma	1907	OK	Oklahoma City	Legislature
Oregon	1859	OR	Salem	Legislative Assembly
Pennsylvania	1787	PA	Harrisburg	General Assembly
Rhode Island	1790	RI	Providence	General Assembly
South Carolina	1788	SC	Columbia	General Assembly
South Dakota	1889	SD	Pierre	Legislature
Tennessee	1796	TN	Nashville	General Assembly
Texas	1845	TX	Austin	Legislature
Utah	1896	UT	Salt Lake City	Legislature
Vermont	1791	VT	Montpelier	General Assembly
Virginia	1788	VA	Richmond	General Assembly[2]
Washington	1889	WA	Olympia	Legislature
West Virginia	1863	WV	Charleston	Legislature[2]
Wisconsin	1848	WI	Madison	Legislature[1]
Wyoming	1890	WY	Cheyenne	Legislature

[1] The lower house is called the Assembly.
[2] The lower house is called the House of Delegates.
[3] The lower house is called the General Assembly.

TERRITORIES AND COMMONWEALTHS

A territory is a geographical area that is governed by another country, but keeps some degree of independence. A commonwealth is a political unit that has control over its local affairs yet is united by choice with another country. The following lists contain information about all U.S. territories and Commonwealths.

Name	Date Acquired	Abbreviation	Capital	Legislature
American Samoa	1899	AS	Pago Pago	Legislature
Canal Zone		CZ	Balboa Heights	Canal Zone Government
Guam	1950	GU	Agana	Legislature*
Midway Islands	1867	—		Administered by U.S. Navy
Northern Mariana Islands	1947	CM	Saipan	Legislature
Puerto Rico	1898	PR	San Juan	Legislative Assembly
Virgin Islands	1927	VI	Charlotte Amalie	Legislature*
Wake Islands	1899	—		Administered by U.S. Air Force

* Legislatures have only one house.

FLOWERS, BIRDS, MOTTOS, AND NICKNAMES

Every state has its own official designations, as the following list shows:

State	Flower	Bird	Motto	Nickname
Alabama	Camellia	Yellowhammer	We dare defend our rights	Heart of Dixie; Camellia State
Alaska	Forget-me-not	Willow ptarmigan	North to the future	The Last Frontier
Arizona	Saguaro	Cactus wren	Diat Deus (God enriches)	Grand Canyon State
Arkansas	Apple blossom	Mockingbird	Regnat populus (The people rule)	Land of Opportunity
California	Golden poppy	California valley quail	Eureka (I have found it)	Golden State
Colorado	Blue columbine	Lark bunting	Nil sine numine (Nothing without providence)	Centenial State
Connecticut	Mountain laurel	American robin	Qui transtulit sustinet (He who transplanted still sustains)	Constitution State; Nutmeg State
Delaware	Peach blossom	Blue hen chicken	Liberty and independence	First State; Diamond State

State	Flower	Bird	Motto	Nickname
District of Columbia	American Beauty rose	Wood thrush	Justitia Omnibus (Justice for all)	Capital City
Florida	Orange blossom	Mockingbird	In God we trust	Sunshine State
Georgia	Cherokee rose	Brown thrasher	Wisdom, justice, and moderation	Empire State of the South; Peace State
Hawaii	Hibiscus	Nene goose	The life of the land is perpetuated in righteousness	Aloha State
Idaho	Syringa	Mountain bluebird	Esto perpetua (It is perpetual)	Gem State
Illinois	Native violet	Cardinal	State sovereignty— national union	Prairie State
Indiana	Peony	Cardinal	Crossroads of America	Hoosier State
Iowa	Wild rose	Goldfinch	Our liberties we prize and our rights we will maintain	Hawkeye State
Kansas	Sunflower	Western meadowlark	Ad astra per aspera (To the stars through difficulties)	Sunflower State
Kentucky	Goldenrod	Kentucky cardinal	United we stand, divided we fall	Bluegrass State
Louisiana	Magnolia	Eastern brown pelican	Union, justice and confidence	Pelican State
Maine	Pine cone and tassel	Chickadee	Dirigo (I direct)	Pine Tree State
Maryland	Black-eyed Susan	Baltimore oriole	Fatti maschii, parole femine (Manly deeds, womanly words)	Old Line State; Free State
Massachusetts	Mayflower	Chickadee	Ense petit placidam sub libertate (By the sword we seek peace, but peace only under liberty)	Bay State; Colony State
Michigan	Apple	Robin	Si quaeris peninsulam amoenam (If you seek a pleasant peninsula, look about you)	Great Lake State; Wolverine State
Minnesota	Showy lady slipper	Common loon	L'Etoile du nord (Star of the north)	North Star State; Gopher State

(continued)

FLOWERS, BIRDS, MOTTOS, AND NICKNAMES (*continued*)

State	Flower	Bird	Motto	Nickname
Mississippi	Magnolia	Mockingbird	Virtute et armis (By valor and arms)	Magnolia State
Missouri	Hawthorn	Bluebird	Salus populi suprema lex esto (The welfare of the people shall be the surpeme law)	Show-Me State
Montana	Bitterroot	Western meadowlark	Oro y plata (Gold and silver)	Treasure State
Nebraska	Goldenrod	Meadowlark	Equality before the law	Cornhusker State
Nevada	Sagebrush	Mountain bluebird	All for our country	Sagebrush State; Battle-Born State
New Hampshire	Purple lilac	Purple finch	Live free or die	Granite State
New Jersey	Purple violet	Eastern goldfinch	Liberty and prosperity	Garden State
New Mexico	Yucca	Roadrunner	Crescit eundo (It grows as it goes)	Land of Enchantment
New York	Rose (any color)	Bluebird	Excelsior (Ever upward)	Empire State
North Carolina	Dogwood	Cardinal	Esse quam videri (To be rather than to seem)	Tar Heel State; Old North State
North Dakota	Wild prairie rose	Western meadowlark	Liberty and union, now and forever, one and inseparable	Peace Garden State
Ohio	Scarlet carnation	Cardinal	With God, all things are possible	Buckeye State
Oklahoma	Mistletoe	Scissor-tailed flycatcher	Labor omnia vincit (Labor conquers all things)	Sooner State
Oregon	Oregon grape	Western meadowlark	The union	Beaver State
Pennsylvania	Mountain laurel	Ruffed grouse	Virtue, liberty and independence	Keystone State
Rhode Island	Violet	Rhode Island hen	Hope	Little Rhody; Ocean State
South Carolina	Carolina jessamine	Carolina wren	Dum spiro spero (While I breathe, I hope)	Palmetto State
South Dakota	Pasqueflower	Pheasant	Under God, the people rule	Coyote State; Sunshine State
Tennessee	Iris	Mockingbird	Agriculture and commerce	Volunteer State

State	Flower	Bird	Motto	Nickname
Texas	Bluebonnet	Mockingbird	Friendship	Lone Star State
Utah	Sego Lily	Seagull	Industry	Beehive State
Vermont	Red clover	Thrush	Freedom and unity	Green Mountain State
Virginia	Flowering dogwood	Cardinal	Sic semper tyrannis (Thus always to tyrants)	Old Dominion
Washington	Rhododendron	Willow goldfinch	Alki (By and by)	Evergreen State
West Virginia	Big rhododendron	Cardinal	Montani semper liberi (Mountaineers are always free)	Mountain State
Wisconsin	Wood violet	Robin	Forward	Badger State
Wyoming	Indian paintbrush	Meadowlark	Equal rights	Equality State

Flowers, Birds, Mottos, and Nicknames of Territories and Commonwealths

Name	Flower	Bird	Motto
American Samoa	Paogo (Ula-fala)		Samoa Muamua le Atua (In Samoa, God is first)
Guam	Puti tai nobio (bougainvillea)	Toto (fruit dove)	Where America's day begins
Puerto Rico	Maga	Reinita	Joannes est nomen eius (John is his name)
Virgin Islands	Yellow elder or yellow trumpet	Yellow breast	—

HOW THE STATES GOT THEIR NAMES

Like people, states had to be named. The following list tells how each state, including your own, got its name:

Alabama Originally the name for "tribal town," the territory of Alabama was later the home of the Alabama, or Alibamon, Indians of the Creek confederacy.

Alaska The Russians adopted the word meaning "great lands" or "land that is not an island" from the Aleutian word *alakshak*.

Arizona The Spanish coined the name either from the Pima Indian word meaning "little spring place" or from the Aztec *arizuma*, meaning "silver-bearing."

Arkansas Once the territory of the Siouan Quapaw (downstream people). *Arkansas* is the French derivative of this Indian name.

California The name of a fictional earthly paradise in *Las Serged de Esplandian*, a sixteenth-century Spanish romance. It is believed that Spanish conquistadors named this state.

Colorado A Spanish word for "red." The name *Colorado* first referred to the Colorado River.

Connecticut The Algonquin and Mohican Indian word for "long river place."

Delaware This version of the name of Lord

De La Warr, a governor of Virginia, was first used to name the Delaware River. It was later used by the Europeans to rename the local Indians, originally called the Lenni-Lenape.

District of Columbia Named for Christopher Columbus in 1791.

Florida In his search for the "Fountain of Youth," Ponce de Leon named this region "flowery Easter" or "feast of flowers" on Easter Sunday, 1513.

Georgia Named for King George II of England, who granted James Oglethorpe a charter to found the colony of Georgia in 1732.

Hawaii Commonly believed to be an English adaptation of the native word for "homeland," *hawaiki* or *owhyhee.*

Idaho A name coined by the state, meaning "gem of the mountains" or "light on the mountains." Originally the name *Idaho* was to be used for the Pike's Peak mining territory in Colorado, and later for the mining territory of the Pacific Northwest. Others believe the name comes from the Kiowa Apache word for the Comanche.

Illinois From the French version of the Algonquin word meaning "men" or "soldiers," *Illini.*

Indiana English-speaking settlers named the territory to mean "land of the Indians."

Iowa The Sioux word for "one who puts to sleep" or "beautiful land."

Kansas Derived from the Sioux word for those who lived south (the "south wind people") of their territory, which was mainly Wisconsin, Iowa, Minnesota, and North and South Dakota.

Kentucky Originally the term for the Kentucky Plains in Clark County, *Kentucky* is believed to derive from the Indian word meaning "dark and bloody ground," "meadow land," or "land of tomorrow."

Louisiana Present-day Louisiana is just a small part of the territory that was named for the French king Louis XIV by Sieur de La Salle.

Maine Originally a French territory, *Maine* was the ancient French word for "province." It is also believed that it refers to the mainland, as distinct from the many islands off the state's coast.

Maryland Named for Queen Henrietta Maria, wife of Charles I of England.

Massachusetts The name of the Indian tribe that lived near Milton, Massachusetts, meaning "large hill place."

Michigan Believed to be from the Chippewa word *micigama*, meaning "great water," after Lake Michigan, although Alouet defined it in 1672 as a clearing.

Minnesota Named from the Sioux description of the Minnesota River, "sky-tinted water" or "muddy water."

Mississippi Probably derived from the Chippewa words *mici* (great) and *zibi* (river). It was first written by explorer La Salle's lieutenant Henri de Tonti as "Michi Sepe."

Missouri Meaning "muddy water," this state is named after an Algonquin Indian tribe.

Montana Derived from the Latin word meaning "mountainous."

Nebraska Descriptive of the Platte River, *Nebraska* is from the Omaha or Otos Indian word for "broad water" or "flat river."

Nevada Spanish word meaning "snowclad."

New Hampshire Captain John Mason named this colony for his home county in England in 1629.

New Jersey Named after the Isle of Jersey in England by John Berkeley and Sir George Carteret.

New Mexico Named by the Spanish for the territory north and west of the Rio Grande.

New York Originally named New Netherland. New York was later named after the Duke of York and Albany, who received a patent to the region from his brother Charles II of England and captured it from the Dutch in 1644.

North Carolina From the Latin name *Carolus*, meaning "Charles." The colony was originally given to Sir Robert Heath by Charles I and was to be called Province of Carolana. Carolana was divided into North and South Carolina in 1710.

North Dakota From the Sioux word meaning "friend" or "ally."

Ohio From an Iroquois Indian word variously meaning "great," "fine," or "good river."

Oklahoma The Choctaw Indian word meaning "red man," which was coined by the Reverend Allen Wright, a Choctaw-speaking Indian.

Oregon Though its exact origin is unclear, one theory maintains that it may have been a variation on the name of the Wisconsin River, which was called *Ouaricon-sint* on a French map dated 1715. Later, the English explorer Major Robert Rogers named a river "called by the Indians Ouragon" in his request to seek a Northwest Passage from the Great Lakes. Another theory derives the word from the Algonquin *wauregan*, meaning "beautiful water."

Pennsylvania Named after the colony's founder, the Quaker William Penn. The translation is "Penn's woods."

Rhode Island Possibly named by Giovanni de Verrazano, who charted an island about the size of the island of Rhodes in the Mediterranean. Another theory suggests Rhode Island was named Roode Eylandt by Dutch explorer Adrian Block because of its red clay.

South Carolina *See* **North Carolina.**

South Dakota *See* **North Dakota.**

Tennessee The state of Franklin, or Frankland, from 1784 to 1788, it was finally named after the Cherokee villages called *tanasi* on the Little Tennessee River.

Texas Also written *texias, tejas,* and *teysas, Texas* is a variation on the Caddo Indian word for "friend" or "ally."

Utah Meaning "upper" or "higher," *Utah* is derived from a name used by the Navajos (Utes) to designate a Shoshone tribe.

Vermont It is believed Samuel de Champlain coined the name from the French words *vert* (green) and *mont* (mountain). Later, Dr. Thomas Young suggested this name when the state was formed in 1777.

Virginia Named for the Virgin Queen of England, Queen Elizabeth I, by Sir Walter Raleigh, who first visited its shores in 1584.

Washington Originally named the Territory of Columbia, it was changed to *Washington* in honor of the first U.S. President because of the already existing District of Columbia.

West Virginia Named when this area refused to secede from the Union in 1863.

Wisconsin A Chippewa word that was spelled *Ouisconsin* and *Mesconsing* by early explorers. Wisconsin was formally named by Congress when it became a state.

Wyoming The Algonquin word meaning "large prairie place," the name was adopted from Wyoming Valley, Pennsylvania, the site of an Indian massacre. It was widely known from Thomas Campbell's poem "Gertrude of Wyoming."

WEATHER CHARTS

Average Precipitation for Selected Cities (in inches)

State	City	Jan/Feb	Mar/Apr	May/Jun	Jul/Aug	Sep/Oct	Nov/Dec
Alabama	Mobile	4.8	6	5.3	7.3	4.6	4.6
Alaska	Juneau	3.7	3.1	3.2	4.6	7.0	5.0

(continued)

Average Precipitation for Selected Cities (in inches) (*continued*)

State	City	Jan/Feb	Mar/Apr	May/Jun	Jul/Aug	Sep/Oct	Nov/Dec
Arizona	Phoenix	0.7	0.6	0.2	0.4	0.6	0.7
California	Los Angeles	3.4	1.8	0.1	0.03	0.3	2.0
	San Francisco	4.0	2.1	0.2	0.08	0.7	3.0
Colorado	Denver	0.6	1.5	2.1	1.7	1.1	0.7
Connecticut	Hartford	3.4	4.1	3.4	3.6	3.7	4.2
Delaware	Wilmington	3.1	3.7	3.4	4.0	3.3	3.4
District of Columbia		2.7	3.3	3.9	4.0	3.2	3.2
Florida	Jacksonville	3.3	3.5	5.2	6.9	5.4	2.3
	Miami	2.1	2.5	7.9	6.5	7.6	2.3
Georgia	Altanta	4.7	5.2	3.7	4.1	2.9	3.8
Hawaii	Honolulu	3.3	2.5	0.9	0.6	1.3	3.3
Idaho	Boise	1.4	1.1	1.1	0.4	0.7	1.3
Illinois	Chicago	1.5	3.2	3.7	3.6	2.9	2.1
Indiana	Indianapolis	2.6	3.7	3.9	3.9	2.6	3.0
Iowa	Des Moines	1.1	2.7	4.1	3.7	2.7	1.5
Kansas	Dodge City	0.5	1.7	3.2	2.8	1.6	0.7
Kentucky	Louisville	3.3	4.4	3.9	3.7	3.1	3.5
Louisiana	New Orleans	5.1	4.6	4.9	6.4	4.3	4.7
Maine	Portland	3.7	4.0	3.2	2.8	3.6	4.6
Massachusetts	Boston	3.9	3.9	3.2	3.2	3.4	4.6
Michigan	Detroit	1.8	2.9	3.1	3.2	2.2	2.4
Minnesota	Duluth	1.1	2.0	3.6	4.1	2.8	1.5
	Minneapolis	0.9	1.9	3.7	3.6	2.2	1.1
Mississippi	Jackson	5.0	5.9	3.9	4.1	3.1	4.8
Missouri	Kansas City	1.0	2.4	3.8	3.4	2.9	1.2
	St. Louis	1.9	3.5	3.6	3.1	2.5	2.4
Montana	Helena	0.6	0.9	1.9	1.1	0.8	0.6
Nebraska	Omaha	0.9	2.4	4.2	3.9	2.3	1.1
Nevada	Reno	1.1	0.6	0.4	0.3	0.3	0.9
New Jersey	Atlantic City	3.3	3.4	2.9	4.2	2.8	3.5
New Mexico	Albuquerque	0.4	0.5	0.5	1.4	0.9	0.5
New York	Albany	2.4	3.0	3.3	3.2	3.1	3.0
	Buffalo	2.7	3.0	2.8	3.6	3.2	3.5
	New York	3.2	3.9	3.5	3.9	3.6	4.0
North Carolina	Raleigh	3.5	3.3	3.7	4.4	3.0	3.0
North Dakota	Bismarck	0.5	1.1	2.6	1.9	1.1	0.5
Ohio	Cleveland	2.4	3.2	3.4	3.4	2.6	2.8
	Columbus	2.5	3.3	3.9	3.9	2.4	2.6
Oklahoma	Oklahoma City	1.2	2.5	4.7	2.7	2.9	1.4
Oregon	Portland	5.1	3.0	1.8	0.8	2.4	5.8
Pennsylvania	Philadelphia	3.0	3.7	3.6	4.0	3.1	3.4
	Pittsburgh	2.7	3.5	3.4	3.6	2.7	2.5
Rhode Island	Providence	3.9	4.2	3.2	3.5	3.7	4.4
South Carolina	Charleston	3.4	3.5	5.5	6.9	3.9	2.7
South Dakota	Huron	0.6	1.6	3.0	2.2	1.4	0.6
Tennessee	Memphis	4.5	5.6	4.4	3.9	3.0	4.6
	Nashville	4.4	5.2	4.2	3.6	3.2	4.1
Texas	Dallas-Ft. Worth	1.8	3.0	3.5	1.9	2.9	1.8

Average Precipitation for Selected Cities (in inches) (*continued*)

State	City	Jan/Feb	Mar/Apr	May/Jun	Jul/Aug	Sep/Oct	Nov/Dec
	Houston	3.3	3.5	4.4	3.5	4.3	3.6
Utah	Salt Lake City	1.4	2.0	1.3	1.3	0.8	1.0
Vermont	Burlington	1.8	2.6	3.3	3.7	3.0	2.6
Virginia	Norfolk	3.5	3.4	3.7	5.3	3.9	3.1
	Richmond	3.2	3.3	3.6	5.1	3.6	3.4
Washington	Seattle	5.1	3.0	1.5	1.0	2.7	5.6
Wisconsin	Milwaukee	1.5	3.0	3.4	3.3	2.6	2.0
Wyoming	Lander	0.6	1.4	2.1	0.6	1.1	0.7

Average Temperatures and Wind Speeds for Selected Cities

All wind speeds are expressed in miles per hour; temperature is expressed in degrees Fahrenheit. T = temperature; W = wind speed.

State	City	Jan/Feb		Mar/Apr		May/Jun		Jul/Aug		Sep/Oct		Nov/Dec	
		T	W	T	W	T	W	T	W	T	W	T	W
Alabama	Mobile	53	10.6	66	10.7	78	8.3	82	6.8	74	8.1	56	19.2
Alaska	Juneau	25	8.6	35	8.8	50	8.1	56	7.6	46	8.9	30	9.0
Arizona	Phoenix	54	5.6	65	6.9	82	7.0	91	6.9	79	6.1	57	5.2
California	Los Angeles	58	7.0	61	8.3	67	8.1	75	7.7	72	7.0	61	6.5
	San Francisco	51	7.8	54	11.2	59	13.6	63	13.1	63	10.2	52	7.0
Colorado	Denver	33	9.1	43	10.1	62	9.3	72	8.4	58	8.1	36	8.7
Connecticut	Hartford	27	9.5	43	10.1	62	9.3	72	8.4	58	8.1	36	8.7
Delaware	Wilmington	32	10.4	47	10.9	67	9.0	76	7.6	62	8.1	41	9.4
District of Columbia		33	10.3	48	10.8	67	9.0	75	8.2	61	8.5	40	9.5
Florida	Jacksonville	54	8.9	64	9.1	77	8.3	81	7.3	74	8.2	58	8.1
	Miami	68	9.8	74	10.6	80	9.0	83	7.9	80	8.8	71	9.4
Georgia	Atlanta	43	10.8	58	10.5	73	8.3	79	7.3	68	8.2	49	9.5
Hawaii	Honolulu	73	10.3	75	10.2	79	9.4	81	8.4	81	8.4	76	8.5
Illinois	Chicago	24	11.6	43	12.0	64	9.9	73	9.3	60	8.1	34	10.9
Indiana	Indianapolis	28	11.0	46	11.6	68	9.1	74	7.3	61	8.4	37	10.5
Iowa	Des Moines	22	11.8	43	13.1	67	10.9	75	8.9	60	10.0	33	11.5
Kentucky	Louisville	35	9.7	51	10.2	70	7.8	77	6.6	64	7.0	42	9.1
Louisiana	New Orleans	54	9.6	65	9.7	78	7.5	82	6.1	74	7.4	58	8.8
Maine	Portland	23	9.4	38	10.0	58	8.6	68	7.5	54	8.0	32	8.9
Massachusetts	Boston	31	14.2	44	13.6	64	11.8	73	10.8	60	11.7	40	13.3
Michigan	Detroit	25	11.6	41	11.3	63	9.5	72	8.2	58	9.2	35	11.3
Minnesota	Duluth	9	11.7	31	12.4	55	1.4	64	9.7	49	11.0	21	11.6
	Minneapolis	15	10.4	38	11.7	64	10.8	72	9.2	56	10.1	26	10.6
Mississippi	Jackson	48	8.6	61	8.8	76	6.6	82	5.7	71	6.4	52	7.8
Missouri	Kansas City	29	11.3	49	12.4	71	10.1	78	8.8	63	9.5	38	11.1
	St. Louis	32	10.7	50	11.7	71	9.1	78	7.8	64	8.3	40	10.1
Nebraska	Omaha	22	11.2	43	11.8	67	10.7	75	9.0	59	9.7	32	10.8
Nevada	Reno	35	5.9	44	7.8	34	7.6	69	6.5	55	5.4	37	5.2
New Jersey	Atlantic City	35	11.8	47	12.2	64	10.0	74	8.6	63	8.7	43	10.9
New Mexico	Albuquerque	37	8.4	30	10.6	70	10.4	78	8.7	63	8.5	40	7.8
New York	Albany	22	9.7	41	10.7	63	8.7	70	7.3	56	7.8	33	9.2
	Buffalo	25	14.2	39	13.2	61	11.4	70	10.2	57	10.9	35	13.1

(*continued*)

Average Temperatures and Wind Speeds for Selected Cities (*continued*)

All wind speeds are expressed in miles per hour; temperature is expressed in degrees Fahrenheit. T = temperature; W = wind speed.

State	City	Jan/Feb T	W	Mar/Apr T	W	May/Jun T	W	Jul/Aug T	W	Sep/Oct T	W	Nov/Dec T	W
	New York	33	10.8	47	10.8	67	8.5	76	7.7	63	8.5	42	9.7
North Carolina	Raleigh	41	8.8	54	9.3	71	7.4	78	6.5	66	7.0	46	8.0
North Dakota	Bismarck	11	10.1	35	11.7	60	11.3	70	9.4	52	10.1	22	9.8
Ohio	Cleveland	27	12.3	43	12.1	63	9.9	71	8.6	59	9.6	37	12.2
	Columbus	29	10.3	46	10.5	66	8.1	73	6.7	60	7.3	37	9.7
Oklahoma	Oklahoma City	39	13.3	55	14.9	73	12.7	82	10.9	68	11.6	45	12.6
Oregon	Portland	41	9.6	48	7.8	60	7.1	68	7.4	59	6.5	44	9.0
Pennsylvania	Philadelphia	32	10.8	48	11.3	68	9.3	76	8.0	63	8.6	41	9.9
	Pittsburgh	28	10.7	45	10.7	64	8.6	72	7.4	59	8.0	37	10.2
Rhode Island	Providence	29	11.6	43	12.2	63	10.7	72	9.4	59	9.6	38	10.8
Tennessee	Memphis	42	10.4	58	10.9	75	8.5	82	7.3	69	7.7	47	9.6
	Nashville	39	9.3	55	9.8	72	7.4	79	6.3	66	6.5	45	8.7
Texas	Dallas-Ft. Worth	47	11.5	61	12.8	78	10.9	86	9.3	74	9.4	52	10.7
	Houston	53	8.5	65	9.3	78	7.9	83	6.4	74	6.7	57	7.7
Utah	Salt Lake City	32	7.9	45	9.4	37	9.4	77	9.6	59	8.8	35	7.7
Vermont	Burlington	18	9.4	36	9.3	60	8.6	69	7.6	54	8.4	30	9.6
Virginia	Norfolk	41	11.7	54	12.0	72	9.9	78	8.8	67	10.0	48	10.8
	Richmond	38	8.2	53	8.9	70	7.5	78	8.8	65	6.7	45	7.5
Wisconsin	Milwaukee	21	12.8	39	13.1	60	11.2	70	9.6	57	11.0	31	12.5

Average Percentage of Possible Sunshine for Selected Cities

State	City	Jan.	Feb.	Mar.	Apr.	May	June	July	Aug.	Sept.	Oct.	Nov.	Dec.	Annual
Alabama	Montgomery	48	54	59	65	65	65	62	64	62	66	56	50	60
Alaska	Juneau	32	32	37	39	39	34	31	32	26	19	23	20	22
Arizona	Phoenix	78	80	83	88	93	94	85	85	89	88	83	77	85
Arkansas	Little Rock	48	55	59	63	69	74	73	73	69	70	57	49	63
California	Los Angeles	69	72	73	70	66	65	82	83	79	73	74	71	73
	Sacramento	45	61	72	81	88	93	97	96	93	85	63	46	77
	San Francisco	56	62	69	73	72	73	66	65	72	70	62	53	66
Colorado	Denver	71	71	70	68	64	71	72	72	75	72	65	67	70
Connecticut	Hartford	57	58	56	57	58	61	64	63	60	57	47	49	57
Delaware	Wilmington	50	54	56	57	56	62	62	62	59	69	52	49	57
District of Columbia	Washington	48	52	55	58	59	65	64	64	62	59	52	47	57
Florida	Jacksonville	58	61	67	71	69	63	61	60	55	58	60	56	62
	Miami	67	65	77	79	70	75	79	75	72	72	66	67	72
Georgia	Atlanta	49	54	58	65	68	67	63	65	64	68	60	51	61
Hawaii	Honolulu	62	64	68	66	68	70	73	75	75	68	61	58	67
Idaho	Boise	39	50	62	67	71	75	87	84	81	68	44	38	64
Illinois	Chicago	45	51	56	63	65	72	74	76	69	68	52	45	63
	Peoria	46	50	51	54	59	66	68	67	65	61	45	40	56
Indiana	Indianapolis	41	50	50	54	60	66	67	70	66	62	43	39	56
Iowa	Des Moines	51	54	54	55	60	68	72	70	66	62	50	45	59

State	City	Jan.	Feb.	Mar.	Apr.	May	June	July	Aug.	Sept.	Oct.	Nov.	Dec.	An- nual
Kansas	Wichita	59	60	60	63	65	70	75	75	68	66	58	58	65
Kentucky	Louisville	42	48	49	54	61	66	66	67	65	61	47	41	56
Louisiana	New Orleans	48	53	57	63	61	67	62	60	63	67	55	53	59
Maine	Portland	56	59	56	55	55	59	64	64	62	58	48	53	57
Maryland	Baltimore	51	55	55	56	56	62	65	62	60	58	51	48	57
Massachusetts	Boston	53	56	57	57	59	64	67	66	64	60	51	52	59
Michigan	Detroit	32	43	49	52	59	65	70	65	61	56	35	32	54
	Sault Ste. Marie	36	46	54	55	57	58	63	58	45	40	24	27	47
Minnesota	Duluth	49	52	55	55	56	58	65	61	52	46	35	39	52
	Minneapolis-St. Paul	52	58	55	56	60	64	71	68	61	55	39	40	57
Mississippi	Jackson	47	56	59	63	63	70	65	64	61	66	55	49	60
Missouri	Kansas City	59	56	58	64	64	69	74	68	65	60	50	50	61
	St. Louis	52	53	54	56	61	67	71	65	64	60	47	42	58
Montana	Great Falls	49	55	65	61	62	64	79	76	68	60	46	44	61
Nebraska	Omaha	54	53	54	57	60	67	74	71	67	65	51	47	60
Nevada	Reno	65	68	76	81	82	85	92	93	92	83	71	64	79
New Hampshire	Concord	52	55	52	53	54	58	63	60	56	54	42	47	54
New Jersey	Atlantic City	49	51	53	55	54	58	60	63	60	56	49	44	54
New Mexico	Albuquerque	72	73	73	77	80	83	76	76	79	79	77	72	76
New York	Albany	45	51	52	53	55	59	63	60	57	51	36	38	52
	Buffalo	32	38	45	52	58	65	68	64	59	51	29	27	49
	New York	50	55	56	59	61	64	65	64	63	61	52	49	58
North Carolina	Charlotte	55	60	63	69	69	70	68	69	67	68	61	58	65
	Raleigh	54	59	62	63	59	61	61	61	59	61	60	55	60
North Dakota	Bismarck	54	54	59	59	62	64	75	73	66	58	45	47	60
Ohio	Cincinnati	41	44	50	55	60	66	68	66	66	58	44	38	56
	Cleveland	31	37	44	52	58	65	67	63	60	53	32	26	49
	Columbus	36	42	43	52	56	60	60	60	61	56	38	31	49
Oklahoma	Oklahoma City	59	61	64	66	66	74	78	79	72	69	61	58	67
Oregon	Portland	27	37	46	52	58	55	70	65	61	42	29	21	47
Pennsylvania	Philadelphia	50	53	55	56	56	62	62	62	60	59	52	49	56
	Pittsburgh	33	38	44	48	52	57	59	57	58	52	38	29	47
Rhode Island	Providence	56	57	56	56	57	60	63	60	61	60	50	52	57
South Carolina	Columbia	57	61	64	69	68	67	67	68	65	67	65	60	65
South Dakota	Rapid City	55	59	61	59	58	62	72	73	69	65	55	53	62
Tennessee	Memphis	50	54	56	64	69	74	74	75	70	70	58	50	64
	Nashville	41	48	51	58	61	66	64	65	63	63	50	42	56
Texas	Dallas-Ft. Worth	53	58	59	64	64	71	81	77	74	61	62	56	65
	El Paso	77	82	85	87	89	89	80	81	82	84	82	78	83
	Houston	43	51	47	51	57	64	66	64	62	61	53	55	56
Utah	Salt Lake City	46	55	63	67	72	79	83	82	83	72	54	43	67
Vermont	Burlington	41	48	50	49	55	59	64	60	54	48	30	32	49
Virginia	Norfolk	56	59	60	65	65	68	64	65	64	58	58	55	61
	Richmond	53	58	60	65	65	68	66	66	64	60	58	53	61
Washington	Seattle	24	37	49	53	56	54	65	64	59	44	29	20	46

(continued)

Average Percentage of Possible Sunshine for Selected Cities (*continued*)

State	City	Jan.	Feb.	Mar.	Apr.	May	June	July	Aug.	Sept.	Oct.	Nov.	Dec.	An-nual
	Spokane	27	38	53	60	63	65	80	77	70	53	28	21	53
West Virginia	Parkersburg	32	37	44	50	56	59	62	59	59	54	37	30	49
Wisconsin	Milwaukee	44	47	50	53	59	64	70	66	59	55	40	37	54
Wyoming	Cheyenne	62	65	65	61	59	65	68	67	68	68	60	59	64
Puerto Rico	San Juan	66	69	74	68	60	61	67	66	60	61	58	58	64

INFORMATION, PLEASE

Altman, Susan R. *Extraordinary Black Americans: From Colonial to Contemporary Times.* Children's Press, 1989.

Chronicle of America. John W. Kirshon, Editor in Chief. Chronicle Publications, 1989.

DeGregorio, William. *The Complete Book of U.S. Presidents.* 2d ed. Dembner/Norton, 1989.

Dowden, Anne Ophelia. *State Flowers.* Crowell, 1978.

Facts about the States. Edited by Joseph Nathan Kane, Steven Anzovin, and Janet Podell. Wilson, 1989.

Findlay, Bruce A. *Your Rugged Constitution: How American's House of Freedom Is Planned and Built.* Stanford University Press, 1974.

Garraty, John. *The American Nation: A History of the United States.* 6th ed. Harper & Row, 1987.

Gilbert, Martin. *Atlas of American History.* Rev. ed. Dorset Press, 1985.

Lawson, Don. *Landmark Supreme Court Cases.* Enslow, 1987.

National Geographic Picture Atlas of Our Fifty States: 1980. National Geographic Society.

Shearer, Benjamin F. *State Names, Seals, Flags, and Symbols: A Historical Guide.* Greenwood Press, 1987.

Smith, Whitney. *The Flag Book of the United States.* Rev. ed. Morrow, 1975.

Waldman, Carl. *Encyclopedia of Native American Tribes.* Facts On File, 1987.

24

THE WORLD

The world's past is divided into two major periods: history and prehistory. Prehistory refers to the period before people left written records. Humans are believed to have first appeared around 40,000 years ago, but our written history began only about 5,000 years ago.

The study of prehistory is conducted by archaeologists, who search for artifacts, such as pieces of ancient pottery or jewelry, that help them reconstruct what life might have been like in prehistoric times. Historians study the world primarily through the written records that people have left behind.

GREAT EVENTS THAT SHAPED OUR WORLD

Some events have proven to be turning points in the development of human history. The world was a different place after they happened than it was before. The list that follows describes some of the great events in prehistory and history.

What's Prehistory?

Prehistory refers to a time before people knew how to write. Once a people learn to write, they begin to record their story. The study of this story is called history.

The term "prehistory" was first used in the midnineteenth century, when people became intensely interested in two relatively new social sciences called anthropology and archaeology.

Prehistory is generally divided into three periods—the Stone, Bronze, and Iron ages—when western Europeans did not read or write. Not all of the world was illiterate at this time, though. For example, during the Iron Age, Greeks and Romans had advanced civilizations with literature that included stories and poetry.

The study of prehistory is especially important because it helped to date the origins of the first humans. Originally, humans were thought to have appeared around 6,000 years ago, but due to the efforts of archaeologists and anthropologists, the special scientists who study prehistory, and also to such new twentieth-century technologies as radiocarbon dating, social scientists have established that humans have been around for at least 40,000 years. Our *Homo sapiens* ancestors, who resembled us in many ways, are thought to date back 250,000 years.

B.C.

1,600,000	Earliest humanlike ancestors.
250,000	Earliest *Homo sapiens*.
70,000	Neanderthals use stone tools and fire.
40,000	Ice Age ends; Cro-Magnons migrate into Europe.
30,000	Neanderthals disappear.
28,000	Asians cross land bridge between Asia and America.
20,000	European cave art exists.
12,000	Dog domesticated from Asian wolf.
8000	Agriculture develops in Near East.
7000	Jericho settled and soon walled to protect from attack.
6500	Wheel invented by Sumerians.
6000	First true pottery made.
5000	Copper, first shapable metal, smelted (melted and worked) in Persia.
4236	Earliest date on Egyptian calendar.
3760	Earliest date on Jewish calendar.
3600	Bronze made in southwest Asia.

3100	Egypt united under first dynasty.
3000	Phoenicians migrate to eastern Mediterranean.
2780	First Egyptian pyramid built.
2700	Cheops builds Great Pyramid at Giza.
2697	Huang-ti becomes "Yellow Emperor" of China.
2640	Legendary Empress Si Ling-chi introduces silk production in China.
2340	Sargon established Semitic and Sumerian civilizations.
2150	Aryans invade Indus Valley.
2000	Bronze age begins in Europe.
1760	Shang dynasty is founded in China.
1750	Hammurabi, Babylonian king, issues code of laws.
1400	Iron Age begins in Asia.
1250	Exodus of Israelites from Egypt.
1193	Greeks destroy city of Troy.
1100	Pa-out-She, Chinese scholar, compiles first dictionary.
1050	Dorian tribes invade Peloponnesus.
1000	Hebrews establish Jerusalem as capital of Israel.
994	Teutons migrate to Rhine River area.

What's Civilization, and When Does It Begin?

The beginning of *civilization* is often seen as a turning point in human history. But when exactly did we become civilized, that is, when did we begin to live in civilizations? And what did we do before civilizations existed?

Although humans have been on Earth for at least 40,000 years, their lives were very limited. Existence consisted mostly of wandering from place to place to search for food. Because of their wandering, humans soon lived on most of the globe, and they soon discovered they could band together to produce a better existence. Around 10,000 B.C. people began to plant food crops to keep domesticated animals.

It took another 5,000 years, till around 5000 B.C., though, before people began to live together in formal groups, where individuals performed different jobs and people had social roles. This is considered the beginning of civilization, and it soon led—for better or worse—to the rise of towns and cities, and the highly complex world we live in today.

815 Carthage is founded by Phoenicians.

776 First Olympic Games are held in Greece.

753 Rome is founded.

580 King Nebuchadnezzar builds Hanging Gardens of Babylon.

563 Buddha is born.

559 Cyrus establishes Persian Empire.

551 Confucius is born.

503 Cleisthenes introduces democratic government in Athens.

460 Pericles establishes democracy in Athens.

450 Herodotus becomes known as father of history.

334 Alexander III, king of Macedonia, begins world conquest.

218 Hannibal leads army from Spain over Alps to Italy.

215 Great Wall of China is built.

63 Cicero, orator, compiles record of Roman life.

55 Julius Caesar conquers Gaul, invades Britain.

27 Caesar Augustus becomes first Roman emperor.

5 Jesus Christ is born.

A.D.

30 Jesus is crucified.

32 Saul of Tarsus begins early Christian missionary work.

64 Rome under Nero is partly destroyed by fire.

79 Eruption of Vesuvius destroys Pompeii.

132 Bar-Kokhba leads revolt against Rome and makes Israel independent.

268 Goths invade Greece.

312 Constantine becomes first Christian emperor of Rome.

370 Asian Huns invade Europe.

391 Augustine begins work as founder of Christian theology.

406 Vandals invade Gaul; Romans leave Britain.

410 Goths sack Rome.

425 Angles, Saxons, and Jutes invade Britain.

433 Attila the Hun begins reign.

476 Goths depose western Roman emperor, Romulas Augustus; Middle Ages begin.

550 Justinian codifies Roman law in Corpus Juris Civilis.

570 Muhammad is born.

630 Muhammad goes to Mecca and founds religion of Islam.

632 Muhammad dies.

634 Muslims begin conquest of Near East and Africa.

711 Moors invade Spain.

768 Reign of Charlemagne begins.

800 Charlemagne is crowned Emperor of the West.

814 Arabic numerals are established.

862 Viking Russ tribe seizes control of northern Russia.

874 Vikings settle Iceland.

900 Spain begins to drive out Moors.

920 Golden Age of Ghana Empire begins in Africa.

932 Printed books from woodblocks are developed in China.

936 Otto I establishes Holy Roman Empire, a successor to Charlemagne's empire.

981 Eric the Red begins settlement of Greenland.

995 Fugiware Michinaga founds Japanese Golden Age.

1000 Vikings begin exploration of North America.

1054 Byzantine Empire breaks with Holy Roman Church; Abdallah ben Yassim spreads Islamic culture in Africa.

1066 Normans, led by William the Conqueror, conquer Britain.

1096 Crusades are launched to oust Muslims from Holy Land.

1156 Civil wars are fought in Japan.

Charlemagne and a United Europe

Charlemagne, also known as Charles the Great and the King of the Franks, was the first person to succeed in uniting Europe. In contrast to the purpose of the European Community today, which is to unite the region economically, Charlemagne's goal was a religiously united Europe, and the religion was Christianity, or more specifically, Roman Catholicism.

Charlemagne, born around A.D. 742, set about conquering Europe in 772. His own kingdom comprised much of France and Germany, and he systematically began taking over much of what is today England, Italy, Poland, Hungary, Austria, the Netherlands, and northern Italy. In subduing local peoples, he left their laws in place and promoted regional diversity. He also organized a body of laws to help the various regions interact with one another. Charlemagne restored Leo III to the papacy, and on Christmas Day, A.D. 800, had himself crowned emperor of the West.

Charlemagne's fame soon made him a romantic figure of medieval legend who was remembered as a great warrior and a wise administrator, as well as a patron of the arts and learning. But it must not be forgotten that to achieve his goal of a religiously united Europe, he waged almost constant war, and that most of his victories were gained through a military might that was at times vicious. In one day in 782 he executed 4,500 Saxons.

1161	Chinese use explosives in warfare.
1162	Thomas à Becket becomes archbishop of Canterbury.
1189	Last recorded Viking voyage to North America.
1190	Genghis Khan begins conquest of Asia.
1204	Crusaders capture and sack Constantinople.
1210	Mongols invade China; Francis of Assisi founds Franciscan religious order.
1215	England's Magna Carta is signed by King John.
1228	Sixth Crusade results in capture of Jerusalem by Christians.
1240	Mongols capture Moscow, destroy Kiev.

The Pied Piper and the Children's Crusade

During the Middle Ages, European Christians undertook a series of military journeys intended to capture the Holy Land, then in the hands of Muslims. One of the journeys was called the Children's Crusade. In 1212, 50,000 French and German children marched off to rescue the Holy Land. The German children were turned back, but the French children were sold into slavery in Marseilles, France.

The old German legend of the Pied Piper is supposed to be about the Children's Crusade. It is the story of a man who appeared in Hamelin, Germany, a town overrun with rats, and offered to play magic pipes to rid the town of the rodents. He did get rid of them, but the people refused to pay him. Out of revenge, the Pied Piper played his magic pipe and lured all the children away from the town. They were never seen again.

Magna Carta: Bedrock of Democracy

As Europe emerged from the Middle Ages, the power of kings and queens grew virtually unchallenged, in part because they played an important role in turning geographic regions into nations. By the thirteenth century, though, the absolute power of rulers was called into question—largely through the abuses of the rulers themselves. King John of England was especially abusive, taxing his people unmercifully and seizing lands that did not belong to him in the name of the Crown.

The barons, whose lands were being seized, forced a meeting with John in June 1215 at Runnymede on the banks of the Thames River, and insisted that he sign a charter reducing his powers.

This charter, which became known as Magna Carta, or Great Charter, was in the eyes of some early historians merely an attempt by the barons to protect their lands from the Crown. But the Magna Carta has been viewed by most of the world's peoples as far more. It is considered to be the charter that founded democracy, by ensuring the freedoms and rights of individual subjects. In it many scholars see the basis of such specific freedoms as the right to a jury trial and the right to produce evidence before convicting someone of a crime. Many legal systems, including that of the United States, have been founded on the principles of the Magna Carta.

1259 Thomas Aquinas develops official Roman Catholic philosophy.

1260 Kublai Khan founds Yuan dynasty in China.

1264 Simon de Montfort founds House of Commons in Parliament.

1270 Gregorius Bar-Hebraeus writes a history of the world.

1271 Marco Polo leaves for China to visit Kublai Khan.

1274 Mongols attempt invasion of Japan but fail.

1291 Crusades end as Muslims force Christians out of Palestine.

1295 King Edward I of England summons first representative Parliament.

1336 Civil war lasting until 1392 begins in Japan.

1337 Hundred Years' War between England and France begins.

1347 Bubonic plague spreads from China to Cyprus.

1348 Black Death (plague) spreads to England.

1351 Plague reaches Russia; Europe's death toll tops 25 million.

1363 Tamerlane begins conquest of Asia.

1368 Mongol dynasty ends in China; Ming dynasty begins.

1390 Turks conquer Asia Minor.

1402 Tamerlane conquers Ottoman Empire.

1419 Henry the Navigator begins period of African exploration.

1431 Joan of Arc is burned as a witch at Rouen.

1453 Hundred Years' War ends; fall of Constantinople ends Byzantine Empire; Middle Ages begin decline; Renaissance begins.

1454 Movable-type printing press is introduced.

1455 England's War of the Roses is fought.

1478 Spanish Inquisition is begun by Ferdinand and Isabella; period of exploration by Europeans begins.

1482 Portuguese colonize African Gold Coast.

1488 Bartholomeu Dias sails around Cape of Good Hope.

1492 Christopher Columbus reaches the West Indies.

Joan of Arc: Girl Warrior

Joan of Arc was born in 1412, when her native France was in the midst of a long struggle with England to decide which country would control the throne of France. This series of wars became known as the Hundred Years' War. In Joan's lifetime, the French heir to the throne was the young dauphin later known as Charles VII.

Having grown up under the shadow of this conflict, at age 13 Joan reported hearing the voices of three saints: St. Catherine, a woman in ancient history who was tortured to death when she refused to marry an emperor who did not share her faith; St. Margaret, believed to have been swallowed by Satan disguised as a dragon; and the archangel St. Michael, the protector of soldiers. They told her to offer support to the dauphin.

Five years later, dressed as a man but escorted like a girl, Joan of Arc finally managed to travel to the French court, where she persuaded the young prince to let her lead the weary, defeated French troops in battle once again. In one month, May 1429, she ended the eight-month siege of Orleans. By age seventeen, she had led French troops in several successful battles and had turned the war in France's favor. When the dauphin was crowned king of France, Joan of Arc was at the height of her power.

Her success was not to endure, however. Captured in battle, she was sold to French forces loyal to England. Turned over to a religious court, Joan of Arc was tried as a witch and religious heretic, or dissenter. Her crimes were wearing men's clothes and claiming direct inspiration from God.

After being tricked into a confession, she was sentenced to life in prison, and when she retracted her confession, she was burned at the stake at the age of nineteen. Charles VII, whom she had helped so much, did nothing to aid her in her time of trouble. Two women who attempted to defend her were also burned at the stake as witches.

Twenty-five years after her death, Charles VII, who didn't want his claim to power to rest on assistance from a witch, supported a retrial that restored Joan of Arc's reputation. In 1920, the Catholic Church made her a saint. Today in France she is a national hero, honored by many statues—virtually all showing her on horseback and in full battle dress.

1497　John Cabot reaches Newfoundland.

1498　Vasco da Gama sails around Cape of Good Hope to India.

1500　Pedro Cabral discovers Brazil.

1502　Columbus discovers Nicaragua.

1505　Portuguese colonize Mozambique.

1507　First world map showing "America" is produced.

1513　Vasco Núñez de Balboa reaches the Pacific Ocean.

1517　Martin Luther's Reformation begins.

1521　Hernando Cortés conquers Aztecs and claims Mexico for Spain.

1522　Crew under Ferdinand Magellan circumnavigates the world.

1531　Francisco Pizarro begins conquest of Peru.

1534　Henry VIII is excommunicated and founds Church of England; John Calvin begins Protestant Reformation in Switzerland; Ignatius Loyola founds Society of Jesus (Jesuits).

1541　Hernando de Soto discovers Mississippi River.

1547　Ivan IV becomes first czar of united Russia.

1557　Portuguese establish colony at Macao.

1558　Elizabeth I becomes queen of England.

1582　Gregorian calendar is introduced.

1588　Spanish Armada is defeated by English fleet.

1595　Dutch colonize Guinea Coast.

Why Henry VIII of England Had Six Wives

Henry VIII of England (1509–1547) is most famous for having had six wives: Catherine of Aragon, Anne Boleyn, Jane Seymour, Anne of Cleves, Katherine Howard, and Catherine Parr. During this king's reign, his subjects even had a saying that helped them keep track of the fates of each of the wives:

Divorced, beheaded, died;
divorced, beheaded, survived.

Henry VIII divorced his first wife after nearly twenty years of marriage because he needed a male heir to succeed him on the throne of England. Without a male heir, England might find itself in the throes of a civil war as competing factions tried to take over the throne. Henry's divorces, though, led to a shocking break between the King of England and the Roman Catholic Church (when the Pope refused to recognize his first divorce) and to the establishment of the Church of England. Today, the reigning monarch of England is still the head of the Church of England.

Jane Seymour, Henry's third wife, gave birth to a son who became Edward VI, but she died, and he went on to take three more wives.

1600 English East India Company is chartered.
1602 Dutch East India Company is formed.
1606 Europeans land in Australia.
1607 English found North American colony of Virginia.
1610 Hudson Bay is discovered.
1618 Thirty Years' War begins as a conflict between Europe's Protestants and Catholics.
1620 English Pilgrims reach Cape Cod, found Plymouth Colony.
1637 Russian explorers reach Pacific coast of Siberia.
1642 French found Montreal in Canada; Charles I battles Parliament in English Civil War.
1652 English and Dutch begin series of wars; Dutch East India Company founds settlement on the Cape of Good Hope.
1661 English take control of Bombay in India.
1664 Manchu dynasty is founded in China.

1686 English establish Dominion of New England.
1696 Peter the Great leads Russian modernization program.
1704 English seize Gibraltar from Spain.
1733 John Kay starts Industrial Revolution with flying sewing shuttle.
1763 Peace of Paris gives Canada to England.
1767 Townshend Acts tax American colony imports; Mason-Dixon line is established.
1770 Boston Massacre occurs; Townshend Acts are repealed except for the tax.
1773 Boston Tea Party occurs.
1774 First Continental Congress of American colonies is held.
1775 War of Independence begins in Massachusetts.
1776 American Declaration of Independence is signed.
1781 English General Cornwallis surrenders at Yorktown.
1783 Treaty of Paris ends American War

of Independence; India Act allows English control of India.

1788 First English convicts are transported to Australia; Sierra Leone is established as a refuge for blacks.

1789 George Washington becomes first U.S. president; U.S. Constitution takes effect; French Revolution begins.

1791 U.S. Bill of Rights takes effect.

1792 France is declared a republic; Denmark becomes the first country to ban slave trade.

1793 Maximilien Robespierre leads French reign of terror; Toussaint L'Ouverture leads revolt, ending slavery by French in Haiti; first free settlers migrate to Australia.

1798 Napoleon Bonaparte invades Egypt, capturing Cairo; Thomas Malthus publishes essay on population explosion.

1803 Louisiana Purchase is completed.

1804 Lewis and Clark begin exploration of American Northwest; Bonaparte crowns himself Napoleon I, Emperor of France.

1806 Napoleon dissolves Holy Roman Empire.

1807 England abolishes slave trade.

1809 David Ricardo develops modern concepts of finance.

1811 Simón Bolívar frees parts of South America from Spanish rule.

1812 War is fought between England and United States; Napoleon invades Russia, occupies Moscow.

1814 Napoleon is exiled to Elba.

1815 Napoleon is defeated at the Battle of Waterloo and exiled again.

1819 Florida is ceded by Spain to United States.

1820 Missouri Compromise on U.S. slave states takes effect.

1821 José San Martin frees Chile and Argentina from Spanish control.

1823 Monroe Doctrine against foreign activity in America is adopted.

1833 England bans slavery and child labor in factories.

1836 Texas secedes from Mexico; battle of the Alamo is fought.

1846 War is fought between Mexico and United States; Irish potato famine occurs, with death toll reaching one million.

1848 Revolutions erupt throughout Europe; Marx and Engels produce *The Communist Manifesto*; Mexico cedes California and New Mexico to the United States.

1854 Crimean War is fought; Japan ends isolation, signs commercial treaty with United States.

1860 Giuseppe Garibaldi begins nationalist movements in Europe.

1861 U.S. Civil War begins; British establish colonial presence in what is now Nigeria.

1863 Emancipation Proclamation declares abolition of slavery in part of the United States.

1865 U.S. Civil War ends; President Lincoln is assassinated.

1867 United States acquires Alaska from Russia; Dominion of Canada is established.

1868 Japan ends 700-year shogun rule, begins modernization.

1869 Suez Canal is completed.

1870 Franco-Prussian War is fought.

1883 Germany introduces first health insurance.

1894 Sun Yat-sen begins move to end Manchu dynasty in China.

1898 War between Spain and United States is fought over Cuba; United States acquires Hawaiian Islands.

1900 Boxer Rebellion erupts in China, where hundreds of Europeans are killed; England and Germany begin arms race.

1902 Boer War ends; England acquires South African states.

1904 Russo-Japanese War is fought; Japan acquires Korea and Manchuria.

1908 William d'Arcy discovers oil in Persian Gulf region.

1909 England introduces first old-age pensions; assembly-line production is introduced in Detroit.

1912 Chinese revolution ends Manchu dynasty, and republic is formed; passenger ship *Titanic* sinks, with 1,513 lives lost; Balkan wars begin.

1914 World War I begins with assassination of Austrian archduke; trench warfare begins, and airplanes are used as weapons; Panama Canal opens.

1915 Poison gas is first used by Germany in warfare.

1916 Tanks are first used by England in warfare.

1917 United States joins Allies in European fighting; Bolsheviks led by Lenin seize power in Russia; Balfour Declaration urges Jewish state in Palestine.

1918 Russia withdraws from World War I fighting; Kaiser of Germany abdicates; Germany forms republic after revolt; armistice ends World War I.

1919 Treaty of Versailles causes heavy German economic losses; League of Nations is founded; Sinn Fein rebellion erupts in Ireland; Benito Mussolini introduces fascism in Italy; Gandhi begins passive resistance movement in India.

1920 Civil war is fought in Ireland.

1921 Irish Free State is established.

1922 Union of Soviet Socialist Republics is established; fascists march on Rome; Mussolini is named prime minister of Italy; Palestine becomes British protectorate under League of Nations.

1923 Adolf Hitler forms National Socialist Party in Germany.

1924 Joseph Stalin succeeds Lenin as leader of Soviet Union; new Chinese government is formed with communist members.

1927 Purge of communists leads to civil war in China.

1929 U.S. stock market crash triggers worldwide depression; fighting begins between Jews and Arabs in Palestine.

1931 Spain becomes a republic; British Empire becomes British Commonwealth.

1933 Adolf Hitler is named chancellor of Germany, and National Socialists (Nazis) get rid of opposition; Stalin gets rid of opposition in Russia.

1934 Hitler assumes title of *Fuhrer*; Mao Tse-tung starts "Long March" of Chinese communists.

1935 Italy invades Ethiopia; Hitler renounces Versailles Treaty and begins open rearmament; John Keynes publishes a book about government's role in the economy.

1936 Germany reoccupies Rhineland and forms "Axis" alliance with Italy; General Franco begins Spanish civil war; King Edward of England abdicates to marry American Wallis Simpson.

1937 Japanese invade China, capturing Peking and Shanghai; German aircraft bomb Spain in support of Franco.

1938 Germany annexes Austria and gains Czechoslovakia's Sudetenland in Munich Pact.

1939 Germany annexes Czechoslovakia; Franco captures Madrid, and Spanish civil war ends; Italy invades Albania; Germany invades Poland, triggering World War II; Russo-Finnish War ends in defeat of Finland.

1940 Germany invades France, Belgium, Denmark, and Norway; Battle of Britain halts German invasion of England; Japan joins Berlin-Rome Axis; Italy invades Greece and joins war against England and France.

1941 Germany invades Russia; Italy and

Germany invade Egypt; Japanese attack U.S. bases in Hawaii; U.S. joins Allies in World War II against Axis powers.

1942 Japanese capture Philippines and much of Southeast Asia; Battle of Midway alters naval balance back to Allies from Japanese in Pacific; Germans begin to retreat in North Africa.

1943 United States begins recapture of Japanese Pacific bases; Allies invade Sicily; Italians surrender; Germans surrender to Russians at Stalingrad.

1944 Allies invade Normandy; German retreat begins; Allies liberate Rome, Paris, and Brussels; U.S. forces defeat Japanese navy in Leyte Gulf.

1945 Yalta Conference is attended by United States. Great Britain, and Soviet Union; Germany surrenders; Mussolini is assassinated; Hitler commits suicide; atom bombs are dropped at Hiroshima and Nagasaki; Japan surrenders, ending World War II; Potsdam Conference discusses postwar settlements.

1946 League of Nations is replaced by United Nations; Ho Chi Minh begins war against French in Indochina; German war crimes trials are held in Nuremberg.

1947 Marshall Plan aids European war recovery; Arabs reject plan for separate Jewish and Arab states; independent states of India and Pakistan are formed.

1948 Nation of Israel is established; war begins between Israel and Arab League; Gandhi is assassinated by a Hindu extremist; communists gain control of Czechoslovakia; Korea is divided into North Korea and South Korea; Berlin is blockaded by Soviet Union.

1949 Mao Tse-tung's communists gain control of China; Nationalist Chinese move government to Taiwan; South Africa establishes apartheid policy; Germany is divided into East Germany and West Germany; North Atlantic Treaty Organization (NATO) is formed.

1950 North Korean troops invade South Korea.

1951 Chinese communists occupy Tibet.

1952 Jawaharlal Nehru is elected first prime minister of India.

1953 Stalin dies; USSR announces development of hydrogen bomb; Vietnamese Viet Minh forces invade Laos.

1954 Viet Minh troops defeat French at Dien Bien Phu; Vietnam is divided into North Vietnam and South Vietnam; South-East Asia Treaty Organization (SEATO) is formed.

1955 European communist states sign Warsaw Pact; Argentine President Juan Perón is exiled.

1956 Soviets crush anti-Russian uprising in Hungary; Egypt nationalizes Suez Canal, and British withdraw; Israel invades Egypt.

1957 Russia launches first artificial satellite, *Sputnik I*; Fidel Castro begins revolution in Cuba; European Common Market is formed.

1958 Egypt, Syria, and Yemen form United Arab States; Charles de Gaulle is elected president of France; United States launches an artificial satellite, *Explorer I*.

1959 Fidel Castro overthrows Fulgencio Batista and becomes Cuban premier.

1960 Many European colonies in Africa gain independence.

1961 Bay of Pigs invasion of Cuba fails; Russian Yuri Gagarin is first man in space; communists build Berlin Wall; United States sends thousands of military advisers to Vietnam.

1962 Soviet missile crisis threatens in Cuba; Algeria gains independence from France; Nelson Mandela is imprisoned in South Africa for anti-apartheid activities, eventually freed in 1991; Cesar Chavez founds the United Farm Workers Union of America, a labor union representing migrant farm workers.

1963 Russian Valentina Kareshkova is first woman in space; President Kennedy is assassinated; United States, Great Britain, and Soviet Union sign nuclear test ban treaty; North Vietnamese boats attack U.S. Navy in Gulf of Tonkin; President Lyndon Johnson orders attack on North Vietnam.

1965 U.S. Marines are sent to Vietnam; U.S. aircraft begin air strikes against North Vietnam.

1966 China undergoes "Cultural Revolution"; Indira Gandhi becomes prime minister of India.

1967 Six-Day War between Israel and Arabs is fought; Israel controls Jerusalem and occupies West Bank of Jordan River.

1968 Martin Luther King, Jr., is assassinated; U.S. senator Robert Kennedy is assassinated; Soviets invade Czechoslovakia to crush uprising; Vietcong stage Tet offensive in South Vietnam; U.S. troop deployment in Vietnam passes 500,000; North Korea seizes U.S. Navy ship *Pueblo*.

1969 U.S. military begins withdrawal from Vietnam; U.S. astronauts land on the moon.

1970 U.S. troops invade Cambodia.

1971 Communist China replaces Taiwan in United Nations; Aswan High Dam completed in Egypt.

1972 President Nixon travels to China to renew relations; Great Britain takes over direct rule of Northern Ireland.

1973 Military coup in Chile overthrows Marxist government; Arabs attack Israel in October War; participants in Vietnam War sign peace agreements.

1974 Watergate scandal ends Nixon term in White House.

1975 Vietnam War ends with communist seizure of Saigon; communists take control of government of Cambodia; U.S. and Soviet spacecraft link up in space.

1978 United States votes to return Canal Zone to Panama in year 2000.

1979 Ayatollah Khomeini gains control of Iran; Shah of Iran leaves; Iranians seize U.S. Embassy in Teheran, holding hostages; Soviet Union invades Afghanistan; Israel and Egypt sign peace treaty; Sandinistas force dictator Somoza to leave Nicaragua.

1980 War begins between Iran and Iraq; Solidarity trade union confronts communists in Poland.

1981 United States begins series of space shuttle flights; assassination attempt is made on Pope John Paul II.

1982 Falklands War between Argentina and England is fought; Israel withdraws troops from Egypt's Sinai.

1983 Soviets shoot down South Korean airliner and 269 are killed; bomb kills 237 U.S. marines in Beirut, Lebanon; U.S. forces invade island of Grenada.

1984 Marines withdraw from Beirut.

1985 Mikhail Gorbachev becomes leader of Soviet Union.

1986 U.S. space shuttle *Challenger* explodes in flight, killing crew; Corazon Aquino is elected president of Philippines; U.S. aircraft raid Libya in retaliation for terrorism; nuclear accident occurs at Soviet Chernobyl power station.

1987 U.S. stock market crashes with 508-point one-day loss; Iran-contra scandal involves U.S. government officials; United States and Soviet Union agree to reduce nuclear arms.

1988 Cease-fire agreement is signed between Nicaraguan government and contras; Iran accepts peace plan offered by Iraq; King Hussein abandons claim to West Bank and gives authority to Palestine Liberation Organization; Palestine Liberation Organization renounces terrorism and recognizes Israel as a state; devastating earthquake in Armenia kills tens of thousands.

1989 Berlin Wall is crumbled, marking the beginning of the end of Soviet communism; Chinese military puts down student protest for freedom and liberty at Tiananmen Square; U.S. troops invade Panama and arrest Gen. Manuel Noriega; Soviet Army withdraws from Afghanistan; Czechoslovakia and Romania hold free elections.

1990 Under Operation Desert Shield U.S. forces go to Saudi Arabia to defend that country after neighboring Kuwait is invaded by Iraq; U.S. stock markets soars to record highs, reaching 3,000 points for the first time.

1991 U.S.S.R. dissolved and reformed as the Commonwealth of Independent States (CIS); all the Soviet satellite nations and several of the republics become independent states; U.S.-led multinational forces fight Persian Gulf War, freeing Kuwait from Iraqi control.

1992 South African whites vote to end minority rule through talks with black majority; Croatia, Bosnia and Herzegovina, and Slovenia are recognized by the European Community and United States; South Africa repeals the Population Registration Act, a basic apartheid law.

FAMOUS PEOPLE WHO CHANGED THE WORLD

Every era has major figures who have made significant contributions to the world and have in one way or another changed it forever. The list that follows describes some of the people who have helped to change our world. They are listed chronologically.

B.C.

2780 Imhotep designs first step pyramid at Saqqara, Egypt.

2700 Cheops builds Great Pyramid at Giza.

2697 Huang-ti becomes legendary "Yellow Emperor" of China.

2640 Si Ling-chi introduces silk production in China.

1750 Hammurabi, Babylonian king, issues code of laws.

1560 Hatshepsut becomes first woman pharoah.

1270 Abulfaraj, Syrian historian, compiles first encyclopedia.

1250 Moses, Hebrew lawgiver, leads Israelites from Egypt to Canaan.

1100 Pa-out-She, Chinese scholar, compiles first dictionary.

1000 David, first king of Judah, establishes Jerusalem as capital.

760 Homer, Greek poet, writes *Iliad* and *Odyssey*.

600 Lao-tze develops Chinese philosophy of Taoism.

563 Siddhartha Gautama develops Buddhist philosophy.

559 Cyrus establishes Persian Empire.

551 K'ung Fu-tzu, also known as Confucius, develops philosophy of Confucianism.

550 Anaximander invents star charts and model of spherical Earth.

540 Pythagoras, mathematician, studies musical harmonics.

485 Aeschylus writes first early Greek tragedies.

480 Sophocles writes early Greek tragic poems.

460 Pericles establishes democracy in Athens.

450 Euripides writes Greek tragedies; Herodotus becomes known as father of history.

440 Greek philosopher Socrates teaches that virtue and knowledge are identical.

400 Aristophanes introduces political satire in Greek comedies; Plato writes dialogues that help shape Western thought.

340 Aristotle contributes to development of logical thought.

334 Alexander the Great begins conquest of known world.

321 Chandragupta forms first great empire in India.

300 Euclid develops deductive system of mathematics; Meng-tse spreads philosophy of Confucius in Orient.

221 Shih Hwang-ti, first emperor of China, begins Great Wall.

220 Archimedes, Greek mathematician, develops physics and mechanics.

218 Hannibal leads army from Spain over Alps to Italy.

78 Julius Caesar begins his climb as ruler of Roman Empire.

63 Cicero, orator, compiles record of Roman life.

51 Cleopatra rules Egypt at time when Roman general Julius Caesar seeks to conquer Egypt.

39 Trung Trac and Trung Nhi, two Vietnamese sisters, lead a rebellion against the Chinese.

38 Horace, Roman poet, writes classic satires.

30 Virgil, Roman poet, writes *Aeneid*.

27 Caesar Augustus becomes first Roman emperor.

5 Jesus of Nazareth, Christian leader, is born.

A.D.

105 T'sai Lun invents paper manufacture.

312 Constantine becomes first Christian emperor of Rome.

391 Augustine begins work as founder of Christian theology.

451 Attila, leader of Huns, invades Europe.

570 Muhammad, founder of Islam, is born.

768 Charlemagne becomes king of the Franks.

786 Harun al-Rashid makes Baghdad center of Islamic culture.

936 Otto I establishes Holy Roman Empire.

995 Fugiware Michinaga founds Japanese Golden Age.

1002 Leif Eriksson establishes North American colony.

1054 Abdallah ben Yassim spreads Islamic culture in Africa.

1066 William the Conqueror establishes Norman culture in Britain.

1096 Pope Urban II begins Crusades to free Holy Land.

1162 Thomas à Becket becomes archbishop of Canterbury.

1190 Temujin (Genghis Khan) begins conquest of Asia and Near East.

1215 King John signs Magna Carta, foundation of modern democracy.

1250 Roger Bacon, English philosopher, invents magnifying lens.

1259 Thomas Aquinas develops official Roman Catholic philosophy.

1271 Marco Polo begins 24-year journey to court of Kublai Khan.

1295 King Edward I of England summons first representative Parliament.

1368 Chu Yuan-chang overthrows Mongols, founds Ming dynasty.

1369 Tamerlane becomes ruler of land from India to Egypt.

1387 Geoffrey Chaucer writes *Canterbury Tales*.

1419 Henry the Navigator of Portugaul begins explorations on coast of Africa.

1429 Joan of Arc, peasant girl, leads

And You Think Skyscrapers Are Big:
Seven Wonders of the Ancient World

We often think that whatever is newest and biggest in our time is the best, yet there were seven wonders of the ancient world that would seem impressive to us even today. Of these, only one—the pyramids of Egypt—has survived, so we can visit it.

The seven wonders of the ancient world were as follows:

1. *Artemision at Ephesus,* the temple of the Greek goddess Artemis (also the Roman goddess Diana), was begun in 541 B.C. at Ephesus (now a site in Turkey) and completed 220 years later. The temple was 425 feet long and 220 feet wide with 127 marble columns, each 60 feet tall. The gates were made of cypress and the ceiling of cedar. The temple was destroyed by the Goths in A.D. 262.

2. *The Colossus of Rhodes,* a 100-foot-tall bronze statue of the sun god Helios, was erected between 292 and 280 B.C. in the harbor at Rhodes. According to legend, it appeared to stand astride the harbor, but it was actually on a promontory overlooking it. The statue was toppled by an earthquake around 224 B.C. and lay in ruins until A.D. 653, when the remains were sold as scrap metal.

3. *The Hanging Gardens of Babylon,* a series of five terraces of glazed brick, each 50 feet above the next, was erected by King Nebuchadnezzar for his wife, Amytis, in 562 B.C. The terraces, featuring rare and exotic plants, were connected by a winding stairway. A pumping device supplied water so the gardens could be irrigated by fountains.

4. *The Mausoleum at Halicarnassus,* a 140-foot-high white marble structure, was built in 352 B.C. at Halicarnassus (now in Turkey) in memory of King Mausolus of Caria. Its massive base contained a tomb and supported 36 columns crowned with a stepped pyramid on which was constructed a marble chariot. It was destroyed so that the stone could be used to build a castle for the Knights of Saint John in 1402.

5. *Olympian Zeus,* a statue of the supreme god in Greek mythology, was created in gold and ivory for the temple at Olympia. The figure of the seated Zeus was 40 feet tall and rested on a base that was 12 feet high. The portions of the statue representing the flesh of the god were covered with marble, and his cloak was made of gold. Golden lions rested near his feet.

6. *The Pyramids of Egypt* were started by Khufu (Cheops) around 2700 B.C. as tombs for the ancient kings. The three largest and finest were erected during the Fourth Dynasty at Giza, near Cairo. The largest of the group is the Khufu Pyramid, built of limestone blocks from a base 756 feet wide on each side and covering an area of 13 acres. It is 482 feet high. Smaller pyramids were built for wives and other members of the royal families.

7. *The Tower of Pharos* was a great lighthouse built on the island of Pharos, at Alexandria, Egypt, during the reign of Ptolemy Philadelphus, 285 B.C. Also called The Pharos, it was 500 feet tall with a ramp leading to the top. Light was produced with a fire and reflectors and could be seen from a distance of 42 miles.

French army against English in Hundred Years' War.

1454 Johannes Gutenberg perfects movable-type printing press.

1478 Ferdinand and Isabella establish Spanish Inquisition.

1482 Leonardo da Vinci, Italian artist and inventor, creates many modern devices.

1492 Christopher Columbus sails to West Indies and South America.

1498 Vasco da Gama sails around Cape of Good Hope to India.

1510 Michelangelo paints ceiling of Sistine Chapel.

1513 Italo Balboa discovers Pacific Ocean at Panama.

1517 Martin Luther begins Protestantism.

1519 Ferdinand Magellan begins first trip to circumnavigate world.

1521 Hernando Cortés conquers Aztecs and claims Mexico for Spain.

1534 Henry VIII is excommunicated and creates Church of England.

1540 Nicolaus Copernicus suggests that the sun, not the Earth, is the center of the solar system.

1547 Ivan IV becomes first czar of united Russia.

1558 Elizabeth I rules England at start of colonization period.

1582 Pope Gregory XIII introduces calendar still in use.

1585 Galileo Galilei develops understanding of many laws of nature.

1588 Francis Drake leads English destruction of Spanish fleet.

1592 William Shakespeare emerges as successful British dramatist.

1605 Francis Bacon, essayist, teaches inductive reasoning.

1607 John Smith founds English colony at Jamestown, Virginia.

1611 Johannes Kepler explains movements of the planets.

1620 Jinga Mbandi, a powerful queen of Angola and much of central Africa who negotiates with the Portuguese and later fights a war against them, is involved in slave trading of her own people.

1631 Rembrandt becomes famous as prodigious portrait painter.

1644 Oliver Cromwell leads revolt against English King Charles I.

1683 Anton van Leeuwenhoek discovers bacteria with microscope.

1696 Péter the Great leads Russian modernization program.

1733 John Kay starts the Industrial Revolution.

1747 Johann S. Bach composes vocal and instrumental music.

1764 Catherine the Great (Catherine II) becomes Empress of Russia and initiates reforms of the Russian legal code; during her reign Russia becomes accepted as a European power.

1769 Wolfgang Mozart begins career as musical composer.

1776 Thomas Jefferson prepares Declaration of Independence; Adam Smith writes *Wealth of Nations*; George Washington leads revolution of English colonies.

1789 Georges Danton leads French Revolution.

1796 Edward Jenner introduces vaccination against smallpox; Napoleon Bonaparte begins conquest of Europe and Mediterranean.

1798 Eli Whitney, cotton-gin inventor, introduces mass production.

1804 Meriwether Lewis and William Clark begin exploration of Louisiana Purchase.

1807 Robert Fulton develops steam-powered water travel.

1811 Simón Bolívar frees part of South America from Spanish rule.

1815 Duke of Wellington crushes Napoleon in battle of Waterloo.

1821 Michael Faraday develops electric motor principle; José de San Martín frees Chile and Argentina from Spanish control.

1823 James Monroe issues doctrine against foreign interference in the Americas.

1825 George Stephenson develops steam-locomotive land travel.

1836 Sam Houston gains independence of Texas from Mexico.

1837 Louis Daguerre invents photography.

1840 Samuel Morse patents electric telegraph system.

1848 Karl Marx and Friedrich Engels produce *Communist Manifesto*.

1854 Matthew Perry ends Japanese isolation with U.S. trade treaty.

1855 Florence Nightingale introduces battlefield nursing care.

1857 Rani of Jhansi, an Indian woman, is one of the leaders of the Indian rebellion against the British.

1859 Charles Darwin publishes *On the Origin of Species*.

1860 Giuseppe Garibaldi begins nationalist movements in Europe.

1863 Abraham Lincoln proclaims abolition of slavery in Confederate states.

1867 Joseph Lister introduces antiseptic practices in hospitals.

1869 Ferdinand de Lesseps completes Suez Canal construction.

1871 Otto von Bismarck defeats France and forms new German Reich.

1874 Paul Cézanne leads Impressionist movement in painting.

1875 Leo Tolstoy becomes established as great Russian author.

1876 Alexander Graham Bell patents the telephone; Crazy Horse, an Oglala Sioux warrior, defeats General George Custer at the Battle of Little Bighorn.

1879 Thomas Edison develops light bulb.

1882 William Jenny designs first "skyscraper" office building; Robert Koch discovers cause of tuberculosis and cholera.

1885 Gottlieb Daimler builds first gasoline-powered automobile.

1894 Sun Yat-sen begins move to end Manchu dynasty in China; Guglielmo Marconi invents wireless telegraphy.

1895 Sigmund Freud develops method of psychoanalysis; Louis and Auguste Lumière introduce motion pictures; Wilhelm Roentgen discovers X rays; Joseph Thomson discovers the electron.

1897 Ferdinand Braun invents the cathode ray tube. Ivan Pavlov conducts conditioned-reflex experiments; Ronald Ross discovers cause of malaria, the mosquito.

1898 Christiaan Eijkman discovers vitamin-deficiency diseases.

1902 Pierre and Marie Curie discover radium.

1903 Orville and Wilbur Wright fly first practical airplane.

1905 Albert Einstein develops special theory of relativity.

1907 Pablo Picasso and Georges Braque found Cubist movement in art.

1913 Henry Ford develops moving assembly line for mass production.

1914 George Goethals completes Panama Canal.

1917 Vladimir Lenin leads Bolshevik revolution in Russia.

1919 Mahatma Gandhi begins passive-resistance campaign in India; Benito Mussolini founds Italian fascist movement.

1920 Woodrow Wilson helps form League of Nations.

1924 Josef Stalin succeeds Lenin as leader of Soviet Union.

1927 Niels Bohr proposes fission of uranium with neutrons; Werner Heisenberg discovers uncertainty principle in physics; Chiang Kai-shek succeeds Sun Yat-sen in China.

1928 Alexander Fleming discovers penicillin.

1931 Vladimir Zworykin invents television camera.

1933 Adolf Hitler becomes dictator of Nazi Germany; Franklin D. Roosevelt becomes thirty-second president of United States.

1934 Mao Tse-tung leads China's communist army on "Long March."

1936 Francisco Franco begins Spanish Civil War.

1940 Winston Churchill becomes prime minister of Great Britain. John Randall invents radar tube.

1942 Enrico Fermi builds first nuclear reactor.

1945 U.S. team work under J. R. Oppenheimer to develop first atomic bomb.

1946 Ho Chi Minh begins war against France in Vietnam.

1947 Charles Yeager is first to fly at supersonic speed.

1948 William Shockley develops transistor; Eleanor Roosevelt, U.S. delegate to the United Nations, oversees the passage of the Universal Declaration of Human Rights, which embodies standards that civilized people should accept as sacred and inalienable.

1950 Harry Truman sends U.S. troops to fight communists in Korea.

1952 Team under Edward Teller develops the hydrogen bomb.

1953 Francis Crick and James Watson map DNA molecule.

1957 Fidel Castro begins communist revolution in Cuba.

1958 Charles de Gaulle becomes president of French Fifth Republic.

1961 Yuri Gagarin becomes first human to orbit Earth.

1962 Cesar Chavez founds the United Farm Workers Union of America, a labor union representing the interests of migrant farm workers.

1966 Indira Gandhi daughter of Jawaharlal Nehru, becomes Prime Minister of India; elected as a figurehead, she proves to be a shrewd and masterful leader and liberates Bangladesh from Pakistan.

1967 Jocelyn Bell discovers pulsars.

1969 Neil Armstrong and Edwin Aldrin walk on surface of the moon; Golda Meir becomes prime minister of Israel.

1978 Patrick Steptoe develops method for developing test-tube baby.

1979 Ayatollah Khomeini leads revolution against Shah of Iran.

1983 Barbara McKlintock, an American geneticist, is awarded Nobel Prize for Medicine and Physiology for her early work on genetics.

1985 Michael Phelps develops positron emission tomography; Mikhail Gorbachev becomes leader of Soviet Union.

1991 Mikhail Gorbachev presides over the dismantling of the Soviet Union; Nelson Mandela, leader of the African National Congress who spent most of his adult life imprisoned for his anti-apartheid stand in South Africa, is freed.

1992 Boris Yeltsin becomes leader of the reorganized Soviet Union, now the Commonwealth of Independent States; Rigoberta Menchu, a Guatemalan Ouiche Indian woman and human rights activist, wins Nobel Peace Prize.

Royal Rulers of Europe and Asia

In some periods of history, the shape of nations has been determined by monarchies—ruling royal families. This was especially true of Europe and Asia starting in the 1100s. Only in the last one hundred years have monarchies fallen into decline as one nation after another has declared itself independent of its royal rulers. The list that follows shows some of the world's monarchies and when they ruled or reigned.

Europe and Russia

Great Britain

William I the Conqueror	1066–1087
William II	1087–1100
Henry I	1100–1135
Stephen	1135–1154
Henry II	1154–1189
Richard I	1189–1199
John	1199–1216
Henry III	1216–1272
Edward I	1272–1307
Edward II	1307–1327
Edward III	1327–1377
Richard II	1377–1399
Henry IV	1399–1413
Henry V	1413–1422
Henry VI	1422–1461
Edward IV	1461–1483
Edward V	1483
Richard III	1483–1485
Henry VII	1485–1509
Henry VIII	1509–1547
Edward VI	1547–1553
Mary I	1553–1558
Elizabeth I	1558–1603
James I	1603–1625
Charles I	1625–1649
(Commonweath period)	1649–1660
Charles II	1660–1685
James II	1685–1688
William III and Mary II	1689–1694
William III (alone)	1694–1702
Anne	1702–1714
George I	1714–1727
George II	1727–1760
George III	1760–1820
George IV	1820–1830
William IV	1830–1837
Victoria	1837–1901
Edward VII	1901–1910
George V	1910–1936
Edward VIII	1936
George VI	1936–1952
Elizabeth II*	1952–

France

Henri I	1031–1060
Philip I	1060–1108
Louis VI	1108–1137
Louis VII	1137–1180
Philip II	1180–1223
Louis VIII	1223–1226
Louis IX	1226–1270
Philip III	1270–1285
Philip IV	1285–1314
Louis X	1314–1316
John I	1316
Philip V	1316–1322
Charles IV	1322–1328
Philip VI	1328–1350
John II	1350–1364
Charles V	1364–1380
Charles VI	1380–1422
Charles VII	1422–1461
Louis XI	1461–1483
Charles VIII	1483–1498
Louis XII	1498–1515
François I	1515–1547
Henri II	1547–1559
François II	1559–1560
Charles IX	1560–1574
Henri III	1574–1589
Henri IV	1589–1610
Louis XIII	1610–1643
Louis XIV	1643–1715
Louis XV	1715–1774
Louis XVI	1774–1792
(First Republic)	1792–1804
Napoleon I	1804–1814
Louis XVIII	1814–1824
Charles X	1824–1830
Louis Philippe	1830–1848
(Second Republic)	1848–1852
Napoleon III	1852–1870
(Third Republic)	1870–1914

Germany

Frederick I	1710–1713
Frederick William I	1713–1740
Frederick II	1740–1786

Frederick William II	1786–1797
Frederick William III	1797–1840
Frederick William IV	1840–1861
William I	1861–1888
Frederick III	1888
William II	1888–1918

Russia

Ivan III	1462–1505
Vasilly III	1505–1533
Ivan IV	1533–1584
Theodore I	1584–1598
Boris Godunov	1598–1605
Theodore II	1605
Demetrius I	1650–1606
Basil IV	1606–1610
Wladyslaw (Polish Prince)	1610–1613
Mikhail Romanov	1613–1645
Alexis I	1645–1676
Theodore III	1676–1682
Ivan V and Peter I	1682–1689
Peter I (alone)	1689–1725
Catherine I	1725–1727
Peter II	1727–1730
Anna	1730–1740
Ivan VI	1740–1741
Elizabeth	1741–1762
Peter III	1761
Catherine II	1762–1796
Paul I	1796–1801
Alexander I	1801–1825
Nicholas I	1825–1855
Alexander II	1855–1881
Alexander III	1881–1894
Nicholas II	1894–1917

China

Yuan (Kublai Khan) dynasty	1260–1368
Ming dynasty	1368–1644
Manchu (Ch'ing) dynasty	1644–1912
Shun Chih	1644–1661
K'ang Hsi	1661–1722
Yung Cheng	1722–1735
Ch'ien Lung	1735–1796
Chia Ch'ing	1796–1820
Tao Kuang	1820–1851

Hsien Feng	1851–1861
T'ung Chi	1861–1875
Kuang Hsu	1875–1898
Tzu Hsi	1898–1908
P'u Yi	1908–1912

Japan

Tokugawa Shogun rule	1603–1868
(Meiji) Mutsuhito	1867–1912
Taishō (Yoshihito)	1912–1926
Shōwa (Hirohito)	1926–1989
Heisei (Akihito)	1989–1992

COUNTRIES AND TERRITORIES OF THE WORLD

For the past two hundred years, the world has been divided into nations. These are, for the most part, political divisions, although a country's economic system, its ethnic background, and even its natural resources and geography often play a role in the creation of its physical shape.

A Note About New Nations

During some historic periods, the world's nations are stable, and few new nations are formed. At other times, the world is in a state of upheaval, and new nations are frequently formed.

One such period occurred in the 1950s in Africa, when many of the countries that had been colonies of England, France, Spain, and Portugal sought freedom and became independent nations.

A second period began just a few years ago and is still underway. The current upheaval in the world's nations was caused by the fall of communism, and caused the breakup of the Soviet Union, now renamed the Commonwealth of Independent States (CIS). Some nations that were formerly of the Soviet Union became part of the CIS, while others broke off to form new countries—often returning to what they were before they became part of the Soviet Union.

Afghanistan
Area: 647,500 km² (249,999 sq. mi.)
Capital: Kabul
Government: In transition
Population: 16,450,304
Languages: Pushtu, Afghan Persian, Turkic languages
Religions: Sunni Muslim, Shi'a Muslim

Albania
Area: 28,750 km² (11,100 sq. mi.)
Capital: Tirana
Government: In transition
Population: 3,335,044
Languages: Albanian, Greek
Religions: Muslim, Greek Orthodox, Roman Catholic

Algeria
Area: 2,381,740 km² (919,590 sq. mi.)
Capital: Algiers
Government: In transition
Population: 26,022,188
Languages: Arabic, French, Berber dialects
Religion: Sunni Muslim

Andorra
Area: 450 km² (174 sq. mi.)
Capital: Andorra la Vella
Government: Coprincipality of France and Spain
Population: 53,197
Languages: Catalan, French, Castilian
Religion: Roman Catholic

Angola
Area: 1,246,700 km² (481,351 sq. mi.)
Capital: Luanda
Government: In transition
Population: 8,668,281
Languages: Portuguese, Bantu dialects
Religions: Indigenous beliefs, Roman Catholic, Protestant

Anguilla
Area: 91 km² (35 sq. mi.)
Capital: The Valley

Government: Dependent territory of U.K.
Population: 6,922
Language: English
Religions: Anglican, Methodist

Antigua and Barbuda
Area: 440 km² (170 sq. mi.)
Capital: Saint John's
Government: Parliamentary democracy affiliated with U.K.
Population: 63,917
Languages: English, local dialects
Religions: Anglican, Methodist, Roman Catholic

Argentina
Area: 2,766,890 km² (1,068,296 sq. mi.)
Capital: Buenos Aires
Government: Republic
Population: 32,663,983
Languages: Spanish, English, Italian, German, French
Religions: Roman Catholic, Protestant, Jewish

Armenia
Area: 29,283 km² (11,306 sq. mi.)
Capital: Yerevan
Government: Republic
Population: 3,305,000
Languages: Armenian, Russian
Religion: Armenian Apostolic

Aruba
Area: 193 km² (75 sq. mi.)
Capital: Oranjestad
Government: Independent territory of Netherlands
Population: 64,052
Languages: Dutch, Papiamento, Spanish, English
Religions: Roman Catholic, Protestant

Australia
Area: 7,686,850 km² (2,967,893 sq. mi.)
Capital: Canberra
Government: Federal parliamentary state affiliated with Great Britain
Population: 17,288,044
Languages: English, native languages

Religions: Anglican, Roman Catholic, other Protestant faiths

Austria
Area: 83,850 km² (32,374 sq. mi.)
Capital: Vienna
Government: Federal Republic
Population: 7,665,804
Language: German
Religions: Roman Catholic, Protestant

Azerbaijan
Area: 86,506 km² (33,400 sq. mi.)
Capital: Baku
Government: In transition
Population: 7,145,600
Languages: Azeri, Russian
Religion: Muslim

The Bahamas
Area: 13,940 km² (5,382 sq. mi.)
Capital: Nassau
Government: Independent commonwealth affiliated with U.K.
Population: 252,110
Languages: English, Creole
Religions: Baptist, Anglican, Roman Catholic, other Protestant faiths

Bahrain
Area: 620 km² (239 sq. mi.)
Capital: Manama
Government: Monarchy
Population: 536,974
Languages: Arabic, English, Farsi, Urdu
Religions: Shi'a Muslim, Sunni Muslim

Bangladesh
Area: 144,000 km² (55,598 sq. mi.)
Capital: Dhaka
Government: Republic
Population: 116,601,424
Languages: Bangla, English
Religions: Muslim, Hindu

Barbados
Area: 460 km² (166 sq. mi.)
Capital: Bridgetown
Government: Parliamentary democracy affiliated with U.K.
Population: 254,626

Language: English
Religions: Anglican, Pentecostal, Methodist, Roman Catholic

Barbuda
See Antigua and Barbuda.

Belgium
Area: 30,520 km² (11,784 sq. mi.)
Capital: Brussels
Government: Constitutional monarchy
Population: 9,921,910
Languages: Flemish, French
Religions: Roman Catholic, Protestant

Belize
Area: 22,960 km² (8,865 sq. mi.)
Capital: Belmopan
Government: Parliamentary democracy affiliated with U.K.
Population: 228,069
Languages: English, Spanish, Maya, Garifuna
Religions: Roman Catholic, Anglican, Methodist

Benin
Area: 112,620 km² (43,483 sq. mi.)
Capital: Porto-Novo
Government: Multiparty democracy
Population: 4,831,823
Languages: French, Fon, Yoruba, tribal dialects
Religions: Indigenous beliefs, Muslim, Christian

Bermuda
Area: 50 km² (19 sq. mi.)
Capital: Hamilton
Government: Dependent territory of U.K.
Population: 58,433
Language: English
Religions: Anglican, Roman Catholic, African Methodist

Bhutan
Area: 47,000 km² (18,147 sq. mi.)
Capital: Thimphu
Government: Monarchy
Population: 1,598,216

Languages: Dzongkha, other Tibetan dialects, Nepalese dialects
Religions: Lamaistic Buddhist, Hindu

Bolivia
Area: 1,098,580 km² (424,162 sq. mi.)
Capitals: La Paz and Sucre
Government: Republic
Population: 7,156,591
Languages: Spanish, Quechua, Aymara
Religions: Roman Catholic, Protestant faiths

Bosnia and Herzegovina
Area: 51,129 km² (19,741 sq. mi.)
Capital: Sarajevo
Government: Republic
Population: 4,116,000
Languages: Serbian, Croatian
Religions: Muslim, Serbian Orthodox, Roman Catholic

Botswana
Area: 600,370 km² (231,803 sq. mi.)
Capital: Gaborone
Government: Parliamentary republic
Population: 1,258,392
Languages: English, Setswana
Religions: Indigenous beliefs, Christian

Brazil
Area: 8,511,970 km² (3,286,472 sq. mi.)
Capital: Brasília
Government: Federal republic
Population: 155,356,073
Languages: Portuguese, Spanish, English, French
Religion: Roman Catholic

British Virgin Islands
Area: 150 km² (58 sq. mi.)
Capital: Road Town
Government: Dependent territory of U.K.
Population: 12,396
Language: English
Religions: Methodist, Anglican, other Protestant faiths, Roman Catholic

Brunei
Area: 5,770 km² (2,228 sq. mi.)
Capital: Bandar Seri Begawan
Government: Constitutional sultanate
Population: 397,777
Languages: Malay, English, Chinese
Religions: Muslim, Buddhist, Christian, indigenous beliefs

Bulgaria
Area: 110,910 km² (42,822 sq. mi.)
Capital: Sofia
Government: In transition
Population: 8,910,622
Language: Bulgarian
Religions: Bulgarian Orthodox, Muslim, Jewish, Roman Catholic

Burkina Faso
Area: 274,200 km² (105,869 sq. mi.)
Capital: Ouagadougou
Government: Military
Population: 9,359,889
Languages: French, Sudanic tribal dialects
Religions: Indigenous beliefs, Muslim, Christian

Burundi
Area: 27,830 km² (10,745 sq. mi.)
Capital: Bujumbura
Government: Republic
Population: 5,831,233
Languages: Kirundi, French, Swahili
Religions: Roman Catholic, indigenous beliefs, Protestant faiths, Muslim

Belarus
Area: 207,718 km² (80,200 sq. mi.)
Capital: Minsk
Government: In transition
Population: 10,200,000
Languages: Byelorussian, Russian
Religions: Russian Orthodox, Baptist

Cambodia
See Kampuchea.

Cameroon
Area: 475,440 km² (183,567 sq. mi.)
Capital: Yaoundé
Government: Unitary republic
Population: 11,390,374
Languages: English, French, African languages

Religions: Indigenous beliefs, Christian, Muslim

Canada
Area: 9,976,140 km² (3,851,788 sq. mi.)
Capital: Ottawa
Government: Confederation affiliated with U.K.
Population: 26,835,036
Languages: English, French
Religions: Roman Catholic, United Church, Anglican

Cape Verde
Area: 4,030 km² (1,556 sq. mi.)
Capital: Praia
Government: Republic
Population: 386,501
Languages: Portuguese, Crioulo
Religions: Roman Catholic and indigenous beliefs

Cayman Islands
Area: 260 km² (100 sq. mi.)
Capital: George Town
Government: Dependent territory of U.K.
Population: 27,489
Language: English
Religions: United Church, Anglican, Baptist, Roman Catholic

Central African Republic
Area: 622,980 km² (240,533 sq. mi.)
Capital: Bangui
Government: Military republic
Population: 2,952,382
Languages: French, Sangho, Arabic, Hunsa, Swahili
Religions: Christian (with animist beliefs), indigenous beliefs, Muslim

Chad
Area: 1,284,000 km² (495,752 sq. mi.)
Capital: N'Djamena
Government: Republic
Population: 5,122,467
Languages: French, Arabic, Sara, Sango
Religions: Muslim, Christian, indigenous beliefs/animism

Chile
Area: 756,950 km² (292,258 sq. mi.)
Capital: Santiago
Government: Republic
Population: 13,286,620
Language: Spanish
Religions: Roman Catholic, Protestant, Jewish

China
Area: 9,596,960 km² (3,705,386 sq. mi.)
Capital: Beijing
Government: Communist
Population: 1,151,486,981
Languages: Mandarin, Yue, Wu, Minbei, Minnan, Xiang, Gan, Hakka dialects, minority languages
Religions: Officially atheist; Confucianist, Taoist, Buddhist, Muslim, Christian

Christmas Island
Area: 135 km² (52 sq. mi.)
Capital: The Settlement
Government: Territory of Australia
Population: 2,278
Language: English
Religions: Buddhist, Muslim, Christian

Colombia
Area: 1,138,910 km² (439,733 sq. mi.)
Capital: Bogotá
Government: Republic
Population: 33,777,550
Language: Spanish
Religion: Roman Catholic

Comoros
Area: 2,170 km² (838 sq. mi.)
Capital: Moroni
Government: Independent republic
Population: 476,678
Languages: Arabic, French
Religions: Sunni Muslim, Roman Catholic

Congo
Area: 342,000 km² (132,046 sq. mi.)
Capital: Brazzaville
Government: Republic
Population: 2,309,444

Languages: French, Lingala, Kikongo
Religions: Christian, animist, Muslim

Cook Islands
Area: 240 km² (93 sq. mi.)
Capital: Avarua
Government: Self-governing in association with New Zealand
Population: 17,882
Language: English
Religion: Cook Islands Christian Church

Costa Rica
Area: 51,100 km² (19,730 sq. mi.)
Capital: San José
Government: Democratic republic
Population: 3,111,403
Languages: Spanish, English
Religion: Roman Catholic

Croatia
Area: 56,524 km² (21,824 sq. mi.)
Capital: Zagreb
Government: Republic
Population: 4,756,000
Language: Croatian
Religion: Roman Catholic

Cuba
Area: 110,860 km² (42,803 sq. mi.)
Capital: Havana
Government: Communist
Population: 10,732,037
Language: Spanish
Religion: Roman Catholic

Czech Republic
Area: Unavailable
Capital: Prague
Government: Republic
Population: 10,500,000
Language: Czech
Religion: Christian

Denmark
Area: 43,070 km² (16,629 sq. mi.)
Capital: Copenhagen
Government: Constitutional monarchy
Population: 5,132,626
Languages: Danish, Eskimo dialects, Faroese, German

Religions: Evangelical Lutheran, other Protestant faiths, Roman Catholic

Djibouti
Area: 22,000 km² (8,494 sq. mi.)
Capital: Djibouti
Government: Republic
Population: 346,311
Languages: French, Arabic, Somali, Afar
Religions: Muslim, Christian

Dominica
Area: 750 km² (290 sq. mi.)
Capital: Roseau
Government: Parliamentary democracy
Population: 86,285
Languages: English, French patois
Religions: Roman Catholic, Methodist, Pentecostal, Seventh-Day Adventist, Baptist

Dominican Republic
Area: 48,730 km² (18,815 sq. mi.)
Capital: Santo Domingo
Government: Republic
Population: 7,384,837
Language: Spanish
Religion: Roman Catholic

Ecuador
Area: 283,560 km² (109,483 sq. mi.)
Capital: Quito
Government: Republic
Population: 10,751,648
Languages: Spanish, Indian languages (esp. Quechua)
Religion: Roman Catholic

Egypt
Area: 1,001,450 km² (386,660 sq. mi.)
Capital: Cairo
Government: Republic
Population: 54,451,588
Languages: Arabic, English, French
Religions: Muslim, Coptic Christian

El Salvador
Area: 21,040 km² (8,124 sq. mi.)
Capital: San Salvador
Government: Republic
Population: 5,418,736
Languages: Spanish, Nahua

Religions: Roman Catholic, Protestant
    Evangelical

Equatorial Guinea
Area: 28,050 km² (10,830 sq. mi.)
Capital: Malabo
Government: Republic
Population: 378,729
Languages: Spanish, native languages
Religions: Christian, indigenous beliefs

Estonia
Area: 45,100 km² (17,413 sq. mi.)
Capital: Tallinn
Government: Republic
Population: 1,573,000
Languages: Estonian
Religion: Lutheran

Ethiopia
Area: 1,221,900 km² (471,776 sq. mi.)
Capital: Addis Ababa
Government: One-party republic
Population: 53,191,127
Languages: Amharic, Tigrinya, Orominga,
    Guaraginga, Somali, Arabic, English
Religions: Muslim, Ethiopian Orthodox, ani-
    mist

Falkland Islands
Area: 12,170 km² (4,699 sq. mi.)
Capital: Stanley
Government: Dependent territory of U.K.
Population: 1,968
Language: English
Religions: Anglican, Roman Catholic

Faroe Islands
Area: 1,400 km² (541 sq. mi.)
Capital: Tórshavn
Government: Self-governing overseas ad-
    ministrative division of Denmark
Population: 48,151
Languages: Faroese, Danish
Religion: Evangelical Lutheran

Fiji
Area: 18,270 km² (7,054 sq. mi.)
Capital: Suva
Government: Military republic
Population: 744,006

Languages: English, Fijian, Hindustani
Religions: Christian, Hindu, Muslim

Finland
Area: 337,030 km² (130,127 sq. mi.)
Capital: Helsinki
Government: Republic
Population: 4,991,131
Languages: Finnish, Swedish, Lapp, Rus-
    sian
Religions: Evangelical Lutheran, Greek Or-
    thodox

France
Area: 547,030 km² (211,208 sq. mi.)
Capital: Paris
Government: Republic
Population: 56,595,587
Languages: French, regional dialects
Religions: Roman Catholic, Protestant
    faiths, Jewish, Muslim

French Guiana
Area: 91,000 km² (35,135 sq. mi.)
Capital: Cayenne
Government: Overseas department of
    France
Population: 101,603
Language: French
Religion: Roman Catholic

French Polynesia
Area: 4,000 km² (1,544 sq. mi.)
Capital: Papeete
Government: Overseas territory of France
Population: 195,046
Languages: French, Tahitian
Religions: Protestant faiths, Roman Catholic

Gabon
Area: 267,670 km² (103,347 sq. mi.)
Capital: Libreville
Government: Republic
Population: 1,079,980
Languages: French, Fang, Myene, Bateke,
    Bapounou/Eschira, Bandjabi
Religions: Christian, animist, Muslim

The Gambia
Area: 11,300 km² (4,363 sq. mi.)
Capital: Banjul

Government: Republic
Population: 874,553
Languages: English, Mandinka, Wolof, Fula, local dialects
Religions: Muslim, Christian, indigenous beliefs

Georgia
Area: 69,699 km² (26,911 sq. mi.)
Capital: Tbilisi
Government: In transition
Population: 5,549,000
Languages: Georgian, Russian
Religion: Georgian Orthodox

Germany
Area: 356,910 km² (137,803 sq. mi.)
Capital: Berlin
Government: Federal republic
Population: 79,548,498
Language: German
Religions: Protestant faiths, Roman Catholic

Ghana
Area: 238,540 km² (92,100 sq. mi.)
Capital: Accra
Government: Military
Population: 15,616,934
Languages: English, Akan, Moshi-Dagomba, Ewe, Ga-Adangbe
Religions: Indigenous beliefs, Muslim, Christian

Gibraltar
Area: 6.5 km² (2.5 sq. mi.)
Capital: Gibraltar
Government: Dependent territory of U.K.
Population: 29,613
Languages: English, Spanish, Italian, Portuguese, Russian
Religions: Roman Catholic, Anglican, Muslim, Jewish

Greece
Area: 131,940 km² (50,942 sq. mi.)
Capital: Athens
Government: Presidential Parliamentary
Population: 10,042,956
Language: Greek
Religions: Greek Orthodox, Muslim

Greenland
Area: 2,175,600 km² (839,999 sq. mi.)
Capital: Nuuk (Godthåb)
Government: Self-governing overseas administrative division of Denmark
Population: 56,752
Languages: Eskimo dialects, Danish
Religion: Evangelical Lutheran

Grenada
Area: 340 km² (131 sq. mi.)
Capital: St. George's
Government: Parliamentary democracy affiliated with U.K.
Population: 83,812
Languages: English, French patois
Religions: Roman Catholic, Anglican, other Protestant faiths

Guadeloupe
Area: 1,780 km² (687 sq. mi.)
Capital: Basse-Terre
Government: Overseas department of France
Population: 344,897
Languages: French, Creole
Religions: Roman Catholic, Hindu, indigenous African

Guatemala
Area: 108,890 km² (42,042 sq. mi.)
Capital: Guatemala City
Government: Republic
Population: 9,266,018
Languages: Spanish, Quiche, Cakchiquel, Kekchi, other native dialects
Religions: Roman Catholic, Protestant, traditional Mayan

Guernsey
Area: 194 km² (75 sq. mi.)
Capital: St. Peter Port
Government: British crown dependency
Population: 57,596
Languages: English, French, Norman-French
Religions: Anglican, Roman Catholic, other Protestant faiths

Guinea
Area: 245,860 km² (94,927 sq. mi.)

Capital: Conakry
Government: Republic
Population: 7,455,850
Languages: French, tribal languages
Religions: Muslim, Christian, indigenous beliefs

Guinea-Bissau
Area: 36,120 km² (13,948 sq. mi.)
Capital: Bissau
Government: Republic
Population: 1,023,544
Languages: Portuguese, Criolo, African languages
Religions: Indigenous beliefs, Muslim, Christian

Guyana
Area: 214,970 km² (83,000 sq. mi.)
Capital: Georgetown
Government: Republic
Population: 749,508
Languages: English, Amerindian dialects
Religions: Christian, Hindu, Muslim

Haiti
Area: 27,750 km² (10,714 sq. mi.)
Capital: Port-au-Prince
Government: Military republic
Population: 6,286,511
Languages: French, Creole
Religions: Voodoo, Roman Catholic, Protestant faiths

Honduras
Area: 112,090 km² (43,278 sq. mi.)
Capital: Tegucigalpa
Government: Republic
Population: 4,949,275
Languages: Spanish, Amerindian dialects
Religions: Roman Catholic, Protestant faiths

Hungary
Area: 93,030 km² (35,919 sq. mi.)
Capital: Budapest
Government: Republic
Population: 10,558,001
Language: Hungarian (Magyar)
Religions: Calvinist, Lutheran

Iceland
Area: 103,000 km² (39,768 sq. mi.)
Capital: Reykjavík
Government: Republic
Population: 259,742
Language: Icelandic
Religions: Evangelical Lutheran, other Protestant faiths, Roman Catholic

India
Area: 3,287,590 km² (1,269,338 sq. mi.)
Capital: New Delhi
Government: Federal republic
Population: 866,351,738
Languages: Hindi, English, Bengali, Telugu, Marathi, Tamil, Urdu, Gujarati, Malayalan, Kannada, Oriya, Punjabi, Assamese, Kashmiri, Sindhi, Sanskrit, Hindustani
Religions: Hindu, Muslim, Christian, Sikh, Buddhist, Jains

Indonesia
Area: 1,904,570 km² (735,272 sq. mi.)
Capital: Jakarta
Government: Republic
Population: 193,560,494
Languages: Bahasa Indonesian, Javanese, English, Dutch
Religions: Muslim, Protestant faiths, Roman Catholic, Hindu, Buddhist

Iran
Area: 1,648,000 km² (636,293 sq. mi.)
Capital: Teheran
Government: Theocratic republic
Population: 59,051,082
Languages: Farsi, Turk, Kurdish, Arabic, Luri, Baloch
Religions: Shi'a Muslim, Sunni Muslim, Zoroastrian, Jewish, Christian, Bahá'í

Iraq
Area: 434,920 km² (167,923 sq. mi.)
Capital: Baghdad
Government: Republic
Population: 19,524,718
Languages: Arabic, Kurdish, Assyrian, Armenian

Religions: Shi'a Muslim, Sunni Muslim, Christian

Ireland
Area: 70,280 km² (27,135 sq. mi.)
Capital: Dublin
Government: Republic
Population: 3,489,165
Languages: Irish (Gaelic), English
Religions: Roman Catholic, Anglican

Israel
Area: (excluding occupied territories) 20,770 km² (8,019 sq. mi.)
Capital: Jerusalem
Government: Parliamentary democracy
Population: 4,264,605 (excluding occupied territories)
Languages: Hebrew, Arabic
Religions: Jewish, Muslim, Christian, Druze

Italy
Area: 301,230 km² (116,305 sq. mi.)
Capital: Rome
Government: Republic
Population: 57,772,375
Languages: Italian, German, French, Slovene
Religion: Roman Catholic

Ivory Coast
Area: 322,460 km² (124,502 sq. mi.)
Capital: Abidjan (also Yamoussoukro)
Government: Republic
Population: 12,977,909
Languages: French, Dioula, tribal languages
Religions: Indigenous beliefs, Muslim, Christian

Jamaica
Area: 10,990 km² (4,243 sq. mi.)
Capital: Kingston
Government: Parliamentary democracy affiliated with U.K.
Population: 2,489,353
Languages: English, Creole
Religions: Protestant, Roman Catholic, spiritualist cults

Japan
Area: 377,835 km² (145,882 sq. mi.)
Capital: Tokyo
Government: Constitutional monarchy
Population: 124,017,137
Language: Japanese
Religions: Shinto, Buddhist, Christian

Jersey
Area: 117 km² (45 sq. mi.)
Capital: Saint Helier
Government: British crown dependency
Population: 84,331
Languages: English, French, Norman-French
Religions: Anglican, other Protestant faiths, Roman Catholic

Jordan
Area: 91,880 km² (35,475 sq. mi.) (excluding West Bank)
Capital: Amman
Government: Constitutional monarchy
Population: 3,412,553 (excluding West Bank)
Languages: Arabic, English
Religions: Sunni Muslim, Christian

Kampuchea
Area: 181,040 km² (69,900 sq. mi.)
Capital: Phnom Penh
Government: Disputed between National Government of Cambodia and the State of Cambodia
Population: 7,146,386
Languages: Khmer, French
Religion: Theravada Buddhist

Kazakhstan
Area: 2,717,428 km² (1,049,200 sq. mi.)
Capital: Alma Alta
Government: In transition
Population: 16,538,000
Languages: Kazakh, Russian
Religion: Muslim

Kenya
Area: 582,650 km² (224,961 sq. mi.)
Capital: Nairobi
Government: One-party republic
Population: 25,241,978
Languages: English, Swahili, local languages

Religions: Protestant faiths, Roman Catholic, indigenous beliefs, Muslim

Kiribati
Area: 710 km² (274 sq. mi.)
Capital: Tarawa
Government: Republic
Population: 71,137
Languages: English, Gilbertese
Religions: Roman Catholic, Protestant, Seventh-Day Adventist, Bahá'í

Korea, North
Area: 120,540 km² (46,540 sq. mi.)
Capital: Pyongyang
Government: Communist
Population: 21,814,656
Language: Korean
Religions: Buddhist, Confucianist

Korea, South
Area: 98,480 km² (38,023 sq. mi.)
Capital: Seoul
Government: Republic
Population: 43,134,386
Language: Korean
Religions: Confucianist, Christian, Buddhist, Shamanist, Chondokyo

Kuwait
Area: 17,820 km² (6,880 sq. mi.)
Capital: Kuwait
Government: Nominal constitutional monarchy
Population: 2,204,400
Languages: Arabic, English
Religions: Sunni Muslim, Shi'a Muslim, Christian, Hindu, Parsi

Kyrgyzstan
Area: 198,509 km² (76,642 sq. mi.)
Capital: Frunze
Government: In transition
Population: 4,372,000
Languages: Kirghiz, Russian
Religion: Muslim

Laos
Area: 236,800 km² (91,428 sq. mi.)
Capital: Vientiane
Government: Communist

Population: 4,113,223
Languages: Lao, French, English
Religions: Buddhist, animist

Latvia
Area: 63,701 km² (24,595 sq. mi.)
Capital: Riga
Government: Republic
Population: 2,681,000
Language: Latvian
Religions: Lutheran, Russian Orthodox, Catholic

Lebanon
Area: 10,400 km² (4,015 sq. mi.)
Capital: Beirut
Government: Republic
Population: 3,384,626
Languages: Arabic, French, Armenian, English
Religions: Muslim and Christian, each divided into sects (17 in all)

Lesotho
Area: 30,350 km² (11,718 sq. mi.)
Capital: Maseru
Government: Constitutional monarchy (military regime)
Population: 1,801,174
Languages: Sesotho, English, Zulu, Xhosa
Religions: Christian, indigenous beliefs

Liberia
Area: 111,370 km² (43,000 sq. mi.)
Capital: Monrovia
Government: Republic
Population: 2,730,446
Languages: English, Niger-Congo languages
Religions: Indigenous beliefs, Christian, Muslim

Libya
Area: 1,759,540 km² (679,358 sq. mi.)
Capital: Tripoli
Government: Military dictatorship
Population: 4,350,742
Languages: Arabic, Italian, English
Religion: Sunni Muslim

Liechtenstein
Area: 160 km² (62 sq. mi.)

Capital: Vaduz
Government: Constitutional monarchy
Population: 28,476
Languages: German, Alemannic
Religions: Roman Catholic, Protestant faiths

Lithuania

Area: 65,190 km² (25,170 sq. mi.)
Capital: Vilnius
Government: Republic
Population: 3,690,000
Language: Lithuanian
Religion: Roman Catholic

Luxembourg

Area: 2,586 km² (998 sq. mi.)
Capital: Luxembourg
Government: Constitutional monarchy
Population: 388,017
Languages: Luxembourgish, German,
  French, English
Religions: Roman Catholic, Protestant
  faiths, English

Macau

Area: 16 km² (6 sq. mi.)
Capital: Macau
Government: Overseas territory of Portugal
  until 1999
Population: 446,262
Languages: Portuguese, Cantonese
Religions: Buddhist, Roman Catholic

Macedonia (former Yugoslav Republic of)

Area: 25,713 km² (9,928 sq. mi.)
Capital: Skopje
Government: Republic
Population: 2,033,964
Language: Macedonian
Religions: Eastern Orthodox, Muslim

Madagascar

Area: 587,040 km² (226,656 sq. mi.)
Capital: Antananarivo
Government: Republic
Population: 12,185,318
Languages: French, Malagasy
Religions: Indigenous beliefs, Christian,
  Muslim

Malawi

Area: 118,480 km² (45,745 sq. mi.)
Capital: Lilongwe
Government: One-party state
Population: 9,438,462
Languages: English, Chichewa, Tombuka
Religions: Protestant faiths, Roman Catho-
  lic, Muslim, indigenous beliefs

Malaysia

Area: 329,750 km² (127,316 sq. mi.)
Capital: Kuala Lumpur
Government: Constitutional monarchy with
  hereditary rulers in peninsular states
Population: 17,981,698
Languages: Malay, English, Chinese dia-
  lects, Tamil, Hakka dialects, tribal lan-
  guages
Religions: Muslim, Buddhist, Hindu, Confu-
  cianist, Christian

Maldives

Area: 300 km² (116 sq. mi.)
Capital: Male
Government: Republic
Population: 226,200
Languages: Divehi, English
Religion: Sunni Muslim

Mali

Area: 1,240,000 km² (478,764 sq. mi.)
Capital: Bamako
Government: Republic
Population: 8,338,542
Languages: French, Bambara
Religions: Muslim, indigenous beliefs, Chris-
  tian

Malta

Area: 320 km² (124 sq. mi.)
Capital: Valletta
Government: Parliamentary democracy
Population: 356,427
Languages: Maltese, English
Religion: Roman Catholic

Man, Isle of

Area: 588 km² (227 sq. mi.)
Capital: Douglas
Government: British crown dependency

Population: 64,075
Languages: English, Manx Gaelic
Religions: Anglican, other Protestant faiths, Roman Catholic

Martinique
Area: 1,100 km² (425 sq. mi.)
Capital: Fort-de-France
Government: Overseas department of France
Population: 345,180
Languages: French, Creole patois
Religions: Roman Catholic, Hindu, indigenous African

Mauritania
Area: 1,030,700 km² (397,953 sq. mi.)
Capital: Nouakchott
Government: Military republic
Population: 1,995,755
Languages: Hasaniya Arabic, French, Toucouleur, Fula, Sarakole, Wolof
Religion: Muslim

Mauritius
Area: 1,860 km² (718 sq. mi.)
Capital: Port Louis
Government: Parliamentary democracy affiliated with U.K.
Population: 1,081,000
Languages: English, Creole, French, Hindi, Urdu, Hakka, Bojpoori
Religions: Hindu, Roman Catholic, Anglican, Muslim

Mayotte
Area: 375 km² (145 sq. mi.)
Capital: Dzaoudzi
Government: Territory of France
Population: 75,027
Languages: Mahorian, French
Religions: Muslim, Christian

Mexico
Area: 1,972,550 km² (761,602 sq. mi.)
Capital: Mexico City
Government: Federal republic
Population: 90,007,304
Language: Spanish
Religions: Roman Catholic, Protestant faiths

Moldova
Area: 33,701 km² (13,012 sq. mi.)
Capital: Kishinev
Government: In transition
Population: 4,341,000
Language: Romanian
Religions: Russian Orthodox, Seventh-Day Adventist

Monaco
Area: 1.9 km² (.7 sq. mi.)
Capital: Monaco
Government: Constitutional monarchy
Population: 29,712
Languages: French, English, Italian, Monegasque
Religion: Roman Catholic

Mongolia
Area: 1,565,000 km² (604,247 sq. mi.)
Capital: Ulaanbaatar
Government: In transition
Population: 2,247,068
Languages: Khalkha Mongol, Turkic, Russian, Chinese
Religions: Tibetan Buddhist, Muslim

Montserrat
Area: 100 km² (39 sq. mi.)
Capital: Plymouth
Government: Dependent territory of U.K.
Population: 12,504
Language: English
Religions: Anglican, other Protestant faiths, Roman Catholic

Morocco
Area: 446,550 km² (172,413 sq. mi.)
Capital: Rabat
Government: Constitutional monarchy
Population: 26,181,889
Languages: Arabic, French, Berber dialects
Religions: Muslim, Christian, Jewish

Mozambique
Area: 801,950 km² (309,633 sq. mi.)
Capital: Maputo
Government: Republic
Population: 15,113,282

Languages: Portuguese, indigenous languages
Religions: Indigenous beliefs, Christian, Muslim

Myanmar (Burma)
Area: 676,550 km² (261,216 sq. mi.)
Capital: Yangon
Government: Military
Population: 42,112,082
Languages: Burmese, ethnic languages
Religions: Buddhist, Christian, Muslim, animist beliefs

Namibia
Area: 824,290 km² (318,258 sq. mi.)
Capital: Windhoek
Government: Republic
Population: 1,520,504
Languages: Afrikaans, German, English, indigenous languages
Religions: Christian, indigenous beliefs

Nauru
Area: 20 km² (8 sq. mi.)
Capital: Yaren
Government: Republic
Population: 9,333
Languages: Nauruan, English
Religions: Protestant faiths, Roman Catholic

Nepal
Area: 140,800 km² (54,363 sq. mi.)
Capital: Kathmandu
Government: Constitutional monarchy
Population: 19,611,900
Languages: Nepali, local languages
Religions: Hindu, Buddhist, Muslim

Netherlands
Area: 37,310 km² (14,405 sq. mi.)
Capital: Amsterdam and The Hague
Government: Constitutional monarchy
Population: 15,022,393
Language: Dutch
Religions: Roman Catholic, Protestant faiths

Netherlands Antilles
Area: 960 km² (371 sq. mi.)
Capital: Willemstad (on Curacao)

Government: Autonomous territory of Netherlands
Population: 183,872
Languages: Dutch, Papiamento, English, Spanish
Religions: Roman Catholic, Protestant faiths, Jewish, Seventh-Day Adventist

New Caledonia
Area: 19,060 km² (7,359 sq. mi.)
Capital: Nouméa
Government: Overseas territory of France
Population: 171,559
Languages: French, Melanesian-Polynesian dialects
Religions: Roman Catholic, Protestant faiths

New Zealand
Area: 268,680 km² (103,737 sq. mi.)
Capital: Wellington
Government: Parliamentary democracy affiliated with U.K.
Population: 3,308,973
Languages: English, Maori
Religions: Anglican, Presbyterian, Roman Catholic

Nicaragua
Area: 129,494 km² (49,998 sq. mi.)
Capital: Managua
Government: Republic
Population: 3,751,884
Languages: Spanish, English, Amerindian dialects
Religion: Roman Catholic

Niger
Area: 1,267,000 km² (489,189 sq. mi.)
Capital: Niamey
Government: Republic (under military control)
Population: 8,154,145
Languages: French, Hausa, Djerma
Religions: Muslim, indigenous beliefs, Christian

Nigeria
Area: 923,770 km² (356,668 sq. mi.)
Capital: Lagos
Government: Military

Population: 122,470,574
Languages: English, Hausa, Yoruba, Ibo, Fulani
Religions: Muslim, Christian, indigenous beliefs

Niue
Area: 260 km² (100 sq. mi.)
Capital: Alofi
Government: Self-governing territory affiliated with New Zealand
Population: 1,908
Languages: Polynesian (Tongan-Samoan dialect), English
Religions: Ekalesia Niue, Mormon

Norfolk Island
Area: 40 km² (15.4 sq. mi.)
Capital: Kingston
Government: Territory of Australia
Population: 2,576
Languages: English, Norfolk
Religions: Anglican, other Protestant faiths, Roman Catholic, Seventh-Day Adventist

Norway
Area: 324,220 km² (125,181 sq. mi.)
Capital: Oslo
Government: Constitutional monarchy
Population: 4,273,442
Languages: Norwegian, Lapp, Finnish
Religions: Evangelical Lutheran, other Protestant faiths, Roman Catholic

Oman
Area: 212,460 km² (82,031 sq. mi.)
Capital: Muscat
Government: Absolute monarchy
Population: 1,534,011
Languages: Arabic, English, Baluchi, Urdu
Religions: Ibadhi Muslim, Sunni Muslim, Shi'a Muslim, Hindu

Pakistan
Area: 803,940 km² (310,401 sq. mi.)
Capital: Islamabad
Government: Federal republic
Population: 117,490,278
Languages: Urdu, English, Punjabi, Sindhi, Pushtu, Baluchi
Religions: Muslim, Christian, Hindu

Panama
Area: 78,200 km² (30,193 sq. mi.)
Capital: Panama
Government: Centralized republic
Population: 2,476,281
Languages: Spanish, English
Religions: Roman Catholic, Protestant faiths

Papua New Guinea
Area: 461,690 km² (178,259 sq. mi.)
Capital: Port Moresby
Government: Parliamentary democracy affiliated with U.K.
Population: 3,913,186
Languages: Motu, local dialects, English
Religions: Roman Catholic, Protestant faiths

Paraguay
Area: 406,750 km² (157,046 sq. mi.)
Capital: Asunción
Government: Republic
Population: 4,798,739
Languages: Spanish, Guarani
Religions: Roman Catholic, Mennonite, other Protestant faiths

Peru
Area: 1,285,220 km² (496,223 sq. mi.)
Capital: Lima
Government: Republic
Population: 22,361,785
Languages: Spanish, Quechua, Aymara
Religion: Roman Catholic

Philippines
Area: 300,000 km² (115,830 sq. mi.)
Capital: Manila
Government: Republic
Population: 65,758,788
Languages: Pilipino (Tagalog), English
Religions: Roman Catholic, Muslim, Buddhist

Poland
Area: 312,680 km² (120,727 sq. mi.)
Capital: Warsaw
Government: Democratic state
Population: 37,799,638

Language: Polish
Religions: Roman Catholic, Russian Orthodox, Catholic

Portugal
Area: 92,080 km² (35,552 sq. mi.)
Capital: Lisbon
Government: Republic
Population: 10,387,617
Language: Portuguese
Religions: Roman Catholic, Protestant faiths

Qatar
Area: 11,000 km² (4,247 sq. mi.)
Capital: Doha
Government: Traditional monarchy
Population: 518,478
Languages: Arabic, English
Religion: Muslim

Réunion
Area: 2,510 km² (969 sq. mi.)
Capital: Saint-Denis
Government: Overseas department of France
Population: 607,086
Languages: French, Creole
Religion: Roman Catholic

Romania
Area: 237,500 km² (91,699 sq. mi.)
Capital: Bucharest
Government: In transition
Population: 23,397,054
Languages: Romanian, Hungarian, German
Religions: Romanian Orthodox, Roman Catholic, Protestant faiths, Greek Catholic

Russia
Area: 17,075,352 km² (6,592,800 sq. mi.)
Capital: Moscow
Government: In transition
Population: 147,386,000
Language: Russian
Religions: Russian Orthodox, Baptist, Jewish

Rwanda
Area: 26,340 km² (10,170 sq. mi.)
Capital: Kigali

Government: Republic (under military control)
Population: 7,902,644
Languages: Kinyarwanda, French, Kiswahili
Religions: Roman Catholic, Protestant faiths, indigenous beliefs, Muslim

St. Helena
Area: 410 km² (158 sq. mi.)
Capital: Jamestown
Government: Dependent territory of the U.K.
Population: 6,695
Language: English
Religions: Anglican, other Protestant faiths, Roman Catholic

St. Kitts and Nevis
Area: 269 km² (104 sq. mi.)
Capital: Basseterre
Government: Constitutional monarchy affiliated with U.K.
Population: 40,293
Language: English
Religions: Anglican, other Protestant faiths, Roman Catholic

St. Lucia
Area: 620 km² (239 sq. mi.)
Capital: Castries
Government: Parliamentary democracy affiliated with U.K.
Population: 153,075
Languages: English, French patois
Religions: Roman Catholic, Protestant faiths, Anglican

St. Pierre and Miquelan
Area: 242 km² (93 sq. mi.)
Capital: Saint-Pierre
Government: Territorial collectivity of France
Population: 6,356
Language: French
Religion: Roman Catholic

St. Vincent and the Grenadines
Area: 340 km² (131 sq. mi.)
Capital: Kingstown

Government: Constitutional monarchy affiliated with U.K.
Population: 114,221
Languages: English, French patois
Religions: Anglican, other Protestant faiths, Roman Catholic, Seventh-Day Adventist

San Marino
Area: 60 km² (23 sq. mi.)
Capital: San Marino
Government: Republic
Population: 23,264
Language: Italian
Religion: Roman Catholic

São Tomé and Principe
Area: 960 km² (371 sq. mi.)
Capital: São Tomé and Principe
Government: Republic
Population: 128,499
Language: Portuguese
Religions: Roman Catholic, Evangelical Protestant, Seventh-Day Adventist

Saudi Arabia
Area: 2,149,690 km² (829,995 sq. mi.)
Capital: Riyadh
Government: Monarchy
Population: 17,869,558
Language: Arabic
Religion: Muslim

Senegal
Area: 196,190 km² (75,748 sq. mi.)
Capital: Dakar
Government: Republic
Population: 7,952,657
Languages: French, Wolof, Pulaar, Diola, Mandingo
Religions: Muslim, indigenous beliefs, Christian

Seychelles
Area: 455 km² (176 sq. mi.)
Capital: Victoria
Government: Republic
Population: 68,932
Languages: English, French, Creole
Religions: Roman Catholic, Anglican

Sierra Leone
Area: 71,740 km² (27,699 sq. mi.)
Capital: Freetown
Government: One-party republic
Population: 4,274,543
Languages: English, Mende, Krio, Temne
Religions: Muslim, indigenous beliefs, Christian

Singapore
Area: 633 km² (244 sq. mi.)
Capital: Singapore
Government: Republic
Population: 2,756,330
Languages: Chinese, Tamil, Malay, English
Religions: Buddhist, Muslim, Christian, Hindu, Sikh, Taoist, Confucianist

Slovakia
Area: 49,035 km² (18,929 sq. mi.)
Capital: Bratislava
Government: Republic
Population: 5,263,541
Languages: Slovak, Hungarian
Religion: Roman Catholic, Greek-Catholic, Protestant faiths, Jewish, Orthodox Eastern

Slovenia
Area: 20,246 km² (7,817 sq. mi.)
Capital: Ljubljana
Government: Republic
Population: 2,000,000
Language: Slovene
Religions: Roman Catholic, Protestant faiths

Solomon Islands
Area: 28,540 km² (10,985 sq. mi.)
Capital: Honiara
Government: Independent parliamentary state within British Commonwealth
Population: 347,115
Languages: Melanesian, pigdin English, local dialects
Religions: Anglican, Roman Catholic, other Protestant faiths

Somalia
Area: 637,660 km² (246,201 sq. mi.)
Capital: Mogadishu

Government: Republic
Population: 6,709,161
Languages: Somali, Arabic, Italian, English
Religion: Sunni Muslim

South Africa
Area: 1,221,040 km² (471,444 sq. mi.)
Capital: Pretoria, Cape Town
Government: Republic
Population: 40,600,518
Languages: Afrikaans, English, Zulu, Xhosa, Tswana
Religions: Christian, Hindu, Muslim

Spain
Area: 504,750 km² (194,884 sq. mi.)
Capital: Madrid
Government: Parliamentary monarchy
Population: 39,384,516
Languages: Castilian Spanish, Catalan, Galician, Basque
Religion: Roman Catholic

Sri Lanka (Ceylon)
Area: 65,610 km² (25,332 sq. mi.)
Capital: Colombo
Government: Republic
Population: 17,423,736
Languages: Sinhala, Tamil, English
Religions: Buddhist, Hindu, Christian, Muslim

Sudan
Area: 2,505,810 km² (967,493 sq. mi.)
Capital: Khartoum
Government: Military
Population: 27,220,088
Languages: Arabic, Nubian, Ta Bedawie, Nilotic and Nilo-Hamitic dialects, Sudanic dialects, English
Religions: Sunni Muslim, indigenous beliefs, Christian

Suriname
Area: 163,270 km² (63,039 sq. mi.)
Capital: Paramaribo
Government: Military republic
Population: 402,385

Languages: Dutch, English, Sranan Tongo, Javanese
Religions: Hindu, Muslim, Roman Catholic, Protestant faiths

Svalbard
Area: 62,049 km² (23,597 sq. mi.)
Capital: Longyearbyen
Government: Territory of Norway
Population: 3,942
Languages: Russian, Norwegian
Religion: Evangelical Lutheran

Swaziland
Area: 17,360 km² (6,703 sq. mi.)
Capital: Mbabane
Government: Independent monarchy within British Commonwealth
Population: 859,336
Languages: English, siSwati
Religions: Christian, indigenous beliefs

Sweden
Area: 449,960 km² (173,729 sq. mi.)
Capital: Stockholm
Government: Constitutional monarchy
Population: 8,564,317
Languages: Swedish, Lapp, Finnish
Religions: Evangelical Lutheran, Roman Catholic

Switzerland
Area: 41,290 km² (15,942 sq. mi)
Capital: Bern
Government: Federal republic
Population: 6,783,961
Languages: German, French, Italian, Romansch
Religions: Roman Catholic, Protestant faiths, Jewish

Syria
Area: 185,180 km² (71,498 sq. mi.)
Capital: Damascus
Government: Military republic
Population: 12,965,996
Languages: Arabic, Kurdish, Armenian, Aramaic, Circassian, French
Religions: Muslim, Christian

Tadzhikistan
Area: 139,909 km² (54,019 sq. mi.)
Capital: Dushanbe
Government: In transition
Population: 5,112,000
Languages: Tadzhik, Russian
Religion: Muslim

Taiwan
Area: 35,980 km² (13,892 sq. mi.)
Capital: Taipei
Government: Republic
Population: 20,658,702
Languages: Mandarin Chinese; Taiwanese and Hakka dialects
Religions: Buddhist, Confucianist, Taoist, Christian

Tanzania
Area: 945,090 km² (364,899 sq. mi.)
Capital: Dar es Salaam
Government: One-party republic
Population: 26,869,175
Languages: Swahili, English
Religions: Christian, Muslim, indigenous beliefs

Thailand
Area: 514,000 km² (198,455 sq. mi.)
Capital: Bangkok
Government: Constitutional monarchy under martial law
Population: 56,814,069
Languages: Thai, English, local dialects
Religions: Buddhist, Muslim

Togo
Area: 56,790 km² (21,927 sq. mi.)
Capital: Lomé
Government: One-party republic
Population: 3,810,616
Languages: French, Ewe, Mina, Dagomba, Kabyè
Religions: Indigenous beliefs, Christian, Muslim

Tokelau
Area: 10 km² (4 sq. mi.)
Capital: None (various local government agencies)

Government: Territory of New Zealand
Population: 1,700
Languages: Tokelauan, English
Religions: Congregational Christian Church, Roman Catholic

Tonga
Area: 748 km² (289 sq. mi.)
Capital: Nuku'alofa
Government: Constitutional monarchy
Population: 102,272
Languages: Tongan, English
Religion: Christian

Trinidad and Tobago
Area: 5,130 km² (1,981 sq. mi.)
Capital: Port-of-Spain
Government: Parliamentary democracy
Population: 1,285,297
Languages: English, Hindi, French, Spanish
Religions: Roman Catholic, Hindu, Protestant faiths, Muslim

Tunisia
Area: 163,610 km² (63,170 sq. mi.)
Capital: Tunis
Government: Republic
Population: 8,276,096
Languages: Arabic, French
Religions: Muslim, Christian, Jewish

Turkey
Area: 780,580 (301,382 sq. mi.)
Capital: Ankara
Government: Republican parliamentary democracy
Population: 58,580,993
Languages: Turkish, Kurdish, Arabic
Religions: Muslim (mostly Sunni), Christian, Jewish

Turkmenistan
Area: 488,000 km² (188,417 sq. mi.)
Capital: Ashkhabad
Government: In transition
Population: 3,621,700
Languages: Turkmen, Russian
Religion: Sunni Muslim

Turks and Caicos Islands
Area: 430 km² (166 sq. mi.)

Capital: Grand Turk (Cockburn Town)
Government: Dependent territory of U.K.
Population: 9,983
Language: English
Religions: Baptist, Methodist, Anglican, Seventh-Day Adventist

Tuvalu
Area: 26 km² (10 sq. mi.)
Capital: Funafuti
Government: Democracy affiliated with U.K.
Population: 9,317
Languages: Tuvaluan, English
Religion: Protestant faiths

Uganda
Area: 236,040 km² (91,135 sq. mi.)
Capital: Kampala
Government: One-party republic
Population: 18,690,070
Languages: English, Luganda, Swahili, Bantu and Nilotic languages
Religions: Roman Catholic, Protestant faiths, Muslim, indigenous beliefs

Ukraine
Area: 603,729 km² (233,100 sq. mi.)
Capital: Kiev
Government: In transition
Population: 51,704,000
Languages: Ukrainian, Russian
Religions: Russian Orthodox, Baptist, Roman Catholic, Jewish

United Arab Emirates
Area: 83,600 km² (32,278 sq. mi.)
Capital: Abu Dhabi
Government: Federation of seven emirates
Population: 2,389,759
Languages: Arabic, Farsi, English, Hindi, Urdu
Religions: Muslim, Christian, Hindu

United Kingdom
Area: 244,820 km² (94,525 sq. mi.)
Capital: London
Government: Constitutional monarchy
Population: 57,515,307
Languages: English, Welsh, Scottish Gaelic

Religions: Anglican, other Protestant faiths, Roman Catholic, Jewish

United States
Area: 9,372,610 km² (3,618,765 sq. mi.)
Capital: Washington, D.C.
Government: Federal republic
Population: 252,502,000
Languages: English, Spanish
Religions: Protestant faiths, Roman Catholic, Jewish, Muslim, Native American

Uruguay
Area: 176,220 km² (68,039 sq. mi.)
Capital: Montevideo
Government: Republic
Population: 3,121,101
Language: Spanish
Religions: Roman Catholic, Protestant faiths, Jewish

Uzbekistan
Area: 447,293 km² (172,700 sq. mi.)
Capital: Tashkent
Government: In transition
Population: 19,906,000
Languages: Uzbek, Russian
Religion: Muslim

Vanuatu
Area: 14,760 km² (5,699 sq. mi.)
Capital: Port-Vila
Government: Republic
Population: 170,319
Languages: English, French, Bislama
Religion: Christian

Vatican City
Area: 0.438 km² (108.7 acres)
Capital: Vatican City
Government: Independent papal state
Population: 738
Languages: Italian, Latin
Religion: Roman Catholic

Venezuela
Area: 912,050 km² (352,143 sq. mi.)
Capital: Caracas
Government: Republic
Population: 20,189,361

Languages: Spanish, Amerindian dialects
Religion: Roman Catholic

Vietnam
Area: 329,560 km² (127,243 sq. mi.)
Capital: Hanoi
Government: Communist
Population: 67,568,033
Languages: Vietnamese, French, Chinese, English, Khmer, tribal dialects
Religions: Buddhist, Confucianist, Taoist, Roman Catholic, indigenous beliefs, Muslim, Protestant faiths

Wallis and Futuna
Area: 274 km² (106 sq. mi.)
Capital: Mata-Utu
Government: Overseas territory of France
Population: 16,590
Languages: French, Wallisian
Religion: Roman Catholic

Western Sahara
Area: 2,860 km² (1,097 sq. mi.)
Capital: None
Government: Moroccan administrative protectorate
Population: 196,737
Languages: Hassaniya Arabic, Moroccan Arabic
Religion: Muslim

Western Samoa
Area: 2,860 km² (1,104 sq. mi.)
Capital: Apia
Government: Constitutional monarchy
Population: 190,346
Languages: Samoan, English
Religions: Congregational, Roman Catholic, other Protestant faiths

Yemen
Area: 527,970 km² (203,849 sq. mi.)
Capital: Sanaa
Government: Republic
Population: 10,062,633
Language: Arabic
Religions: Muslim, Christian, Hindu

Yugoslavia, Federal Republic of
(consists of Serbia, the largest republic of pre-independence Yugoslavia, and Montenegro, the smallest republic)
Area: 134,563 km² (51,995 sq. mi.)
Capital: Belgrade
Government: Republic
Population: 10.5 million
Languages: Serbian, Hungarian (Vojvodina), Albanian (Kosovo), Montenegrin
Religions: Serbian Orthodox, Muslim, Roman Catholic

Zaire
Area: 2,345,410 km² (905,563 sq. mi.)
Capital: Kinshasa
Government: Republic
Population: 37,832,407
Languages: French, Lingala, Swahili, Kinwana, Kikongo, Tshiluba
Religions: Roman Catholic, Protestant faiths, Kimbanguist, Muslim, indigenous beliefs

Zambia
Area: 752,610 km² (290,583 sq. mi.)
Capital: Lusaka
Government: Multi-party state
Population: 8,445,724
Languages: English, local languages and dialects
Religions: Christian, Muslim, Hindu, indigenous beliefs

Zimbabwe
Area: 390,580 km² (150,803 sq. mi.)
Capital: Harare
Government: Parliamentary democracy
Population: 10,720,459
Languages: English, Shona, Sindebele
Religions: Indigenous/Christian beliefs, Christian, indigenous beliefs, Muslim

MAJOR WORLD CITIES

Every country has a capital city, but some cities are what we might call "world capitals." They are important because they are centers of commerce or industry, or because they are cultural centers. The following list describes the major cities of the world.

Major World Cities

City	Population
Addis Ababa, Ethiopia	1,739,130
Capital since 1896	
Ahmedabad, India	2,059,725
Founded in 1411	
Alexandria, Egypt	2,893,000
Founded by Alexander the Great, 332 B.C.	
Algiers, Algeria	1,523,000
Founded in tenth century on Roman site	
Amman, Jordan	900,000
Site of biblical city of Ammonites	
Amsterdam, The Netherlands	693,209
Founded in 1300	
Ankara, Turkey	2,541,899
Capital of Galacia around 300 B.C.	
Athens, Greeece	885,737
Ancient Greek city-state in 700 B.C.	
Auckland, New Zealand	150,000
Founded 1840, original capital	
Baghdad, Iraq	1,984,142
Center of Islamic culture since 813	
Baku, Azerbaijan	1,741,000
Founded in ninth century	
Bandung, Indonesia	1,462,637
Founded in 1810	
Bangalore, India	2,628,593
Founded in sixteenth century	
Bangkok, Thailand	4,697,071
Capital since 1782	
Barcelona, Spain	1,667,699
Founded by Carthaginians around 300 B.C.	
Barranquilla, Colombia	917,486
Inland seaport since 1935	
Beijing	5,531,460
Founded around 1122 B.C.	
Beirut, Lebanon	474,870
Site of ancient Phoenician settlement	
Belgrade, Serbia, Yugoslavia	1,087,915
Site of Singidunum, ancient Roman camp	
Belo Horizonte, Brazil	2,122,073
Cattle and cotton-trading center	
Berlin, Germany	3,022,000
Founded in thirteenth century; capital of Germany 1871–1945, of United Germany since 1990	

City	Population
Birmingham, England	993,695
Market town since before thirteenth century	
Bogotá, Colombia	4,176,769
Founded by conquistadors in 1538	
Bombay, India	8,243,405
Established in early Christian era	
Brisbane, Australia	1,215,300
Founded in 1824 as a penal colony	
Brussels, Belgium	139,678
Capital since 1530	
Bucharest, Romania	1,975,508
Capital since 1861	
Budapest, Hungary	2,109,173
Site of Aquincum, second-century Roman camp	
Buenos Aires, Argentina	11,125,554
Settled by conquistadors in 1536	
Cairo, Egypt	6,075,836
Site of seventh-century Arab military camp	
Calcutta, India	3,305,006
Developed from 1690 English factory site	
Calgary, Alberta, Canada	706,000
Originally (1875) Northwest Mounted Police post	
Cali, Colombia	1,369,331
Founded by conquistadors in 1536	
Cape Town, South Africa	776,617
Founded in 1652 as Dutch naval base	
Caracas, Venezuela	1,246,677
Founded by conquistadors in 1567	
Casablanca, Morocco	2,408,600
Site of ancient city of Anfa	
Chicago, Illinois	2,977,520
Originally portage site for fur traders	
Chittagong, Bangladesh	1,388,476
Portuguese tradng post in 1600s	
Chongging, China	2,673,170
Former capital of Nationalist China	
Cologne, Germany	934,375
Site of Roman (A.D. 50) Colonia Agrippina	
Copenhagen, Denmark	469,706
Capital since 1443	
Córdoba, Argentina	1,134,086
Founded in 1573; university founded 1613	

City	Population
Damascus, Syria	1,343,000

City of Egyptians and Hittites before 1000 B.C.

Delhi, India	4,884,234

Thirteenth-century capital of northern India

Dhaka, Bangladesh	3,458,602

Capital since 1971 secession from Pakistan

Dnepropetrovsk, Ukraine	1,182,000

Founded in 1787 at Cossack village site

Donetsk, Ukraine	1,090,000

Founded in 1870; called Stalino until 1961

Dresden, Germany	515,892

Originally (A.D. 922) a Slavonic settlement

Dublin, Ireland	502,749

Originally a ninth-century Viking base

Düsseldorf, Germany	567,372

Rhine River port since eleventh century

Edmonton, Alberta, Canada	803,500

Originally (1795) Hudson Bay trading post

Essen, Germany	619,981

Ruhr Valley city founded in ninth century

Frankfurt, Germany	623,724

Site of ancient Roman military camp

Fukuoka, Japan	1,203,729

Thirteenth-century seaport on Hakata Bay

Genoa, Italy	742,442

Roman settlement in third century B.C.

Glasgow, Scotland	703,186

Founded by sixth-century missionaries

Gorky, Russia	1,425,000

Founded in 1221; renamed for Maxim Gorky

Guadalajara, Mexico	1,626,152

Originally founded in 1530

Guatemala City, Guatemala	754,243

Founded as capital in 1776

Guayaquil, Ecuador	1,572,615

Founded by conquistadors in 1535

Hamburg, Germany	1,595,255

Founded in ninth century by Charlemagne

Harbin, China	2,519,120

Village until linked by railroad in 1898

City	Population
Havana, Cuba	2,077,938

Founded in 1519 as Spanish navy base

Ho Chi Minh City, Vietnam	2,700,938

Formerly Saigon, ancient Khmer village

Hyderabad, India	2,093,488

Founded as Golconda; capital in 1589

Hyderabad, Pakistan	751,529

Founded in 1768 as capital of Sind

Ibadan, Nigeria	847,000

Founded around 1830 as military camp

Istanbul, Turkey	6,293,397

Until A.D. 300, Byzantium; until 1930, Constantinople

Jakarta, Indonesia	7,885,519

Founded in 1619 as Batavia; renamed 1971

Jerusalem, Israel	493,000

Capital of ancient kingdoms of Israel and Judah

Johannesburg, South Africa	632,369

Founded as gold-mining camp in 1886

Kanpur, India	1,481,789

Village until ceded to British in 1801

Karachi, Pakistan	5,180,562

Founded in 1725 as Hindu trading center

Kharkov, Ukraine	1,587,000

Founded in 1654 as outpost of Moscow

Kiev, Ukraine	2,544,000

Russian "Mother of Cities," founded 882

Kinshasa, Zaire	2,653,558

Founded in 1881 as Leopoldville; renamed 1966

Kobe, Japan	1,447,547

Ancient fishing village until 1868

Kuala Lumpur, Malaysia	919,610

Founded as tin-mining settlement in 1857

Kuibyshev, Russia	1,280,000

Founded in 1586; temporary Russian capital in World War II

Lagos, Nigeria	1,060,848

Former slave trading center; now the capital

Lahore, Pakistan	2,952,689

Capital of Mogul sultans in eleventh century *(continued)*

Major World Cities (*continued*)

City	Population
La Paz, Bolivia	976,800
Founded in 1548; capital since 1898	
Leipzig, Germany	538,860
Founded in eleventh century; Bach was organist here	
Lima, Peru	6,233,800
Site of oldest university of Americas (1551)	
Lisbon, Portugal	806,167
Ancient Phoenician, Carthaginian trading center	
Liverpool, England	469,642
Chartered in 1207 by King John	
Lodz, Poland	857,485
Founded in 1423; belonged to Russia until 1919	
London, England	6,735,353
Established in A.D. 43 as Roman town of Londinium	
Los Angeles, California	3,362,710
Founded in 1781 as capital of Spanish colony	
Madras, India	3,276,622
Founded in 1640 as British outpost	
Madrid, Spain	2,991,223
A Moorish fortress until 932	
Managua, Nicaragua	608,020
Established as capital in 1855	
Manila, Philippines	1,728,441
Founded by Spanish in 1571	
Marseilles, France	876,260
Originally Massilia, Ionian Greek colony, in 600 B.C.	
Mecca, Saudi Arabia	366,801
Birthplace of Muhammad in 570	
Medellín, Colombia	1,452,392
Mining center founded 1675	
Melbourne, Australia	2,965,600
Founded 1835 by Tasmanian settlers	
Mexico City, Mexico	8,831,079
Aztec capital until captured by Cortés in 1521	
Milan, Italy	1,548,580
Ancient Celtic town captured by Romans in 222 B.C.	

City	Population
Minsk, Belarus	1,543,000
Eleventh-century city on Moscow–Warsaw rail link	
Monterrey, Mexico	1,084,696
Founded in 1579; invaded by U.S. troops in 1846	
Montevideo, Uruguay	1,251,647
Settled by Spanish in 1726; capital since 1828	
Montreal, Quebec, Canada	3,021,300
Site of Indian encampment; founded by French in 1642	
Moscow, Russia	8,818,000
Founded in 1147; became capital around 1340	
Munich, Germany	1,206,394
Founded in 1158; birthplace of Nazi movement, 1923	
Nagoya, Japan	2,147,667
Buddhist temple site in second century	
Nanjing, China	2,091,400
Founded in 1368; twice capital in twentieth century	
Naples, Italy	1,207,750
Named Neapolis (New City) by Greek settlers around 600 B.C.	
New York City, New York	7,352,700
Founded in 1609 as New Amsterdam by Dutch; renamed 1664	
Novosibirsk, Russia	1,423,000
Founded in 1893 on Trans-Siberian Railway; called "Chicago of Siberia"	
Odessa, Ukraine	1,141,000
Founded by Tartars in fourteenth century	
Osaka, Japan	2,644,691
Founded in sixteenth century as capital city	
Ottawa, Ontario, Canada	853,200
Selected as capital in 1858 by Queen Victoria	
Palermo, Italy	714,246
Founded by Phoenicians in eighth century B.C.	
Paris, France	2,188,960
Grew from pre-Roman settlement named Lutetia Parisiorum	

City	Population
Port-au-Prince, Haiti	461,464

Founded by sugar planters in 1749; capital since 1804

Pôrto Alegre, Brazil	1,275,483

Founded in 1742 by settlers from the Azores

Prague, Czech Republic	1,209,149

Grew from tenth-century trading center

Pusan, South Korea	3,514,798

Originally a fishing village; opened to trade in 1443

Pyongyang, North Korea	1,250,000

Existed as Heijo, a cultural center, in 1100 B.C.

Quebec City, Quebec, Canada	615,400

Site of Indian settlement visited by explorer Cartier in 1535

Quezon City, Philippines	1,546,019

Founded in 1940 as site of future capital

Quito, Ecuador	1,137,705

Originally camp of the Quitos; captured by Incas in 1470

Recife, Brazil	1,289,627

Settled by Portuguese in 1535

Rio de Janeiro, Brazil	5,615,149

Founded by Portuguese in 1502; capital since 1889

Riyadh, Saudi Arabia	666,840

One-time center of classic Arabic architecture

Rome, Italy	2,828,692

According to legend, founded in 753 B.C. by Romulus and Remus

Rosario, Argentina	1,071,384

City in La Pampa region; founded in 1730

Rotterdam, The Netherlands	575,266

North Sea port chartered in 1328

St. Petersburg, Russia	4,948,000

Founded in 1703; named Leningrad from 1924 to 1991

Salvador, Brazil	1,811,367

Founded in 1549 as Bahia

Santiago, Chile	4,099,714

Founded in 1541 by conquistadors

City	Population
Santo Domingo, Dominican Republic	673,470

Oldest continuous European settlement in Americas, founded in 1496

São Paulo, Brazil	10,099,086

Founded in 1554 by Jesuit missionaries on native campsite

Sapporo, Japan	1,621,418

Founded in 1869 in government plan to develop Hokkaido Island

Seoul, South Korea	9,639,110

Originally named Keijo, a Korean capital since 1392

Seville, Spain	653,533

Originally Hispalis, a Phoenician trading center

Shanghai, China	6,292,960

Existed as Hu-tsen in Sung dynasty, in eleventh century

Shenyang, China	3,944,240

Formerly Mukden, capital city of twelfth-century Tartars

Singapore, Singapore	2,704,000

Originally Singhapura, destroyed in 1365; refounded in 1819

Sofia, Bulgaria	1,127,527

Founded as Sardica by second-century Romans; capital since 1879

Stockholm, Sweden	666,810

Originally a fishing village, founded in thirteenth century

Surabaja, Indonesia	2,027,913

Grew from seventeenth-century Javanese trading post

Sverdlovsk, Russia	1,331,000

Founded in 1721 as Ekaterinburg; renamed in 1924

Sydney, Australia	3,531,000

First British settlement in Australia, in 1788

Taipei, Taiwan	2,270,983

Settled in eighteenth century by Chinese mainland immigrants

Tashkent, Uzbekistan	2,124,000

Ancient central Asian city; existed in first century B.C.

(continued)

Major World Cities (*continued*)

City	Population
Tbilisi, Georgia	1,194,000
Also called Tiflis; settled in fourth century B.C.	
Teheran, Iran	6,042,584
Settled in thirteenth century by refugees from Mongol invasion	
Tianjin, China	5,152,180
Also called Tientsin, ancient trading center	
Tokyo, Japan	8,323,699
Founded in twelfth century as fortress for warlord	
Toronto, Ontario, Canada	3,666,600
Originally Fort Rouille, 1749; York, 1793; renamed 1834	
Tripoli, Libya	551,477
Founded as Oea by Phoenicians in seventh century B.C.	
Tunis, Tunisia	596,654
Pre-Carthaginian city with access to Mediterranean	
Turin, Italy	1,059,505
Ancient Roman city of Augusta Taurinorum	
Valencia, Spain	718,750
Former city of Romans, Visigoths, and Moors	

City	Population
Vancouver, British Columbia, Canada	1,506,000
Originally settled in 1875 as Granville; renamed 1886	
Vienna, Austria	1,486,963
Capital of the Austro-Hungarian Empire 1278–1918; now capital of the Austrian republic	
Volgograd, Russia	988,000
Founded in 1589 as Tsaritsyn; later Stalingrad; renamed 1961	
Warsaw, Poland	1,673,688
Settled in eleventh century; capital since 1596	
Washington, D.C.	617,000
Founded in 1790 on site selected by George Washington	
Wellington, New Zealand	135,400
Founded in 1840; replaced Auckland as capital in 1865	
Yangon, Myanmar	2,513,023
Existed as fishing village in sixth century; formerly Rangoon, Burma	
Yokohama, Japan	3,151,087
Feudal fishing village until opened to foreign trade in 1859	

WORLD COOPERATION: THE UNITED NATIONS

The United Nations was promoted during World War II as a successor to the League of Nations, which was formed after World War I.

President Franklin D. Roosevelt suggested the name in 1941, and it was officially adopted the next year. The United Nations was formally organized on June 26, 1945. UN headquarters are located in New York City, although its specialized agencies are located in cities throughout the world.

The United Nations is composed of six general bodies, and many specialized agencies, committees, and commissions. An agency or committee may specialize in a region, such as sub-Saharan Africa, or in a topic, such as women's issues or child nutrition.

The six general bodies are as follows:

- *General Assembly* This is the deliberative body of the UN, with representatives from all member nations. Although the General Assembly cannot pass laws, it makes recommendations to the Security Council on social, political, and economic issues. Located in New York.
- *Security Council* Its primary task is to preserve world peace. Composed of fifteen members, the Security Council has five permanent, ones: the United States, the Russian Federation (formerly part of the Soviet Union), China, France, and the United Kingdom. Ten other mem-

Secretaries General of the United Nations

1946	Trygve Lie, Norway
1953	Dag Hammarskjold, Sweden
1961	U Thant, Burma
1972	Kurt Waldheim, Austria
1982	Javier Pérez de Cuellar, Peru
1992	Boutros Boutros-Ghali, Egypt

bers hold nonpermanent seats for two-year terms. The Security Council votes on major issues, and has the power to impose an economic sanction or to take military action when there is a threat to world peace or military aggression by one nation on another. Located in New York.

- *Economic and Social Council* This 54-member body, elected by the General Assembly, investigates economic and social issues and presents its findings to the General Assembly. It also coordinates and oversees the work of the specialized agencies. Located in New York.
- *Secretariat* This body carries out the administrative tasks that support the other bodies and agencies. It is headed by the Secretary-General, who is elected to a five-year term. Located in New York.

- *International Court of Justice* Fifteen judges sit on this court, and nine must be present in order to render a decision. The court handles disputes among member states involving questions of international law. Located at The Hague.
- *Trusteeship Council* The Trusteeship Council (along with the Special Committee on Decolonization, formed in the 1960s) assists colonies or territories of other countries in becoming independent countries. It helps them figure out what kind of government they want. For example, the council aided many of the African nations that became independent in the 1950s and 1960s. Located in New York.

The chart that follows shows the organization of the UN:

A Better Halloween: Children Helping Children

In addition to collecting candy, some U.S. and Canadian children collect money for UNICEF on Halloween. UNICEF, which stands for United Nations International Children's Fund, is the one organization at the UN devoted to working exclusively with children and adolescents around the world. UNICEF brings relief to children in devastated areas, those suffering under war or famine, for example.

UNICEF began life as the Children's Emergency Fund and was intended to help children whose lives were torn apart by World War II. Since then it has expanded to help children all over the world. It brings food and medical supplies directly to children and adolescents who need them, and also helps to develop nutritional and educational programs in regions of the world that need this assistance. In 1965, UNICEF was awarded the Nobel Peace Prize.

If you are interested in collecting for UNICEF at Halloween, have one of your parents or your teacher call 1-800-252-KIDS and ask for Halloween collection boxes. If you don't trick-or-treat, UNICEF has many other programs throughout the month of October that let you help other children.

The United Nations System

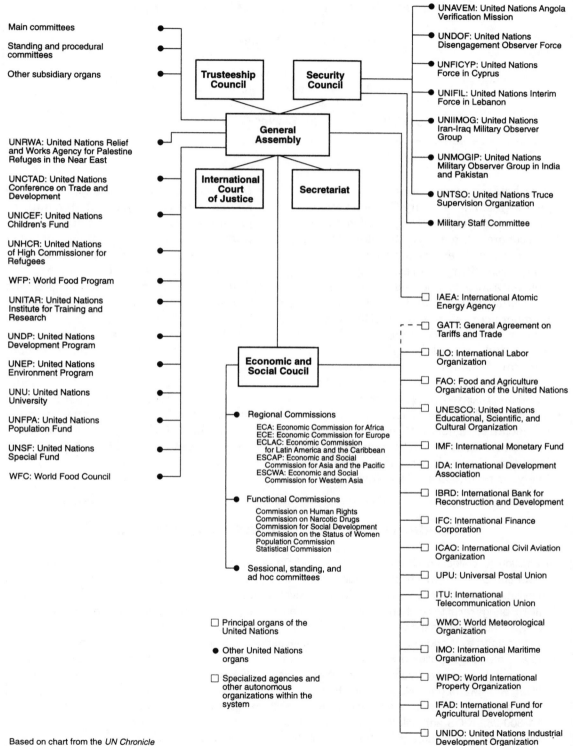

UNAVEM: United Nations Angola Verification Mission

UNDOF: United Nations Disengagement Observer Force

UNFICYP: United Nations Force in Cyprus

UNIFIL: United Nations Interim Force in Lebanon

UNIIMOG: United Nations Iran-Iraq Military Observer Group

UNMOGIP: United Nations Military Observer Group in India and Pakistan

UNTSO: United Nations Truce Supervision Organization

Military Staff Committee

Main committees

Standing and procedural committees

Other subsidiary organs

Trusteeship Council

Security Council

General Assembly

UNRWA: United Nations Relief and Works Agency for Palestine Refuges in the Near East

UNCTAD: United Nations Conference on Trade and Development

UNICEF: United Nations Children's Fund

UNHCR: United Nations of High Commissioner for Refugees

WFP: World Food Program

UNITAR: United Nations Institute for Training and Research

UNDP: United Nations Development Program

UNEP: United Nations Environment Program

UNU: United Nations University

UNFPA: United Nations Population Fund

UNSF: United Nations Special Fund

WFC: World Food Council

International Court of Justice

Secretariat

Economic and Social Coucil

Regional Commissions

ECA: Economic Commission for Africa
ECE: Economic Commission for Europe
ECLAC: Economic Commission for Latin America and the Caribbean
ESCAP: Economic and Social Commission for Asia and the Pacific
ESCWA: Economic and Social Commission for Western Asia

Functional Commissions

Commission on Human Rights
Commission on Narcotic Drugs
Commission for Social Development
Commission on the Status of Women
Population Commission
Statistical Commission

Sessional, standing, and ad hoc committees

☐ Principal organs of the United Nations

● Other United Nations organs

☐ Specialized agencies and other autonomous organizations within the system

IAEA: International Atomic Energy Agency

GATT: General Agreement on Tariffs and Trade

ILO: International Labor Organization

FAO: Food and Agriculture Organization of the United Nations

UNESCO: United Nations Educational, Scientific, and Cultural Organization

IMF: International Monetary Fund

IDA: International Development Association

IBRD: International Bank for Reconstruction and Development

IFC: International Finance Corporation

ICAO: International Civil Aviation Organization

UPU: Universal Postal Union

ITU: International Telecommunication Union

WMO: World Meteorological Organization

IMO: International Maritime Organization

WIPO: World International Property Organization

IFAD: International Fund for Agricultural Development

UNIDO: United Nations Industrial Development Organization

Based on chart from the *UN Chronicle*

478

INFORMATION, PLEASE

Everyone's United Nations: A Handbook on the Work of the United Nations. 10th ed. United Nations, 1986.

Reader's Digest Guide to Places of the World. Reader's Digest Association, 1987.

The New International Atlas. Rand McNally, 1993.

The Timetables of History: A Horizontal Linkage of People and Events. Simon & Schuster, 1987.

Worldmark Encyclopedia of the Nations: A Practical Guide to the Geographic, Historical, Social, and Economic Status of All Nations. Wiley, 1988.

INDEX